Inside Generic CADD™

Randall S. Newton

NEW RIDERS PUBLISHING

New Riders Publishing, Carmel, Indiana

Inside Generic CADD

By Randall S. Newton

Published by:
New Riders Publishing
11711 N. College Ave., Suite 140
Carmel, IN 46032
USA

Printed in the United States of America 1 2 3 4 5 6 7 8 9 0

Library of Congress Cataloging-in-Publication Data

Newton, Randall S., 1955-
Inside Generic CADD / Randall S. Newton.
p. cm.
Includes index.
ISBN 1-56205-001-X : $29.95
1. Computer graphics. 2. Generic CADD (Computer program)
I. Title.
T385.N49 1991
620'.0042'02855369—dc20 91-24731 CIP

Publisher
David P. Ewing

Product Director
Brad Koch

Managing Editor
Tim Huddleston

Production Editor
Margaret Berson

Editors
Merry Carlson
Peter Kuhns
Rob Lawson
Rich Limacher
Mark Montieth
Nancy Sixsmith
Christine Steel
Rob Tidrow

Technical Editor
Ralph Ferrin

Editorial Secretary
Karen Opal

Book Design and Production
William Hartman,
Hartman Publishing

Proofreaders
Suzanne Tulley
Rob Lawson
Nancy Sixsmith
Rob Tidrow

Indexed by
Jeanne Clark

Composed in Bookman, Helvetica, and Courier by
William Hartman,
Hartman Publishing

About the Author

Randall S. Newton is Publications Manager for Generic Software, Inc., an Autodesk company. Mr. Newton is editor of the award-winning *Generic Software News*, and has written three other books on the use of Generic CADD. His writing has appeared in many other publications, including *Computer Graphics Report, Plot and Print, San Francisco Chronicle*, and *Columbiana*. Mr. Newton also has served as Director of Academic Computing for Heritage College. He and his wife Teresa have six children.

New Riders Publishing extends special thanks to the following contributors to this book:

Sheldon F. Simpson, who contributed Chapters 11 and 13. Mr Simpson is an AutoCAD trainer who also has developed third-party software and symbol libraries for CADD programs. In 1988, he became one of the first third-party developers for Generic CADD. He currently develops predrawn bathroom, kitchen, deck, and other architectural plans for Generic CADD 5.0.

C. Scott van der Linden, who contributed Chapters 8 and 17. Mr. van der Linden attended Western Washington University and has worked as a repair technician, customer support specialist, testing engineer, and technical writer. He is in charge of Generic CADD on-line support on BIX, Genie, and CompuServe. He can be reached on BIX and Genie as ScottV, and his CompuServe number is 76702,533.

Donald L. Archer, who contributed Chapters 15 and 16. Mr. Archer is the founder of CDP Systems, a consulting, design, and programming firm. He has 39 years of drafting experience and has used CADD systems for twelve years. Mr. Archer has used Generic CADD for three years.

Acknowledgments

New Riders Publishing would like to express its sincere thanks to the following people, for their contributions to this book:

The staff of Generic Software, Inc., whose invaluable assistance made this project possible.

Ralph Ferrin of Generic Software, for technical editing.

Rusty Gesner, for initial development.

Tim Huddleston, for managing us all.

Production editor Margaret Berson, for taking on a project of such depth and breadth at the last possible moment, and for pulling together all the pieces and players.

Editors Merry Carlson, Peter Kuhns, Rob Lawson, Rich Limacher, Mark Montieth, Nancy Sixsmith, Christine Steel, and Rob Tidrow, for their careful and rapid work, and for their valuable input.

Bill Hartman of Hartman Publishing, for the design effort and expeditious handling of materials.

Randall Newton would like to thank his wife Teresa and his children for their patience and understanding.

Trademark Acknowledgments

New Riders Publishing has made every attempt to supply trademark information about company names, products, and services mentioned in this book. Trademarks indicated below were derived from various sources. New Riders Publishing cannot attest to the accuracy of this information.

AutoCAD is a registered trademark of Autodesk, Inc.

Generic and Generic CADD are registered trademarks of Generic Software, Inc.

Hewlett-Packard and LaserJet are registered trademarks of Hewlett-Packard Co.

1-2-3 and Lotus are registered trademarks of Lotus Development Corporation.

Microsoft and MS-DOS are registered trademarks of Microsoft Corporation.

Trademarks of other products mentioned in this book are held by the companies producing them.

Warning and Disclaimer

This book is designed to provide information about the Generic CADD computer-aided drafting and design program. Every effort has been made to make this book as complete and as accurate as possible, but no warranty or fitness is implied.

The information is provided on an "as is" basis. The author and New Riders Publishing shall have neither liability nor responsibility to any person or entity with respect to any loss or damages arising from the information contained in this book or from the use of the disks or programs that may accompany it.

Table of Contents

Introduction

With the release of Generic CADD version 5.0, a product that started out as a trim, relatively simple $99 computer-aided drafting program has become a robust, powerful $495 program. With all the extra power of its many new features, learning to take full advantage of the program is no longer an afternoon's diversion. As software complexity increases, so does the task of mastery. *Inside Generic CADD* is written with one goal in mind: to make it easier to master Generic CADD version 5.0.

How Inside Generic CADD Is Organized

This book has been organized to unfold the features of Generic CADD in a natural sequence. It starts with setting up the program to match your needs and the task at hand. Next come introductions to the basics of drawing and editing. (Editing in CADD is modifying the objects you have drawn. Editing is as important as drawing in the creation of the final product.) Explanations of the more powerful features follow, like dimensioning (placing measurements on the drawing) and the use of attributes (database-type information attached to objects in the drawing). The book ends with chapters on how to customize Generic CADD to further automate your drafting and design work.

What this book won't do is to teach you the fundamentals of drafting or to show you how to become a contractor, architect, engineer, facilities manager, or designer. In other words, to take full advantage of both Generic CADD and *Inside Generic CADD*, you need to have an application in mind, and you need to know what end result you're trying to achieve. After all, CADD stands for "Computer Aided Drafting and Design," not "Computers replAce Drafters and Designers."

Each chapter will follow the same format. The topic of the chapter will be introduced, allowing you to become familiar with any new concepts or features. Each aspect of the topic is covered with an explanation and then an exercise.

The Explanations

Each command or feature covered in *Inside Generic CADD* has its own explanation. This section will give you a framework for using the command in the context of your drawing and editing. Many Generic CADD commands share a common logic, which will be noted in the explanation, making it easier for you to learn the new feature by comparing it to one you have already covered.

The Exercises

After the introductory explanation, an exercise follows, providing an opportunity to apply the knowledge gained from the discussion of the command or feature. Only a genius can simply read a software manual and then immediately be productive. Most users need to work through commands and procedures, becoming comfortable gradually. It is one thing for your brain to understand a software command, but quite another for your fingers to become equally knowledgeable. The exercises in *Inside Generic CADD* are designed to bridge the gap.

Some of the exercises are progressive. You will start a task in the beginning of the chapter and build on it as the chapter progresses. In other chapters, the exercises will be separate, concentrating on one or two commands only. Additional explanations may sometimes follow the exercise, adding new insights that will make more sense once the exercise has been completed.

The exercises consist of three columns. The first column shows the Generic CADD prompt in computer-style type. The middle column instructs you. Characters you type are shown in boldface type. If all you need to do is to type something and then press Enter, we just show the input you need to type in bold—remember to press Enter after typing it. The third column gives a description of the action the computer will take.

When the exercise tells you to click somewhere in the drawing window, press the first mouse button. If you don't have a mouse or digitizer, press Enter to achieve the same effect. Sometimes you will be asked to "click" in the menu. Always use the second mouse button to select items in the menu; use the Home key if you lack a pointing device.

Where the exercise shows `Command:`, you should see the prompt `Enter a command >` just below your drawing window. If you see an ellipsis (three periods) in the leftmost column, it means that we are showing only part of a prompt that displays more than one option. The option listed is the one you're going to choose; for example, the Text Spacing command displays six options after you first invoke the command. So you would see `...Justification (left)` in the exercise if you were going to select justification.

Exercise Format

Prompt	*Input*	*Description*
`Command`	**RE**	Starts the Rectangle command
`Enter one corner of rectangle`	Click	Starts drawing first corner of rectangle
`Enter opposite corner`	Move cursor to opposite corner, then click	Draws the rectangle

The Optional Inside Generic CADD Disk

There is an optional disk available from New Riders Publishing to accompany this book. It contains finished versions of all the drawings and exercises in this book. If you are unsure that your work matches the description in the book, or if you want to skip some exercises to concentrate on difficult material, having these completed drawings available will make it easier to follow the exercises in the book. The disk is not required to benefit from using *Inside Generic CADD.*

How to Use Inside Generic CADD

Just as no two individuals learn in the same way, no two readers of *Inside Generic CADD* will use this book in the same way. To keep this book from being too lengthy, however, it is organized to be used in two ways.

Using Inside Generic CADD as a Tutorial

Most Generic CADD users will buy *Inside Generic CADD* because they want detailed help in learning to use the program. To make sure that as many people as possible benefit, computer jargon is kept to an absolute minimum, and CADD jargon (a necessary evil) is defined on first usage and again in the glossary. True to our word, we've already defined "editing," "dimensions," and "attributes" as they apply to Generic CADD. These definitions will be repeated and expanded later, because some people don't read introductions.

Using Inside Generic CADD as a Reference

Some people will buy *Inside Generic CADD* as a supplementary reference work. To help them, in addition to the Table Of Contents and the Index, there is a glossary of CADD vocabulary and two complete listings of Generic CADD commands—one as organized in the Generic CADD menus, and a second one following the organization of this book. The reader buying *Inside Generic CADD* as a supplementary reference may need only the explanations and the guides to be successful.

Two Important Tips to Learning Generic CADD

Reading this book and following the exercises are important, but true mastery of Generic CADD will require a little more bravery on your part. To really benefit from your *Inside Generic CADD*, follow these two tips:

Learn To Use Two-Letter Commands

Generic CADD commands can be entered by using the on-screen menu, typing additional information as needed. But the real power in CADD comes from using the two-letter commands, such as ZA for Zoom All, RE for Rectangle, and CP for Component Place. Most of the two-letter commands are mnemonic, easy to remember once you use them.

Play with the Commands

After you work through the exercises in each chapter, erase your work and start fresh on a drawing of your own choosing. The verb "play" is not used here by accident. "Play" implies that you are doing the activity for fun and enjoyment, without pressure or obligation. Play with the commands until you gain familiarity with them, then put them to work.

What You Will Need

This book makes a few assumptions about the program in use, the reader's knowledge, and the computer equipment available.

Generic CADD Version 5.0

Inside Generic CADD is based on version 5.0 of Generic CADD. This version, released in September 1990, is substantially more powerful than any previous release of the program. Many new features were added, the logic of editing was substantially reworked, and functions that once resided outside the main drafting program have been integrated within CADD. This book is not intended to be used with Generic CADD Level 3 or Generic CADD 3.0.

Basic Working Knowledge of MS-DOS

While *Inside Generic CADD* assumes no prior knowledge of Generic CADD or a specific method of drafting, you need a basic working knowledge of DOS, the computer's operating system. In particular, you should know:

- What directories and subdirectories are, and how to move between them.
- What files are, and how to copy or delete them.
- How to start programs from the DOS prompt.

In addition, you need to know how to use a word processor or text editor to create ASCII text files. Reference will also be made to the use of database management programs and spreadsheets, but you will not need to know how to use a particular program.

Required Computer Equipment

Generic CADD requires a computer with a minimum of 640 kilobytes of RAM memory, a hard drive, and a video display device capable of showing graphics. Unlike most powerful CAD programs, Generic CADD will still run on a PC or an XT that otherwise meets these requirements. (At this writing, for example, the DOS version of AutoCAD Release 11 requires an AT-compatible computer with a 80386 processor. A version supporting 80286 processors is said to be in the works, but Autodesk does not plan to support the use of AutoCAD on PC- and XT-level computers.)

In addition to the hardware required by Generic CADD, this book assumes that you have a mouse or a digitizer for use as a pointing device. While it is possible to use Generic CADD without a pointing device, it is not a productive use of one's time. The most efficient way to use Generic CADD is to combine the two-letter commands with a pointing device. (If you just bought Generic CADD and need to buy a mouse, be sure to get one with three buttons.)

Summary

If you are standing in the aisle of a bookstore reading this introduction, it's decision time. This book will help you become comfortable and productive with Generic CADD version 5.0. It offers explanations in real English, and exercises that are easy to follow. This book will serve you now as you learn Generic CADD, and later when you need to review a command or feature. There is an optional disk available, showing the completed versions of all exercises. All in all, it's a pretty good deal.

Welcome aboard! We'll meet in Chapter One.

1

Getting Started

This chapter covers the basics of getting Generic CADD 5.0 up and running on your computer. It discusses the computer hardware you need and the pitfalls of hardware incompatibility. The installation of Generic CADD 5.0 on your computer is also covered. Then the chapter introduces the Generic CADD display screen and explains how to execute commands. The number one question of new users—"What if I make a mistake?"—is answered (the quick answer, of course, is "Don't worry about it"). The basics of loading and saving drawings are explained.

Just as you will use Generic CADD to *design* things, the way Generic CADD operates is by *design*. From the start, and throughout the book, we will refer to the logic behind the operation of Generic CADD. This will make it easier for you to understand commands as they are presented, and even to correctly anticipate how new features work.

Setting Up Generic CADD

If you haven't already done so, take the time right now to install your copy of Generic CADD 5.0 on your computer. If you have purchased additional hardware for your system to use with Generic CADD, such as a mouse, a hard drive, or a new video display system, install it first and make sure it is working properly.

Although the installation of Generic CADD 5.0 is straightforward, the program has to work with literally hundreds of possible combinations of peripheral devices, those pieces of equipment one connects to the computer. Despite the fact that the IBM clone is an industry "standard," incompatibility between devices sometimes happens.

Generic CADD has an uncanny ability to root out the otherwise hidden incompatibilities between devices. One of the computers used to write this book was an example. By CADD standards, it was a modest machine: a 12-Mhz AT-compatible with a 40M hard drive, one 1.2M floppy drive, 640K of RAM memory on the motherboard, and another 2M of RAM memory on an add-in board. The system also sported one serial port, one parallel printing port on a separate card, a 16-bit VGA video adapter board, a fax/modem board, and a math coprocessor. The version of MS-DOS in use was 3.3.

The system was assembled and seemed to work fine for word processing and telecommunications; then Generic CADD 5.0 was installed. At first Generic CADD could not complete the installation process. Several hours of analysis later, it turned out that the file COMMAND.COM, part of MS-DOS 3.3, had been tampered with. (The size of the file did not match that of other versions of MS-DOS or PC-DOS 3.3.) After the DOS was replaced, the Generic CADD installation program ran through to completion.

Next, the CADD program itself would not run. An error message appeared in response to typing **CADD** at the DOS prompt. Pressing any key returned the computer to the DOS prompt. Several hours more analysis revealed that the fax/modem board, the parallel printer port card, the serial port/RAM card, and the math coprocessor were all stepping on each other's toes. (The problem involved IRQ interrupts and other internal entanglements). Remove any one of the devices, and CADD would operate just fine. But with all of them installed, CADD balked. Since telecommunications and the use of the printer were essential, and the mouse was connected to the serial port, the math coprocessor was sacrificed for the cause of IRQ-interrupt peace inside the computer. Now CADD runs without a hitch, albeit a little slow without the math coprocessor.

There is no bug in Generic CADD that caused this unfortunate string of events—the problems were elsewhere. Generic CADD was just the messenger of bad tidings. If the conflict had not been rooted out by Generic CADD, sooner or later this problem would have erupted, probably in the middle of some crucial task.

TIP

Buying a new computer? Make sure that it runs Generic CADD with all devices installed *before* you buy it!

Hardware conflicts are not the only problems Generic CADD has brought to the surface. Several users of Generic CADD have called Generic Software to thank the company because the program helped them discover viruses lurking within their computers. CADD stopped working, and investigating why led to discovering the viruses. Although such timely discoveries may have saved each user hundreds of dollars, Generic Software has no plans to advertise CADD as a virus catcher.

Installing Generic CADD 5.0

The minimum hardware requirements for Generic CADD 5.0 are a 100 percent IBM-compatible computer with 640K of RAM memory, one hard drive and one floppy drive, DOS version 3.0 or later, and a video graphics display adapter. These should be considered as *absolute* minimums; CADD performance improves dramatically with better hardware. A word processor works at about the same speed on an XT or an 80486, but CADD will look like two different programs. If you are looking to boost performance by buying new equipment, do so in this order (the higher on the list, the more benefit to CADD performance).

1. Math coprocessor
2. Faster CPU with matching math coprocessor
3. Faster, larger hard drive
4. Faster, high-resolution video display adapter
5. More RAM memory

Despite the power user advantages of better hardware, one of the beauties of Generic CADD is that it will run on a very modest computer. An XT-compatible computer with 640K of RAM, a 20M hard drive, one floppy drive, a math coprocessor, and a monochrome graphics display adapter and monitor can be purchased new for less than $700. Add $495 for Generic CADD and you have a great introductory drafting station, ideal for students, moonlighters, or anybody on a budget who still wants to use a professional CAD program.

TIP

By the way, an XT with a math coprocessor runs Generic CADD *faster* than an AT without a math coprocessor.)

Whether your computer system is state-of-the-art or state-of-the-budget, the installation of Generic CADD 5.0 should go smoothly. Before you begin, make sure you know what devices are installed in the computer, how much RAM memory you have, and whether or not any is being used as EMS memory. For safety's sake, make backup copies of all the Generic CADD 5.0 disks before you start, and use the backups for installation.

Also, before you start, fill out and send in the registration card. When you register, you are eligible for unrestricted, free technical support (you pay for the phone call). Generic Software's technical support staff are extremely knowledgeable and helpful. This means you can rely on them, but it also means they are hard to reach. The best times to get through are after 4 p.m. Pacific time weekdays, or between 9 a.m. and noon Pacific time on Saturdays. Registering your purchase of Generic CADD also puts you on the mailing list to receive *Generic Software News*, a 16-page tabloid filled with technical tips, user profiles, new product announcements, CADD upgrade notices, letters from users, and the occasional odd rambling from yours truly.

For now, follow the program's recommendations for the creation of directories on the hard drive. If you are installing Generic CADD on the C drive, the installation program will create a directory called CADD5, and four subdirectories: CMP, for components; DWG, for drawing files; FNT, for fonts; and HCH, for hatch pattern files. (See figs. 1.1 and 1.2.)

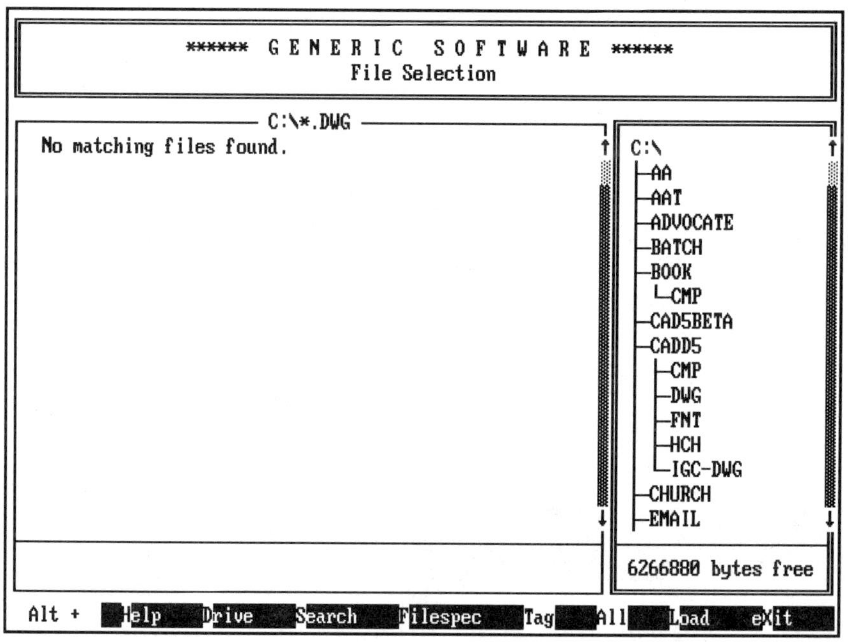

Figure 1.1: *A typical DOS directory with Generic CADD installed.*

When the installation process is complete, you'll see a screen listing your video adapter and mouse. If these don't seem correct, just press Enter anyway. (If you exit at this point, you'll have to start over again.) Next a screen will appear with four configuration options, as shown in figure 1.2.

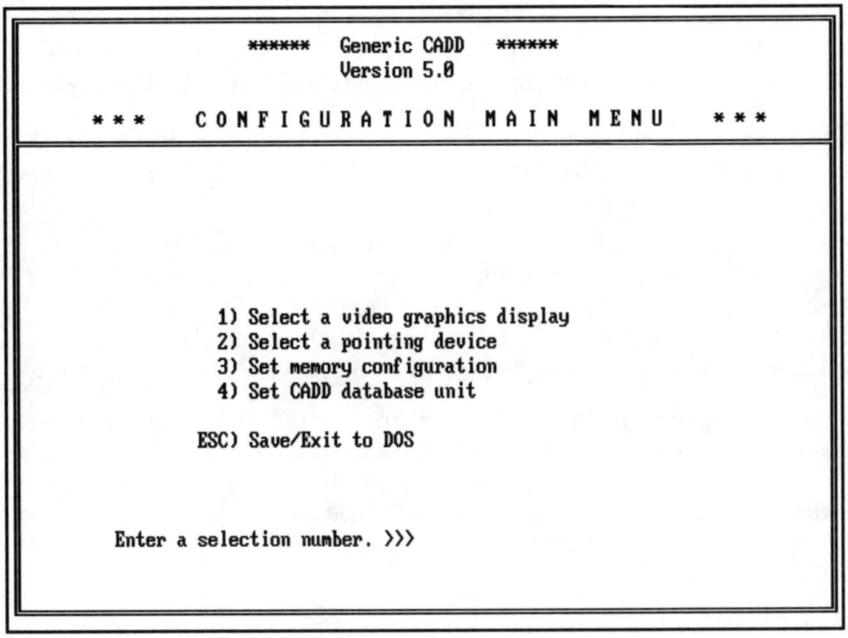

Figure 1.2: *The configuration screen.*

You must respond to the first two options to complete the installation of Generic CADD. Press the number of the option you want to set, and press Enter.

For the video graphics display option, press 1, then Enter. Look through the list of supported video devices. If your particular video board isn't listed, choose one that is compatible. For most VGA cards, the IBM VGA option is the best choice.

CAD programs are very demanding of a video board's capabilities, and the mark of a conscientious video board manufacturer is the distribution of specialty video drivers for various CAD programs, including Generic CADD. (A video driver is a software program that acts as the go-between for the program and the video board.)

If your video display device is CGA-compatible or MCGA-compatible, you will not have color when you use Generic CADD. This is not a bug in CADD, but a limitation of the video display device. CGA and MCGA systems cannot access enough memory to display CADD adequately unless they are used in their monochrome modes.

If you have an EGA monitor, you may be able to achieve higher resolution with Generic CADD than you can with most programs. Refer to Appendix A in the *Generic CADD 5.0 User's Guide* for a discussion of higher resolution for EGA devices.

When you have selected the video display option that best matches your hardware, move on to selecting a pointing device; press 2, (then Enter) at the configuration screen.

If you have a mouse, it has either two or three buttons. (If you have yet to buy a mouse, be sure to get one with three buttons. Generic CADD can take advantage of all three keys, even though most programs on the market only use two buttons.) If you have a two-button mouse, you'll still be able to do all the things you could with the third button, by holding down Shift and pressing the first button.

The MOUSE.COM driver option that matches your mouse is the best option to select in most cases. For this selection to work, you must use the MOUSE.COM program that came with your mouse. It must be loaded *before* you use Generic CADD. The best approach is to have your AUTOEXEC.BAT file load MOUSE.COM into memory when your computer starts up. Refer to your DOS manual if you need help in creating an AUTOEXEC.BAT file.

Option 3 allows you to customize Generic CADD's use of the memory in your computer. The five options are shown in figure 1.3:

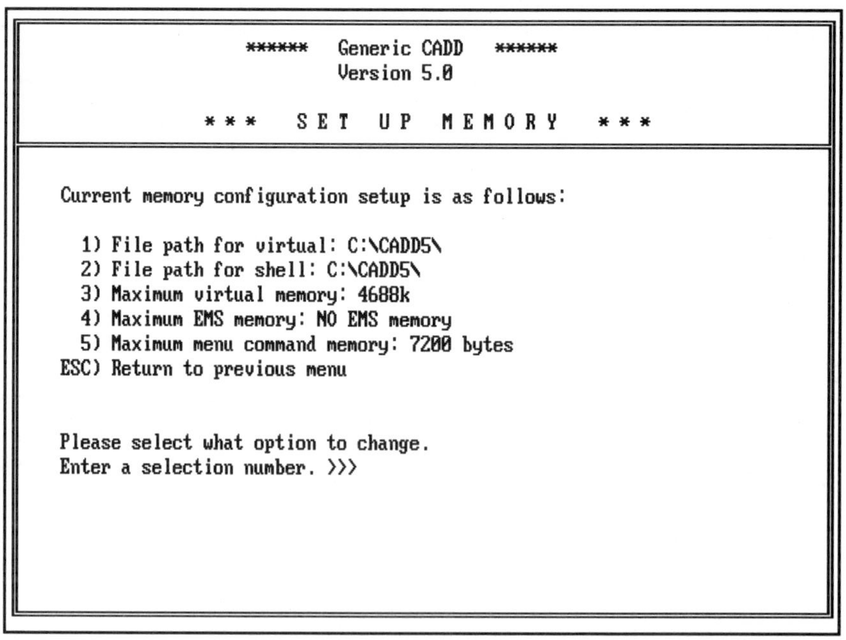

Figure 1.3: *The memory configuration screen.*

The first option allows you to set what drive and directory will be used by Generic CADD's virtual memory capability. Virtual memory is a "trick" whereby CADD uses a portion of the hard drive as if it were RAM memory. When virtual memory is in operation, your drawings can be larger than the amount of RAM memory in your computer. (This one new feature alone was reason enough for many hard-core Generic CADD users to upgrade to version 5.0 when it was first released.) If you do not change the setting, CADD will use the CADD5 directory for the virtual memory file. If you have another hard drive (D, for example) with more room on it than on your C drive, you may want to choose to have the virtual memory file created on that drive and directory instead of the CADD5 directory. The file that is created by the virtual memory function is temporary, and it is erased by CADD when you close the program.

The second option sets the drive and directory where Generic CADD stores a "placeholder" file when you shell out of CADD. To *shell* is to freeze the execution of CADD and run another program. When you finish with the other program, you can return to CADD and continue as if you had never left. Unless you have more room on another drive, it is best to leave this option as-is. Like the virtual memory file, the file created by the shell routine is temporary, and it is erased when you close Generic CADD.

Option three allows you to decide how much room to devote to virtual memory (see fig. 1.4). When CADD starts up, it scans the hard drive and determines how much room is available for virtual memory. You may choose to use all of this amount, or a percentage.

```
                ******   Generic CADD   ******
                         Version 5.0

            * * *   S E T   U P   M E M O R Y   * * *

 Virtual memory status: Available = 6160k, Maximum useable = 4688k, 76%

   1)   0%
   2)  25%
   3)  50%
   4)  75%
   5) 100%
   6) User selectable (in kilobytes)
 ESC) Return to previous menu

 Please select what option to change.
 Enter a selection number. >>>
```

Figure 1.4:
Virtual memory size options.

The fourth option controls the amount of EMS memory used by Generic CADD, if you have EMS memory installed. As with virtual memory, you may choose to use a percentage of the available memory, or set a specific size in kilobytes.

The last setting is the amount of RAM memory reserved by Generic CADD for its menu. To the new user, it may seem odd to want to control the memory needed for one part of the program's command structure, but there is good cause. As we will learn in a later chapter, Generic CADD's menus are customizable. You can add new features or menus. To conserve RAM, the default setting for the amount of memory used by CADD's menu is just enough for the standard menu. If you make any changes, you should come back to this option and increase the memory. We will walk through that when we cover Generic CADD's menus in detail.

After finishing with all the memory settings, the next item on the configuration menu is: Set CADD database unit. Unless you need to work in metric units, or your work will be exclusively in a field such as surveying, it is best to leave the Units setting in inches. This setting controls how Generic CADD stores data within files. If you switch back and forth between various units using this setting, CADD must recalculate all units used in drawing files, and roundoff errors are sure to occur. This command does not affect the display of distances on-screen, as we shall see below.

Once all the configuration options have been set, you may press the Escape key, which we will abbreviate from now on as Esc. A prompt will appear on the screen asking `Do you wish to keep the changes? (Y,N) >>`. If you are satisfied, press **Y**; if you need to make a change, press **N** and go back to the item above you want to review. It is not necessary to press Enter after pressing **Y** or **N**.

After you press **Y**, the configuration program will ask if you want Generic CADD to update your AUTOEXEC.BAT file. If you say yes, it will add two lines to your AUTOEXEC.BAT file that assist the program in using your video display to best advantage. If you say no, you will need to add these lines yourself. A listing of the possible lines is found in Appendix A of the *Generic CADD 5.0 User's Guide*. Although it is wise to protect your AUTOEXEC.BAT file zealously, it is safe to let Generic CADD change it. Just as a precaution, the existing AUTOEXEC.BAT file will be renamed to AUTOEXEC.BAK and saved separately before a new AUTOEXEC.BAT is created.

Creating a Subdirectory for Exercises

Once the installation and configuration of Generic CADD 5.0 is complete, you will need to create a subdirectory on your hard drive, which we will use to save the drawings you will create while using *Inside Generic CADD*.

When the configuration program ended, your DOS prompt should be at a directory called C:/CADD5. Type the following line:

```
md IGC-DWG
```

DOS will create a new subdirectory called IGC-DWG, which is within the CADD5 directory. (See fig. 1-5.)

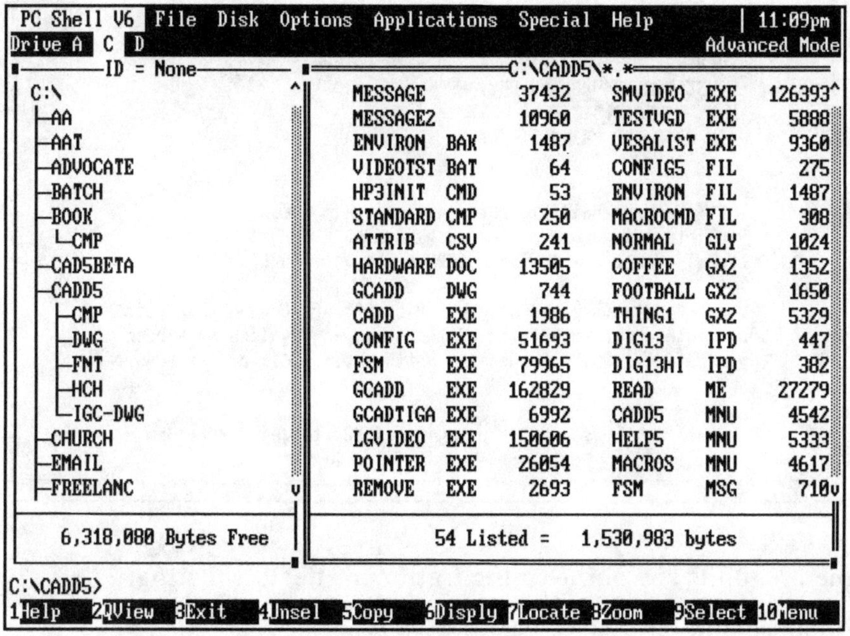

Figure 1.5: Modified DOS directory.

Installing the Optional Inside Generic CADD Disk

If you have purchased the optional disk that accompanies this book, copy its contents to this new directory. From the C:\CADD5\IGC-DWG directory prompt, type the following:

```
COPY A:*.*
```

If you placed the floppy in your B drive, substitute B: for A: in the line above.

Communicating with Generic CADD

We're ready to start Generic CADD and take a look at how it operates. From the DOS prompt of the \CADD5 directory, type:

```
CADD
```

After a few seconds (the actual time depends on the speed of your computer), the opening screen will appear (see fig. 1.6).

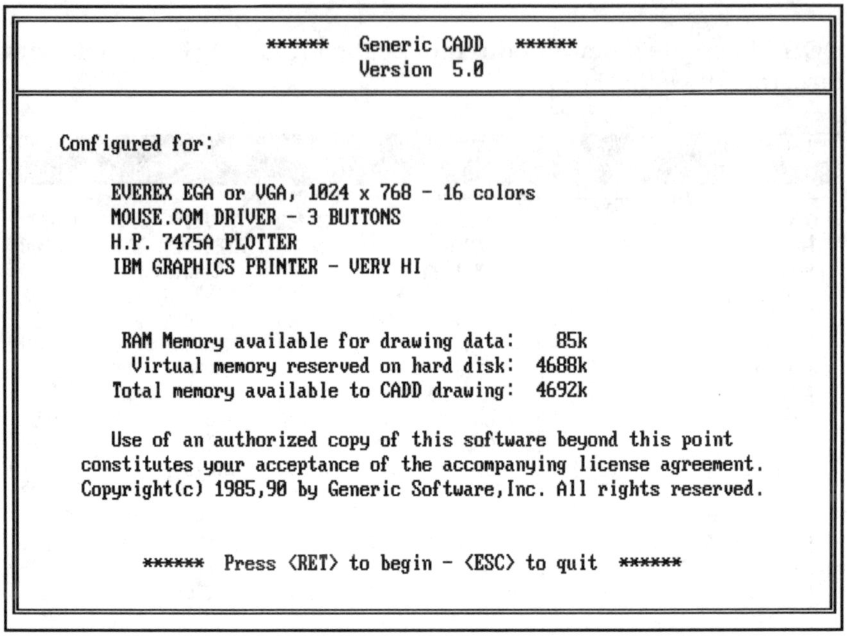

Figure 1.6: *Generic CADD 5.0 opening screen.*

The opening screen reminds you of the configuration in effect, by listing:

- the video display adapter in use
- the resolution of the video display
- the number of colors that can be displayed
- the pointing device driver installed
- the plotter installed
- the dot matrix or laser printer installed, and its resolution
- available RAM memory
- available virtual memory
- total memory available for CADD drawings

If you notice that one of these settings is incorrect, you can press Esc and return to the DOS prompt. From there, type CONFIG, which runs the program we used during the installation routine to set the video, the memory, and so on.

Don't bother to add the available RAM memory and available virtual memory to see if they equal total memory—they usually don't. The "total memory" is calculated differently.

The first time you use CADD, there will be a default setting for the plotter and printer. You must configure for your particular output devices from within Generic CADD. Configuring for your printer and/or plotter is covered in Chapter 8.

If all the settings are fine, press Enter to continue.

Understanding Screen Informational Displays

While some CADD programs start off with a screen full of menus, Generic CADD takes you straight to the drawing screen. This is home base for everything you do in Generic CADD. If you leave this screen to print or plot, or to search the hard drive for files, you will always return to this screen. Figure 1.7 shows you: the drawing window (1), the drawing cursor (2), the coordinate display (3), the ROOT menu (4), the menu bar (5) the prompt line (6), and the status lines (7).

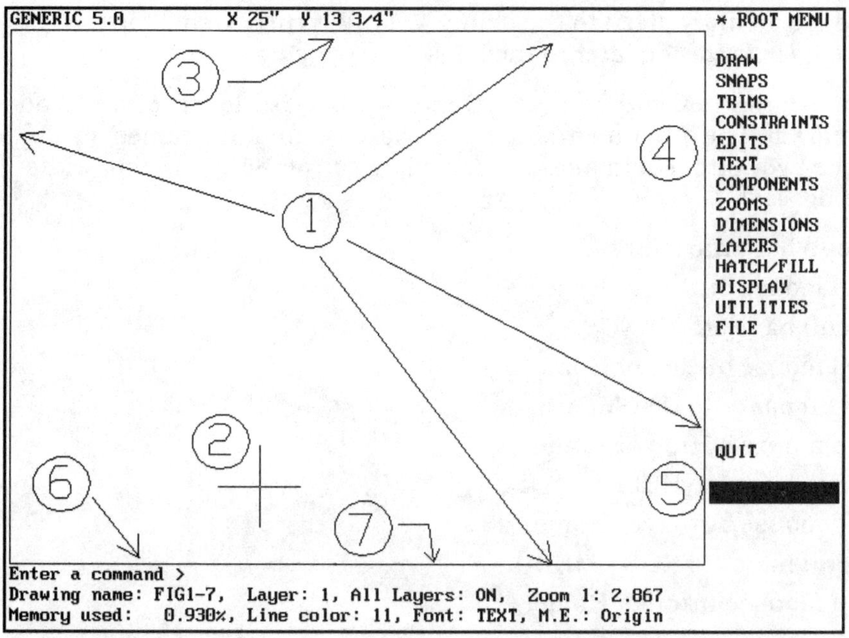

Figure 1.7: The Generic CADD drawing screen.

The largest portion of the screen is the drawing window. This is where you create and edit your drawings. The crossed lines in the drawing window form the drawing cursor. When you move the pointing device or the arrow keys, the drawing cursor responds. From now on, we will refer to it simply as the cursor.

At the top of the screen is the coordinate display, item (3) in figure 1.7. The coordinate display gives a continuous readout of the location of the cursor, using a Cartesian coordinate grid as a frame of reference. There will be more on the coordinate display later, when we discuss the concept of real scale.

Using Generic CADD's Menus

Along the right side of the screen is the ROOT menu, item (4) in figure 1.7. Each of the items on this menu is actually the topic of one or more submenus. To select an item from the menu, move the pointing device or press an up or down arrow key. The menu bar (item [5] in fig. 1.7) moves as the cursor moves. When the menu bar is on the item you want, press the second pointer button or the Home key on the keyboard. To return to this menu from any submenu, select the ROOT MENU option, always found at the bottom of any submenu. If you just want to look at the various submenus without selecting commands, press the PageUp or PageDown keys on the keyboard. The Generic CADD menu is like a belt on rollers: if you move through it far enough, you return to the beginning.

When configuring Generic CADD, you had the option of increasing the amount of memory reserved for the menu. You don't need any more than is already allocated now, but if you customize the menu or add symbol library menus later, you may need to increase the memory given to the menu. We will return to this topic when we discuss menu customization later in the book.

The menu that appears when you first start Generic CADD 5.0 is one of two available with the program. The other menu has abbreviated command names, to make room for the two-letter commands. To switch to the other menu, follow the steps below (see fig. 1.8).

Move the menu bar onto DISPLAY.

Press second mouse button or Home.

Move the menu bar onto MENUS.

Press second mouse button or Home.

Move the menu bar onto New Menu.

Press second mouse button or Home.

Move the menu bar onto HELP5.

Press second mouse button or Home.

Move the menu bar onto ROOT MENU.

Press second mouse button or Home.

Using Two-Letter Drawing Commands

At the bottom of the screen are the prompt line (item [6] in fig. 1.7) and the status lines (item [7]). While it is possible to execute most commands in Generic CADD by using the menu, experienced CADD users often find it faster to use Generic CADD's two-letter commands. When you type in a two-letter command, it appears on the prompt line. If Generic CADD 5.0 requires any additional information from you to complete the command, the prompt line will display the request.

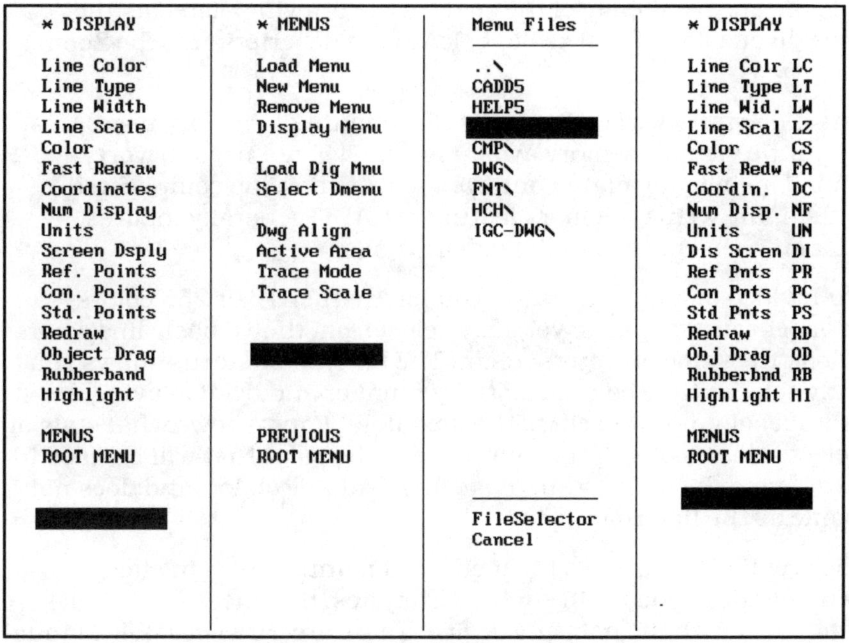

Figure 1.8: *Selecting a new menu for CADD.*

Now you can see the two-letter abbreviations for each command as you use the menus.

The two-letter commands are almost all mnemonic in nature (LI for Line, ZP for Zoom Previous), which makes them easy to learn. We will always provide the two-letter commands as we describe new features, and of course they are now listed in the CADD menu if you loaded the HELP5 menu as explained above.

Below the prompt line are the two status lines. When you are not in the middle of executing a command, these lines display the status of a variety of settings. If you have given a name to the drawing you are working on, or if you have loaded a drawing from disk, the name will appear after Drawing Name. The number after Layer refers to the drawing layer in use. Generic CADD drawings can be divided into as many as 256 layers, numbered 0 through 255. Think of layers as sheets of clear plastic that we can draw on, adding or removing sheets at will. We will devote some time later to the efficient use of layers.

The next item in the first status line shows the status of the All Layers Edit command. If All Layers is on, then you can edit any item that appears on the screen. If All Layers is off, then only the items which are on the current layer may be edited; items on other visible layers may not be edited. As a new Generic CADD user, it may be hard for you to imagine when you would need such a feature, but it comes in handy quite often.

After All Layers is the status display of the scale of the drawing, listed as the Zoom. Refer to the discussion of real scale, below, for a description of the Zoom Status.

The second status line starts with a display of the amount of memory used. Unless you have very little virtual memory available, you will not need to worry about the amount of memory available until you start to develop complicated drawings. Even then, the virtual memory feature of CADD generally insures plenty of space for even the most complicated drawings.

Depending on your video display hardware, you have either 16 or 256 colors available. (On monochrome displays, you may select from the 16 basic line colors, but they will all look the same on your screen.) The Line Color status shows you what the currently selected line color is, both by number and by displaying the number in the actual color it represents. The next item, Font, shows what style of font has been selected. The color of the font name is the color that will be used to place text in the drawing. It can be adjusted to any available color, and does not have to be the same as the line color.

The last item, the cryptic M.E., shows the method of manual entry in effect. Manual entry is using the keyboard to enter coordinates, distances, and angles instead of drawing them with the pointing device. There are three possible Manual Entry settings: Origin, Relative, and Basepoint. An introduction to these settings follows in Chapter 2, and a full discussion of these options will be presented in Chapter 5. While mice and digitizers are wonderfully useful drawing tools, sometimes it is more efficient to enter the length, location, or angle of an object from the keyboard.

Drawing in Real Scale

If you have been trained in drafting procedure, you are at home with the concept of drawing scale and you know its importance when drafting manually. But CADD changes the rules, making drawing scale a seldom-considered aspect of the drawing process. To understand why, consider the following example.

A football field is 100 yards long and 50 yards wide. If you want to draw it on a piece of paper, you need to calculate at what scale to draw it so that it is an accurate representation. If you choose to draw so that 1" on the paper represents 12" of real football field, you need a piece of paper 300" wide. Setting 1" on paper equal to 36" (one yard) will require a page 100" wide. Setting the scale at 1" on paper equal to 360" (10 yards) of real football field will require a page 10" wide. Finally, a manageable size to work with. To draw the first side line, you would calculate the scale (100 yards divided by 10 equals 10 inches on paper) and draw the line.

Now consider the same project being done in Generic CADD. The sidelines are, in real life, 100 yards long. So in CADD the first thing to do would be to draw a line 100 yards long—no calculating scale, no worrying about making it fit. Just draw the line.

If you think we skipped a step, you're wrong. When drawing in CADD, always draw the real-world size of an object. The drawing window is not a fixed size like the sheet of paper: it is a viewport, a window into a flat, two-dimensional universe that can be as big or as small as anything in our three-dimensional world.

Take a moment to look out the nearest window. Can you see things larger than the pane of glass in front of you? Of course you can, because of the distances involved. CADD, being limited to two dimensions, doesn't have distance, but it offers a good substitute. It is called the Zoom factor. If you are drawing the drain in a sink, you can set the screen to have the drain fill the screen. You can then adjust the view and have the sink, the kitchen, or even the entire house fill the screen just as easily as the drain filled the screen. Like a television camera at a baseball game that provides a close-up view of the batter even though the camera sits in center field, Generic CADD can easily "zoom" to any required viewpoint.

Follow the steps below to draw the outline of a football field at real scale. We will use manual (keyboard) entry. Throughout the book, we will use the format presented below for exercises. In the left column will be the Prompt, the message Generic CADD offers. The center column is labeled Input, which is what you should type or otherwise execute. The third column will list the Description of the action required. When the on-screen prompt reads `Enter a command >`, we will shorten it to `Command:` in the listings.

Drawing a Football Field

Prompt	*Input*	*Description*
`Command`	**RE**	Invokes Rectangle command
`Enter one corner of the rectangle`	**0,0**	Starts one corner of the rectangle at coordinate location X 0" Y 0" (see fig. 1.9)
`Enter opposite corner`	**300',162'**	Sets the opposite corner of rectangle at X 300', Y 162', and draws four lines of the rectangle (see fig. 1.10)
`Command`	**ZA**	Zoom All command redraws the screen to view rectangle (see Fig. 1.11)

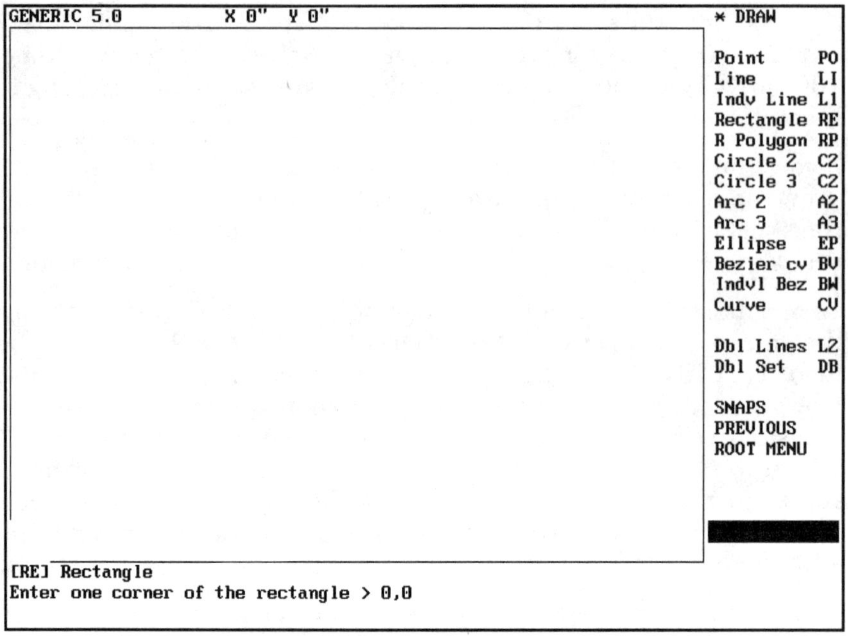

Figure 1.9: *Entering the first corner of the rectangle.*

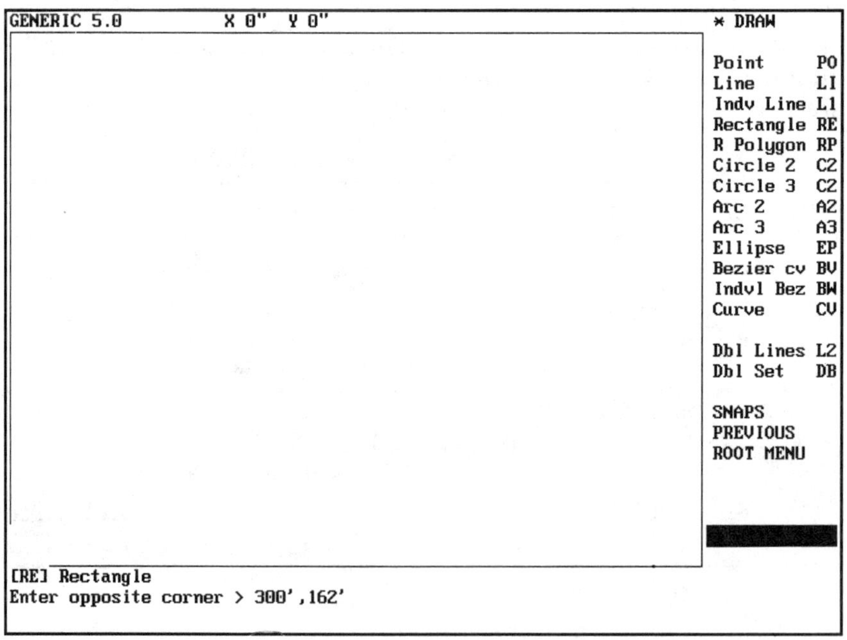

Figure 1.10: *Entering the opposite corner of the rectangle.*

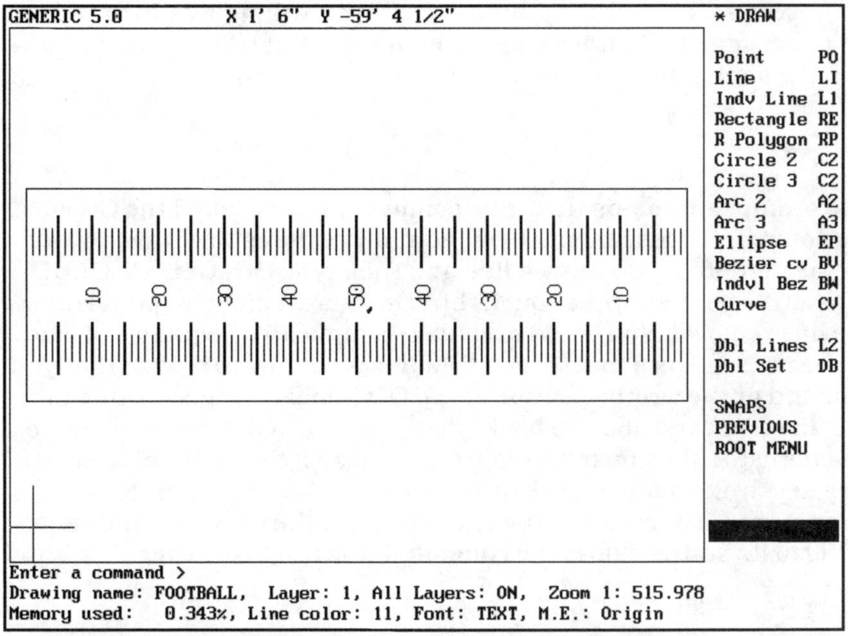

Figure 1.11. *The completed rectangle, with field marks added.*

In the exercise above, you drew two lines that for all practical purposes are each 100 yards long, and two more that are 53 1/3 yards long, to represent the dimensions of a football field. In the database that CADD creates to store drawing data, these lines are listed as being those dimensions. There is no consideration given to scale. When you type ZA for Zoom All, Generic CADD automatically adjusts the view on the monitor so you can see the entire football field.

If you are in the habit of drawing everything to scale from years of manual drafting, try to relax and enjoy the new freedom of drawing to real scale. But don't worry that we've forgotten scale completely. We will return to it when we print our drawings, because the drawings we place on paper usually need to be printed at specific scales.

Handling Errors

Now that you've broken the ice and actually drawn something in Generic CADD, feel free to put your hand on the mouse or the arrow keys (the poor man's mouse, they say), and doodle. Move the cursor and press the first button on the mouse (or the Enter key), to automatically start a line. Move the cursor again and press the first button (or Enter) again to finish the line. Note that CADD will continue on, drawing another line. If you wish to disconnect from the last point you placed on the screen, press the Esc key or move the menu bar to a blank menu line and press the second mouse button. Try drawing lines all over the football field.

This is a risk-free exercise, requiring nothing except your willingness to draw. But it is a good time to become familiar with four commands that will get you out of a jam if you ever make a mistake in a future exercise.

Undo (OO)

Typing **OO** at the prompt summons the Undo command (often called the Oops! command). This command does not erase but actually restores the drawing as it was before your last action. If you draw a line and then type OO, Generic CADD removes the line. This seems simple enough, but Undo is much more powerful than just simple line removal. You could execute a complicated sequence of commands that had been saved as a macro on a function key, only to realize that you started the command at the wrong location. Type OO (repeat it for each step of the macro, up to 25 steps) and you are back where you started before the macro was executed. Generic CADD remembers your actions as if they were placed on a list, keystroke by keystroke, mouse click by mouse click. When you undo something, CADD refers to the list, removes the last step from the drawing, and restores the drawing to its status before the command was originally executed.

Redo (UU)

Yes, sometimes even using the Undo command can be a mistake. That's why Generic CADD offers its opposite, Redo. If you type OO only to say "Oops!" because of it, type **UU** and breathe a sigh of relief.

Undo and Redo are not infinitely powerful. Each can reach back a total of 25 actions, which can be a lot of drawing and editing. If you use the Pack Data, Definition Unload, Window Text, or Drawing Remove commands, Generic CADD's undo/redo list is wiped clean. (These commands will be covered later, when we are ready to take full advantage of them.)

Erase Last (EL)

Less powerful than Undo, Erase Last is handy nonetheless. By typing **EL** at the prompt (or selecting it from the EDITS menu), you erase the last object drawn on the screen. If you use RE to draw a rectangle, and then type EL to erase last, only the fourth line of the rectangle will be erased, because the rectangle is made of four objects (straight lines, in this case).

UnErase (UE)

Used Erase Last by mistake, did you? Don't fret. Just type **UE** or select UnErase from the EDITS menu, and all is forgiven. Erase Last and UnErase can be used repeatedly to "undraw" or redraw your work. They are limited to removing or replacing simple objects. If you perform a more complicated editing command, and need to reverse the action, use Undo or Redo.

Saving and Loading Drawings

If you want to quit for now, but return to your doodled-on football field later, you need to know how to save the drawing on disk and how to retrieve it later. There are several options for each action.

Options for Saving a Drawing

When you save a drawing to disk, you can choose to save the entire drawing, or only a portion of it. The commands are:

Save (SA)

Save, found in the FILE menu, is an all-purpose command. When you type **SA** or click on it in the menu, you can choose to save not only a drawing file, but several other file types as well, as shown in figure 1.12. We will not concern ourselves with these other save options now. To save your doodling, follow the steps below.

Saving Your Drawing

Prompt	*Input*	*Description*
`Command`	**SA**	Initiates Save command
`Save`	**D**	Save a drawing file
`Save file as`	**C:\CADD5\IGC-DWG\ FOOTBALL**	Expects name of drive, directory, and file
`Saving file`		
`Save is complete`		

Drawing Save (DS)

Save can be used to save files other than standard drawing files. Since it is a good habit to save often, no matter what software application you use, Generic CADD offers a shortcut to bypass the steps involved in using Save. When you type **DS** for Drawing Save, Generic CADD immediately knows you want to save the current drawing file. It displays the name of the file. If it is correct (you can choose to rename it at this point), press Enter. If there is already a version of the drawing on disk, CADD will ask if you want to overwrite the version on disk, or rename the version on disk to filename.BAK. Type **O** or **R** to answer, and the drawing is saved.

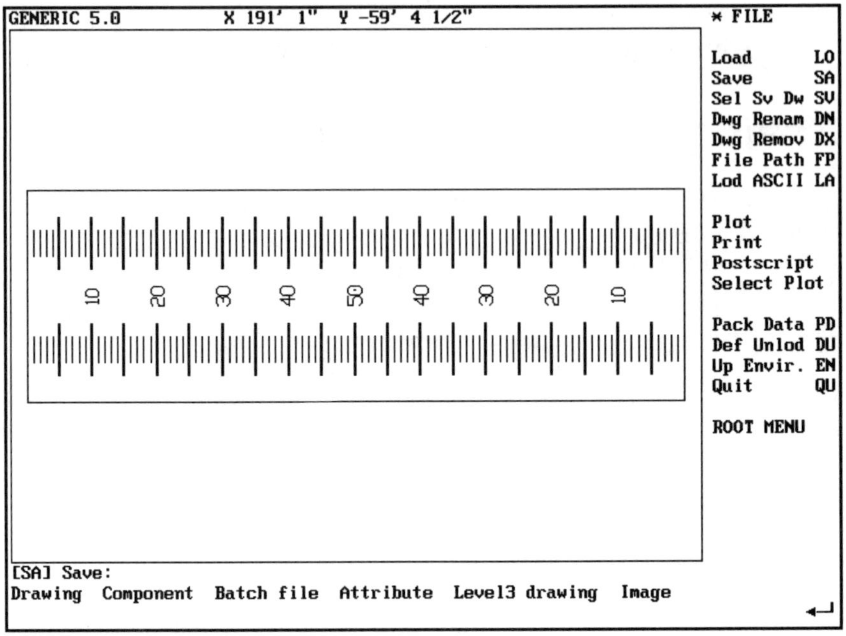

Figure 1.12: *Options available using the Save command.*

Even though using the Rename command means taking up more room on the hard drive, it is a good idea to have a version saved as a backup file (filename.BAK). If Generic CADD should happen to crash (rare but possible, and sometimes not CADD's fault), the current drawing file could be corrupted or lost. The version renamed to filename.BAK would still be safe.

Selection Save (SV)

If you ever want to save certain objects in a drawing in their own drawing file, use Selection Save (SV) and choose Drawing. It allows you to pick and choose those objects to be saved; all others will not become part of the file recorded on disk (see fig. 1.13). A complete understanding of the options in the Selection Save Drawing command will keep until we cover the selection process in detail (Chapter 10). Generic CADD uses the selection process extensively; you will become thoroughly familiar with it by the end of this book.

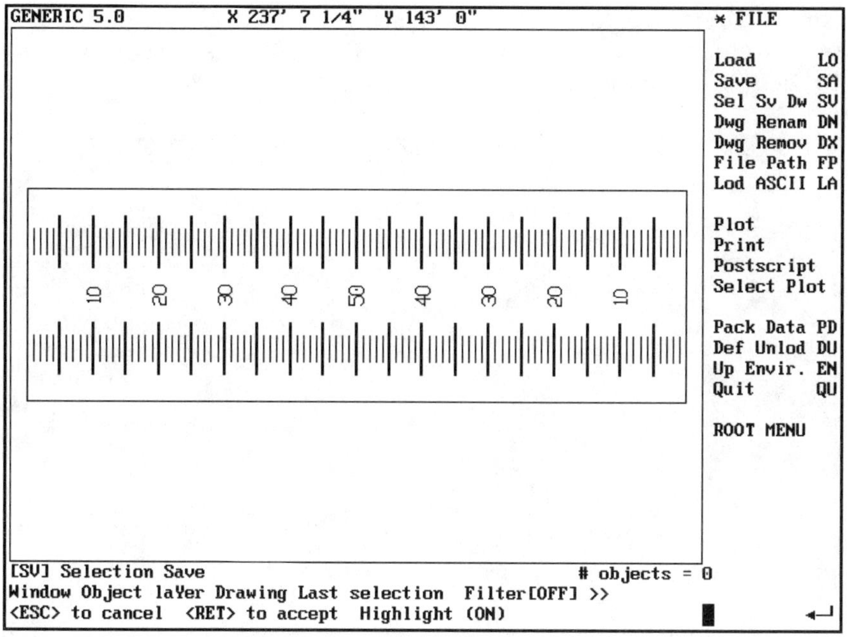

Figure 1.13: *Options available with Selection Save (SV) command.*

Layer Save (YS)

If you have divided a drawing into a number of different layers, it is possible to save the contents of an individual layer as a separate drawing file, using Layer Save (YS), found in the LAYERS menu. Selection Save Drawing also allows you to save the contents of a layer, but the two are not redundant commands. Layer Save will only save one layer, while Selection Save Drawing will let you choose several layers, plus select objects in other ways. When you use Layer Save, the command will automatically name the drawing, using either the number of the layer or the name if you have named the layer. We will come back to Layer Save when we discuss layers in detail (Chapter 10).

Options for Loading a Drawing

Once you have a drawing saved to disk, sooner or later you will want to print it, or retrieve it and make changes. Use one of the following Load commands.

Load (LO) and File Selector

Load, in the FILE menu, is the all-purpose opposite of Save. All of the file types that can be saved to disk with Save can be loaded from disk with Load. If you look near the bottom of the menu in figure 1.14, you'll see the words `File Selector`. When you select this item from the menu, Generic CADD switches away from the drawing screen to the File Selector.

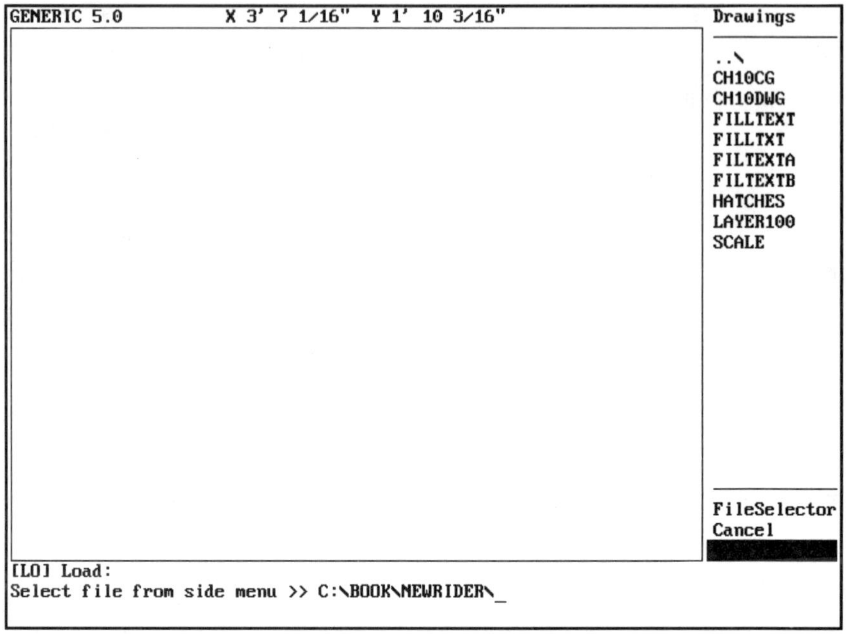

Figure 1.14. *Options available using the Load command.*

File Selector may be used to view the contents of any directory on your hard drive, making it easier to search for files. Individual files in each directory can be highlighted, with information on the file displayed at the bottom of the screen. Once you find the file you seek, File Selector can retrieve it for you. The File Selector (fig. 1.15) is available in the menu during any file loading operation. (If you are looking for the two-letter command for switching to the File Selector, don't bother. There isn't one.) As we progress, we will find other uses for File Selector, and we'll return to it often.

Drawing Load (DL)

Just as Save has an all-purpose opposite in Load, Drawing Save has a function-specific opposite in Drawing Load. If you know the name of the file you need to retrieve from disk, type **DL**, the name of the file (and directory, if different from the one listed), and press Enter. If you type **DL** and then forget the name of the file, look in the menu. All the drawing files of the current directory are listed. To select one, move the menu bar onto it, and press the second mouse button or the Home key, just as if it were a command. You may also choose to summon the File Selector, if you prefer.

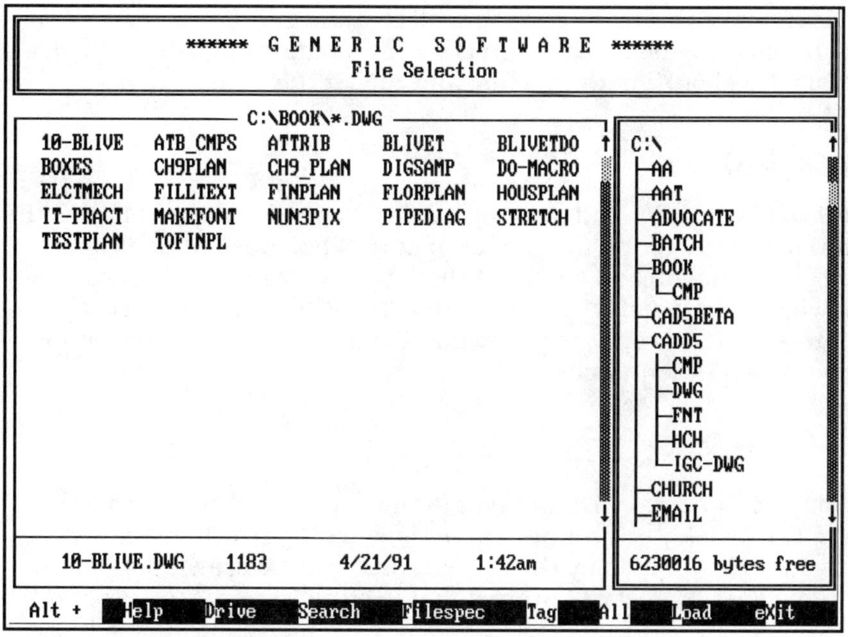

Figure 1.15. The File Selector screen.

Layer Load (YL)

If you want to add material to an existing drawing, a good way to do it is with the Layer Load command, on the LAYERS menu. When selected, Layer Load asks for a drawing file, then asks what layer of the current drawing this new drawing should be written to. Use the menu to select an unused layer, or type in a layer number at the prompt line.

Moving From One Drawing to the Next

With Generic CADD 5.0, you may often work on one drawing for a while, then switch and work on another. There are two commands that speed up this process.

Remove Drawing (DX)

To quickly and completely eliminate whatever is on-screen, use Remove Drawing, found in the FILE menu. But be absolutely sure you want to say good-bye forever to this material. Once you type **Y** to say yes to CADD's warning (`Do you really want to remove the current drawing? (Y/N) >`), the drawing is gone forever, unless you had saved it previously.

A common sequence of events for the experienced Generic CADD user can be summarized like this: Draw some, save with DS, draw some more, DS again, draw some more, DS then DX, load a new drawing, and repeat the cycle.

Drawing Rename (DN)

If you are working on a drawing, and want to create a second version of it, use the Drawing Rename command, found in the FILE menu. When used, it does not change the name of the drawing on disk, but the next time you save the drawing on the screen, it will be saved using the new name. If you are extremely concerned about protecting your work, use Drawing Rename to save several versions of the file under several different names.

Quit (QU)

If you wish to end your Generic CADD session for now, use the Quit command. Type **QU**, and CADD will ask if you want to save the current drawing. If you press **Y** for Yes, the prompt line will display the current name of the drawing. If it is correct, press Enter. Then CADD will prompt you to either press **Q** to quit or **C** to continue.

Summary

At the beginning of this chapter, we mentioned the consistent logic behind how Generic CADD commands operate. Now that you have been exposed to several commands, perhaps a bit of that logic is evident. Generally, the two-letter commands correspond directly to the name of the command or to a description of what it does. There are all-purpose commands that provide a broad range of services (Load and Save are two), and there are function-specific commands that complement the general-purpose commands (Drawing Load, Drawing Save, Layer Load, and Layer Save all focus on particular aspects of the Load/Save process). This division of labor between all-purpose commands and function-specific commands is a common theme in Generic CADD, and it provides a great deal of flexibility in how a user can get the job done.

2

Getting Ready To Draw

Nobody enjoys digging for worms before going fishing, but it is a necessary task. Some of the settings and operations we will look at in this chapter are the CADD equivalent of digging worms. We will become familiar with them, find out the best way to utilize them, and quickly move on to catching the big ones.

This chapter covers the commands and functions that have everything to do with how the drawing looks and how you organize your work, even though they don't actually create a drawing. By learning to use these commands before moving on to the actual tools of drawing, you can save some time once you start to draw.

Wise Generic CADD users take advantage of the program's layer structure, which allows a drawing to be divided up into to 256 separate layers. Using layers to organize the information in a drawing makes it easier to prepare custom versions of the drawing, and speeds up editing.

Generic CADD 5.0 offers a myriad of display options that affect color, size, visibility, and response to user input. The best use of each of these will be explained. This chapter also discusses the commands that set the units of measurement and other construction settings. Before you reach for the headache medicine, you should know that Generic CADD offers an easy way to maintain the settings you like so they may be easily repeated from project to project. This feature is known as the CADD environment, and becoming familiar with it will make your CADD work easier.

Many of the commands in this chapter function as toggle commands. Selecting the command sets its status to the opposite of what it was. For example, to turn

All Layers off, type **AL** or select the command from the Layers menu. To turn All Layers on again, type **AL** again.

Preparing Generic CADD for Use

If you are familiar with manual drafting, you know that before you draw, steps need to be taken and decisions need to be made. Choosing a sheet size, selecting the pen widths, and choosing a drawing scale are three typical decisions. Preparing to draw with Generic CADD is similar in some ways, but it's different, too. You don't select a sheet size, for example, but you do set the screen limits. Instead of pen widths, we will choose the line color and width and decide if we need to set the line type and line scale. And, as mentioned in Chapter 1, you don't need to be concerned now about drawing scale. We must also consider other aspects that have no counterpart in manual drafting. The best use of layers is one of these areas. Such things as setting elements of the screen display also have no equivalent in manual drafting.

Setting the Screen Limits (LS)

When you start a new drawing project, you generally have a good idea of the real-world size of what you are going to draw. Whether it's a house plan or a gasket, you know how big it is before you start. Generic CADD has a setting called Limits, in the UTILITIES menu, which sets the size of the on-screen view (see figs. 2.1 and 2.2). The default setting is 24" wide x 36" long. This means that when you start Generic CADD, a rectangle drawn to those dimensions will bump against the left and right sides of the screen and have some room top and bottom.

If you are drawing something small that will fit within a 24" x 36" area, then you don't need to adjust the limits unless the object is extremely small. But if you are drawing a house plan, you may want to adjust the screen limits to a multiple of 24" x 36" that will fit your entire drawing on the screen at one time. In figure 2.3, a 20' x 20' cabin fits inside a Limits setting of 240" x 360", leaving room for notations and dimensioning.

Setting the Limits provides a quick way to gain a zoomed view of the entire drawing. Generic CADD executes the Zoom Limits command faster than the Zoom All command. With Zoom Limits, CADD knows to set the screen so that it matches the size you defined with the Limits command. With Zoom All, the program must take the time to calculate the size of everything in the drawing and where it lies on the coordinate plane, and then draw the screen at a scale that will show everything. Beyond this, Limits does not limit you in any way. You can still draw anywhere on the coordinate plane, whether it appears on-screen when you do a Zoom Limits or not.

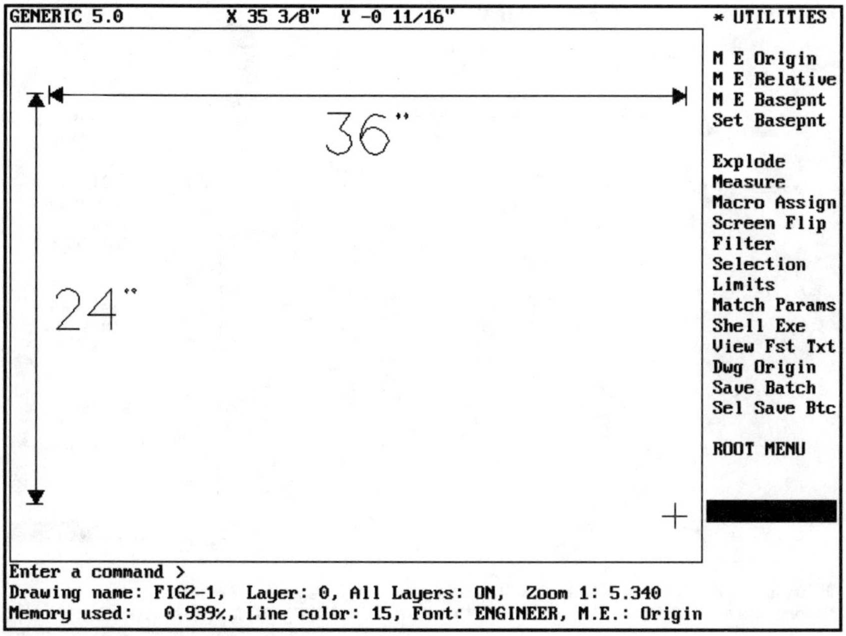

Figure 2.1: *The default screen limits are 24" x 36".*

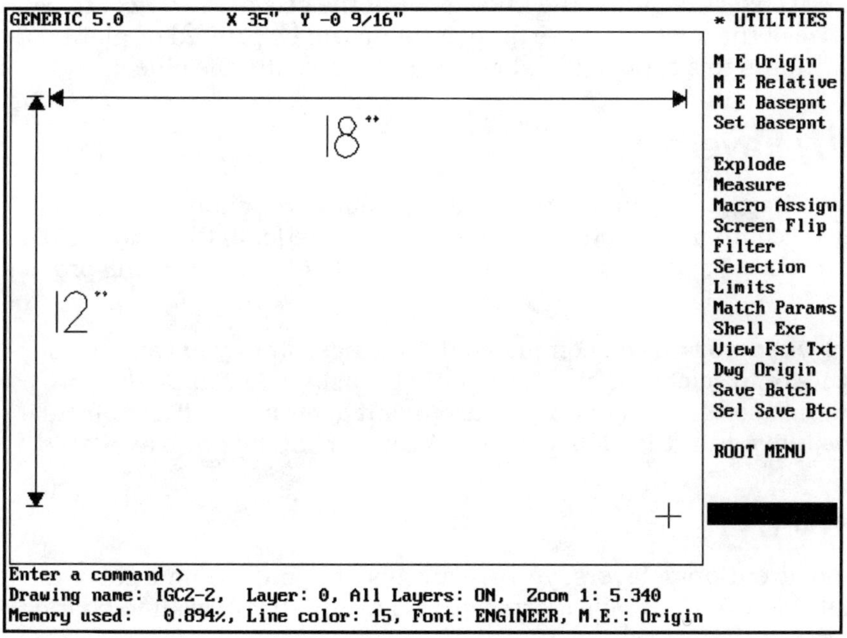

Figure 2.2: *Changing the screen limits to 12" x 18" for a small item.*

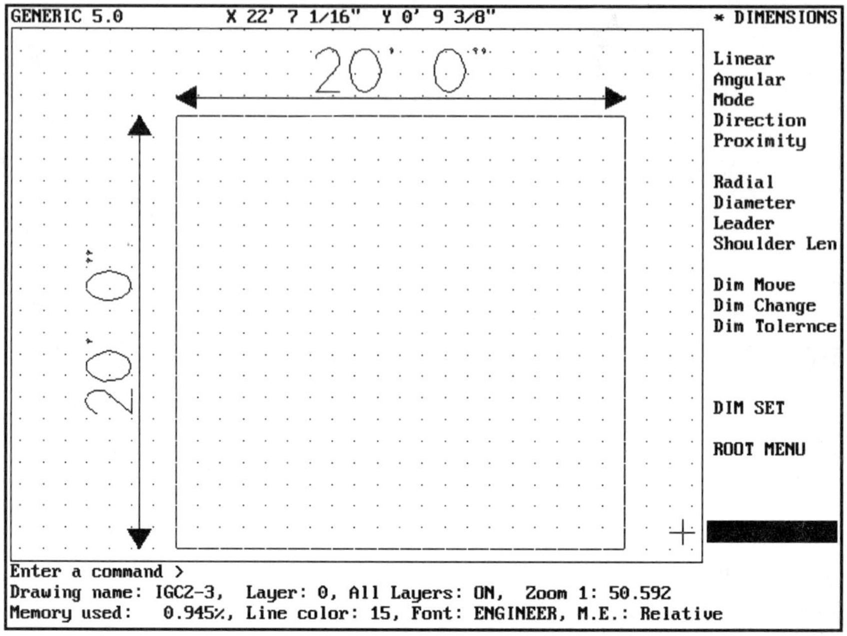

Figure 2.3: *Changing the screen limits to 240" x 360".*

Some Generic CADD users combine the knowledge of the size of the object to be drawn with the size of the sheet that the final drawing will be printed or plotted onto, and set the Limits to a ratio of the sheet size that also fits the object.

Organizing by Layers

One of the big advantages computer-aided drafting offers over manual is the use of layers. Earlier we compared layers to sheets of clear plastic. In Generic CADD, you can give each "sheet" a name, which makes it easy to divide a drawing project logically.

Layers are useful when working on complicated drawings, since you can choose to display all layers or to select which ones should be visible. Additionally, you can choose to edit all visible layers or only the current layer in use. The objects on a layer may be individually loaded or saved. A total of 256 layers is available.

Set Current Layer (YC)

Even if you pay no attention to layers, you are always drawing on some particular layer. The default that CADD always starts with is Layer 0. If you wish to change to a different layer, type **YC** or select Current Layer from the LAYERS menu. Type the number of the layer you wish to switch to, and press Enter. Any drawing you do now will be on the newly selected layer.

When you type **YC**, the menu will change to show a list of all the layers available in CADD, which is several screens long (see fig. 2.4). Instead of typing the number of the layer you wish to switch to, you can select it from the menu by moving the menu bar onto it and pressing the second button on your mouse or the Home key. This feature is best when combined with the use of Named Layers, explained below.

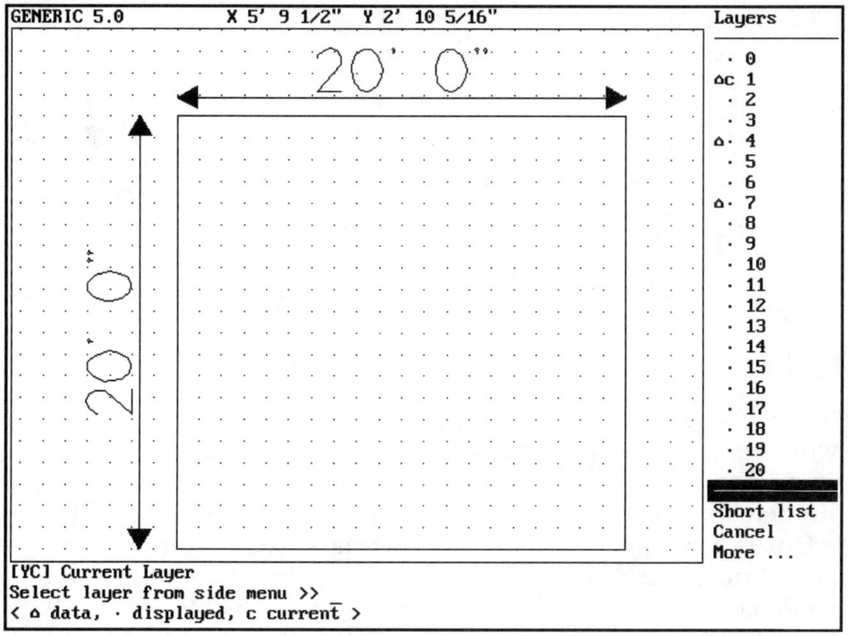

Figure 2.4: *The list of available layers.*

Since you probably don't need to see all 256 layers, you can switch the menu display to the Short List by selecting it from the menu (as in fig. 2.5). Then only the layers that have been drawn upon or named, plus the current layer, will appear in the list.

Generic CADD uses a shorthand in the menu layer list to provide you with additional information. The layer with a "c" in front of it is the current layer. Any layer with information on it will have a delta mark (Δ) in front of it. Any layer visible on-screen will have a raised dot in front of it. If you choose to use the short list, CADD ignores visible layers that lack data.

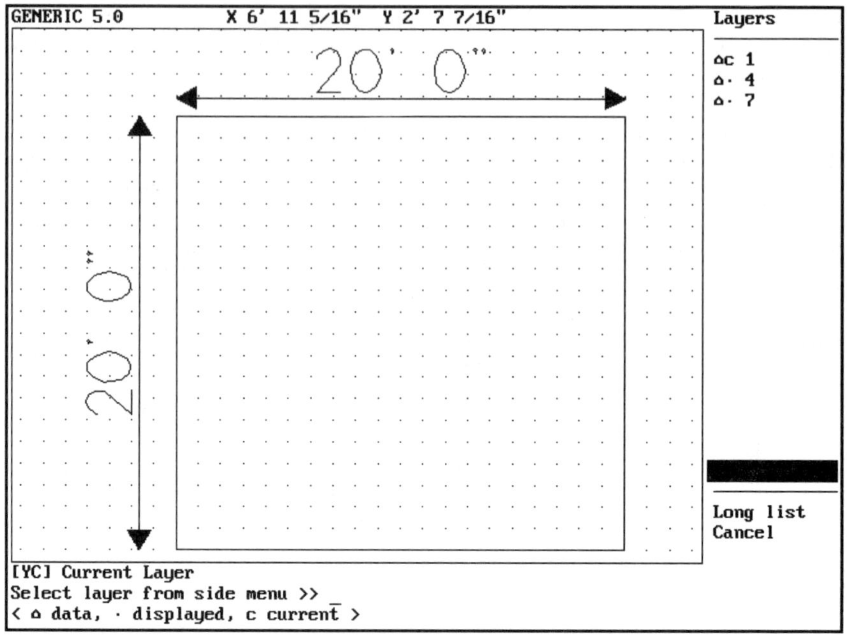

Figure 2.5. Switching to the short menu list.

All Layers Edit (AL)

As your drawing becomes more complex, you will have data on a variety of layers. (To you, it is drawings or objects—to the computer, it is data—which is why the terms are often used interchangeably in this book.) You may want to see several layers but not edit them or have to worry about affecting them as you draw. When you start Generic CADD, the All Layers Edit (AL) command is set to on; you can see that in the status lines. The items you draw will go on the current layer, but if you draw on several layers, you will be able to edit anything visible. When All Layers is off, you can still see every visible layer, but you are now limited to editing objects on the current layer.

All Layers is one of the many toggle commands in Generic CADD. To turn All Layers off, type **AL** or select the command from the Layers menu. To turn All Layers on, just type **AL** again.

Name Layer (YN)

The ability to name layers is new to Generic CADD with the release of version 5.0. It makes organizing complicated drawings much easier. Instead of drawing the plumbing on layer 5, now you can put it on the PLUMBING layer. If a layer has been named, the name shows up in the menu list instead of the number when the menu switches to display layers. If a named layer is the current layer, the name instead of the number will appear in the status lines at the bottom of the screen.

To name a layer, type **YN** or select Name from the LAYERS menu (see fig. 2.6). The prompt will ask you to select a layer to be named. Type the number or select it from the menu. Next you will be prompted to type a name for the layer, which must not exceed eight characters. Press Enter when you have typed the name.

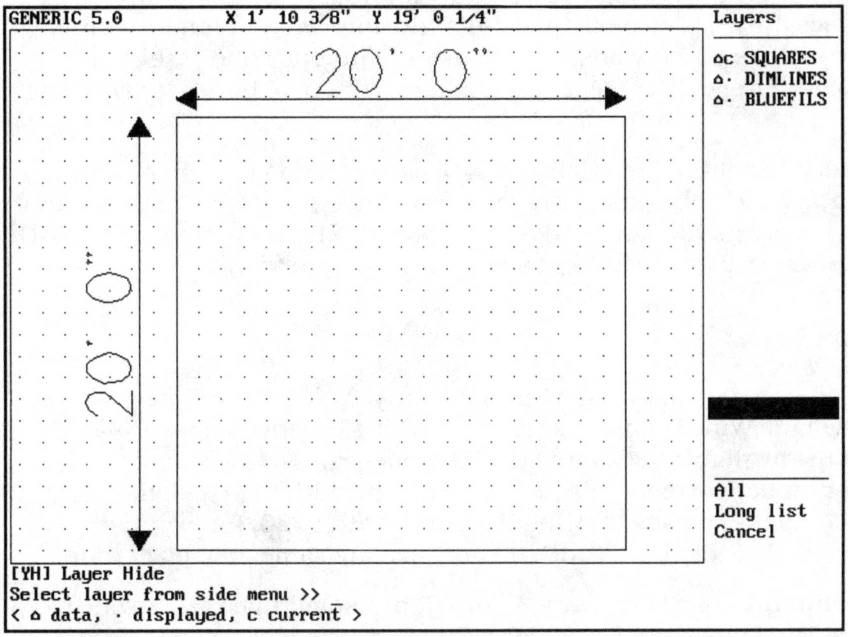

Figure 2.6. *The name of the layer appears instead of the number.*

TIP

If you plan to divide a drawing into a number of separate layers, name them ahead of time. That way, you can pre-organize the layer structure to match your needs.

Setting Entity Display Options

After you have chosen a plan for the use of layers in CADD, turn to the more visible aspects of work in CADD—how lines and other objects will be displayed.

Line Color (LC)

Unless you are using a monochrome monitor, the most obvious display setting is the line color. Most color monitors have 16 colors available; a few have 256 colors. To select a line color, type **LC** or select Line Color from the DISPLAY menu. A chart of the available colors will appear in the menu, along with the number of each color. Type the number of the color you want and press Enter, or select it from the menu. All lines drawn after you set the Line Color command will be in the new color; lines drawn previously in a different color will remain the same. To change the color of lines already on the screen, you must use one of the Change commands (Object Change, Change, Layer Change, Window Change, or Drawing Change).

It is not a good idea to set the Line Color to 0, because that is the color of the screen background on which you are drawing. Any lines you draw in Line Color 0 will be invisible on screen, but they can print to paper. (Hmmm... invisible CADD ink—doesn't appear until printed. What would that be good for?)

Line Width (LW)

Color is not the only way to distinguish lines visually. The width of lines can be adjusted with the Line Width command, in the DISPLAY menu. There are 256 possible line widths available in Generic CADD. Some samples are illustrated in figure 2.7. Each number corresponds to an on-screen width in pixels, the points of light that make up the display. Setting the Line Width to 20, for example, creates a line 20 pixels wide. Line Width 0 and 1 are the same, one pixel wide.

For most work, you will want to use Line Width 0, but sometimes other widths are of value. Very large line widths aren't very appealing to look at on-screen, beyond a certain point. The ends don't connect smoothly. Illustrators who use Generic CADD seem to have more use for very wide lines than contractors, architects, and most engineers.

The exact width of lines when printed or plotted depends on the hardware in use.

Line Type (LT)

The thin solid line is far and away the most commonly used line in CADD, but many other choices are available. The Line Type command, available in the DISPLAY menu, controls the setting of line types. Available line types are numbered 0 through 255. The default is Line Type 0, the ubiquitous thin solid line. When you select this command, the patterns of Line Types 0 through 9 appear in the menu, as shown in figure 2.8.

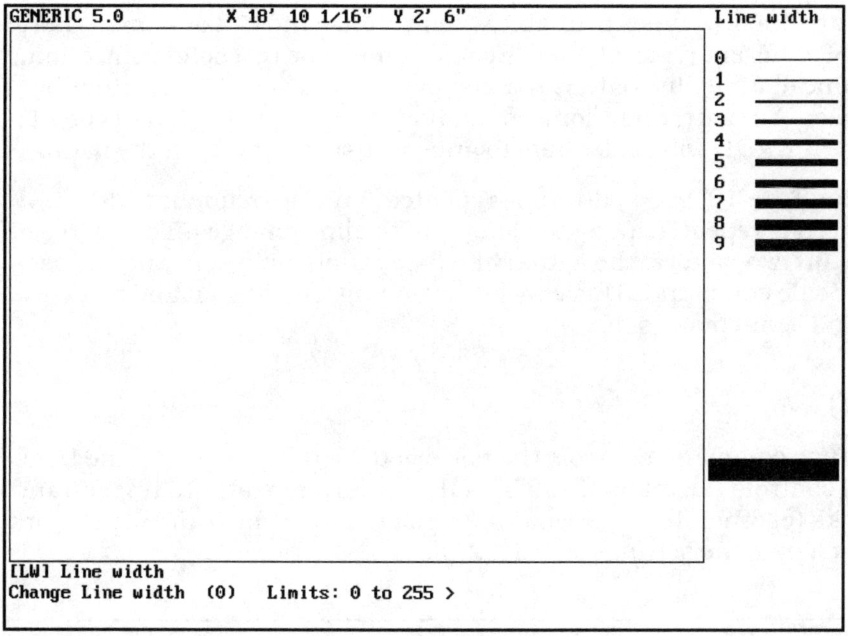

Figure 2.7: *Several possible line widths in Generic CADD.*

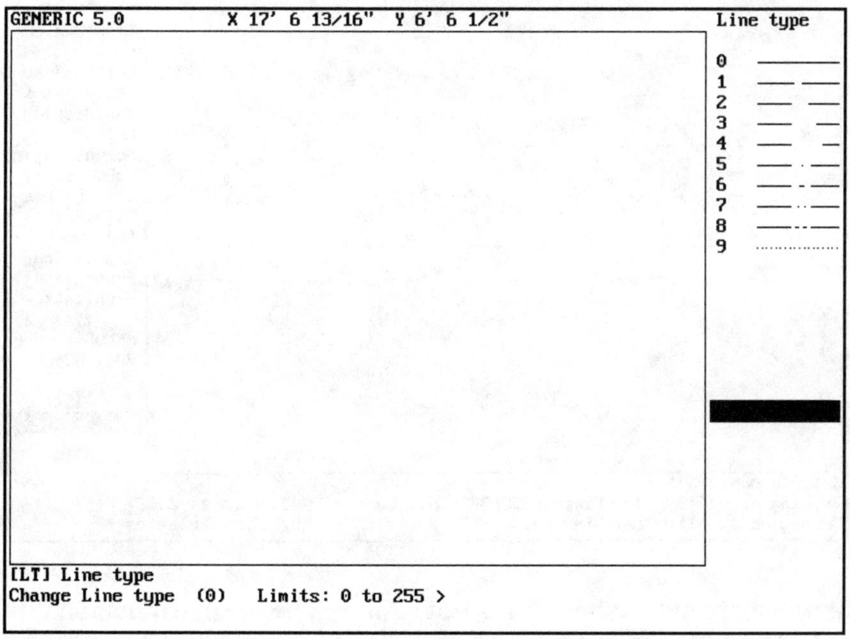

Figure 2.8: *Line Types 0 through 9, as displayed in the menu.*

Although there are 256 line types available when you use the LT command, there are not really 256 different types of lines. Besides Line Type 0, a solid continuous line, there are nine distinct line patterns. Each pattern is a specific combination of lines and spaces. No matter how long you make your lines using Line Types 1 through 9, Generic CADD will scale them to appear just as they do in the menu.

Starting with Line Type 10, each pattern is repeated, but the frequency with which each pattern is repeated along the length of the line changes. The degree of change depends on two factors: the actual line type number chosen, and the setting of the Line Scale command. This can get confusing, so hang on and work through it all, and it will make sense.

Line Scale (LZ)

While the Line Type command controls the pattern to be used for a line, the Line Scale command controls the interval at which the pattern repeats. To understand how all this works together, let's see what happens to Line Type 5 and some of its multiples as we change the settings (see fig. 2.9).

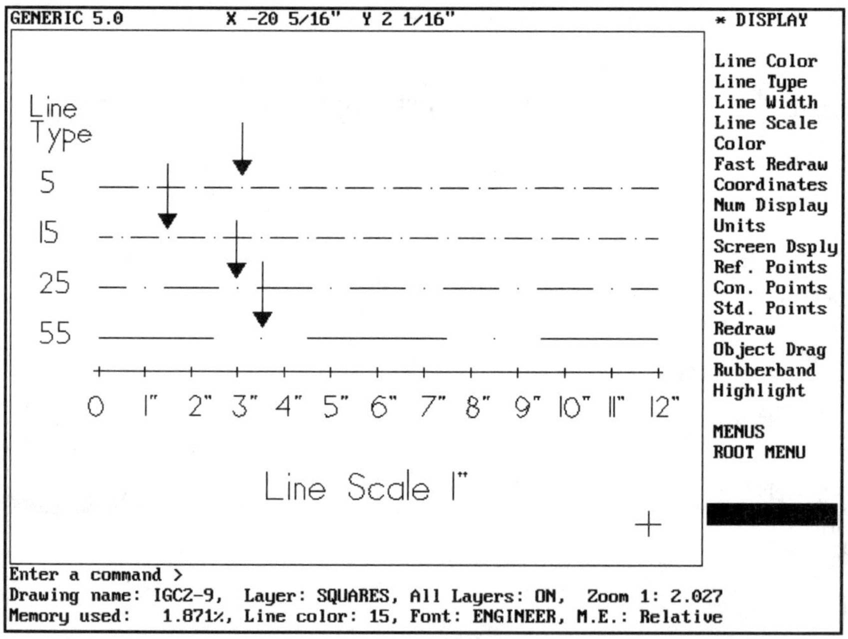

Figure 2.9: *Line types drawn using the default Line Scale setting of 1".*

Line Type 5 is a pattern of long dashes with a dot centered between each dash. Line Type 15 is the same pattern, except that now each repetition of the pattern (the dash-dot) measures one "unit" (an inch for now). To understand the meaning of line type numbers above 9, multiply the tens-place number by the basic Line Type. For example, Line Type 15 repeats its pattern every 1 unit (1"). Line Type 25 repeats one repetition of the pattern in 2 units (2")—two times Line Type 5. Line Type 55 repeats one repetition of the pattern in 5 units (5")—five times Line Type 5. Notice the arrows pointing to a dot on each line in figure 2.9 to compare the repetitions of the patterns.

Now let's add Line Scale to this. When a Line Type is selected, it looks to the Line Scale setting to determine what a "unit" is, to know how often to repeat the pattern. In figure 2.9, the unit is the default Line Scale of 1". But in figure 2.10, the Line Scale has been changed to 2". The arrows pointing to the dots have not moved, but look at how the change of Line Scale affected the lines.

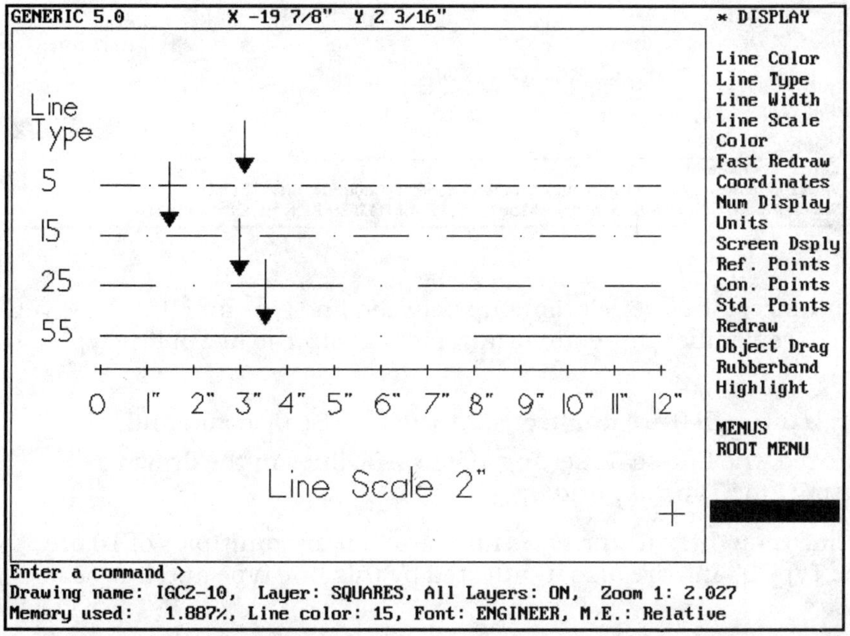

Figure 2.10: *Line types drawn using a Line Scale setting of 2".*

With a Line Scale setting of 2", each unit of repetition has doubled. Line Type 15 now repeats the dot-dash pattern one time over a distance of two inches, not one inch as it did when Line Scale was 1". Line Type 55 now repeats the pattern once over a distance of 10" instead of 5" (five times Line Type 5 times 2"). For one more example, take a look at figure 2.11, which shows the same lines as they appear under the influence of a Line Scale setting of 4".

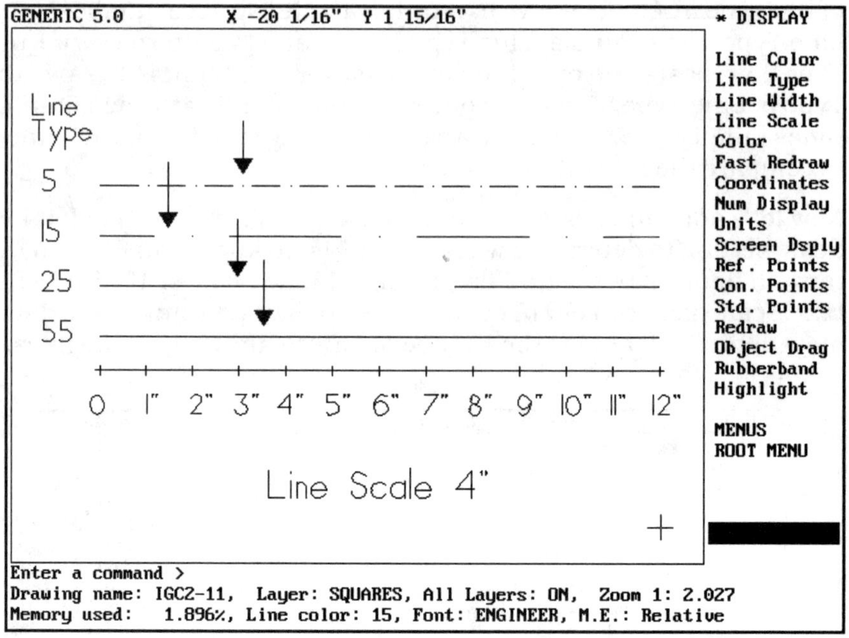

Figure 2.11: *Line types drawn using a Line Scale setting of 4".*

Even if you don't understand the relationship between line type and line scale yet, it is easy enough to remember these important facts about the use of line type and line scale.

1. Line Types 0 through 9 are unaffected by the Line Scale command.
2. When changed, the line scale setting affects ALL lines in the drawing created using Line Types 11 and up.

Here's a comforting thought: the line type numbers that are multiples of 10 are the same as Line Type 0, and are also unaffected by this line type and line scale business.

Other Color Settings (CS)

Now for something a little easier. Earlier we met the Line Color command, but there are other things in CADD that require a color setting besides lines. The Color Settings (CS) command, on the DISPLAY menu, is an all-purpose control device for color. Use it to set the color of text, dimensions, attributes, hatches, and fills as well as lines, if you like.

Setting Program Display Options

Certain commands let you customize the "look and feel" of Generic CADD. Some of these are valuable drawing aids; others appeal to personal style preferences. Since the real use of some of these settings requires an application, we will briefly explain their purpose now, and return to them as we work through the book.

Screen Display (DI)

The Screen Display command, in the DISPLAY menu, controls the color and size of the cursor and the color of the status lines (see fig. 2.12).

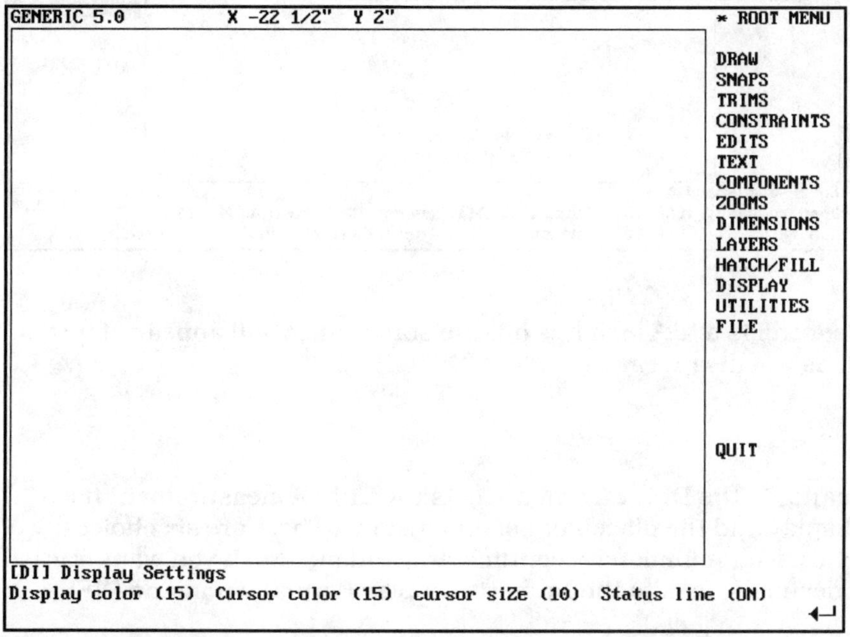

Figure 2.12: Command options available with Screen Display (DI).

Cursor size may be set to any number between 0 and the number that displays on your screen when you use this command (it varies depending on your video display hardware). The numbers refer to pixels, so a cursor size of 1 creates a cursor one pixel high and one pixel wide—in other words, barely visible. Setting the cursor size to 0 creates a cursor that stretches from top to bottom and side to side, as shown in figure 2.13.

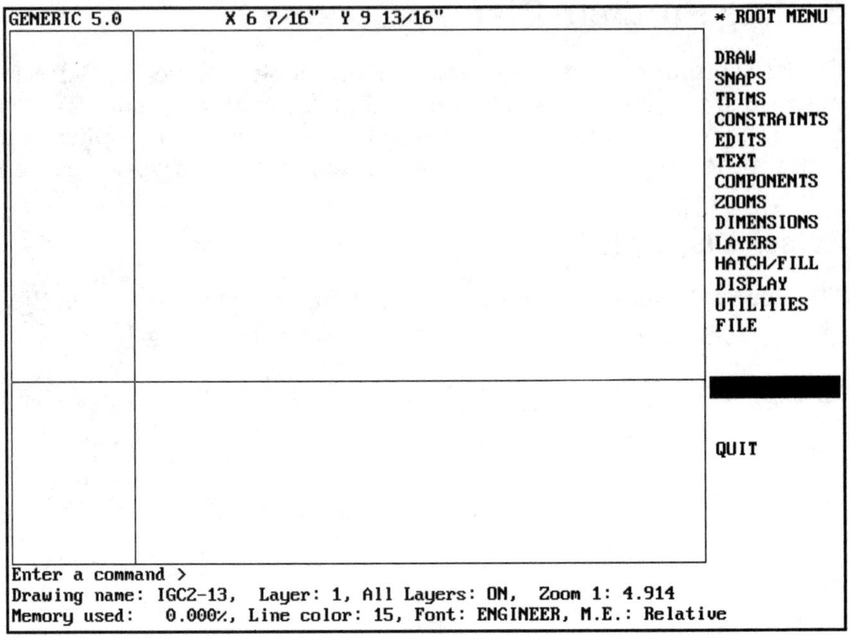

Figure 2.13: *Cursor size set to zero.*

The status line control is a toggle; if it is on, the status lines will appear. If it is off, the status lines will disappear.

Units (UN)

The Units command, in the DISPLAY menu, sets the unit of measurement used for coordinate display and the placement of dimensions. There are six choices: inches, feet/inches, feet, millimeters, centimeters, and meters. If you want fractions instead of decimals, look to the Numeric Display Format command (NF) below.

You should match the units of measurement set with this command to the choice of units you made when you configured Generic CADD. If you selected inches or another English unit of measurement, then select only English units with the Units command. If you selected a metric unit, use metrics now. It is possible to select a metric measurement for the coordinate display when an English measurement has been specified during installation. However, this can lead to roundoff errors when CADD converts between the two. The amount of error will be in the range of 1/100,000th of a unit. If your work depends on extreme accuracy, try to avoid mixing the two unit systems.

Numeric Display Format (NF)

This command controls how numbers and angles are displayed on screen, as well as the appearance of numbers placed when using CADD's dimensioning commands (see fig. 2.14).

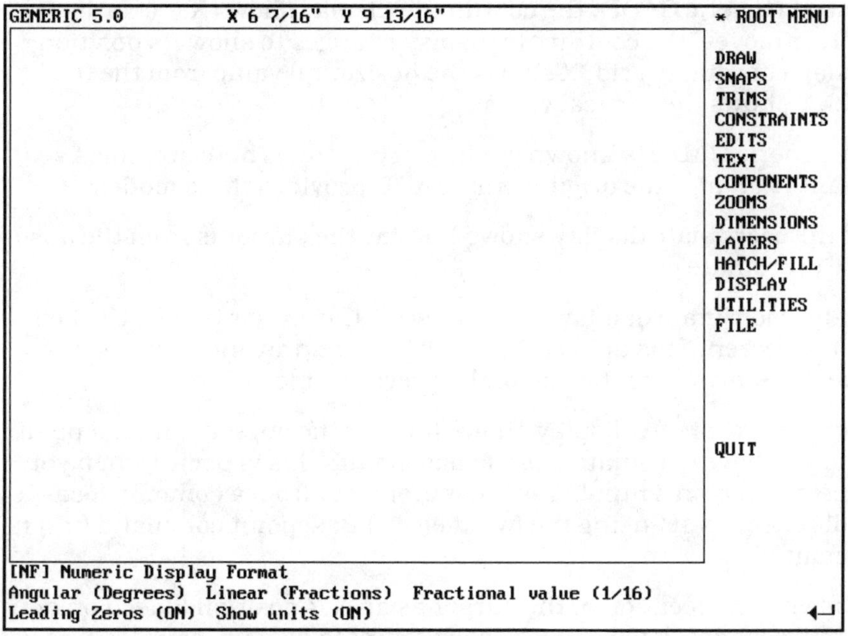

Figure 2.14: *Control options for Numeric Display Format.*

In brief, the choices and their options are:

Angular: Degrees or Deg:Min:Sec

Linear: Decimal or Fractional display

Decimal Value: (available only if Linear is set to Decimal) Sets the number of decimal places displayed, from 0 to 6.

Fractional Value: (available only if Linear is set to Fractional) Sets the choice of fractional units from 1/2" to 1/64".

Leading Zeros: A toggle. 0.112" is Leading Zeros on; .112" is Leading Zeros off.

Show Units: A toggle. Controls the display of the units sign, such as the double quote marks for inches.

Coordinate Display (DC)

The Coordinate Display command, in the DISPLAY menu, controls the setting of the coordinate display. There are two types of display and three possible reference points for either display.

When you first start Generic CADD, the coordinate display shows X,Y coordinates. As the cursor moves, the coordinate display changes to show its position along the Cartesian coordinate grid: X shows the horizontal value from the 0,0 center of the grid, Y shows the vertical value.

The 0,0 point in Generic CADD is known as the origin point. There are times when you will want to change the origin point. CADD provides three modes:

Absolute mode: the coordinate display shows how far the cursor is from the absolute center of the coordinate grid.

Relative mode: the coordinate display shows how far the cursor is from the last point placed on the screen. This mode is handy if you are drawing from a set of notes, where one line starts from the end of the previous line.

Basepoint mode: the coordinate display shows how far the cursor is from a point on the grid which you have designated as the basepoint. This is useful when you are drawing objects based on a number of measurements from a common location. The basepoint itself is set using the (what else?) Basepoint command (BP) in the UTILITIES menu.

In addition to showing the location of the cursor as an X,Y position (based on one of the three reference modes listed above), the coordinate display may also be set to polar coordinate display. Polar coordinates show the distance and angle of the cursor from the origin. As with X,Y coordinates, polar coordinates may be in absolute, relative, or basepoint mode.

For now, leave the coordinate display as it is, set to X,Y display in absolute mode. We will take advantage of the other options later.

Reference Points (PR)

Points in Generic CADD are made from small lines. There are three types of points, each with a different meaning (see fig. 2.15). The command for each is a toggle, meaning the display of the point type is either on or off.

Reference points identify text, components, solid color fills, hatches, attributes, dimensions, and the 0,0 point of the screen. If Reference Points are on, an asterisk-type marker will identify any of these items on the screen. Any item marked by a reference point may be erased, copied, scaled, moved, or changed simply by including the reference point in the command—the entire item does not have to be located first.

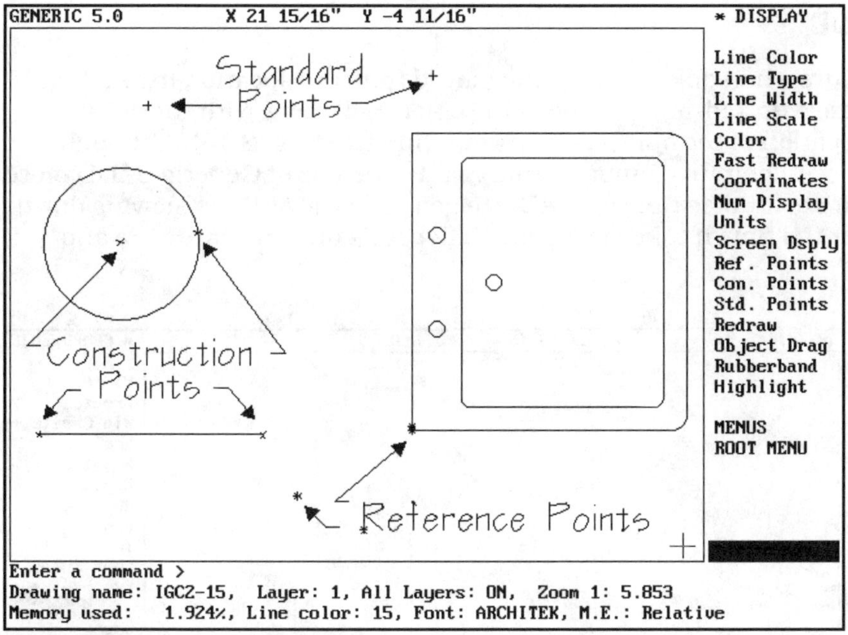

Figure 2.15: The three styles of points in Generic CADD.

Construction Points (PC)

If Construction Points are on, little x-shaped symbols will show up on the screen as you draw. They identify the endpoints of lines, the end and midpoints of arcs, the center and radius of circles, and various construction parts in curves and ellipses. It is useful to turn Construction Points on when editing, since you will often want to connect to these points to carry out various commands. They can get distracting fast, however, and are better left off unless needed.

Standard Points (PS)

Standard Points are cross-shaped symbols that may be placed anywhere by the user. They are handy to mark temporary locations you may need while drawing. Of the three styles of points, standard points are the only ones that will appear if the drawing is printed or plotted. If Standard Points are off, however, they will stay hidden.

TIP

When any of the three points are changed from off to on or vice versa, the screen must be redrawn for the change to take effect. Use Redraw (RD), located in the DISPLAY menu.

Object Drag (OD)

Object Drag occurs when objects are being moved from one location to another. If Object Drag is on, a dotted-line outline of the object will move with the cursor while the new location of the object is being identified (see fig. 2.16). Although Object Drag is a very helpful command that makes the use of Generic CADD more visual and intuitive, it takes time for CADD to generate the outline, slowing down editing. Whether the time it takes is too much depends on your hardware and your patience.

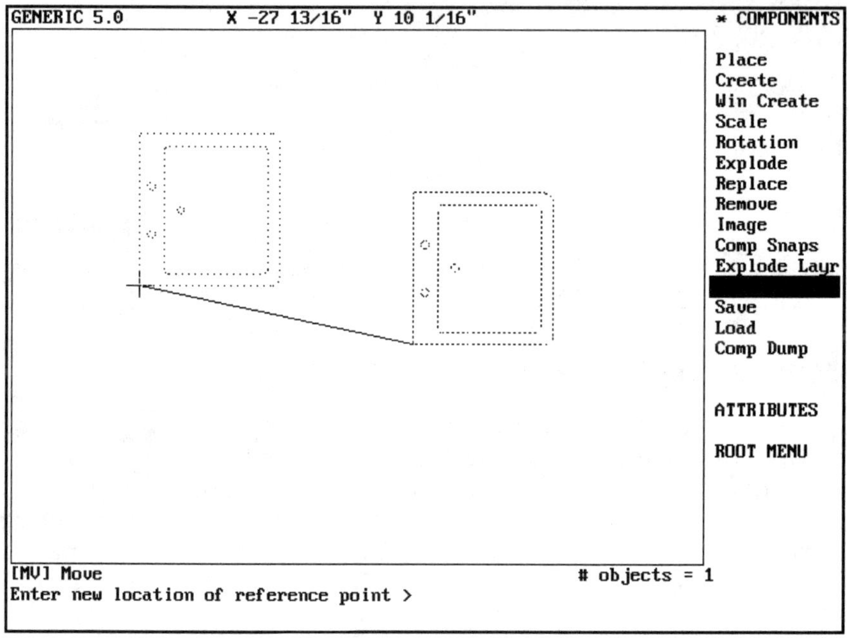

Figure 2.16: *Object Drag in use.*

Rubber-Banding (RB)

Rubber-banding occurs as you draw with the cursor. If Rubber-banding is on, a line is attached to the cursor whenever you are drawing. This helps you to see the placement of a line before you finish placing it on screen. Since Generic CADD's default operation is drawing a line, having Rubber-banding on shows you if a line will be drawn if you click the first mouse button or the Enter key to place a point. Most CADD users leave Rubber-banding on, except when running elaborate macros or batch files.

Highlight (HI)

Highlighting occurs when objects are being selected for an editing function. If Highlight is on, all selected items appear with dotted lines instead of their normal line type. As with Object Drag and Rubber-banding, Highlight makes using CADD more visual and intuitive, but it can slow the system down. Unless it bothers you, leave Highlight on.

Deleting the Menu

If you ever feel that you don't need the menu, you can remove it from the screen. Since there are times when even the most experienced CADD users rely on the menus, this may never happen to you. But we'll show you how anyway.

Display Menu (VM)

Display Menu is a toggle command. If the menu is visible when you type **VM**, the menu will disappear. If it is invisible when you type **VM**, the menu will reappear.

Remove Menu (VX)

The difference between this command and Display Menu is that Remove Menu deletes the menu from memory. Once this command is used, you must use the Load Menu (LV) command to bring it back. Remove Menu is generally used when switching from one of CADD's standard menus to a custom menu, when you don't want the custom menu to append to the standard menu. First you will remove the standard menu with Remove Menu, then load the new one.

Integrating CADD Environment Settings

If you have been reading through this long list of settings, wondering if you will have to adjust all of these every time you draw, the answer is a resounding and reassuring NO. If you know that you want to change any of these settings from their defaults, you may do so, comfortable in the knowledge that they will stay set for you. A feature of Generic CADD known as the environment is the key to your reassurance.

What Is the CADD Environment?

The CADD environment is the sum total of all settings in a drawing, except the actual objects in the drawing. When you save a drawing on disk, all the settings in effect at that time are saved with it. When you bring this drawing back into CADD again, the settings in effect when you saved it are returned to the program, even if you had previously set some of them to something else.

An exception to this rule occurs if you are loading a drawing and there is already a drawing on the screen. Generic CADD will not replace an active environment with another. This remains true even if a font is loaded into memory or erased objects are in CADD's memory available to be redrawn with the Undo or Unerase commands.

System settings, like file paths and the setting for printing and plotting, are not saved with the display and drawing control settings. They are saved in a separate file on disk, called ENVIRON.FIL.

Environment Save (EN)

If you want the settings you have specified to be active whenever you start a new drawing, use the Environment Save command, located on the FILE menu. This command saves all display and drawing control settings to a file on disk called GCADD.DWG. Whenever you start Generic CADD without specifying a drawing to be loaded, CADD looks to GCADD.DWG to know what settings should be in effect.

Environment Save When Quitting

In addition to saving the current environment with the Environment Save command, it is possible to save the environment when quitting CADD. After you type **QU** for Quit, and you have answered **Y**es or **N**o to saving the current drawing, Generic CADD asks you to type **Q** to quit the program and return to DOS, or to type **C** to continue to use CADD. There is a third option that is not shown on the screen. Type **E** and CADD will ask you if you want to save the current environment. Type **Y** for yes, and the environment will be saved as part of the current drawing, as well as updating the GCADD.DWG file. You may then proceed to exit CADD.

Using Multiple Environments

If you regularly switch between two or more distinct environments as your knowledge of CADD increases, it will save you time if you create a dummy drawing file for each one. Draw one line on the screen, then set all the settings just the way you want. Save the drawing, and the settings will be part of it. For each distinct style of environment you need, create a dummy drawing file for each. When you need a particular environment for a project, load the correct dummy file, erase the one line, and go to work on your drawing. Use the Drawing Rename (DN) command to change the name of the dummy file to another name.

Summary

While a variety of settings control how Generic CADD looks and how it responds to your input, they are all linked in what is known as the CADD environment. Once you determine your needs and preferences, you can use the CADD environment to transfer this look and feel to every project. You do not have to set each possible display and response command before you start to use Generic CADD 5.0. The defaults provided are usually acceptable.

We are done with the preliminaries. Starting with the next chapter, we move on and begin actually drawing. Understanding these preliminary steps before you draw gives you a feeling for the context of the drawings you will create.

3

Graphic Entities

Enough of display settings and multiple environments. You bought Generic CADD for drawing, so let's draw. In this chapter, you will become familiar with the basic commands that actually draw all the objects you will ever create in Generic CADD. In later chapters, you will learn to edit, embellish, and annotate, but here is where it all starts.

Manual drafting can be considered the stepchild of formal geometry. The building blocks of drafting are primitive objects defined by their geometric characteristics: lines, arcs, circles, ellipses, rectangles, regular polygons, and curves. Using the computer's ability to calculate rapidly, CADD programs are able to automate the construction of these primitive objects. In Generic CADD 5.0, the name of the object and the name of the command are one and the same, although in some cases there is more than one way to draw the objects (Two-Point Arc or Circle and Three-Point Arc or Circle are examples). Commands to draw straight lines, arcs, circles, ellipses, polygons, Bézier curves, and complex curves are all available in Generic CADD.

DRAW Menu Commands

This will be a relatively short chapter, because the basic drawing commands are limited in their usefulness without a knowledge of Generic CADD's many drawing aids. A few drawing aids will be introduced in this chapter, but many more are waiting. Nonetheless, a firm understanding of drawing tools in Generic CADD is the key to your success. These commands, all located on the DRAW menu, are the essence of Generic CADD.

The Point of Points

In the last chapter, you saw that Generic CADD has three kinds of points that are displayed on the screen: construction points, reference points, and standard points. Construction and reference points are by-products of the objects with which they associate, but standard points exist in a drawing only because you place them there. They can be used as markers, to locate a position you need to identify to draw something else, or perhaps to show the corners of a sheet.

While standard points are primarily for your benefit, construction points and reference points are as much for CADD's benefit as they are for yours. Every object that you draw using the draw tools is stored by CADD in a database (think of it as the drawing file). When you draw a line, CADD records the type of object and the coordinate locations of each end of the line. The construction points that gleam at each end of the line (if the display of construction points is turned on) mark the position of the points that CADD needs to know in order to save the position and nature of the object in the drawing database. For circles, CADD records the location of the center and the endpoint of the radius, again needing only two points to create the object. For arcs, CADD needs three points: the center of the arc and the beginning and end points of that portion of the circumference which makes up the arc.

Reference points, which identify objects and drawing elements that will be discussed, are also stored in the database to identify the location of the object on the coordinate grid.

When Points Become Lines

If you haven't already done so, start up Generic CADD. When you get to the drawing screen, move the cursor to about the center of the screen and press Enter or the first mouse button. Generic CADD places a construction point at that spot. Keep moving the cursor, and notice that a line trails behind the cursor, connected to that first construction point (that's the rubber-banding described in the last chapter). Type **RB** to turn this rubber-banding feature on or off.

Now press Enter again. You have just drawn a line. Whenever two points are located on the screen, and Generic CADD is given no additional information, the program places a line between them. Thus the Line command is Generic CADD's default operation.

Line (LI)

If you want to specifically tell Generic CADD to draw a line, you can do so by using the Line command. Despite the fact that most of the objects in nearly every CADD drawing are straight lines, this command is seldom invoked in Generic

CADD. That's because it is much easier to use the default line-drawing mode, moving the cursor and pressing Enter or the first mouse button.

Line is unique among Generic CADD commands in that once invoked, it continues to operate until you specifically stop it or execute another command. Again, that's because it is the default command. To end Generic CADD's automatic line-drawing mode, press Esc or "click" with the second mouse button on a blank line in the menu, which sends a Pen Up command. If you like using two-letter commands, you can type **PU** at the keyboard at any time to end automatic line-drawing mode.

NOTE

To make things simpler in the rest of the book, add "click" to your CADD vocabulary. Whenever the instructions tell you to click somewhere in the drawing window, press mouse button number one. Press Enter to achieve the same effect if you don't have a mouse or digitizer. Sometimes you will be asked to "click" in the menu. Always use the second mouse button to select items in the menu; use the Home key if you lack a pointing device.

Individual Line (L1)

You can draw a straight line in Generic CADD without having to turn off the command when finished. Individual Line draws just one straight line—no continued rubber band after the second point is placed, no need to press Esc or type **PU**. Individual Line is handy when selecting commands from the draw menu with the mouse, and you need to draw one (just one!) line. It's fast to click on the command name in the menu, place the points, and move on to the next task without having to turn off the Line command.

As you go through the introductions to the draw commands, take time to experiment with them. A few tricks, which really belong with the information in the chapters ahead, will also be presented to make life easier.

The Individual Line Command (L1)

Prompt	*Input*	*Description*
`Command`	**DXY**	Erases all objects on screen
`Command`	Click on DRAW in ROOT menu	Moves to DRAW menu
`Command`	Click on Individual Line	Selects the command

The Individual Line Command (L1)—continued

Prompt	*Input*	*Description*
`Starting point`	Move cursor to left side of screen and click	Places first point of line
`Enter next point on line`	Move cursor to top right portion of screen and click	Places endpoint of line

Watch what happens when you draw a line this time, taking advantage of a Generic CADD drawing technique. The results are shown in figure 3.1.

`Command`	Press Spacebar	Repeats the last command (L1)
`Starting point`	Move cursor a little below the start of first line and click	Places first point of new line
`Enter next point on line`	Hold down Ctrl as you move cursor to right side of screen and click	Places endpoint of second line

Holding down the Control key (Ctrl) is a way to constrain the cursor temporarily. When Ctrl is down, the cursor can only move at right angles. This useful function is part of Generic CADD's ortho mode features, described in detail later.

Generic CADD is designed to take advantage of three-button mice. So far, you have used the first button to place points on the drawing, and the second button to select items from the menu. Now use the third button. What, your mouse only has two buttons? Don't worry. Generic CADD is sensitive to the needs of handicapped mice. You can compensate for the missing third button by holding down the Shift key and clicking the first mouse button whenever the exercises call for the use of the third mouse button.

Now draw a line to connect the start points of the two lines on the screen. To create clean connections, try a snap command, Snap to Nearest Point (NP), available on the third mouse button. Snap is a command that causes the cursor to seek a specific place and connect to it. In this case, tell the cursor to connect to the nearest construction point. Doing this when drawing a line has the same effect as pressing the first button: it causes the line to start or end at that point.

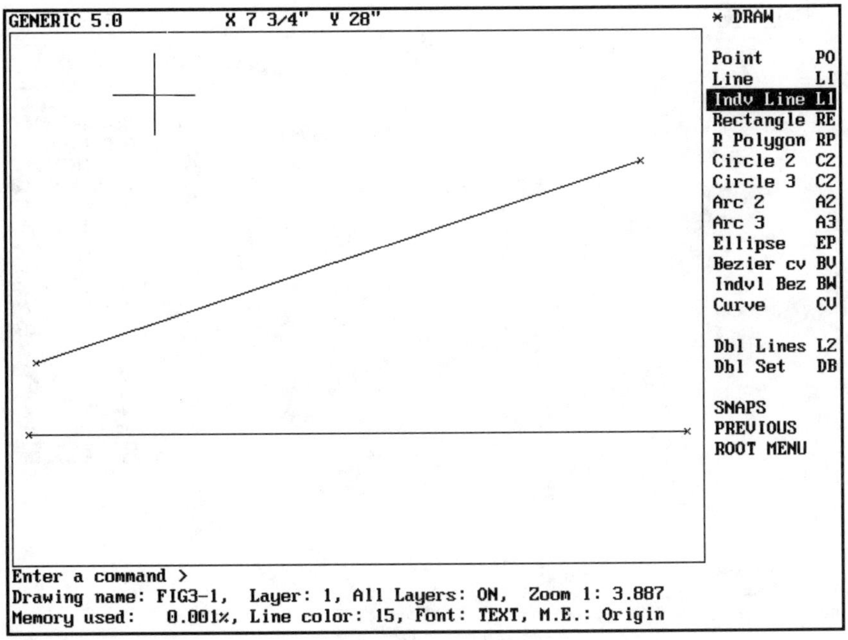

Figure 3.1: *Two lines drawn using the Individual Line (L1) command.*

Remember, if you have a two-button mouse, press Shift and the first mouse button instead when asked to click the third mouse button. If you have no pointing device, type **NP**.

Drawing a Line

Prompt	*Input*	*Description*
`Command`	Press Spacebar	Repeats the last command (L1)
`Starting point`	Move cursor close to starting point of first line and press third mouse button	Starts the new line by snapping to the left end of the first line drawn
`Enter next point on line`	Move cursor down to the starting point of second line and press third mouse button	Finishes this line by snapping to the bottom line on the screen (see fig. 3.2)

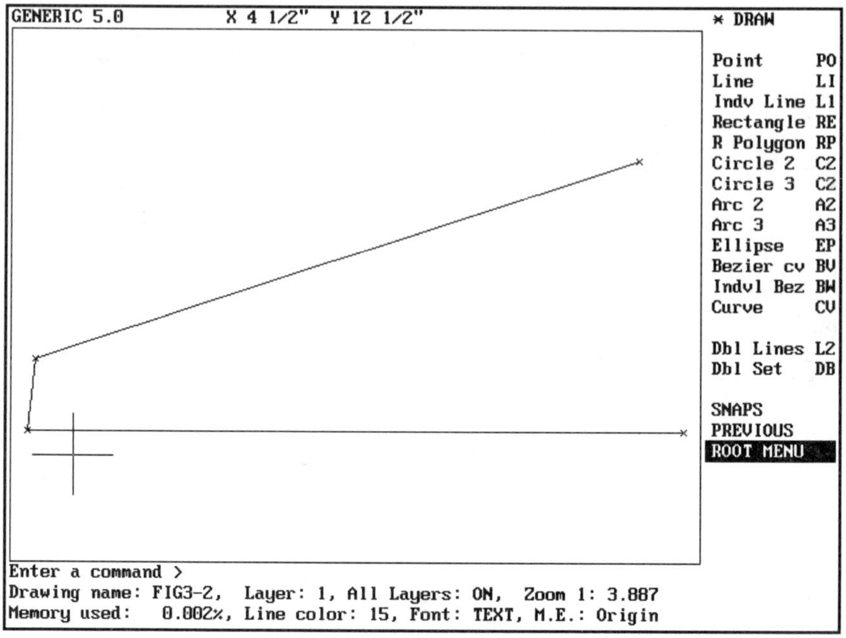

Figure 3.2: *Using Snap to connect the first two lines with a third.*

Drawing Arcs and Circles

A straight line, you may remember from geometry classes, is the shortest distance between two points. Another way to connect two points is by placing them on the path of a circle. Such a line, if it does not form a complete circle, is known as an arc.

Generic CADD offers three ways to draw an arc. One of them, the Four-Point Arc command, is not documented in the *Generic CADD Reference Manual* or listed in the DRAW menu.

Two-Point Arc (A2)

The Two-Point Arc command is used to draw an arc when you know the length of the arc's radius. To use this command, you start by selecting the center of the radius (Snap to Nearest Point is often used for this). Next, move the cursor to the location where the arc is to begin, and click to set the start of the arc. To finish the arc, move the cursor to the point where you want the arc to end, and click to select the end point.

Now try placing an arc on the screen, using the Two-Point Arc command. You'll also learn another drawing technique, one you can use in a variety of situations.

Using the Two-Point Arc Command

Prompt	*Input*	*Description*
`Command`	Type **A2** or move the menu bar to 2-Point Arc and click	Starts the Two-Point Arc command
`Enter center of arc`	Move cursor to center of screen and click	Sets the location of the center of the arc (see fig. 3.3)
`Enter start of arc`	Hold down Ctrl while using the left arrow key to move cursor left a little: type **10**, press Enter	Sets the radius to be 10" long
`Enter the end of the arc`	Hold down Ctrl and use the right arrow key or mouse to move cursor just to right of arc, and click	Sets the direction and end of the arc

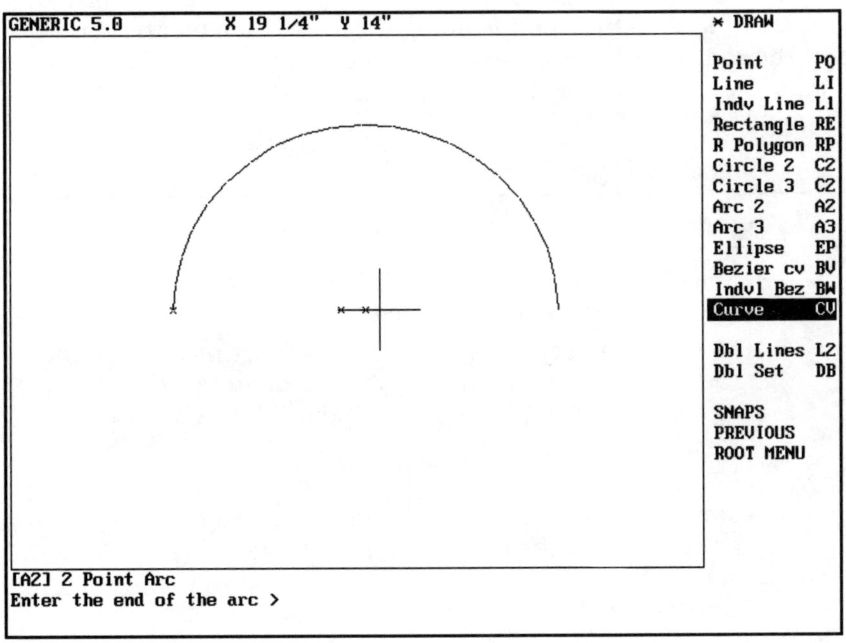

Figure 3.3: *Setting the end-point of an arc using Two-Point Arc.*

You typed a number to set the radius, defining it precisely. Any time the cursor needs to move from one point to another and you know the exact distance, you can type the number. CADD uses the direction you move the cursor towards as the true direction, or heading, of the line and then travels the distance you specify. Using this technique with Two-Point Arc does the same job as the drawing tip associated with Two-Point Arc in the *Generic CADD Reference Manual*, but in fewer keystrokes.

Notice that it was not necessary to define the endpoint of the arc with precision. Generic CADD already knew the radius, so there was no question as to the path of the arc. All you had to do was move the cursor to a location that would define a line between the center point and the endpoint. CADD then drew the arc so it stopped at a point on that line.

Two-Point Arc is designed to be used when you know the radius of the arc and the two endpoints. The next arc, Three-Point Arc, is for situations where you don't know the radius exactly.

Three-Point Arc (A3)

In drawing an arc using the Three-Point Arc command, you identify a point that is the start of the arc, a point that is somewhere along the arc, and an endpoint for the arc. You are literally placing three points along the arc, which means you don't need to know the radius as long as you know where you want the arc to go. In the steps that follow, you will draw a Three-Point Arc that attaches to two points along the first arc (see fig. 3.4).

Drawing a Three-Point Arc

Prompt	*Input*	*Description*
`Command`	Select Arc 3 from the menu, or type **A3**	Starts the Three-Point Arc command
`Enter the start of the arc`	Move the cursor toward the construction point along the first arc; press the third mouse button or type **NP**	Sets the starting point of the arc by attaching to the midpoint of the first arc
`Enter a point on the arc`	Move the cursor down a little toward the right end of first arc; press Enter or click	Sets a point along the span of the arc
`Enter the end of the arc`	Move the cursor to the right end of the first arc; press the third mouse button or type **NP**	Attaches the end of the arc to the right end of the first arc

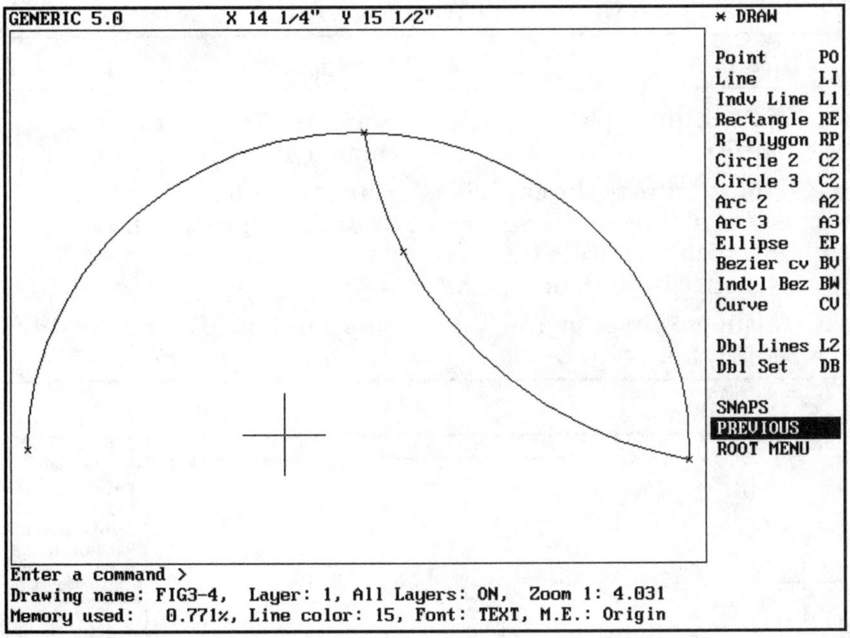

Figure 3.4: *Using Three-Point Arc to draw an arc.*

Four-Point Arc (A4)

This command was dropped as a documented command with the release of version 5.0 of Generic CADD; it existed in previous versions. In virtually every situation where you might use it, Three-Point Arc will also work, and with fewer keystrokes. When requested (by typing A4, since it is not on the menu), the command asks for the center of the arc (same as A3). It then asks for the start of the arc (same as A3), then requests that you identify a point along the arc. Finally the command asks you to enter the end point of the arc (same as A3). The only difference in operation between Three-Point Arc and Four-Point Arc is the request for a point along the arc. Since you have defined the radius, this point may or may not be accurate. Generic CADD will adjust the points you enter so that the arc remains a true portion of a circle when drawn.

Two-Point Circle (C2)

Two-Point Circle works just like Two-Point Arc, except you don't have to specify an endpoint. Just click to set the center of the circle, and move the cursor to show the radius and set a point.

You will use the construction method you used with Two-Point Arc to draw a circle with this command (see fig. 3.5). The right end of the arc is the center of the circle.

Drawing a Circle with Two-Point Arc

Prompt	*Input*	*Description*
`Command`	Click on "2-point circle" in the menu or type **C2**	Starts the Two-Point Circle command
`Enter center of circle`	Move cursor close to left end of largest arc on screen and press third mouse button, or type **NP**	Sets the center of the circle by snapping to the end of an arc
`Enter a point on the circle`	Nudge cursor in any direction, type **5**	Sets a radius of 5", draws the circle

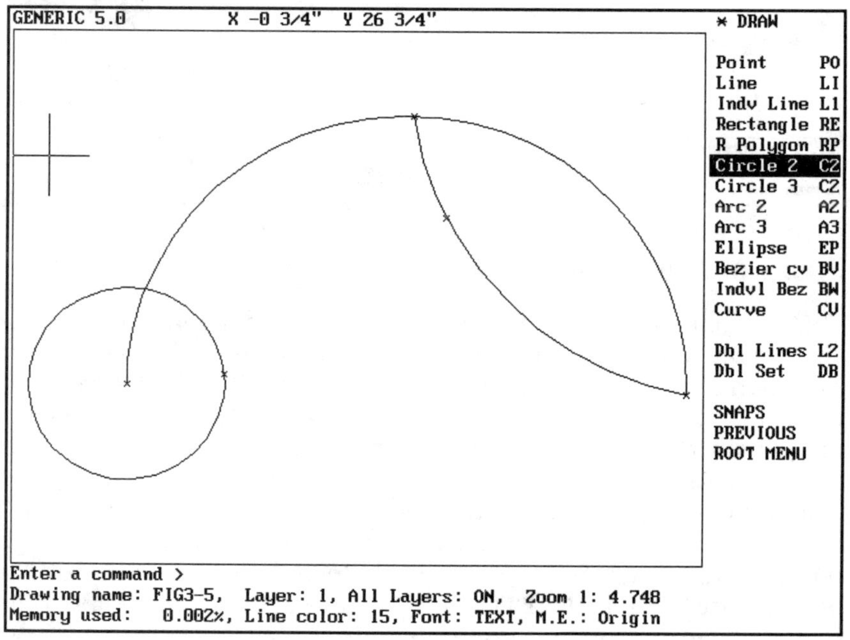

Figure 3.5: *Drawing a circle using Two-Point Circle command.*

Three-Point Circle (C3)

Three-Point Circle is useful when you know part of the path for the circle, but you don't know the location of the center point (which means you don't know the radius). When you enter this command, Generic CADD prompts you to enter three points, one at a time. After you place the first two, CADD's rubber-banding effect shows you what the circle will look like if the location of the cursor is the third point placed. When the third point is entered, Generic CADD draws the circle.

Be careful that you don't enter three points in a straight line. This can have unpredictable results. If the three lines are *almost* in a straight line, you will define a very large circle.

Drawing a Three-Point Circle

Prompt	*Input*	*Description*
`Command`	**DXY**	Erases the previous drawing
`Command`	**C3**	Starts the Three-Point Circle command
`Enter first point on circle`	Move cursor to left side of screen, click or press Enter	Places the first point on the circle on the left side of the screen
`Enter second point on circle`	Move cursor to the right, click or press Enter	Places a point that will be on the circumference of the circle
`Enter third point on circle`	Move cursor up, click or press Enter	Places a third point, which defines the circumference of the circle

Drawing Ellipses (EP)

The ellipse is an interesting shape. It isn't just a closed curve, and yet it isn't a circle, either. Geometrically, the ellipse is defined by the path of a point moving so that it is always the same distance from two points. The ellipse is a popular entity in engineering applications, and it finds some use among architects and construction professionals to define the shape of basins.

There is only one Ellipse command, and only one way to define the points on the ellipse, but two choices in how the ellipse is defined in the CADD database. To place an ellipse when you select the Ellipse command, you define two axes. The first is called the major axis, and it sets the length of the ellipse. The actual ellipse will pass through the endpoints of this axis line. The second axis, which Generic CADD defines as the minor axis, sets the width of the ellipse. You may draw the minor axis anywhere up and down the length of the major axis. When you have defined the width, select the point, and Generic CADD draws the ellipse.

Construction Ellipse

When you have defined both axes of the ellipse, Generic CADD asks if you want the ellipse to be a True ellipse or a Construction ellipse. If you select the Construction option, Generic CADD draws the ellipse using four connecting arcs. The advantage of selecting a Construction ellipse is that the endpoints of each arc can be selected later for editing the shape of the ellipse. Additionally, the arc lines can be broken if necessary, a CADD editing technique in which part of a line is removed.

True Ellipse

A True ellipse is constructed from one line and cannot be broken later. Both the True and Construction ellipses can be filled with solid color using Generic CADD fill commands or cross-hatched using the hatch routines. The advantage in using the True option is that the Construction ellipse compromises the true ellipse shape to allow for construction by four arcs. If you draw a construction ellipse, then change line colors or line types and draw a true ellipse over the top of it (using Snap to Nearest Point to select the endpoints of the axis), you will see that the Construction ellipse is too narrow on the sides, too pointed on the ends. Figure 3.6 shows the two types of ellipses. On the right a True ellipse has been drawn, in dotted lines, over the top of a Construction ellipse, in solid lines.

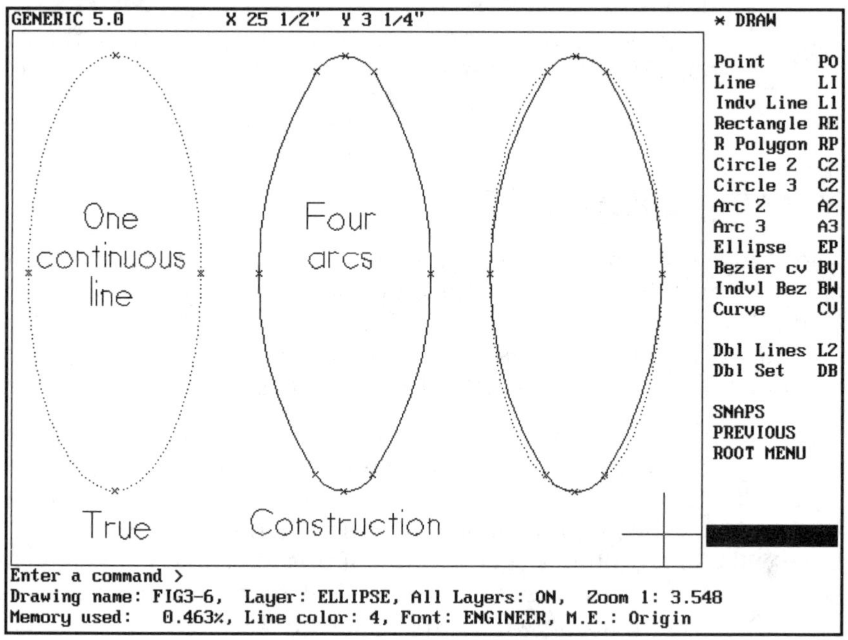

Figure 3.6: *The two types of ellipses, True and Construction.*

Drawing Curves

Because of the precise, mathematical nature of Generic CADD, and the precision drawing it can do, the program lacks a freehand drawing mode. This is somewhat compensated for, however, by the two curve commands available: Bézier Curve and Complex Curve.

Bézier Curves (BV) and (BW)

Bézier curves are named after the French mathematician who first described them. They are ideal for creating shapes where the curves are irregular (see fig. 3.7). Each segment of the curve has two control points, not on the curve. These control points help to define the shape of the curve; if you later move these control points with commands like Move Point (MP) or the special Bézier Edit (BE) command, you can change the shape of the curve. When you draw a Bézier curve, Generic CADD's rubber-band feature makes placing the curves a visual, intuitive process; the curves flex and bend as you move the cursor. There are two Bézier curve commands. Bézier Curve (BV) is used to draw a series of curves, as in the exercise below. Single Bézier (BW) is for drawing one curved segment. Compare the use of these two commands to the use of Line (LI) vs. Individual Line (L1).

Drawing a Bézier Curve

Prompt	*Input*	*Description*
`Command`	Type **BV** or select Bézier Cv from the menu	Starts the Bézier Curve command
`Enter first point`	Move cursor to left side of screen and click	Sets first point on curve
`Enter next point`	Move cursor down and click	Sets next point, draw first curve segment.
`Enter next point`	Continue moving the cursor and clicking to set points (press Esc to stop)	Draws a curve with many segments (see fig. 3.7)

Complex Curves (CV)

Complex curves are also known as *spline* curves. They are the automated equivalent of using splines, flexible wooden or plastic strips, to create curves. While Bézier curves are good for irregularly shaped curved lines, use the Complex Curve command to create smoother, more natural-shaped curves. The command is simple to use. After typing CV or selecting Complex Cv from the menu, click to place points on the screen that will define sections of the curve. When you're finished, type **PU** for Pen Up (clicking a blank line in the menu also issues the Pen Up command). You cannot press Esc to end the Complex curve as you did for Bézier. The reason is that the complex curve you are drawing is one object, while the Bézier command drew several curves in succession. Pressing Esc to end the Bézier Curve command only stopped the last curve from being drawn. If you pressed Esc to finish the complex curve, the last curve drawn—the ONLY curve—would be reversed, and you would be left with nothing.

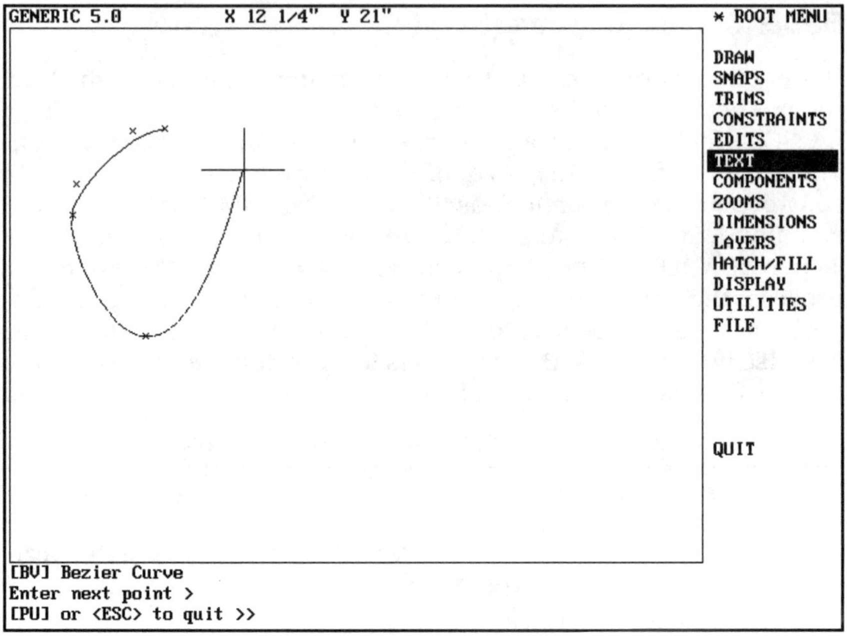

Figure 3.7: *Completed Bézier curves.*

Drawing a Spline Curve

Prompt	*Input*	*Description*
`Command`	Type **CV** or select Complex Cv from the menu	Starts the Complex Curve command
`Enter a point on the curve`	Move the cursor and click	Sets the first point on the curve
`Enter a point on the curve`	Continue moving cursor, clicking to place points (to finish the curve, type **PU** or click on a blank line in menu)	Completes the curve (see fig. 3.8)

Drawing Polygons

Generic CADD provides two commands for drawing polygons: Rectangle and Regular Polygon. The Rectangle command is heavily used, since so many things seem to have four-sided objects in them. It has one limitation, which Regular Polygon can overcome.

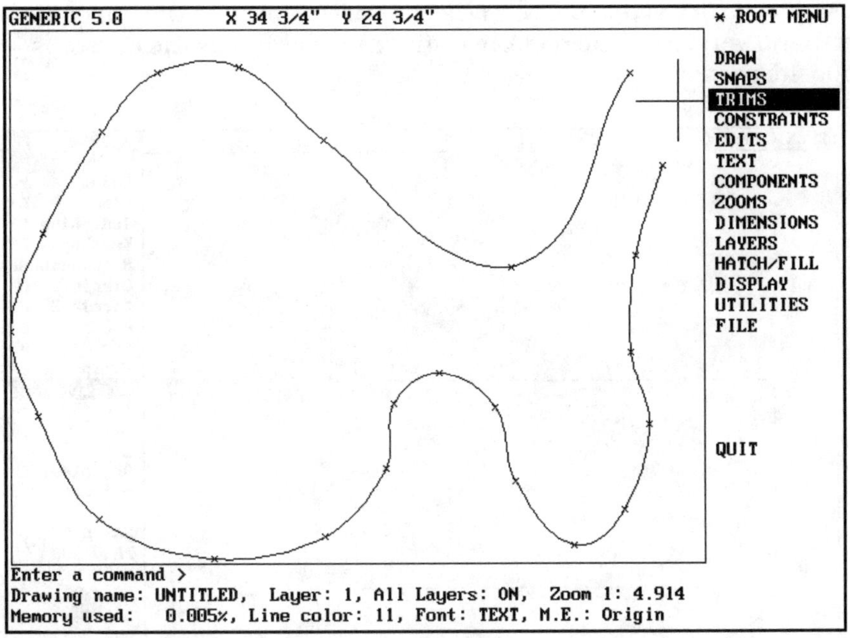

Figure 3.8: *Drawing a complex curve.*

Rectangle (RE)

To use Rectangle, type **RE** or select Rectangle from the DRAW menu. The prompt will ask you for one corner of the rectangle. Move the cursor to where one corner of the rectangle will sit and click to set the point. Next CADD prompts you to enter the opposite corner. Move the cursor up or down, left or right as required, and click to set the point. Notice the rubber-banding rectangle stretching behind as you move the cursor.

Drawing a Rectangle

Prompt	*Input*	*Description*
`Command`	Type **RE** or select Rectangle from the DRAW menu	Starts the Rectangle command
`Enter one corner of the rectangle`	Move the cursor to the lower left of the screen and click	Sets the first corner of the rectangle
`Enter opposite corner`	Move the cursor up and to the right; click to set the opposite corner	

In figure 3.9, first one corner is placed, then the cursor is moved to the opposite corner. A rubber-band version of the rectangle stretches behind as the cursor is moved to the opposite corner.

Figure 3.9: Drawing a rectangle.

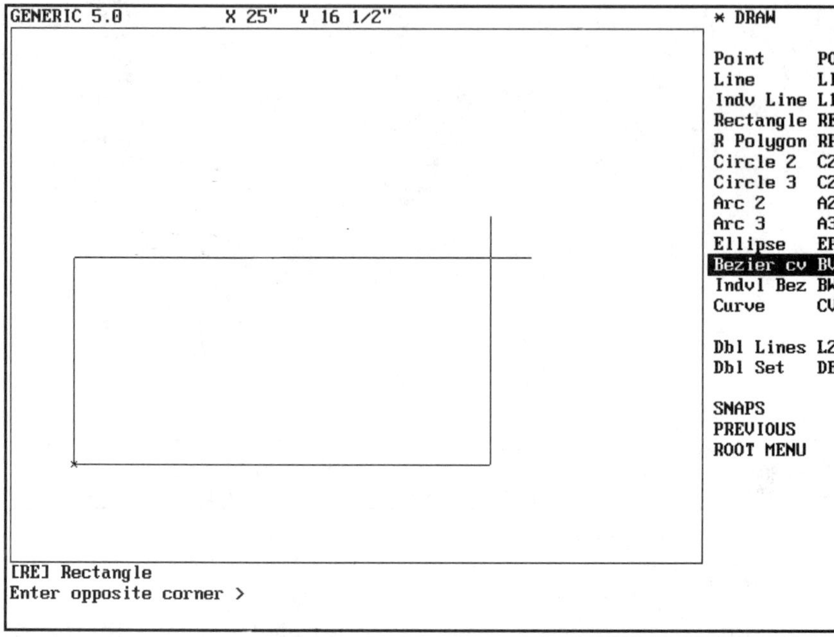

TIP

When using the Rectangle command, you are limited to creating a rectangle that is vertical or horizontal in placement; this command cannot place a rectangle on the screen rotated at an odd angle. If you need to rotate a rectangle already in the drawing, use the Rotate command. If you have yet to draw the rectangle, use the Regular Polygon command.

Regular Polygon (RP)

Use the Regular Polygon command to make closed objects having anywhere from 3 to 255 sides, each side of equal length, all angles the same. The first thing you will be asked to do when using this command is to set the number of sides. If the number in parenthesis is the number of sides you want, just press Enter.

There are two options to choose when you use this command: Center construction or Side construction. Center construction defines the polygon by having you define the length from the center of the polygon to one corner. Side construction defines the polygon by having you define the length of one side. If one side of the polygon must adjoin another object, Side construction is easier. Use Center construction for free-standing polygons, unless you have a situation that calls for a polygon but a circle could fit as well (three points being connected by the polygon instead of a circle is one possibility).

Drawing a Regular Polygon

Prompt	*Input*	*Description*
`Command`	Type **RP** or select R Polygon from the DRAW menu	Starts the Regular Polygon command
`Change number of sides (5) -- Limits: 3 to 255`	**6**	Sets the command to draw a hexagram (six-sided polygon)
`(Center construction) or Side Construction`	**C**	Selects Center construction
`Enter center of polygon`	Move cursor to desired location, press Enter	Sets the center point of the polygon
`Enter one corner of the polygon`	Move the cursor to set one corner, click to draw the polygon	

Notice the rubber-band effect as you move the cursor to set the corner point. You can move the cursor in any direction from the center point, which causes the rubber-band polygon to spin around the center point until the corner is located. See figure 3.10.

`Command`	Press Spacebar	Repeats the Regular Polygon command
`Change number of sides (6)`	Press Enter	Draws a six-sided polygon again
`(Center Construction) or Side Construction`	**S**	Uses Side Construction method
`Enter one point on the polygon`	Move the cursor away from the first polygon, press Enter	Places the starting point of one side

Drawing a Regular Polygon—continued

Prompt	*Input*	*Description*
`Enter an adjacent corner of the polygon`	Hold down Ctrl while moving the cursor; press Enter when the side is the desired length	Defines the length of one side of the polygon
`Enter polygon location`	Move cursor left or right to select polygon orientation; press Enter to finish	Which side of the line should the polygon be on? (see fig. 3.11)

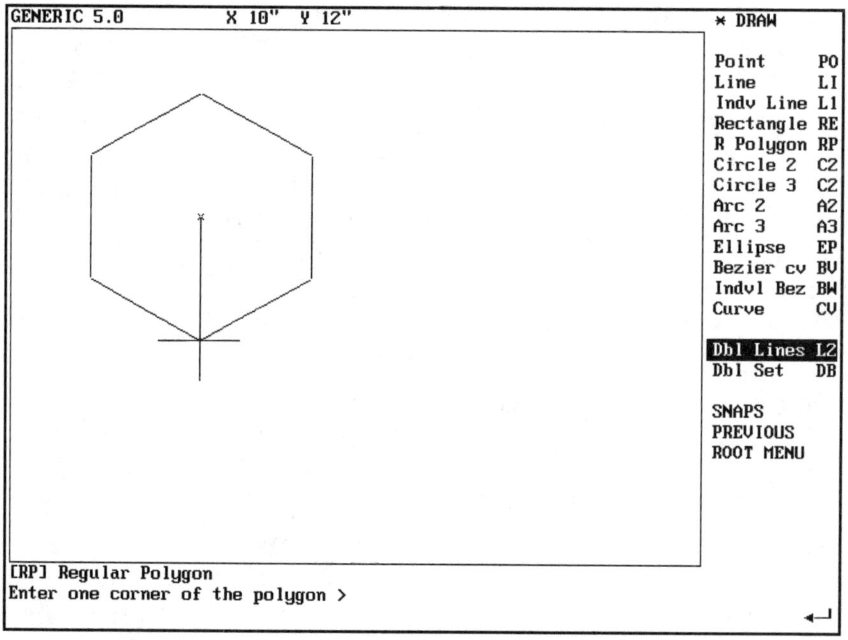

Figure 3.10: *Drawing a regular polygon using the Center construction option.*

Drawing Double Lines and Solid Lines

It is not uncommon to need to draw two lines side by side (parallel). The most obvious example is when drawing floor plans—double lines show the thickness of the walls.

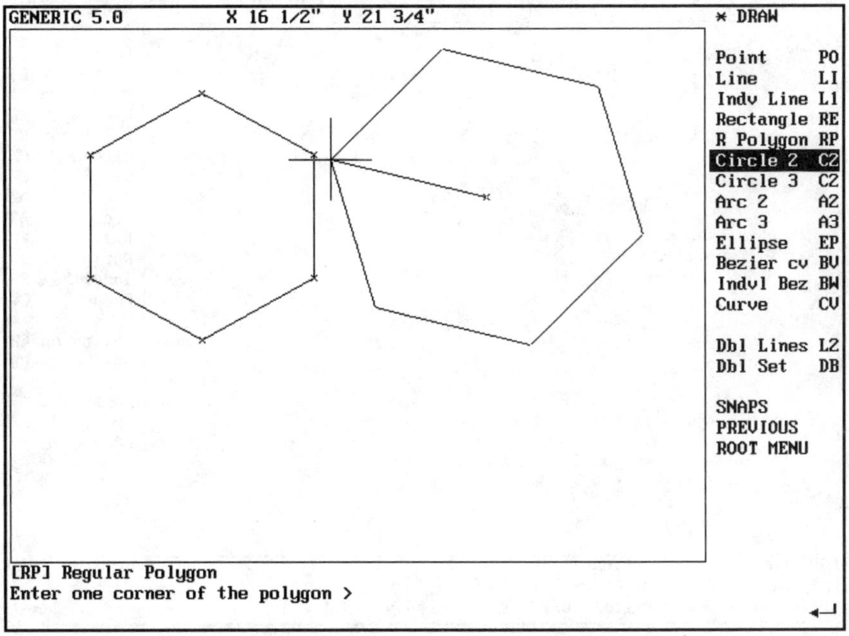

Figure 3.11: *Drawing a regular polygon using the Side construction option.*

The Double Lines command (L2) will draw a succession of double lines, just as the Line (LI) command will draw a succession of single lines. The width is set using the Double Line Settings command (DB).

Double Line Settings (DB)

The Double Lines command can be set to draw parallel lines, any distance apart. The lines can be drawn to appear as one solid line, and you can choose whether or not the corners are filleted, which means to place an arc where the two lines meet to form a corner. As shown in figure 3.12, all these options may be set from the Double Line Settings menu, which appears in the prompt lines when you type **DB** at the keyboard, or select Double Set from the DRAW menu.

To set the distance between the two lines, use either the right or left offset, or both together. Each offset controls how far the line is from the cursor and the point placed on the screen. Setting both offsets at 3", for example, would draw a 6" wide double line. You could achieve the same effect by setting the right offset at 6" and the left offset at 0.

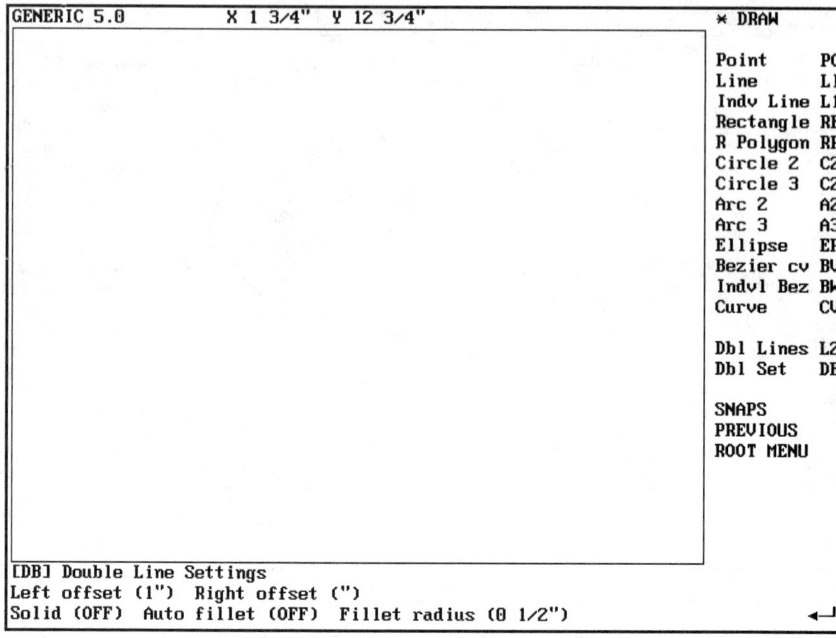

Figure 3.12: *Available settings using the Double Line Settings command.*

The way you adjust these settings depends on the way you plan to use the command. If you want one of the lines of the pair to follow a set path, set it at 0 and achieve the distance by setting the other line offset to 6" (or whatever distance). An example of this would be drawing a foundation from a set of measurements. You want one line to be the outer edge of the foundation, which is what the measurements indicate, so you set the left offset at 0 and the right offset at 6".

If instead you wanted both lines to be the same distance from the points you select, set the right and left offsets to be the same distance apart.

The Solid option, if on, uses the solid color fill capabilities of CADD to fill the space between the lines with solid color. The color of the fill is controlled by the Color Settings (CS) command, or the shortcut Fill Color (FK).

If Autofillet is on, each corner will have an arc inserted into it. You can set the size of this arc with the Fillet Radius option. The inside arc of the pair (remember, two lines, two arcs) will be of the size indicated by this setting, the outside arc will be drawn parallel to the first.

Double Lines (L2)

Experiment with the Double Lines command. Use it as you would the Line command, moving the cursor and clicking. To end the command, press Esc, type **PU** or click on a blank menu line. Some examples of double lines are shown in figure 3.13.

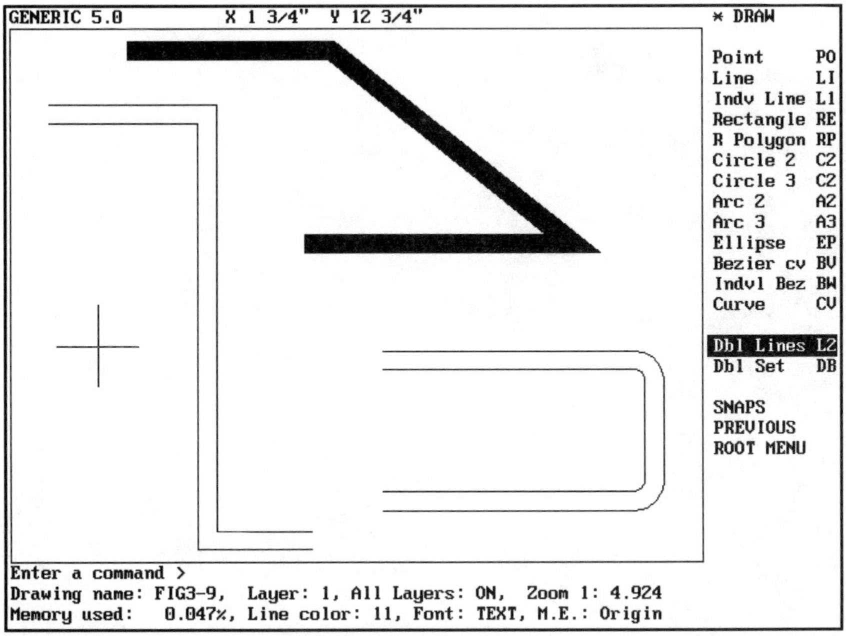

Figure 3.13: *Variations using double lines.*

Summary

You have now seen all of Generic CADD's elementary drawing commands. By themselves they may not seem too impressive, but you have only begun to tap the real power of Generic CADD. Starting with the next chapter, which discusses snaps, you'll begin to build on these basics.

Even without the added utility and convenience of snaps and other drawing tools, the commands on the DRAW menu represent a substantial improvement over manual drafting methods. The objects are geometric entities and are constructed in Generic CADD using mathematical formulas. Once the math has been done to draw the object, the fruit of that bit of computer labor can be used over and over. This is unlike drawing manually, where the drafting technician doubles as the calculator, and each step that requires the application of geometric principles means starting over.

4

Tools for Accuracy

Computer users often ask about the differences between paint programs and CADD programs. While from a technical standpoint they are very different, the differences can be summarized in one word: precision. A program like Generic CADD 5.0 allows the user to draw with mathematical accuracy of up to six decimal places. A paint program offers no such equivalent. There is no direct correspondence between the size of objects in a paint program and in the real world, so there is no specific scale size for objects in the drawing. In Generic CADD, just the opposite is true. Everything is drawn to its real-world size and can be printed out at any proportional scale the user chooses.

Such precision is fundamental to CADD and is why it can successfully replace manual drafting.

Drawing with Precision

Generic CADD can draw with extreme accuracy because everything is located on the coordinate grid. Every point on every object has a unique coordinate address, expressed in terms of its horizontal and vertical distance from the center of the grid (point 0,0). By using these coordinates to identify the exact locations of objects, you are able to draw with extreme accuracy. In most cases, you do not need to know these exact locations to draw accurately; Generic CADD 5.0 will calculate them for you. The Snap command's job is to locate exact points on objects. Snap Midpoint, for example, will look for the exact midpoint on a line and "snap" the cursor to it.

Controlling the Screen Grid

The grid facilitates the operation of the snap commands by providing a reference to all locations in the drawing. You can make the grid visible, which makes it easier to place points on-screen. Like graph paper, the screen grid gives you a visual understanding of the distances between objects. But the grid offers more than just visual guidelines. The grid itself can limit the movement of the cursor to increments that you can specify.

Grid Size (GS)

The grid consists of dots that appear on-screen at a set distance. You control the spacing of the dots with the Grid Size command, found on the CONSTRAINTS menu. The horizontal and vertical spacing may be controlled separately, as illustrated in figures 4.1 and 4.2. To set the grid size, type **GS** or select Grid Size from the CONSTRAINTS menu. The prompt will ask you for the X (horizontal) and Y (vertical) spacing. For each entry, type a distance and press Enter.

Three pre-set grid sizes are available from the CONSTRAINTS menu: 1.0, .5, and .25 inches. No two-letter commands are available for these three options; they are menu commands only, provided for your convenience. If the grid is not visible when the Grid Size command is used, it will become visible when you finish.

Figure 4.1: Grid set to a horizontal and vertical distance of 1".

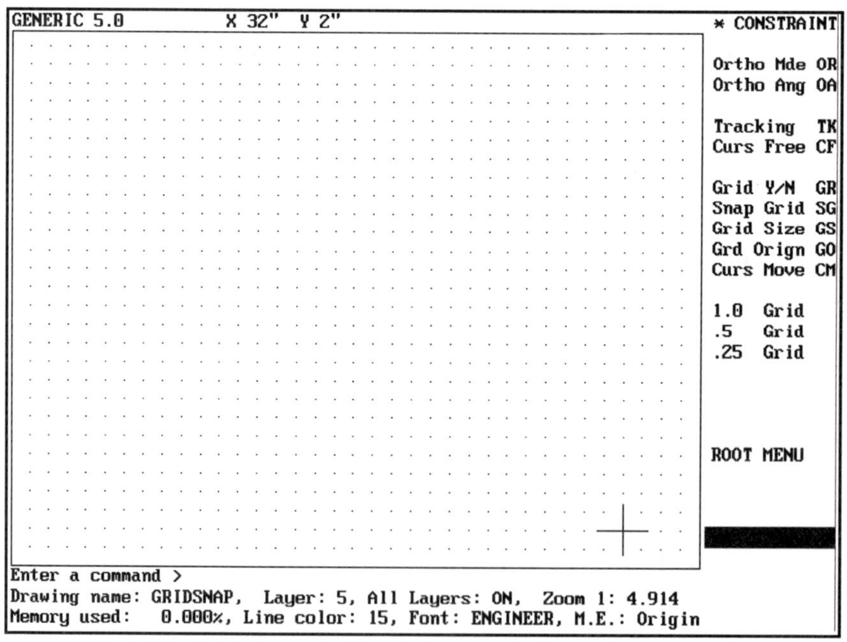

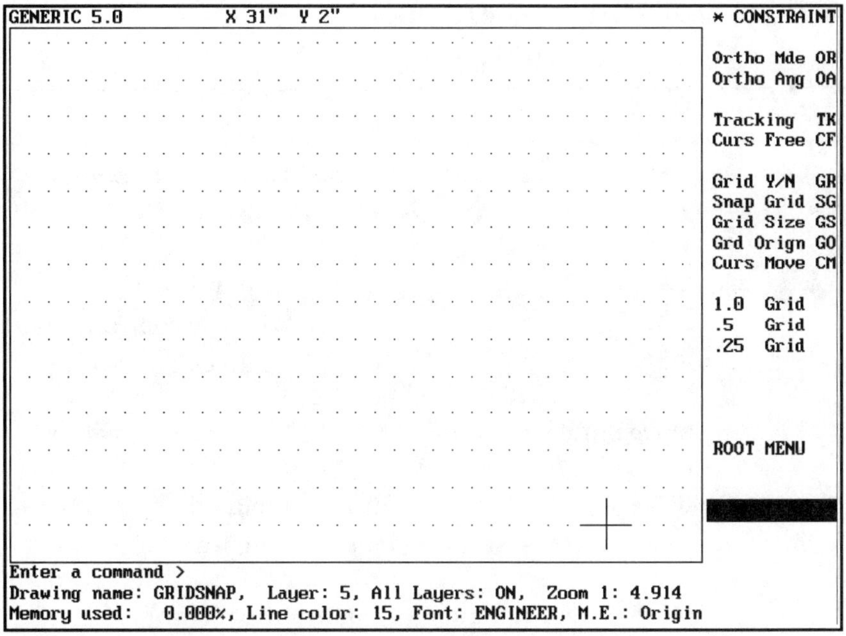

Figure 4.2: *Grid set to horizontal distance of 1", vertical distance of 2".*

Grid On/Off (GR)

If you want to hide the grid temporarily, or if you haven't been using it and you want to make it visible, use the Grid On/Off command, found on the CONSTRAINTS menu. Grid On/Off is a simple toggle that turns the grid display on or off, whatever is opposite of its status when you execute the command.

Snap To Grid (SG)

You can limit the cursor's movement to the points on the grid. To do so, use the Snap To Grid command from the CONSTRAINTS menu. This is one of three snap commands that works as a toggle (the other two are Snap To All Layers [SY] and Component Snap [GC]). If the cursor moves freely about the screen when you type SG, it will then be limited to moving from point to point. Once Snap To Grid is on, typing SG again will shut it off.

Start the exercise that follows by turning on the grid, setting its size, and enabling Snap To Grid. In this exercise, you'll use relative coordinate display, which shows the distance the cursor has moved from the last point placed on the screen.

If you haven't already done so, start Generic CADD.

Drawing a Rectangle

Prompt	*Input*	*Description*
`Command`	**GS**	Starts Grid Size command
`Change Grid Size X` `Change Grid Size Y`	**1** **1**	Sets Grid size to 1" x 1"
`Command`	**SG**	Turns on Snap To Grid
`Command`	**DC**	Turns on display coordinates
`...Relative (ON)`	**R**	Toggles relative display on (see fig. 4.3)
`Command`	Move cursor to lower left of the screen	
`Command`	**RE**	Starts a rectangle
`Enter one corner of the rectangle`	Click or press Enter	Places first corner of rectangle
`Enter opposite corner`	Move cursor up and right until coordinate display reads ΔX 8" ΔY 8" and press Enter	Finishes the rectangle

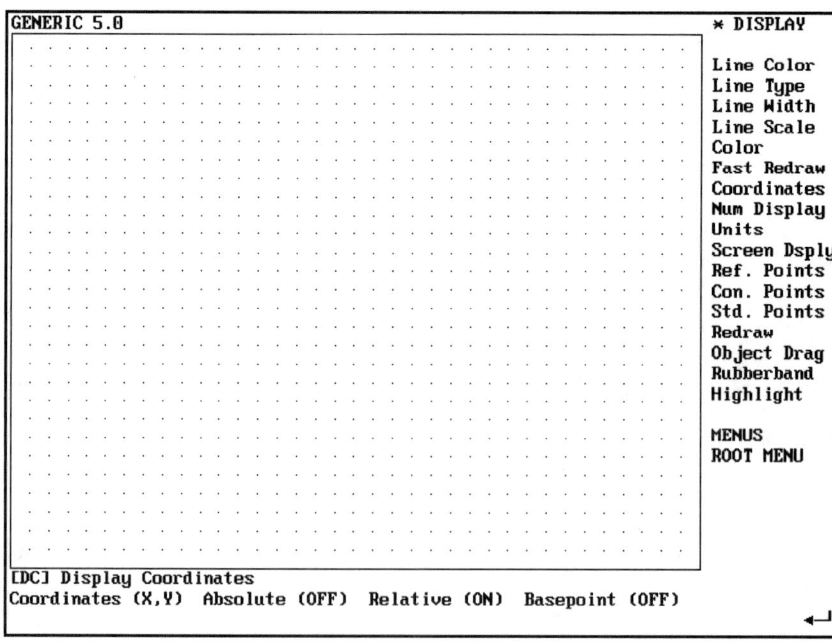

Figure 4.3: Turning relative coordinate display on.

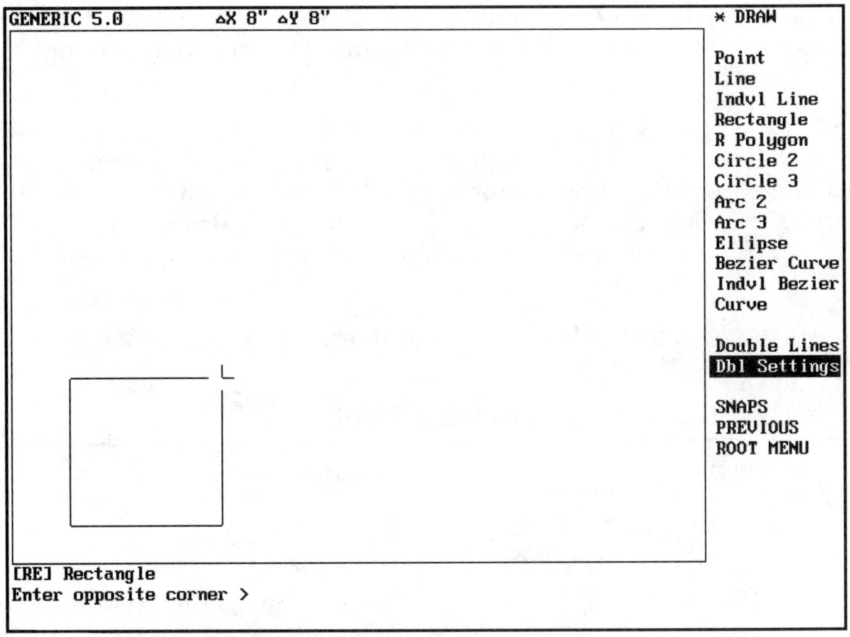

Figure 4.4: Drawing with relative display coordinates and Snap To Grid.

It was easy to draw an 8" x 8" square using relative coordinate display. The first corner of the rectangle became the 0,0 point in the coordinate display, so to finish the figure, you moved up 8" and over 8", using both the grid and the coordinate display as guides (see fig. 4.4).

Using Snaps for Accuracy

The previous chapter covered the basic objects that can be drawn in Generic CADD 5.0. But rarely would these objects be drawn in isolation from each other. Normally, one uses a combination of lines, arcs, curves, and other objects to create a drawing. The snap commands, found on the SNAPS menu, make it easy to place these objects where you want them. They may be used whenever CADD prompts you to place a point on the screen. This makes it possible to use snap commands in the middle of any drawing command. Also, because the Line (LI) command is the default operation in Generic CADD, when the prompt says `Enter a command`, you can enter a snap command to start a line.

Snap To Nearest Point (NP)

Perhaps the most commonly used snap command is Snap To Nearest Point. If you have a three-button mouse, the third button should be programmed to issue this command. This command was used in the last chapter, so you already have experience with it. Snap To Nearest Point looks for the construction point nearest the cursor, and attaches to it the object being drawn. You do not need to know the exact coordinates of this location—the Snap command figures them out for you.

If you have looked at the SNAPS menu, you may have noticed that Snap To Nearest Point is not there. It would be hard to pick the command from the menu with a mouse, because the cursor also moves when you select items from the menu and the cursor probably would not be where you needed it to be when the command was issued. Keep this in mind during the discussion of Snap To Closest Point.

If you have a two-button mouse, hold down Shift and press the first mouse button to issue Snap To Nearest Point.

Using Snap to Nearest Point

Prompt	*Input*	*Description*
`Command`	Move cursor near top left corner of square	
`Command`	**C2**	Starts a two-point circle
`Enter center of circle`	**NP**	Cursor snaps to top left corner of square (see fig. 4.5)
`Enter a point on the circle`	Move cursor right until coordinate display reads ΔX 2" ΔY 0 and press Enter	Draws a circle with 2" radius as shown in figure 4.6 (Snap To Grid helps set the radius accurately)

Snap To Closest Point (SC)

Like Snap To Nearest Point, Snap To Closest Point also snaps the cursor to an existing point. But the difference between this command and Nearest Point is that Closest Point asks which Point you want before it snaps. Because of this extra step, you can use Snap To Closest Point from a menu. If you would rather select commands from the menu than type them at the keyboard, or if you don't have a mouse, you may find yourself using Closest Point most often.

Snap To Midpoint (SM)

Snap To Midpoint locates and snaps the cursor to the exact center point of a straight line or an arc. This is a frequently used snap because the midpoint of one line often is the starting place for another object. You also can use Snap Midpoint to draw an arc that connects to a line on both ends. To draw this, you would make a two-point arc and use Snap to Midpoint to define the midpoint of the line as the center of the arc.

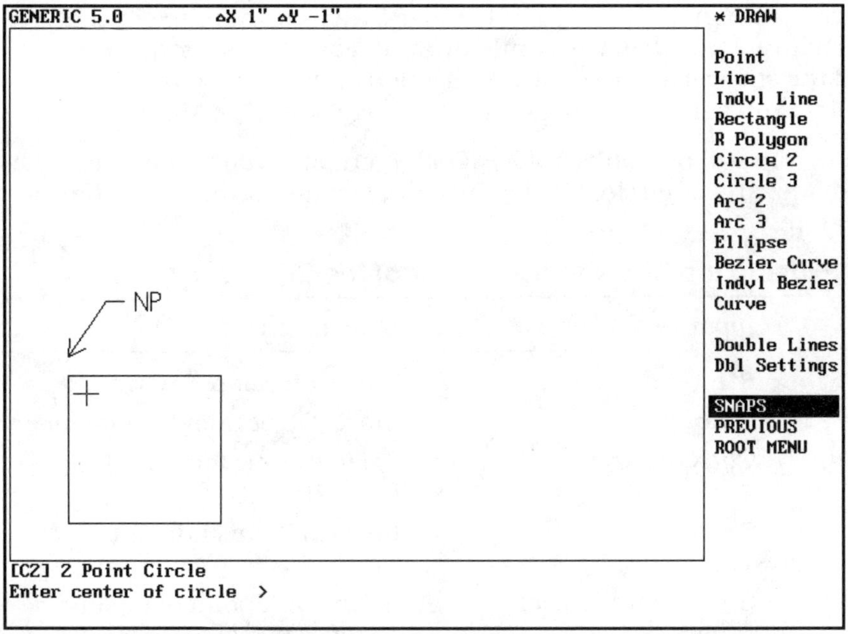

Figure 4.5: *Using Snap To Nearest Point to start the two-point circle.*

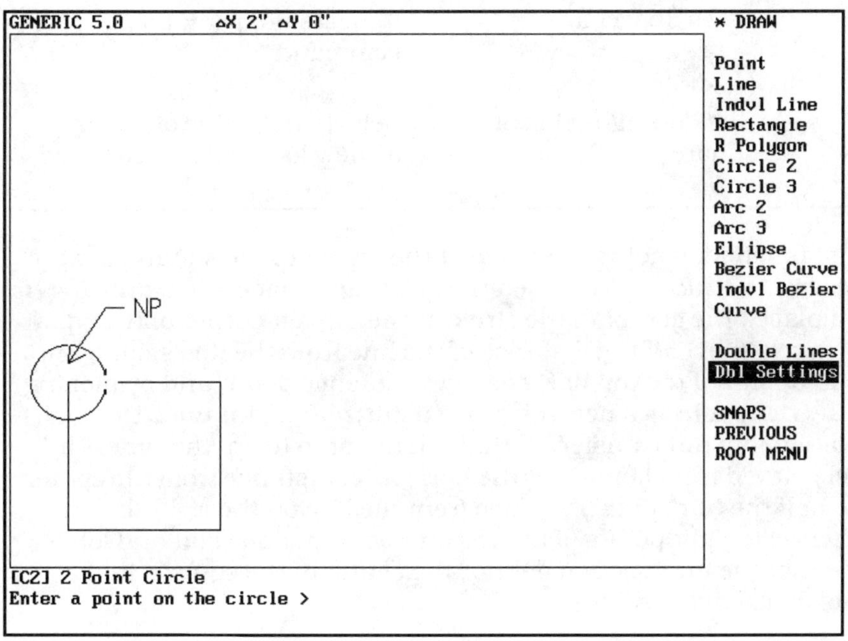

Figure 4.6: *Setting the radius of the two-point circle.*

In the next exercise, use Snap To Midpoint to move the circle to the exact center of the square. In manual drawing, you would draw diagonal lines connecting opposite corners of the square, and use the intersection of the diagonals to locate the square's center. You can bypass these steps by using Snap To Midpoint.

To move the circle, you will use Object Move (OM). It enables you to move a single object, such as a line, arc, or circle, displaying a drag image as you move the object to a new location.

Moving the Circle to the Center of the Square

Prompt	*Input*	*Description*
`Command`	**SG**	Turns off Snap To Grid
`Command`	**OM**	Starts Object Move command
`Pick Object`	Click on circle	Selects circle for move (see fig. 4.7)
`Enter a reference point`	**SM**	Invokes Snap Midpoint
`Midpoint of`	Click on top line of square	Selects midpoint of top line as reference point for move (see fig. 4.8)
`Enter new location of reference point`	Press Spacebar	Repeats Snap Midpoint command
`Midpoint of`	Click on right side of square	Selects right side of square as new location for reference point (see fig. 4.9)

The steps you just finished, placing the circle at the center of the square, are an example of *geometric construction*. You used the existing geometry in a drawing to draw or edit. You placed the center of the circle at the top left corner of the square (the center of the circle was half the distance of the line from the line's midpoint). By selecting the midpoint of the top line as a new reference point, and by picking the midpoint of the right side as a new reference point, you maintained the "half-the-distance" relationship but transferred that relationship to another line. The center of the circle moved from being half the horizontal distance from the center of the top line, to half the horizontal distance from the line on the right. If you draw lines connecting the midpoints of the top and bottom, and right and left lines, you will see that the intersection defines the center of the square, just as the intersection of diagonal lines does.

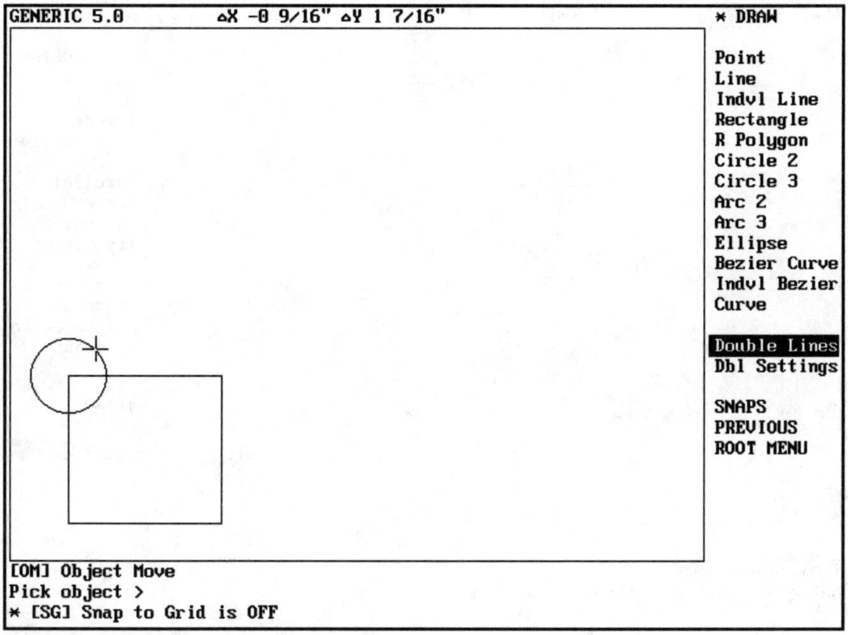

Figure 4.7: *Starting the Object Move command.*

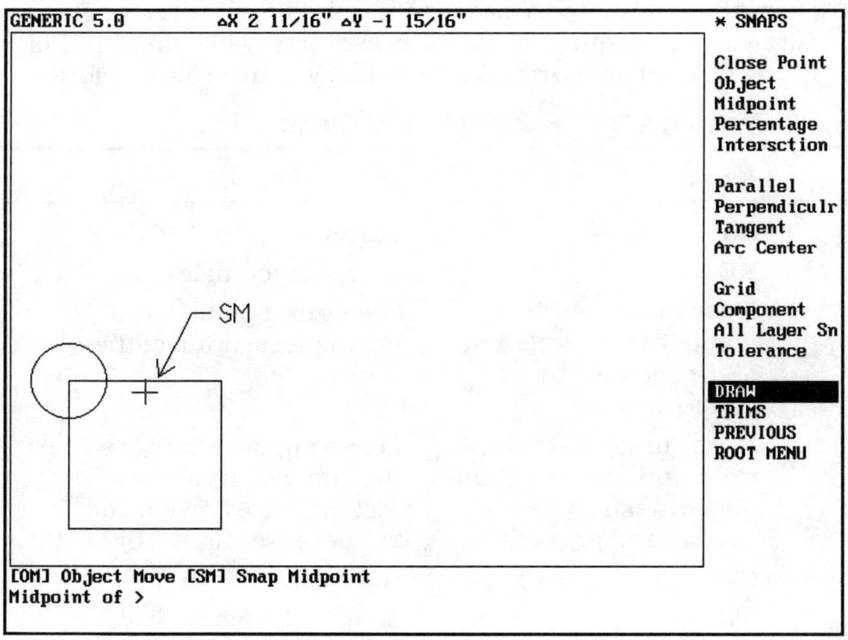

Figure 4.8: *Locating the midpoint by clicking on the top line.*

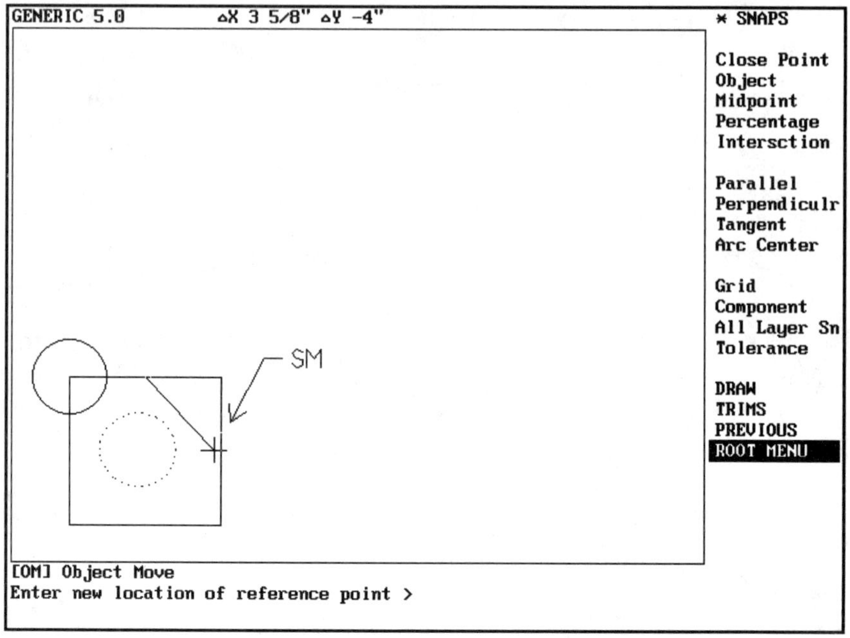

Figure 4.9: *Moving the circle to its new location.*

Draw a rectangle again and put a circle inside it. Use another snap command to copy the circle to a point half the distance between the middle of the rectangle and the top. A new drawing technique, setting the cursor free, will help with this part of the exercise. You also will use Ortho Mode, which you have used before.

Drawing a New Rectangle and Circle

Prompt	*Input*	*Description*
`Command`	**SG**	Turns Snap To Grid on
`Command`	**RE**	Starts a rectangle
`Enter one corner of the rectangle`	Move the cursor to a point near the top right of the screen and press Enter	Places first point of the rectangle near top of the screen
`Enter opposite corner`	Move cursor down and right until the coordinate display reads ΔX 6" ΔY -22" and press Enter	Places opposite corner so the dimensions of the rectangle are 6" wide and 22" deep (see fig. 4.10)
`Command`	**C2**	Draws another circle
`Enter start of circle`	**SM**	Snap To Midpoint places the center of the circle
`Midpoint of`	Click on left side of rectangle	Select left side of rectangle (see fig. 4.11)

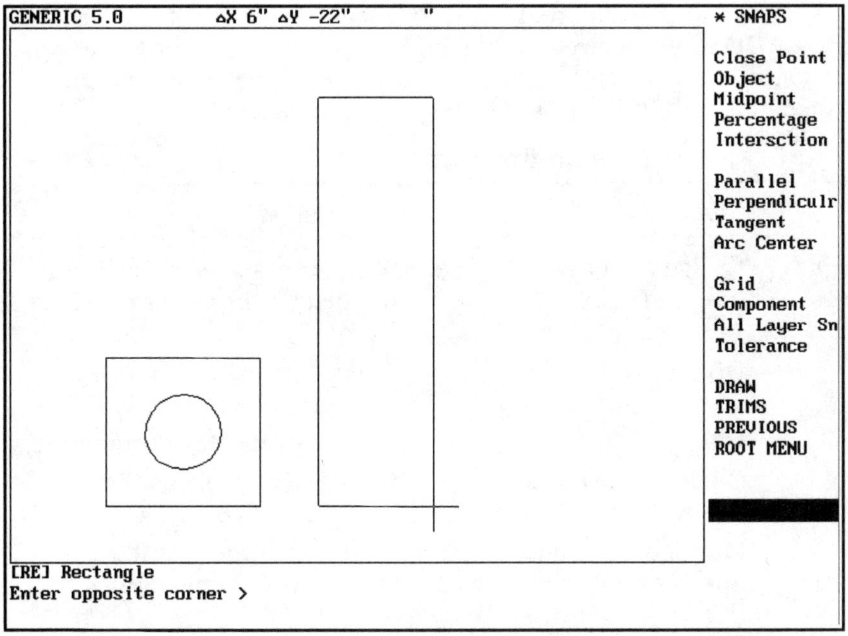

Figure 4.10: *Drawing the second rectangle.*

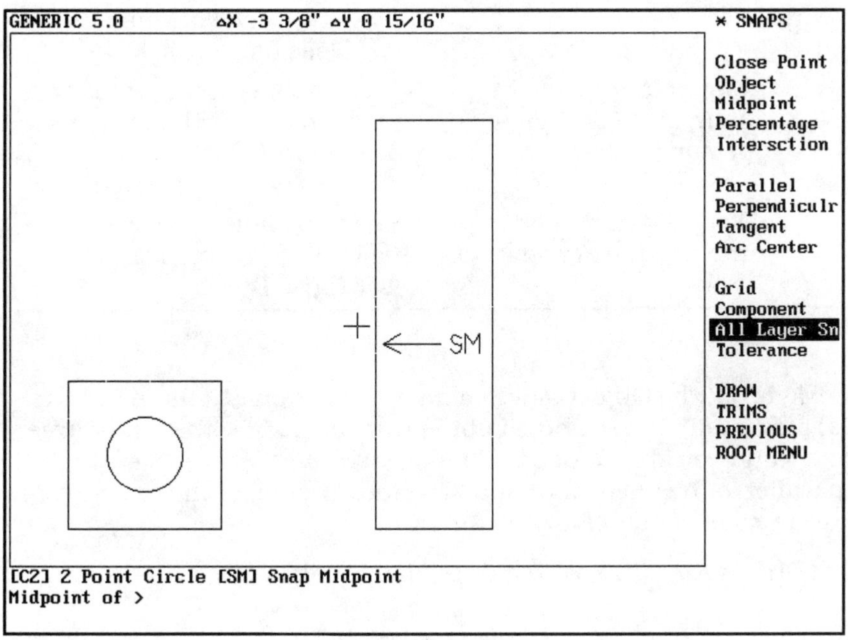

Figure 4.11: *Placing the circle on the left side of the rectangle.*

In the next exercise, use Snap To Nearest Point to select the center of the circle. Whenever Generic CADD draws a circle, it places a construction point at the center. If you set Construction Points to on (PC), you can see the point on-screen. Whether or not the construction point is visible, you can snap to it.

Freeing the Cursor

Prompt	*Input*	*Description*
`Enter a point on the circle`	Nudge the cursor up the line and type **1.5**	Sets radius of circle at 1.5 inches; draws the circle (see fig. 4.12)
`Command`	**OR**	Turns Ortho Mode on to limit cursor's movement
`Command`	**OM**	Starts Object Move command
`Pick object`	Click on the circle	Selects the circle as the object to move
`Enter a reference point`	Move cursor inside circle and type **NP** or click with third mouse button to Snap To Nearest Point	Snaps to circle's center to select a reference point
`Enter new location of reference point`	**KF**	Frees cursor from restriction by Ortho Mode or Snap to Grid (see fig. 4.13)
`Cursor Free is ON`	Move cursor to right, then up to the top of rectangle	Circle's movement is still restricted by Ortho Mode and Snap To Grid, but cursor's is not restricted
	Type **SM** and click on the top line of rectangle	Snap To Midpoint selects new center point of circle (see fig. 4.14)

By turning Ortho Mode on, the Object Move command's action is limited to vertical and horizontal movement. When you combined Ortho Mode with Cursor Free in the last exercise, you were able to use the midpoint of the top line to move the circle to a point parallel to the line's midpoint. The intersection of the top and side midpoints locates the exact center of any rectangle.

A full discussion of Cursor Free (KF), with more examples of its use, is in Chapter 5.

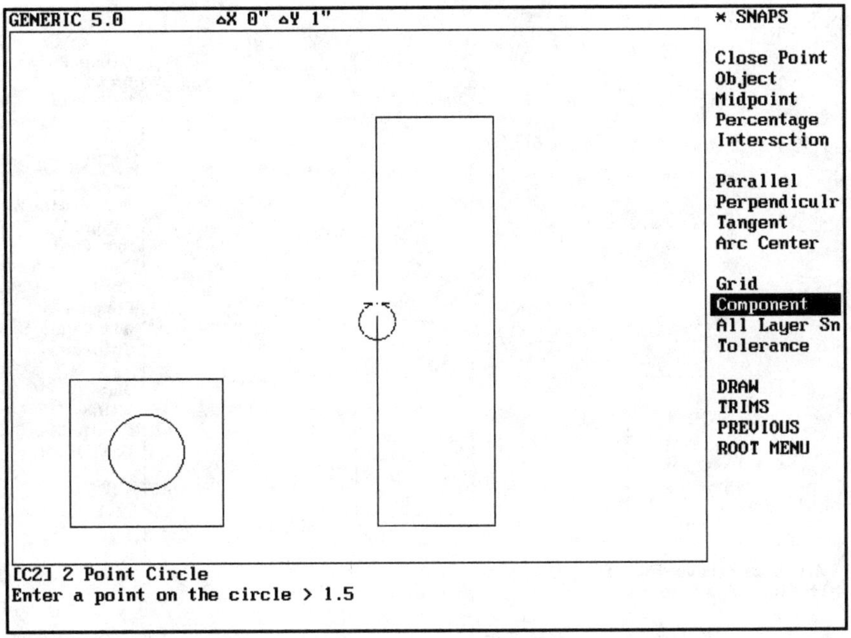

Figure 4.12: *The finished circle.*

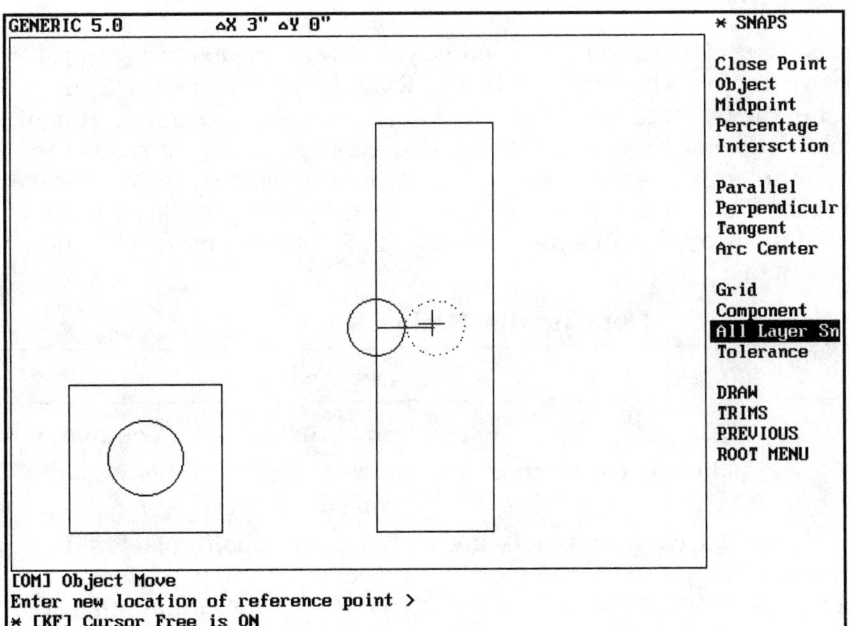

Figure 4.13: *Turning on Cursor Free (KF).*

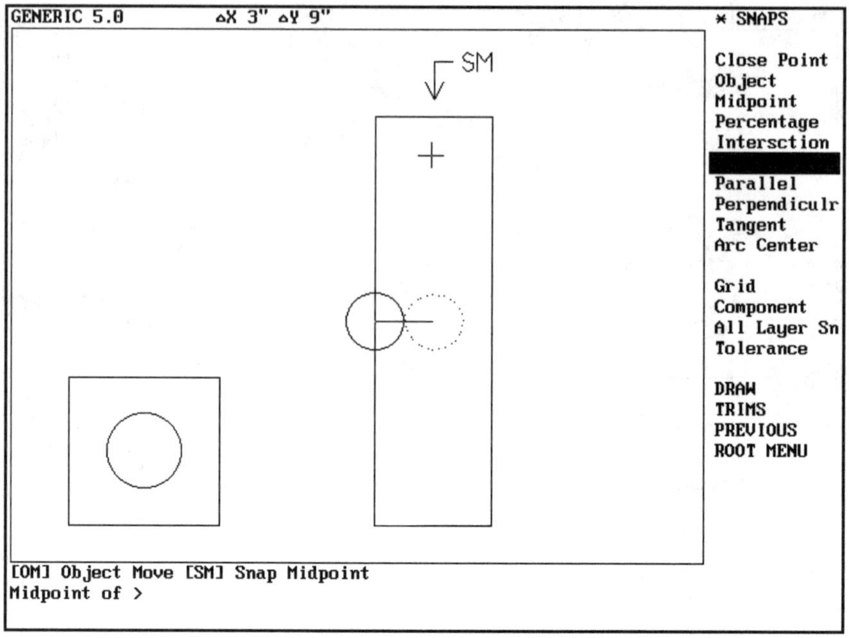

Figure 4.14: *Using the top line's midpoint as a reference for placing circle.*

Snap Percentage (SR)

Try making a copy of the circle and place it midway between the existing circle and the top of the rectangle. The center of this new circle will be on a line that bisects the center of the existing circle and the midpoint of the top and bottom of the rectangle. To do this, use Snap Percentage. Like Snap Midpoint, it reads the distance of a line or arc and locates a point along its length. But Snap Percentage enables you to set the distance as a percentage of the line's length. (Snap To Midpoint, by comparison, always locates the point that is 50 percent of the distance between the endpoints.)

Copying the Circle

Prompt	*Input*	*Description*
`Command`	**OC**	Starts Object Copy command
`Pick object`	Click on the circle	Selects circle as object to be copied
`Enter a reference point`	Move cursor to left line of rectangle and type **SM**	Selects midpoint of left side of rectangle as the reference point for copy command (see fig. 4.15)

Copying the Circle—continued

Prompt	*Input*	*Description*
`Enter a new reference point or offset`	**SR** or select Percentage from the SNAPS menu	Uses Snap Percentage to locate new reference point
`Pick object for Snap Percentage`	Click on the top half of left line	Selects left line of tall rectangle as object to measure for the Snap Percentage command (see fig. 4.16)
`Change percent-age (25.000)`	If 25.000 is in parentheses, press Enter. If any other number is listed, type **25**	The reference point for the copy of the circle uses a point 25 percent of the distance from the endpoint of the line (see fig. 4.17) In figure 4.17, the current value is in parentheses. To accept it without change, press Enter.
`Enter number of copies`	**1**	Makes one copy of the circle (see fig. 4.18)

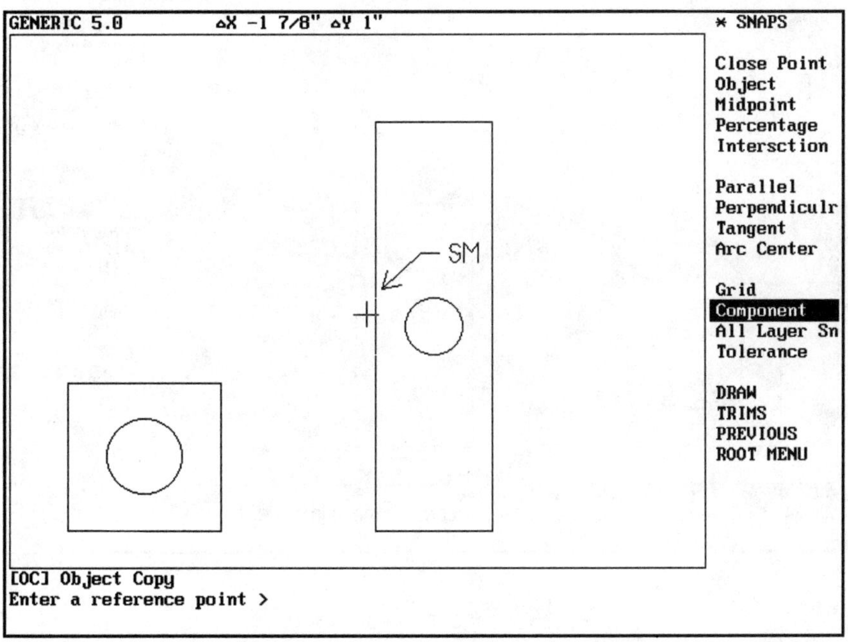

Figure 4.15: Selecting the midpoint of the rectangle's left side.

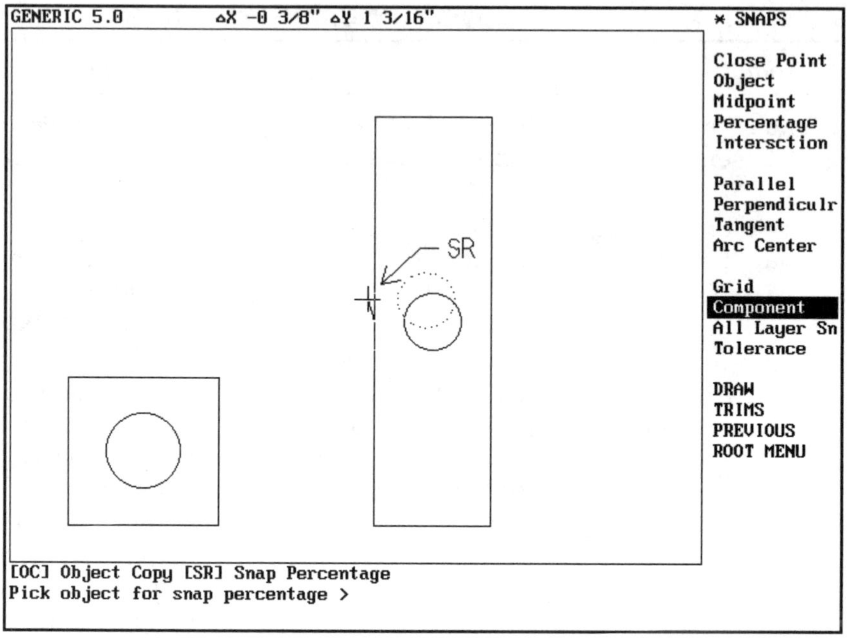

Figure 4.16: *Entering the Snap Percentage command.*

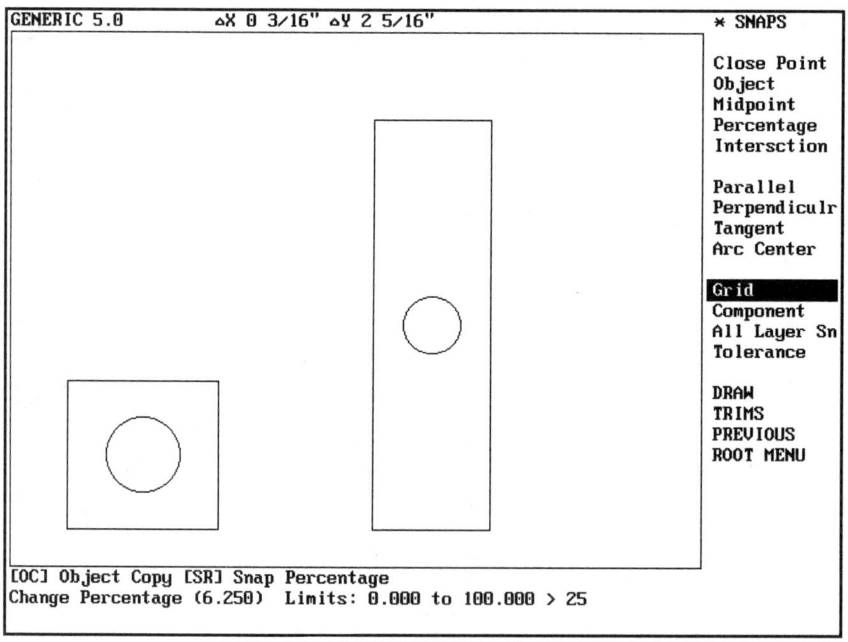

Figure 4.17: *Setting the percentage value for Snap Percentage.*

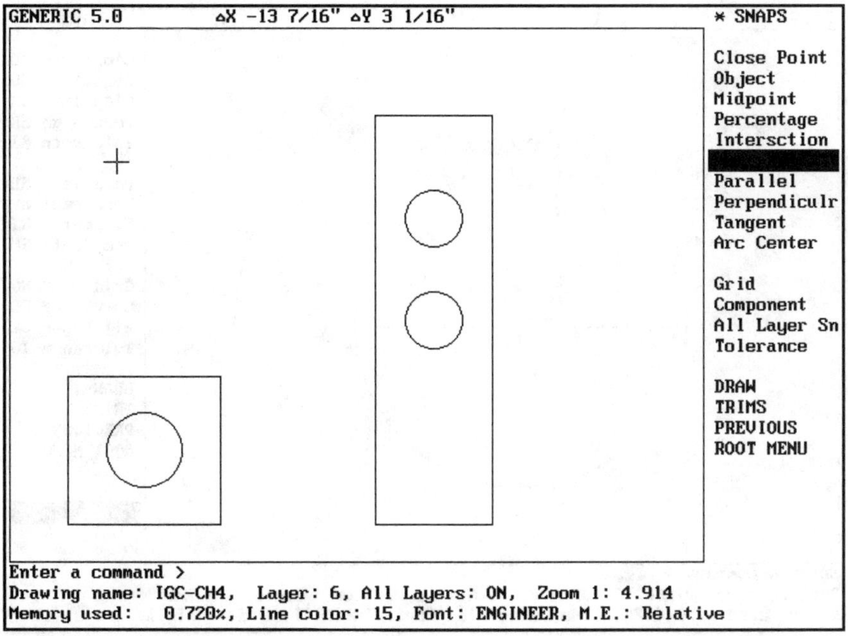

Figure 4.18: *Placing the copy halfway between the rectangle's midpoint and top.*

When you use the Snap Percentage command, Generic CADD looks to the end-point closest to the point you click on when you select the line. In the previous example, you wanted to snap to a point one-quarter (25 percent) of the way down the line from the top. You clicked on the upper section side of the line. Generic CADD calculated the location for the snap using the upper end of the line as the beginning point.

Use Snap Percentage to make quick work of drawing pie charts. Generic CADD always starts with the point on the circle that is at 0 degrees—the point straight to the right of the center. From there, it measures counterclockwise. Figure 4.19 shows a circle divided into sections using Snap Percentage. To do this on your own, start each line by using Snap To Nearest Point to snap to the center point of the circle. Then type **SR** for Snap Percentage. Click on the circle to identify it (anywhere is fine), then type in the percentage that matches the size of the wedge you want to draw. Repeat this sequence to mark off additional wedges.

Snap Tangent (ST)

A tangent line is a line that touches a circle or arc without intersecting it. Typical tangent lines are shown in figure 4.20. Note that the two lines *touch* the two circles and the arc, but never at more than one point.

Figure 4.19: *Using Snap Percentage to make a pie chart.*

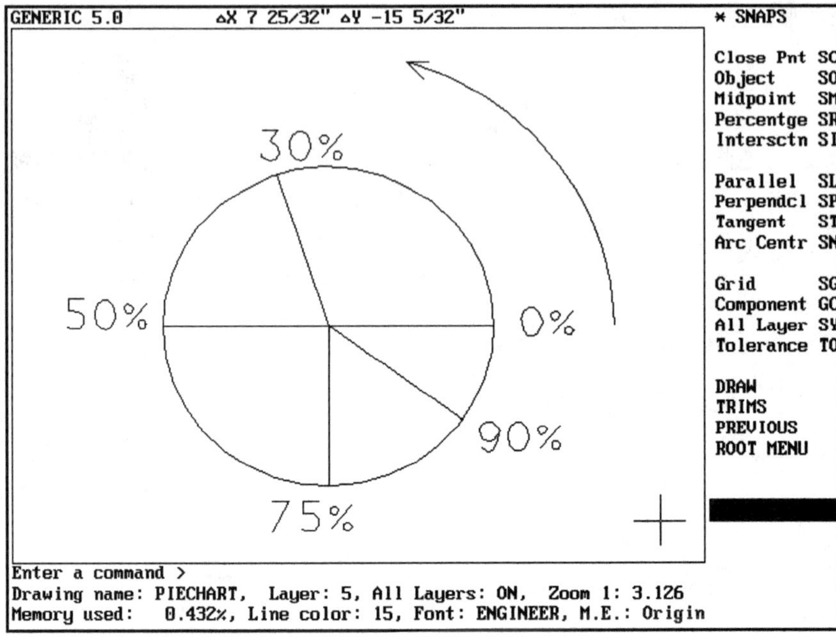

Figure 4.20: *Tangent lines touch circles and arcs without intersecting them.*

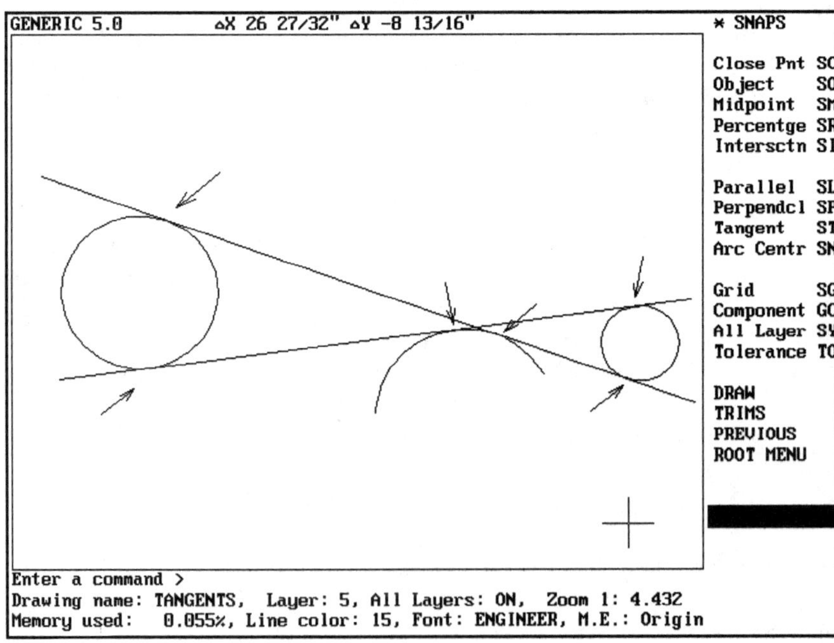

Draw a tangent line from each circle in the tall rectangle to the circle inside the square.

Drawing Tangent Lines

Prompt	*Input*	*Description*
`Command`	Move cursor to circle inside the square; type **ST**	Starts a new line using the Snap Tangent command to place the first point
`Tangent to`	Click on top of circle	Selects circle as the starting point of the tangent line (see fig. 4.21)
`Enter start point`	Click again at the same place	CADD makes the line tangent to this circle, no matter where it goes
`Enter next point on line`	Move cursor to top circle inside tall rectangle; type **ST**	Identifies top circle in tall rectangle as destination of tangent line (the line also will be tangent to this circle)
`Tangent to`	Click on upper side of top circle	Draws a line, tangent to a circle on each end (see fig. 4.22)
`Command`	Click on a blank line in the menu (second mouse button)	Ends the Line command
`Command`	Move cursor back to circle inside square and type **ST**	Starts the next line
`Tangent to`	Click on the circle	Identifies circle as the object of the Snap Tangent command
`Enter start point`	Click again on the circle	Line begins at a point tangent to the circle
`Enter next point on line`	Move cursor to top of middle circle in tall rectangle and type **ST**	Identifies the middle circle as the endpoint of the line being drawn
`Tangent to`	Click on middle circle	Draws a line, tangent to the circle on each end (see fig. 4.23)

Drawing Tangent Lines—continued

Prompt	*Input*	*Description*
`Command`	Click on a blank line in the menu (or second mouse button)	Ends the Line command
`Command`	Move cursor to bottom of circle in square and type **ST**	Starts the third line
`Tangent to`	Click on the circle	Identifies the circle as starting point of the line being drawn
`Enter start point`	Click again on circle	Begins line at a point tangent to the circle
`Enter next point on line`	Move cursor to bottom circle in tall rectangle; type **ST**	Identifies the bottom circle as the destination of the line being drawn (see fig. 4.24)
`Tangent to`	Click on bottom circle	Draws the line
`Command`	Click on a blank menu line	Ends the Line command

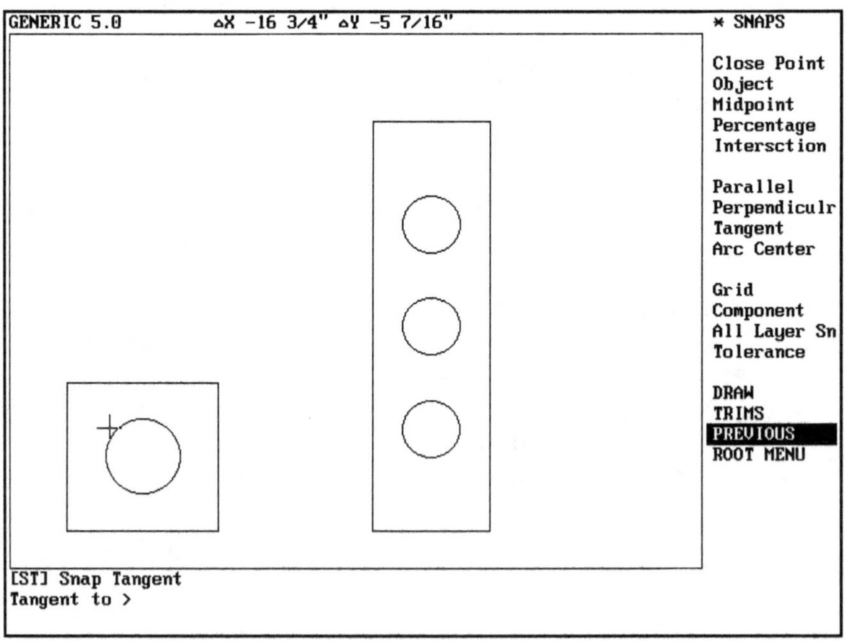

Figure 4.21: *Click on the top of the circle for the Snap Tangent command.*

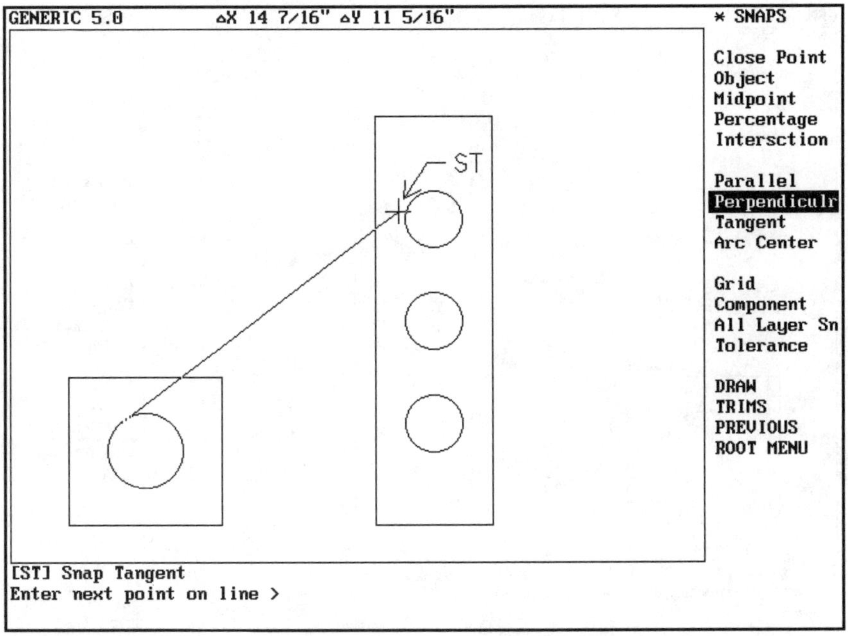

Figure 4.22: *Drawing a line tangent to both circles.*

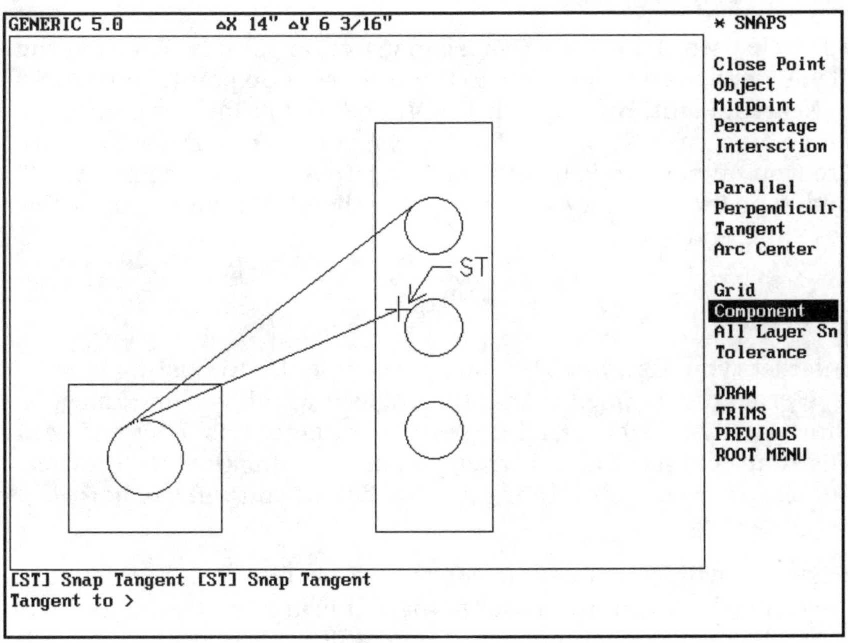

Figure 4.23: *Drawing a line tangent to the middle circle.*

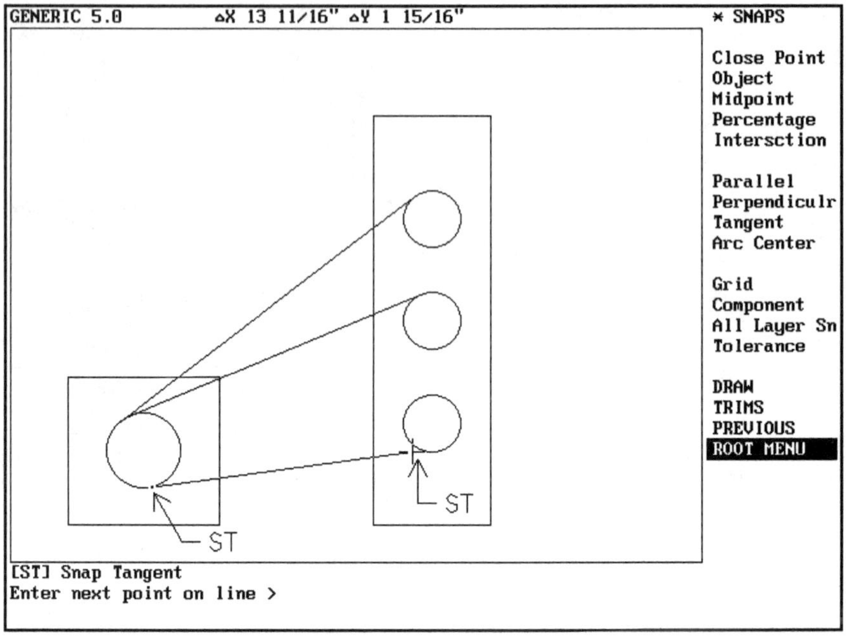

Figure 4.24: Drawing a line tangent to two circles.

Snap To Arc Center (SN)

When you draw a circle with Generic CADD, a construction point is placed at the circle's center. If you need to connect a line to the construction point, you can just use Snap To Nearest Point. But Generic CADD does not grant this courtesy to arcs, even though an arc is a segment of a circle. If you need to know the center point of an arc, you must snap to it with the Snap To Arc Center command. To use this command, type **SN** or select Arc Center from the SNAPS menu, then click on the arc whose center you need.

Snap Perpendicular (SP)

Snap Perpendicular lets you draw lines that are perpendicular to existing lines, arcs, and circles. (Perpendicular means that the angle at which two lines meet is 90 degrees. If a line is truly horizontal, a line perpendicular to it is truly vertical.) You can enter this snap command either when you are starting the line, or when you are looking to place the endpoint. In the section below, you will use both methods.

In the next exercise, you will draw an arc in the top left portion of the screen. Then you will draw a line between the center point of this arc and the top tangent line, making the new line perpendicular to the tangent line.

After drawing a line perpendicular to the top tangent line that connects to the center of the arc, you will attach a perpendicular line one inch long to the middle tangent line.

Drawing Perpendicular Lines

Prompt	*Input*	*Description*
`Command`	**OR**	Turns Ortho Mode off
`Command`	**KF**	Turns Cursor Free off
`Command`	**A3**	Starts a three-point arc
`Enter start of arc`	Move cursor to top left of screen; click to set first point	Places the starting point of the arc
`Enter a point on the arc`	Move cursor up and right; click to set a point	Sets the direction of the arc
`Enter the end of the arc`	Move cursor right and down; click to finish the arc	Completes the arc (see fig. 4.25)
`Command`	Type **SN** or select Arc Center from SNAPS menu	
`Center of`	Click on arc just drawn	Identifies the arc just drawn by rubberbanding a line from it to cursor
`Command`	**SP** or select Perpendicular from SNAPS menu	Starts a perpendicular line connecting center of arc to top tangent line
`Perpendicular to`	Click on top tangent line	Selects a base line, draws a line perpendicular to it, ending at the center of the arc (see figs. 4.26 and 4.27)
`Command`	**SP** or select Perpendicular from SNAPS menu	Starts a line with Snap Perpendicular command
`Perpendicular to`	Click on middle tangent line	Selects the base line for next perpendicular line (see fig. 4.28)
`Enter start point`	**SM**	Selects the midpoint of the middle tangent line as the starting point for the perpendicular line
`Enter next point on line`	Nudge the cursor upwards and type **1"**	Tells program to draw a one-inch line from the point placed (see fig. 4.29)
`Command`	Click on a blank menu line or press Esc	Ends the Line command

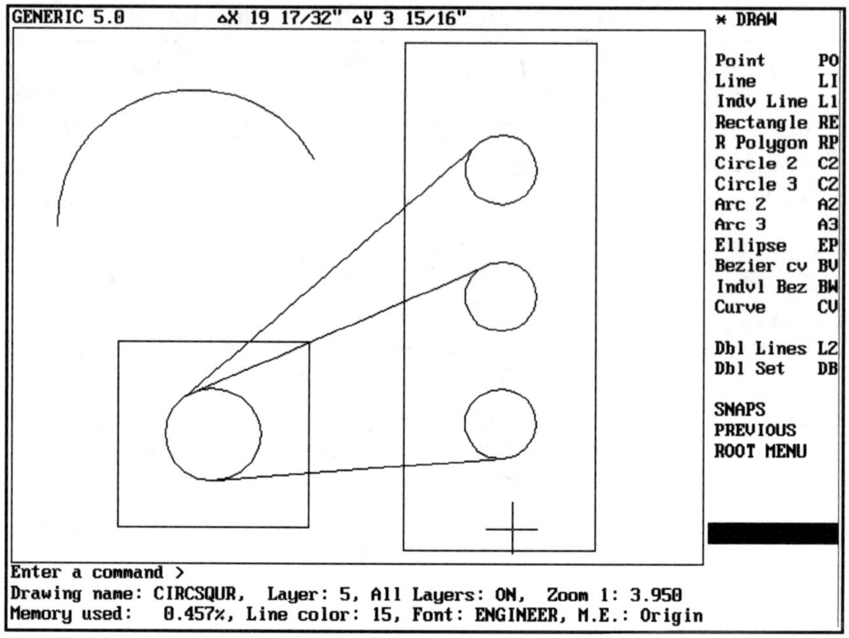

Figure 4.25: *Adding an arc to the drawing.*

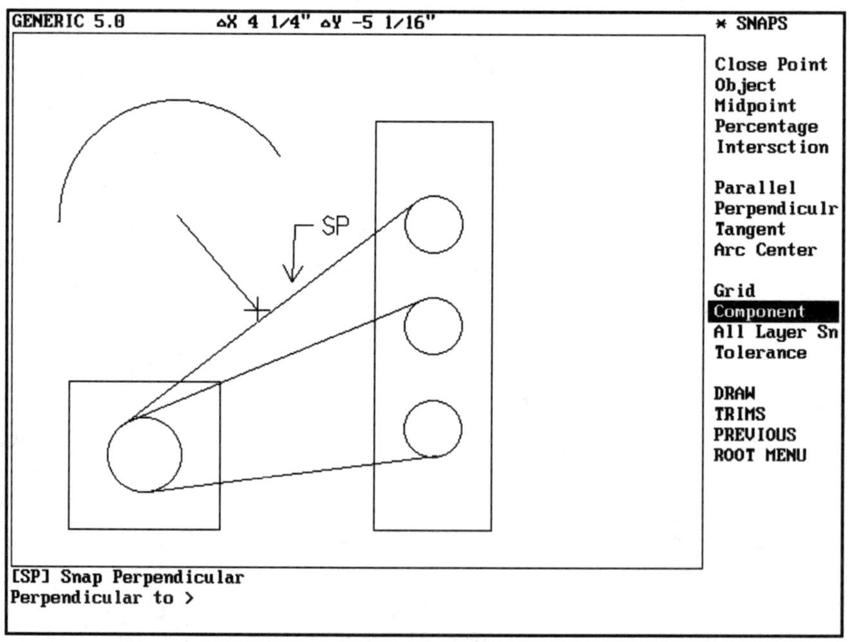

Figure 4.26: *Selecting the top tangent line, draw a line perpendicular to it.*

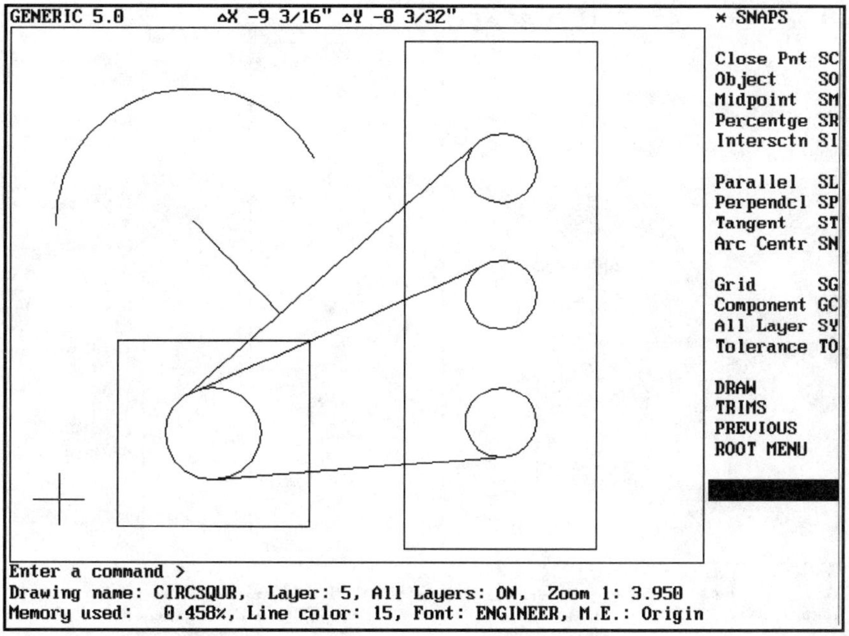

Figure 4.27: *Drawing a line perpendicular to the top tangent line.*

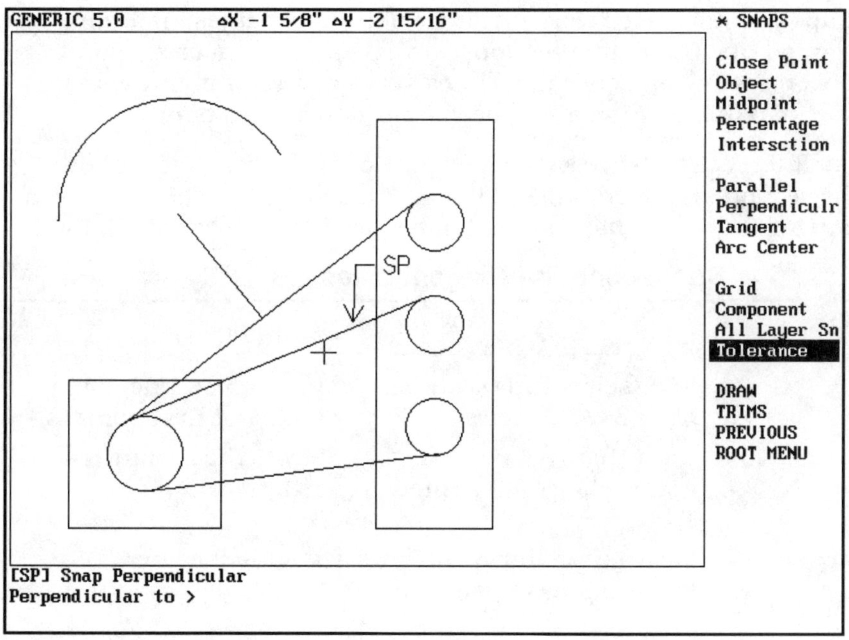

Figure 4.28: *Click on the line that will be the base for the perpendicular line.*

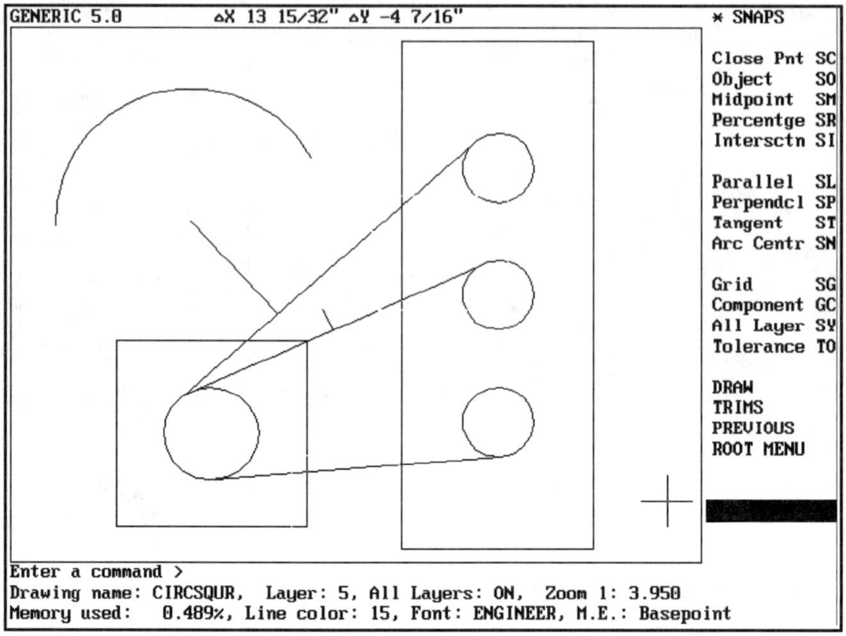

Figure 4.29: *The completed 1" perpendicular line.*

Snap Intersection (SI)

So far, all the snaps you have used work on single objects like lines (including arcs and circles) or points. Snap Intersection is an exception. It places a point where two objects cross. The objects can be lines, arcs, or circles in any combination. You can use Snap Intersection any time you need to place a point.

You will use Snap Intersection twice in the next section to draw a diagonal line that connects the second and third tangent lines. You also will see how to save a keystroke when using the same snap command to place two consecutive points.

Connecting the Tangent Lines

Prompt	*Input*	*Description*
`Command`	**SI** or select Intersection from SNAPS menu	Starts a new line using SI to place first point
`Pick intersection`	Using figure 4.30 as a guide, click on top intersection	Selects the first intersection
`Place next point on line`	Move cursor down and left and press Spacebar	Extends the line

Connecting the Tangent Lines—continued

Prompt	*Input*	*Description*
`Pick intersection`	Using figure 4.30 as a guide, click on bottom intersection	Places the endpoint of the line at the lower intersection
`Command`	Click on a blank menu line or press Esc	Ends the Line command

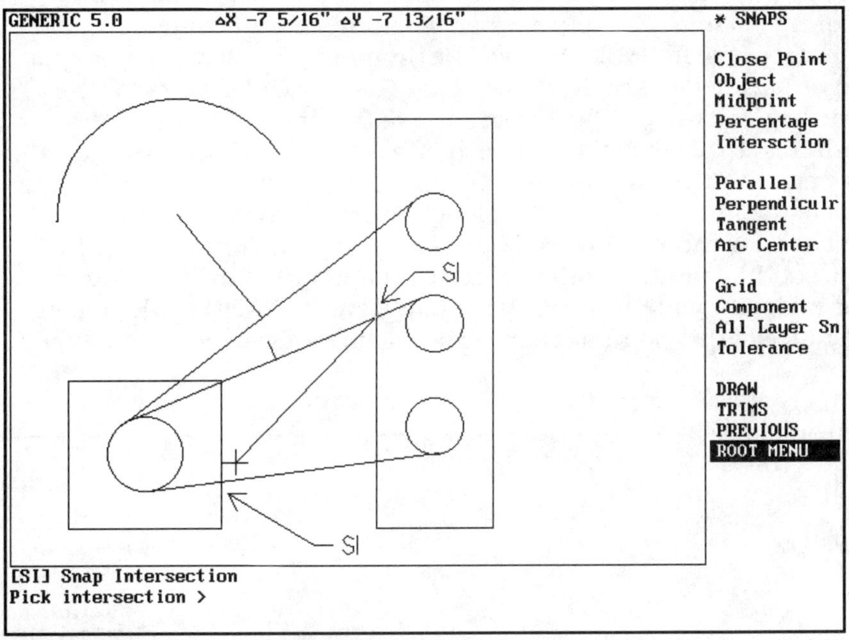

Figure 4.30: Drawing a diagonal line using Snap Intersection.

Any time you are placing points in a drawing and you want the same snap command you just used, press Spacebar to repeat it. The last command used is always the command available by pressing Spacebar. Once you have entered another command, however, you will need to type the snap's two-letter code or select it from the SNAPS menu.

Snap Parallel (SL)

Two lines that are the same distance from each other along their entire lengths are parallel. To manually draw a line parallel to another line, you measure a start point and an endpoint, both the same distance from the first line, and then connect the points. Using Snap Parallel is much faster.

There are two ways to use Snap Parallel. The first is when you have already started a line that you want to make parallel to an existing one. The second method is when you identify a line about to be drawn as a parallel line.

Figures 4.31, 4.32, and 4.33 show how to use Snap Parallel after the line has been started. After you type SL or select Parallel from the SNAPS menu, the prompt line asks you to select which line the new line will be parallel to (see fig. 4.31). Click on the line. Then the program asks you to enter the endpoint of the line (see fig. 4.32). Place the point, using a snap to identify the point if necessary (see fig. 4.33).

Figures 4.34, 4.35, 4.36, and 4.37 show how to use Snap Parallel *before* you place the first point on a line. Use this method when the new line must be a specified distance from the first line. You will be prompted to select the line that the new line will be parallel to (see fig. 4.34). Next, Generic CADD asks for the distance that the new line will be offset from the existing line. If the number shown in parentheses is the distance you need, press Enter. Otherwise, type in the new distance and then press Enter (see fig. 4.35). Next, the prompt asks you to enter the start of the line. This will be for length only, because you already have determined how far the new line will be from the existing line (see fig. 4.35). Click (or snap) to set this point, and then place the endpoint of the line (see fig. 4.37). Again, the endpoint you place only will show Generic CADD the length of the line—the distance of this point from the existing line was set when you typed an offset distance.

Figure 4.31. *Click on the existing line.*

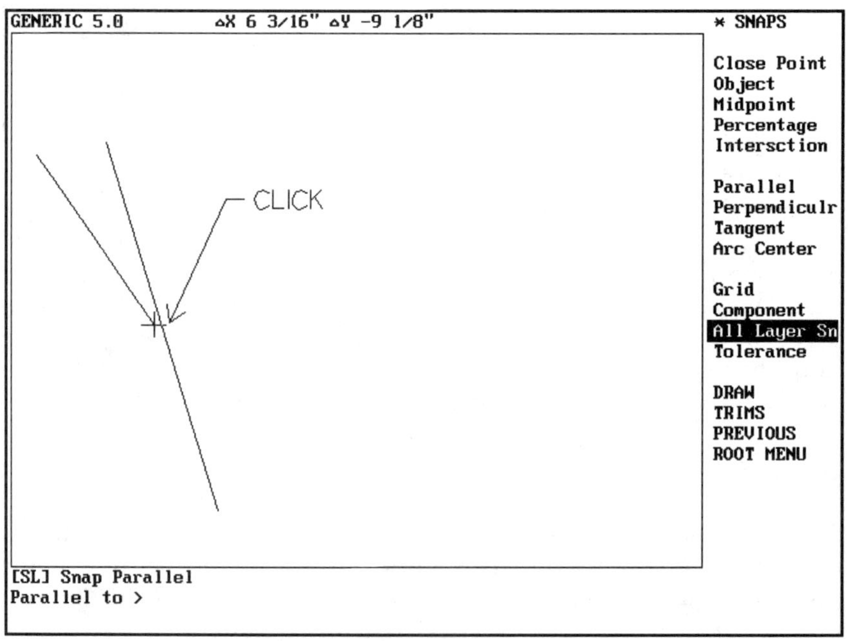

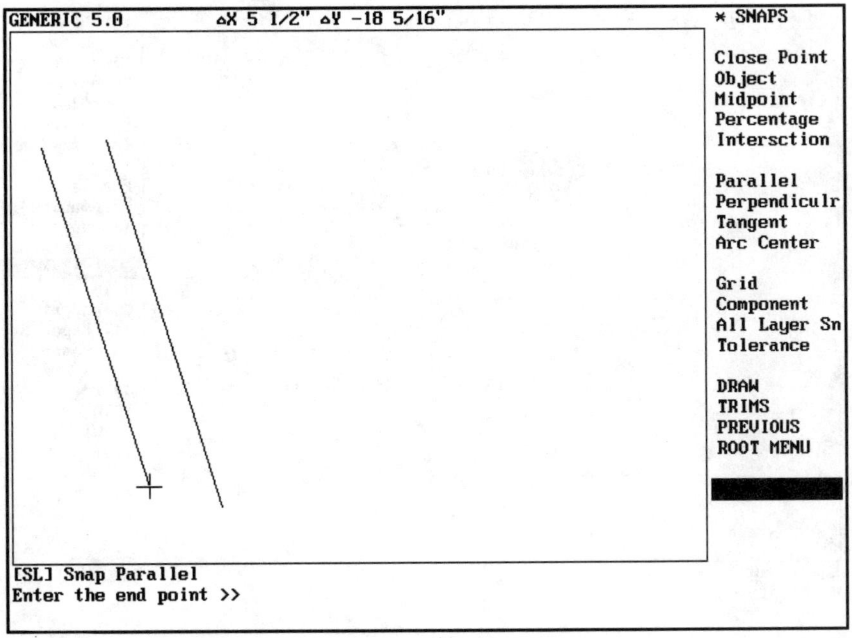

Figure 4.32: *Enter the end-point of the parallel line.*

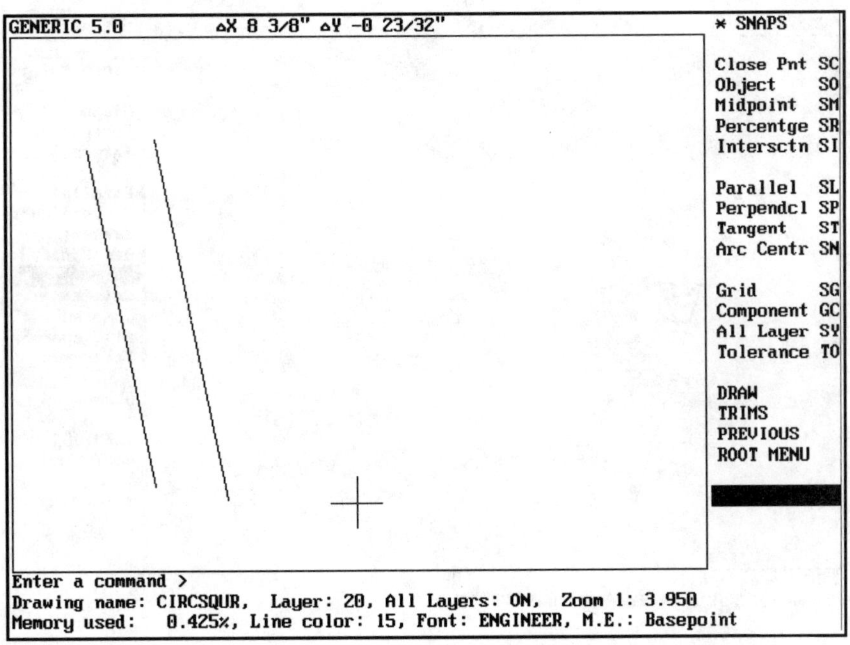

Figure 4.33: *The finished parallel line.*

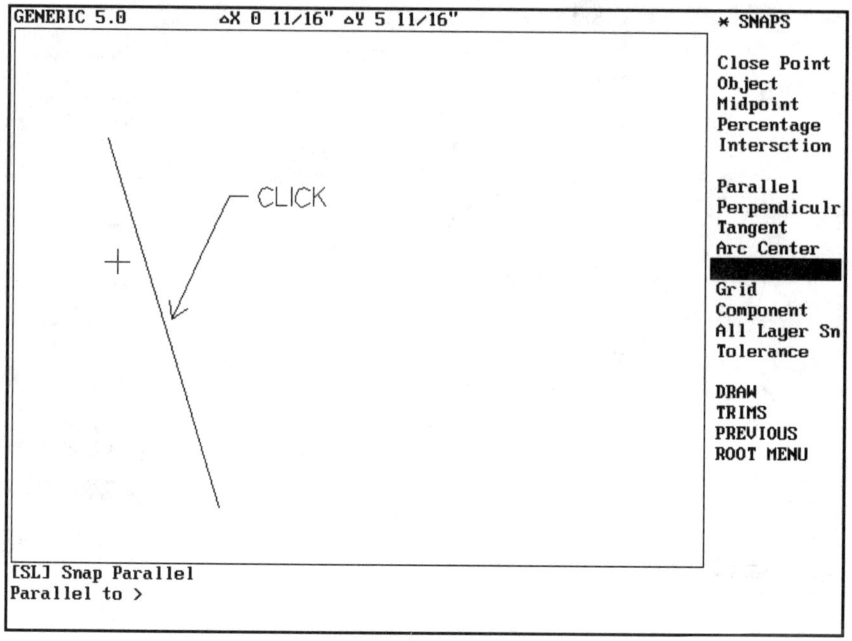

Figure 4.34: *Click on the line that will be parallel to the new line.*

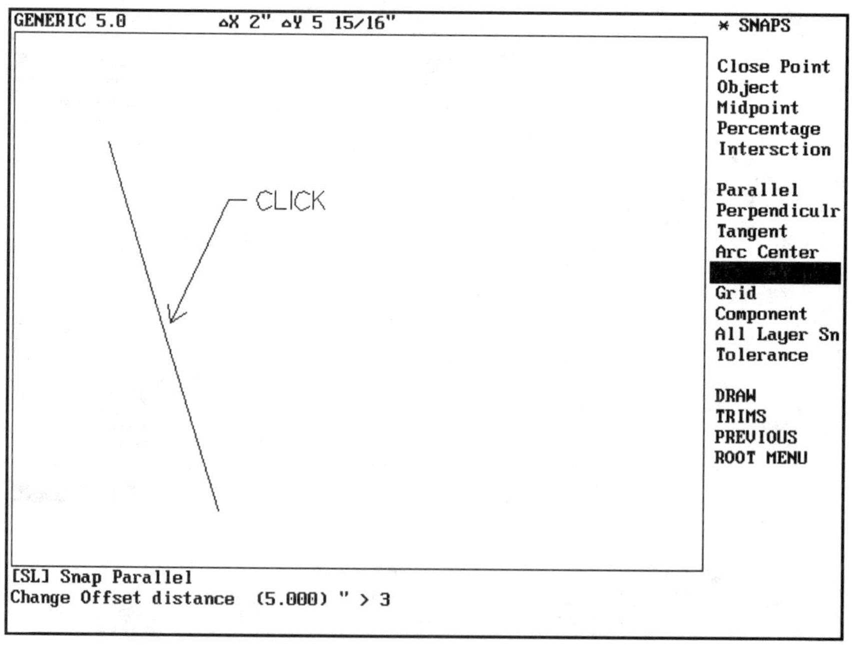

Figure 4.35: *Set the offset distance.*

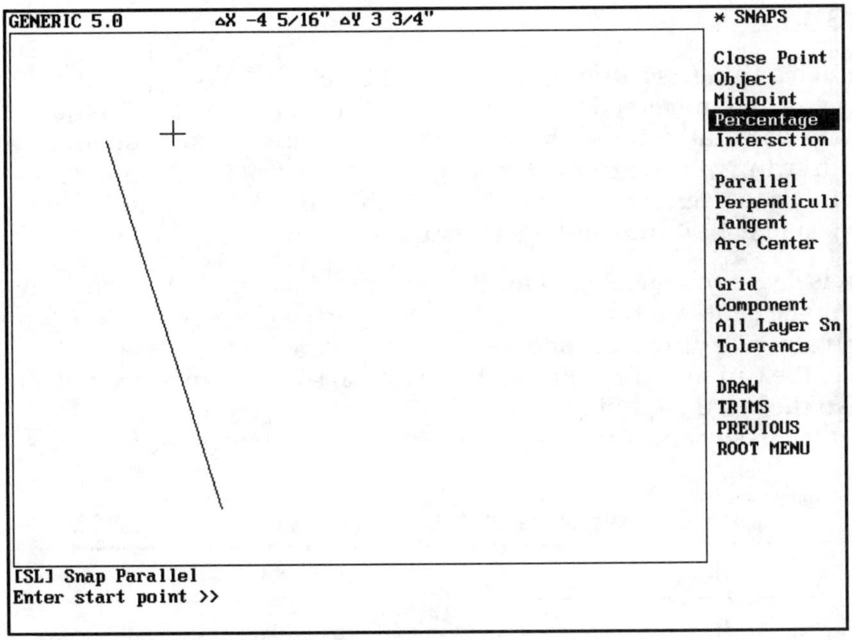

Figure 4.36: *Enter the start of the parallel line.*

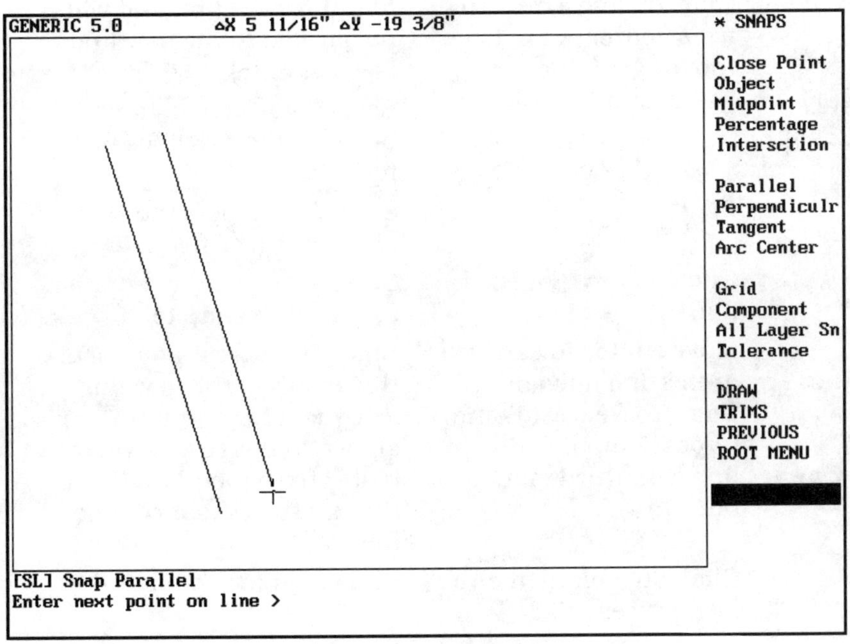

Figure 4.37: *Place the end-point of the parallel line.*

Snap Object (SO)

If there can be such a thing as a dumb snap, Snap Object is it. It doesn't calculate a midpoint or a percentage. It doesn't orchestrate the placement of a parallel line or do anything else that's reasonably sophisticated. It just makes sure that the line you are drawing will connect to the object you select. It is not limited to a construction point or to a reference point; it can snap to any point on the selected object (Snap Object may be dumb, but it's not stupid).

In the next exercise, you will use Snap Parallel to draw a line parallel to the one that extends from the center of the arc at the top left part of the screen to the top tangent line. You also will draw a second arc, parallel to the first one. You will take advantage of the Cursor Free (KF) command again, so make sure it is still on (type **KF** and read the status—either it will say off, which means you'll have to type KF again, or it will say on). You also will use another Snap command, Snap Object (SO).

Snapping to Points with Snap Object

Prompt	*Input*	*Description*
`Command`	**SL**	Starts a line, using the Snap Parallel command to define its location
`Parallel to`	Click on line extending from center of arc to top tangent line	Identifies the line that will be parallel to the new line (see fig. 4.38)
`Change Offset distance (X.000)`	**2"**	Sets a two-inch distance between the two lines (see fig. 4.39)
`Enter start point`	**SO**	Snap Object sets the start of the line (see fig. 4.40)
`Object to snap to`	Click on top tangent line	Selects the top tangent line as object to snap to
`Enter next point on line`	Move cursor toward top of existing line and Snap To Nearest Point (type **NP** or click on line with third mouse button)	Snap To Nearest Point sets the length of the new line as equal to the first line as shown in figure 4.41 (note restricted rubberband even though the cursor can move freely)
`Command`	Click on a blank menu line or press Esc	Ends the Line command

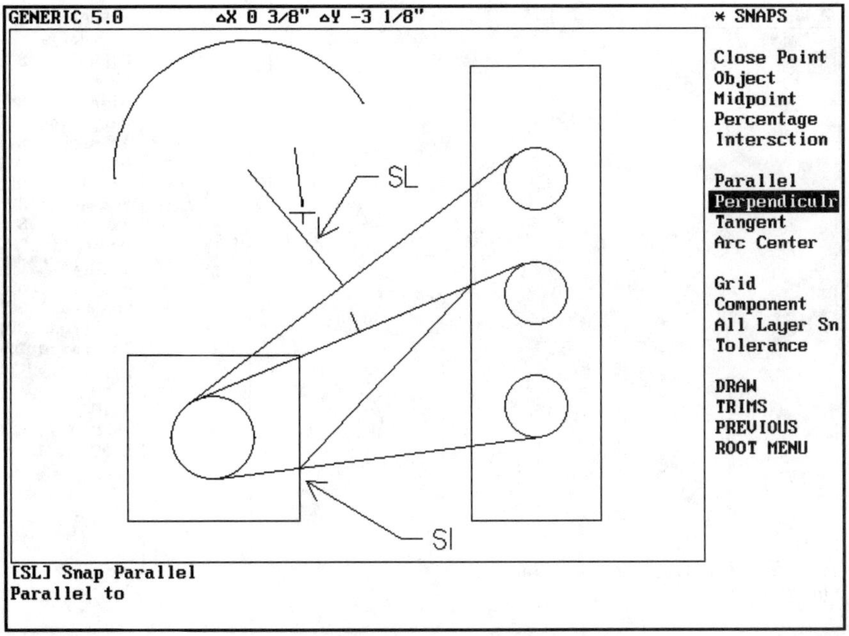

Figure 4.38: *Click on the line that will be parallel to the new line.*

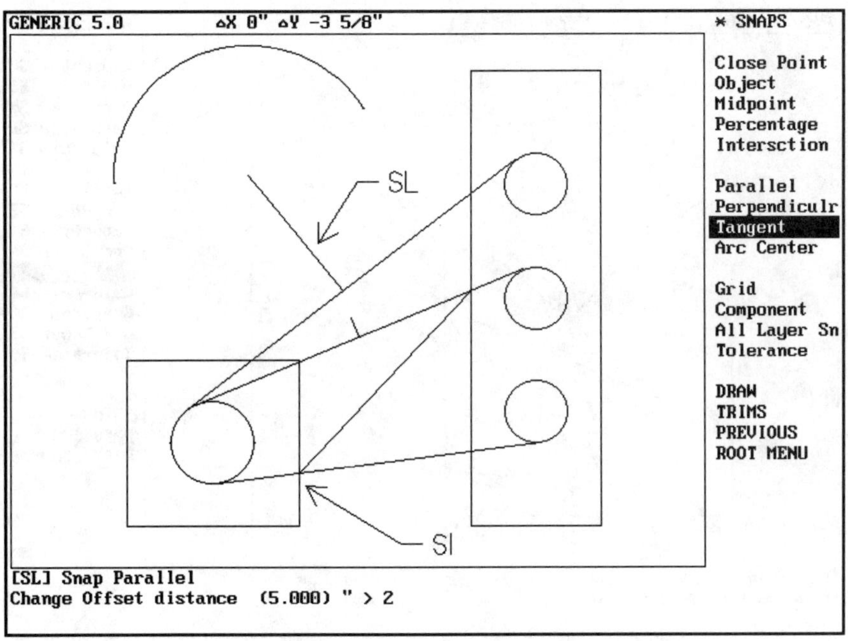

Figure 4.39: *Set the distance between the two parallel lines at two inches.*

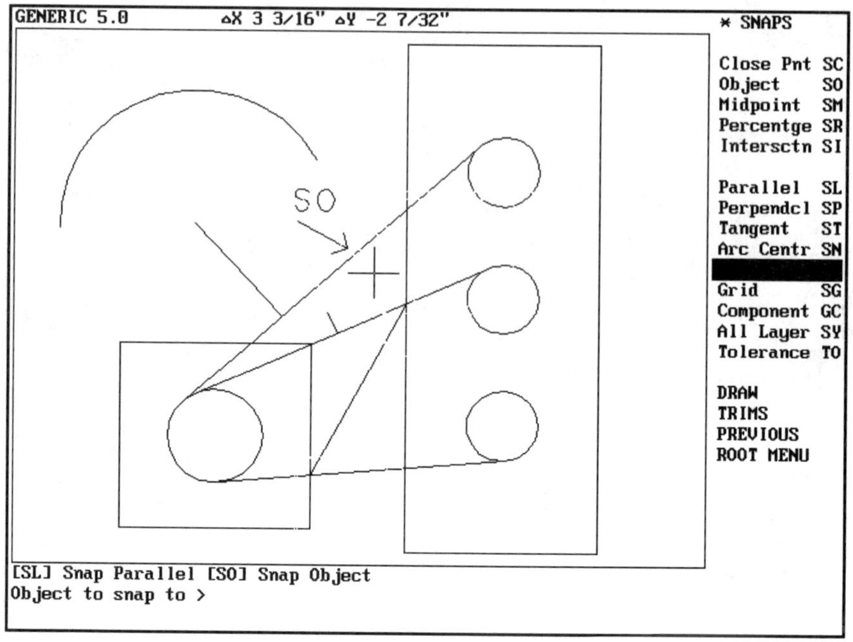

Figure 4.40: *Using Snap Object to identify the starting point.*

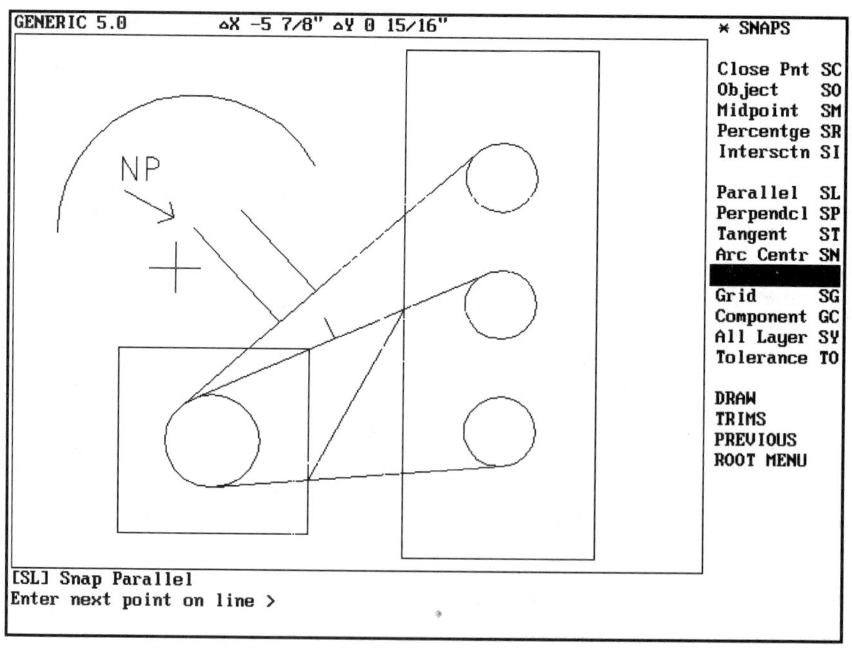

Figure 4.41: *Use Snap To Nearest Point to set the distance.*

Component Snaps (GC)

Component Snaps is a toggle. If it is on, you may snap to construction points on objects that are part of a component. If it is off, the only point on a component that can be snapped is the reference point that identifies it as a component. This command will be explored in more detail in the chapter on components.

Snap To Non-Editable Layers (SY)

The All Layers Edit command (AL) was mentioned in Chapter 2. If it is on, any object on the screen may be edited. If All Layers is off, only the objects on the current layer may be edited. Snap to Non-Editable Layers modifies this slightly by enabling you to snap to objects on *visible* non-editable layers. If you have hidden the objects on a layer with Layer Hide (YH), they cannot be snapped to, regardless of the status of Snap To Non-Editable Layers.

Like All Layers Edit, Snap To Non-Editable Layers is a toggle; each time you use it, the status switches between on and off.

Redrawing the Screen for Clarity

The bits of light on your monitor that display everything you see are known as pixels. Sometimes, as you draw, a few pixels will be unintentionally erased or left on-screen. When you draw a window around an object to erase, for example, your window may erase a bit of a line it crosses even though the line itself is not erased. The redraw commands can clear up unwanted clutter and restore missing pixels.

Redraw (RD)

Redraw, found on the DISPLAY menu, normally is the command to use to restore objects to their normal clarity. When you type RD or select Redraw from the menu, Generic CADD removes and redraws everything in the drawing window. The size of objects does not change (no change in the display scale). The speed of the redraw depends on the speed of your computer equipment and the size of the drawing. Large drawings take more time to redraw than small ones. Having construction points and/or reference points turned on also can slow down the redraw, because their presence means more pixels to display.

Backward Redraw (BR)

If you have a large drawing and you find yourself needing to redraw the screen quite often, you may save time by turning on Backward Redraw, found on the ZOOMS menu.

Backward Redraw is a toggle command. When it is off, the screen redraws items in the order they were drawn. In other words, the first line drawn is the first redrawn. When Backward Redraw is on, and the Redraw command is used, the last line drawn becomes the first line redrawn. The redraw process continues in reverse order until the first line drawn becomes the last line redrawn.

The reason Backward Redraw can be a time-saver is that you usually edit the material most recently drawn. If you must do a redraw before you edit something on-screen, turn Backward Redraw on and issue the Redraw command. The items you drew last will redraw first. When everything you need to see is back on the screen, press any key to stop the redraw process. All the objects that don't make it back onto the screen are safe—CADD just didn't redraw them. On a slower computer, you could save a minute or more if the drawing is large just by using Backward Redraw and stopping screen redraw when the objects you need are on-screen.

TIP

To gain additional speed in the redraw process, try hiding some of the layers in the drawing.

Window Redraw (WD)

At times, only a small portion of the screen may show stray pixels or have missing pixels. If this is the case, try Window Redraw (WD), found on the ZOOMS menu. You can use it to redraw only the portion of the screen that you draw a window around.

Fast Redraw (FA)

Redrawing large drawings can eat up a lot of time, time you'd rather not spend watching Generic CADD redraw what you have created every time you change the zoom factor. The Fast Redraw command, on the DISPLAY menu, can help you out.

Fast Redraw has five options, each one a toggle. With Fast Redraw, you can do the following:

- ❑ Have text redrawn as standard points
- ❑ Have arcs redrawn as line segments
- ❑ Have all line widths and linetypes display as width and type zero
- ❑ Hide hatch patterns
- ❑ Hide solid color fills

If you select the Arcs option, you have an additional choice to make. The number of line segments displayed when Fast Arcs is on can be adjusted. The default is 3, which means circles will be displayed as triangles. You can set Fast Arcs to any number of segments between 3 and 12, but the more segments you choose, the less benefit the command offers.

If you use Fast Redraw to change any of these settings, the new status will not take effect until the next time the screen is redrawn.

Summary

The techniques and tools of manual drafting were developed to serve a specific need—the precise, accurate visual display of design information. To improve upon manual drafting, a CADD program must not only display objects with precision and accuracy but also offer the user the benefits of automation to make the accurate drawing of objects easier than doing it at the drafting table.

Generic CADD 5.0 provides a variety of commands to automate and simplify the task of drawing with precision. The on-screen grid provides a visual perspective of relative sizes and interacts with the drawing cursor like a magnet, limiting movement to specific locations. Snap commands use complex mathematics to identify specific locations instantaneously. The various snap commands offer many ways to find the locations of specified points and parts of the basic types of drawing objects. Generic CADD also offers a number of redraw commands to improve the clarity of the on-screen image, including Window Redraw and Fast Redraw.

5

Drawing Techniques

The chapters so far have covered the fundamentals of drawing objects on the screen, controlling their display, and using snap commands to move them to precise locations. As you build a drawing, sometimes a new object to be drawn shares a common point or a common length with another object. Taking advantage of these situations in your drawing is known as using existing geometry. The snap commands are all about using existing geometry, and much of the drawing we did in Chapter 4, including placing the circles inside the rectangles, made use of existing geometry. You'll be doing more of this kind of drawing throughout the later chapters.

In this chapter, you will learn more about placing objects in drawings accurately and efficiently. This will include using the various types of keyboard entry to place objects on-screen, more drawing aids, and a few tips for good measure. You will see in this chapter that there is always more than one way to draw in Generic CADD; the trick is to use the most efficient method.

When using manual entry, you have three modes available. You also have a variety of ways of controlling the cursor. You can constrain it in several ways, you can have it track where you've been, you can shut off the default rubberbanding, or you can operate the cursor without a mouse or digitizer.

Coordinate Entry Fundamentals

When you draw a line on the screen, it has a start point, a length, a heading (the direction it points), and an end point—and each of these elements has a location.

At times, you may not care about any of these aspects; at other times, you may want to be in control of each of these aspects when you draw the line. To sketch a design idea, for example, using the mouse to place lines (combined with the occasional use of Snap To Nearest Point) may be all you need. But if you have to draw an object based on measurements written in a notebook, you will find it easier to type in the location of each line at the keyboard. Generic CADD calls this manual entry.

Everything you draw goes on the coordinate grid, and the location of the cursor on the grid is always displayed in the coordinate display. In Chapter 2, you saw how the Display Coordinates (DC) command switched the display between absolute, relative, basepoint, and polar coordinates. Figure 5.1 shows the possible settings in the prompt line. Now you'll see how to use each one for drawing.

Absolute Coordinates and Manual Entry Origin

The default coordinate display mode is Absolute Coordinates. If the coordinate display is set to Absolute and reads X 3" Y 3", this means the cursor is at a location on the grid that is three inches up from the 0,0 point, and three inches right of the 0,0 point. This is because the default method of manual entry (keyboard entry) is Origin. This means that every coordinate typed at the keyboard is understood to be in relation to the 0,0 point of the grid, also known as the *Origin Point.* If you press Enter and then move the cursor to the location X 6" Y 6", you create a line as shown in figure 5.2. Follow the steps below to set your display coordinates and manual entry method to draw this line.

Using Absolute Coordinates

Prompt	*Input*	*Description*
`Command`	**SG**	Sets Snap To Grid off (if prompt says ON after you type this command, retype it)
`Command`	**GR**	Sets Screen Grid off (if prompt says ON after you type this command, retype it)
`Command`	**MO**	Sets Manual Entry, Origin on
`Command`	**DC**	Sets your display coordinates to match figure 5.1
`Command`	**LS**	Sets the screen limits
`Change height limit (X.000)`	**12**	Sets the new height to 12"
`Change width limit (X.000)`	**18**	Sets the new width to 18"

Using Absolute Coordinates—continued

Prompt	*Input*	*Description*
Command	**ZL**	Sets the screen view to match the limits
Command	**LW8**	Sets line width to 8 (note we typed in new line width without waiting to read prompt)
Command	**0,0**	Moves the cursor to coordinate location X 0 Y 0
Command	**PU**	Issues Pen Up command, so next movement of cursor will not draw a line
Command	**3,3**	Moves the cursor to coordinate location X 3" Y 3"
Command	**6,6**	Moves the cursor to coordinate location X 6" Y 6", and draws a line from X 3" Y 3" to here

Draw another line using keyboard entry, but first make a change. For the first line, set Manual Entry to Origin (MO). This means that every coordinate location typed at the keyboard is understood to be so many X units and so many Y units away *from the 0,0 point of the grid.* This 0,0 never changes, so you can refer to Manual Entry Origin as creating *absolute* coordinates.

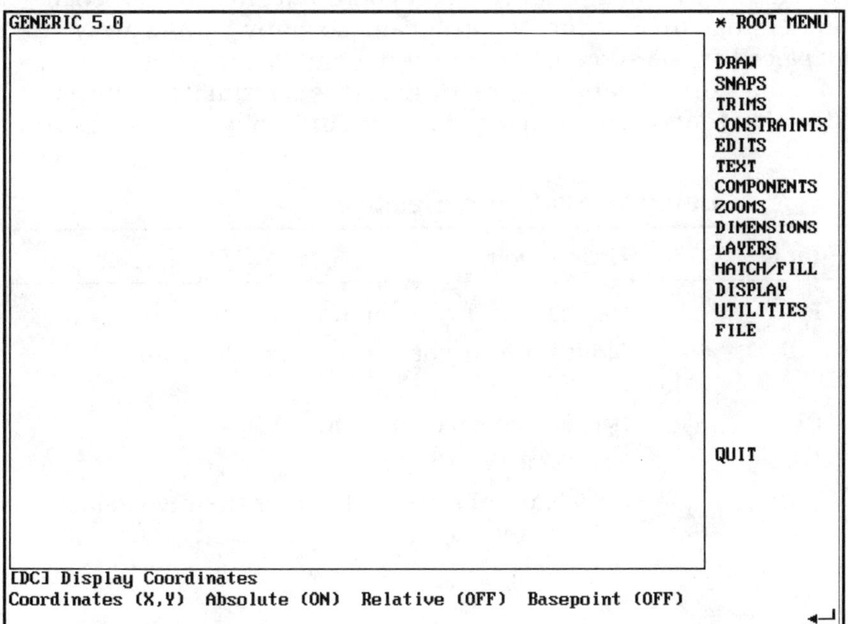

Figure 5.1: *Settings for the Display Coordinates command.*

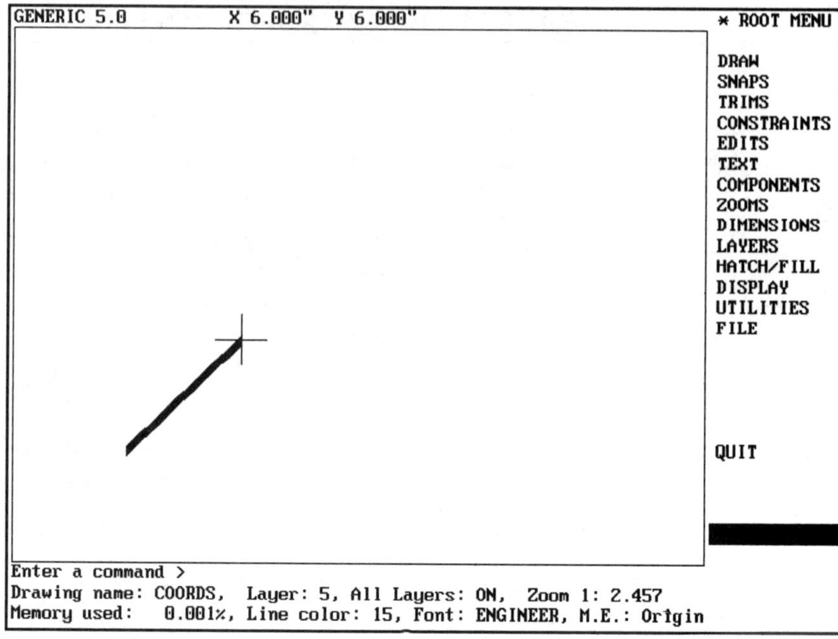

Figure 5.2: *A line drawn with Manual Entry Origin.*

Manual Entry Relative

When you set Manual Entry to Relative (MR), every coordinate location typed at the keyboard is understood to be so many X units and so many Y units away from the *last point placed* on the screen. Since the 0,0 point is always changing, you can refer to Manual Entry Relative as creating *relative* coordinates. This is an important distinction that can make a big difference in what you draw, as you will see.

Using Manual Entry Relative

Prompt	*Input*	*Description*
`Command`	**PU**	Issues Pen Up command
`Command`	**0,0**	Moves the cursor to coordinate location X 0 Y 0
`Command`	**PU**	Issues Pen Up command
`Command`	**LWO**	Sets Line Width to zero
`Command`	**MR**	Sets Manual Entry to Relative (relative to last point entered)

Using Manual Entry Relative—continued

Prompt	*Input*	*Description*
Command	**3,3**	Moves the cursor three inches up and three inches right of last point placed (X 0 Y 0)
Command	**6,6**	Moves cursor six inches up and six inches right of last point placed

In figure 5.3, you see a line drawn using the same coordinates, but it looks quite different with Manual Entry Relative in effect.

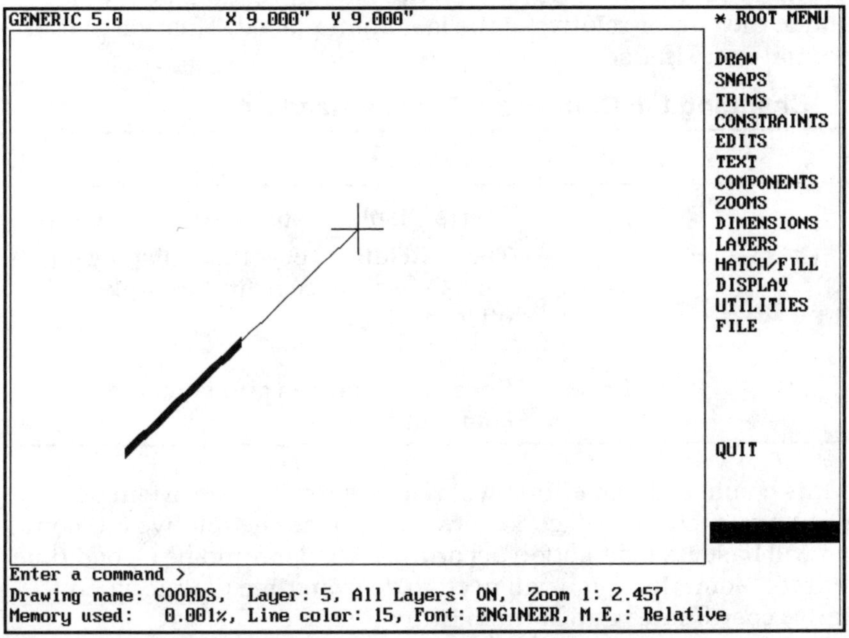

Figure 5.3: *The same line with Manual Entry Relative.*

Notice the difference? When the first line was drawn, Generic CADD interpreted everything from the keyboard using only absolute coordinates. When the second line was drawn, Generic CADD interpreted everything from the keyboard using only relative coordinates. With absolute, every coordinate was a set distance from the 0,0 point on the grid. With relative, every coordinate was a set distance from the last point placed.

There is one oddity here. Although you used the Manual Entry Relative (MR) command to tell Generic CADD how to interpret what you typed at the keyboard, you never told it to change how it displays coordinates at the top of the screen. Did you notice in figure 5.3 and in your drawing that the coordinate display at the top of the screen says X 9" Y 9"? The display is still telling you where the cursor sits using absolute coordinates, even though the keyboard commands are interpreted as relative coordinates. You can change the coordinate display so that it matches the manual entry method in operation.

Relative Coordinates

When you're drawing with Manual Entry Relative, it can be confusing to type in 6,6 and have the coordinate display read X 9" Y 9". You can use the Display Coordinate (DC) command to change the coordinate display readout so that it shows the position of the cursor relative to the last point placed. This will match the method of manual entry in use.

Changing the Coordinate Display Readout

Prompt	*Input*	*Description*
`Command`	**DC**	Starts Display Coordinates command

`Coordinates (X,Y)`
`Absolute (ON)`
`Relative (OFF)`
`Basepoint (OFF)`
	R	Turns Relative coordinate display on, turns Absolute coordinate display off (see fig. 5.4)

`...Relative (ON)`	Press Enter	Saves the changes and ends the command

When you finish this command, the cursor will relocate itself to the origin point (absolute 0,0). But be warned—it still considers X 9" Y 9" as the relative 0,0 point on the screen and will base its next action accordingly. This would be a good time to re-orient the cursor, something you will need to do from time to time when drawing with relative coordinates and Manual Entry Relative.

Re-Orienting the Cursor

Prompt	*Input*	*Description*
`Command`	Press Enter	Makes the current cursor location the last point placed
`Command`	**PU**	Issues Pen Up command (automatic Line command status is off)

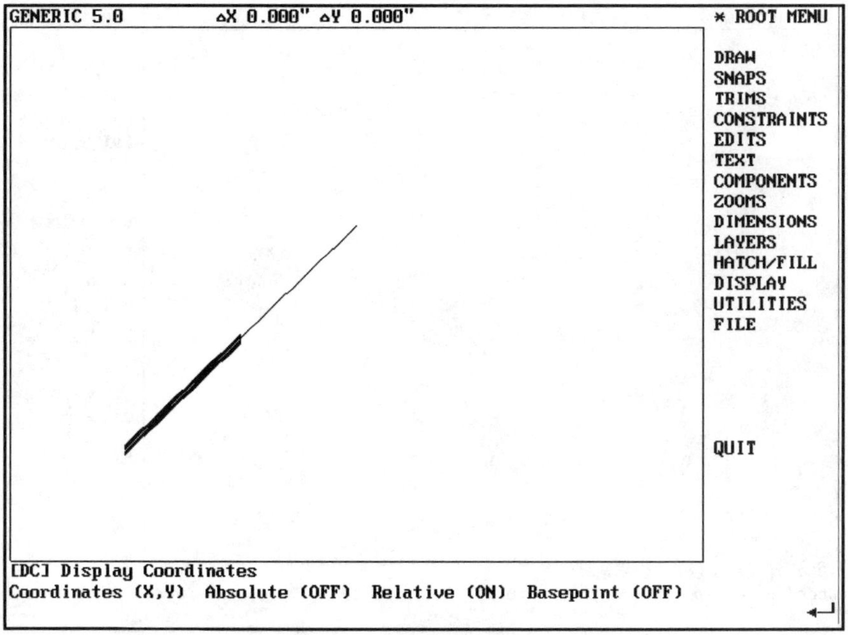

Figure 5.4: *Display coordinates now show relative coordinates.*

Polar Coordinates

The Cartesian coordinates you have used so far, both absolute and relative, identify a *position.* Polar coordinates identify a *distance* and a *heading.* Switch the screen to display polar coordinates, so you can explore how the polar readout works.

Setting Polar Coordinates

Prompt	*Input*	*Description*
`Command`	**DC**	Initiates Display Coordinates command
`Coordinates (polar) ...Absolute (OFF)`	**C**	Changes coordinates to Polar (see fig. 5.5)
`...Coordinates...`	Press Enter	Ends command

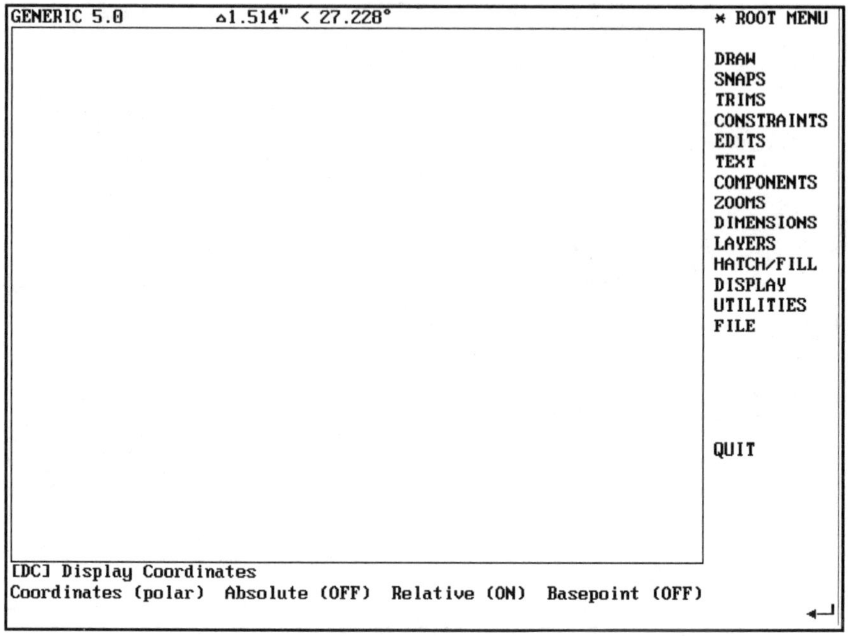

Figure 5.5: *Polar coordinates as the active coordinate method.*

Like Cartesian coordinates, polar coordinates can be absolute (based on the origin point of the drawing) or relative (based on the last point placed). When they are relative, the readout on the screen identifies the distance and heading of the cursor based on the last point placed. When polar coordinates are absolute, the readout on the screen identifies the distance and heading of the cursor based on its distance and angle from the origin point. Either way, zero degrees always points to 3 o'clock, and the headings proceed counterclockwise around the circle. Figure 5.6 shows several polar headings.

Follow the steps below to gain practice using polar coordinates.

Using Polar Coordinates

Prompt	*Input*	*Description*
`Command`	**DXY**	Erases the drawing
`Command`	Use the mouse to move the cursor to the middle of the screen and press Enter	Places the start point of a new line
`Command`	**3,<90**	Moves the cursor 3" on a 90-degree heading from the last point placed; draws a line

Using Polar Coordinates—continued

Prompt	*Input*	*Description*
`Command`	**2,<45**	Moves the cursor 2" on a 45-degree heading from last point placed; draws a line
`Command`	**4,<180**	Moves the cursor 4" on a 180-degree heading from last point placed; draws a line
`Command`	**2,<315**	Moves the cursor 2" on a 315-degree heading from last point placed; draws a line
`Command`	**3,<270**	Moves the cursor 3" on a 270-degree heading from last point placed; draws a line

Your screen should look like the one in figure 5.7. Save this drawing as SHAPE1.DWG. You will use it in a later chapter.

`Command`	**DS**	Issues the Drawing Save command
`Save File as`	Name the file SHAPE1	Saves the drawing as SHAPE1.DWG

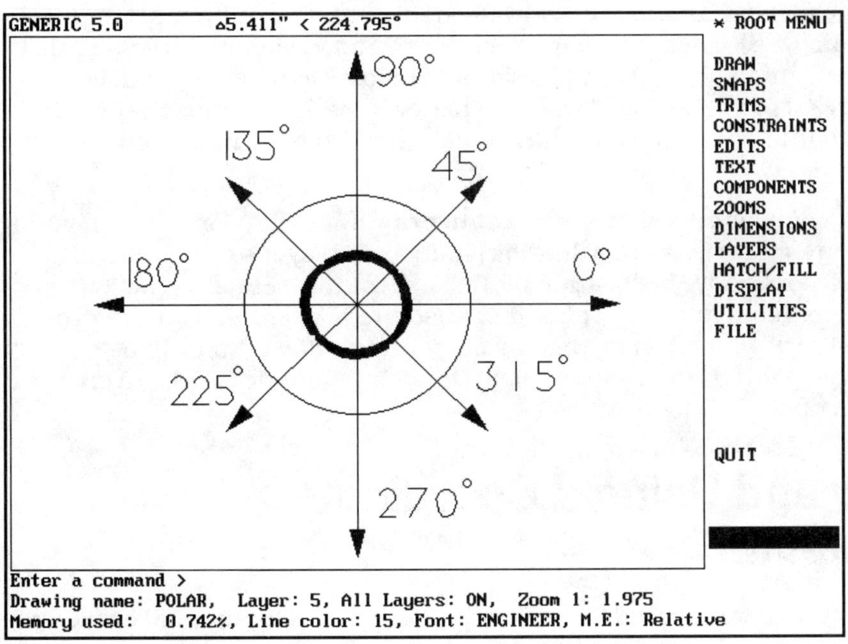

Figure 5.6: *Examples of polar headings.*

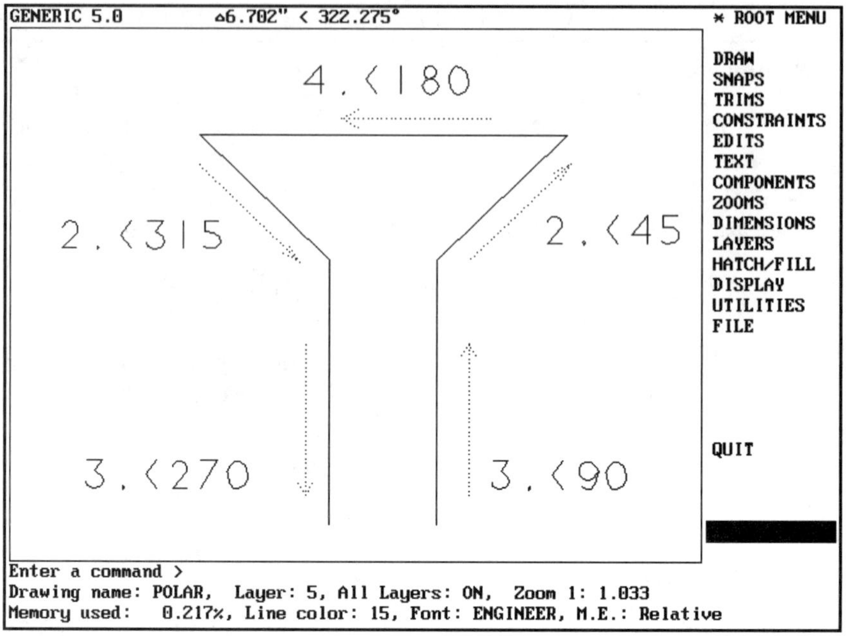

Figure 5.7: *A shape drawn by typing polar coordinates.*

Basepoint Coordinates and Manual Entry Basepoint

A basepoint in Generic CADD is a temporary origin point you can place anywhere on the coordinate plane. It remains essentially non-existent until you set Manual Entry to Basepoint (MB). Then it becomes active, and all keyboard entry is evaluated using the current basepoint. The coordinate display can be set to show either Cartesian (X,Y) or polar coordinates. Whenever Manual Entry is set to Basepoint, the coordinate display will have a diamond (◆) in front of each number.

Using the basepoint is handy when you want to draw lines that connect to a point off-screen or to enter a series of coordinates (such as surveyor's data) that all relate to a specific location. The location of the basepoint is set using the Basepoint (BP) command and is expressed in absolute X,Y terms, no matter the mode of manual entry or coordinate display currently in effect. You will use Manual Entry Basepoint in the chapter on customizing Generic CADD, to create a command you'll call Snap Basepoint.

Choosing and Using a Coordinate Display Method

Here are a few points to remember when choosing a method for manual entry and setting the status of the display coordinates.

- ❑ When you select absolute, relative, or basepoint display using the Display Coordinates command, be careful how you make the selection. When you turn a selection on, the alternative selections are automatically turned off. But if you turn off a setting that is on, it will switch to off and the others will stay off, too, leaving you with no coordinate display format in effect.
- ❑ Be careful to match the manual entry method with the appropriate coordinate display. It would be confusing to have manual entry set to relative, for example, but have the coordinate display show absolute coordinates.
- ❑ Choosing a manual entry method is usually a three-step process. First you choose the manual entry method (Origin, Relative, or Basepoint). Then you choose the appropriate coordinate readout to match (polar or Cartesian). Then you select the display type to match the manual entry method you selected (Absolute for Origin, Relative, Basepoint). If you plan on entering only one or two lines using a manual entry method, and you don't need to rely on the coordinate display, it is safe to skip this process. Just don't forget to return the manual entry method back to Origin!

Controlling the Cursor

The shy star of this chapter is the drawing cursor. Earlier, this chapter covered the various ways to describe the location of the cursor on the coordinate plane. Generic CADD gives you several ways to limit the movement of the cursor.

Using Cursor Control Commands

The cursor control commands discussed here are all in the CONSTRAINTS menu. In addition to these commands, the grid commands (Grid On/Off, Grid Size, and three grid settings) are on the CONSTRAINTS menu.

Ortho Mode (OR)

You're already familiar with Ortho Mode. When Ortho Mode is on (it's a toggle), all lines entered into the drawing will be limited to increments of 90 degrees. If you are drawing something with all horizontal and vertical lines, Ortho Mode is an easy way to keep the lines straight.

The Ctrl key works with the Ortho mode as a temporary toggle. If you press Ctrl while drawing, the status of Ortho mode is reversed. If Ortho mode is on, and you need to draw one diagonal line, don't bother to turn Ortho mode off. Just press Ctrl, draw the diagonal, then release Ctrl. If you need one perfectly horizontal line, but Snap to Grid and Ortho mode are off, press Ctrl to make Ortho mode active temporarily. Ortho mode is a powerful drawing tool that you will return to again and again throughout the rest of this book.

Ortho Angle (OA)

It is possible to adjust the angles used by Ortho mode. They will still be in increments of 90 degrees, but you can rotate the base heading of Ortho mode from 0 degrees (3 o'clock) to any other angle. If you create isometric drawings, set Ortho Angle to 30 degrees to help you draw lines at the proper angle.

In figure 5.8, the square on the left was drawn using Ortho Angle at zero degrees. The one on the right was drawn with Ortho Angle at 30 degrees.

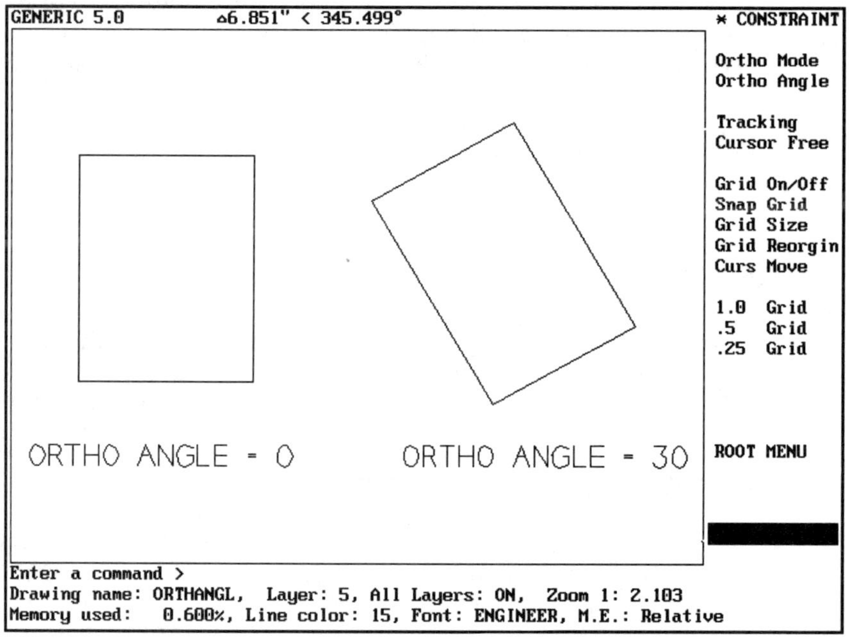

Figure 5.8: Two squares drawn with Ortho mode on.

Tracking (TK)

Tracking lets you move from one point to another, leaving a trail as you go, in search of a specific point on the screen. It is available anytime you must enter a point, by typing TK at the prompt. As you move from point to point using Tracking, a line extends back to the last point you placed. When you click to select another point, Tracking forgets about any previous points selected while in Tracking mode and attaches the line to the latest point placed. When you have found your way to the point you need, type **PU** to end Tracking. The position of your cursor after you end Tracking will be the point you need to finish when you started Tracking.

Tracking is used most often when moving objects and placing components. Hands-on examples showing the use of Tracking will be found in Chapters 9, 10, and 11.

Cursor Free (CF)

Normally when you draw in Generic CADD, there is a "rubberband" attached to the cursor. If you are placing the end point of a line, this rubberband stretches back to the first point placed. If Cursor Free is on (it's a toggle), it detaches the cursor from the rubberband. As you saw in Chapter 4, this enables you to use Snap commands that would otherwise be unavailable. You can limit the placement of lines with Ortho mode, and still use nearby points as references to snap to.

Cursor Movement (CM)

If you do not have a mouse or digitizer and must rely on the arrow keys as your only method of cursor movement, you need to be familiar with Cursor Movement. Users who have pointing devices will never need it. If you are using the screen grid and moving the cursor with the arrow keys, Cursor Movement will force the cursor to move only one grid point at a time. Cursor movement is a toggle, which you should turn on if you are using the arrow keys and Snap To Grid.

Summary

This chapter focused on cursor movement and the various ways to identify the position of the cursor. The cursor is only the means to our ends, but knowing the position and heading of the cursor helps us to use more than one way to place objects in the drawing.

In this chapter, you learned how to draw by typing in coordinates at the keyboard. This is referred to in Generic CADD as manual entry. Manual entry takes three forms, depending on what you use as a reference for your data. Manual Entry Origin uses the 0,0 point of the coordinate grid to calculate the locations of objects; Manual Entry Relative uses the last point placed as a reference. And Manual Entry Basepoint uses a temporary 0,0 point (that you designate) as a reference.

Generic CADD offers two ways to show the location of the cursor on the drawing screen—by using X,Y coordinates (Cartesian coordinates) or by using polar coordinates, which show the heading of the cursor and its distance from point 0,0. What either coordinate method defines as 0,0 depends on the style of operation you choose—Absolute (Origin), Relative, or Basepoint.

In addition to the various methods of manual entry and coordinate display, there are ways to control the movement of the cursor. Ortho mode limits the cursor to increments of 90 degrees. Ortho Angle sets the base angle for Ortho mode. Cursor Free allows the cursor to separate from the rubberband line, and Tracking lets you move from one point to the next in the middle of a drawing command without drawing anything, leaving a temporary trail in its path.

As you progress in your knowledge of Generic CADD 5.0, you will find ways to take advantage of each of these systems.

The next chapter detours from the techniques of drawing to focus on the techniques of adding text to drawings. A few well-placed words of explanation can make the difference between a good drawing and a great one.

6

Labeling and Explaining the Drawing

When most people see Generic CADD for the first time, they are impressed by the program's many ways to draw and reshape objects. They applaud the program's capability to place dimensions in the drawing automatically, and they are duly impressed to see on-screen dimensions recalculate when the object changes shape. Show them text in drawings, however, and most people respond with a shrug. After all, text is text. You type in some words, and they appear in the drawing. No big deal, right? Wrong.

The capability to create and place text in a drawing is one of Generic CADD's best time-saving features. If you had to create legible text by drawing each character, it would take you hours to annotate a drawing. And what style, or typeface, would you use? Could you maintain consistency from letter to letter?

Generic CADD is not a word processing program; it is a graphics program. Text that you place in a CADD drawing is not the same as the text you are familiar with in word processing programs. Generic CADD uses the computer's graphics environment, rather than the text-based environment most word processing programs use. Any text that appears inside the drawing window is actually drawn with lines and curves. The look of the text must conform to generally accepted type styles, called *fonts*.

Text Fundamentals

The purpose of text in a CADD drawing is to convey information. This sounds simple enough, but information can be conveyed in many ways. The right fonts for displaying text are a powerful enhancement to any drawing. Consider the following examples of what you can do with fonts.

- **Draw attention.** Bold fonts (wider lines or a more "outspoken" font style) focus attention on specific portions of documents.
- **Organize information.** The careful selection of fonts can help to show the relative importance of information, as the use of italic and bold text does in a manuscript.
- **Impart a theme.** Documents created for specific clients often have greater appeal if a type style identified with the client can be used, aiding in visualization of the completed project.
- **Display a logo.** Many clients, especially those working on joint projects, want their company name included on the final documents in the type style of their choice.
- **Convey an emotion.** Advertisers have long used type styles to arouse emotion or convey an attitude. Type styles can look whimsical, formal, traditional, or state-of-the-art to set the tone of the document.
- **Perpetuate a tradition.** Sometimes fonts are chosen simply because documents have always been done that way. Some of the fonts included with Generic CADD 5.0 match lettering styles that have been taught in drafting courses for generations.
- **Greater simulation of the actual product.** By using the actual production type style in a design document, instrumentation and panel labeling can be accurately designed, evaluated, and modified for full effectiveness.

Generic CADD 5.0 includes three basic steps for using text: selecting the font, setting placement and size options, and placing the text in the drawing. Commands are available to execute these steps, as well as to edit text already placed in a drawing, to import text from other files, and to create new fonts for use in Generic CADD.

Using Font Select (FS)

Before you place text in a Generic CADD drawing, you must select the font you wish to use. The program is shipped with eight fonts, and two volumes of additional fonts are available from Generic Software. You can also create your own fonts, which will be discussed later in this chapter. Figure 6.1 shows each of the eight fonts available in Generic CADD 5.0.

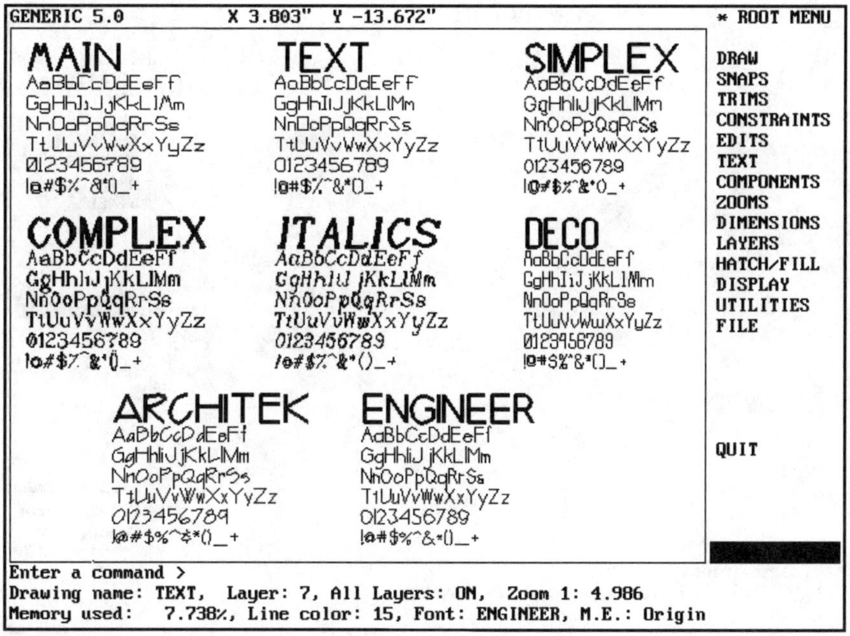

Figure 6.1: *Fonts distributed with Generic CADD 5.0.*

When you use Generic CADD for the first time, the default font for text in the drawing is Main. Text for dimensions and attributes also selected using Font Select will be discussed in Chapters 13 and 14.

If you have not done so already, start Generic CADD 5.0; then follow the steps below to change the font for text placed in the drawing.

Changing a Font

Prompt	*Input*	*Description*
`Command`	**FS**	Starts the Font Select command (see fig. 6.2)

`Text (MAIN)`
`Dimension (ENGINEER)`
`Attribute (ENGINEER)`
	T	Changes font for regular text

`Select file from side menu`	Move menu bar to Engineer and click second mouse button, or press Home	Selects Engineer as the new font for text in the drawing

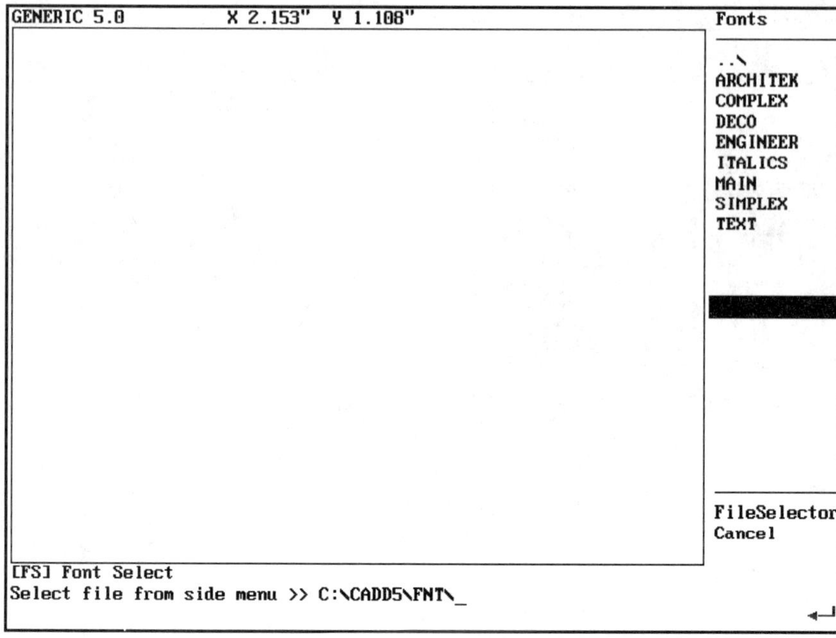

Figure 6.2: *Fonts are displayed in the side menu.*

Text Placement Settings (TS)

Once you have selected the font you want, using Font Select, you must choose the size of the text in the drawing and set a number of style and placement options. Most of these options are included in the Text Spacing command found on the TEXT menu, and a few have their own two-letter commands. Each option is described in detail. Many of these settings are seldom changed from their defaults; others you will change every time you place text in a drawing. If you place text in a drawing and then change any of these settings, only the text that you place *after* changing the setting will be affected. The text already in the drawing will stay as it is. (To change the font of text already a part of the drawing, use the Text Change command, discussed later.)

Many of the options found in the Text Spacing prompt (see fig. 6.3) take their cue from the Text Size (TZ) command (see fig. 6.4). When preparing to place text in a drawing, you should determine the appropriate size before you adjust the other settings.

If you plan to print or plot your drawing at a certain scale, set the text size accordingly. If, for example, you need to print the drawing at a scale of 1" = 1' (1/12 scale), and you want your text to be 1/4" tall on paper, set your text size to 3" (1/4" × 12). A required scale on paper of 1/4" = 1' (1/48 scale), with text 1/4" high on your print-out would require a text size of 12" (1/4" × 48).

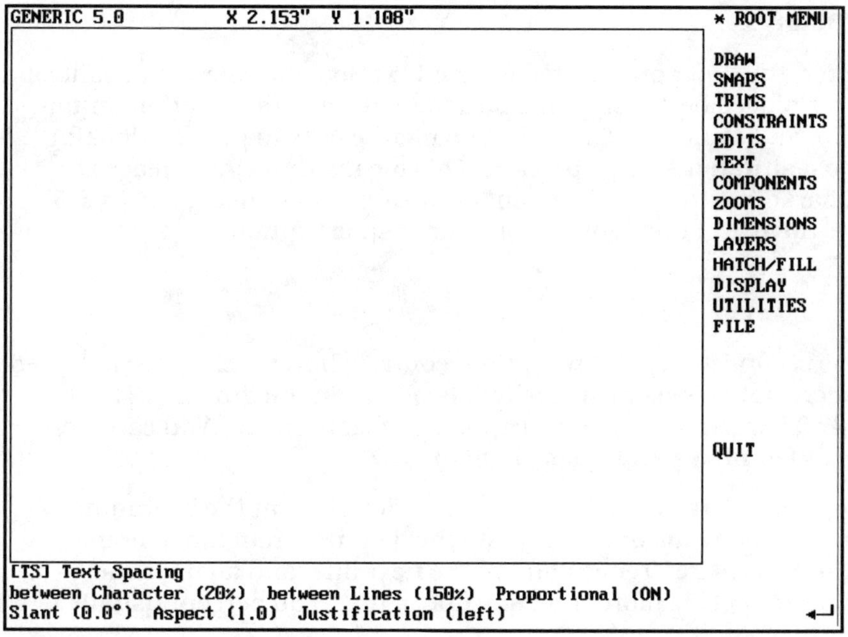

Figure 6.3: *The Text Spacing command.*

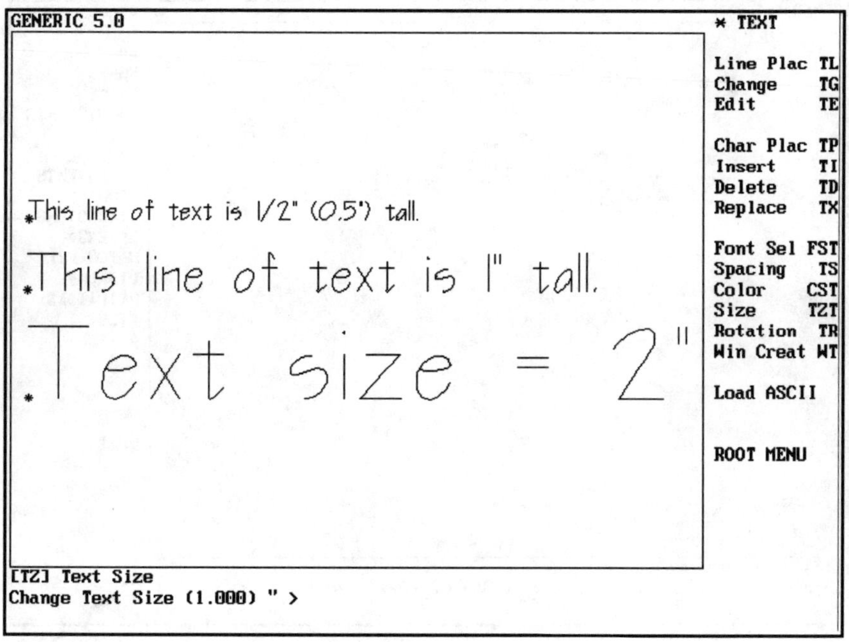

Figure 6.4: *The Text Size command.*

Between Character

Between Character, the first option listed for the Text Spacing command, controls how much space is placed between each character (characters are letters, numbers, punctuation, and symbols). The default, which results in the best-looking placement for most situations, is 20 percent. This means that CADD places a space between characters that is 20 percent of the text size in use. Figures 6.5 and 6.6 illustrate the use of the Between Character space option.

Between Line

Between Line, the second Text Spacing option, controls how much space is placed between lines when more than one line of text is placed in the drawing. The default spacing is 150 percent, using text size as the measurement. You can see some samples of different spacing effects in figure 6.7.

Each line of text placed in the drawing has a reference point at the beginning of the first line. The Between Line option adjusts the distance from the reference point of the first line to the reference point of the next line, and all lines thereafter. When you need to place more than one line of text, 150 percent usually is the best choice.

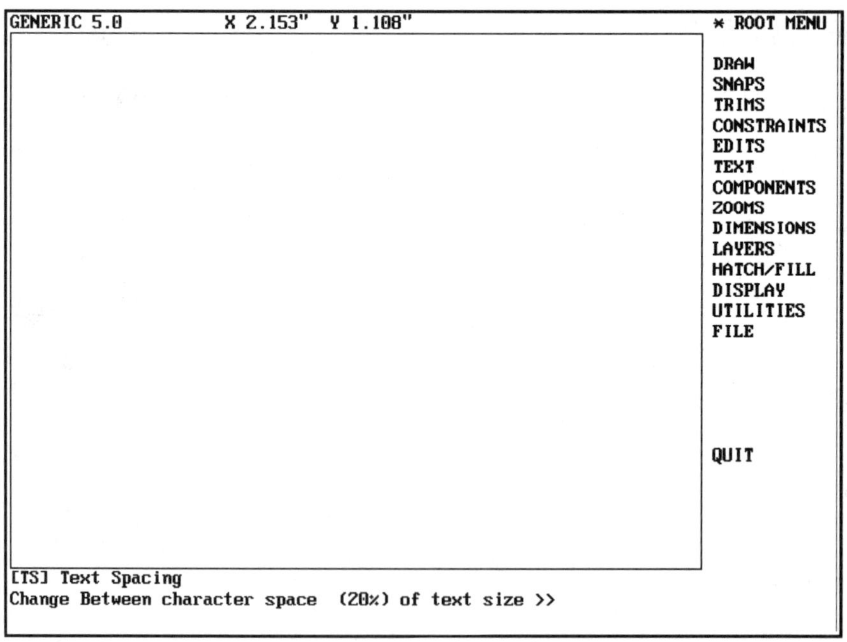

Figure 6.5: *Type percentage of text size at the Between Character spacing prompt.*

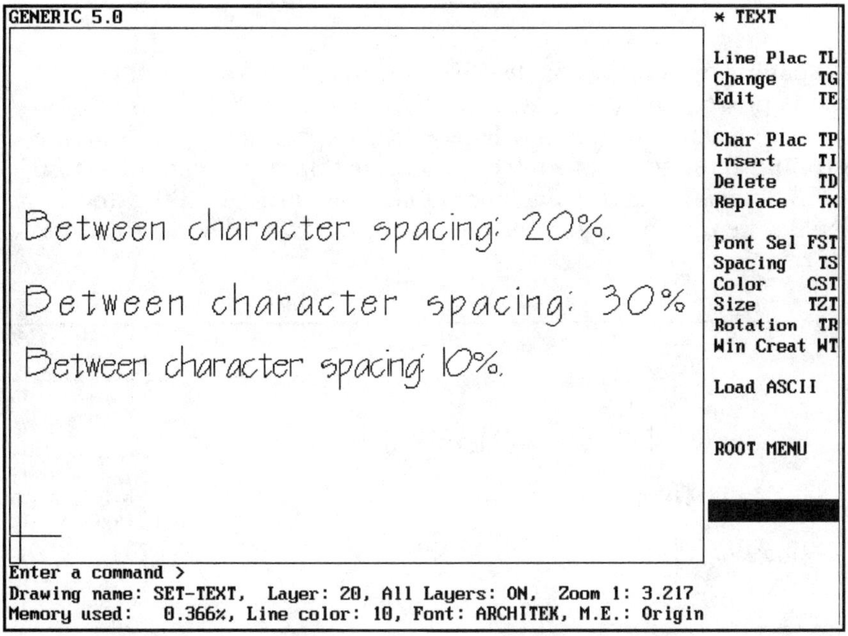

Figure 6.6: *Different spacings using the Between Character option.*

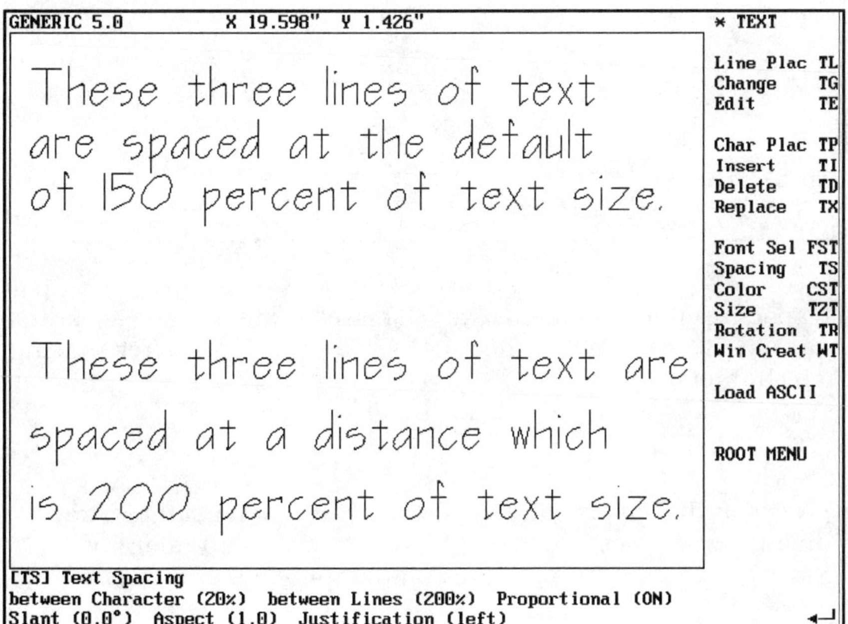

Figure 6.7: *Different line spacing effects.*

Proportional

The Proportional spacing option is a toggle. The default setting is on, which means that as text is placed (using the Text Line command only; more on that shortly) the spacing between characters will be varied to produce more readable text. The Between Character space of each character is taken into consideration by Generic CADD in determining the placement of each character in the line. An "i," for example, will take up less space on the line than a "w." Observe the difference in figure 6.8.

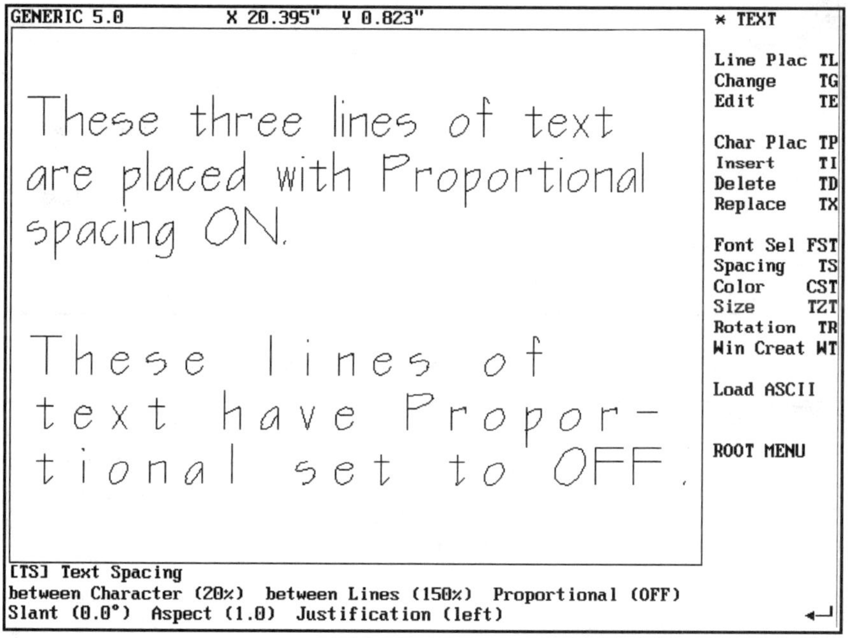

Figure 6.8: *The Engineer font, showing proportional spacing on and off.*

If the Proportional spacing option is off, all text will be set in monospace, meaning an "i" will take up as much space on the line as a "w." Between Character spacing is the same for each character.

Slant

The Slant option gives you the opportunity to have each character slant forward or backward, for an italicized effect (see fig. 6.9). You can adjust the slant between negative 45 and positive 45 degrees. The default, for text standing straight up, is zero degrees.

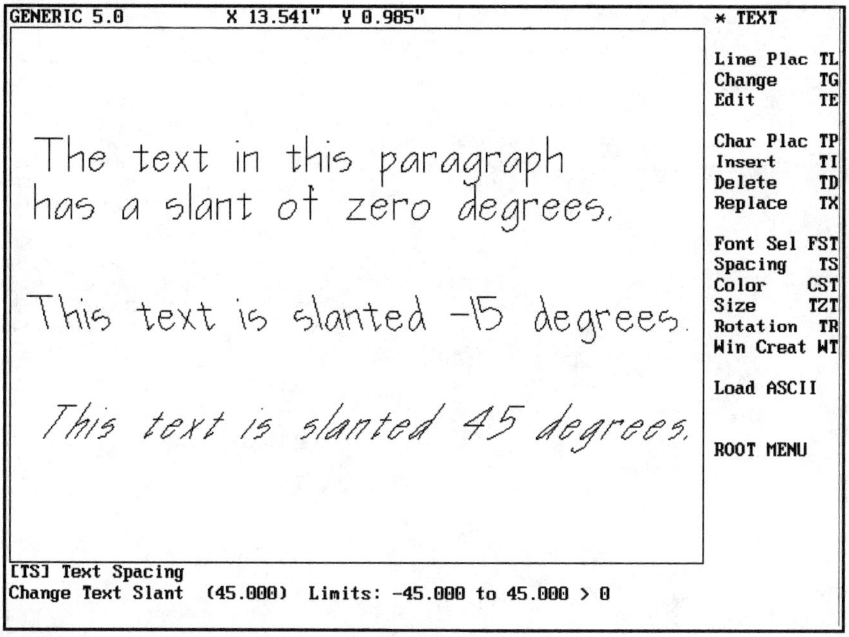

Figure 6.9: *Type the number of degrees desired to slant text.*

Aspect

Aspect is the width of each character and can be set independently of the Text Size (TZ) command, which controls the height of text. The default setting is 1, meaning that text will be the width it was when the font was defined. Setting the Aspect at 2 would double the width of each character (see fig. 6.10). The maximum value for Aspect is 10 and the minimum is .1. Assigning a negative value to Aspect would cause each character to be placed backwards.

If space is limited, Aspect can sometimes be used to create display text that is no taller than other text in the drawing but stands out because of the width change.

Justification

The Justification option does not control the size or look of individual characters; it is used to place blocks of text in the drawing. You have three choices: Left, Center, and Right. When you use the Text Line command to place a block of text (a block being one or more lines), you are asked to select a starting point, also known as the insertion point. Justification uses the insertion point to determine where to place the text.

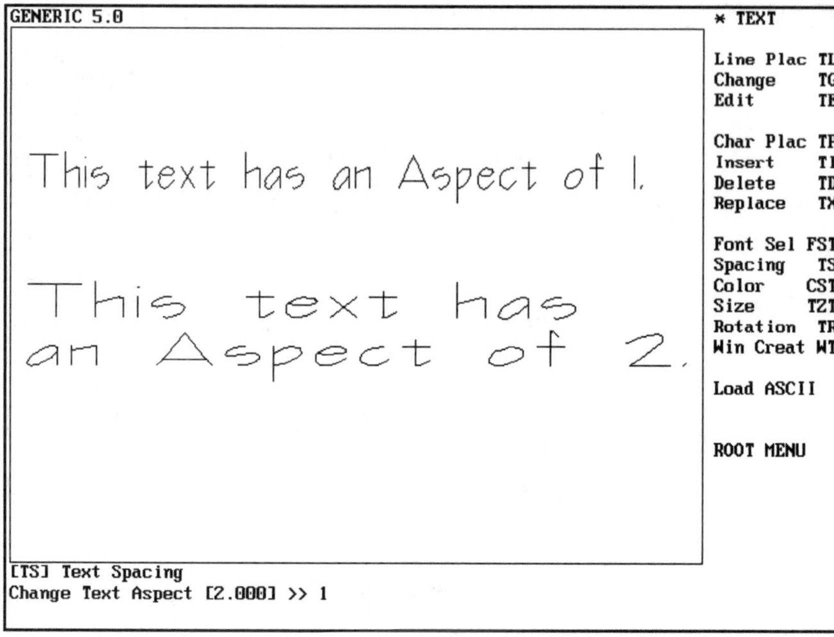

Figure 6.10: *Type in a value between .1 and 10 to change Text Aspect (width).*

Left justification means that the text will be lined up in a straight line along the left edge, as with the text you are reading now. The insertion point will be the leftmost point of the line, and the reference points of all other lines in the block will line up immediately below the first point. All of the text will be placed to the right of the point.

Center justification means that for every line of text placed in the drawing, half of the line will be to the left of the insertion point and half will be to the right.

Right justification means that the text will be aligned in a straight line along the right edge. The first line's insertion point will be the rightmost point of the first line, and the reference points of all other lines will be immediately below the first line reference point.

Figure 6.11 illustrates how an identical paragraph of text will look if placed using each of the three justification options.

Text Rotation (TR)

Lines of text may be placed at any angle in Generic CADD with the Text Rotation command. Positive numbers give an upward slant; negative numbers give a downward slant. The default is zero degrees. Figure 6.12 shows some of the effects you can achieve.

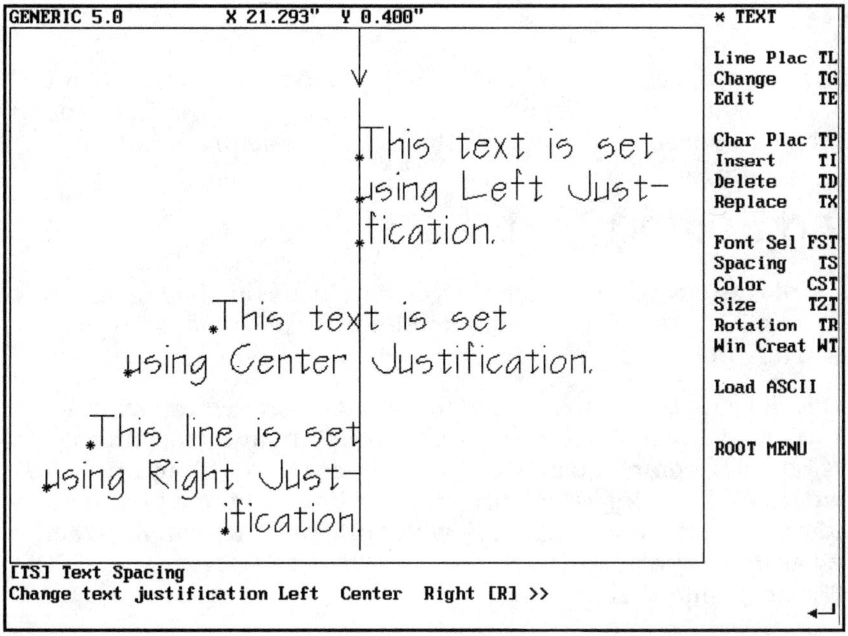

Figure 6.11: *Three justification options.*

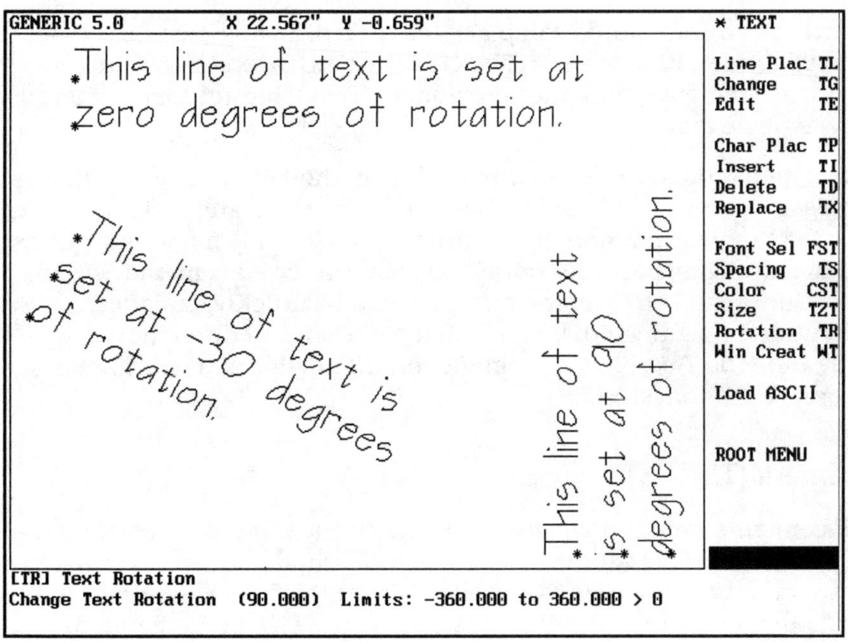

Figure 6.12: *Examples of text rotation.*

Text Color (TC)

Any color available on your system in Generic CADD can be used as the color for text, through the Text Color option. Type **TC**, or select Color from the TEXT menu and click on the color you desire (or type the color number and press Enter).

Placing and Editing Text

Once you have set all the text spacing options, you can focus on placing text in your drawing. Generic CADD 5.0 provides two methods for placing text in your drawing: as lines of text placed as one unit or as individual characters.

Each line of text placed with the Text Line command is considered by Generic CADD 5.0 to be one entity. Each line has one reference point at the beginning of the line. The Text Edit (TE) command is used to edit lines of text, if required. Justification and proportional spacing work only with text lines, not text placed as individual characters. The other settings work with both styles of text placement. To edit text placed as individual characters, use Text Insert (TI), Text Delete (TD), or Text Replace (TX), explained below.

Placing Text

As mentioned earlier, two commands will place text in a drawing: Text Line Placement (TL) and Text Character Placement (TP). Generic CADD version 5.0 introduced the Text Line Placement command; previously, Text Character Placement was the only way to place text.

The Text Line Placement command is the preferable method of placing text in a drawing. Text lines are more easily edited, they can be justified and proportionally spaced, and they take up less memory in the drawing file. If only a few characters are being placed in a drawing, consider using Text Character Placement instead. It is easier to move individual characters, and they can be quickly exploded (which means they can be reduced to lines, which can then be edited individually). Text placed using the Text Line Placement command also can be exploded, but this requires an additional step.

Text Line Placement (TL)

The Text Line Placement command allows you to enter one or more lines of text. CADD will treat each line as a single entity, not as individual characters or as lines, arcs, and so on. When you type **TL** or select Text Line from the TEXT menu, the `Enter starting point` prompt will appear. Move the cursor to the place where you want the first line to start and click your mouse to select the point. Then type each line of text, pressing Enter to place the line in the drawing. As you type, the text appears at the bottom of the screen in the prompt line. A rectangle called a *bounding box* is drawn to represent the text. If you need to change what you have typed, and it still is in the prompt line, press Backspace or your arrow keys to move through the text. Pressing Backspace will delete one character to the left, just as it does in most word processors. When you press Enter at the end of the line, the bounding box is replaced by the text. To overwrite existing text, press Insert, and type new characters over the existing ones.

When you have typed your last line of text, press Enter to place the line, then press Esc to end the Text Line Placement command. Usually the Pen Up (PU) command works whenever you need the Esc key, but not when entering text. If you typed PU, the letters would be placed in the drawing, not interpreted as a command.

Now try a few text operations. In the following exercise, you will set up a grid and place a left-justified paragraph on the upper part of an 8.5" by 11" rectangle. When you're finished, your screen should look like figure 6.13.

Placing the First Paragraph

Prompt	*Input*	*Description*
`Command`	**GS**	Places a grid on the screen
`Change grid size X`	**.5**	Sets the grid width spacing to .5"
`Change grid size Y`	Press Enter	Accepts .5" as height spacing for grid
`Command`	**SG**	Starts Snap To Grid command; if response shows "off," type **SG** again
`Command`	**TZ**	Starts Text Size command

`Text (1.0")`
`Dimension (1.0")`
`Attribute (1.0")`
	T	Sets the size of drawing text

`Change Text Size`	Type **.25**, press Enter twice	Sets size to 1/4", then ends the command
`Command`	**RE**	Draws a rectangle
`Enter one corner of the rectangle`	**0,0**	Sets the bottom corner at coordinate location X 0, Y 0
`Enter opposite corner`	**8.5, 11**	Sets the top corner at coordinate location X 8.5", Y 11"
`Command`	**TL**	Starts the Text Line Placement command

Placing the First Paragraph—continued

Prompt	*Input*	*Description*
`Enter starting point`	**.5,10**	Places insertion point at X .5", Y 10"
`>`	Type **This text is one-quarter inch tall. If** (press Enter) **printed at full size, it will be one-quarter** (press Enter) **inch tall on paper.**	Displays and places the text in the drawing (press Enter at the end of every line and press Esc to end the command)

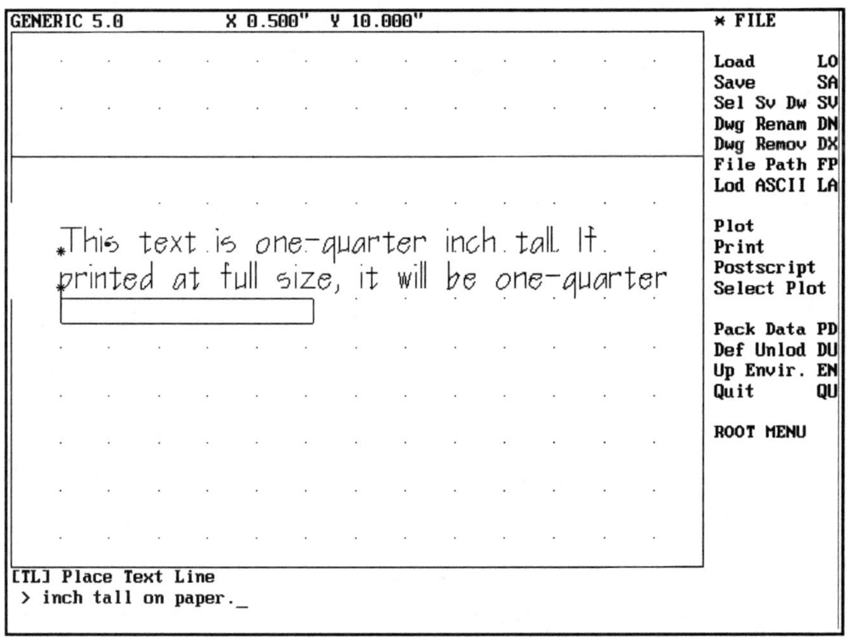

Figure 6.13: *Place the first paragraph at the top of the drawing.*

By typing three characters at once, you can go quickly into a command, choosing an option at the same time. You'll use this technique in the next exercise as you change text slant and size and place a second paragraph of text. The results are shown in figure 6.14.

Placing the Second Paragraph

Prompt	*Input*	*Description*
`Command`	**TSS**	Starts Text Spacing Slant command
`Change Text Slant`	**15**	Changes slant to 15 degrees
`Command`	**TZT**	Starts Text Size Text command
`Change Text Size` (0.250)	Type **.5** and press Enter twice	Changes text size to .5"
`Command`	**TL**	Starts the Text Line Placement command
`Enter starting point`	Move cursor to X .5 Y 8 and press Enter	Places insertion point at X .5", Y 8"
`>`	Type **This text is one-half** (press Enter)**inch tall, placed at a** (press Enter) **slant of 15 degrees.** (press Enter and Esc)	Displays and places the text in the drawing in the drawing

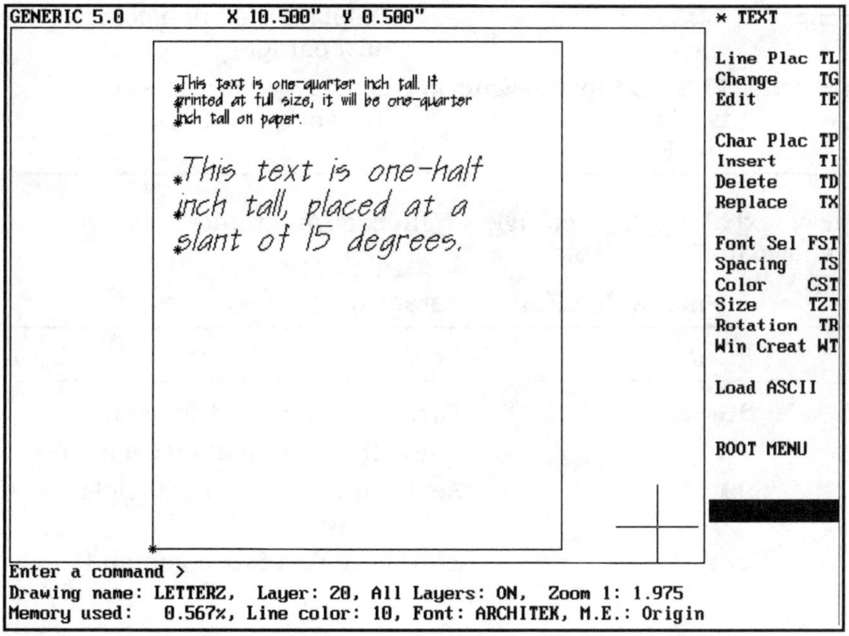

Figure 6.14: *Add the next paragraph of text.*

The next paragraph's text is a full 1" tall and centered in the rectangle. Don't try to put too many words on a line. Figure 6.15 shows the resulting text.

Placing the Third Paragraph

Prompt	*Input*	*Description*
`Command`	**TSS**	Starts Text Spacing Slant command
`Change Text Slant`	**0**	Returns text slant to normal (zero degrees)
`...Justification (Left)`	**J**	Justifies text
`Change text justification`	Type **C**, press Enter twice	Centers text and ends command
`Command`	**TZT**	Starts Text Size Text command
`Change Text Size`	Type **1**, press Enter twice	Displays new text size as 1" and ends command
`Command`	**SG**	Turns off Snap To Grid command
`Command`	**TL**	Starts Text Line Placement command
`Enter starting point`	**4.25,4.5**	Displays insertion point for next paragraph
`>`	**This text** (press Enter) **is 1" tall** (press Enter and Esc)	Displays and places two lines of centered text

Finally, put a line of text along the rectangle's right edge and rotate it at a 90-degree angle, as shown in figure 6.16.

Placing the Fourth Paragraph

Prompt	*Input*	*Description*
`Command`	**SG**	Turns on Snap To Grid again
`Command`	**TR**	Starts the Text Rotation command
`Change Text Rotation`	**90**	Sets new text placement angle at 90 degrees
`Command`	**TZT**	Starts the Text Size command

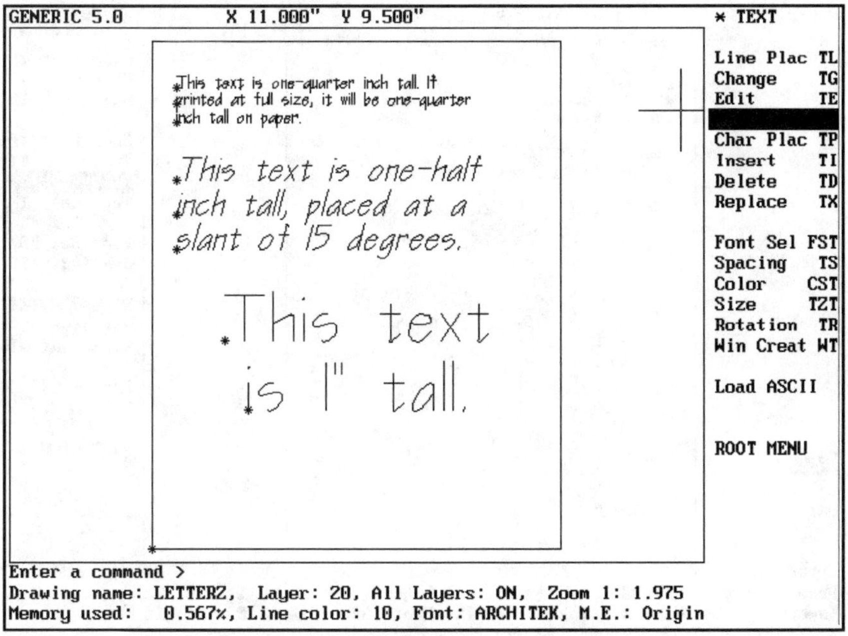

Figure 6.15: *Enter two lines of centered text.*

Placing the Fourth Paragraph—continued

Prompt	*Input*	*Description*
`Change Text Size`	Type **.25** and press Enter twice	Sets new Text Size at .25"
`Command`	**TSJR**	Starts the Text Spacing Justification Right command
`Command`	**TL**	Starts the Text Line Placement command
`Enter starting point`	**8,10.5**	Sets insertion point at X 8" Y 10.5"
`>`	**This text is one-quarter inch tall, and is rotated 90 degrees** and press Enter and Esc	Displays and places one line of right-justified text

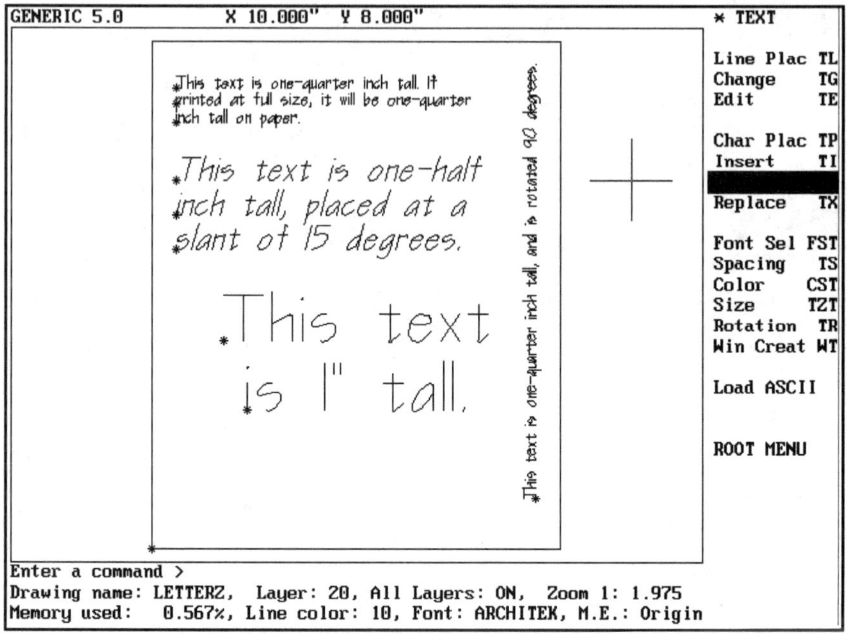

Figure 6.16: *Place a line of text along the right edge of the sheet.*

Text Character Placement (TP)

Use the Text Character Placement command when you do not want the text you place to be tied together as a single entity, as it is with the Text Line Placement (TL) command. All of the Text Spacing options apply to Text Character Placement, except Justification and Proportional spacing.

With Text Line Placement, once you identify an insertion point you are stuck with that location for the text you need to place. The Text Character Placement command, however, gives you the option of moving the insertion point for each character you place, if you choose. This feature will be used to place a number at each corner of a rectangle in the next exercise.

The sequence of commands is: after typing TP or selecting Char Place from the TEXT menu, move the cursor to the location in the drawing where you want the first character placed. Press Enter or the first mouse button to identify the location. Type the character you need (in this case, the numeral 1). Instead of pressing Enter or Esc, press the first mouse button. An I-shaped cursor will appear, replacing the normal Text Character Placement cursor (a flat line). When the I-shaped cursor is on the screen, you may use the mouse to move it to any other location on the screen (see fig. 6.17). Click at the new location, and the text placement cursor returns. Type the required characters. When you are finished entering text with Text Character Placement, press Esc.

Changing to the I-shaped Cursor

Prompt	*Input*	*Description*
`Command`	**RE**	Draws a rectangle
`Enter one corner of the rectangle`	Move cursor to X 2, Y 2 and press Enter	Places upper left corner of the rectangle
`Enter opposite corner`	Move cursor down and right to X 6, Y .5 and press Enter	Places lower right corner of the rectangle
`Command`	**TRO**	Sets Text Rotation to zero degrees
`Command`	**TP**	Starts Text Character Placement command
`Enter text starting point`	Move cursor near top left corner of rectangle and click first mouse button or press Enter	Sets starting point for text placement
`Enter a character`	Click first mouse button; text placement cursor is replaced by I-shaped cursor	Displays I-shaped cursor; starting point may be changed or text settings altered

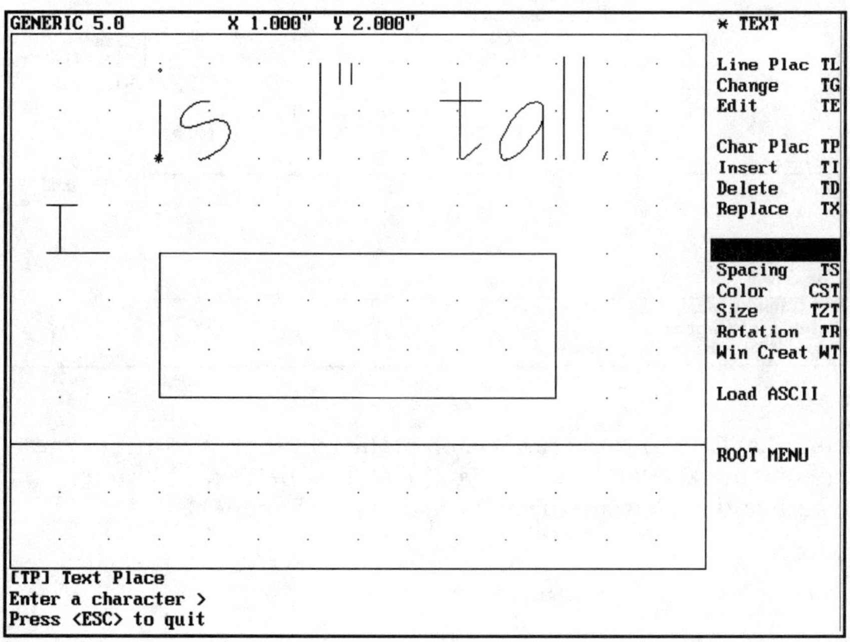

***Figure 6.17:** The I-shaped cursor used with Text Character Placement command.*

Text settings can be changed when the I-shaped cursor is on the screen, as in the following exercise (see fig. 6.18).

Changing Text Settings

Prompt	*Input*	*Description*
`Enter a character`	Type **TSA2** and press Enter twice	Changes Text Spacing Aspect to double width
`Enter a character`	Click first mouse button	Returns to text placement cursor
`Enter a character`	**1**	Places the numeral 1 at the top left corner of the rectangle
`Enter a character`	Click first mouse button	Switches to I-shaped cursor

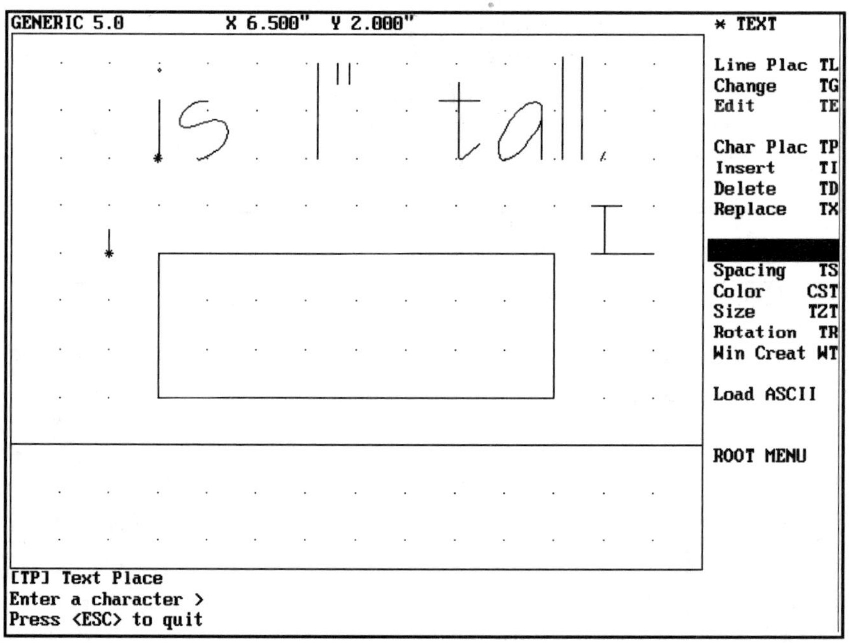

Figure 6.18: *Using the I-shaped cursor to select a new placement point.*

In the next exercise, you'll put a numeral at each of the rectangle's corners. The results are shown in figure 6.19. Notice that you're still in the Text Character Placement command, and you'll remain so until you press Escape.

Numbering the Rectangle's Corners

Prompt	*Input*	*Description*
`Enter a character`	Move I-shaped cursor to top right corner of rectangle	Selects new placement point for text
`Enter a character`	Click first mouse button and type **2**	Identifies new placement point for text; places numeral 2 at top right corner of rectangle
`Enter a character`	Click first mouse button	Switches to I-shaped cursor
`Enter a character`	Move I-shaped cursor to bottom left corner of the rectangle and click first mouse button	Selects new placement point at bottom left corner of rectangle
`Enter a character`	**3**	Places the numeral 3
`Enter a character`	Click the first mouse button; move I-shaped cursor to bottom right corner of the rectangle and click first mouse button	Selects new placement point at bottom right corner of the rectangle
`Enter a character`	**4**	Places the numeral 4
`Enter a character`	Press Esc	Ends Text Character Placement command

Editing Text

Changes are frequently necessary when working with computer text. Text in Generic CADD 5.0 is no exception, so it is important to become familiar with the various text editing commands available.

Each of the two text placement commands has corresponding editing commands. Text Edit (TE) is for text placed using Text Line Placement, while Text Insert (TI), Text Delete (TD), and Text Replace (TX) are for text placed with Text Character Placement.

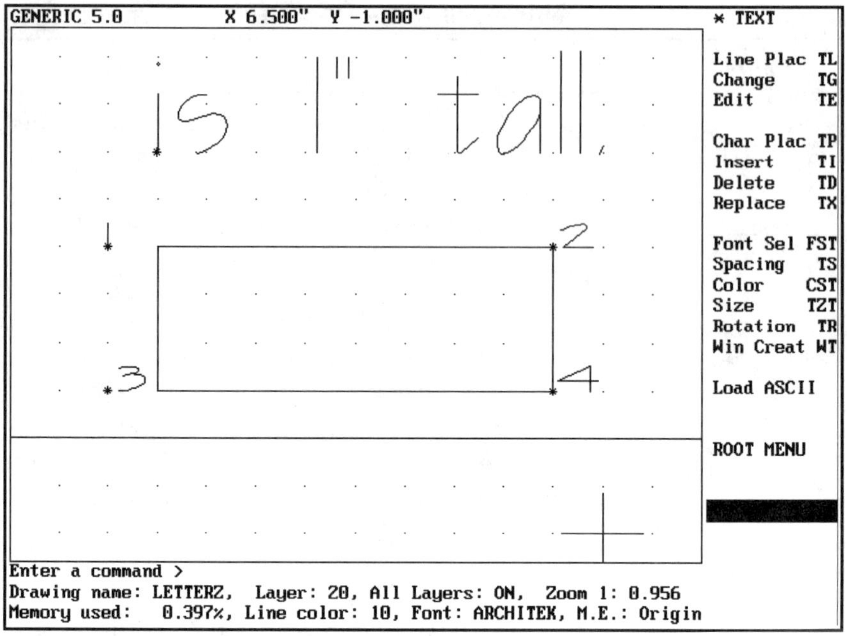

Figure 6.19: *Each corner has been numbered.*

In Generic CADD, editing also means changing objects in the drawing. The lines that make up text characters can also be edited. The Text Change (TG) command is a special version of the Change command that is exclusively for text placed using Text Line Placement. The Explode command, discussed in Chapter 10, must be used when editing text placed with Text Character Placement.

Text Edit (TE)

The Text Edit command, found in the TEXT menu, is used to make changes to text placed in a drawing with the Text Line Placement command. To use Text Edit, type **TE** or select Text Edit from the TEXT menu, and click on or very near the reference point of the line you wish to edit. Just use the first mouse button; the use of Snap to Nearest Point is not required. A bounding box will appear around the line, and the text will appear in the prompt line at the bottom of the screen. Use Backspace, the left- and right-arrow keys, and Delete to make changes to your text, just as you would in a word processor. When finished, press Enter.

When first used, Text Edit will be in insert mode. This means that if you move the text cursor to the middle of the line and type in letters, the characters to the right will move to make room for the new text. If you prefer to use overtype mode, which means that any new text will replace old text, press Insert. The small text cursor will be replaced by a large one. To return to insert mode, press Insert again. (The Insert key toggles between the two choices. No menu command or two-letter command for this function is available.)

The Fast Redraw (FA) command was introduced earlier in the book. One of its features, Fast Text, can be used to speed your work with text. Follow the steps below to edit the second paragraph on the screen.

Preparing Text for Editing

Prompt	*Input*	*Description*
`Command`	**FA**	Displays Fast Redraw options
`fast Text (OFF)`	Type **T**, press Enter	Turns on Fast Text and exits command
`Command`	**ZW**	Starts the Zoom Window command
`Place window`	Draw a window around the second paragraph of text (which begins "This text is one-half...")	Provides a close-up view of the paragraph to be edited (see fig. 6.20)
`Command`	**TV**	Starts Text View command, to redraw Fast Text so it is readable
`Place window`	Draw window around the reference points of the three lines in the second paragraph	Redraws the second paragraph to make it readable; leaves other text in Fast Text mode (see fig. 6.21)

In the next exercise, you'll edit the first line of the second paragraph. When you click on the reference point of a line with the first mouse button, the line to be edited appears in the prompt line and a bounding box surrounds the text on-screen.

Editing Text

Prompt	*Input*	*Description*
`Command`	**TE**	Starts Text Edit command
`Pick text line to edit`	Move cursor to the reference point of the first line in paragraph; click	Selects the first line of the second paragraph for editing
`>`	Use Backspace to erase "one-half" and type **1/2**	Edits line

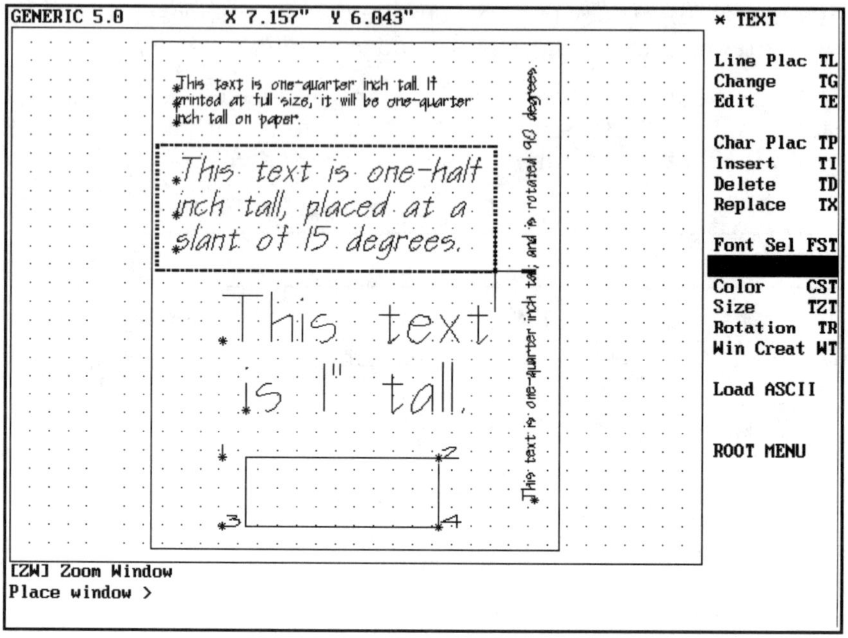

Figure 6.20: *Drawing a Zoom Window around the second paragraph.*

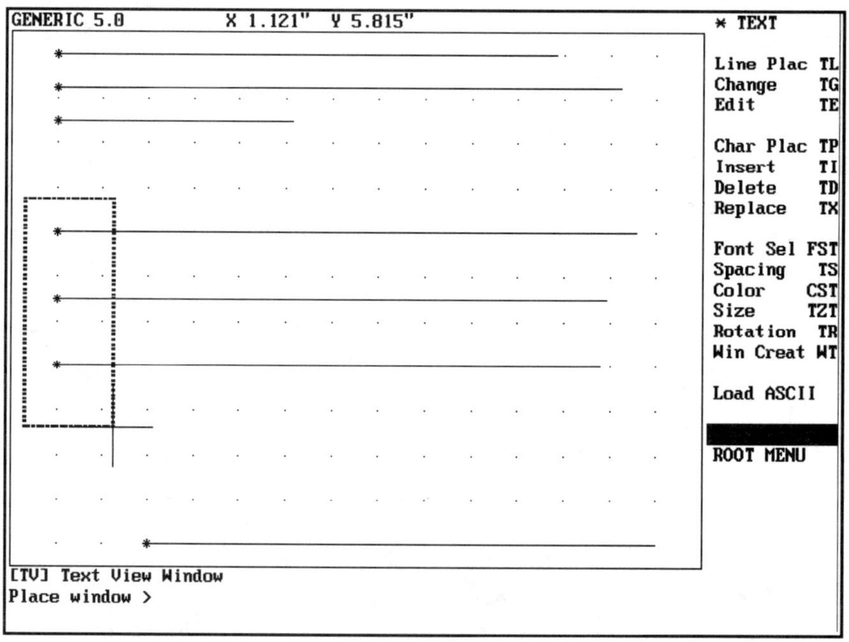

Figure 6.21: *Draw the Text View window around reference points of the lines.*

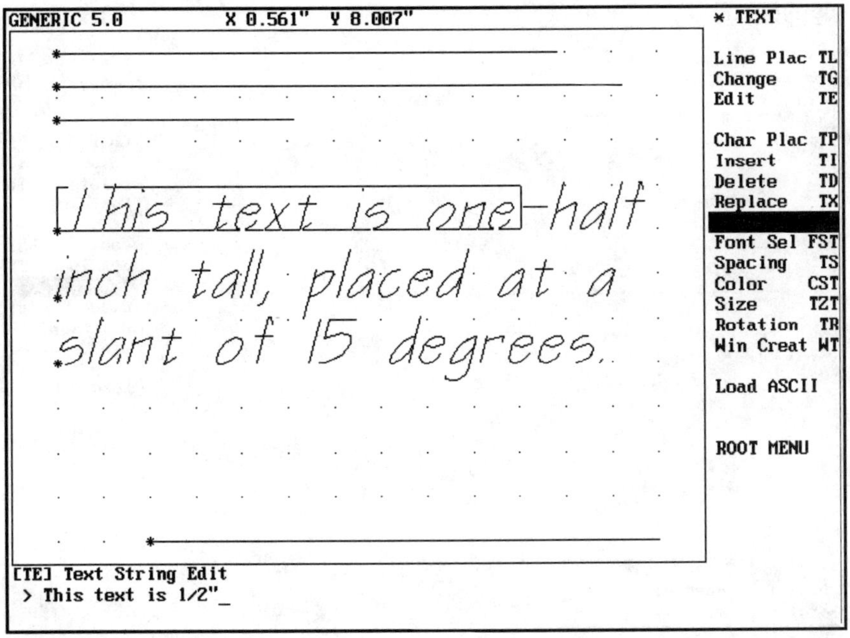

Figure 6.22: Press Backspace to erase old text, then type in new text.

Note that when you select the line to be edited, a bounding box appears on the screen to surround the line, but the line itself remains on-screen. After you make the changes and press Enter, the text line is redrawn. Because the Fast Text command is on, only a straight line will appear, and the old text will remain (stray pixels, so to speak). Use the Redraw command (RD) to restore the screen.

Editing Another Line

Prompt	*Input*	*Description*
`Command`	**RD**	Redraws the screen
`Command`	Type **TV** and draw a window around the paragraph	Uses Text View to view the second paragraph
`Command`	**TE**	Displays the Text Edit command
`Pick text line to edit`	Click on or near the reference point of the of the second line in the second paragraph	Selects the second line of the second paragraph
`>`	Place cursor under the t in tall, then press Backspace to erase inch and press Enter	Removes the word inch from the beginning of the second paragraph (see fig. 6.23)

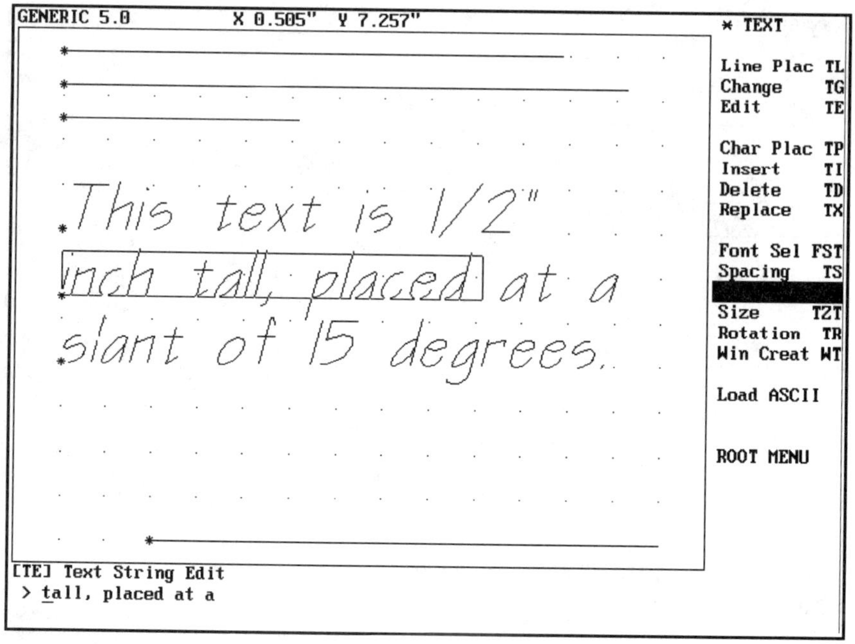

Figure 6.23: *Use Text Edit to erase the word "inch" from the second line.*

Text Change (TG)

The Text Change command is used when you want to change the appearance of the text, but not the context. Text Change is a special version of the Change (CG) command for text; it allows you to change the font, the justification, and the between-character spacing of text placed with the Text Line Placement (TL) command. You can also switch proportional text to monospaced (and vice-versa) and change the slant and aspect of text already in the drawing using Text Change.

The Text Change command will not work with text placed using Text Character Placement. To change text placed as individual characters, use the Explode command to reduce the text to lines, arcs and so on, and then use the Change (CG) command. This will be discussed in Chapter 10.

In the next exercise, try changing fonts, as shown in figure 6.24.

Changing Fonts with the Text Change Command

Prompt	*Input*	*Description*
`Command`	**RD**	Redraws the screen
`Command`	Type **TV** and draw a window around the second paragraph	Redraws the second paragraph
`Command`	Type **TG** or select Change from the TEXT menu	Displays the Text Change command
`Window...`	Type **W** or click on "Window" in the prompt line	Uses Window selection to identify the text to change
`Place window`	Draw the window around the three reference points of the three lines in the second paragraph	Selects the second paragraph as the text to be changed
`<RET>to accept...`	Press Enter or click on <RET>urn in the prompt line	Ends selection process
`...Font...`	**F**	Changes the font of selected text
`Select font from side menu`	Move menu bar to Engineer, click second mouse button	Selects Engineer as new font for the selected text
`Command`	**FAT**	Uses the Fast Redraw command to turn off Fast Text
`Command`	**RD**	Redraws the screen

Text Insert (TI)

Text Insert, found in the TEXT menu, is the first of three commands for editing text placed using Text Character Placement (TP). Use it to place a letter within an existing line. When you type **TI** or select the command from the menu, you are prompted to identify a character. Generic CADD will move this character (and all those following) one space to the right. You then type the character to be added to the line.

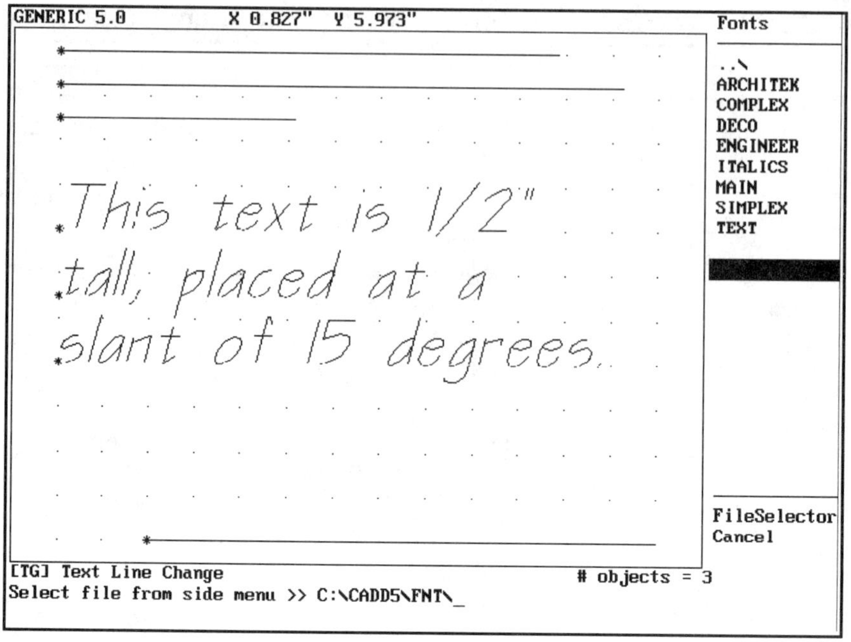

Figure 6.24: *Select Engineer as the new font for the selected text.*

Editing with the Text Insert Command

Prompt	*Input*	*Description*
`Command`	**ZA**	Starts the Zoom All command
`Command`	Type **ZW** and draw a a window around the rectangle at screen bottom; be sure to include the number at each corner	Provides a close-up view of the rectangle
`Command`	**FAT**	Starts the Fast Redraw command and turns off Fast Text
`Command`	**RD**	Redraws the screen; text is visible again
`Command`	**TI**	Starts the Text Insert command
`Point to insert location`	Move cursor to the numeral 1 and click on the reference point	Places another character in front of the numeral 1
`Enter character to insert`	**#**	Places the pound sign in front of the numeral 1 (see fig. 6.25)

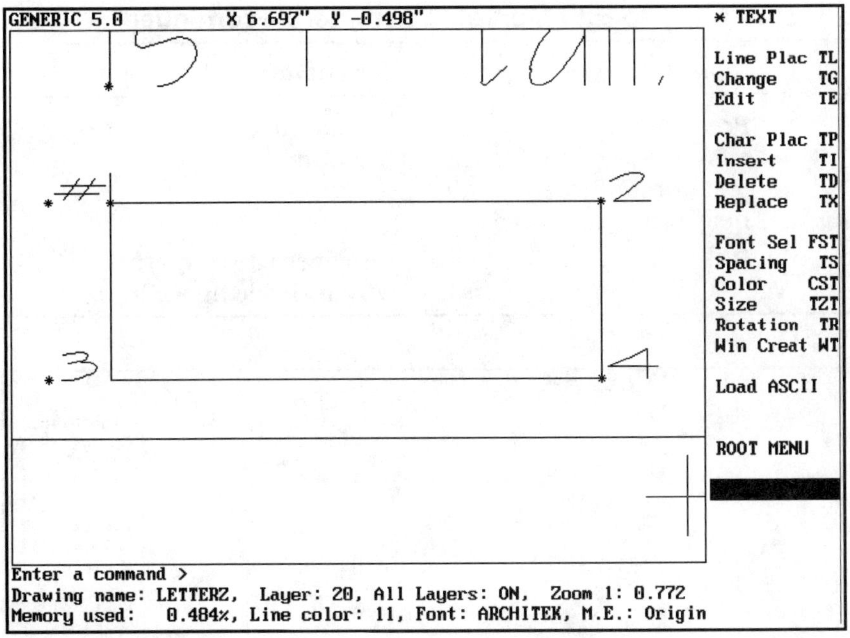

Figure 6.25: Text Insert is used to place "#" in front of "1".

Text Replace (TX)

Of the three commands used to edit single-entity text (text placed with Text Character Placement), Text Replace is the only one that can affect more than one character. When you type **TX** or select Replace from the TEXT menu, you are prompted to select the character to be replaced. Click on a character; a text cursor appears underneath the character. Type a letter, number, or other character to replace it. The new character replaces the old, and the cursor moves on to the next space. You may continue to replace characters or add new text if no other characters are present. If you press Enter, the text cursor moves down a line from where you started, and you may continue to enter new text. To finish, press Esc.

Using Text Replace to Edit Multiple Characters

Prompt	*Input*	*Description*
`Command`	**TX**	Starts the Text Replace command
`Enter Text Starting Point`	Move the cursor to the numeral 3	Selects the 3 as the character to be replaced
`Enter a character`	**A**	Replaces the numeral 3 with an A

Using Text Replace to Edit Multiple Characters—continued

Prompt	*Input*	*Description*
`Enter a character`	Press the right arrow key eight times, bringing the text cursor directly underneath the numeral 4	Moves the text cursor to the numeral 4
`Enter a character`	**B**	Replaces the numeral 4 with a B (see fig. 6.26)

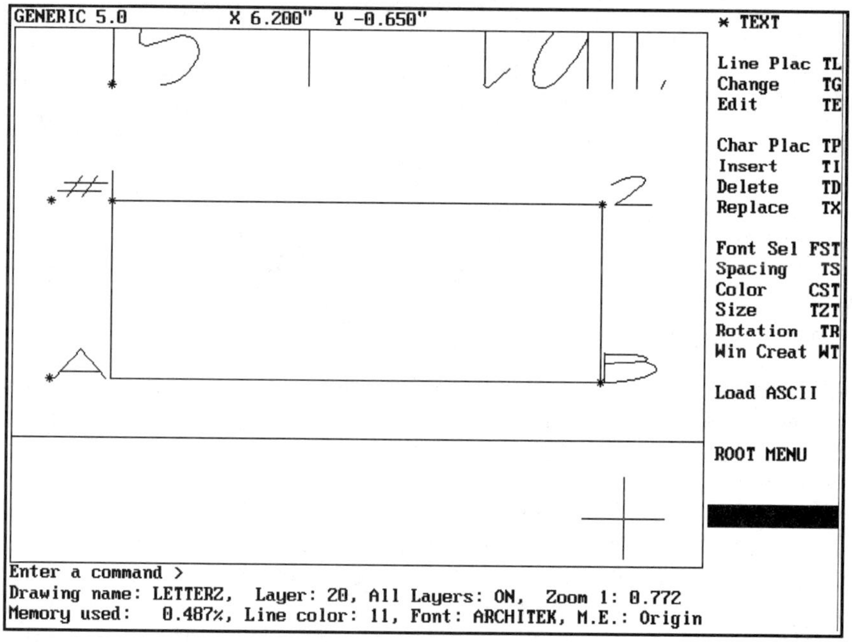

Figure 6.26: *Using Text Replace to replace numbers with letters.*

Text Delete (TD)

The Text Delete command is very straightforward. Type **TD** or select Delete from the TEXT menu, and click on the character you wish to delete. The character will disappear. If it was part of a row of characters placed at the same time, the characters to the right of the deleted character will move one space to the left to fill the gap. Feel free to try it to eliminate any of the text characters surrounding the rectangle in the previous exercise.

Loading Text Files into a Drawing

Although Generic CADD makes it as convenient as possible to place text in a drawing, it is a drafting and design program, not a word processor. If you need to place a significant quantity of text in a drawing, it would be easier to prepare the text in a word processor first, then import it into CADD. The Load ASCII (LA) command allows you to do so.

ASCII is a standard format for text files. Virtually all word processors and text editors, plus most spreadsheets and database programs, can save text in ASCII format, even if they normally save text in a different format. Any text file which has been saved in ASCII format can be imported into Generic CADD using the Load ASCII command.

Some of the files Generic CADD uses to store configuration data are in ASCII format. In the following example, load one of them into a drawing.

Loading an ASCII File

Prompt	*Input*	*Description*
`Command`	**DS**	Saves the drawing
`Save file as`	**TEXT**	Establishes TEXT as name of the file
`Command`	**DXY**	Removes the drawing
`Command`	**LA**	Starts the Load ASCII command
`Select file from side menu: C:\CADD5\`	**CONFIG5.FIL**	Loads file CONFIG5.FIL from the CADD5 directory (see fig. 6.28)
`Enter placement point`	When bounding box appears, move cursor so the entire box is visible; click to select the placement point	The bounding box represents the size of the text file when drawn on the screen (see fig. 6.27)
`Command`	**ZA**	Starts the Zoom All command

While the bounding box is on-screen, before you click to select a placement point, you can change the rotation, slant, spacing, or aspect of the text using the commands previously discussed in this chapter.

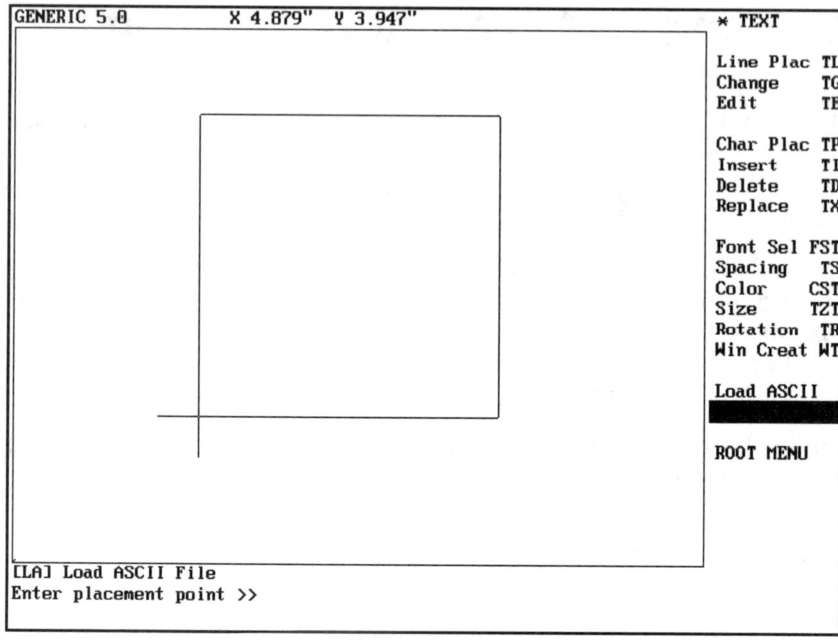

Figure 6.27: *Text first appears as bounding box, showing text block size.*

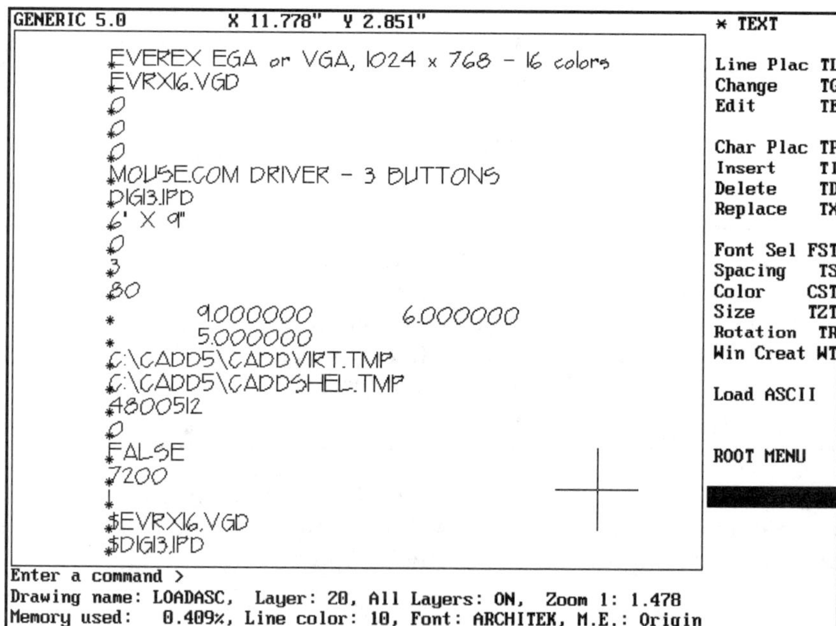

Figure 6.28: *Complete CONFIG5.FIL file. (Yours may be different.)*

Placing a Schedule in a CADD Drawing

The Load ASCII command has many uses. For many users, the ability to import ready-made schedules (such as construction or purchase details that relate to the objects in the drawing) will be a real time-saver. While the details of creating a schedule depend greatly on the type of drawing to be done (ranging from designing machine parts to drafting home remodeling projects), some fundamentals should be kept in mind.

The Load ASCII command brings text into the drawing as text lines. It determines the length of a line as one paragraph, using the end-of-paragraph marks invisibly embedded within the text file to identify lines. You can save time by setting the length of the lines before you import the file by editing the text into short paragraphs within your word processor.

If you need to place the text inside a legend box, take time to consider the line spacing before you import the text. Is 150 percent of text size as a between-line spacing the correct distance, or do you need to adjust it higher or lower? Also take time to consider the between-character spacing.

Be sure to put the text on a layer by itself, so that it is easy to hide or erase. To do so, change the current layer (with YC, Layer Current) to an empty layer before you import the text file with Load ASCII.

Creating New Fonts

If you need a special look for your text and none of the fonts in Generic CADD are appropriate, you can create your own font. Creating a complete font is a time-consuming task and requires much planning. The letters must conform to a common style, and they should blend well. The letters also should contain as few arcs or Bézier curves as possible, if you are concerned about redraw speed.

New text characters must not contain any existing text characters or components unless they have been exploded first to reduce them to separate objects.

Saving new characters as a font might be confusing the first time you try it. Generic CADD will save the character you create to the file of the *currently active* font, as named by the use of the Font Select command. So that you don't ruin an existing font by redrawing some of its characters, use the Font Select command *before* you create a new character to name a font not already defined.

The following steps show how to save an object as a character in a new font.

Saving a New Font Character

Prompt	*Input*	*Description*
`Command`	**DXY**	Erases the drawing
`Command`	Type **C2** and draw a modest circle	Draws a circle as part of a new text character to be created
`Command`	Type **RE** and draw a square around the circle	Draws a square to complete the object to be made into a new text character
`Command`	**FST**	Selects text font
`Select font`	**DODO**	Names the new font
`File C:\CADD5\FNT\DODO.FNT Not Found!! Is this a new font?`	**Y**	Tells CADD that DODO is to be considered a new font
`Selected font is DODO`		Any objects now saved as a character will be part of a font called DODO
`Command`	**WT**	Starts Window Create command
`Draw window`	Draw the window around the circle and the square	Identifies the objects to be saved as a text character
`Enter the character to be defined`	**O** (capital O)	Object becomes capital O in the new font (see fig. 6.29)
`Enter a point at the lower left of character`	Move the cursor to the lower left corner and click	Identifies the location of the new character's reference point
`Command`	**TP**	Tests the new font
`Select text starting point`	Move the cursor anywhere and press Enter	Selects where the text should go
`Enter a character`	**O**	New character appears on-screen

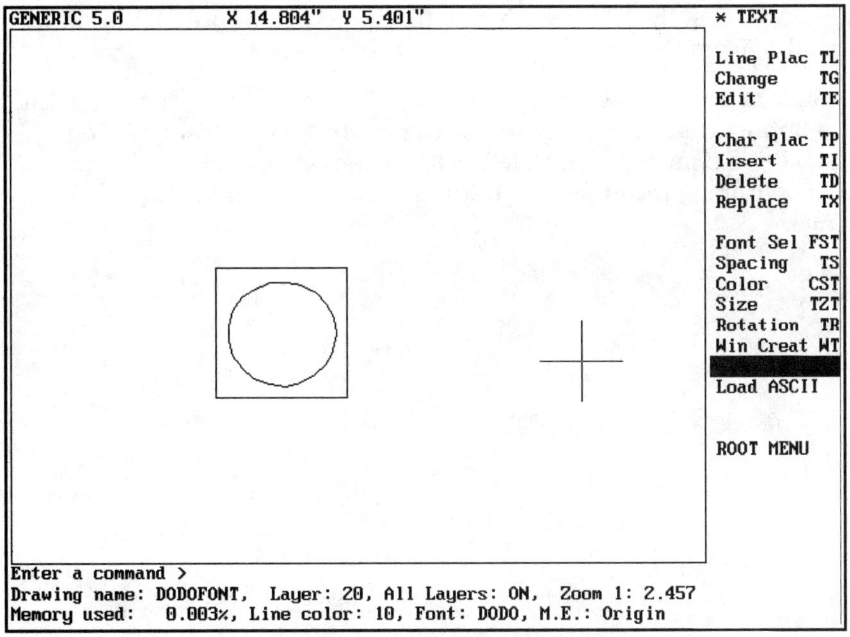

Figure 6.29: *The circle in the square is a new font.*

Summary

The ability to add text to a Generic CADD drawing should not be taken for granted. If text in a CADD drawing had to be drawn character by character, as it does in manual drafting, it would add hours to the process.

Text in Generic CADD has special properties that distinguish it from the other types of objects used to create drawings. Text may be placed as lines or as single characters, and special editing comands are available for each type of text. Because Generic CADD sees text as an entity different from other objects in the drawing, most editing commands used when drawing do not work on text.

Placing text as lines allows the use of proportional spacing and a choice of justification styles. Placing text as individual characters makes it possible to easily change the placement of one letter without affecting others in a line. CADD text is not the same as text used by your word processor. In many instances, it needs to conform to the traditional look of drafting text. All text characters in Generic CADD are made from lines, arcs, circles, and curves, linked together by the program to create a font, a style of text. If one of the eight fonts shipped with the program does not match a style you need, you can create a new font. Additional fonts are also available from Generic Software and other sources.

Knowing how to place and edit text is an important step on the road to mastering Generic CADD, as important as learning to use the basic drawing and editing commands. The next two chapters take the basics you have learned so far and amplify them into two important areas: adjustment of the screen display and the printing of drawings.

7

Getting around the Screen

Your drawings will become increasingly complex as you progress in Generic CADD 5.0. As a result, you may want to examine small portions of a drawing to be sure all objects are precisely constructed.

Most of the items you draw will have a real-scale size larger than the screen display, although drawings by machinists and electronic engineers are exceptions. The ability to view a segment of a drawing close up is vital to ensure accuracy. To avoid distraction, restricting the view to certain objects is also helpful.

Generic CADD 5.0 provides a variety of ways to view a drawing and to adjust the view to suit your needs. These commands will be explored in this chapter, using SHAPE1.DWG, which you created in Chapter 5.

Controlling Screen Display

Most of the commands for controlling the screen display are found on the ZOOMS menu. Although these commands control the display scale for objects on the screen, only one of them requires you to choose a specific scale.

Think of your computer monitor as the eyepiece on a video camera. You can "zoom" in for a close-up view or "zoom" back for a wide-angle shot. You don't have to calculate a specific scale to get these views with the video camera; you just press the button to adjust the lens.

In addition to the zoom commands, you can use the layer commands to limit what appears on your screen. Chapter 6 already reviewed the benefit of dividing the drawing into several layers. If you are drawing a complicated schematic or construction plan with many overlapping sets of information, draw related portions on their own layer to make them easy to hide or display.

Once you experiment with these commands, you will see how easy and convenient they are. They will quickly become essential to your CADD work.

Using Zoom Commands

All the zoom commands are found in the ZOOMS menu, as displayed in figure 7.1. If you learn only a few of the two-letter commands, some of the zoom commands should be among them. Flipping back and forth through the menus to change the view on the screen can be tedious without the two-letter commands.

If you haven't already done so, load SHAPE1.DWG, which you created in Chapter 5. (A copy of SHAPE1.DWG is on the optional disk available for use with *Inside Generic CADD.*)

Loading the SHAPE1 Drawing

Prompt	*Input*	*Description*
`Command`	**LO**	Starts the Load command
`Load`	**D**	Six choices are listed; choose D to load a drawing
`Select from side menu`	**A:\SHAPE1**	Loads drawing from optional disk

If you want to load a drawing from a previous drawing session instead of a drawing from the optional disk, use the menu to locate the directory of the drawing and select the drawing with the menu bar.

Prompt	*Input*	*Description*
`Rename working drawing (Y/N)?`	Type **Y** for yes, or click first mouse button	Uses the name of the drawing as the working name
`Working file name?`	Press Enter	Accepts the existing name of the drawing
`Enter an insert origin. Press <RET> for 0,0`	Press Enter	Places the origin drawing at 0,0 point on screen

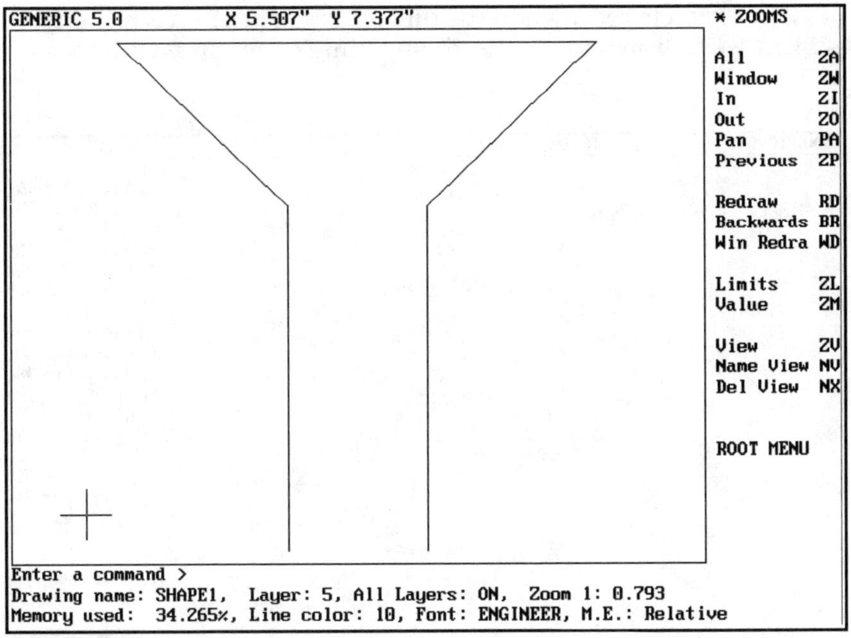

Figure 7.1: *The ZOOMS menu in Generic CADD 5.0, with SHAPE1.DWG loaded.*

Zoom All (ZA)

When you load the SHAPE1.DWG file, the entire drawing fills the screen, as in figure 7.1. This is the same view provided by the Zoom All command. Whenever you use one of the other commands and want to see the entire drawing again, you can type **ZA** and CADD will display it.

If you want to know the scale of the drawing as it appears on the screen, the current scale is always visible in the prompt lines, listed as the ZOOM. For the current view of SHAPE1, the zoom scale is 1:0.793. This means that one unit in the real world of the drawing (inches, in this case) equals 0.793 inches on the screen. The exact scale on your monitor may vary due to the size of the screen and the resolution it provides.

Zoom Limits (ZL)

The Limits command was discussed early in the book; it is used to define a boundary for your work. The Zoom Limits command will redraw the screen to show the limits you have chosen. If your entire drawing fits inside the limits, then it will be visible, although not necessarily at the same scale as drawn by the Zoom All command.

When you type **ZL**, the screen is redrawn to the dimensions of the screen limits. Figure 7.2 shows SHAPE1 redrawn using the Zoom Limits command, with the limits set to 12" x 18".

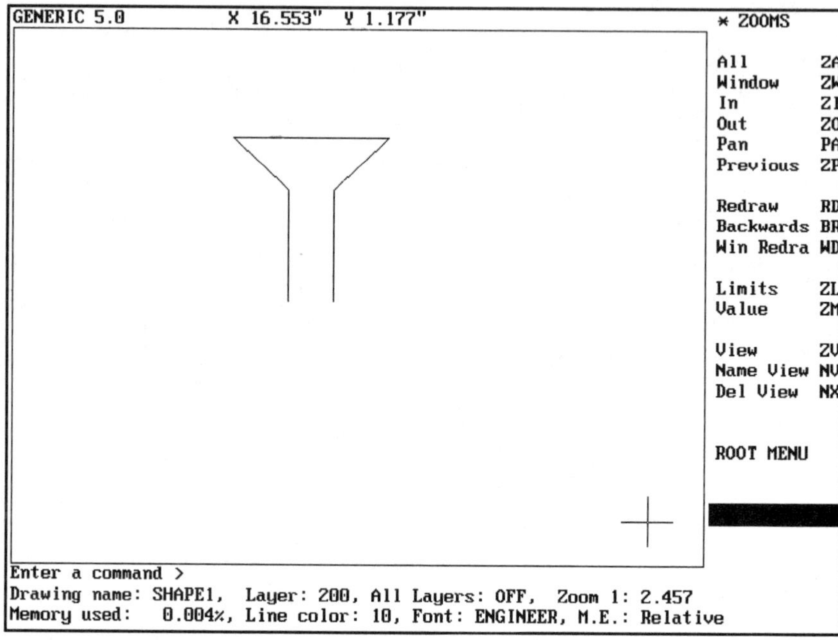

Figure 7.2: SHAPE1.DWG redrawn using the Zoom Limits command.

Zoom Window (ZW)

At times, you will want to get a close-up view of a small portion of the drawing. The easiest way is to use the Zoom Window command. When you type **ZW** or select Window from the ZOOMS menu, you are prompted to draw a window around the portion of the drawing that you want to see close up. Your first mouse click sets the first zoom window corner. When you click the mouse the second time to set the opposite corner of the window, Generic CADD calculates the zoom scale needed to draw only the objects inside the window and displays them on the screen. Figure 7.3 shows where to place the window when following the steps below; Figure 7.4 shows a view of the top left corner of SHAPE1.DWG after the Zoom Window command has been completed.

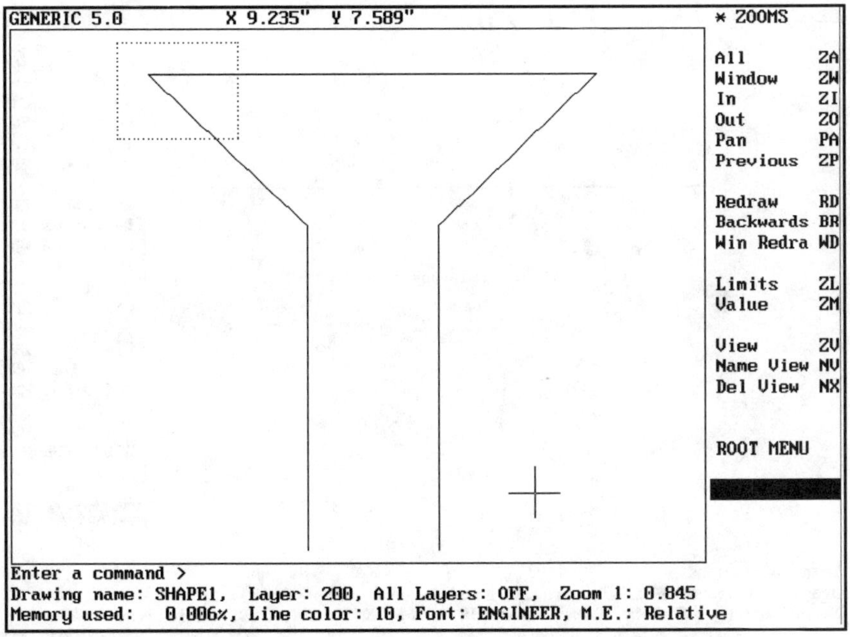

Figure 7.3: *Where to place the window to execute the Zoom Window command.*

Placing a Zoom Window

Prompt	*Input*	*Description*
`Command`	**ZA**	Starts Zoom All command
`Command`	**ZW**	Starts Zoom Window command
`Place Window`	Move cursor above and left of corner and click to set set first point; move cursor down and right to draw window; click again to finish window and execute the Zoom Window command	Identifies the part of drawing to be zoomed

Zoom Previous (ZP)

You just completed a Zoom Window command. The zoomed view on the screen previous to this was a Zoom All view of the drawing. If you wanted to go back to the Zoom All view, you could type **ZA** again, for Zoom All. Typing **ZP**, for Zoom Previous, would be a better choice, however.

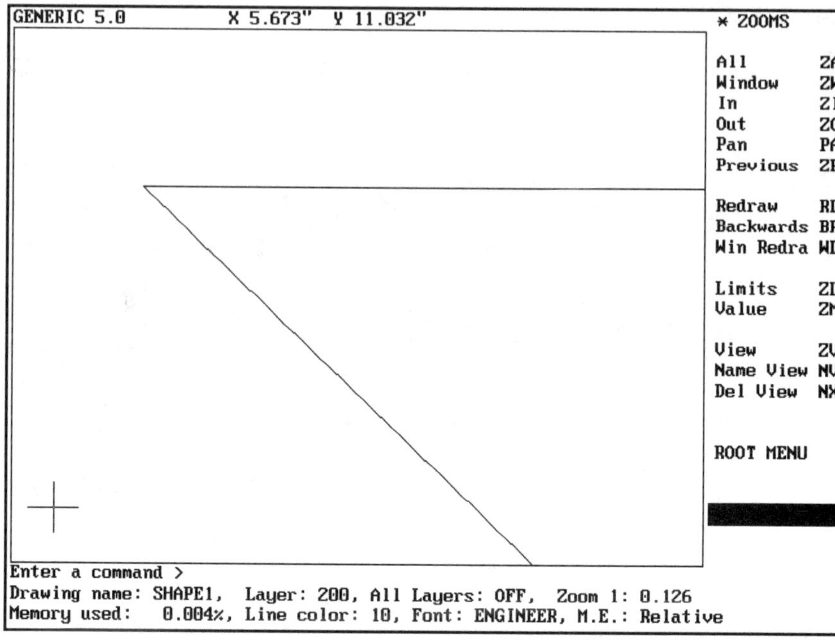

Figure 7.4: *The view after completing the Zoom Window command.*

Why is Zoom Previous a better choice? When Zoom All is invoked, it must calculate the dimensions of the drawing, and then calculate how best to fit the drawing onto the screen. The Zoom Previous command does not calculate anything; it just knows the coordinates of the last zoom and adjusts the screen to match. If you have a very complicated drawing, one that takes a long time to redraw, use Zoom Previous instead of a zoom command that requires calculation, and you'll save time. Using SHAPE1.DWG, the redraw time of the two commands is virtually the same because the drawing is small. The time difference is greater if the drawing is complicated, however.

TIP

The Zoom Previous command is also helpful if you need to switch back and forth between two views. Use Zoom Window or any of the other zooms to set one view, and use Zoom Previous to return to the first view. Once you do so, you can keep using Zoom Previous to switch between the two views.

Zoom In (ZI) and Zoom Out (ZO)

The Zoom In and Zoom Out commands are like two sides of one coin. Zoom In will redraw objects at *twice* the currently displayed size; Zoom Out will redraw objects at *half* the currently displayed size.

The key to these two commands is the placement of the cursor. Each command prompts you to select the center of the new view. Do this by moving the cursor to the location you want and clicking the first mouse button (or pressing Enter). If the center of this new view is any kind of point (construction, standard, or reference), you can use Snap to Nearest Point (NP or third mouse button) to select that point as the center of the zoom. Generic CADD then recalculates the zoom value, either doubling or halving it, and makes your chosen location the center of the display.

To gain an ever-tighter or ever-wider view of a portion of the drawing, use either command several times in succession. Each time the displayed view will be half as large (Zoom Out) or twice as large (Zoom In) as the previous view. Figure 7.5 shows where to click when using the Zoom In command; Figure 7.6 shows the new view after you use the Zoom In command on the last view.

If you have used older versions of Generic CADD, you may be familiar with the Zoom Up and Zoom Back commands. Zoom In and Zoom Out are those same commands, renamed. If you want to use the old two-letter commands, ZU and ZB, they are still available.

Zooming with Zoom In

Prompt	*Input*	*Description*
`Command`	**ZI**	Starts Zoom In command
`Enter center of zoom`	Move cursor to corner and type **NP**, or press third mouse button	Selects the corner as the center of the new view

Zoom Value (ZM)

If you need to see objects on the screen at a certain scale size, use the Zoom Value command. A setting of 2 will make objects appear at half their actual size (two inches in the drawing will display as one inch on the screen). This command can be used in a pinch when you need to measure something but do not have a ruler. First, draw a ruler using the Copy command to mark off sixteenths of an inch along a line seven inches long. Use the Zoom Value command to redraw the line at a 1:1 view, so that one inch on the screen equals one inch in real-world units. Then place your object on the screen and measure it against the CADD ruler you have just created. Voilà! Instant ruler! Perfect measurement!

Figure 7.7 shows the display after using the Zoom Value command to set the screen to a 1:1 view, with the corner as the center of the display.

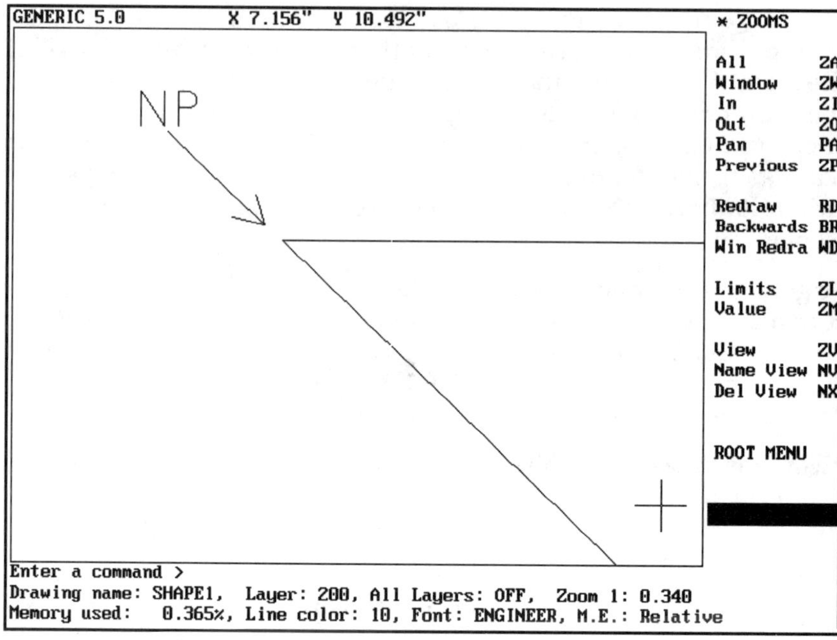

Figure 7.5: *Snap to Nearest Point sets center of new view for Zoom In command.*

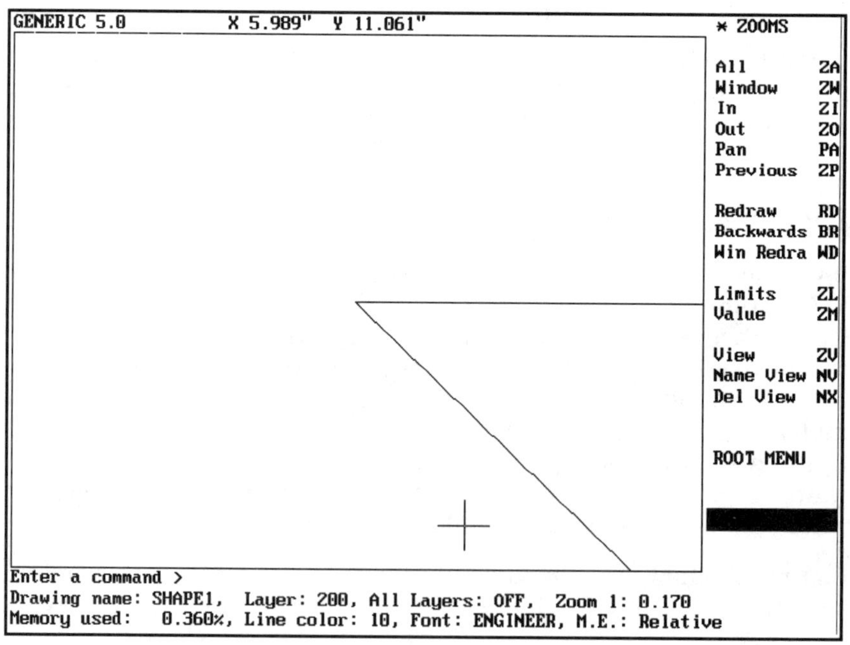

Figure 7.6: *The view after using Zoom In command.*

Setting the Screen to a 1:1 View

Prompt	*Input*	*Description*
`Command`	**ZM**	Starts the Zoom View command
`Enter zoom value 1`	**1**	Sets new zoom value at 1:1
`Enter new center of screen`	Move cursor to corner and type **NP** or press third mouse button	Identifies center of new display

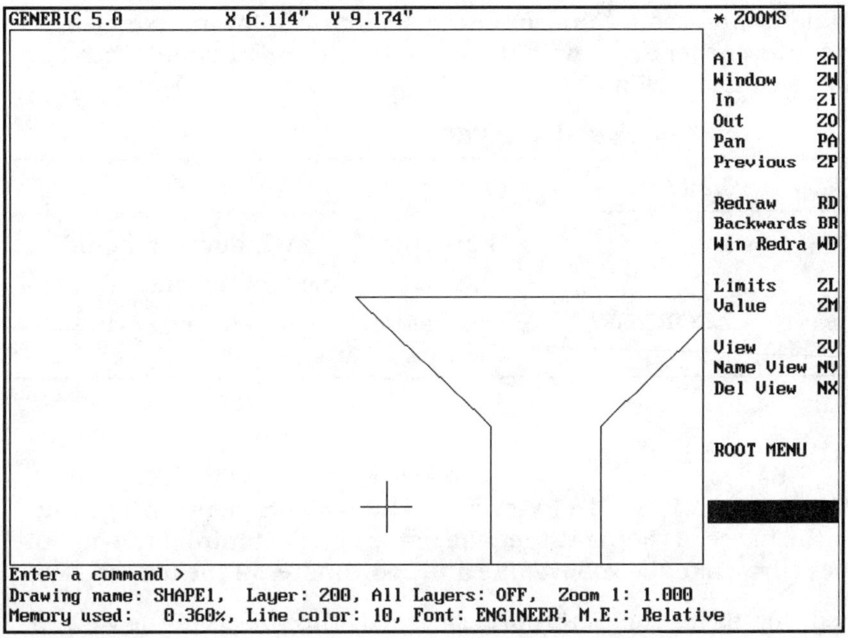

Figure 7.7: *Set a zoom value of 1 to display the object at full scale.*

Pan (PA)

Sometimes you may want to slide the display without changing the zoom value. The Pan command shifts the view without changing the zoom value. To use it, type **PA** or select Pan from the ZOOMS menu. Click on a location and Generic CADD will calculate how to adjust the display so that the point you select becomes the center of the display, without changing the zoom factor.

Pre-Selected Views

If you are working with a large drawing, you may want to return to several locations within the drawing many times, either while you are creating it or after you have finished. You can define these special locations as views and bring them to the screen using the Zoom View (ZV) command. The views are saved using the Name View (NV) command. When you no longer need a saved view, delete it with the Delete View (NX) command.

Name View (NV)

The first step in using a pre-selected view is to name it. Use any of the zoom commands to set the screen the way you want it, then use the Name View command to save the coordinates and zoom value for later use. In the following exercise, you will zoom in on the corner again with the Zoom Previous command, then save the close-up view as a named view.

Naming a View

Prompt	*Input*	*Description*
`Command`	**ZW**	Starts the Zoom Window command
`Command`	**NV**	Starts the Name View command
`Enter view name`	**LCORNER**	Names the current display, saving the view for future use

Zoom View (ZV)

To use a Named View, type **ZV** or select View from the ZOOMS menu. When you are prompted for the name of the view, type the name or select it from the menu. The screen will be redrawn to the zoom value and coordinates of the named view.

Note that a named view saves the *view*, not necessarily the *objects* in the view. If you save a view and then erase something within that view, it will no longer be visible when you summon the named view.

Delete View (NX)

If you decide you don't need a particular pre-selected view, use the Delete View command to remove it from the drawing. Type **NX** or select Delete View from the ZOOMS menu. Type the name of the view to be deleted, or select the name of the view from the menu.

Using Zooms from Other Commands

All the zoom commands can be used as nested commands, which means you can use them while doing something else. Anytime you can place a point on the screen or move the cursor, you can use a zoom command to change the display on the screen.

In the steps that follow, a line will be drawn connecting the left corner with the bottom right of the object on the screen. You will start with a tight view of the corner, then change the view in the middle of the Line command to view the lower right portion of the object. To set up the drawing for the following exercise, change the current layer before drawing the line.

Zooming from within the Line Command

Prompt	*Input*	*Description*
`Command`	**YC100**	Changes current layer to Layer 100
`Command`	Move cursor to top left corner, type **NP** or press third mouse button	Starts a new line at the corner (see fig. 7.8)
`Command`	**ZA**	Starts Zoom All command to see entire drawing
`Command`	Move cursor to bottom right of object and press third mouse button or type **NP**	Finishes the line by connecting to the bottom right of the object
`Command`	Press Esc or click a blank line in the menu with the second mouse button	Ends the Line command

Taking Advantage of Your Layer Organization

Using the zoom commands makes it easy to get a close-up or wide-angle view of a drawing. Occasionally, however, you will need to control what appears within a specific view. If you have planned ahead and divided the drawing into various layers, you can hide and display layers as you choose.

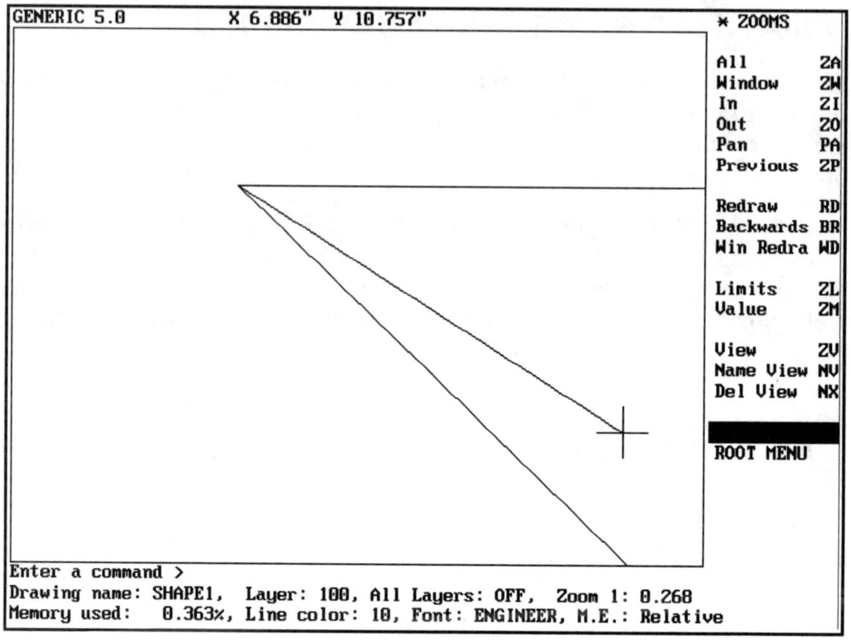

Figure 7.8: *Start a line by using Snap To Nearest Point.*

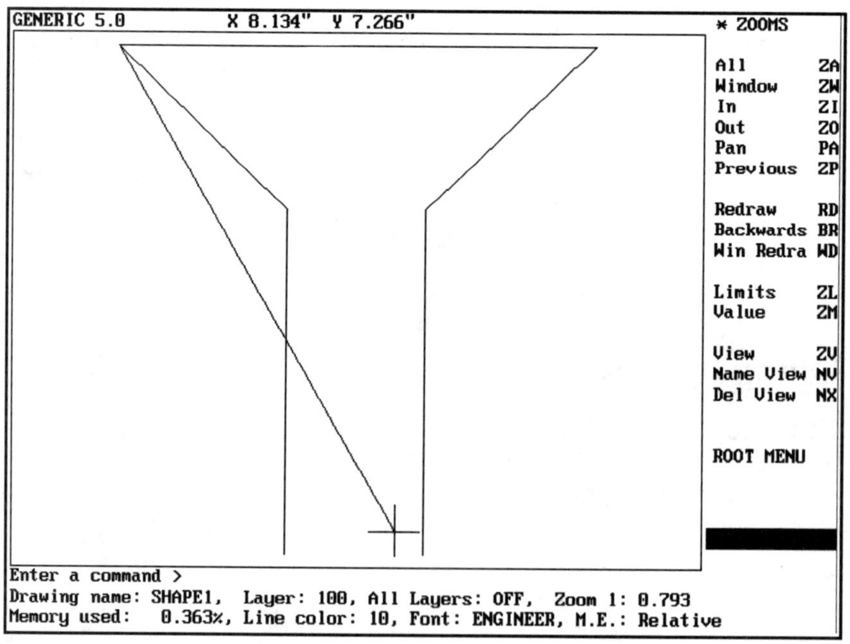

Figure 7.9: *A "Zoom All" view, executed in the middle of drawing a line.*

Layer Hide (YH)

To remove objects on a specific layer, use the Layer Hide command found on the LAYERS menu. When you select the command, a list of layers that have data on them appears in the menu. Click on the layer you want to hide, and it disappears from the screen. You can continue selecting layers, or you can press Enter to end the command. You cannot hide the currently active layer.

Layer Display (YD)

To restore a hidden layer, use the Layer Display command, also found on the LAYERS menu. It works just like Layer Hide, except that the layer(s) you select are displayed, not hidden. Press Enter without selecting a layer to end the command.

Both Layer Hide and Layer Display act as toggles, but only within the command. If you use Layer Hide to hide a layer, for example, it immediately disappears from the display. If you then select the same layer again before ending the Layer Hide command, the layer will reappear.

Resetting Origin Points

The coordinate grid is at the heart of Generic CADD 5.0. Every object in a drawing is saved in memory using coordinate reference points. You will find it necessary on occasion, however, to change the origin point of the drawing, or adjust where the on-screen grid starts.

Grid Re-Origin (GO)

If you turn on the grid when objects are already on the screen, they may not line up with the grid. You can adjust the origin point of the grid with the Grid Re-Origin command, in the CONSTRAINTS menu.

In the exercise below, you will turn on the grid, setting it to 1/4" spacing, then move the grid so it lines up with the drawing. In figure 7.10, the screen grid is set at 1/4" x 1/4" spacing. The view is zoomed to the bottom of the object. Note that the grid points do not line up with the end points of the lines. In figure 7.11, the origin of the grid has been moved to the bottom left of the object. Note how the grid points and the endpoints of the lines now match up.

Moving the Grid

Prompt	*Input*	*Description*
`Command`	**GS**	Initiates Grid Size command
`Change Grid Size X`	**.25**	Sets the grid spacing height to .25"
`Change Grid Size Y`	**.25**	Sets the grid spacing width to .25"
`Command`	**GO**	Starts the Grid Re-Origin command
`Enter new origin`	Move cursor to the bottom left of the object and type **NP**, or click third mouse button	Uses Snap To Nearest Point to move the origin point of the screen grid to the bottom left of the object

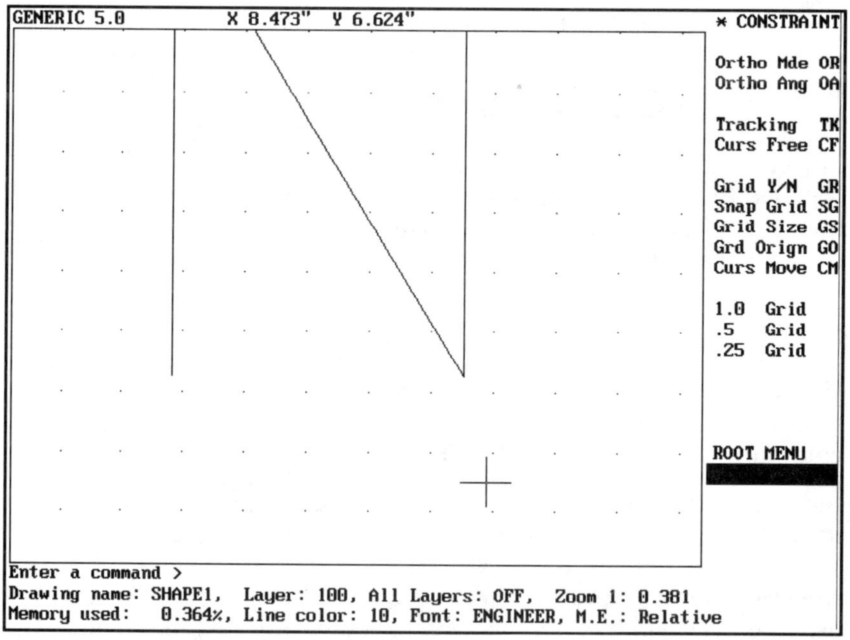

Figure 7.10: *The screen grid set at 1/4" x 1/4" spacing.*

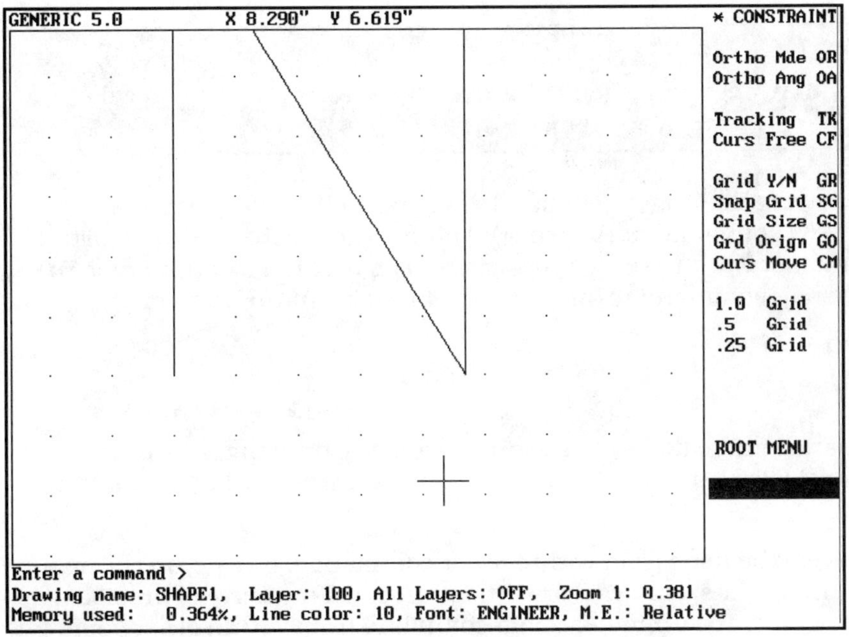

Figure 7.11: *Grid origin moved to the bottom left of the object.*

Drawing Re-Origin (DO)

The Drawing Re-Origin command is found on the UTILITIES menu. It changes the location of the 0,0 origin point of the drawing. This command should be used *rarely*, and its use should be carefully considered.

It may sound like no big deal to move the 0,0 location, but it can have far-reaching effects. When you create a named view, it saves the center of the view as a coordinate location relative to the origin point. The Zoom Limits command uses the origin point as the lower left corner of the new display. If you change the location of the origin point, all these settings will be affected.

Why would Generic CADD offer such a command? Sometimes, changing the drawing origin is the easiest way to achieve harmony in a drawing. If you are combining two completed drawings to make one new one, you may have to adjust the origin to properly align the two. Be sure, however, that you won't regret changing the origin, because it is not reversible using the Undo command. To change the origin, type **DO** and locate a new 0,0 point, either by moving the cursor and clicking or by typing a coordinate location.

NOTE

If you type a location, be sure you are not typing what you believe to be an absolute coordinate location when Manual Entry Relative is on—you will get the wrong location as the new origin.

If you use the Drawing Re-Origin command, give yourself a safety net. Place a Standard Point (PO) command at the true 0,0 of the drawing before you start. If you goof, or if you just want to return the origin to its original location, type **DO** again and use a snap command to snap the origin to the standard point.

Summary

The zoom commands make it easy to see any part of the drawing, at any scale. You can zoom up close for a tight view or look at the entire drawing, no matter how large it is.

Zoom commands can be used from within other commands, giving you the opportunity to adjust the view as you draw or edit, for an extra measure of precision and control. This ability to summon a zoom command from within other commands is an example of what is called nested command structure in Generic CADD. Being able to change the view while drawing helps the user to focus on the work to be done, not on the settings and zoom scale of the display.

Generic CADD offers 256 possible layers to draw on. Planning ahead to take advantage of layers offers a variety of benefits, including the ability to quickly modify the view on-screen using Layer Hide and Layer Display. Any combination of layers may be visible or hidden at any time.

Understanding the use of zooms and layer display prepares you for success in the next chapter, which covers the printing of drawings. Any view you can create on the screen may be sent to your printing or plotting device. Knowing how to create the right view makes it easier to create the right printed version of your work.

8

Printing and Plotting

All plotting and printing operations in Generic CADD are activated from the Output menu. Most of the functions of this menu are the same no matter what type of output device you select; Generic CADD considers all output to be plotting. This is reflected in the terminology of the menus, such as Plot Scale and Start Plot. The menu choices and commands used to set up the page, to determine the style of plot, and to preview the plot are the same for plotters, printers, and PostScript. The choices under the options portion of the menu will vary with the output device you select.

The Output menu, which is not located on the ROOT menu, can be accessed by two-letter commands or from the side menu. The Plot (PL) command uses the selection interface, which allows you to plot all or a portion of your drawing. After selecting the parts of the drawing to be plotted, you will see the main Output menu (see fig. 8.1). The Drawing Plot (DP) command automatically selects all objects on all currently displayed layers and immediately places you in the Output menu. The FILE menu contains macros for Plot, Print, and PostScript, which can be selected with the second button of your pointing device.

Choosing an Output Device

The first line of the Output menu, `Output menu for`, indicates the specific device to which output will be sent. Select the device—a plotter, a dot-matrix or laser printer, or a PostScript printer—from the first menu option.

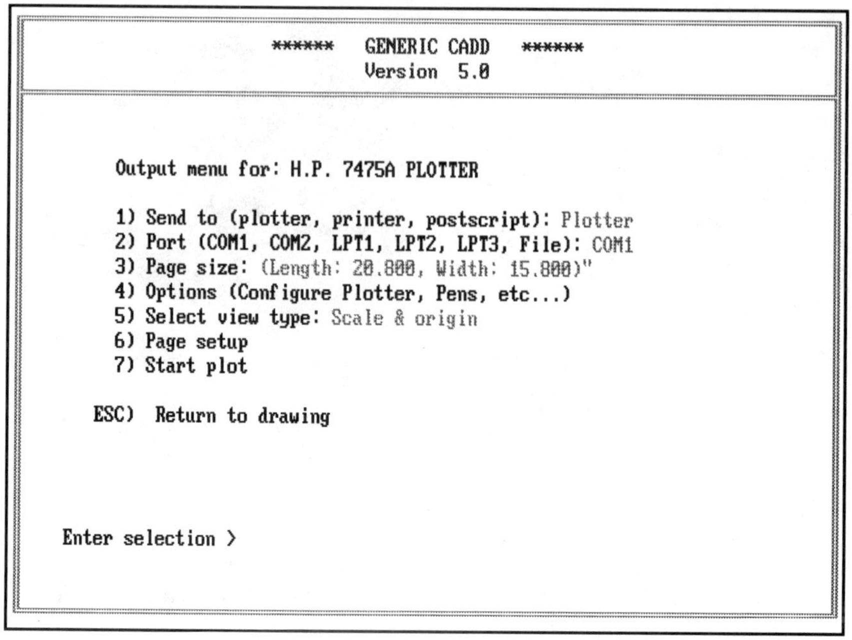
```
****** GENERIC CADD ******
Version 5.0

Output menu for: H.P. 7475A PLOTTER

1) Send to (plotter, printer, postscript): Plotter
2) Port (COM1, COM2, LPT1, LPT2, LPT3, File): COM1
3) Page size: (Length: 20.000, Width: 15.000)"
4) Options (Configure Plotter, Pens, etc...)
5) Select view type: Scale & origin
6) Page setup
7) Start plot

ESC) Return to drawing

Enter selection >
```

Figure 8.1: *The Generic CADD 5.0 Output menu.*

If you access the Output menu using either the DP or PL two-letter commands, the first line is for the device that was used most recently. Generic CADD remembers all the settings for each type of device. Whenever you switch from one device to another, Generic CADD recalls settings such as the type of plotter printer, the output port, the number of plotter pens, and so on.

If you used one of the macros on the FILE menu, the device will be set automatically, and the first line of the output menu and default value shown for the first option reflects this.

Plotters

Plotters fall into two broad categories, Pen/Pencil and Raster. Pen plotters use pens (or sometimes pencils) to physically draw the plot, line by line. They require more time, but they normally can accept a wide range of media, such as paper, transparency film, Vellum, and Mylar. Color is limited only by the pens available.

The Raster category includes electrostatic plotters, thermal plotters, dot-matrix plotters, and laser printers with plotter emulation capabilities. The plotters in this category typically buffer the plot data and then draw the entire plot at once. These devices usually generate a complicated plot in less time, but often they are limited in the types of media they can accept. Many plotters in this category are not capable of color output.

All plotters are sent data in a "plotter language" which describes the drawing in vectors or lines. This language is closer to Generic CADD's method for storing drawing data than to the bit-map language of dot-matrix printers. As a result, Generic CADD can generally create plotter code faster and more easily than printer code.

If you have a laser printer that can emulate a plotter, such as a Brother HL-8e or a Hewlett Packard LaserJet III, you should take advantage of this capability and configure Generic CADD for a plotter instead of a printer. This also is true if you use a product such as Plotter in a Cartridge with a printer such as the Canon LBP-8II or the HP LaserJet II. In these cases, treating the printer as a plotter speeds output, and, in the case of the HP LaserJet III, improves quality.

To select a plotter as the output device, choose option `1) Send to (plotter, printer, postscript)` from the main output menu. The output format menu will then appear. Select `1) Plotter`. Generic CADD automatically returns you to the main output menu after you make your choice.

To configure your plotter's specific brand and model, select `4) Options` from the main output menu. This places you in the Options: Plotter menu. Then select `1) Configure new plotter`. Generic CADD may prompt you to enter a path to the PLOTTERS.TPL file. This file contains all the plotter configuration choices and normally is stored in your default CADD directory (C:\CADD5). Type **C:\CADD5** (or the drive and directory where you installed Generic CADD 5.0), and press Enter. As figure 8.2 demonstrates, Generic CADD presents you with a list of plotters to choose from, 30 per screen..

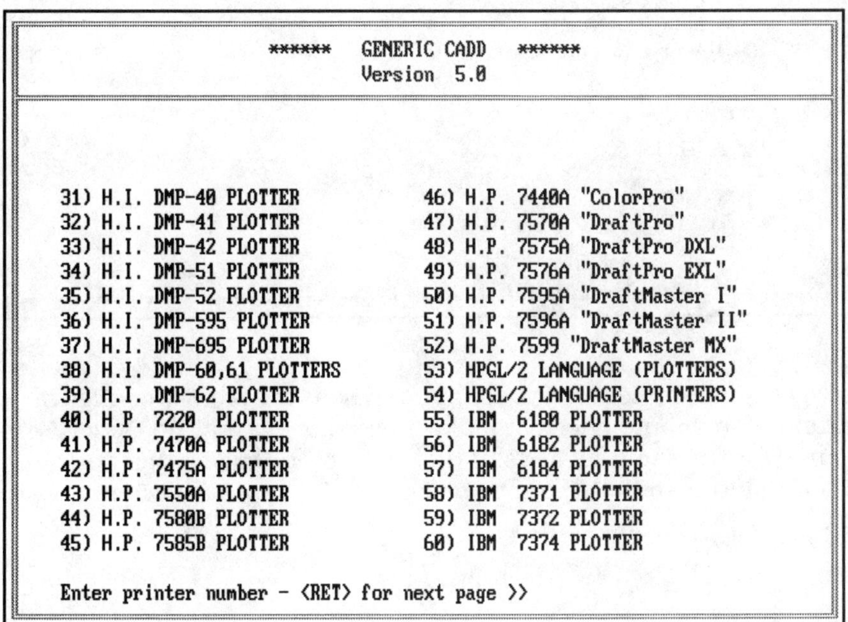

Figure 8.2: Selecting a plotter.

If you do not see your plotter listed on the first page, press Enter and you see the next 30 options. When you find your plotter, type its corresponding number and press Enter. For the HP LaserJet III, choose the option labeled `HPGL/2 LANGUAGE (PRINTERS)`. If you do not see your plotter listed, refer to your plotter manual to see what other plotters it emulates. Many plotters emulate one of the Houston Instrument or Hewlett-Packard models (indicated on the menu as H.I. or H.P.).

After you choose a plotter, you are returned to the Options menu. Press Esc to return to the main output menu. Now, you must tell the program how the plotter you selected is connected to your computer. Choose `2) Port (COM1, COM2, LPT1, LPT2, LPT3, File)` from the main output menu. Most plotters use a serial connection and are thus connected to either COM1 or COM2. Select the number that represents the port to which your plotter is connected and press Enter. If you selected a COM port, Generic CADD will now prompt you, as figure 8.3 shows, to confirm the configuration of the serial port.

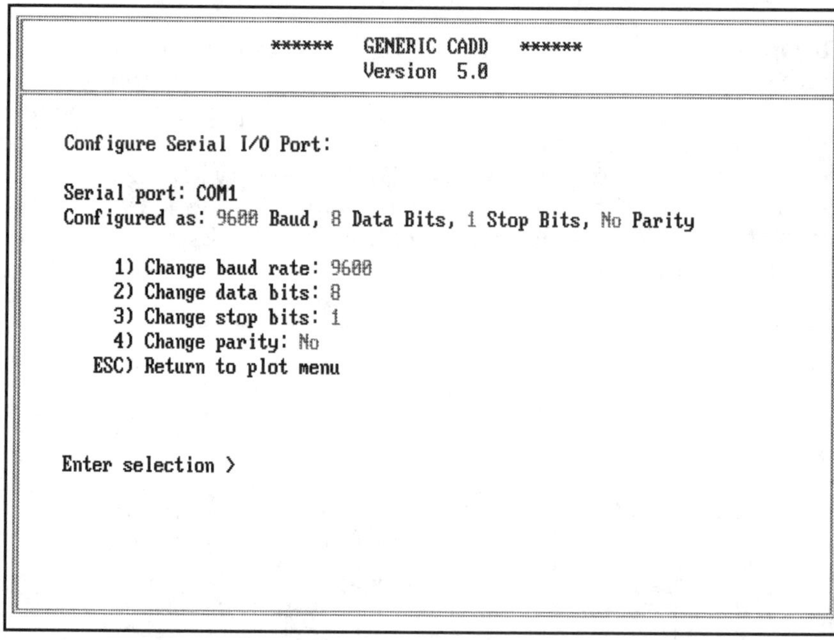

Figure 8.3: *Serial port parameters.*

Generic CADD suggests parameters that usually represent the factory configuration for most plotters. You should check to make sure your plotter and Generic CADD are configured for the same settings. If they are not, change either your configuration or your plotter so that the settings match. Your plotter will not operate correctly if the serial port settings for Generic CADD and your plotter are different. See the *Generic CADD 5.0 Users Guide* for more information on default settings for most plotters. When the settings are correct, press Esc to return to the main output menu.

NOTE

Normally, you only need to configure for a plotter once. When you exit Generic CADD using the Quit (QU) command, or update the environment with the Environment Update (EN) command, Generic CADD saves your plotter settings and recalls them the next time you use the program.

Dot-Matrix and Laser Printers

Dot-matrix printers and laser printers form images on paper by printing a series of dots. This technique is referred to as raster or bitmap graphics. For Generic CADD to plot a drawing on this type of printer, it must convert the drawing from its own object/vector format into a raster image. Generic CADD then converts the raster image into printer code and sends it to the printer. This process often involves the calculation of millions of dots, which are then sent to the printer. The calculation and transmission of this volume of information to the printer can be time-consuming.

Many laser printers can emulate plotters or support the PostScript page description language. Plotter languages and the PostScript language are vector-based and do not require Generic CADD to convert the drawing to a raster image. For this reason, laser printers that can emulate plotters should be treated as plotters by Generic CADD. Similarly, printers that are PostScript-compatible should be configured as PostScript devices.

To select a printer as the output device, choose `1) Send to (plotter, printer, postscript)` from the main Output menu, then select `2) Printer` from the output format menu. Generic CADD automatically returns you to the main output menu after you make your choice.

Configuring for the specific brand and type of printer is much like configuring for a plotter. Select `4) Options` from the main output menu. This will place you in the Options: Printer menu. Next, select `1) Configure printer`. Generic CADD may prompt you to enter a path to the .TPR files. Just as with the plotter configuration files, these files contain all the printer configuration choices. These files are normally stored in your default CADD directory (C:\CADD5). Type **C:\CADD5** (or the drive and directory where you installed CADD 5.0) and press Enter. Generic CADD will display a list of printer brands, like the one displayed by figure 8.4, to choose from.

```
                ******   GENERIC CADD   ******
                         Version 5.0

1) AMT-Advanced Matrix Technology   16) OKIDATA
2) BROTHER PRINTERS (Epson mode)    17) PANASONIC PRINTERS
3) CANON                            18) RADIO SHACK (TANDY)
4) Citizen                          19) SHARP
5) C.ITOH                           20) TEXAS INSTRUMENTS
6) KODAK DICONIX                    21) TOSHIBA
7) EPSON and COMPATIBLES            22) XEROX
8) FUJITSU                          23) OTHER GRAPHICS PRINTERS
9) HEWLETT PACKARD
10) HEWLETT PACKARD
11) IBM
12) JDL
13) MANNESMANN TALLY
14) NEC
15) NEWGEN SYSTEMS

Enter printer number - <RET> for next page >>
```

Figure 8.4: *Selecting a printer brand.*

Type the number that corresponds to your printer and press Enter. If you do not see your printer brand listed, refer to your printer manual to see what printers it is compatible with. Most 24-pin printers, for example, emulate one or more of the Epson 24-pin (LQ) model printers.

After you choose a brand of printer, Generic CADD displays a list of models and resolutions as shown in figure 8.5. Most printers fall into broad categories such as 8/9-pin or 24-pin (8- and 9-pin printers are really the same, because most 9-pin printers only use 8 pins when printing graphics). Usually, you see several listings for each type of printer, each listing a different resolution. Most printers are capable of printing at several resolutions. If in doubt, start with the low resolution choice and run a test print; then try the other options. Higher resolutions yield higher quality output but take longer to print. You may want to configure for a low or medium resolution for draft-quality check prints and reconfigure to high or very high resolution for presentation-quality output.

After choosing a printer, you need to tell Generic CADD how that printer is connected to your computer. Choose `2) Port (COM1, COM2, LPT1, LPT2, LPT3, File)` from the main output menu. Most printers use a parallel connection and thus are connected to LPT1, LPT2, or LPT3. Select the number that represents the port to which your printer is connected and press Enter. If you have a serial printer and you select a COM port, Generic CADD prompts you to confirm the configuration of the serial port (see fig. 8.3).

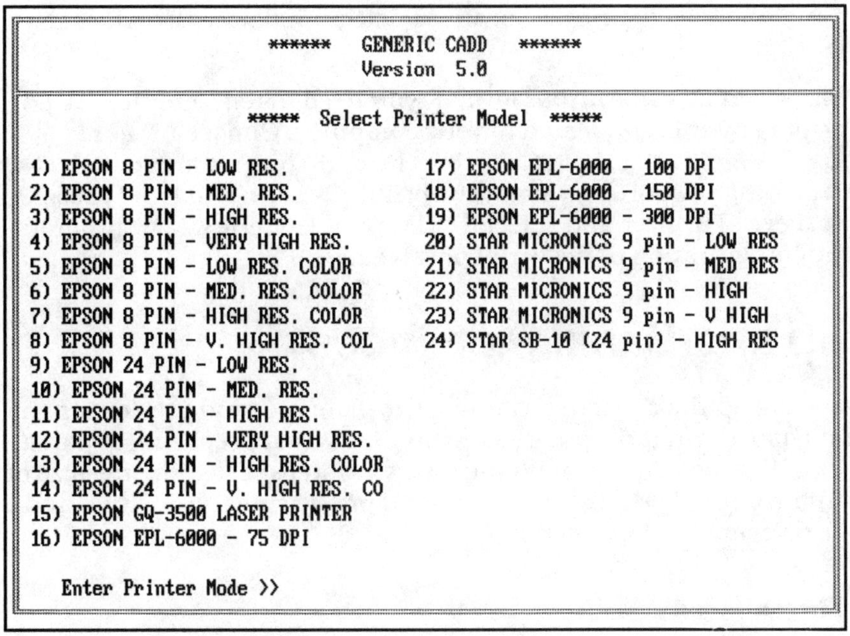

Figure 8.5: *Selecting a printer type and resolution.*

Most serial printers use the 9600 baud, 8 data bits, 1 stop bit, and no-parity settings. Make sure your printer and Generic CADD are configured for the same settings. If not, change your configuration for either Generic CADD or your printer so that the settings match. Your printer will not operate correctly if the serial port settings for Generic CADD and your printer are different. When the settings are correct, press Esc to return to the main Output menu.

As with plotting, you do not need to configure for a printer each time you run Generic CADD, except when you switch resolutions. When you exit Generic CADD using the Quit command, or update the environment with EN, Generic CADD saves your printer settings and recalls them the next time you use the program.

PostScript Printers

If you have a printer, such as the Apple LaserWriter or NEC Colormate PS, which supports the Adobe PostScript language, you should configure Generic CADD for PostScript output.

To select a printer as the output device, choose `1) Send to (plotter, printer, postscript)` from the main output menu, then select `3) Postscript` from the output format menu. Generic CADD automatically returns you to the main output menu after you make your choice. You do not need to configure for the individual brand or model of printer because PostScript devices are the same in Generic CADD.

After choosing PostScript as your output format, you need to tell Generic CADD how your PostScript printer is connected to your computer. Choose `2) Port (COM1, COM2, LPT1, LPT2, LPT3, File)` from the main output menu. Select the number representing the port to which your printer is connected and press Enter. If you have a serial printer and select a COM port, Generic CADD prompts you to confirm the configuration of the serial port (see fig. 8.3).

Page Setup and Basic Plot Types

The process for setting up the page, determining the plot type, and previewing the plot is the same no matter what output device you use. When preparing to plot a drawing, you normally need to go through the following steps: selecting the size of paper, selecting the type of plot (view, fit, scale), and previewing the position and appearance of the drawing on the paper.

Setting the Page Size

The first step in plotting a drawing is setting the page size. The page size represents the area that Generic CADD is allowed to use when plotting your drawing. The page size you set in Generic CADD should be smaller than the actual size of the paper being used. It is aesthetically pleasing to allow for a little white space around your drawing, and, more importantly, most output devices have a maximum image size that is smaller than the physical paper size.

Plotters have a safety margin at the front and back of the page, and those plotters that move the paper during plotting need an area at the sides of the sheet for the pinch rollers. Laser printers also have pinch rollers and usually cannot print within a quarter-inch of either side of the sheet. Unless you override the settings, most lasers also have a default top and bottom margin of one-half inch.

To select a page size, choose `3) Page size` from the main output menu. Generic CADD will prompt you to choose from a selection of standard sizes. If you are configured for a plotter, the sizes listed represent the maximum allowable plot area for standard architectural and engineering sheet sizes (A, B, C, and so on). If you are configured for a dot-matrix printer, Generic CADD suggests two standard sizes for narrow and wide carriage paper.

Choose one of the sizes listed and press Enter. If you want to specify a size that is not listed, choose the option labeled `User selected size`, and Generic CADD prompts you for the width and length of the paper. Remember, do not enter the physical size of the paper itself unless your device is capable of printing to the entire sheet.

Current View

Choose `5) Select view type` from the main output menu, and Generic CADD will prompt you to select the type of view you want to plot. figure 8.6 depicts Generic CADD's three standard plot view types. After you choose one of the three options, Generic CADD returns you to the main output menu. The `Fit full drawing` and `Specify scale & origin` options also can be activated when in page preview mode.

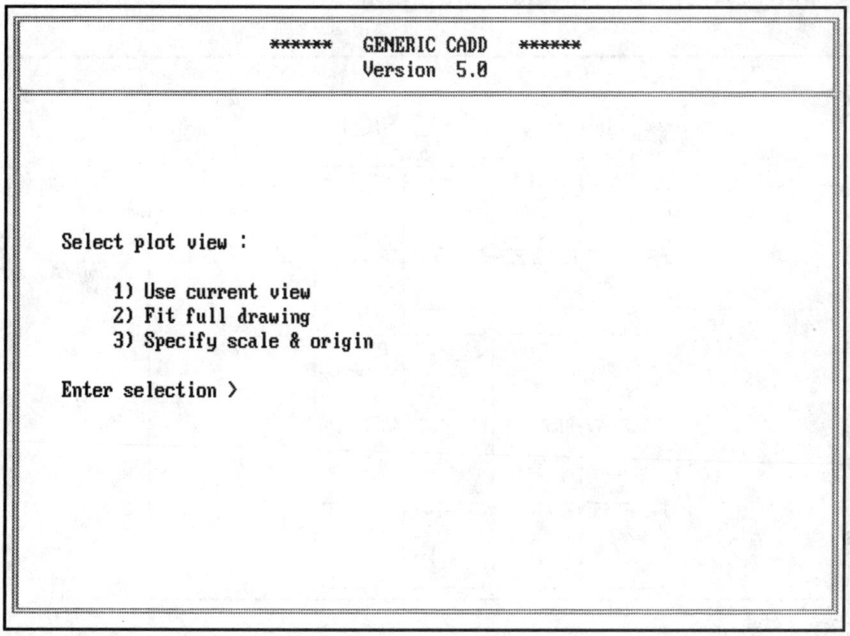

Figure 8.6:
Plot view types.

The first of the three view options is `Use current view`. This option tells Generic CADD to take the current view on the drawing screen and plot it to fit the page size you have selected. What you get on the paper does not match what is seen on the screen because the height and width ratio of your screen and your page size are rarely the same. This usually results in extra material at the top and bottom of the plot that was not visible on the screen.

This option is desirable when you want a quick printout of some portion of your drawing at no specific scale. This plot type is one of the easiest to do, but it offers the least amount of control over the plot that is created. You should use one of the other two options for more serious plots.

Start in the drawing screen and use one of the zoom commands to center a portion of your drawing on the screen. Then type **DP** to get to the Output menu and choose the `Use current view` option after verifying that the output device, port, and page size are correct.

To preview what will be plotted, choose `6) Page setup` from the main Output menu. Generic CADD prompts you with `Fast redraw? (Y/N)`. Press **N** or click your second mouse button. As figure 8.7 shows, Generic CADD then shows your drawing and a solid box (drawn using the cursor color) that represents the area to be plotted. Press Enter to return to the main output menu.

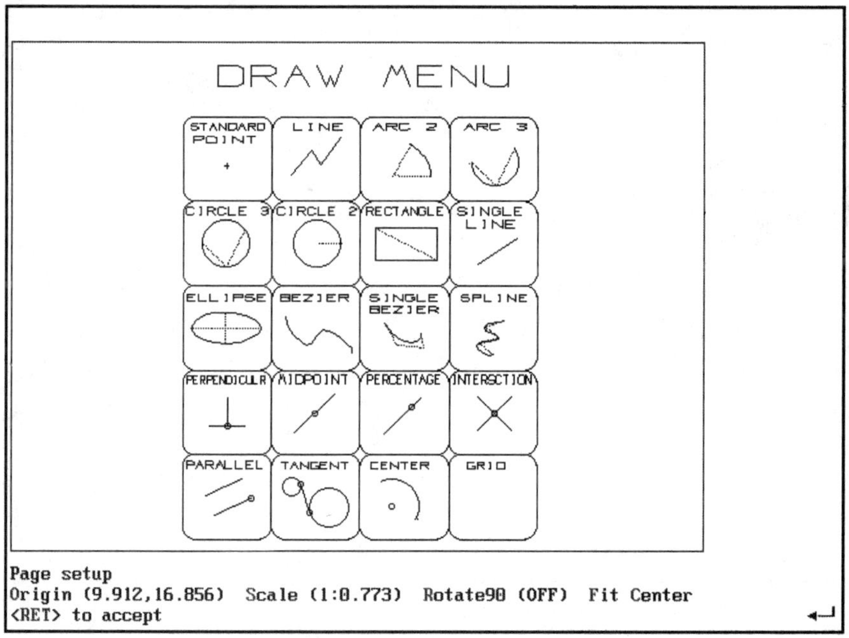

Figure 8.7: *Page preview.*

If all your other settings (plotter type, output port, paper size and so on) are correct and your output device is loaded with paper and on-line, select `7) Start plot` and Generic CADD begins plotting your drawing.

Fit Full Drawing

The second plot view type is `Fit full drawing`. When you select this option, Generic CADD calculates the plot scale required to plot your entire drawing as large as possible on the page size you have selected. Generic CADD automatically centers your drawing on the page, but it does not calculate what rotation will result in the largest plot. This option is most useful when you want to plot your entire drawing and the scale of the resulting plot is not important.

Because Generic CADD does not calculate the best orientation, it is often a good idea to use the Page setup option to see if the drawing would plot larger if rotated. Choose `6) Page setup` from the main output menu. Generic CADD prompts you with `Fast redraw? (Y/N)`; press **Y,** or click with your first mouse button. Generic CADD then shows a light blue dashed box with an X drawn from the cornersas depicted by figure 8.8. The dashed box represents the extent of your drawing and fits around the outermost objects in your drawing. A solid box (drawn using the cursor color) is placed over the dashed box. The solid box represents the area that will be plotted.

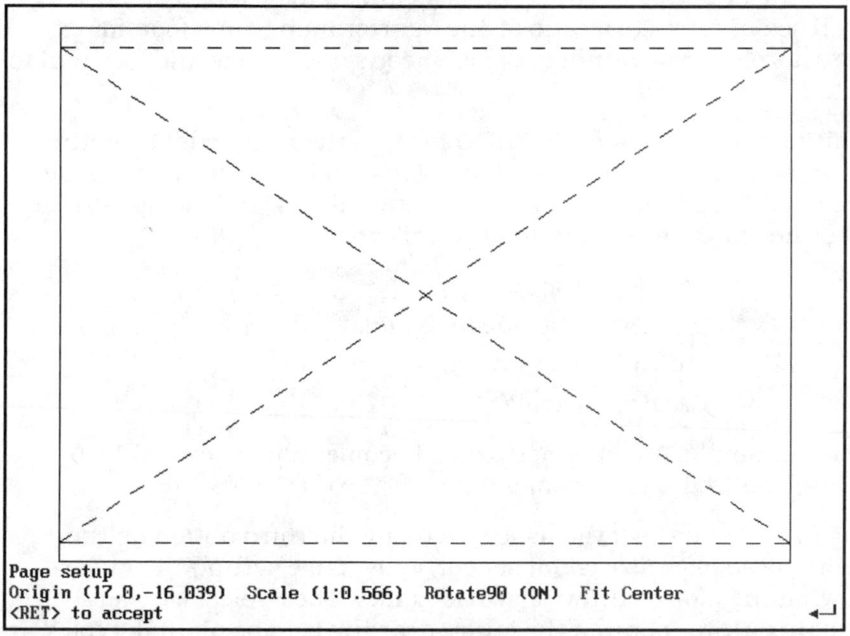

Figure 8.8: *Page preview, fast redraw mode.*

If you believe the drawing would fit better on the page if it was rotated 90 degrees, press **R** and Generic CADD rotates the dashed box that represents your drawing and aligns the lower left corners of the two boxes. If you press **F**, Generic CADD fits and centers your drawing to the paper using the new rotation. If you liked it better the first way, press **R** and then **F** again to rotate the drawing back to the prior view. When you are satisfied with the orientation and fit, press Enter to return to the main output menu.

If all your other settings (plotter type, output port, paper size, and so on) are correct and your output device is loaded with paper and on-line, select `7) Start plot` and Generic CADD begins plotting your drawing.

Plotting to Scale

Most drawings of real-world objects (as opposed to charts or schematic diagrams) must be plotted to scale to be useful to others. Generic CADD expresses the plot scale as a ratio of 1:*nn*, where one unit measured on the plotted drawing is equal to *nn* units in the real world. The units on both sides of the ratio are assumed to be the same and are therefore not shown. Thus, the ratio can be inches to inches or feet to feet, but not inches to feet.

Architects and surveyors typically express scale as a ratio of Y inches to X feet. In many cases, one or the other side of the ratio is assumed to be one. The expression "quarter-inch scale" refers to a ratio of one quarter inch to one foot, for example. The expression "one to a hundred scale" means one inch would be equal to one hundred feet.

To convert a traditional scale to Generic CADD format, the ratio must be in the same units (feet or inches, for example) on both sides. You then bring the value on the left side to one. The process to convert traditional 1/4" to 1' scale into Generic CADD plot scale, for example, would be as follows:

1. 1/4": 1'	Starting ratio
2. 1/4": 12"	Convert right side to inches
3. 4 × 1/4": 4 × 12"	Multiply both sides by 4
4. 1": 48"	CADD plot scale

Following the above example, "eighth-inch scale" becomes a plot scale of 1:96, while "one inch to a hundred feet" becomes a plot scale of 1:1200.

To plot a drawing to scale, first set the page size using the third option on the main output menu. If the page size is not set correctly, page setup will not correctly represent what the plotted drawing will look like. Then select `6) Page setup` from the main output menu. If the entire drawing is to be plotted, type **Y** at the `Fast redraw? (Y/N)` prompt. If only a portion of the drawing is to be plotted, answer **N** to this prompt.

After Generic CADD has drawn the page setup screen (see fig. 8.9), press **S** to set the scale. Generic CADD will indicate the current plot scale and prompt you to enter a new value. Enter only the right half of the plot scale and press Enter. Generic CADD will redraw the page setup screen and will align the lower left corners of the drawing and the page outline.

If the drawing will fit better on the page rotated, press **R** to rotate the drawing. Generic CADD will again redraw the screen and align the lower left corners. If the entire drawing is to be plotted, press **C** and Generic CADD will center the drawing on the page. If the entire drawing does not fit on the page, you will need to choose a new plot scale (press **S**) and center the drawing on the paper again.

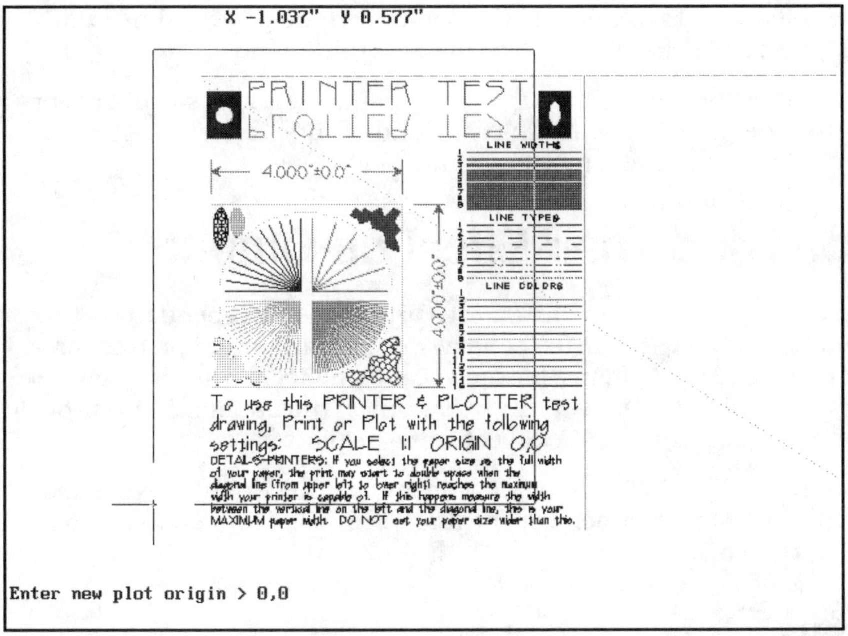

Figure 8.9: Page preview, setting scale, and origin.

If only a portion of the drawing is to be plotted, press **O** to locate the origin for the page outline. You may now use your pointer to drag the page outline and position it over the portion of the drawing that you want to plot. While dragging the page frame, you can use commands such as Zoom In (ZI), Zoom Out (ZO), Zoom Window (ZW), and Pan (PA) to better position the page outline properly. The origin in this case refers to the lower left corner of the page outline. If it helps, think of the page outline as a viewfinder; whatever is located inside the page frame will be plotted.

You may also use manual entry to position the page frame at a specific location in your drawing. After pressing **O** to locate the plot origin, type **MO** to ensure that manual entry values are relative to the origin of the drawing.

Positioning the plot origin with the manual entry set relative to last point or relative to basepoint can be very frustrating. If rotation is off, enter manual entry coordinates as you usually would and press Enter. If rotation is on, it gets a little trickier. Because the drawing is rotated, you have to rotate the coordinate values in order to properly position the page outline. To rotate the coordinates, transpose the X and Y values and multiply the Y value by -1. For example, to place the corner of the page outline at 2,5, you would enter **5,-2**. This is necessary only if the drawing has been rotated to fit on the paper.

When you are satisfied with the scale and the position of the page outline relative to your drawing, press Enter to return to the main output menu.

If all your other settings (plotter type, output port, paper size, and so on) are correct and your output device is loaded with paper and on-line, select `7) Start plot`, and Generic CADD will begin plotting your drawing.

Plot Options and Their Effect on Output

The choices available under `4) Options` on the Output menu depend upon the output device you have selected. The first choice on the printer and plotter versions of this menu is used to configure for the specific model of printer or plotter that is connected to Generic CADD. All three versions of the options menu provide a choice that lets you select the number of copies to be plotted.

The other choices generally allow you to tailor the output in various ways, such as selecting the number of plotter pens or the line width used for PostScript output.

Plotter Options

The plotter options menu provides choices to configure the plotter, draw arcs and circles, configure the plotter pen settings, import a plotter command file, and set the number of copies to be plotted (see fig. 8.10).

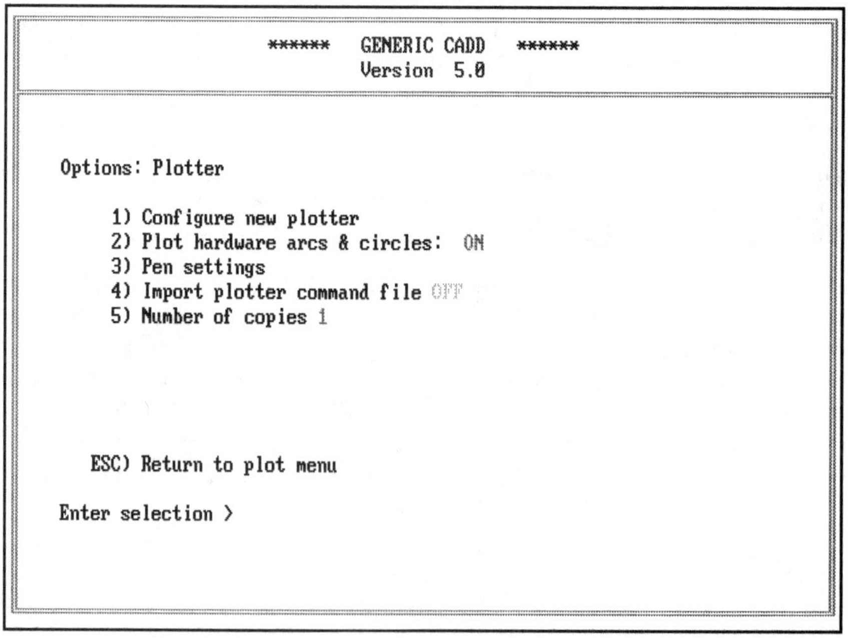

Figure 8.10: *The options menu for plotter output.*

Configure New Plotter

Selecting `1) Configure new plotter` allows you to change the specific model of plotter being used, as discussed earlier.

Plot Hardware Arcs & Circles

Selecting `2) Plot hardware arcs & circles` will toggle the support of hardware arcs on or off. This option is not supported on all plotter types. Some plotters support internal functions to draw arcs and circles. These are commonly referred to as hardware arcs because the arc is drawn by the plotter. Generic CADD 5.0 will indicate "not supported" if your plotter does not support accurate internal routines to draw arcs and circles.

Plotters that use the DM/PL protocol support hardware arcs, but the accuracy level is too low to be used effectively with Generic CADD because they round the arcs to the nearest degree.

Plotters that support internal arc and circle functions usually draw these entities using a relatively small number of line segments, or facets (256 for a full circle). If you have relatively large arcs or circles in your drawing, you often will be able to see the individual line segments. Generic CADD uses a larger number of line segments, which usually results in a smoother arc. Hardware arcs should be enabled only if you are creating a plot file that will be used to import your drawing into another graphics program. For everyday plotting, it is usually best to leave this option set to off.

Pen Settings

Choosing `3) Pen settings` will display a separate menu with the various pen settings options (see fig. 8.11). These options are used to control the pen speed, width, number of pens, and so on.

The first choice under pen settings is `1) Pen speed`. If you are using an electrostatic, thermal, pencil, or laser printer in plotter emulation mode, this option should be set to 50, which is the maximum possible value. You may need to use a lower pen speed in order to prevent skipping or fading, depending upon the pens and media you are using. Some plotters will sense the pen type and adjust automatically. The optimum pen speed varies with both the type of pen and the media, so you will need to experiment to find what speed works best with a given combination of pens and media.

Roller ball pens generally can be run at full speed without much difficulty. Fiber-tip and ceramic-tip pens require a fast to medium speed. Technical or drafting pens usually work best at a medium to slow setting. Transparency pens require a very slow setting.

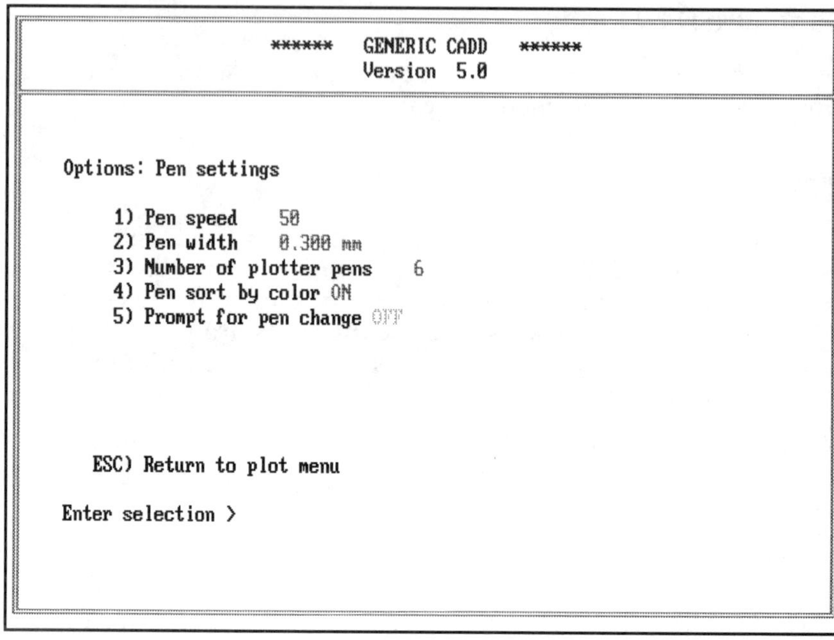

Figure 8.11: *The options menu for pen settings.*

The second option is `2) Pen width`. This is normally specified in millimeters. Generic CADD takes the pen width into account when drawing line widths and fills. If the width is set too wide, gaps will appear between the lines. If the width is set too narrow, the lines will overlap and the paper may become saturated with ink.

Most plotter pens are labeled with the width of the pen in millimeters. If you do not see a decimal point, assume that the value is tenths of millimeters. Fiber pens typically come in .3mm and .7mm widths. Typical sizes for drafting pens are .15, .25, .5, and .7 millimeters. The pen width normally should be set to allow a very slight overlap to assure that wide lines and fills appear solid. This may not be necessary for fiber-tip pens becuase their tips often flatten out. For technical pens, this means specifying a value a few hundredths less than the rated width of the pen. Roller ball pens often plot much narrower than their rated width, sometimes requiring a pen-width setting 30-50 percent narrower than the pen's official width.

TIP

The pen width setting is especially important for laser printers in a plotter emulation mode. Laser printers are capable of producing very fine lines, sometimes requiring a pen width setting as small as .08 or .07 millimeters.

The value for the third option, `3) Number of plotter pens`, is set automatically when you configure the plotter. You may need to reset it if you have an optional pen changer installed on your plotter, or if you are using fewer than the maximum number of pens your plotter supports.

This option works in conjunction with the fourth option, `4) Pen sort by color`, and the fifth option, `5) Prompt for pen change`.

If the prompts for pen change and pen sort are both set to yes, Generic CADD will pause for you to change the plotter pens after it has plotted with the last pen available. Generic CADD then plots the next series of colors, and, if necessary, pauses again for you to change the pens. If the number of plotter pens is set to 6, for example, Generic CADD will prompt you to change the pens after plotting all objects drawn using colors 1-6. It will pause again after plotting all objects drawn, using colors 7-12.

If `Prompt for pen change` is set to no or n/a, Generic CADD will start over with the first pen after using the last available pen. If `Number of pens` is set to 8, for example, Generic CADD will plot colors 1-8 using pens 1-8, then will use pen 1 for color 9, pen 2 for color 10, pen 3 for color 11, and so on.

Choosing `Pen sort by color` toggles this setting between on and off. When `Pen sort by color` is on, Generic CADD will plot all objects drawn using color 1, then all objects drawn using color 2, and so forth. This decreases plot time by minimizing the number of times the plotter needs to pause to change pens.

If `Pen sort by color` is off, Generic CADD will plot objects in the order in which they appear in the drawing database. If you are plotting to an electrostatic or laser printer that is emulating a plotter, this may reduce plot time slightly because Generic CADD only has to process the drawing database one time. Setting this option to off also changes `Prompt for pen change` to a setting of n/a, indicating that the choice is not available. Generic CADD will only prompt for pen changes if `Pen sort by color` is on.

Choosing `Prompt for pen change` toggles this setting between on and off. When `Prompt for pen change` is on, Generic CADD will prompt you to change pens as described above under `Number of pens`.

Import Plotter Command File

Plotter command files are used when you need to send extra command codes to the plotter during initialization (before plotting) and/or after a plot is finished. When you choose `4) Import plotter command file`, Generic CADD will prompt you for the name of a plotter command file. Plotter command files are ASCII files that contain keywords recognized by Generic CADD and plotter commands in the language of your plotter. The keywords tell Generic CADD when to send the plotter commands which follow the keyword.

Plotter command files are useful when a roll-feed or sheet-feeding plotter is used and when you need to send a command after plotting which tells the plotter to advance to the next page or plot frame. Refer to the *Generic CADD 5.0 User Guide* for a list of the keywords, and to your plotter reference manual for a list of the plotter command codes.

Number of Copies

When you choose `5) Number of copies`, Generic CADD will prompt you to enter the number of copies you want to be plotted. This option is useful if you need to generate a number of identical plots. When you tell Generic CADD to start plotting, it will ask if you need it to pause for paper changes between plots. This prompt only occurs if the number of copies is set to a value greater than one.

If you are using an electrostatic or laser printer, it is often possible to set the number of copies via the control panel on the device. This is normally a more desirable option because Generic CADD generates additional copies by repeating the entire plot. Generic CADD takes much longer to generate the data for each plot than the plotter or printer does to generate additional copies once it has the plot data in its own memory. The `Number of copies` option should only be used for devices that cannot generate additional copies on their own.

Printer Options

Printing is a relatively simple process. The printer options menu has only two printer options available, as shown in figure 8.12.

Configure New Printer

Selecting `1) Configure new printer` allows you to change the model of printer being used, as explained earlier.

Number of Copies

When you choose `2) Number of copies`, Generic CADD prompts you to enter the number of copies you want. This option is most useful if you need to generate a number of identical prints. With a laser printer, you can often set the number of copies through the control panel on the printer. Normally, this is a more desirable option because, as with plotting, Generic CADD generates additional copies by repeating the entire printing process. It takes Generic CADD much longer to generate the raster data for each plot than it does to have the printer generate additional copies once it has the plot data in its memory. The `Number of copies` option should only be used for those printers that cannot generate additional copies on their own.

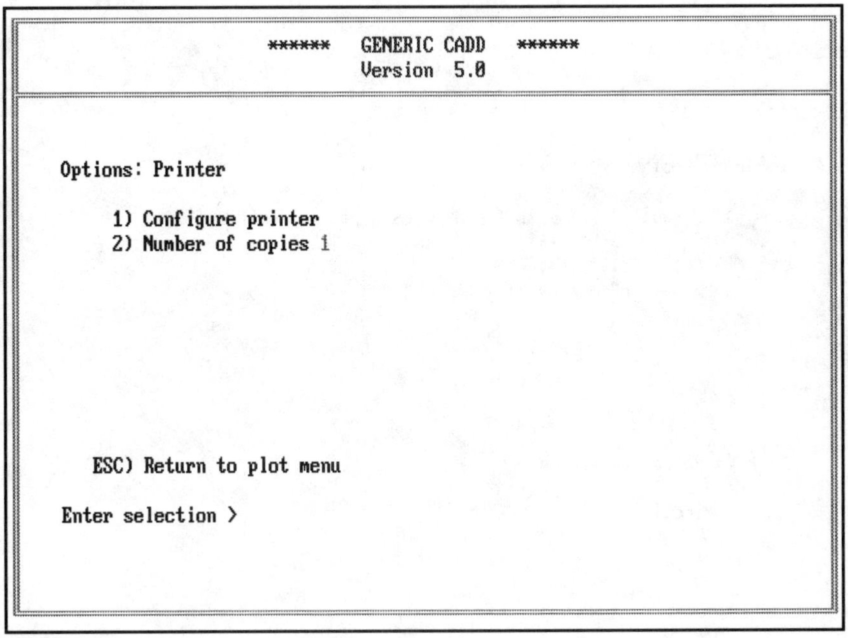

Figure 8.12: *The options menu for printer output.*

PostScript Options

The PostScript options menu (see fig. 8.13) provides options for setting the line width, greyscale, color, and number of copies.

Default Line Width

The PostScript language is based upon *points*, a unit of measurement used in typesetting and page layout. A point is 1/72". The `1) Default line width` option sets the base PostScript line width used when plotting your drawing. Generic CADD line widths of 0 and 1 are plotted using the base line width setting, line width 2 is plotted using 2 times the base width, line width 3 is plotted at 3 times the base width, and so forth.

When you choose this option, Generic CADD will prompt you for a new line default line width. Enter a value from 0 to 25. Note that 25 points is a very wide line, more than one-third of an inch wide. If you enter a value of 0.00, the PostScript printer will draw the thinnest possible lines. With 300dpi printers, such as the Apple LaserWriter, this can result in quality output. With PostScript devices, such as Linotronic typesetters, this will result in a line so fine that it is almost impossible to see. If you are plotting to a high resolution (greater than 300dpi) printer, values from .1 to .3 points are recommended.

Figure 8.13: The options menu for PostScript output.

```
                    ******  GENERIC CADD   ******
                            Version  5.0

Options: Postscript

     1) Default line width ( 0.00 - 25.0 pt.):  (0.007 pt.)
     2) Grayscale for filled objects:  (Variable)
     3) Color PostScript OFF
     4) Number of copies 1



  ESC) Return to plot menu

Enter selection >
```

Greyscale for Filled Objects

When using black-and-white PostScript for output, Generic CADD allows options for printing fills. Fills may be printed using variable greyscaling based on the color number of the fill: color 1 gives the darkest fill and color 15 the lightest. The other option is for all fills to be printed using the same greyscale level.

When you choose the `2) Greyscale for filled objects` option, Generic CADD will toggle between a variable and a number indicating the greyscale level between 0 (darkest) and 1 (lightest). Typically, you would enter a decimal value such as .5 or .75.

If the `Color PostScript` option is activated, `Greyscale for filled objects` is automatically changed to read `Color PostScript` as well, indicating that fills will be plotted using their screencolors.

Color PostScript

Choosing `3) Color PostScript` toggles this option on or off. When `Color PostScript` is off, Generic CADD prints all lines in black and fills are printed according to the setting of greyscale for filled objects. When `Color PostScript` is on, Generic CADD prints all objects in color. The effect of this setting varies depending on whether you are printing on a black-and-white or a color PostScript printer.

If you have a color PostScript printer, the objects in your drawing print according to their screen colors. Some colors, such as 6 and 7, may not print well on some printers. You should make a test plot with various colors of lines at various angles to see what works best with your printer. Depending upon your printer, as many as 256 colors may be printed. Generic CADD sets the PostScript color palette to match the standard VGA hue and saturation palette. This may not match the default palette on some more advanced video cards.

If you have a black-and-white PostScript printer, the objects in your drawing print use greyscales. The greyscales attempt to represent the brightness of the screen color; color numbers such as 1, 5, 8, and 9 come out in a fairly dark greyscale, while colors such as 3, 7, 11, and 14 are represented by relatively light grey values. Color 15 (white) is printed as solid black instead of white, which would be invisible on white paper. All color values greater than 15 print as solid black.

TIP

Because PostScript printers print greyscales using a dither pattern, some fine lines may drop out entirely on black-and-white printers. This effect is worse on 300dpi printers, such as the Apple LaserWriter than on the much higher resolution Linotronic printers. When printing color PostScript on a black-and-white printer, increase the default line width. PostScript line widths of .5 points to 1.5 points work relatively well on 300dpi printers.

Number of Copies

When you choose `4) Number of copies`, Generic CADD prompts you to enter the number of copies you want plotted. This option is most useful if you need to generate a number of identical prints. As of this writing, Generic CADD 5.0 generates additional copies by repeating the entire printing process. Because each copy takes as long to print as the first copy, you may simply want to use a photocopier to make extra copies. Hopefully, in the future, Generic CADD will support generating extra copies through the PostScript command that tells the printer the number of copies to print.

Generic CADD also asks if you want it to pause between prints. This is rather unusual, because virtually all PostScript printers do not require paper to be loaded manually for each print.

Plotting to a File

Generic CADD 5.0 can direct plotting and printing output to a file on disk. You might want to direct output to a file for several reasons:

- Exporting drawing data to a word processor or desktop publishing program via HPGL or EPS files.
- Printing or plotting drawings when the output device is off-site or attached to another computer.
- Printing or plotting multiple copies of a drawing without tying up CADD.
- Exporting drawing data to another drawing program that can read plotter files or PostScript code.

The file that is created on disk contains all the data that normally would be sent to the output device, so it can be used to print or plot independently of Generic CADD by simply using the DOS Copy command to copy the file to the proper output port. This can be very useful because printing or plotting tasks that take a long time to complete. The file can be carried to another computer on a floppy disk, and that system can be used to plot the drawing. A less powerful computer with a high density disk drive, for example, can be used as a plot server in offices where several people share a plotter.

To plot to a file, select `2) Port (COM1, COM2, LPT1, LPT2, LPT3, File)`. Generic CADD will prompt you to select an output port or file. Select the option for file, and Generic CADD will prompt you to enter a name for the file. Generic CADD will suggest the name of the current drawing, followed by an extension indicating the type of file. Type a name for the plot file, or simply press Enter to accept the suggested name. Generic CADD uses the following extensions to denote file types:

Extension	*File*
DPF	Disk Plotted File (a plotter file)
PRF	PRinter file
DEV	PostScript DEVice file
EPS	Encapsulated PostScript file

If your configurations have been set for PostScript output, Generic CADD will offer you a choice of two files: DEV and EPS. A device (DEV) file contains PostScript code just as it would be sent to the PostScript printer, and it may be copied directly to a PostScript device to plot a drawing. An Encapsulated PostScript file (EPS—often called EPSF on Macintosh systems) is a special type of PostScript file, designed to be imported into another document, which is then printed to a PostScript printer. Encapsulated PostScript files are an excellent means of importing Generic CADD graphics into a word processor or page layout program (such as PageMaker or Ventura Publisher), provided that the final output will be printed on a PostScript printer.

Plotter files in Hewlett Packard Graphics Language (HPGL) also are often used to import Generic CADD drawings into a word processor or page layout program. This option is routinely used when the final document will not be printed with a PostScript printer. To create an HPGL file, you should first configure for an HP plotter, such as the HP model 7475. Some programs expect plot files to have the extension PLT; if this is the case, you can either tell Generic CADD to save the file with this extension or use the DOS Rename command to change the name of the file if needed.

To plot or print a file from disk, use the DOS Copy command. If the device is connected to a serial port, you will first need to use the DOS Mode command to set the serial port to the proper baud rate, parity, and so on (refer to your DOS manual for details on using the Mode command). To copy a file to a printer or plotter, use the following command:

COPY filename port /B

Filename is the name of the file, such as HOUSE.DPF, and *port* is the DOS device name for the port to which your printer or plotter is connected. DOS uses the following device names for the following output ports.

Device	*Output ports*
COM1	Serial Communications Port 1
COM2	Serial Communications Port 2
LPT1	Parallel (printer) Port 1
LPT2	Parallel (printer) Port 2
LPT3	Parallel (printer) Port 3

To send a printer file called PIECHART.PRF to Parallel Port 1, for example, you would type:

COPY PIECHART.PRF LPT1 /B

The /B parameter tells DOS that the file contains binary codes. This may not be needed with PostScript or some plotter files, but it is usually mandatory with printer files. This is because printer files may contain values that DOS could interpret as an End Of File (EOF) mark, which could cause DOS to copy only a portion of the file to the printer. The /B parameter tells DOS to ignore any EOF values it might encounter in the middle of the file. For this reason, this parameter always should be included.

Plotting Part of a Drawing

Occasionally you might want to plot only some of the entities in your drawing—specific layers, for example. Generic CADD 5.0 offers two ways of doing this.

If the objects you want to plot happen to be on one or more layers, the Drawing Plot (DP) command is the easiest to use. First, use the layer commands to set your Current Layer (YC), and then apply the Hide (YH) or Display (YD) layer commands until your plotted drawing appears as you want it. Use the Zoom All (ZA) command to be sure everything is correct, and then enter the DP command. DP will plot only those layers that were displayed in the drawing screen when you issued the command. Finally, set up your page size options and select `Page setup` to preview the plot.

If the objects you want to plot are not segregated by layers, you can use the Selection Plot (PL) command. This command, as the name implies, selects the parts of the drawing you want to plot. You may select a variety of objects using several methods, including the Entity Filter command. (Generic CADD's standard selection interface is described in Chapter 10.) Once you have selected the objects you want plotted, press Enter to confirm your choices and proceed with plotting as usual.

Using Colors in Plotted Drawings

If you are using a plotter, the colors of the objects in your drawing can be plotted in a number of ways. The most obvious is for plotting the drawing with different colors. This results in an appealing drawing that is easy to read. Most drafting style plotter pens are available in a minimum of four colors (black, red, green, and blue), and fiber-tip pens come in a wider range of colors.

You also can use color to control the width of objects. Most plotter pens come in several widths, or *line weights*. Many users overlook this and plot entire drawings using different pen colors of the same line weight.

Generic CADD associates color numbers with pen numbers when it plots. Generic CADD does not know if you insert a .7mm pen in one pen holder and a .25mm pen in another pen holder. The only occasion in which the pen width matters to Generic CADD is when it draws fills or line widths. This allows you to choose any configuration of colors and pen widths. All you need to know is that Generic CADD will draw all objects drawn with color 1 using pen 1. This enables you to change the colors and line weights used for your plot simply by rearranging the pens.

After the last available pen is used, Generic CADD can either prompt you to install a new set of pens or automatically start using the pens again in order. You can easily determine what pen numbers will be used for which color numbers; just remember that whenever Generic CADD runs out of pen numbers, it starts over with pen 1. If you have a 6-pen plotter and 15 colors in your drawing, for example, it works out as follows:

Color No.	*Pen No.*
1, 7, 13	1
2, 8, 14	2
3, 9, 15	3
4, 10	4
5, 11	5
6, 12	6

Most black-and-white plotters (such as electrostatic plotters and laser printers in plotter emulation mode) enable you to assign different width pens to different logical pen numbers. If all your colors are black, for example, differently numbered pens can plot in different line weights.

Using color numbers to control line widths has two primary advantages: it takes less time to plot, and it results in cleaner corners between wide lines.

When Generic CADD plots a wide line, it does so by drawing several parallel lines. When output is to a plotter, Generic CADD always uses an odd number of strokes, offset evenly from the center of the line (with the X,Y coordinates denoting the ends of the line). Figure 8.14 shows wide lines made by stroking a .25mm pen three times, as opposed to a single line drawn with a .7mm pen.

If you plot heavier line weights by using a particular color with a wider pen in the appropriate pen holder, your plots will be finished faster because Generic CADD does not have to draw as many lines. You also can plot faster by using wider pens for fills so that they, too, can be formed with fewer plotter strokes. Remember to use the plotter options menu to set the pen width accordingly.

Speed is important, but appearance is paramount for many users. Wide lines create a notch when they meet at a corner. A wide pen, however, makes a clean corner because of the pen's round shape. Using colors mapped to pen weights results in a cleaner and sharper plot than using Generic CADD's line widths feature.

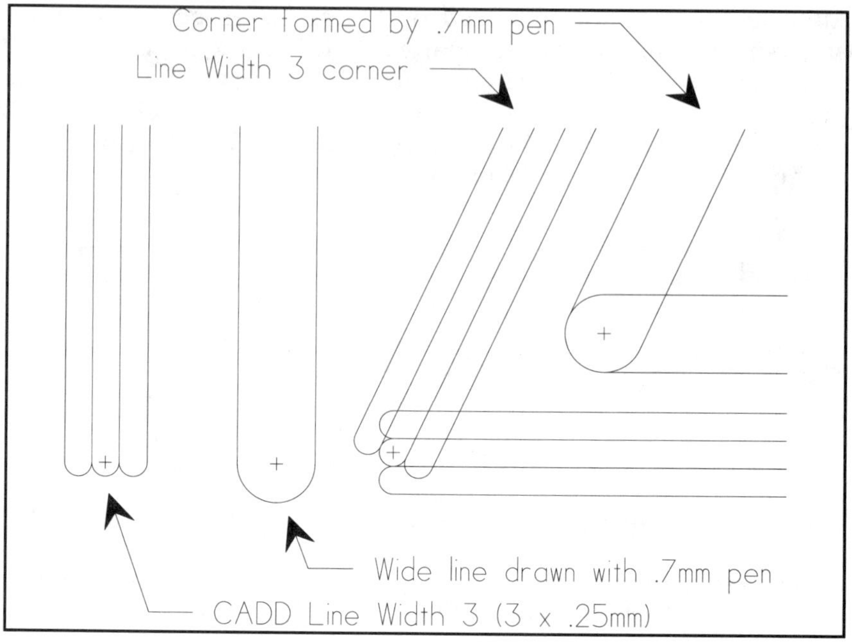

Figure 8.14: *Wide lines drawn by Generic CADD as opposed to pen widths.*

Some users eschew the use of Generic CADD's line widths altogether. They take full advantage of the 15 line colors offered on most display systems and use specific colors for wider lines and place heavier line weight pens in those pen holders. Generic CADD's Solid Double Lines option can be used for particularly bold lines, such as borders. Specific colors can be used for fills, which again are associated with a wider pen. This approach requires planning, but results in cleaner, more readable drawings that also plot faster.

Your choice of pens and media will greatly influence the appearance of a finished plot. The best plotter in the world cannot overcome cheap pens and rough, inconsistent paper. You can get surprisingly good output with inexpensive plotters if you use quality materials, however. And Generic CADD can produce plots that rival those of far more expensive systems if a quality plotter and quality materials are used.

Summary

The end result of any drawing is usually a finished plot. Generic CADD 5.0 permits a variety of plotting methods, from quick plots of what appears on your screen to output that is accurately scaled to hundredths of an inch. Regardless of the output device you use, Generic CADD uses the same interface for setting up and previewing the plotted drawing.

As you have seen in this chapter, Generic CADD 5.0's output menu provides all the functions needed when plotting or printing a drawing. You access CADD's output menu using either the Plot (PL) command (which uses the selection interface) or the Drawing Plot (DP) command. You also can access the output menu through three macros on the FILE menu.

Plotting a drawing normally consists of six steps: choosing the output device and port, changing the paper size, setting plot options, choosing the type of plot, previewing the plot, and starting to plot.

You also have seen how the various plot options are used to control the appearance of the finished plot and how colors on the screen can be related to pen widths as well as colors.

In the next chapter, you'll take a look at the many ways to edit your drawings in Generic CADD.

9

Editing Individual Objects

Some dyed-in-the-wool manual drafters take their first suspicious look at a CADD system and sniff with indignation that they can draw faster than "that machine." Even if they are correct, these folks are missing the point. Perhaps an experienced draftsperson can lay down the original lines as fast as someone using a CADD program, but what happens at revision time? The CADD system can make changes to a drawing much faster than someone restricted to a drafting table.

Erasing lines or changing their length, moving an endpoint, copying lines or other objects, filleting or chamfering corners, and much more is easily accomplished on the CADD screen. These processes are known as editing. When you use CADD for editing as well as drawing, the end result won't be a sheet filled with poor erasures, and you won't need a vacuum cleaner to remove the crumbs of rubber from the table.

No matter what the specific application, the one thing common to all professions that rely on the use of scale drawings is that there will be changes. Using Generic CADD is a crucial step toward ensuring that the process of change through editing is rapid.

Basic Editing Tools

When you look at Generic CADD's ROOT menu, you see not just the menus, but also a logical division of CADD commands. The ROOT menu is organized to complement the way most people work. Three menus have a direct bearing on the editing process: SNAPS, TRIMS, and EDITS, but most of the other menus contain commands that apply to editing as well.

Generic CADD has two basic types of editing. The first type of editing occurs as part of the drawing process, via editing commands that add detail as well as ensure precision and eliminate unnecessary construction lines. The second type of editing occurs when revising a "finished" drawing in order to accommodate changes to the original design.

In this chapter, you will learn editing commands that apply to single objects you draw. Chapter 10 covers editing commands that operate on groups of objects simultaneously. Single-object editing commands are used most frequently for adding detail and precision while constructing the drawing. Multiple-object editing commands are used for revising a drawing. So stay with Chapter 9 to learn about the editing commands necessary to create a drawing, and turn to the next chapter when you are ready to revise your efforts.

Several of the commands covered in this chapter are found in a Generic CADD 5.0 menu called SHORTCUTS. Until version 5.0, most of the more powerful multiple-object editing commands did not exist. As you'll see in Chapter 10, many of the multiple-object editing commands involve an extra step. Rather than eliminate the older, single-object editing commands, the program designers retained them for continuity with older versions of CADD. These single-object editing commands, now found in the SHORTCUTS menu, can be used when you don't need the power of multiple-object editing commands. Dividing the commands between single- and multiple-object editing wasn't part of the plan, but it has worked out that way. Some of the SHORTCUTS commands will be discussed here; others will be discussed in Chapter 10.

To aid in the introduction of editing commands, you need a drawing to work on. Start Generic CADD and follow the steps below to begin a drawing. The object to be drawn will vaguely resemble something a mechanical engineer might draw; don't worry if it isn't what you would normally draw. The skills you will learn are what count.

First, take care of the necessary environment settings before starting to draw.

Setting Up the Environment

Prompt	*Input*	*Description*
`Command`	**LS**	Starts the Set Limits command
`Change height limit`	**24**	Sets new limits height to 24"
`Change width limit`	**36**	Sets new limits width to 36"
`Command`	**ZL**	Starts Zoom Limits command

Setting Up the Environment—continued

Prompt	*Input*	*Description*
`Command`	**GS**	Starts Grid Size command
`Change Grid Size X`	**1"**	Sets grid width to 1"
`Change Grid Size Y`	**1"**	Sets grid height to 1"
`Command`	**MO**	Starts Manual Entry Origin command
`Command`	**GO**	Sets Grid Origin
`Enter new origin`	**0,0**	Ensures that your grid matches this one
`Command`	**UNI**	Sets units to inches
`Command`	**NF**	Gives numeric display
`...Linear (Decimal)` `Decimal Value (3)`	Set Linear to Decimal and Decimal Value to 3	Sets these settings to match figure 9.1
`Command`	**SG**	Sets Snap to Grid on

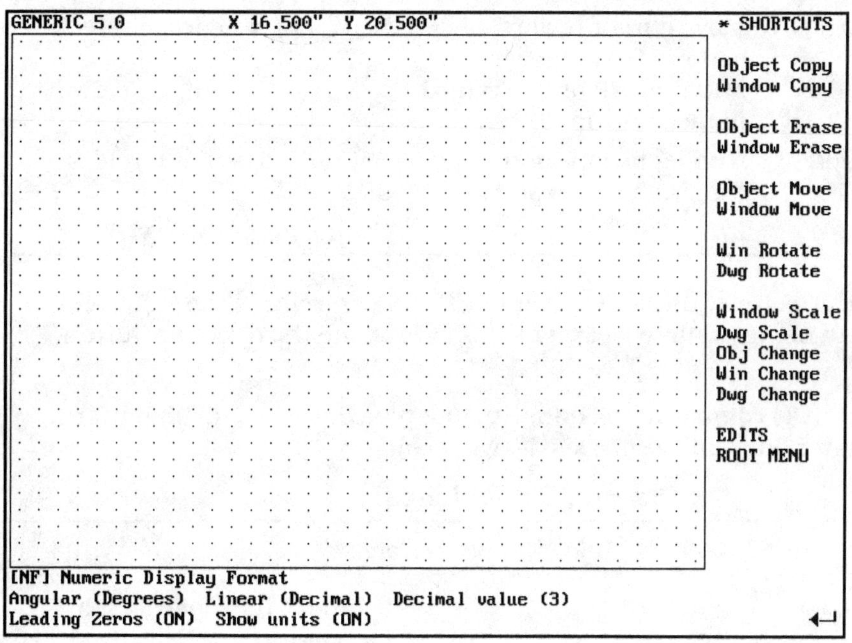

Figure 9.1: *Settings for the Numeric Display Format command.*

Now that your environment is ready, make a rough outline of an object to edit.

Drawing Circles

Prompt	*Input*	*Description*
`Command`	**C2**	Starts a two-point circle
`Enter center of circle`	Move cursor to X 16" Y 16" and click	Sets the center of circle
`Enter a point on the circle`	Move cursor up a nudge and type **5**	Uses direct distance command to set length of radius and draw circle
`Command`	Press space bar	Repeats last command (C2)
`Enter center of circle`	Move cursor to center of circle and click third mouse button or type **NP**	Uses Snap to Nearest Point to identify center of existing circle as start point of a new circle
`Enter a point on the circle`	Move cursor up a nudge and type **4**	Uses direct distance command to set length of radius and draw second circle
`Command`	Press space bar	Repeats last command (C2)
`Enter center of circle`	Move cursor toward center of existing circles and type **NP** or click third mouse button	Sets center of new circle
`Enter a point on the circle`	Nudge the cursor in any direction and type **1"**	Set radius of new circle at 1"
`Command`	**ZA**	Zooms for a better view

When adding a third circle, the center point of all three circles is the same and can be snapped to using Snap to Nearest Point (NP) or the third mouse button. See figure 9.2.

Use the Line Type (LT) command to change to line type 5, the dot-dash pattern. Then put two center lines on the circles drawn so far.

Drawing Center Lines

Prompt	*Input*	*Description*
`Command`	**LT5**	Sets line type to dot-dash pattern
`Command`	**OR** (be sure status line reads "Ortho Mode is on")	Turns on Ortho Mode

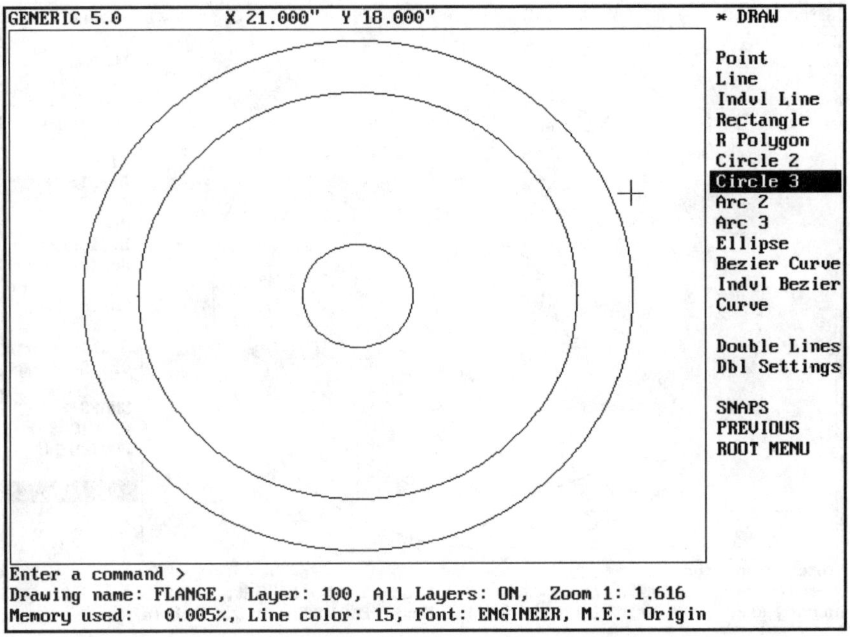

Figure 9.2: *Three circles drawn with Two-Point Circle command.*

Drawing Center Lines—continued

Prompt	*Input*	*Description*
`Command`	Move cursor to center of circles, press third mouse button	Starts a new line
`Command`	Nudge cursor up and type **6**	Draws construction line from the center up (see fig. 9.3)
`Command`	Press Esc	Disconnects cursor from the line
`Command`	**ZA**	Redraws screen to get a complete view of all objects

Object Copy (OC)

All the activity in this chapter so far has been to create objects on which to use editing commands. Copying objects is a crucial activity in CADD, and the next exercise has you copy the construction line with the Object Copy command. When you type **OC** or select Object Copy from the SHORTCUTS menu, CADD asks for the object to be copied. Select it by clicking anywhere on it. Using Snap to Nearest Point is often a good way to select an object. But the process isn't over yet.

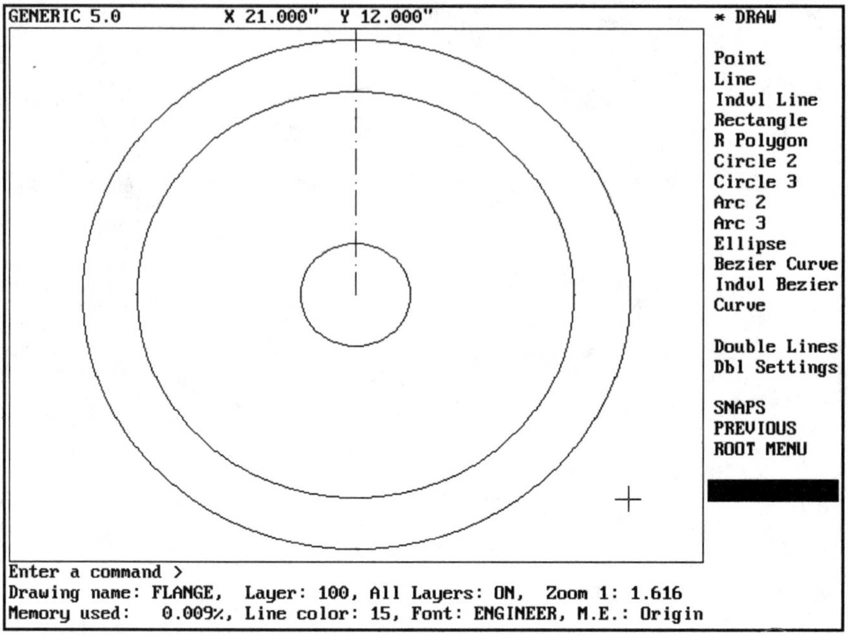

Figure 9.3: *Draw a construction line up from the center of the circles.*

Next, CADD asks for a reference point. CADD will use this reference point as the "from" location. The reference point can be anywhere on-screen; usually, but not always, the reference point is on the object you are copying. After you select the reference point, CADD asks for an offset. This is the "to" location. In essence, you are telling CADD, "Take the object I have selected and draw a new copy of it. Space the new copy the same distance from the original as the spacing between the reference point and the offset." As you move the cursor to set the offset, a dotted-line image of the object to be copied moves along with the cursor. This helps you see how the copy of the object will fit its new location.

Once you have selected the offset, CADD will prompt you for the number of copies you need. If you ask for more than one copy, each additional copy will be placed the same distance from the previous copy as the first copy is from the original. You may select from one to 99 copies.

Using the Object Copy Command

Prompt	*Input*	*Description*
`Command`	**OC**	Starts the Object Copy command
`Pick object`	Move the cursor to anywhere on the line; click	Selects line as the object to be copied
`Enter a reference point`	Move cursor to X 16" Y 22" and press third mouse button	Uses Snap to Nearest Point to select top of line as reference point
`Enter new reference point or offset`	Move cursor to bottom of original line (X 16" Y 16") and press third mouse button	Sets distance for Object Copy command
`Enter number of copies (1-99)`	**1**	Makes one copy of line (see fig. 9.4)
`Command`	**ZA**	Redraws screen for a complete view of all objects

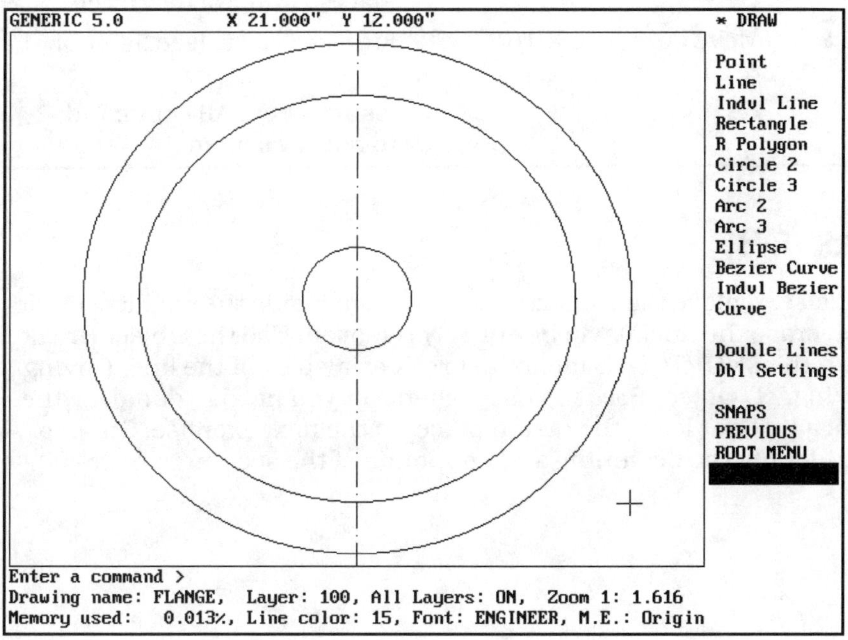

Figure 9.4: *The first line has been copied to extend its length.*

Next, add one more circle to the object. It will fit between the two larger circles.

Adding Another Circle

Prompt	*Input*	*Description*
`Command`	**LTO**	Changes line type back to zero, a solid line
`Command`	**GS**	Starts Grid Size command
`Change Grid Size X (1.000)`	**.5**	Sets new grid width to .5
`Change Grid Size Y (0.500)`	Press Enter	Accepts .5" as new grid height
`Command`	**ZW**	Redraws screen for a close-up view of top of largest circle
`Place Window`	Move cursor to X 14" Y 21.5", click; move cursor to X 18" Y 19.5", click	Draws window to change the view
`Command`	Move cursor to X 16" Y 20.5"	Moves to center of new circle
`Command`	**C2**	Places center of new circle
`Enter a point on the circle`	Move cursor to X 16" Y 21", press Enter	Finishes circle (see fig. 9.5)
`Command`	**ZA**	Issues Zoom All command to redraw screen

Object Break (OB)

For the next exercise, remove the construction line from inside the smallest circle. Notice that if you erase the line, it will be entirely removed. Use the Object Break command, also in the SHORTCUTS menu, to break away part of the line, leaving the rest behind. In fact, Object Break is used whenever you need to cut away the middle section of a line but leave the rest in place. In the next exercise, Snap to Grid will help to identify the beginning and endpoints of the section to be removed.

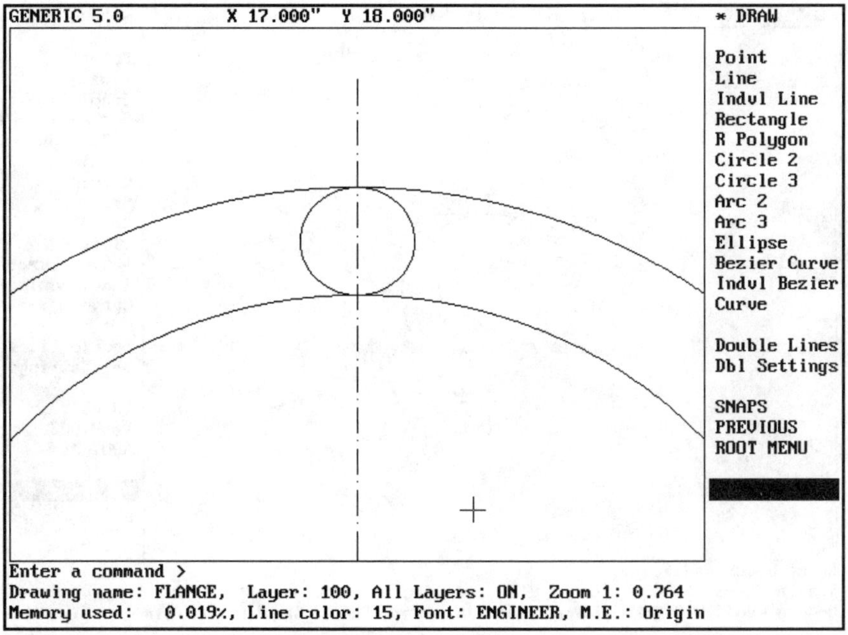

Figure 9.5: *A fourth, smaller circle has been added to the drawing.*

Using the Object Break Command

Prompt	*Input*	*Description*
`Command`	Move cursor to X 16" Y 20.5"	Moves to destination
`Command`	**OB**	Starts Object Break command
`Enter a point on the object to break`	Press Enter or click	Selects line as object to be broken
`Enter first break point`	Move cursor to X 16" Y 21", press Enter or click	Starts in the line at this point
`Enter second break point`	Move cursor down to X 16" Y 20", press Enter or click	Sets length of gap

In figure 9.6, the construction line no longer intersects the smallest circle, after using Object Break to cut away the line from inside the circle.

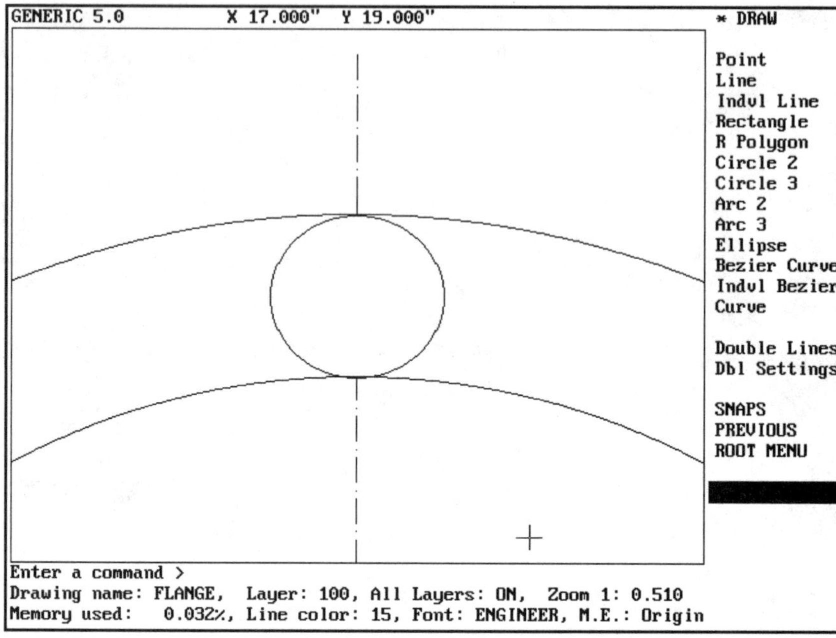

Figure 9.6: *Object Break has cut away the line.*

Trim (RM) and Extend (XT)

Sometimes a line does not extend far enough or extends too far. Trim and Extend, both found on the TRIMS menu, are the handy pair of commands that ensure lines are always just the right length.

Both commands work in a similar fashion. First you identify the line to be shortened or extended; then click on a line or other object that represents the correct length. The first line is extended to the second line (Extend) or cut off at the second line (Trim).

Follow the steps in the next exercise to draw two lines flanking the small circle. Since Snap to Grid is still on, the lines you draw will initially be too short. Use Extend to remedy this problem.

Using Trim and Extend

Prompt	*Input*	*Description*
`Command`	Move cursor to X 15.5" Y 20.5", press Enter or click	Starts a line
`Command`	Move cursor to X 15.5" Y 20", press Enter or click	Sets opposite end of line

Using Trim and Extend—continued

Prompt	*Input*	*Description*
`Command`	Press Esc or click on blank line in menu bar	Ends Line command
`Command`	**SG**	Turns off Snap to Grid
`Command`	**XT**	Extends line to touch circle
`Object to extend`	Move cursor to any point on line just drawn and click	Identifies line to be extended
`Extend to`	Move cursor down to the circle just beyond end of line and click	Identifies object that line will extend to (see fig. 9.7)
`Command`	**SG**	Turns Snap to Grid on
`Command`	**OC**	Copies line to other side of circle
`Pick object`	Make sure cursor is at X 15.5" Y 20"; press Enter or click	Identifies object to be copied
`Enter a reference point`	Press Enter	Identifies point where copying starts
`Enter new reference point or offset`	Move cursor right to X 16.5" Y 20", press Enter or click	Identifies point where copying will move to
`Enter number of copies (1-99)`	**1**	Copies line once to flank both sides of circle

In figure 9.8, the line has been copied to the other side of the small circle. Note that both lines extend to the larger circle below.

Now try the same command on a circle.

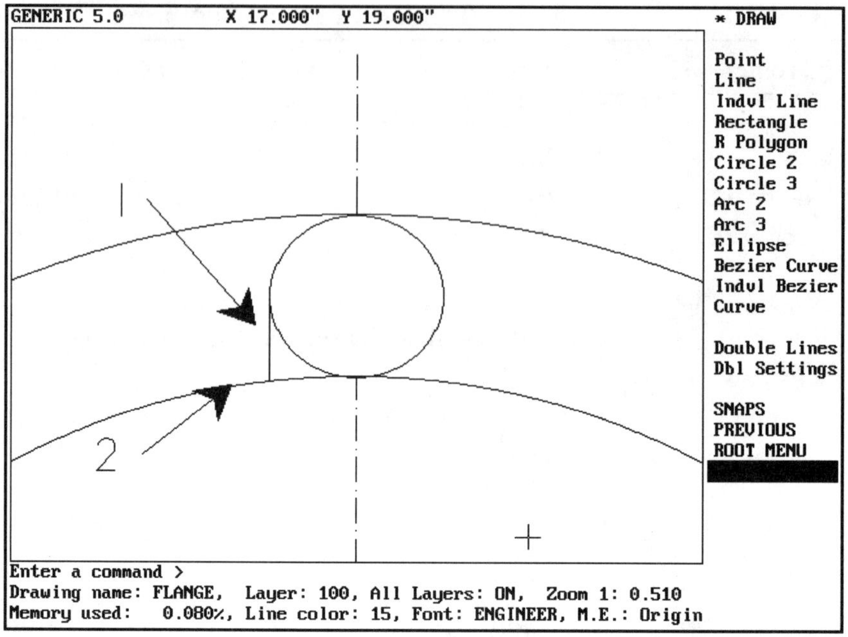

Figure 9.7: *Identify line to extend (1) and distance to extend (2).*

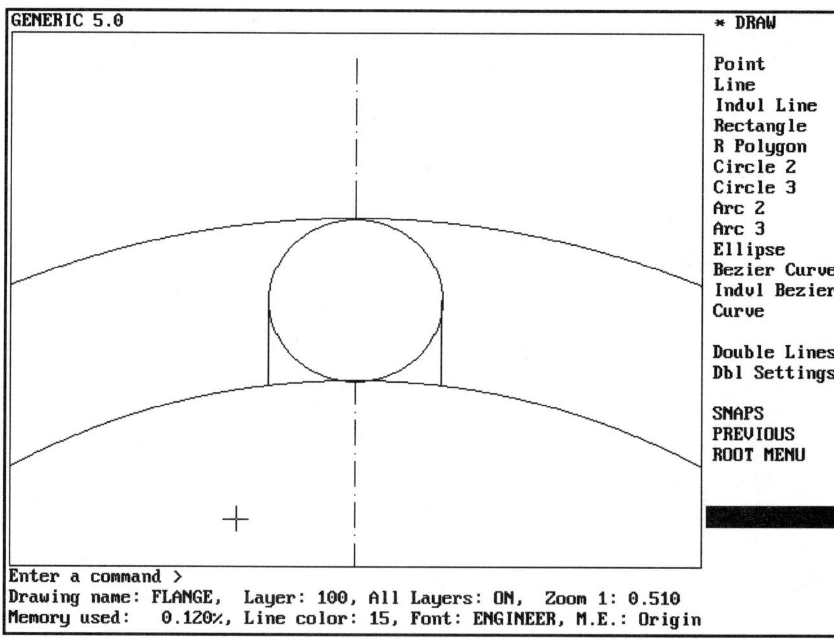

Figure 9.8: *The copied line.*

Breaking Up a Circle

Prompt	*Input*	*Description*
`Command`	**SG**	Turns Snap to Grid off
`Command`	**OB**	Starts Object Break command
`Enter a point on the object to break`	Move cursor to a point on the circle	Identifies circle as the object to break
Be sure the cursor is not close enough to any other object to mistakenly select it instead. Then click to identify the circle.		
`Enter first break point`	**SG**	Turns Snap to Grid on
`Enter first break point`	Move cursor to X 15.5" Y 20.5", press Enter or click	Starts gap in the circle at this point
`Enter the end of the arc`	Move the cursor to X 16.5" Y 20.5", press Enter or click	Sets length of gap along circumference of circle (see fig. 9.9)
`Command`	**ZA**	Redraws screen for complete view
`Command`	**SA**	Starts the Save command
`...Drawing`	**D**	Selects Drawing
`Save File As`	**FLANGE**	Saves drawing as FLANGE.DWG

Keep this drawing for use in Chapter 10. You are finished with it for now.

In the next exercise, you will erase the drawing you just made, start a drawing that represents a simple floor plan. The results are shown in figure 9.10. Drawing the walls will go faster if you use the Double Line (L2) command. To set the distance between the two lines, use Double Line Offset (TH). Also, set the units to feet and inches.

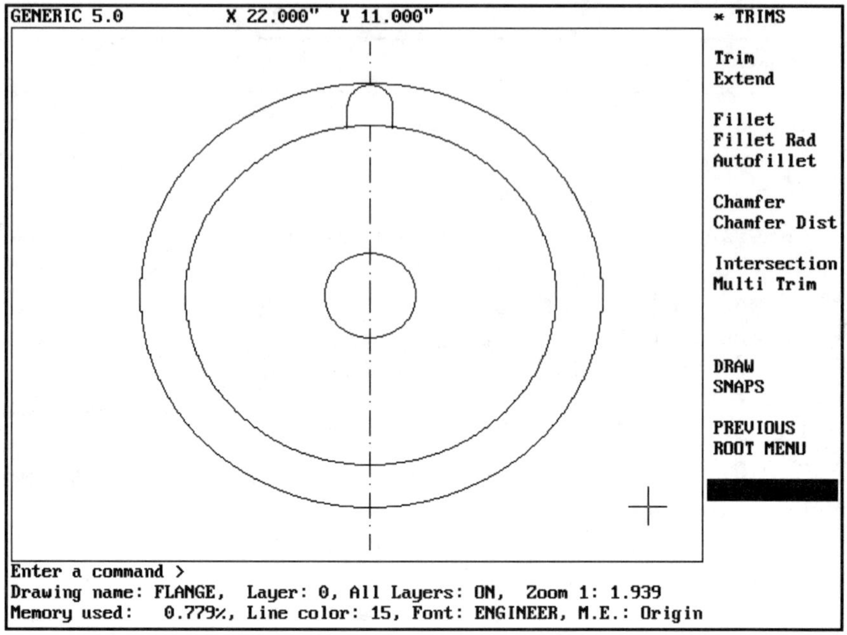

Figure 9.9: *The small circle has been broken using Object Break.*

Drawing a Floor Plan

Prompt	*Input*	*Description*
`Command`	**DXY** (if you still have FLANGE.DWG on screen)	Erases drawing
`Command`	**LS**	Sets new limits
`Change height limit (24)`	**48'**	Sets new height limit to 48 feet
`Change width limit (36)`	**72'**	Sets new width limit to 72 feet
`Command`	**ZL**	Starts Zoom Limits command
`Command`	**GS**	Starts Grid Size command
`Change Grid Size X (.5)`	**6"**	Sets grid height to 6"
`Change Grid Size Y (6)`	Press Enter to accept 6" for Y size	Sets grid width to 6"
`Command`	**TH**	Sets Double Line Offset
`Change Left Offset`	**6"**	Left side of double line is 6" from point placed

Drawing a Floor Plan—continued

Prompt	*Input*	*Description*
`Change Right Offset`	**0**	Right side of double line is at point placed
`Command`	**UNF**	Sets Display Units to Feet/ Inches
`Command`	**RE**	Starts Rectangle command
`Enter one corner of the rectangle`	Type **1',1'** or move cursor to X 1'Y 1' and click	Sets first corner of rectangle
`Enter opposite corner`	Move cursor to X 70' Y 36' and click or type **70',36'**	Finishes rectangle
`Command`	Press space bar	Starts another rectangle
`Enter one corner of the rectangle`	**1'6",1'6"**	Sets first corner of rectangle
`Enter opposite corner`	**69'6",35'6"**	Finishes rectangle
`Command`	**ZA**	Redraws screen

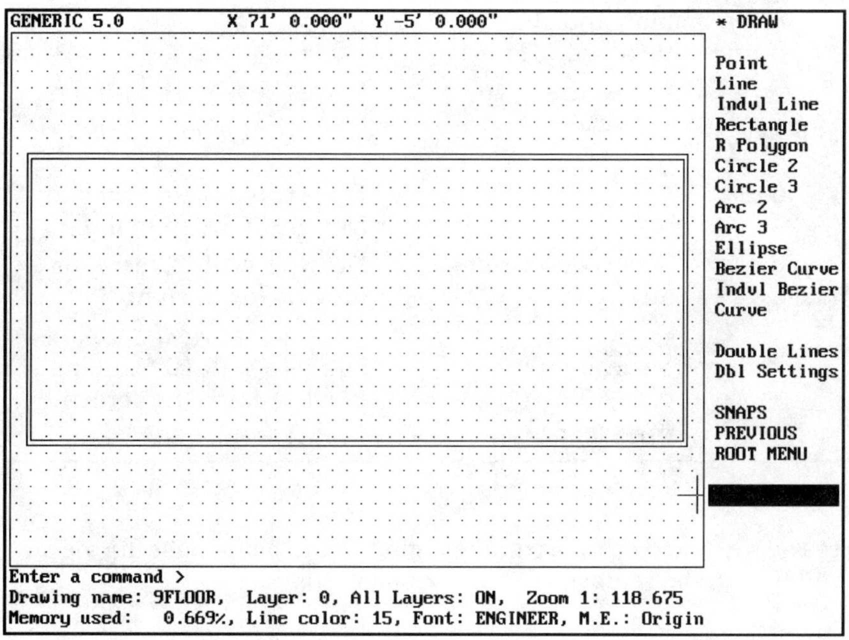

Figure 9.10: *The outline of a basic floor plan.*

Tracking (TK)

Although it isn't strictly an editing command, Tracking is useful when editing. Tracking is found on the CONSTRAINTS menu. There will be many times when you want to draw or place an object a certain distance away from a specific location.

Tracking can be used any time Generic CADD requests the location of a point. Use it to place components, to locate the first point of an object break, or to start drawing a new object.

In the next exercise, a room is drawn in the lower left corner of the floor plan, using Tracking and Double Line (see fig. 9.11). The wall starts 10 feet up from the bottom left corner of the floor plan.

Using Tracking To Draw an Interior Wall

Prompt	*Input*	*Description*
`Command`	**L2**	Starts Double Line to draw interior walls
`Enter start point`	**TK**	Starts Tracking command
`Enter point to start tracking from`	Move cursor near inside lower left corner of floor plan and click third mouse button	Starts tracking from inside lower left corner
`You are now tracking - type PU to end tracking`	Move cursor up, type **10'**	Moves cursor up wall ten feet
`...type PU to end tracking`	**PU**	Ends tracking, returns to Double Line command
`Double Line: Enter next point`	Move cursor right and type **12'**	Draws a wall 12 feet long moving to the right
`Enter next point`	Move cursor down, type **10'**	Draws a wall 10 feet long moving down the screen
`Enter next point`	**PU**	Ends Double Line mode

Before going on to the next step, stop and take a moment to get a close-up view of some lines that will have to be removed in the room you just drew.

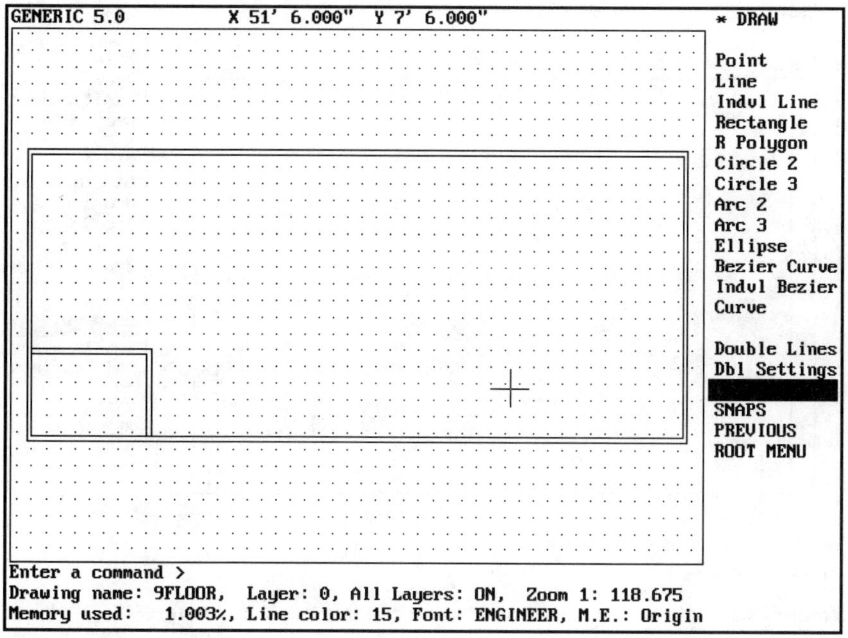

Figure 9.11: *The room drawn with Tracking and Double Line.*

Zooming in for a Close-Up View

Prompt	*Input*	*Description*
`Command`	**ZW**	Starts Zoom Window command
`Place window`	Move cursor above and left of the room just drawn (approx. X 0' Y 13'6") and click	Starts the zoom window
`Place window`	Move cursor below and right of the room (about X 17'Y -2') and click	Finishes window and redraws screen with new view (see fig. 9.12)

Intersection Trim (IT)

The intersections of the floor plan walls shown in figure 9.12 need to be trimmed. If Object Break was the only tool available, it could be used here. But a special editing command exists just for situations like this. Intersection Trim can open up the intersections of sets of lines. It is used whenever you need to trim all of the lines coming into an intersection, as long as the sets of lines are parallel or near-parallel. Given a set of intersecting line pairs, Intersection Trim can create an X-shaped, T-shaped, or L-shaped intersection.

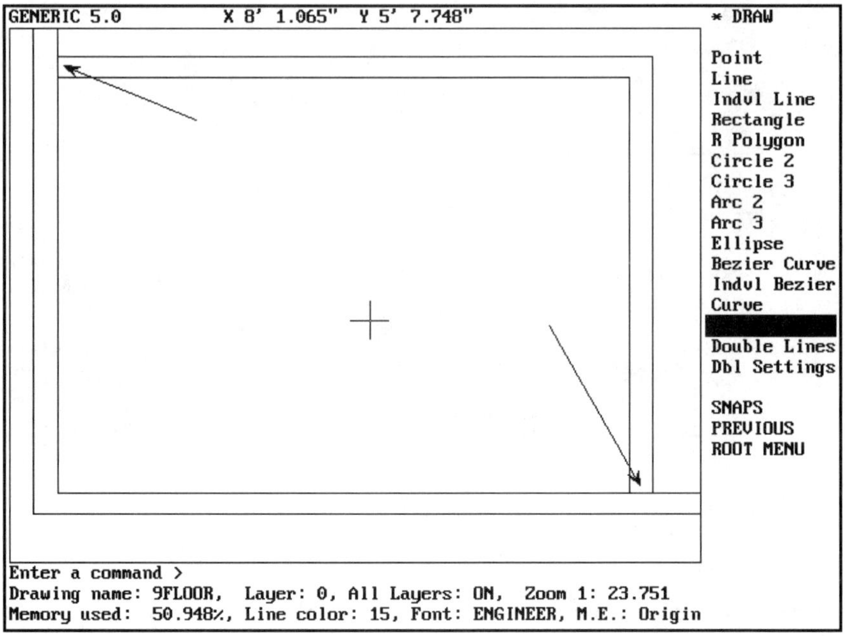

Figure 9.12: *Close-up view of the room, showing lines to be removed.*

Intersection Trim can create three possible intersections from the same set of intersecting lines (see fig. 9.13). Using Intersection Trim requires clicking twice; the arrows show where to click to create each type of intersection.

To use Intersection Trim, you must click once inside the intersection to identify it for Generic CADD. The next click shows the program how you want the intersection to be cleaned. Notice when you use the command that the possible trims appear on the screen as you move the cursor around. When the intersection is the way you want it, click again and the trim is completed.

Follow the steps below to trim the two intersections in the floor plan. The two corners of the interior walls intersecting the outside walls in figure 9.14 have been trimmed using Intersection Trim.

Trimming an Intersection

Prompt	*Input*	*Description*
`Command`	**SG**	Turns Snap to Grid off
`Command`	**IT**	Starts Intersection Trim
`Enter a point inside the intersection`	Move the cursor to about X 1'3" Y 11'9" and click	Identifies inside of intersection to trim

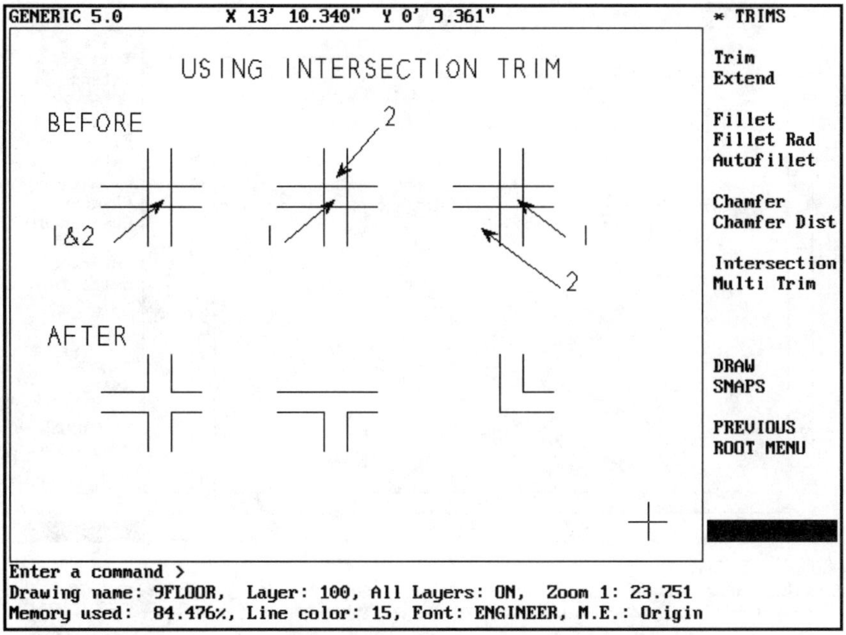

Figure 9.13: *Using Intersection Trim.*

Trimming an Intersection—continued

Prompt	*Input*	*Description*
`Enter a point outside corner`	Move the cursor straight left, to about X 0'6", Y 11'9" and click	Finishes trimming the intersection
`Command`	Press space bar	Repeats the Intersection Trim command
`Enter a point inside the intersection`	Move cursor to about X 13'9" Y 1'2" and click	Identifies inside of intersection to be trimmed
`Enter a point outside corner`	Move the cursor straight down to X 13'9" Y 0'6" and click	Finishes trimming the intersection

Fillet (FI) and Chamfer (CH)

Fillet and Chamfer, both on the TRIMS menu, are similar to each other in that they trim corners. Fillet cuts away the corner and replaces it with an arc, while chamfer replaces the corner with a beveled edge. The size of both the arc and the bevel are predetermined by Fillet Radius (FR) and Chamfer Distance (CA).

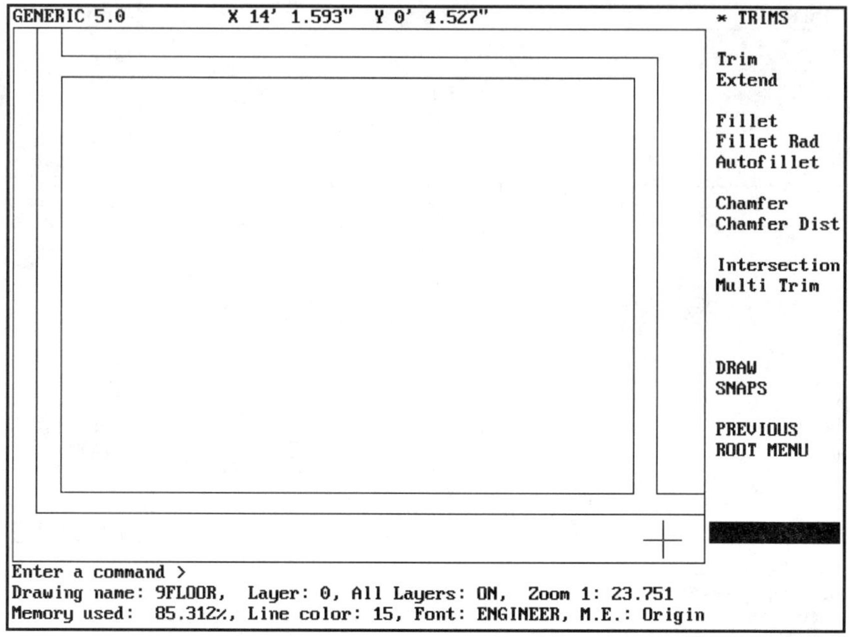

Figure 9.14: *Two corners trimmed with Intersection Trim.*

To use either command, simply click on each line of the intersection. Generic CADD then finds the intersection and replaces the corner as appropriate. The lines to be filleted or chamfered can either terminate or overlap at their intersection.

Figure 9.15 shows fillet and chamfer trim corners made from overlapping lines and from lines that terminate at the intersection. Fillet replaces the corner with an arc, and Chamfer replaces the corner with a beveled edge.

Fillet Radius (FR)

The size of the arc used by Fillet is set by the Fillet Radius (FR) command, also found on the TRIMS menu. The default setting for Fillet Radius is 0. You may set it to any size; experiment with it in your own CADD work to find the most useful settings.

If you use Fillet on an intersecting set of lines with Fillet Radius set to zero, Fillet cuts off the overlapping lines and leaves a clean intersection. This means you can use Fillet (and likewise Chamfer, see below) as a “corner clean” command for single sets of intersecting lines in the same way you use Intersection Trim for double sets of intersecting lines.

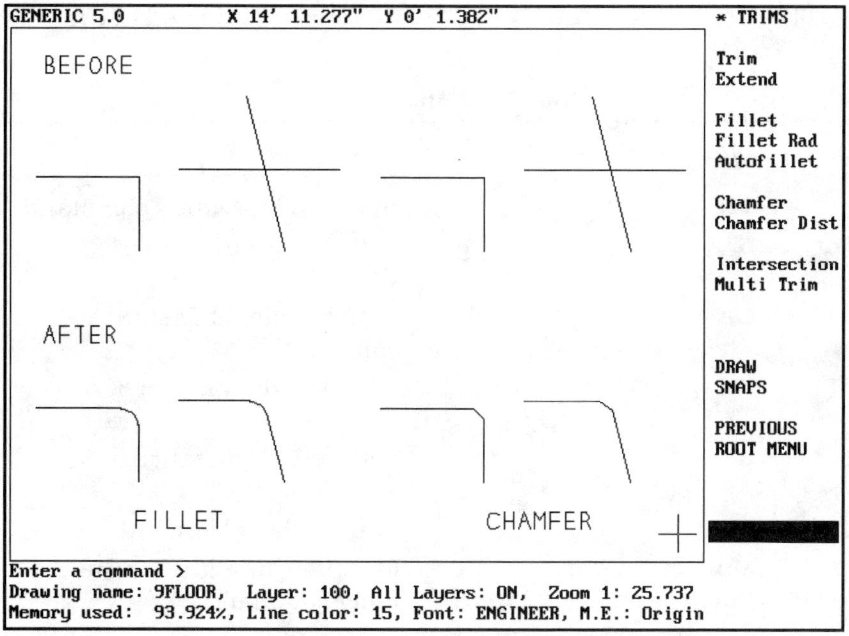

Figure 9.15: *Fillet and Chamfer trim corners.*

Autofillet (AF)

Autofillet, on the TRIMS menu, is a command that toggles on and off. When Autofillet is on, any lines drawn with the Double Line (L2), or the Line command to draw continuous lines, are automatically filleted as you draw them. (To have Autofillet work with single lines, you must start by typing the LI command; just moving the cursor and clicking won't cause Autofillet to take effect.) When Autofillet is off (the default mode), corners created when you use LI or L2 to draw continuous lines are at the angle you draw them, without a radius inserted.

Chamfer Distances (CA)

When Chamfer trims a corner, a line is inserted and the corner redrawn to create a beveled edge. The Chamfer Distances command provides Chamfer with the information necessary to create a beveled edge.

Chamfer Distances holds two values. Each value is the distance from one corner to the point where the beveled edge connects with one existing line. Normally you would set both values of Chamfer Distances to the same number in order to create an even edge. For a special effect, set the two values to differing numbers.

If both Chamfer Distance values are set to zero, Chamfer can also be used to trim single pairs of intersecting lines, as explained above for Fillet.

The interior walls of the room just drawn will be chamfered and filleted in the next exercise.

Filleting the Walls

Prompt	*Input*	*Description*
`Command`	**FR**	Starts Fillet Radius command
`Change Fillet Radius`	**5"**	Sets Fillet Radius to 5"
`Command`	**CA**	Starts Chamfer Distances command
`Change chamfer distance 1"`	**3"**	Sets first distance to 3"
`Change chamfer distance 2"`	**3"**	Sets second distance to 3"
`Command`	**FI**	Starts Fillet command
`Enter a point on the object to fillet`	Move cursor to top inside line, at about X 12'0" Y 12'0", and click to identify line	Identifies first line for the Fillet command
`Enter second object`	Move cursor down to outside right line, at about X 14'0" Y 10'0" and click	Identifies second line for Fillet command, completing the sequence
`Command`	Press space bar	Repeats Fillet command
`Enter a point on the object to fillet`	Move cursor to lower line of the top interior wall at at about X 12'0" Y 11'6" and click	Identifies the first line for the Fillet command
`Enter second object`	Move cursor to intersecting line, at about X 13'6" Y 10'0" and click	Inserts arc at the intersection of the two lines (see fig. 9.16)

Now try chamfering each line of the intersection between the right interior wall and the bottom exterior wall. The results are shown in figure 9.17.

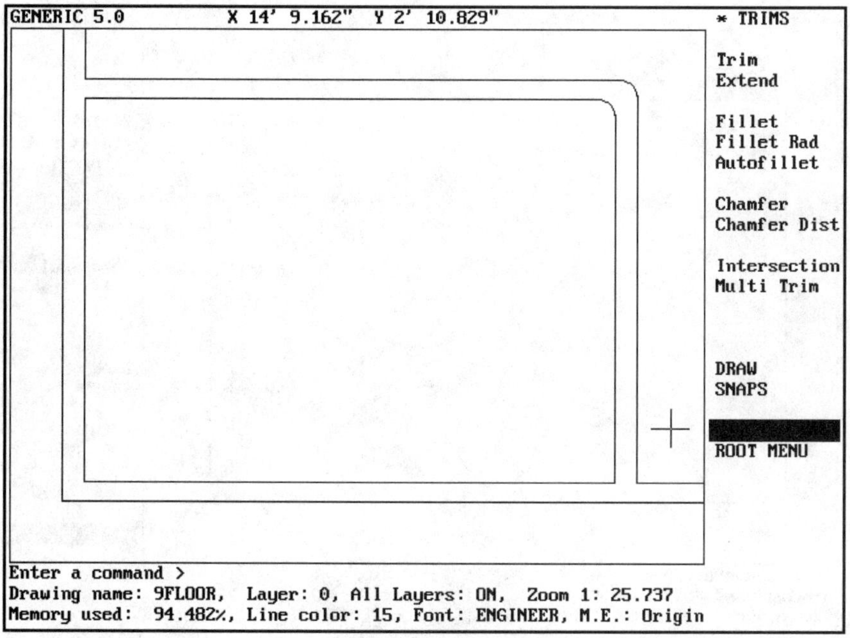

Figure 9.16: *The top right corner of the room has been filleted.*

Chamfering the Walls

Prompt	*Input*	*Description*
`Command`	**CH**	Starts Chamfer command
`Enter a point on first object to be chamfered`	Move cursor to inside line of right wall, at about X 13'6" Y 3'0" and click	Identifies first line for the Chamfer command
`Second object`	Move cursor to inside line of bottom wall, at about X 12'0" Y 1'6" and click	Inserts a beveled edge at the intersection
`Command`	Press space bar	Repeats Chamfer command
`Enter a point on first object to chamfer`	Move cursor to about X 14'0" Y 2'0" and click	Identifies first line
`Second object`	Move cursor to about X 15'0" Y 1'6" and click	Inserts a beveled edge at the intersection

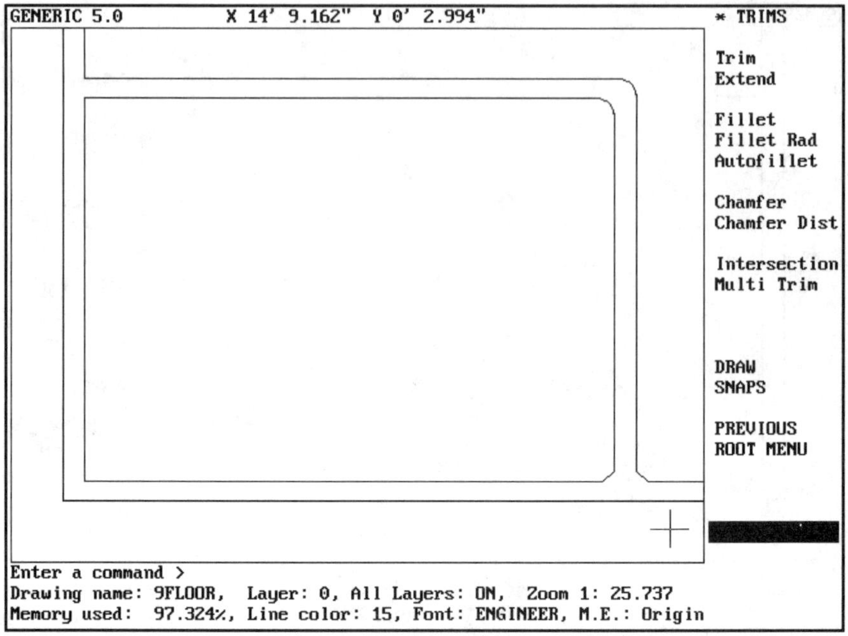

Figure 9.17: *Lines at intersection have been chamfered.*

Follow the steps below to draw a series of lines, which will be used to explain additional editing commands.

Continuing the Floor Plan

Prompt	*Input*	*Description*
`Command`	**ZA**	Redraws screen for complete view
`Command`	Move the cursor and click to draw lines inside floor plan (see fig. 9.18)	Exact lengths are not important; press Esc to end; Ortho Mode should still be on

Object Erase (OE)

The most common editing need is erasing. There always seem to be a few objects that just don't belong. If the line or other object you need to erase is the last one drawn, you can use Erase Last (EL). But if the object was drawn earlier, you can send it to oblivion by using Object Erase on the SHORTCUTS menu.

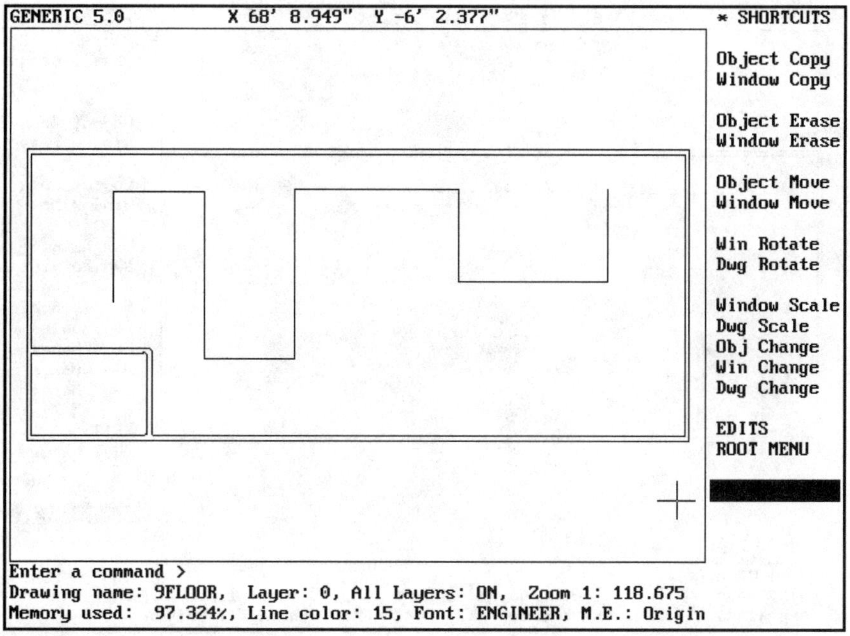

Figure 9.18: *Draw the pattern of lines shown inside the floor plan.*

Using Object Erase is simple; type **OE** or select the command from the menu. Generic CADD prompts you to identify the line; click on it, and it is immediately erased. If you goof and click on the wrong object, you can immediately bring it back with either Unerase (UE) or Undo (OO).

Erasing Objects

Prompt	*Input*	*Description*
`Command`	**OE**	Starts Object Erase command
`Pick object`	Move cursor to first vertical line in pattern just drawn; click on it to erase	Erases the first vertical line
`Command`	Press space bar	Repeats Object Erase
`Pick object`	Repeat Object Erase as needed to erase all vertical lines in pattern	Erases vertical lines (see fig. 9.19)

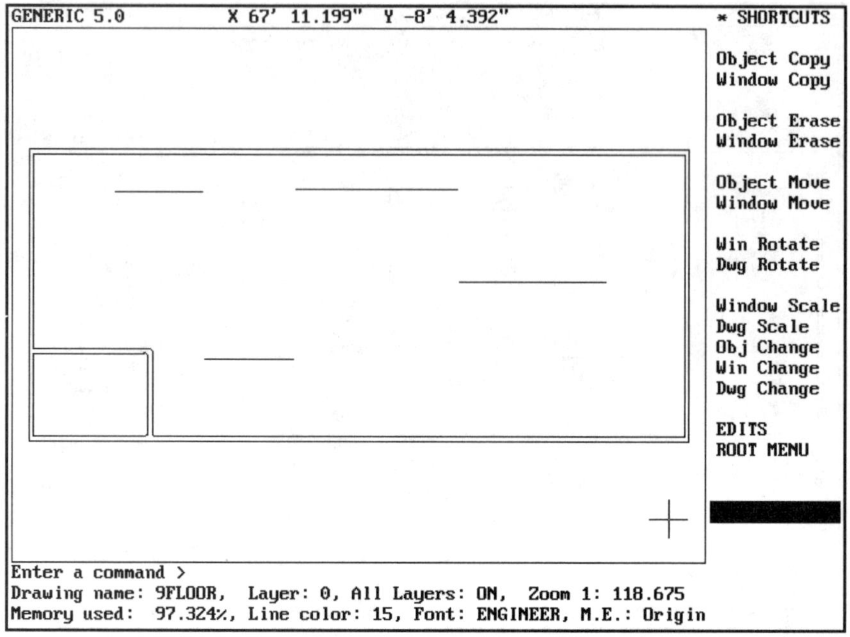

Figure 9.19: *All vertical lines in pattern erased one by one.*

Object Change (OG)

You often need to change the width, type, or color of a line. If you want to change only one object, it is faster to use Object Change, from the SHORTCUTS menu, than to use the more powerful Change (CG) command. When you use Object Change, any or all of these attributes may be changed: layer, color, type, or width.

Try using the Object Change command in the following exercise. Figure 9.20 shows the top left horizontal line changed to Line Type 9, Line Width 6.

Changing Objects

Prompt	*Input*	*Description*
`Command`	**OG**	Starts Object Change command
`Pick object`	Move cursor to first horizontal line on left and click	Selects horizontal line on the left as the object to be changed
`Line Width (0)`	**LW**	Starts Line Width command
`Enter Line width`	**6**	Changes to line width 6
`...Limits: 0 to 255`	**LT**	Changes line type of object
`Enter Line type`	**9**	Changes to line type 9
`...Limits: 0 to 255`	Press Enter	Accepts the setting; changes the selected object

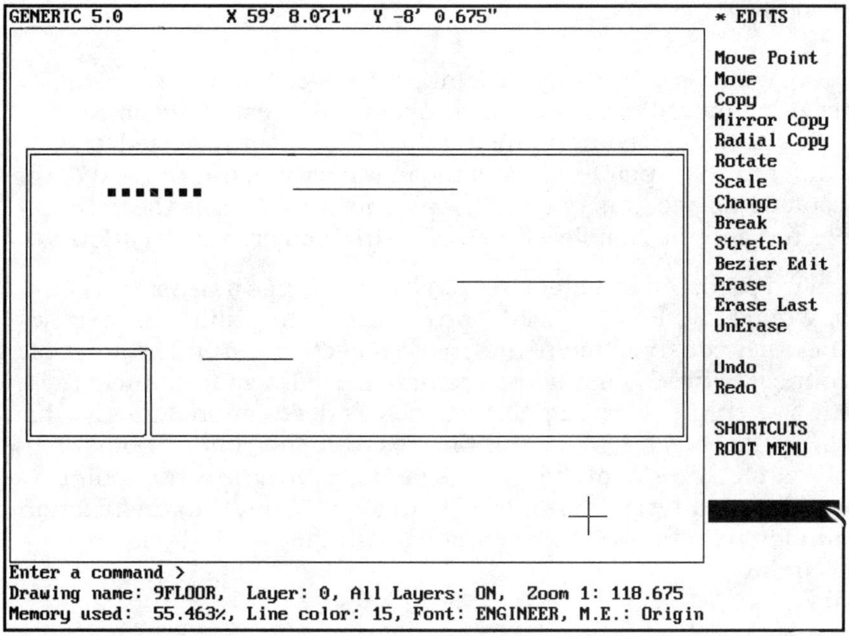

Figure 9.20: The top left horizontal line changed with Object Change.

Object Move (OM)

Object Move, on the SHORTCUTS menu, works very much like Object Copy, except that it moves the original to a new reference point, instead of the first copy. When the object for the Object Move command is selected, Generic CADD asks for a first reference point, then for a new reference point or offset. As soon as the new reference point is selected, the object is moved to its new location. In the program's eyes, the point identified as the reference is moved to the new reference point, and the rest of the object connected to that point moves with it.

You may wish to practice the use of Object Move on your own, moving the other vertical lines inside the floor plan.

Reshaping Entities

Three of the trim commands used earlier in the chapter (Trim, Fillet, and Chamfer) can change the shape of an object by cutting off portions of its lines, while Extend changes the shape of a line by lengthening it. There are two other editing commands that can reshape an object without cutting it: Move Point (MP) and Bézier Edit (BE).

Move Point (MP)

Earlier, Object Move from Generic CADD's point of view was defined by saying that the reference point moved to the new location, and the rest of the object came along with it. When Move Point (found on the EDITS menu) is used, the effect is slightly different. The point moves to the new location, but the rest of the object remains rooted in place. It may stretch, contract, or rotate as the point is moved, but it does not become completely detached from its original location.

Except for a standard point, every object in Generic CADD has at least two construction points. When Move Point is used, one of these points shifts to the new location, while the other construction points in the object stay still. The parts of the object that connect between points (the vectors) are redrawn to connect the construction points when the selected point reaches its destination. Exactly what happens depends on the object. If Move Point moves the construction point on the circumference of a circle, the size of the circle is changed but the center point remains the same. If the center point is moved with Move Point, the construction point on the circumference stays rooted, changing both the size and relative placement of the circle.

Bézier Edit (BE)

Bézier Edit, found on the EDITS menu, is strictly for changing the shape of Bézier curves. Like Bézier Curve, this command takes a little getting used to. If you use Bézier curves on a regular basis, you will eventually gain an intuitive understanding of how they behave, making it easy to draw and edit these special curves.

To use the Bézier Edit command on a series of connected Bézier curves, type **BE** or select Bézier Edit from the EDITS menu. Responding to Generic CADD's prompts, click on two segments which you want to reshape. When you select each curve segment, the control points for that curve become visible. CADD then prompts you to select a point to be moved. This point can be a construction point on one of the curve segments you have selected, a control point, or even a construction point on a third Bézier curve segment. The point selected can make a big difference in the nature of the reshaping; you may need to press Esc and try again if the combination you have selected will not let you bend the lines the way you want.

Try drawing a series of Bézier curves (BV, on the DRAW menu), then practice reshaping the curves with Bézier Edit using various combinations of construction points and control points. There is no one right way to achieve the end result.

Figure 9.21 shows two curves selected for Bézier Edit. The control points extend out from the curves as dotted lines. The arrows point to the curve segments selected for the edit.

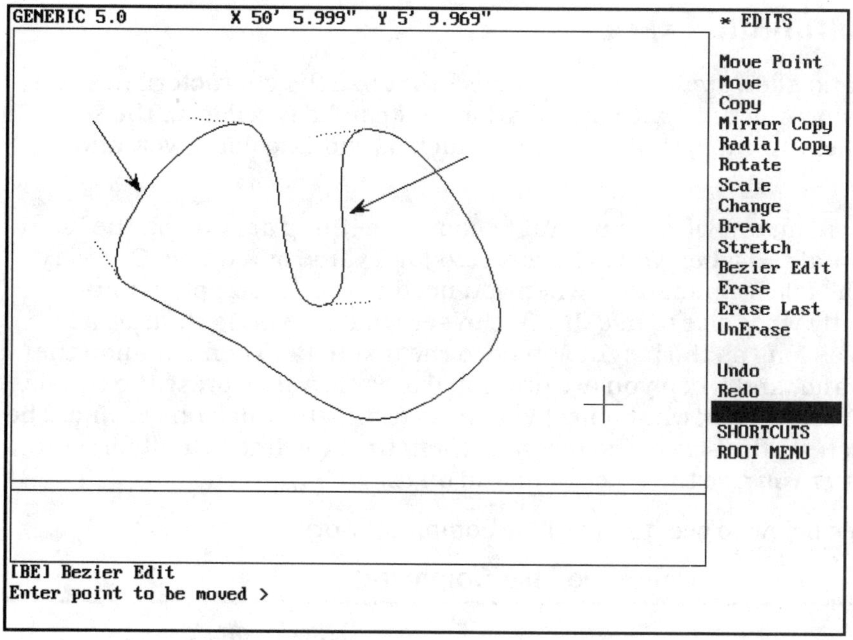

Figure 9.21: *Two curves selected for Bézier Edit.*

CADD Mimicry

The whole idea behind using a CADD program to draw working plans is to give someone a pattern to follow when creating an object. It is one thing to ask someone to manufacture a nickel-plated widget, but quite another to give him a set of pictorial instructions in the form of a CADD drawing, detailing the size and characteristics of the widget. For the experienced widget machinist, reading the drawing becomes a form of mimicry. The machinist can take the ideas in the drawing and create an object just like the one pictured.

The CADD user can take advantage of a little self-induced mimicry to be more productive while drawing. The information already available in the drawing, including such things as line type or width, color, and size, can be used as a reference for drawing new objects.

Three commands in Generic CADD allow the copying of information; only one has a two-letter command and a place in the menu. All three commands (the Like command, Show By Example, and Match Parameters) can be used, at various times, when you feel the urge to mutter, "I want it just like *that* one."

The Like Command (=)

The Like command allows you to copy an object that has the characteristics you need, and it is generally used with information that can be typed from the keyboard. Using Like, you can specify attributes such as width, color, layer, and length of a line.

To use the Like command when you want to copy something already on the screen, press equals (=) when you are prompted for a value or a name. One very handy use for the Like Command is when you need to set the size of text but don't know exactly what size to use. If you can see what size is right, draw a line segment that is as long as the height you need the text to be. Then summon the Text Size command, and when you are prompted for a new size, press the equals key. Generic CADD will ask what object you are referring to. Click on the line. The program will then set the size of the text to the length of the line. (Don't forget to erase the line after you use the Like command on it.)

Try the examples below to see how the Like command works.

Using the Like Command

Prompt	*Input*	*Description*
`Command`	**ZA**	Redraws screen
`Command`	**OR**	Turns Ortho Mode off
`Command`	Draw a line on the screen to represent the size text you want	
`Command`	**TZ**	Starts Text Size command
`Text (1.0")...`	**T**	Sets size of regular text
`Change Text Size`	Press =	Summons the Like command
`Like what object`	Click on the line just drawn	Generic CADD measures the line and uses the value as the new size for text
`Text (1.0)"`	Press Enter	

It is possible to take advantage of Like in ways you might not think of at first. For example, you can set text size by "liking" an arc. Generic CADD will measure the radius of the arc and use that distance to set the text size. You can use the color of any object to set the color of any other object, and you can specify a scale reduction by "liking" something that has a specified scale—a component, for example. If you need to match the rotation of something in a drawing, use Like when asked for the rotation. CADD will measure the angle at which the object sits and use that value to set the rotation of the new object. Setting the rotation of text equal to other rotated objects in a drawing becomes an easy task using the Like command.

TIP

You can even use Like to specify a name when selecting a font, a component, or a specific attribute. If the item you need already exists in the drawing, click on it using Like and Generic CADD will take the name of the object and use it to finish the task at hand.

Show By Example

Show By Example is a more limited version of the Like command. Show By Example is available only when setting distances (Show Distance) or angles (Show Angle).

Show Distance

Any time Generic CADD asks for a distance, you can use the length of an existing object on the screen to provide the value with Show Distance. Instead of typing in the value, type **D**. Generic CADD will ask you to enter two points. It will then calculate the distance and use that value as the distance requested when you typed D. The most precise way to select the two points is to use Snap to Nearest Point (NP or the third mouse button) to select each end of the object.

Show Distance is only useful for setting straight distances when a value (not a coordinate) is requested. For example, you can't use it to draw a circle or even a line when using C2 or LI. These commands require coordinate locations rather than distance values. Don't try to use Show Distance to set scale factors, either. Valid situations in which to use Show Distance include Text Size, Double Line settings, Grid Size, Text Spacing, and Dimension settings. If you use Show Distance to provide a value for a command needing an angle, the length will be translated as an angle. (This may be a useless bit of information, but at least you have been warned.)

Show Angle

Use the Show Angle commands whenever you are prompted for an angle, as when setting the angle of rotation for a component. When you need to type in the value, type **A** or **V** instead. Option A gives a two-point angle, otherwise known as a heading. If you select this option, CADD will prompt you for two points and measure the heading of the line between the two points, starting with the first point you place and moving toward the second point. CADD will use the heading of this "line" as the value needed to complete the command.

Use the V option when you want a three-point angle. In Chapter 10, you'll use the V option, along with Radial Copy, to bisect one angle into two equal angles.

Match Parameters (MH)

Found on the UTILITIES menu, Match Parameters is a powerful feature new to Generic CADD 5.0. Similar commands return one value, but Match Parameters can return *all* the values related to an object.

Here's a typical scenario that makes good use of Match Parameters. Imagine that most of the lines in a drawing are width 0, type 0, but one line is obviously wider and of a different line type—and you need to draw a circle using those characteristics. You could use Screen Flip (SF) to find the line and read what line type and line width it uses, or you could use Match Parameters. Follow the steps below to try it out. In a previous exercise, line width and line type were changed from zero to other values; now they will be reset to zero using Match Parameters.

Using Match Parameters to Choose Line Width and Line Type

Prompt	*Input*	*Description*
`Command`	**C2**	Starts a circle
`Enter center of circle`	Move cursor to an open area on screen and click	Sets center of circle
`Enter a point on the circle`	**MH**	Uses Match Parameters to set characteristics of the circle
`Select object to match`	Click the cursor on any line of width 0, type 0	CADD responds "line matched"
`Enter a point on the circle`	Move cursor to set size of circle and click	Draws circle using line type 0, line width 0

After you finish Chapters 11 and 13 on components and dimensioning, come back to this discussion of Match Parameters.

TIP

If you know you will be using more than one set of options for dimensioning on a regular basis, save an example of each type as a component. When you need to dimension a drawing, place the component that holds the dimensioning style you need. Explode the component, then use Match Parameters on the sample dimension. This will change all the dimensioning settings to match the characteristics of the sample.

Placing components is another situation in which Match Parameters comes in handy. If you are placing components in a variety of scale factors and rotations, use Match Parameter to identify a component placed using the same rotation and scale factors you need for the next component to be placed.

Match Parameters can also save you time when placing text (use MH to match the font, size and rotation of text already on the screen), using hatch patterns (select the pattern and the scale), and using attributes (match the settings of attributes already in the drawing).

Summary

In writing, editing means to modify the text to improve clarity and accuracy; it means the same thing in Generic CADD. Some editing commands help to clarify the message of the drawing by eliminating unnecessary objects (or parts of objects). Commands like Erase Last, Object Erase, and Object Break are used to improve clarity. Some editing commands help improve accuracy by modifying existing objects. Included in this group are Trim, Extend, Intersection Trim, Fillet, Chamfer, Move Point, and Bézier Edit. A third set of editing commands improve accuracy and increase clarity by moving or copying objects: Object Move and Object Copy.

In addition to the commands listed above, several commands make it easier to find location and adjust settings while editing. These include Tracking, Show By Example, the Like command, and Match Parameters.

The commands in this chapter, for the most part, work on only one object. They are handy when you need to make quick small changes. In the next chapter, you will become familiar with the more powerful multiple-object editing commands. After you learn how to use the entire range of editing commands, you will have mastered much of what gives Generic CADD the edge over manual drafting. After all, how fast *can* you erase?

10

Editing Groups of Objects

Chapter 9 introduced the use of single-object editing commands. While these commands are quick and handy, they are limited in their effectiveness. The editing commands covered in this chapter are more robust, thanks to new features in Generic CADD 5.0 known as selection and filtering.

As you work through the exercises in this chapter, think of selection and filtering as the lever and pulley of CADD. Simple tools, perhaps, but they make it easy to amplify your efforts, achieving maximum work from minimum effort. Instead of moving one object, move twelve objects with only one or two extra keystrokes. Use selection and filtering to pick and choose objects that match specific criteria (all red circles of line width 3 on layers 14 and 38, for example). Selection and filtering can be used to identify objects as well as to edit them, making it possible to explore the status of the drawing file.

Selection and Filtering

To understand the difference between the single-object editing commands in Chapter 9 and the multiple-object editing commands in this chapter, consider Object Copy (OC) and its counterpart Copy (CO). Object Copy enables you to select and copy one object. Copy allows you to select several objects, gathering them as a group, and then copy this group all at once. You can select by using a window, by clicking on objects one at time, by identifying a layer (all the objects on the layer will be selected), or even by selecting every object in the drawing. If you goof while selecting objects, you can deselect members of the group before executing the Copy command. Using filtering, you can even specify that only the objects matching certain criteria are to be selected for the Copy command.

In Generic CADD, multiple objects can be selected by one of three methods: *active selection*, used as part of the editing commands to be covered here (and with other commands in other chapters, as well); *passive selection*, used only to select objects—not edit them; and *entity filtering*, which selects entities according to a set of user-defined parameters.

Active Selection within Editing Commands

Active selection works the same way with every command that uses it. When the command is chosen, a list of options appears in the prompt line. All multiple-object editing commands share the same active selection methods, and they display the same prompt choices (see fig. 10.1). Items may be chosen for the edit using one or all of these choices. As illustrated, the options are:

Window **O**bject la**Y**er **D**rawing **L**ast selection **F**ilter

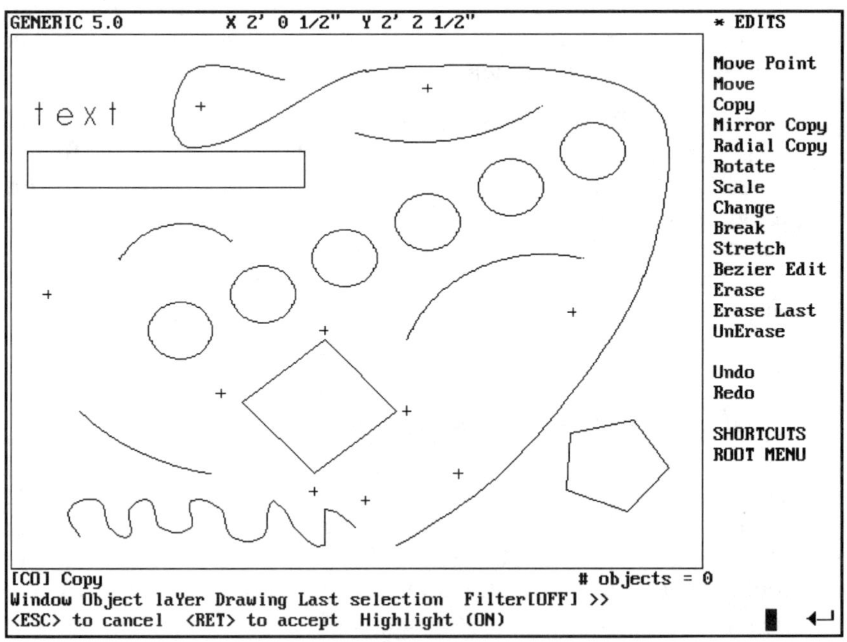

Figure 10.1: *Multiple-object editing commands.*

If you needed to copy the two circles on the left in figure 10.1, you could type **O** for Object, click on one of the circles to select it, and then copy both. Or, you could type **W** for Window and draw a selection window around the two circles.

Only objects that are *completely* inside the window will be selected. As illustrated in figure 10.2, only the circles will be selected; the arc and the polygon will not.

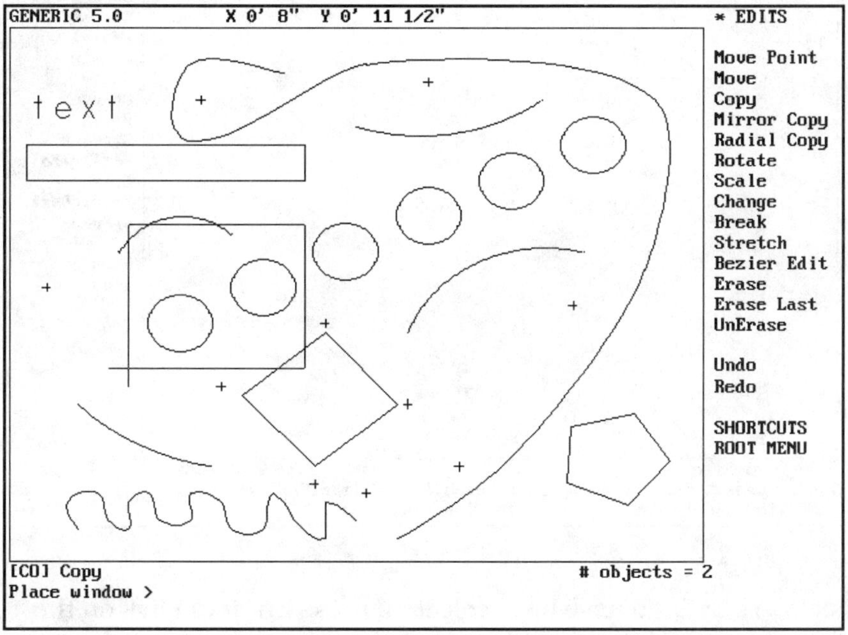

Figure 10.2: *A selection window around two circles.*

The number of objects you select is recorded on the lower right portion of the screen, just below the drawing window. In figure 10.2, the number of objects is two, for the two circles selected (`# objects = 2`).

A component is counted as one item, even if it has 100 lines within it. Lines of text placed with the Text Line Placement command are counted as one for each line; characters placed using the Text Character Placement command are counted as one for each character. A Bézier curve is made of individual segments. To select a complete curve you will have to select each segment. A complex curve, however, is considered to be one item. In figure 10.3, six objects have been selected: the two circles, one complex curve (the squiggly line at the bottom of the drawing), one section of the Bézier curve (highlighted at the bottom of the screen), the line of text at top left, and one standard point (at the right corner of the diamond).

All of the zoom and redraw commands are available when you are using one of the active selection options, making it easier to zero in on what you select. It may be hard to draw a window around the object you need with a Zoom All view, but the same objects can be easily selected with a window by using Zoom In to get up close first.

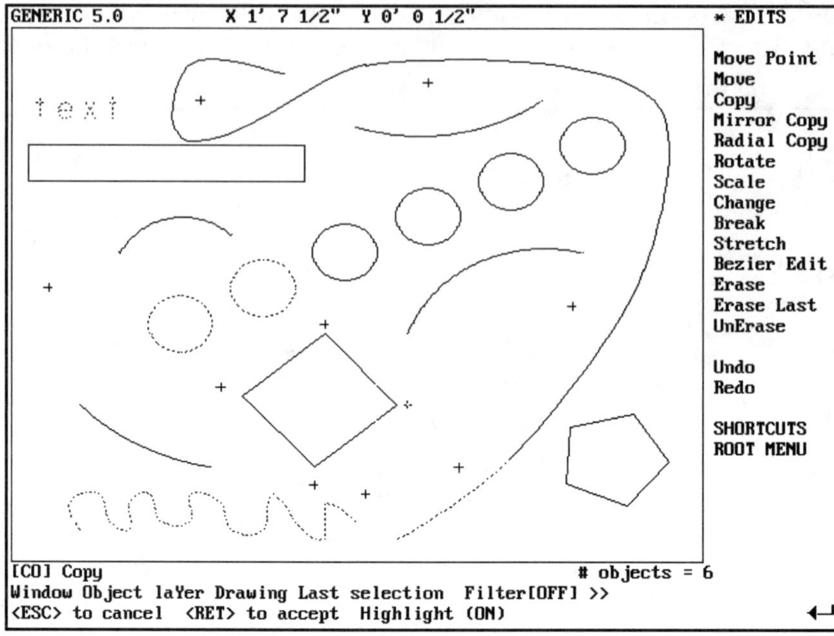

Figure 10.3: *Six items selected using active selection.*

When all the objects to be edited have been selected, press Enter or click on the statement `<RET> to accept` in the status line. What happens after that depends upon the editing command in use.

If you have a slow computer, you might want to turn off the Highlight. To do so, click on it in the status line, or type **H** whenever the Active Selection options appear. Highlight is a toggle and can be set by typing HI whenever CADD will accept a two-letter command from the keyboard.

The All Layers Active (AL) command affects what items can be selected. If AL is off, then only the items on the current layer can be selected, unless you use the Drawing selection option, which overrides AL, or use the Layer command, which will select all items on the specified layer no matter what the status of AL is.

Generic CADD remembers what objects you selected (unless they have been erased) until you select new objects with another command that relies on active selection. The Last selection option lets you take advantage of CADD's memory. If, for example, you want to rescale, rotate, and change the color of the six objects you are about to copy, you can select them with one keystroke each time you perform an editing operation by using the Last selection option. Be warned, though, that when you copy objects, both the originals *and* the copies are remembered and selected by the Last selection option. (If you want to rescale, rotate, change, and copy the same items, copy them last).

Passive Selection (SE)

You also can employ the Last selection option by using the Selection command first. This command, found on the UTILITIES menu, uses the same selection methods as the active selection editing commands. All it does is select objects, however; it does not edit them.

The value of passive selection is that commands such as Selection Save Batch (BS) and Selection Save Drawing (SV) can refer to the listed items identified using Selection. The Selection command also can be used for selecting items to be edited more than once (using Last selection). Items that can be retrieved using Last selection can be combined with other items, using any of the other selection devices. Other uses for Selection require that it be combined with the Entity Filter (EF) and Screen Flip (SF) commands, discussed below.

Entity Filter (EF) Selection

Selecting by entity filter is the third method of multiple object selection in Generic CADD. The Entity Filter command is found on the UTILITIES menu. The Generic CADD manuals refer to it only as Filter (or *the* Filter), but calling it Entity Filter makes it easier to remember its two-letter command and provides a better description of its purpose.

As stated earlier in this chapter, you can be very selective about what items are to be edited. The Entity Filter command makes this possible. It can select every entity that can be drawn in CADD, as shown in figure 10.4. Rectangles and regular polygons are stored in the CADD database as lines only, so they are not mentioned by name. Ellipses created with the Construction option are stored in the CADD database as arcs and will show up as such in the Entity Filter command.

The Entity Filter command is off when first selected. The top status line, just below the drawing screen, displays `Filter = OFF` when the Entity Filter command is started. "Off" means no objects (entities) have been chosen for the filter. When you select an entity type, the filter status changes to show the name of the entity selected.

The drawing used as an example in this chapter includes several standard points. Imagine that each point represents an outcropping of rocks in a field. You want to know how many such outcroppings have been recorded in the drawing, and you want to move these markers to their own layer. This drawing only has a few outcroppings, and it would be relatively easy to count them manually. But what if the drawing contained 50 outcroppings, or 500? The Entity Filter command can count them for you.

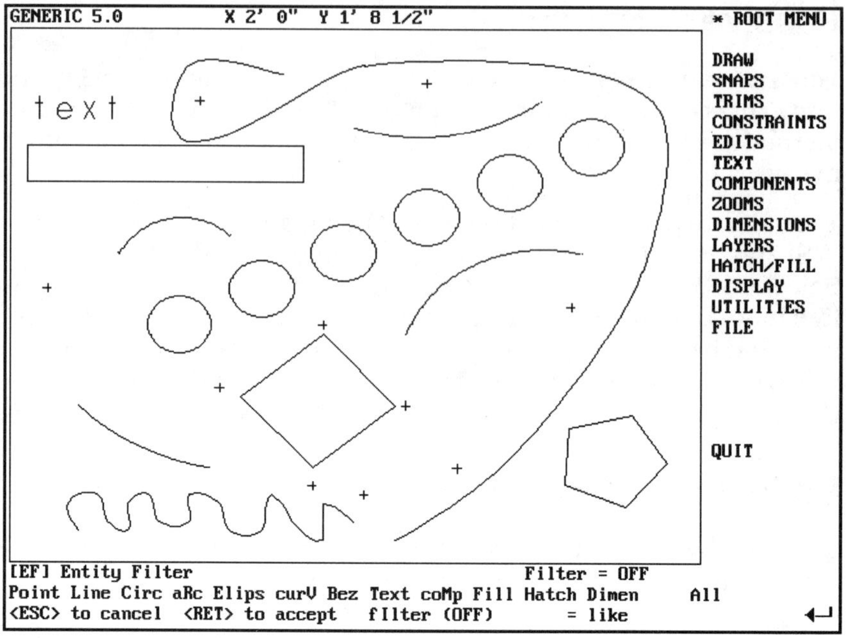

Figure 10.4: *Selecting entities with the Entity Filter command.*

Take a few minutes to re-create the drawing shown here. (If you have the optional disk, the drawing, called CH10.DWG, is on it.) The exact placement of items is not important, but be sure it includes 10 standard points, a long Bézier curve (the exact number of sections is not important), a complex curve, six circles, four arcs, a line of text placed using the Text Line Placement (TL) command, and 13 line segments. Use Line Type 0, Line Width 0, and Line Color 15 (unless you must use a different color on your monitor). In the drawing shown in figure 10.4, all the line segments were placed using the Rectangle and Regular Polygon commands, but the placement method is up to you. When you have created the drawing on your screen, follow the steps below to become more familiar with the Entity Filter command.

Using the Entity Filter Command

Prompt	*Input*	*Description*
Command:	**EF**	Starts the Entity Filter command
`Point...`	**P**	Selects Points as the entity type
`Select characteristics to filter`	**A**	Selects all characteristics
`Select characteristics to filter`	Press Enter, or click on <RET> in status lines	Selects points of all colors, widths, layers; ends command

The Entity Filter command ends abruptly once you have made your choices. The information is stored in CADD's memory and no further action is required, so it returns to the command prompt. But the next time you use a selection command, Generic CADD will limit its search to the entities that match the description you gave when using the Entity Filter command. The Selection command is used in the following exercise to find only those objects the filter allows to be selected.

Using the Selection Command

Prompt	*Input*	*Description*
`Command:`	**SE**	Starts the Selection command
`...Drawing...`	**D**	Selects all objects in the drawing that match the filter's criteria

In figure 10.5, the Selection command has been used to select all objects in the drawing that match the criteria set by the Entity Filter command. The top status line shows `# objects = 10`.

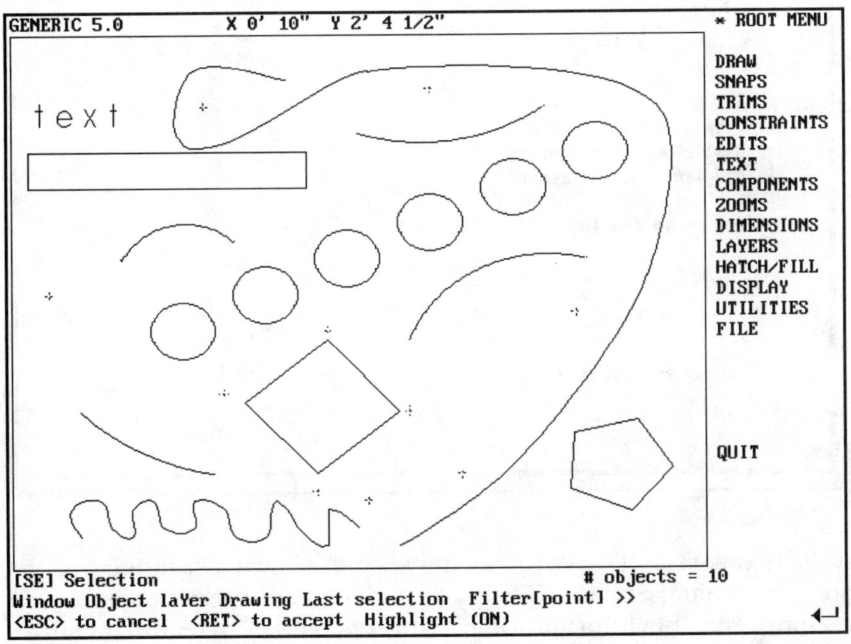

Figure 10.5: *The Selection (SE) command selects 10 points as specified.*

If you only need to know how many points are in the drawing, using the Selection command after setting the Entity Filter gives you the answer. It appears at the top line of the status lines, where it says `# objects = 10`. (See fig. 10.5.) If you want even more information, however, use the Screen Flip command.

Checking the Database

There may be times when you need to know some of the information stored in Generic CADD's database. The Screen Flip command, found on the UTILITIES menu, gives you access to this information. It also provides a convenient, one-stop view of all program settings.

Screen Flip (SF)

This command is named Screen Flip because the display screen "flips" to become a text-only screen, rather than a graphics screen. (The File Selection screen is also a text screen.) When you type **SF** or select Screen Flip from the UTILITIES menu, a list of choices appears (see fig. 10.6).

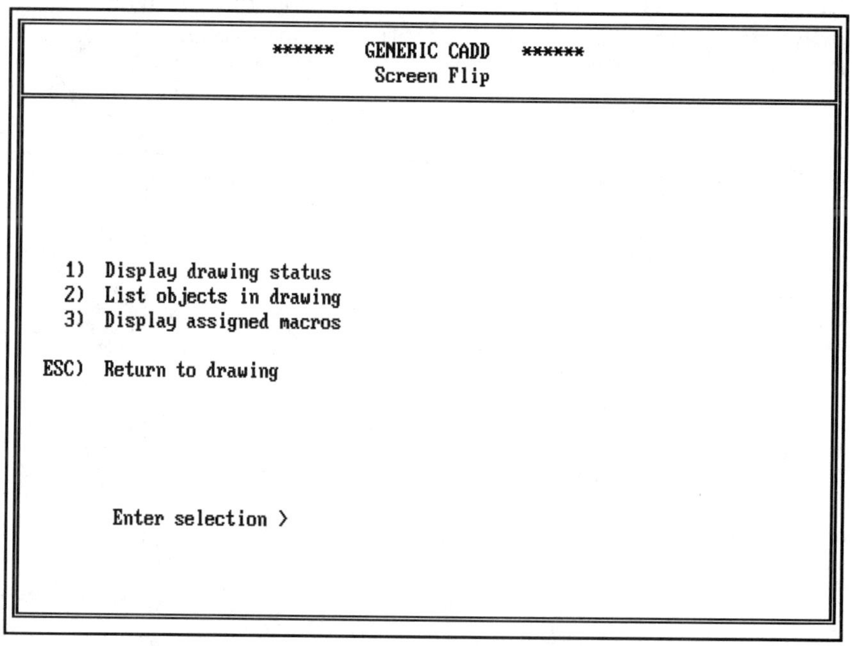

Figure 10.6: *The list of options in the Screen Flip command.*

The first item on the text screen, Display drawing status, shows a summary of settings and reports on memory usage. If you are curious about the internal workings of your computer, this information will interest you. The technical support people at Generic Software often ask their callers to use this screen to report on the status of their memory, disk space, and other possible problem areas. A sample Drawing Status screen appears in figure 10.7. If you need to create a large drawing, looking at the Drawing Status screen might help you to decide whether you need to make room on your hard drive or switch virtual memory to another drive.

```
                    ******   GENERIC CADD   ******
                           Drawing Status

Drawing name: CH10DWG
Drawing extents min: 3 , 2 "  max: 35 , 29 "

Point records: 202 , Entities: 42 , Definitions: 3
Memory available: 35,960 Mem used: 2,020 Mem remaining: 33,940
Basepoint: 0 , 0 " from drawing origin.

Database unit: Inches      Display unit: Feet & Inches
Disk space: C:\ 23,050,240  D:\ 13,484,032  E:\ 1,556,480
Current drive & directory:  D:\CADD5\
Virtual memory drive: D:\

Tolerance: 0                  Current layer:    9
Trace mode: OFF,  Ortho mode: OFF
Grid size: 1 , 1 " , Grid display: OFF, Grid snap: ON


Press <RET> to exit >
```

Figure 10.7: *The Drawing Status screen.*

Try out the Screen Flip command's second option, List objects in drawing, in the following exercise.

Listing Objects in a Drawing

Prompt	*Input*	*Description*
`Command:`	**SF**	Starts the Screen Flip command
`...2) List objects in drawing..`	**2**	Selects List objects in drawing option
`List objects in current: ... View Drawing Selected_list`	**S**	Displays those objects previously selected

After you type **S** for `Selected_list`, your display should look similar to the one pictured in figure 10.8. Every item in this list matches the criteria set by the Entity Filter command and was logged in Generic CADD's memory by the Selection command. You already knew the drawing included 10 points, but now you can see all the characteristics of each point. If the points were assigned various colors or layers, you could see that as well. (Basalt rock outcroppings, for example, could be in Color 14 on Layer 14 and limestone rock outcroppings could be in Color 6 on Layer 6.) If the points were assigned such characteristics, you could use the Entity Filter and Selection commands to further refine your list.

****** GENERIC CADD ******
List Objects

Item	Description	Type	Width	Color	Layer
117	point	0	0	15	9
119	point	0	0	15	9
121	point	0	0	15	9
123	point	0	0	15	9
125	point	0	0	15	9
127	point	0	0	15	9
129	point	0	0	15	9
131	point	0	0	15	9
133	point	0	0	15	9
135	point	0	0	15	9

<PgDn> Next pg <PgUp> Previous pg <->> Goto <Home/End> - <ESC> exit

__Figure 10.8:__ The list of items selected, as displayed by Screen Flip.

The third Screen Flip option, Display assigned macros, is discussed in Chapter 15.

Options for Editing Groups of Objects

The selection process allows you to use a variety of editing commands. You now will explore them one by one. Use the current drawing to experiment with some of them.

Stretch (SS)

The Stretch command, found in the EDITS menu, is used to reshape objects by moving their construction points. It is the multiple-object counterpart of the Move Point command. As with Move Point, construction points are the key, not the objects drawn using them. New users may be confused by the Stretch command until they understand this difference. The lines on the screen connect construction points. Move one of the construction points in an object, and the object changes shape.

The first step of the Selection process is to identify the *objects* to be affected (selection doesn't acknowledge construction points). Once the objects are selected, the Stretch command prompts the user to draw a window to show which *construction points* are to be moved. If you want to stretch a line, for example, and have selected it, the window would be drawn only around the construction point on the end of the line to be stretched; the construction point on the other end of the line would not be included in the window.

A reference point is then chosen and moved to a new location. All the construction points found inside the previous selection window move along with the reference point, and the objects are redrawn to correspond with the construction points in the drawing.

Follow the steps below to stretch the pentagon in the lower right corner of the drawing. (If you drew something else, follow along as best you can. Be sure that your selection window completely includes the object you plan to stretch.)

Stretching the Pentagon

Prompt	*Input*	*Description*
`Command:`	**SS**	Starts the Stretch command
`Window...`	**W**	Selects Window option
`Place Window`	Draw selection window around entire pentagon, selecting each line (see fig. 10.9)	Encircles the pentagon
`Window...`	Press Enter	Completes selection
`Place window around points to be moved`	Draw window around top two lines of pentagon; bottom window line should intersect next two lines of pentagon (see fig. 10.10)	Moves all the points on the top two lines
`Enter a reference point`	Move cursor to top corner of pentagon; type **NP** or click third mouse button	Uses Snap to Nearest Point to select the pentagon as the reference point

Stretching the Pentagon—continued

Prompt	*Input*	*Description*
`Enter new location of reference point`	Move cursor slightly upward, stretching pentagon out of shape (see fig. 10.11)	Moves the construction points upward as the reference points move; connecting objects stretch as points move
`Enter new location of reference point`	Move cursor to new reference point and press Enter	Completes the stretch

The Stretch command is often used to change the dimensions of a floor plan or the dimensions of a room within a floor plan. You can use the Tracking, Direct Distance, or Manual Entry Relative commands to select the new location of the reference point.

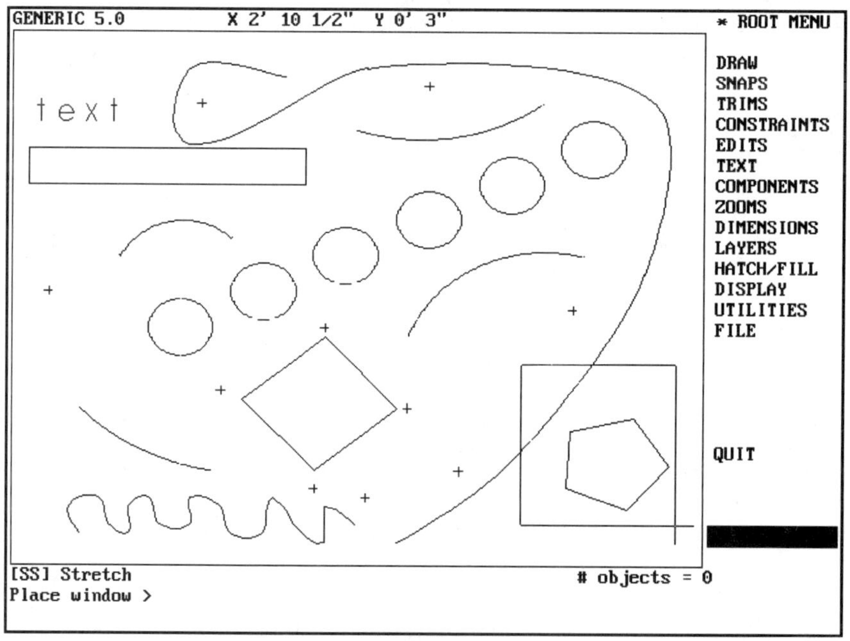

Figure 10.9: *Drawing a selection window around the pentagon.*

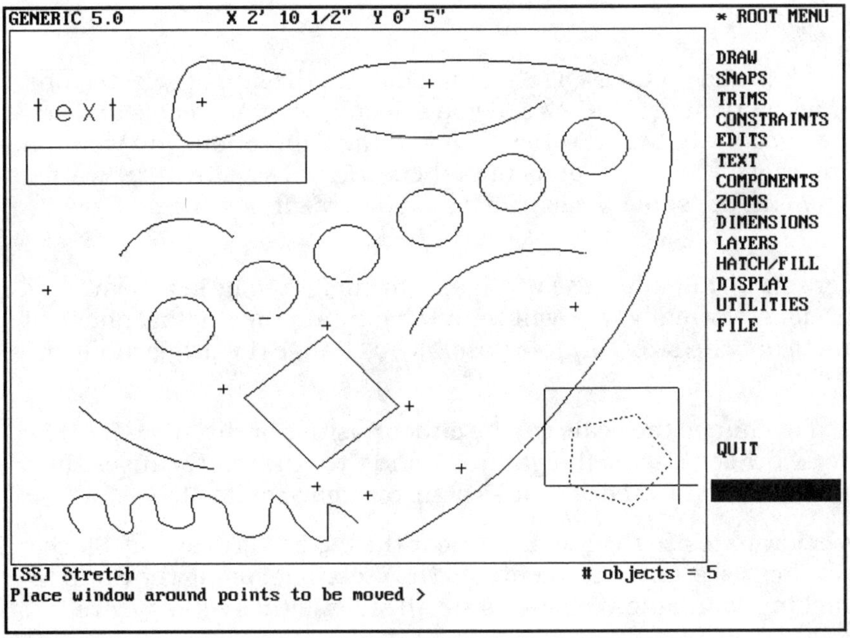

Figure 10.10: *Selecting the pentagon's top two lines.*

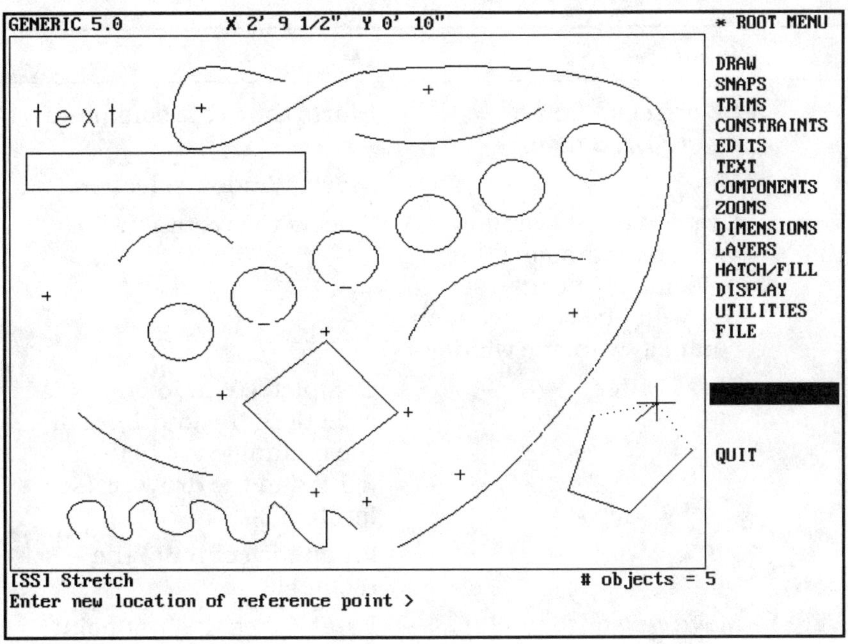

Figure 10.11: *Moving the reference points stretches the objects attached to them.*

Scale (SZ)

The Scale command, found on the EDITS menu, changes the size of selected objects by a percentage of their original size. If you selected several objects and set the scale of change to 1 for both the X direction and the Y direction, you would be telling CADD to redraw them at 100 percent of their original size. In other words, their size would remain the same. A scale of 2 is 200 percent; a scale of .5 is 50 percent.

Some CADD programs do not allow the width and the height to be set separately, as Generic CADD does. Normally, you will want to maintain the original shape of the object, changing only its size. But it is possible to change the proportions of the object(s).

The numbers used to change the scale can be either positive or negative. Setting either the X scale (width) or Y scale (height) to -1 and the other to 1, causes the object to stay the same size but redraws it as a mirror image of itself.

Follow the steps below to resize the rectangle near the top of the drawing. Place the reference point for rescaling at the center of the rectangle, using the Snap to Midpoint and Tracking commands to make sure all sides of the rectangle are drawn evenly.

Resizing the Rectangle

Prompt	*Input*	*Description*
`Command:`	**SZ** or select Scale from EDITS menu	Starts the Scale command
`Window...`	**W**	Starts Window selection
`Place window`	Draw selection window around rectangle; other objects may be intersected, but won't be selected if not completely inside window	Selects the rectangle
`# objects = 4`	Press Enter	Completes Window selection; the four lines of the rectangle are highlighted in the drawing (see fig. 10.12)
`Enter a reference point`	**TK**	Finds the center of the rectangle
`Enter point to start tracking from`	Move cursor to top line of rectangle and type **SM**	Establishes the first point for tracking

Resizing the Rectangle—continued

Prompt	*Input*	*Description*
`Midpoint of`	Click on top line of rectangle	Cursor snaps to midpoint of the top line
`You are now tracking`	**OR** and make sure that Ortho mode is on; if prompt indicates Ortho mode is off, type **OR** again	Constricts the movement of the tracking line
`You are now tracking`	Move cursor to center of rectangle, then to left	Moves toward the next temporary point

Figure 10.13 shows a close-up view of the rectangle. The tracking line points straight down, but the cursor is free to move toward the left side of the rectangle. Snap to Midpoint will be used to find the midpoint of the left side, placing the end of the tracking line in the exact center of the rectangle.

Prompt	*Input*	*Description*
`You are now tracking`	**SM**	Starts the Snap to Midpoint command
`Midpoint of`	Move cursor onto left side of rectangle and click	Executes the Snap to Midpoint command
`You are now tracking`	**PU**	Ends the Tracking command; the last point identified will be the reference point for the Scale command
`Enter new X scale`	**.5**	Reduces width by one-half
`Enter new Y scale`	**.5**	Reduces height by one-half; redraws rectangle (see figure 10.14)

Move (MV)

Even the most carefully prepared plans sometimes need to be changed. Fortunately, Generic CADD has a Move command, which relocates objects in a drawing. You select the objects, set a reference point, and move the point to a new location. All the selected objects will move as a unit, along with the reference point.

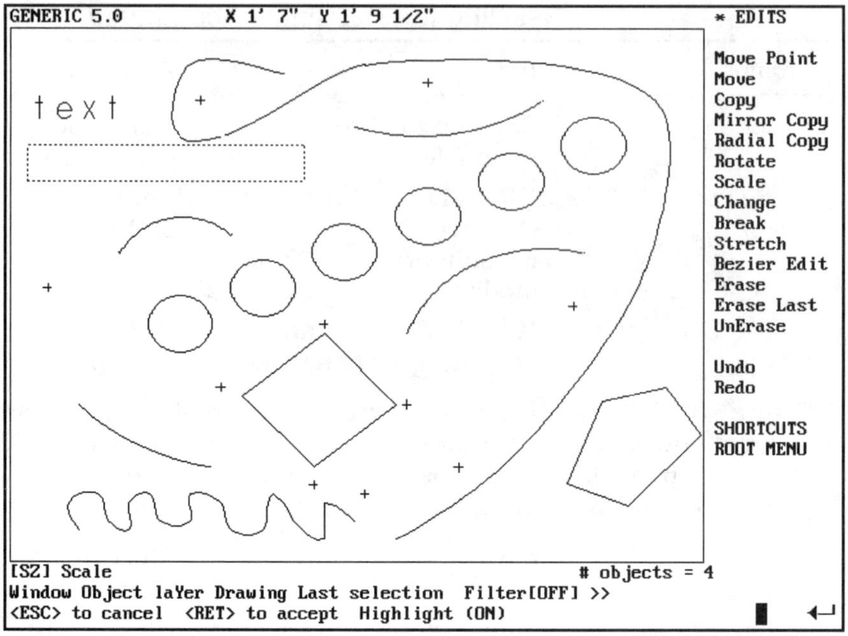

Figure 10.12: *The lines of the selected rectangle appear dotted (highlighted).*

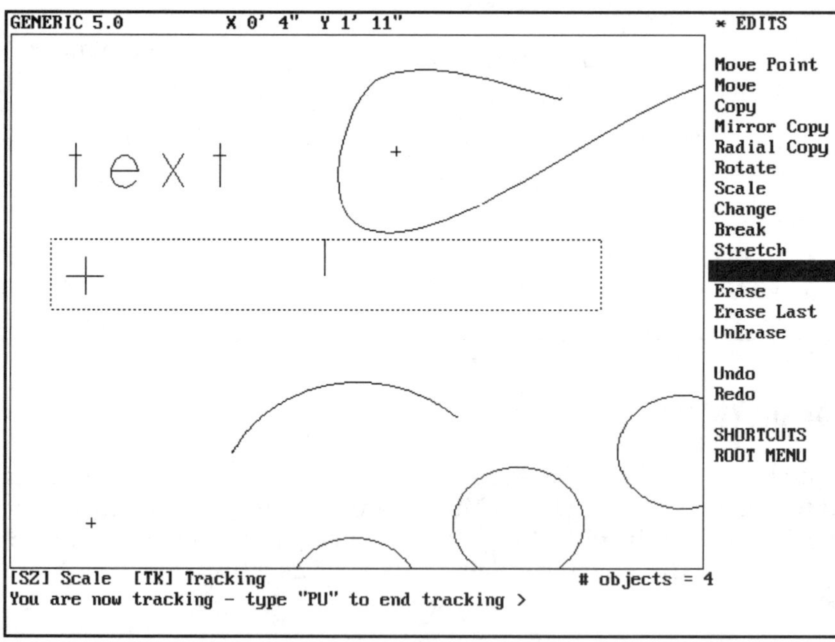

Figure 10.13: *A close-up view of the rectangle.*

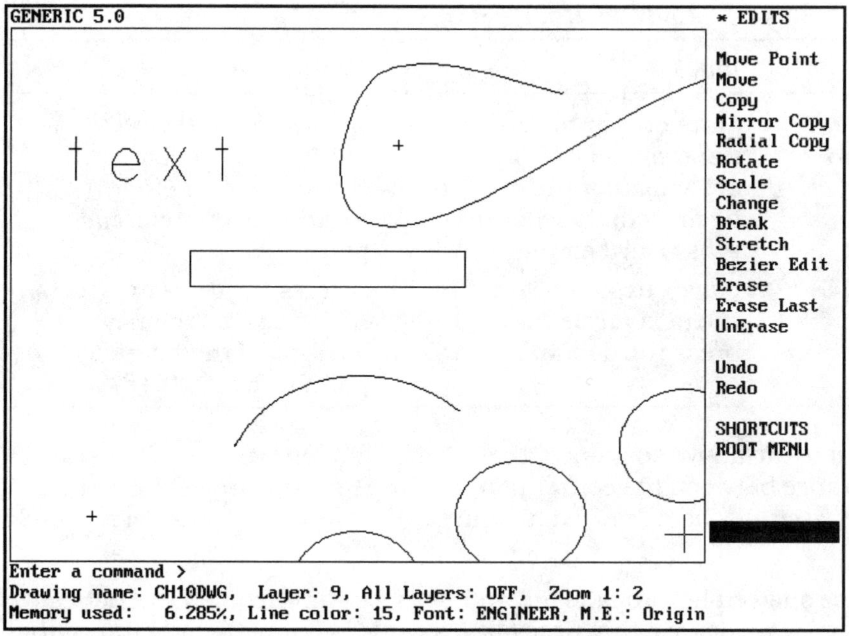

Figure 10.14: *The rectangle redrawn at one-half original size.*

In the following exercise, you will move three of the selected circles down and left, away from the other three. To keep all six circles in line, take advantage of existing geometry when choosing the reference point and its new location.

Moving Circles

Prompt	*Input*	*Description*
`Command:`	**MV**	Starts the Move command
`Window...`	**W**, or click on Window	Selects the Window option
`Place window`	Draw selection window around lower three circles	Selects the lower three circles

If your drawing matches the one in fig. 10.15, a point will also be inside the selection window. To make the selection window large enough to contain all three circles at once, a standard point also is included (# objects = 4, instead of the desired three).

Prompt	*Input*	*Description*
`Window...`	Press Ctrl and type **W**	Uses the window to *deselect* the point
`Place window`	Draw small window around previously selected point; press Enter	Eliminates the point; three objects should remain; then selects objects

Moving Circles—continued

Prompt	*Input*	*Description*
`Enter a reference point`	Move cursor to center of uppermost circle in drawing (not the ones to be moved); type **NP** or press third mouse button	Uses Snap to Nearest Point to select center of the uppermost circle as location of the reference point
`Enter new location of reference point`	Move cursor to center of the next circle in row and press third mouse button	Selects the center of the next circle as the new location of the reference point (see fig. 10.16)

When you complete the above sequence, the selected circles are moved a distance equal to the distance between the center points of the top two circles. Note the images of the three circles being moved in figure 10.16, as dotted-line versions of the originals.

The last sequence showed how to take advantage of existing geometry to help as you draw. The goal was to move the three circles while keeping them in line with the other three. It was not possible to use the Show By Example Angle command because it cannot be used when specifying coordinate locations.

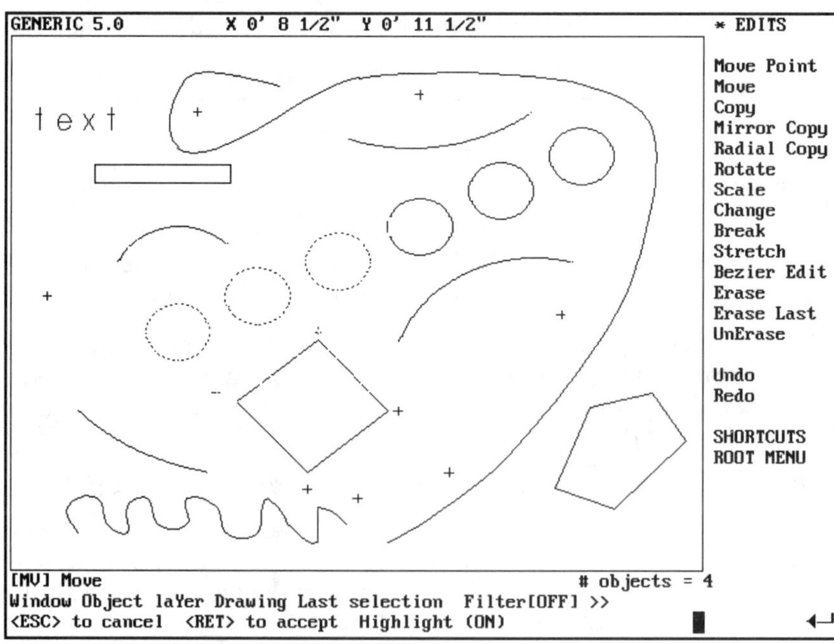

Figure 10.15: *Selecting lower three circles.*

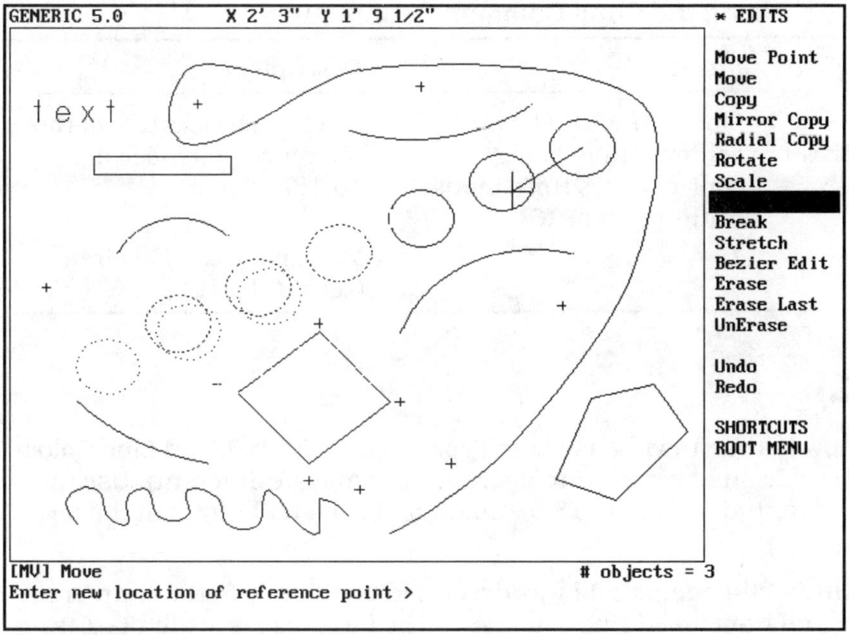

Figure 10.16: Setting the new location of the reference point.

Copy (CO)

The Copy command, found in the EDITS menu, is simply a more flexible version of the Object Copy (OC) or Window Copy (WC) commands. You will use it in the following exercise to add a circle to the row, placing the new copy in the gap created when the others moved.

Using the Copy Command

Prompt	*Input*	*Description*
`Command:`	**CO**	Starts the Copy command
`...Object...`	**O**	Selects Object option
`Pick object`	Move cursor to circle just below gap created by the Move command; click anywhere on circle and press Enter	Selects circle to be copied
`Enter a reference point`	Move cursor to center of circle below circle being copied; type **NP** or press third mouse button	Selects new reference point (see fig. 10.17)

Using the Copy Command—continued

Prompt	*Input*	*Description*
`Enter new reference point`	Move cursor up toward center of item being copied; press third mouse button or type **NP**	Selects new location of the reference point (see fig. 10.18)
`Enter number of copies`	**1**	Makes one copy of circle (see fig. 10.19)

Change (CG)

All the objects now in the drawing use Line Type 0, Line Width 0, and Line Color 15, and they all reside on Layer 9 (your layer number may be different). Use the Change command, found in the EDITS menu, to make a few changes in the following exercise.

The use of the Entity Filter command was described previously in the chapter as a separate command from an editing command. The filter also is available during the selection process. You can use it to select the items you want quickly. All circles, arcs, and Bézier curves will be selected in the following steps, using the filter at times to speed the selection process.

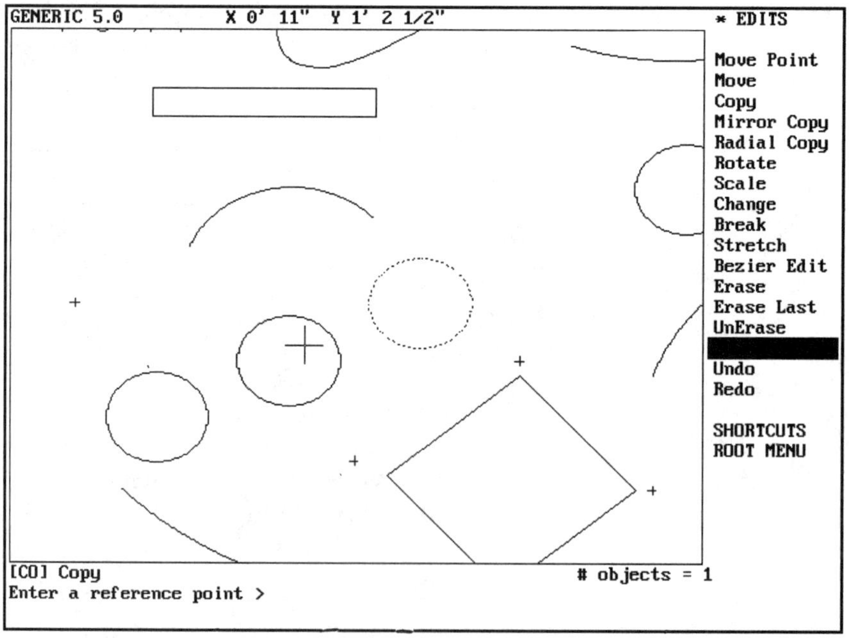

Figure 10.17: *Use the center point as the reference point.*

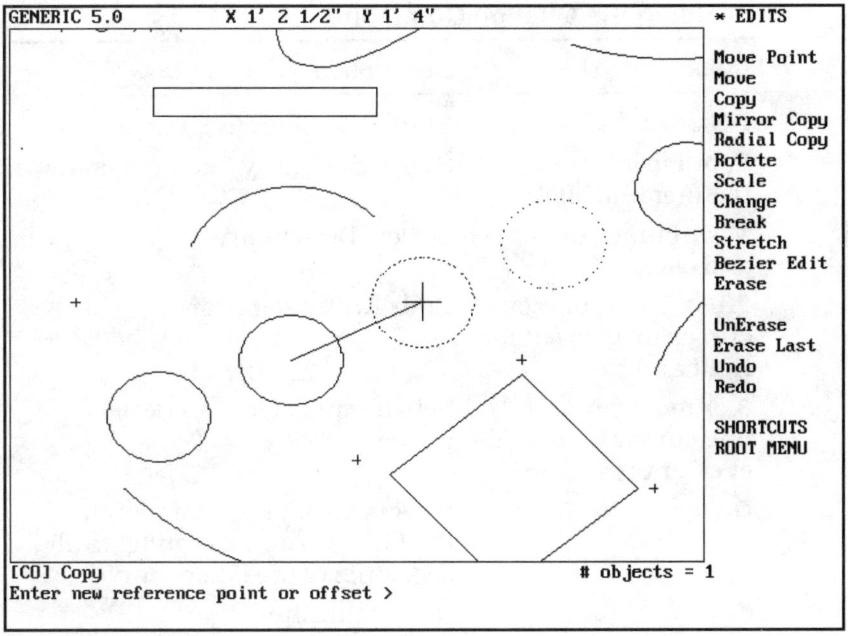

Figure 10.18: *Selecting another reference point and adding a new circle to the line.*

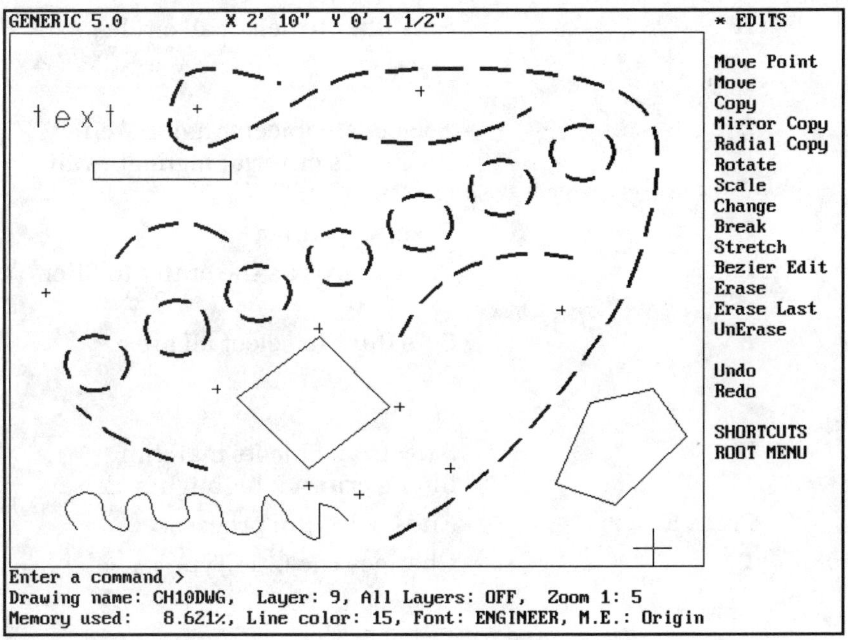

Figure 10.19: *The Bézier curves redrawn.*

Using the Change Command

Prompt	*Input*	*Description*
`Command:`	**CG**	Starts the Change command
`...Filter[OFF]`	**F**, or move cursor to Filter and click	Starts the Entity Filter command
`Select entity to filter`	Move cursor to Bez and click	Selects Bézier curves
`Select entity to filter`	Press Enter, or move cursor to arrow at far right and click	Ends Entity selection
`Select characteristic to filter`	**A** or move prompt line cursor to All and click or press Enter	Sets filter to select all Bézier curves
`...Drawing...`	**D**	Selects all objects that match the filter's criteria; highlights all segments of the Bézier curve
`...FILTER[OFF]`	**F**	Resets the filter
`Select entity to filter`	**C**	Selects circles as the entity to filter
`Select characteristics to filter`	**A**	Sets filter to select all circles
`...Drawing...`	**D**	Selects all objects that match the filter's criteria; highlights all circles
`...FILTER[OFF]`	**F**	Resets the filter
`Select entity to filter`	**R**	Selects arcs as the entity to filter
`Select characteristics to filter`	**A**	Sets filter to select all arcs
`...Drawing...`	**D**	Selects all objects matching filter's criteria; highlights all arcs
`Window...`	Press Enter	Ends selection process
`Change objects to:`	**T**	Changes the Line Type

Using the Change Command—continued

Prompt	*Input*	*Description*
`Enter Line Type`	**2**, or move menu bar to Line Type 2 and press second mouse button	Selects Line Type 2
`Change objects to:`	**W**	Changes the Line Width
`Enter Line width`	**3**, or move menu bar to Line Width 3 and press second mouse button	Selects Line Width 3
`Change objects to:`	Press Enter	Redraws objects with new characteristics (see fig. 10.22)

Rotate (RO)

The Rotate command just rotates objects around a reference point, but the location of that reference point is very important. With the Rotate command, you can place the reference point so that the object spins in place, or shifts to a new portion of the drawing. Take a look at the following illustrations, and then try the Rotate command on your own.

The diamond in the figures that follow will be rotated 45 degrees—in two different ways.

The arrow in figure 10.20 displays the reference point for the first rotation; figure 10.21 shows the result, using a point of rotation inside the diamond. The diamond stays in the same portion of the drawing. The arrow appears again in figure 10.22, to show where the reference point will be placed for the second rotation; figure 10.23 shows the result using a point of rotation located away from the diamond. The diamond's new location in the drawing is dramatically different.

The Rotate command is a good candidate for the use of Show by Example. If you want to rotate an object so that it sits at the same rotation in the drawing as another object, type **A** (for two-point angle) when CADD prompts for the angle of rotation. Click to show the base of the angle, then click again to show the heading. CADD will rotate your selected object(s) to match the rotation of the object used for the Show by Example command.

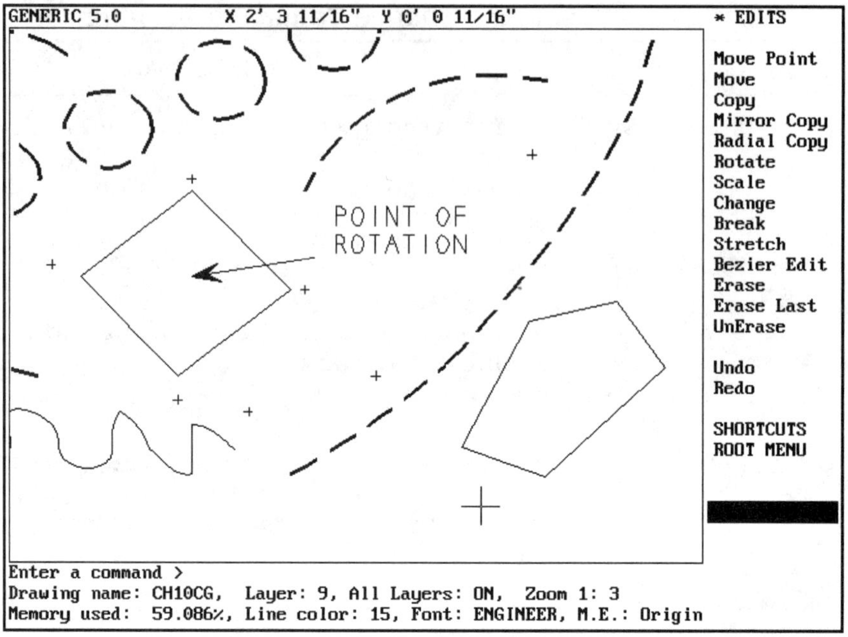

Figure 10.20: *The first point of rotation for the diamond.*

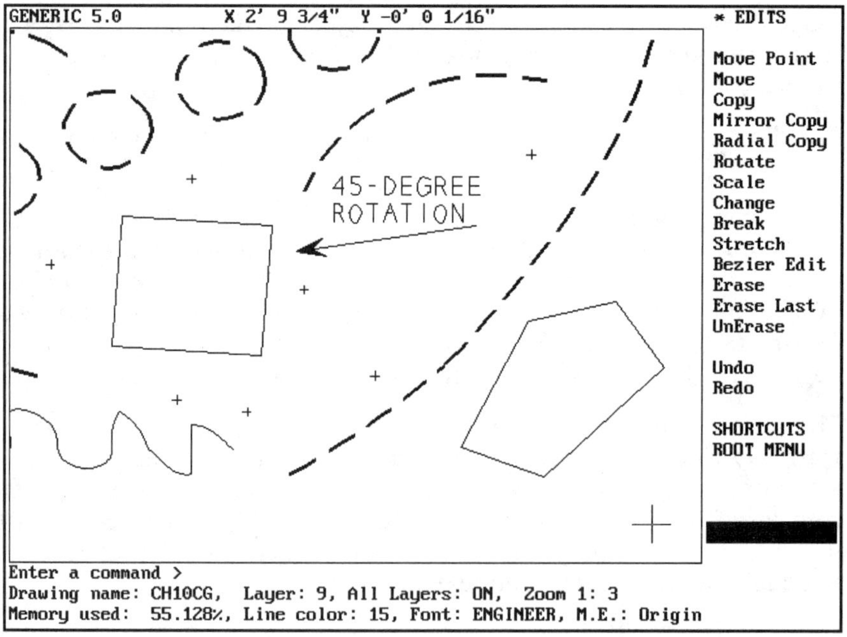

Figure 10.21: *Rotating the diamond with internal point of rotation.*

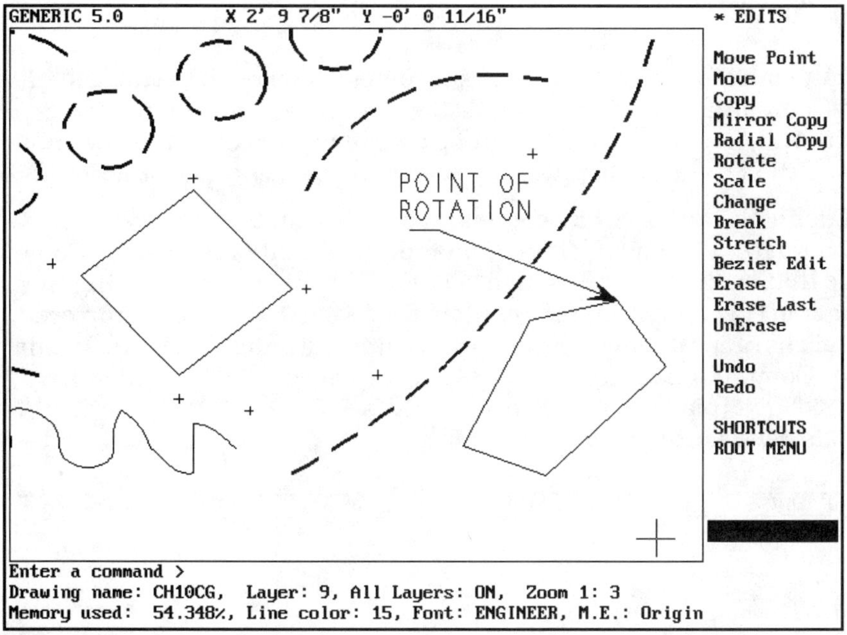

Figure 10.22: *The second point of rotation.*

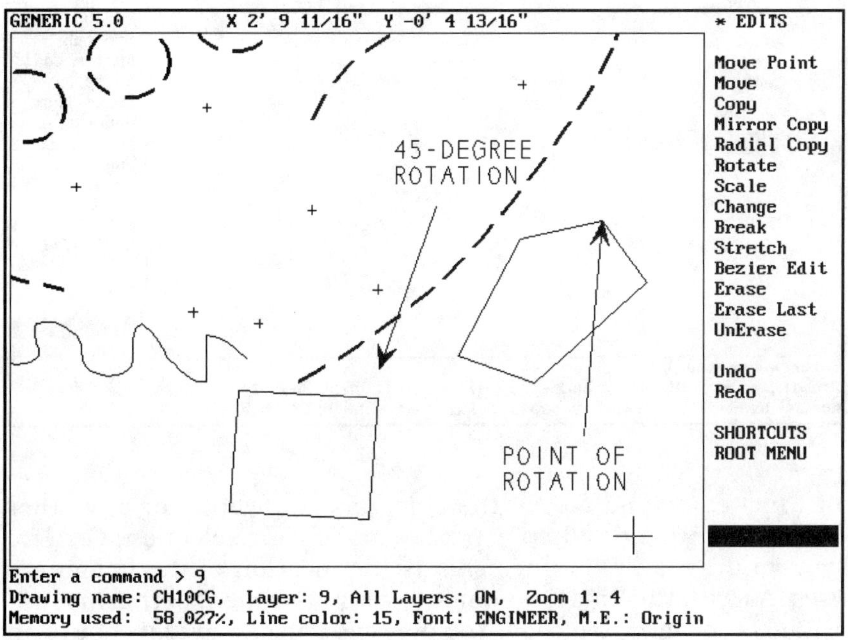

Figure 10.23: *Rotating the diamond with external point of rotation.*

Mirror Copy (MI)

The Copy command makes from one to 99 exact copies of the objects you select. The Mirror Copy command, found on the EDITS menu, makes one *mirror-image* copy of the selected objects. If you are designing a symmetrical object, draw only half the object and then use the Mirrow Copy command to create the other half.

Take care when using the Mirror Copy command with text. If the text was placed using the Text Character Placement (TP) command, the result of the Mirror Copy command will be that each *character* is inverted. If the text was placed using the Text Line Placement (TL) command, the result is that each *line* of text is mirrored, but the individual characters remain readable as a line, although they are upside down. The Mirror Copy command treats lines of text (placed with TL) and individual characters of text (placed with TP) differently (see fig. 10.24). The dotted line shows the axis used for the mirror command.

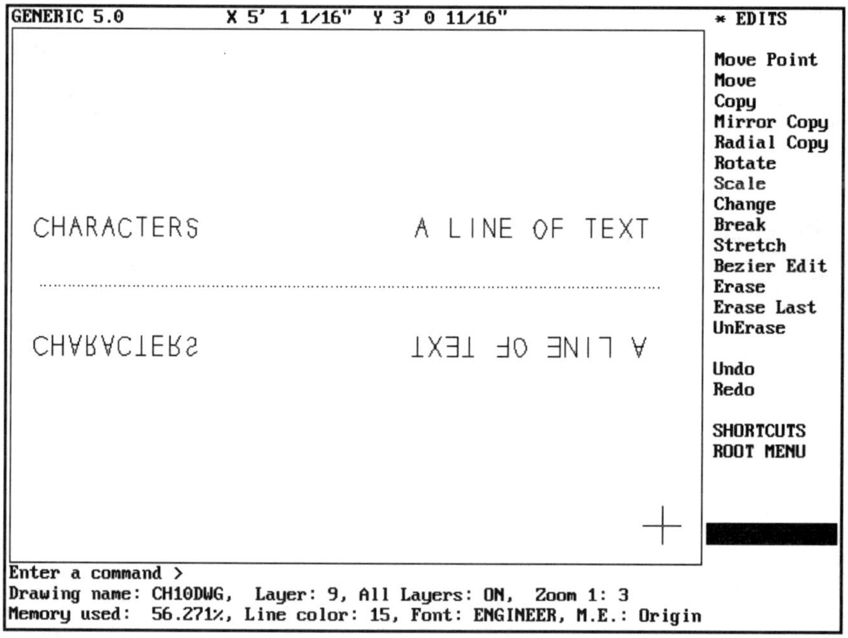

Figure 10.24: *The Mirror Copy command treats character and line text differently.*

To use the Mirror Copy command, select the object as you would for any other multiple-object editing command. When you have made your selection, Generic CADD prompts you to draw an axis line. This is the location of the imaginary "mirror" CADD uses. As with the Rotate command, your placement of this line will determine the location of the mirrored copy. You may even place a mirror copy of an item on top of the original by drawing the axis line through the original object.

You are finished with the drawing used so far in this chapter. You may erase it if you like.

Multi-Trim (MT)

The Trim (RM) command, introduced in Chapter 9, has a multiple-object sibling in Multi-Trim (MT), found on the TRIMS menu. The Multi-Trim command uses the same selection process as the editing commands covered so far, but then trims the objects selected to line up with another line. It works only with lines, arcs, and circles, not with Bézier curves or true ellipses.

Follow the steps below to set up a situation, and then try the Multi-Trim command.

Using the Multi-Trim Command

Prompt	*Input*	*Description*
`Command:`	**DXY**	Erases the current drawing
`Command:`	Draw one vertical line on left side of screen; use Ortho Mode command or press Ctrl	Draws a vertical line
`Command:`	**OC**	Initiates Object Copy command
`Pick object`	Move cursor to the line; click on it with first mouse button	Selects the line as the object to be copied
`Enter a reference point`	Move cursor near top of line; type **NP** or press third mouse button	Selects the top of the line as the reference point for the copy
`Enter new reference point or offset`	Move cursor to right about 1/2" and click; use Ortho mode to move reference point to right	Moves the image of the original to set the distance for the Copy command
`Enter number of copies`	**10**	Makes 10 copies of the original line
`Command:`	**A3**	Initiates a 3-Point Arc command
`Enter start of arc`	Move cursor to bottom of first line; type **NP** or press third mouse button	Places start of the arc at bottom of first line
`Enter a point on the arc`	Move cursor to top of sixth line; type **NP** or press third mouse button	Places the midpoint of the arc on top of the middle line
`Enter the end of the arc`	Move cursor to bottom of last line; type **NP** or press third mouse button	Places the end of the arc at bottom of last line (see fig. 10.25)

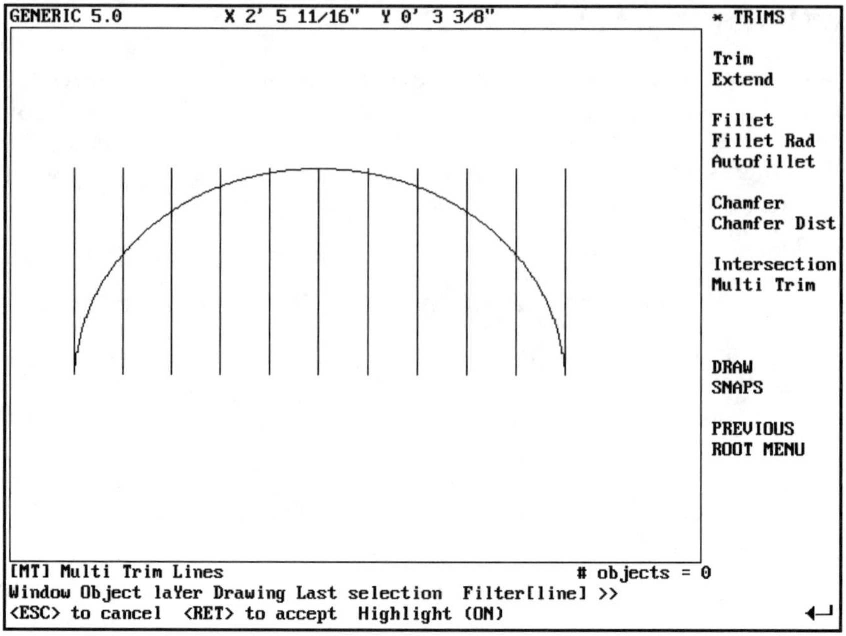

Figure 10.25: *Eleven lines intersected by an arc.*

Multi-Trim with Lines

Prompt	*Input*	*Description*
`Command:`	**OE**	Starts the Object Erase command
`Pick object`	Move cursor to last line and click on it	Erases the last line
`Command:`	Press Spacebar	Repeats the Object Erase command
`Pick object`	Move cursor to first line and click on it	Erases the first line
`Command:`	**MT**	Starts the Multi-Trim Lines command
`...Drawing...`	**D**	Selects all objects in the drawing and completes the selection process
`Trim to`	Move cursor to arc and click anywhere on it	Selects the arc as the object to which the lines will be trimmed

Multi-Trim with Lines—continued

Prompt	*Input*	*Description*
`Enter sides to keep`	Move cursor inside span of arc and click	Displays images of the lines to show you how the lines will be trimmed; selects side of arc to trim lines on (see fig. 10.26)

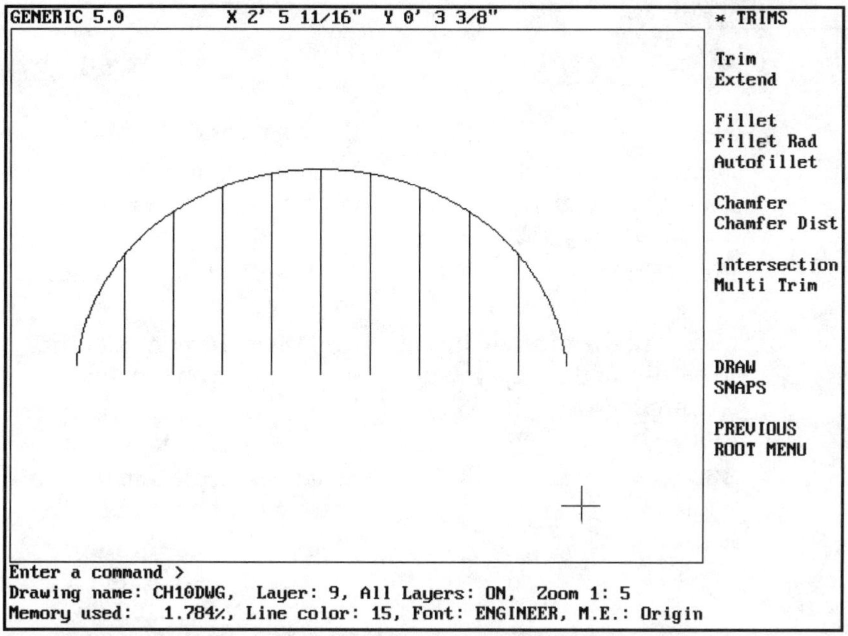

Figure 10.26: *The lines have been trimmed to the arc.*

Radial Copy (RC)

Two copy commands have been introduced in this chapter: Copy (CO) can create from one to 100 exact copies in a straight line, and Mirror Copy (MI) can draw one mirror-image copy. The Radial Copy command, found in the EDITS menu, is a third multiple-object copy command. It copies objects in a circular (radial) pattern around an axis. The number of items and the angular span of the copies are adjustable.

To practice this command, load the drawing that was created in Chapter 9. It looks as if it might have been created for a machine shop; you may have called it FLANGE.DWG. If you didn't create and save the drawing, use figure 10.27 as a guide for drawing it now.

To use the Radial Copy command, select the objects to be copied. Next, select an axis point. The objects you selected will be copied around this point. Now select the degrees of the span. A positive number will copy in a counterclockwise direction, a negative number will copy in a clockwise direction. The final step is to specify the total number of items in the copy. This number includes the original, so be careful to provide the correct number.

Follow the steps below to copy the hole near the edge of the flange around the circle.

Using the Radial Copy Command

Prompt	*Input*	*Description*
`Command:`	**RC**	Starts the Radial Copy command
`Window...`	**W**	Draws a window
`Place window`	Draw selection window around hole at top of object (see fig. 10.27)	Selects the hole to be copied (# objects = 3)
`Window...`	Press Enter	Ends selection of objects to be copied
`Enter an axis point`	Move cursor to small circle in center of flange; type **NP** or click with third mouse button	Identifies the center of the small circle as the axis
`Enter total degrees to span`	**360**	Determines placement of items to be copied
`Enter total number of items in span`	**6**	Places six holes around the circle, distributed evenly (see fig. 10.28)

You may use the Object Break command to remove the construction line from the bottom hole, bringing balance to the object in the drawing. Save the changes to the drawing just completed, if you like, and clear the screen.

Use the Show by Example and Radial Copy commands to bisect (evenly divide) an angle. Draw two lines, as shown in figure 10.29, that come together at a common point. This will be the angle to bisect. The steps that follow start with the assumption that you have already drawn the lines.

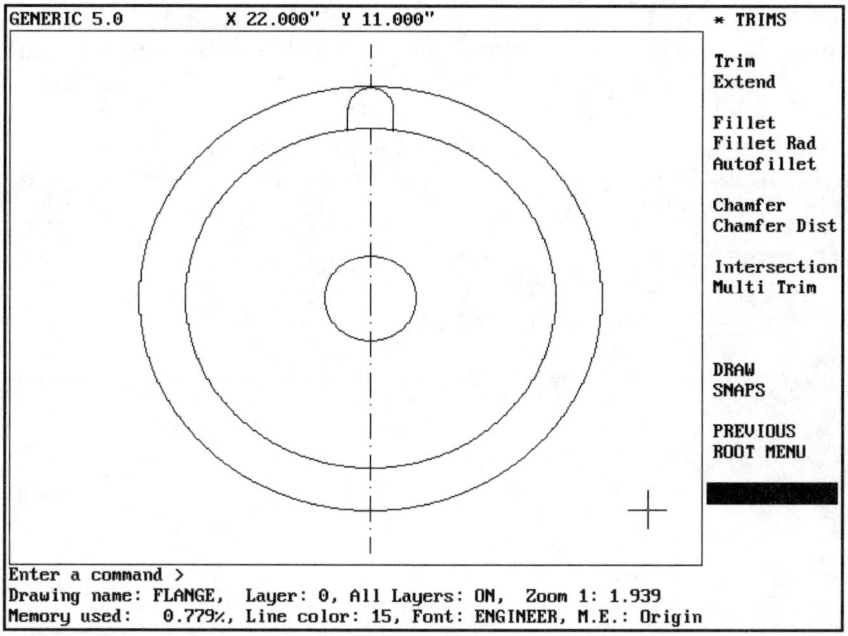

Figure 10.27: *FLANGE.DWG created in Chapter 9.*

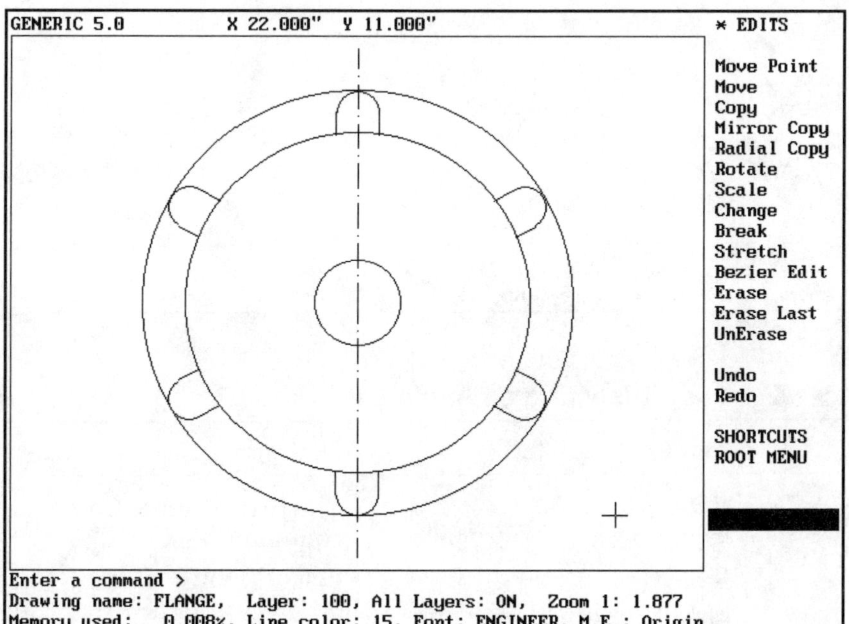

Figure 10.28: *Radial Copy makes five additional copies of the hole.*

You could automatically bisect an angle without the Radial Copy and Show by Example commands, but it would take more steps: Measure 3-point Angle would first be used to measure the angle between the two lines. Measure 2-point Angle would then be used to determine the exact heading of one of the lines. Using a direct distance command, a line would then be drawn from the intersection of the two lines, out at a heading that would bisect the existing angle. The method you are about to use is much simpler.

This procedure creates an extra line; the last step will be to erase the extra line and redraw the screen. The angle between the two original lines will be bisected using the Radial Copy and Show by Example commands.

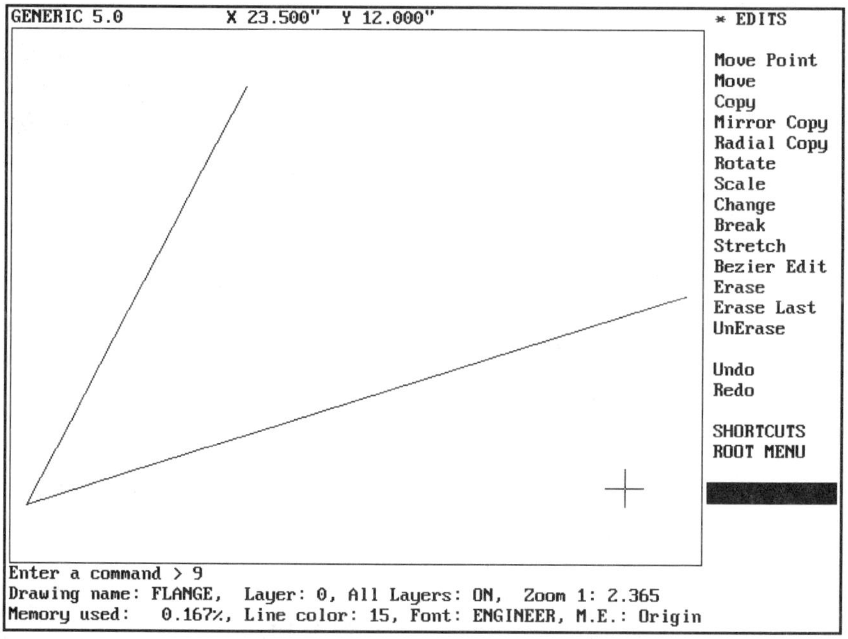

Figure 10.29: *Draw two lines that meet at a common point.*

Bisecting an Angle

Prompt	*Input*	*Description*
`Command:`	**RC**	Starts the Radial Copy command
`...Object...`	**O**	Selects Object option
`Pick object`	Move cursor to lower line and click; press Enter	Selects the bottom line to be copied

Bisecting an Angle—continued

Prompt	*Input*	*Description*
`Enter an axis point`	Move cursor to base of angle; type **NP** or click with third mouse button	Selects base of the angle as axis for copy function
`Enter total degrees to span`	**V**	Determines the number of degrees to span
`Enter base of angle Show vertex by example (3 pts)`	Move cursor to base of angle; type **NP** or click with third mouse button	Selects the base of the angle
`Enter a point on the ray`	Move cursor to endpoint of bottom line; type **NP** or click with third mouse button	Selects the first line of the angle
`Enter next point`	Move cursor to endpoint of top line; type **NP** or click with third mouse button	Selects the second line of the angle (lines must be selected in counter-clockwise fashion)
`Enter total number of items in span`	**3**	Places line evenly between the beginning and the end of span
If you input 2 instead of 3 at the prompt shown above, the program would put one line at the beginning and one at the end of the angle.		
`Command:`	**ELRD**	Erases the last item and redraws screen (see fig. 10.30)

Explode (EX)

The Explode command is one multiple-object command that is not an editing command; it is a utility that sometimes must be used in order to edit objects. The Explode command is on the UTILITIES menu and causes linked objects to revert to the individual pieces they were made from. Except for text, you have yet to learn about the entities that can be exploded in Generic CADD: dimensions, components, and attributes. Remember this discussion of exploding text when you get to sections on other entity types.

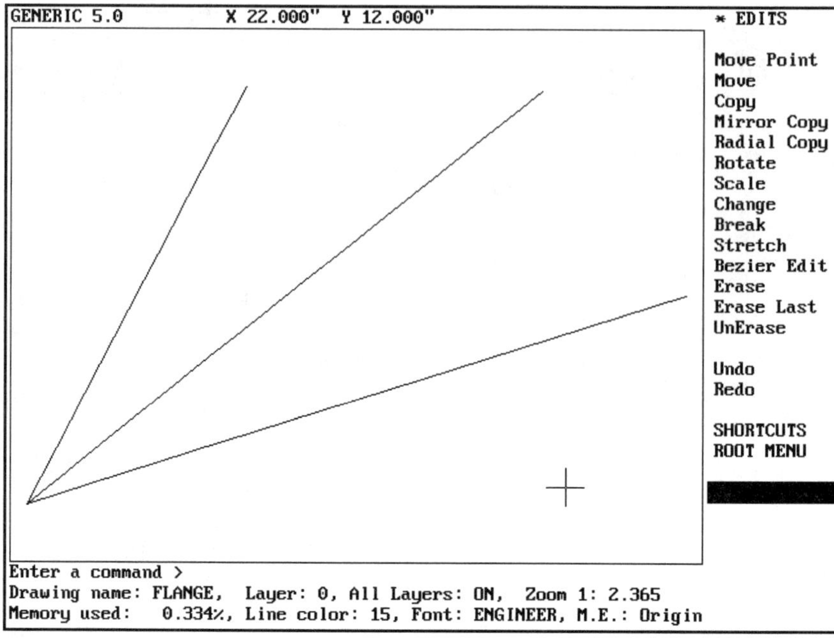

Figure 10.30: *The completed bisection.*

You might explode text for two reasons: to move individual characters that had been placed using the Text Line Placement (TL) command, and to change the shape of characters for a special look.

When a line of text placed with the Text Line Placement command is exploded, it reverts to individual characters, as if it had been placed with the Text Character Placement command. When individual characters are exploded, they revert to lines, arcs, curves and so on; then they can be edited like any other graphic object in the drawing. After erasing the angle on your screen, use the steps in the following exercises to place a line of text on the screen and then explode it twice.

Placing a Line of Text

Prompt	*Input*	*Description*
`Command:`	**TL**	Starts the Text Line Placement command
`Enter starting point`	Move cursor to left side of and click	Sets the starting point for a line of text
`>`	Type **Generic CADD**; press Enter and Esc	Places a line of text (see fig. 10.31)
`Command:`	**ZA**	Starts the Zoom All command

Placing a Line of Text—continued

Prompt	*Input*	*Description*
`Command:`	**PR**; if the prompt says reference points are off, type **PR** again	Turns on reference points
`Command:`	**RD**	Redraws the screen

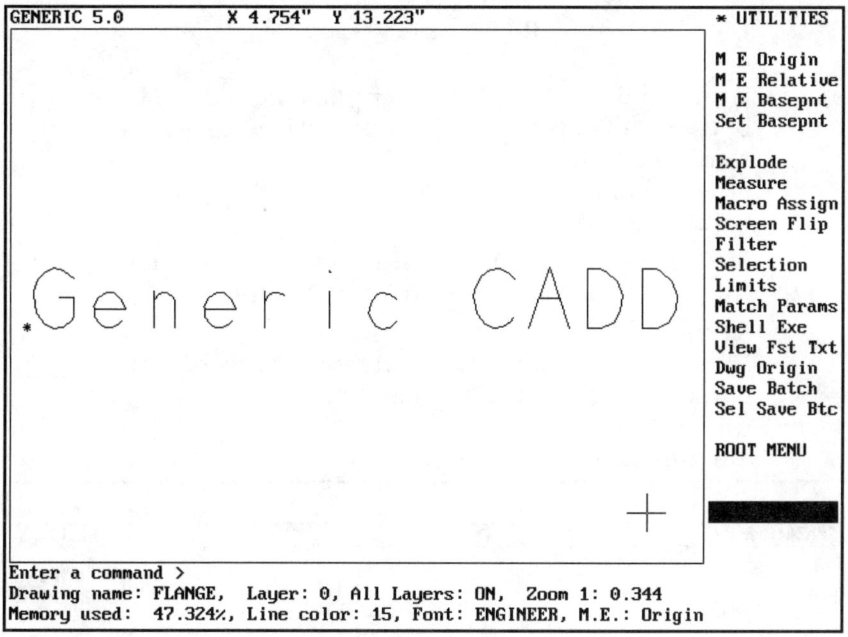

Figure 10.31: *The text "Generic CADD" placed with Text Line Placement.*

Exploding the Text Line

Prompt	*Input*	*Description*
`Command:`	**EX**	Starts the Explode command
`...Drawing...`	**D**	Selects the entire drawing; explodes line of text into individual characters (see fig. 10.32)
`Command:`	Press Spacebar	Repeats the last command (Explode)
`...Drawing...`	**D**	Selects the entire drawing; explodes each text character

Exploding the Text Line—continued

Prompt	*Input*	*Description*
`Command:`	**PCRD**	Starts the Construction Point and Redraw commands (see fig. 10.33)
`Command:`	**SS**	Starts the Stretch command
`Window...`	**W**	Starts a window
`Place window`	Draw window around the word CADD; press Enter	Selects the word CADD
`Place window around points to be moved`	Draw window around bottom half of the word CADD; include crossbar of the letter A within window	Identifies the section to be stretched (see fig. 10.34
`Enter a reference point`	Move cursor to top of the A in CADD and click with third mouse button	Selects the top of the A as the reference point
`Enter new location of reference point`	Press Ctrl and move cursor straight down until satisfied with amount of stretch; click	Stretches the word CADD (see fig. 10.35)

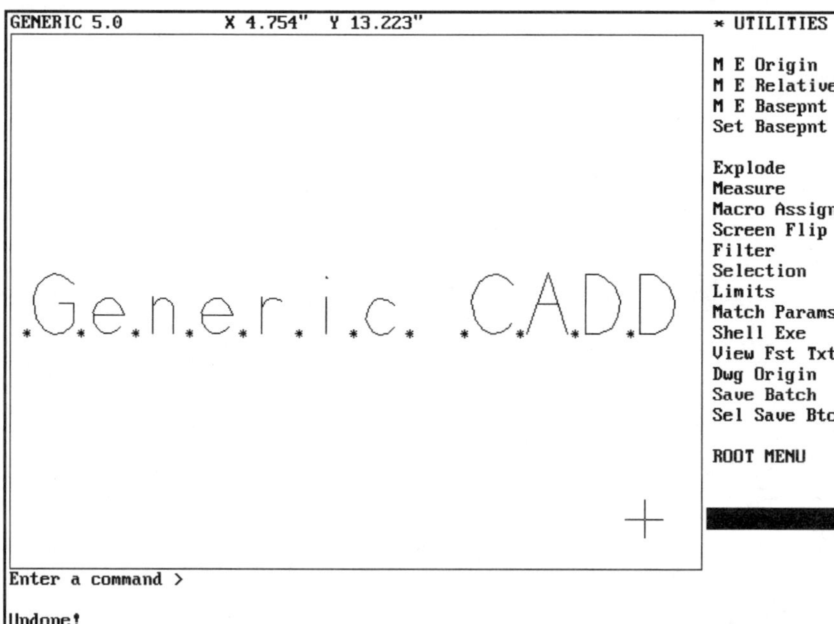

Figure 10.32: *Text is now individual characters with individual reference points.*

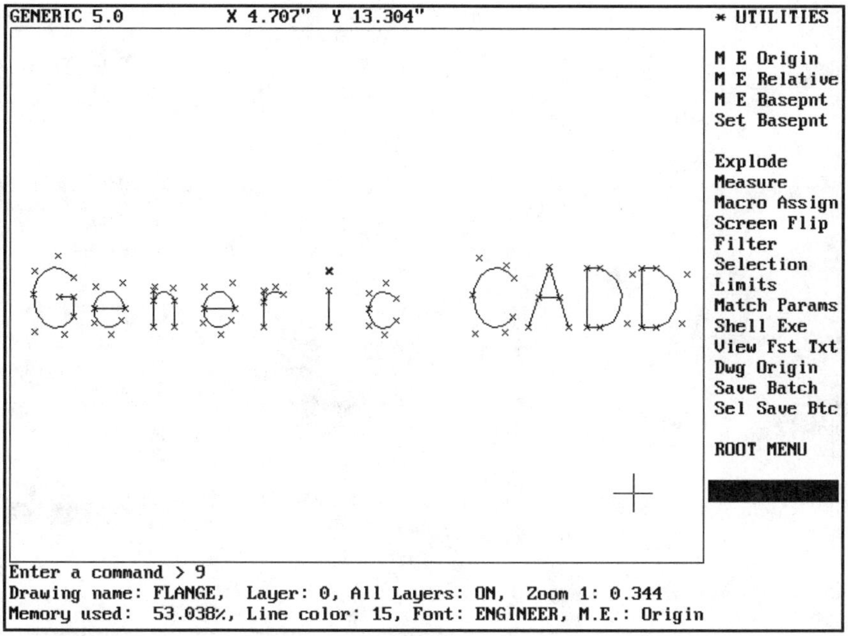

Figure 10.33: Text reduced to individual objects.

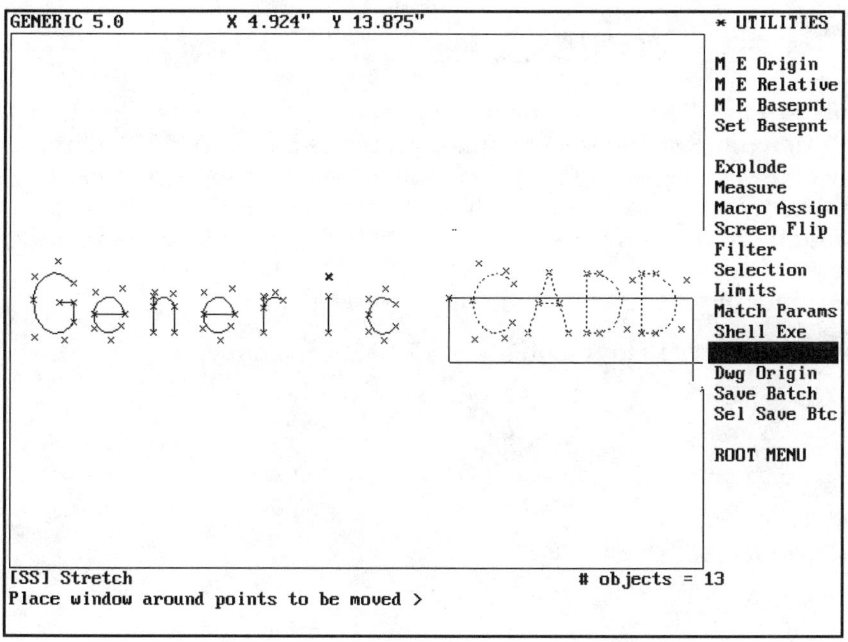

Figure 10.34: The construction points to be moved for the Stretch command.

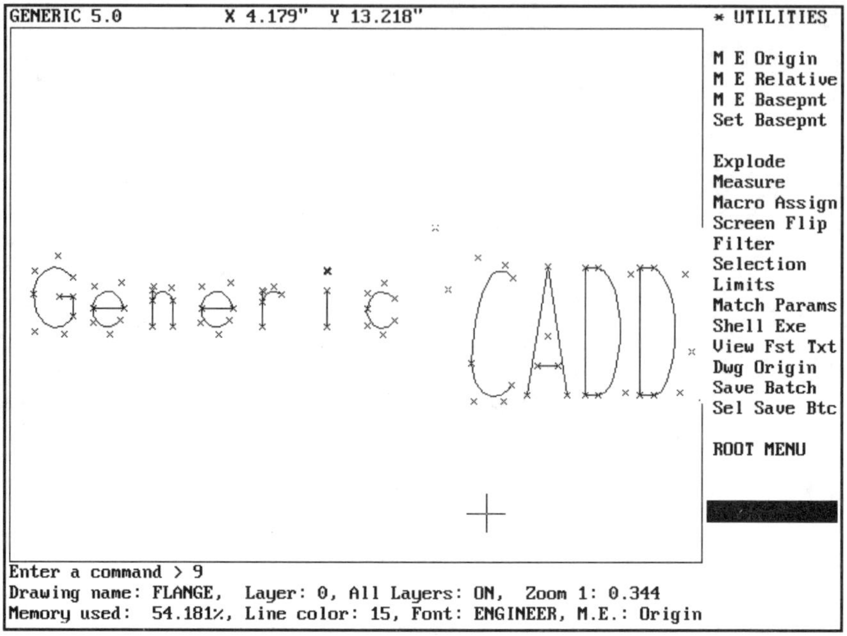

Figure 10.35: *The word "CADD" has been stretched.*

Multiple Object/Single Selection Editing

Now that you have studied both the single-selection editing commands (in Chapter 9) and the multiple-object selection commands (in this chapter), you will understand the use of the many editing commands that fall somewhere between the two categories. Some editing commands allow one chance to choose what is to be edited, yet allow for more than one object to be selected. These editing commands select either one window, one layer, or the entire drawing. They do not use the selection process, and the filter and highlighting are not available.

The commands listed below are found on the SHORTCUTS menu:

Window Copy (WC)
Window Scale (WZ)
Window Erase (WE)
Window Move (WM)
Window Rotate (WR)
Drawing Rotate (DR)
Drawing Change (DG)

The following commands are found on the LAYERS menu.

Layer Scale (YZ)
Layer Erase (YE)
Layer Rotate (YR)
Layer Change (YG)

The methods are the same as for their single-object and multiple-object counterparts, so a detailed description of each is not provided. Practice using them, if you like, on the exploded line of text used above.

Summary

With only a few keystrokes, the multiple-object editing commands provide a virtually unlimited number of ways to select objects for editing. Commands like Copy (CO), Move (MV), Scale (SZ), and Radial Copy (RC) are not limited to acting on only one object. They can be used to perform the same action on many objects at one time.

Selection and filtering are at the heart of the multiple-object editing commands. Selection allows you to pick and choose which objects should be edited, and filtering fine-tunes the selection process by providing a precise definition of what kinds of objects can be selected.

Some of the multiple-object editing commands are comparable to what one might do if using manual drafting, including Copy and Move. But other editing commands have no direct manual equivalent, unless one invests in a fast electric eraser (Stretch, Rotate, and Multi-Trim are examples). The power of automation is also obvious when using Screen Flip, which makes it possible to examine the nature of the drawing file as it resides in memory, and Explode, which reduces linked objects to their individual pieces.

The selection and filtering technology used by the multiple-object editing commands turns up elsewhere in Generic CADD, in commands like Explode (EX), Selection Save (SV), and Selection Save Batch (BS).

Another way of speeding up your work with Generic CADD is to use components. The next chapter will introduce you to the basics of working with components in Generic CADD.

11

Components

A component is an entity or a group of entities that are used to define a single object. This single object is given a name and a reference point (called an *insert point*). The reference point is the only point associated with the object.

Although they can be saved to disk, components are not drawings. They're groupings of entities. When a component is selected, it acts like a single drawing entity. However, the user has more control over it than with a single drawing entity. With the press of a key or the click of the mouse, a component can be scaled, rotated, imaged, exploded, replaced, and removed—all of which is discussed in this chapter.

In manual drafting, the draftsperson draws every line, arc, and circle from scratch. In CADD, inserting components helps to construct the final drawing. Individually-created lines, arcs, and circles, usually make up only a portion of the drawing. Components make up the rest. You can complete drawings much more quickly by using components as often as possible.

For example, you draw a sink using circles and lines. When it is completed, it is considered a single component (a sink), but it is actually a group of circles and lines (see fig. 11.1). You can save the sink under a component name and then insert it into any drawing.

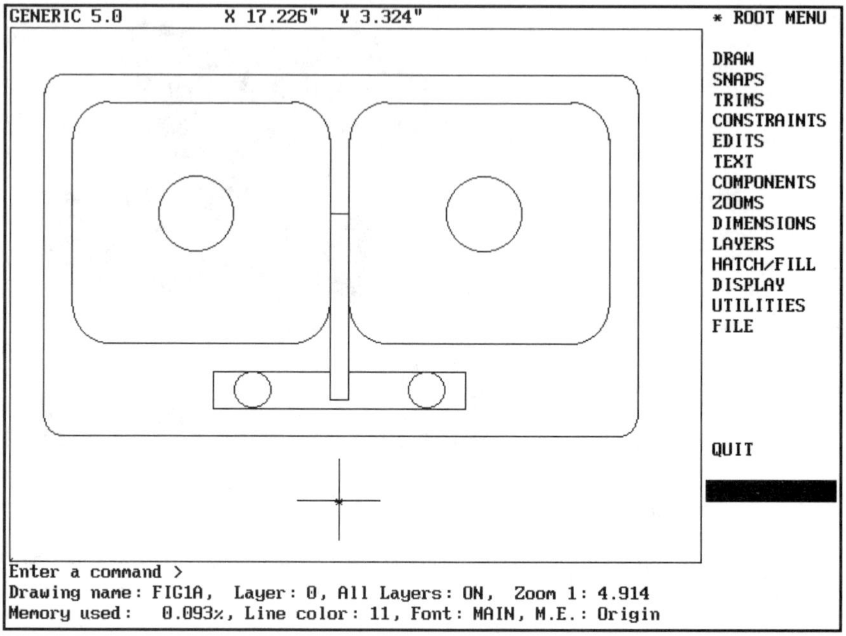

Figure 11.1: *This sample component is a sink used in house plans.*

Component Power

As you learned the edit commands in Chapter 10, the potential speed of computer-aided drafting vs. manual drafting probably became evident to you. Now comes the component, which will help you to develop drawings quickly on the screen. This is what CADD is all about.

Because a component is drawn once and used many times, you can afford to put more effort and artistry into each one. The kitchen range, shown in figure 11.2, reflects this asset. Shadow lines are visible. The kitchen range has a lockset, leaded glass lines, and a brick sill. The construction of the range itself is equally important. The lines start and stop exactly where they should, with no overruns or gaps. This extra attention to detail is possible when you use components.

Components improve the accuracy of a drawing. In manual drafting, the little details develop subtle differences over time. Perhaps a line is drawn a little longer, the text is slightly different, or, worst of all, a critical portion of the detail is forgotten. This cannot happen with components. Once a component exists, it is exactly the same whether it is used once or a million times.

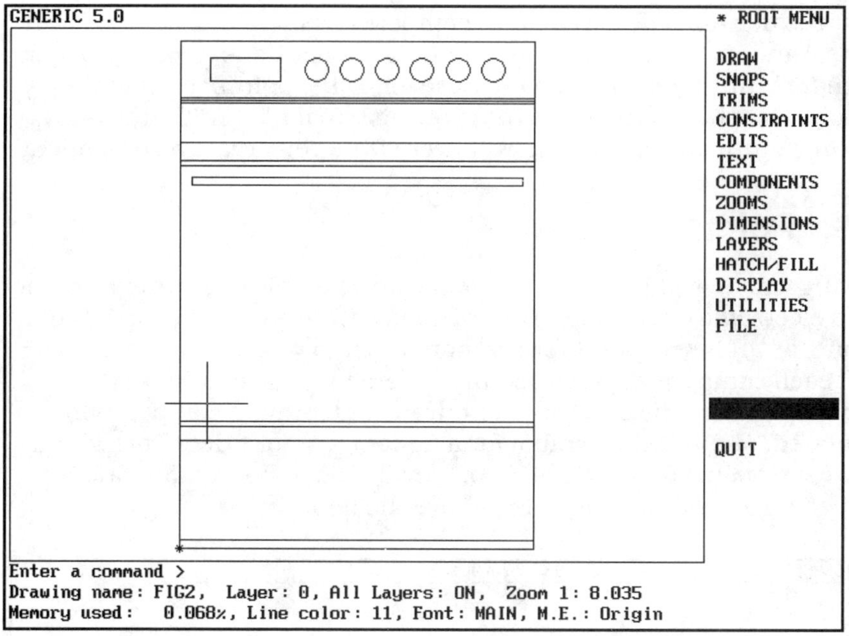

Figure 11.2: *A kitchen range component.*

Components may be either *current* or *permanent*. Current components are those used only while a drawing (or set of drawings) is under development, such as the components you will construct for this chapter. They will not be used later; therefore, you can delete them, when the exercise is completed, to save space on your hard drive. Permanent components are those that will be used many times. The kitchen sink in figure 11.1 or the oven door in figure 11.2 can be permanent components for someone who designs houses, for example. Components can be saved to disk and re-used as many times as you want. Remember CADD's golden rule: *Never* draw the same thing twice.

Some components develop as specifically created parts, while others are taken from larger drawings. In either event, Generic CADD 5.0 makes component creation easy. A dozen or so commands control the entire powerful process.

Creating Components

Creating components requires only two commands. The first command is Window Create (CW), which is quicker. The second command is Component Create (CC), in which objects can be selected and deselected in various ways to produce a component. The first step in creating a component, however, is not deciding which of these two easy commands to use, but thinking through a plan of consistent style.

Nothing will sour the use and effectiveness of components more quickly than random insert points, random rotation, random naming conventions, and the lost or forgotten parts that result. Read and consider the following points; then write down a simple policy for the components that you wish to make. Attach this policy to the side of your monitor and follow it every time you create a component.

Picking Insert Points

The type of drawing you do will probably influence how you pick your insert point (see fig. 11.3). An electronic drafter, for example, may always pick the top left pin, or pin number one, as an insert point for components. Flow chart users may select the center of each component. Architectural users may have two insert points, depending upon the type of component drawn. Floor plan components that are never rotated, such as the symbol for a light or a smoke detector, would have a centered insert point. Window and door elevation symbols could have an insert point located on a centered point 6'8" above the floor line.

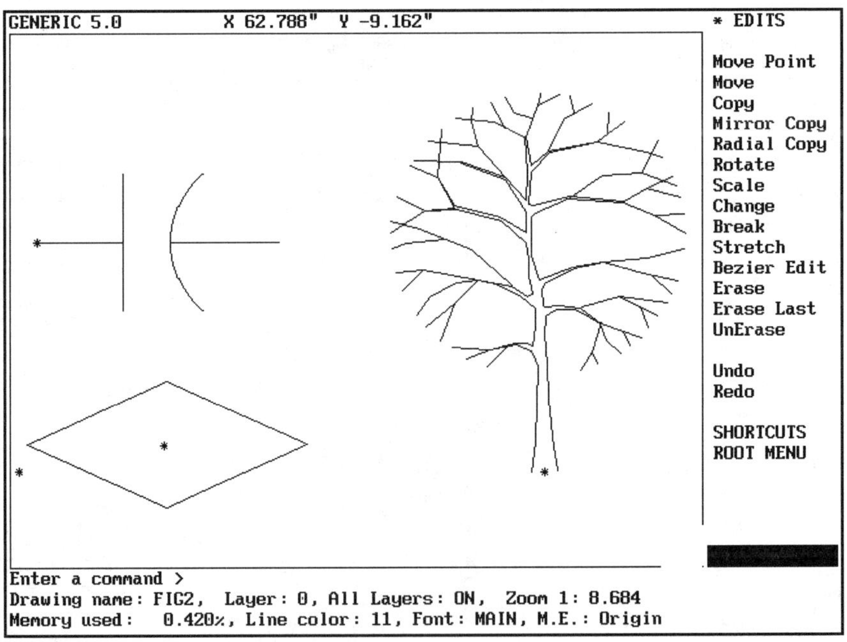

Figure 11.3: *Typical insert points.*

In certain situations, you may not want to have an insert point that is located on the component itself. Such an insert point is called an offset insert point. For example, a lavatory bowl should be located a certain distance from a wall to place it at a consistent distance from the front edge of a countertop. Depending upon the size of the lavatory component, the insert point may be located two, three, or four inches from the back edge of the bowl.

To locate the insert point in the example above, draw a line from the midpoint of the back of the bowl to a point that is two, three, or four inches away from the bowl. When creating the component, take care not to select this line. When the screen prompt asks for the insert point, type **SC**, for Snap to Closest Point, and pick the far end of the line. Since the insert point is several inches away, you can pick the wall line rather than guess the location of the bowl in the countertop. See figure 11.4 for a graphic representation.

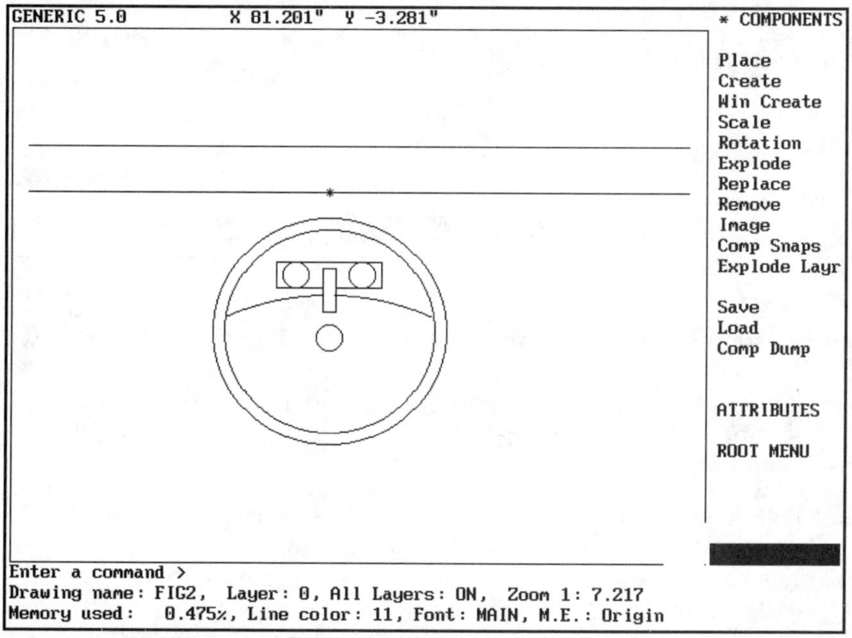

Figure 11.4: *Using an offset insert point to place a lavatory bowl.*

Rotating Components

In some drafting situations, a component can be correctly inserted in only one way. An example would be the decision symbol used in flow charting. In other drafting situations, only two rotations, 0 degrees and 90 degrees, are used 99 percent of the time. Most of the time, a capacitor is shown as horizontal or vertical. In architectural drafting, the symbol for a switch or outlet can be shown in any of 360 different degrees of rotation. It is generally shown as 0, 90, 180, or 270 degrees of rotation, however (see fig. 11.5).

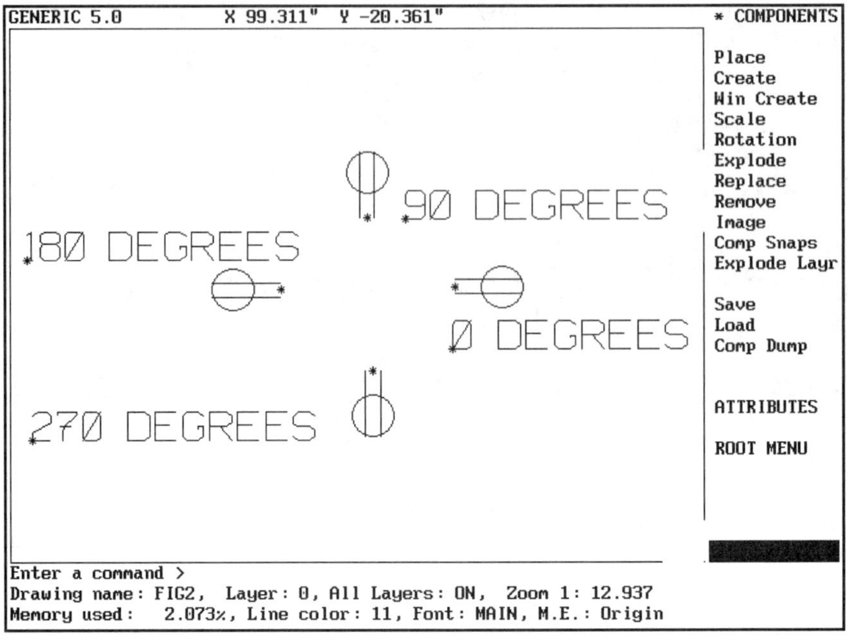

Figure 11.5: *Sample symbol rotation.*

Suppose you drew the switch component pointing toward 0 degrees and you drew the outlet pointing to 90 degrees. Then you created a door bell button pointing toward 270 degrees and you added a chime symbol rotated at another angle. As you add components, it becomes increasingly difficult to remember how much rotation to give each symbol.

This problem has a logical solution. If a symbol normally sits in a certain position, then draw it that way. Door front elevations and electronic components are examples; door fronts stand up and electronic components are usually horizontal. If the symbol is typically rotated in a variety of positions, however, such as the plan view switch symbol in architectural drafting, create the component pointing toward zero rotation (see fig. 11.6). When you insert the symbol later and want it to point upward, you can rotate it 90 degrees.

Naming Components

Component names can be up to eight characters long (Generic CADD can use 12-character component names internally, but when you save the component, the name is limited to eight characters). You should avoid bland or erratic names, however. It might seem logical to name a collection of chair components chair1, chair2, and so on (see fig. 11.7), but later you might become confused. Name the chairs specifically, such as arm chair, rocker, or lounge chair.

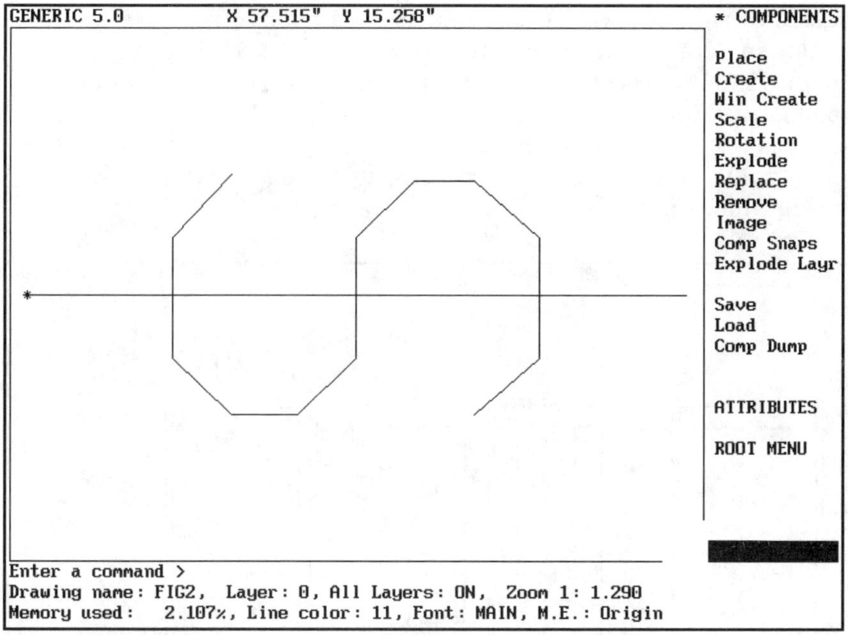

Figure 11.6: *Suggested drawing rotation of the switch symbol.*

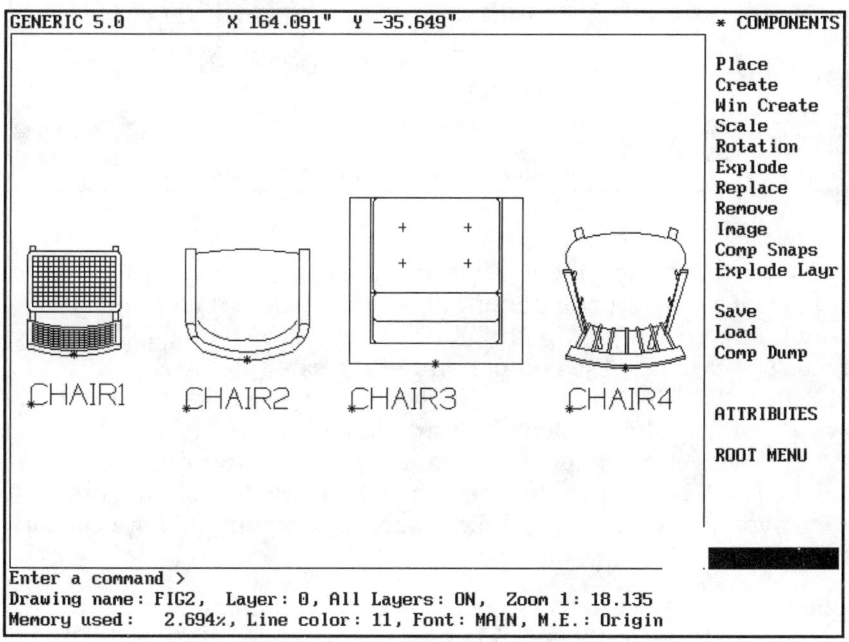

Figure 11.7: *Components with bland names.*

Using subtly different or random names can also wreak havoc. Suppose you have developed a collection of door elevation components and given them a variety of names (see fig. 11.8). This is worse than using bland names. You might not remember what a particular door is called, and then you'd lose the use of that component. Remember that over time you are likely to create hundreds of different components. You do not want to have to search through this multitude of names to find a door whose name you forgot.

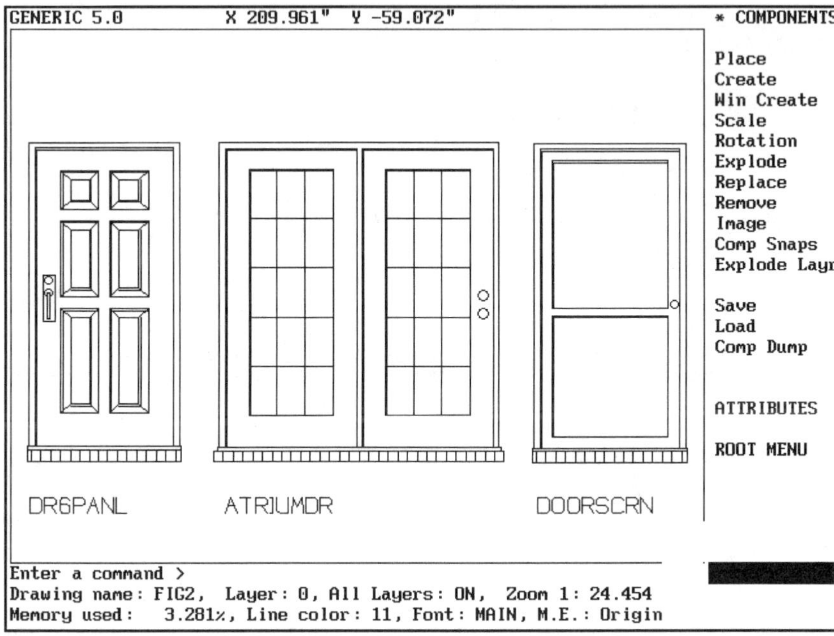

Figure 11.8: *Similar components with a wide variety of names.*

Here is a possible solution to the problem. First, decide whether the newly created component is going to be a current component or a permanent component. If it is a current component, use "JUNK" as the first four letters of the name, followed by up to four more letters to describe the component. Some examples are JUNKOUTL, JUNKSINK, JUNKWALL, and JUNKROOM. Days, weeks, or months from now, when you decide to "houseclean" your disk, you can issue the command **DEL JUNK*.***. Since you probably would not begin the name of a permanent component with JUNK as the first four letters, you would be deleting only unnecessary files. Or you could use any prefix to denote components for a certain project.

Permanent components can be named by type. All light components, for example, could have LIT as the first three letters of the name. Doors could start with DR, windows with WDW, and so on. This reduces the time spent finding a particular component.

If size is important, by all means use it in the title. A collection of single-hung window components could be named SH2030, SH2040, SH2050, and SH2060 (see fig. 11.9). These would be grouped by type and then by size, to allow you to recall them easily.

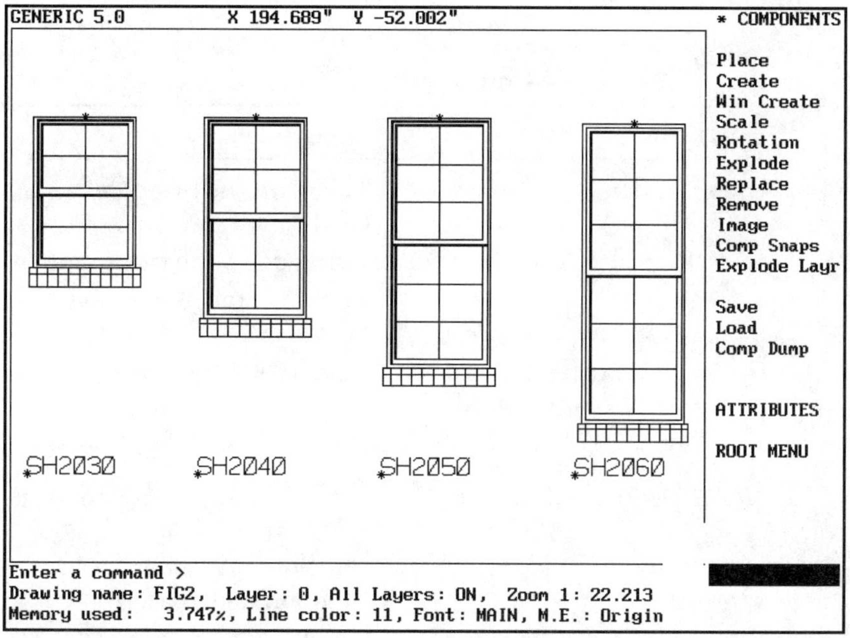

Figure 11.9: *Single-hung window components.*

Still, remembering the names of hundreds of components is extremely difficult. For now, write down the name of every component you create. A better solution—the use of special menus—will be presented in Chapter 16.

Using the Component Creation Commands

Once you've planned how you will insert, rotate, and name your components, you're ready to draw them. The next section will cover the component-creation commands.

Window Create (CW)

This two-letter command defines a portion of a drawing as a component. Place a window around the lines, arcs, circles, and so on that make up the component that you wish to create. A screen prompt will ask for the component name and request an insert point. It's that simple.

Remember that a component can be created from anything on the screen, as long as it is visible and on the active layer. If some of the entities possibly are on different layers, turn on the All Layers (AL) command.

In the following exercise, you will create a component (see fig. 11.10). Later, you will bring it back into a drawing and use the various component edit commands on it.

Creating a Component

Prompt	*Input*	*Description*
`Command`	**SG**	Turns on the Snap To Grid command
`Command`	**OR**	Turns off Ortho command
`Command`	**PR**	Turns Display Reference Points on
`Command`	Type **LI**; draw a line 4" down the screen and then 10" to right, then draw the line back at an angle to finish where you started	Starts the Line command
`Command`	**CW**	Starts the Window Component Create command
`Place window`	Place window around drawing	Identifies component
`Enter component name`	**JUNKSTUF**	Names component
`Enter component reference point`	**SM**	Snaps to midpoint (see fig. 11.11)
`Midpoint of`	Pick vertical line	Sets reference point
`<RET> to complete`	Press Enter	Finishes command

You should check to see if your component was really defined by selecting the Component Place command from the component menu. A list of components appears on the side menu. Do you see JUNKSTUF? You have now created a component that points to zero rotation. You will see later how simple this makes insertion rotation.

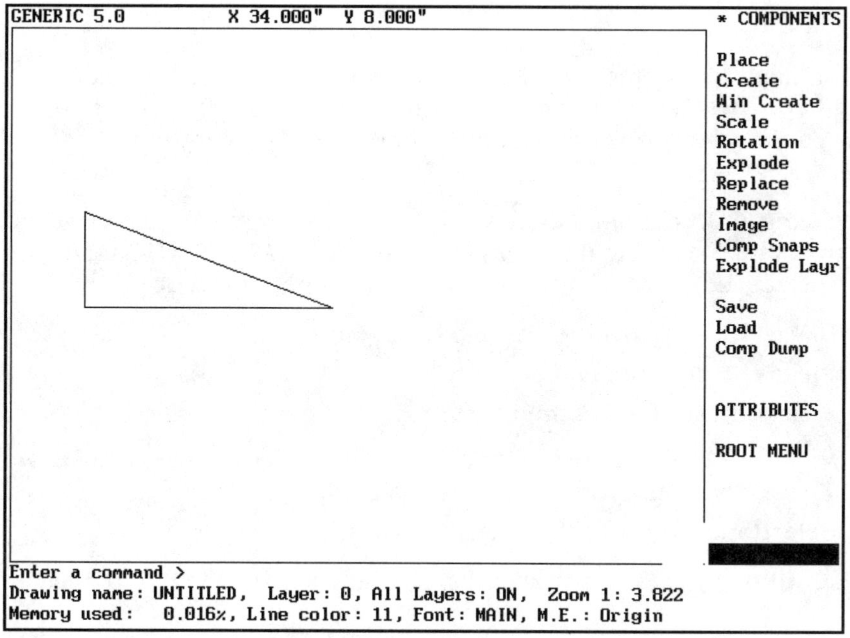

Figure 11.10: *JUNKSTUF component.*

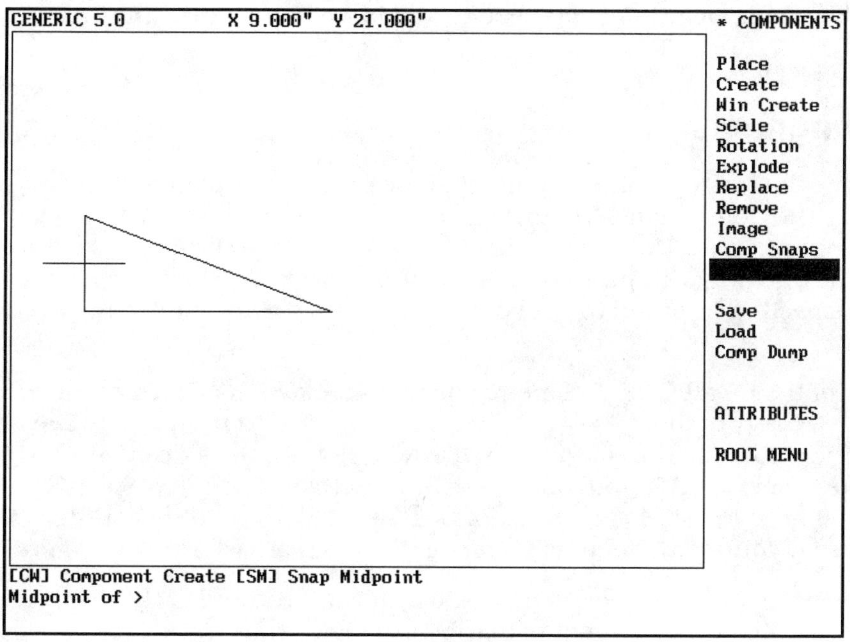

Figure 11.11: *Snapping to midpoint of JUNKSTUF.*

Component Create (CC)

This command is almost identical to the Window Component Create (CW) command; the only difference is how objects are selected. With Window Component Create (CW), you could select only one window at one time. This method is fast but also limiting.

The Component Create (CC) command allows entities to be selected in various ways. Once you select the Component Create command from the COMPONENTS menu, or type **CC**, you can select the objects you want to use in a component by typing:

Window	Places window around entities for a component.
Object	Picks entities for a component.
la**Y**er	Picks entities for a component by layer.
Drawing	An entire drawing becomes a component.
Last	The last selection becomes part of a component.
Filter	Selection is initiated by characteristics.

You can deselect entities by pressing Ctrl and typing any of the above boldfaced letters.

You may use any combination of selection devices and deselection devices. Once you are satisfied with what is shown on the screen, press Enter. The entire selection is ready to be a component; all you need to add is a component name and an insert point.

Saving Components

You might assume that once you have completed the Create Component Window (CW) command or the Component Create (CC) command, your new component is installed on your hard drive. This is not true; it is only stored in the current drawing. If you quit the drawing without saving, the component will be lost. Even current components need to be saved to the hard drive if they are to be used in another drawing.

Near the bottom of the COMPONENTS menu you will see Save (SA,C). Once Save has been selected, the prompt is `Select component from side menu`. Use the second mouse button to pick the component JUNKSTUF from the side menu. Once this is done, Generic CADD 5.0 offers a default path and name to accept or alter. This prompt is `Save file as >> C:\CADD5\CMP\JUNKSTUF`. Press Enter to accept this line; now your component is stored on the hard drive for future use.

The alternate method of saving components is to wait until the end of the drawing session and save all the new components to the hard disk at one time. This is efficient, but you might forget to do this and then lose all your work. The command to save all the components is Component Dump (CD). This command calls up the new components one at a time and gives you the option to save each one or not.

Working with Components

Now that you have made a component, it's time to start working with it. You can place, scale, and rotate a component. Components can be treated as individual entities by using the Component Image, Component Explode, Explode Object, and Component Snap commands.

Placing Components

Generic CADD 5.0 inserts a component with the Component Place (CP) command. Once this command is picked from the COMPONENT menu or typed in, a prompt asks you for the component name. You can respond by typing the name or picking it from the side menu. If the component is not listed on the side menu because it is in another subdirectory, pick the Look On Disk option to find the subdirectory and then the component name. The final prompt to answer concerns the insert point. This location can be picked on the screen or typed in as coordinates from the keyboard.

Sometimes it is easy to accurately pick a spot on the screen to locate a component. Other times, this amounts to a stab in the dark because you cannot accurately place what you cannot see, especially if you cannot remember the location of the insert point. To solve this problem, Generic CADD 5.0 has the Object Drag (OD) command. When this is turned on, an outline of the component appears on the screen with the cursor locked on the component's insert point. As you move the cursor across the screen, the component drags with it. This allows you to see exactly where you wish to place the component. Once the component is properly positioned, pick that point on the screen.

Inserting a Component

Prompt	*Input*	*Description*
`Command`	**OD**	Turns Object Drag on
`Command`	**CP**	Starts the Component Place command
`Select component from side menu`	**JUNKSTUF**	Picks a component to place
`Enter placement location`	Drag in JUNKSTUF	Drags in a component (see fig. 11.12)
`Type [IP] to change insert point`	**IP**	Changes insert point (see fig. 11.13)

Inserting a Component —continued

Prompt	*Input*	*Description*
`Temporarily place component`	Pick a point on the screen	Parks the component temporarily while you change the insert point
`Enter new location of reference point`	**SC**	Snaps to closest point
`Closest point to`	Pick top of vertical line	Sets temporary reference point
`Enter placement location`	**SC**	Snaps to closest point
`Closest point to`	Pick right end of line in original drawing	Places component (see fig. 11.14)

Component Load (LO)

This command loads components stored on the hard drive into the current drawing. If you want to load certain components or all of the components in a particular subdirectory, you can tag multiple components to load in the File Selector.

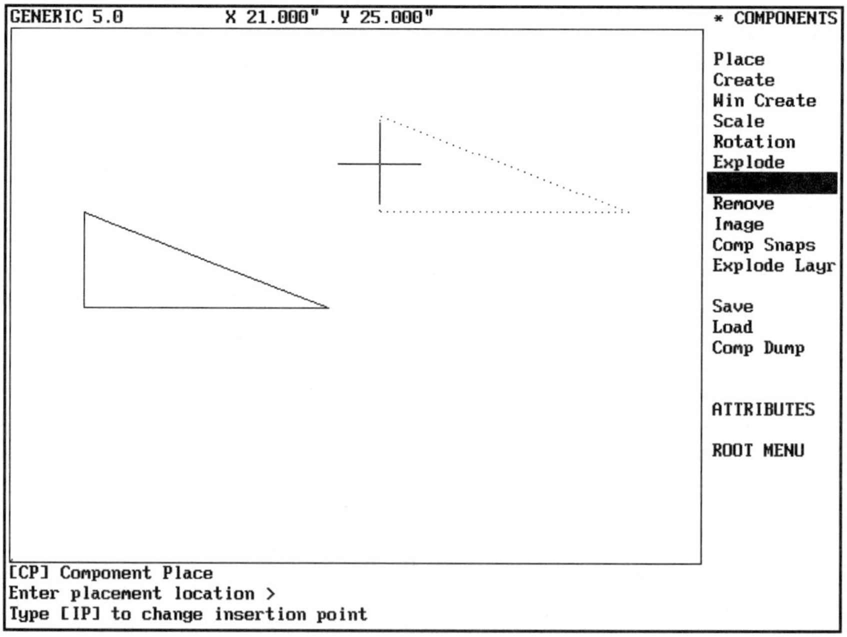

Figure 11.12: *Dragging in JUNKSTUF.*

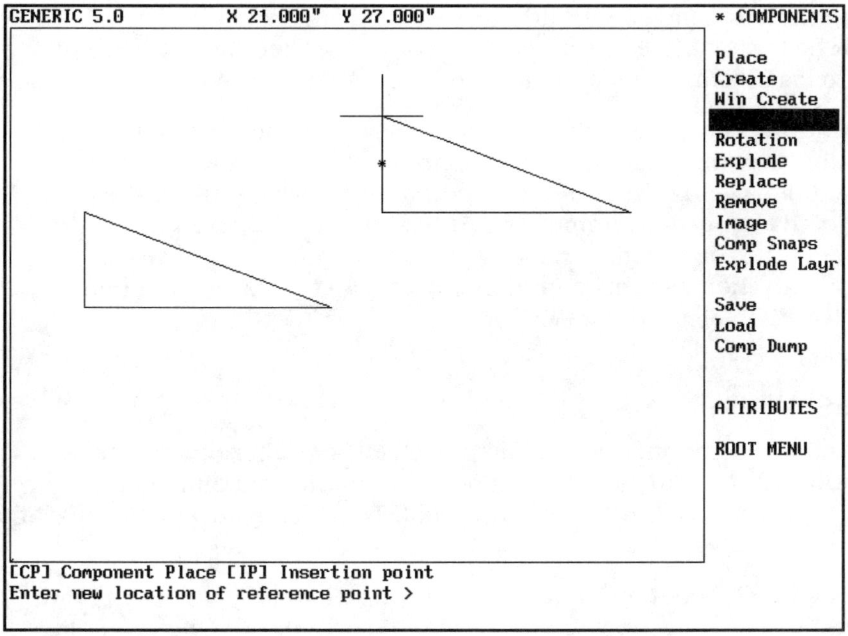

Figure 11.13: *Changing insert point.*

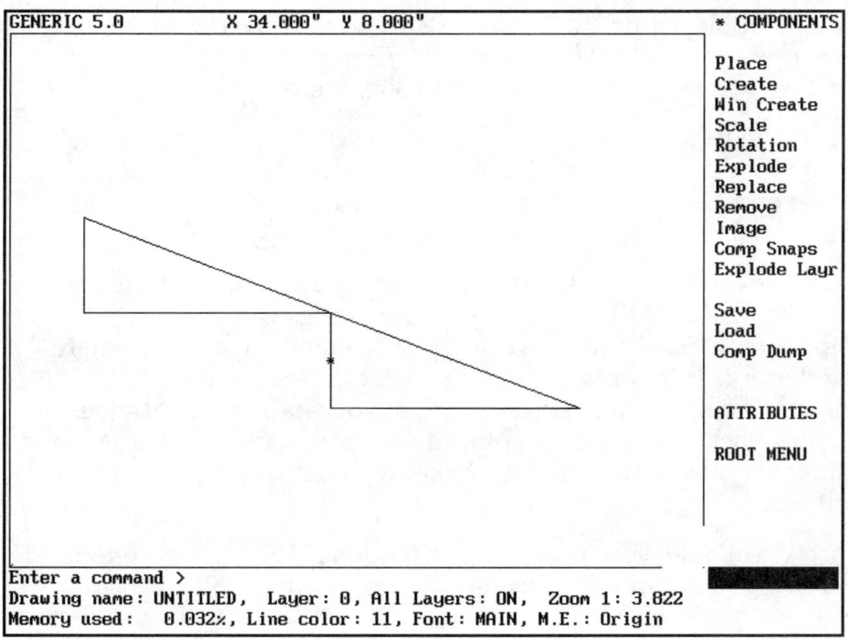

Figure 11.14: *Your screen should look like this.*

You start the Component Load command by selecting Load from the COMPONENTS menu, or by typing **LO**. The Component option is Selection. You can pick the component to load from the side menu or by typing it in.

From a practical standpoint, this command is not useful if you need to bring a component into the drawing—using the disk search option of the Component Place (CP) command makes more sense. This command works in two instances: in a script file that loads needed components into a drawing to save time, or to put the components that are needed in a certain drawing into their own subdirectory. You can then use this command to load all of those components at once, if you use the File Selector.

Component Scale (CZ)

This command enables components to be displayed either larger or smaller than the original component. In addition, it has a powerful additional dimension: X (horizontal) and Y (vertical) scaling can be changed. This alters the appearance of a component.

The Component Scale (CZ) command has many applications. If you drew 1" widgets but now need 1 1/4" widgets, you would use this command. Once you place the stretched widget, explode it and make a new component. In an architectural drawing, for example, you might have a plan view 1-foot wide window as a component. Your next application requires a 3-foot wide window. Type **CZ**. At the prompt for X scaling, enter "3". At the prompt for Y scaling, enter "1". Type **CP** and place the window. It is now rescaled to three feet wide.

The Scale command can be selected from the COMPONENTS side menu or by typing **CZ**. The first prompt asks for an X scaling factor. The second prompt asks for a Y scaling factor and uses your newly entered X scaling factor as the default. This can be accepted by pressing Enter, or another value can be entered.

Several rules should be remembered about this command. If you rescale a component by giving it different X and Y factors, interesting things will happen if you explode that component. Circles and arcs that were stretched to ellipses will return to normal circles and arcs, while stretched lines will remain stretched. This command must be used before placing a component you wish to alter. It does not work after the fact by rescaling a component that already exists in the drawing. Scaling factors always apply to the original component size. If you use negative numbers, you will get a mirror image.

The following exercise will take you through the Component Scale (CZ) command. Refer to figure 11.15 if you doubt the outcome of what you got in the drawing.

Using the Component Scale Command

Prompt	*Input*	*Description*
`Command`	Select Scale from Components menu	Displays the component scale
`Enter new X scale`	**2**	Doubles the X scaling (1.000)
`Enter new Y scale`	**.5**	Halves the Y scaling (2.000)
The Y scaling default matches the X scaling factor you inputted.		
`Command`	From side menu, pick "Place"	
`Select component from side menu JUNKSTUF`	Press Enter	Selects JUNKSTUF
`Enter placement location`	Pick a point in drawing (see fig. 11.15)	Places component
Notice how radically different the component looks now. After issuing the Undo command, you may want to repeat this exercise several times. Try using negative numbers and combinations of negative and positive numbers. When you are through experimenting, remember to reset the X and Y factors to 1.		
`Command`	**OO**	Undoes the last command
`Command`	**CZ**	Resets the scale command
`Enter new X scale (2.000)`	**1**	Resets X to normal
`Enter new Y scale (1.000)`	Press Enter	Accepts new default value

Component Rotation (CR)

This command rotates components around its insert point. It is used prior to selecting the Component Place (CP) command. Once a value is set, all future placements of components will have this rotation until it is changed. Changing the rotation back to 0 restores the original rotation.

The Component Rotation command is found on the COMPONENTS menu. The prompt will ask for a change in component rotation. It limits rotation from negative 360 degrees to positive 360 degrees. Negative numbers rotate the component clockwise, while positive numbers rotate it counterclockwise.

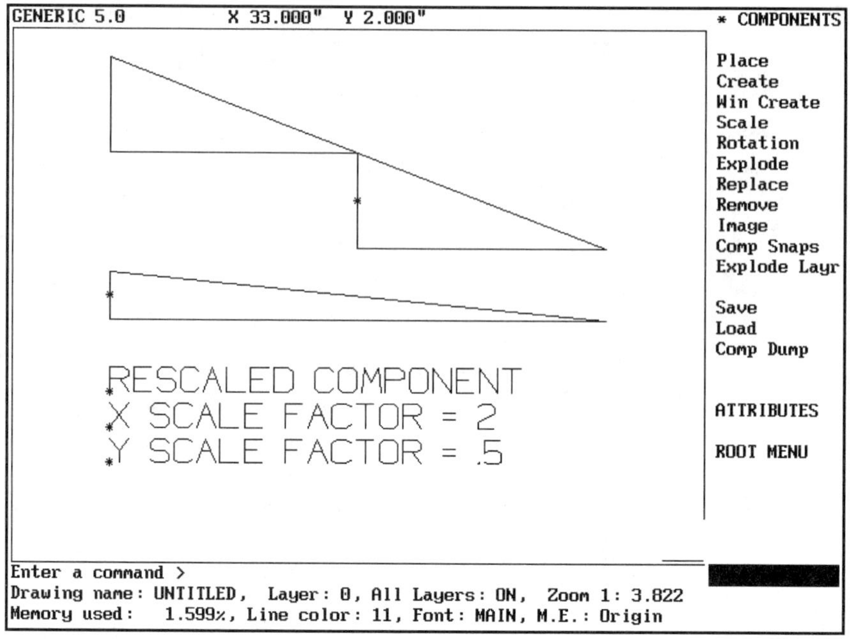

Figure 11.15: *JUNKSTUF with changed scale factors.*

If a component already exists in the drawing and you want to change its rotation, you have two choices: erase the component, use the Component Rotation command, and then reinsert the component; or use the Rotate (RO) command on the EDITS menu.

In the following exercise, JUNKSTUF will be rotated.

Using the Component Rotate Command

Prompt	*Input*	*Description*
`Command`	From Components side menu, pick Rotation	Displays the Component command
`Change component rotation (0.000) Limits -360.000 to 360.000`	**90**	This rotates JUNKSTUF 90 degrees
`Command`	From Components, side menu, pick Place	Places a component
`Select component from side menu >> JUNKSTUF`	Press Enter	Selects JUNKSTUF

Using the Component Rotate Command—continued

Prompt	*Input*	*Description*
`Enter placement location`	Pick a point in drawing (see fig. 11.16)	Places component
`Command`	**OO**	Undoes last command
`Command`	**CR**	Resets the rotation command
`Change component rotation (0.000) Limits -360.000 to 360.000`	**0**	Restores JUNKSTUF to its original orientation

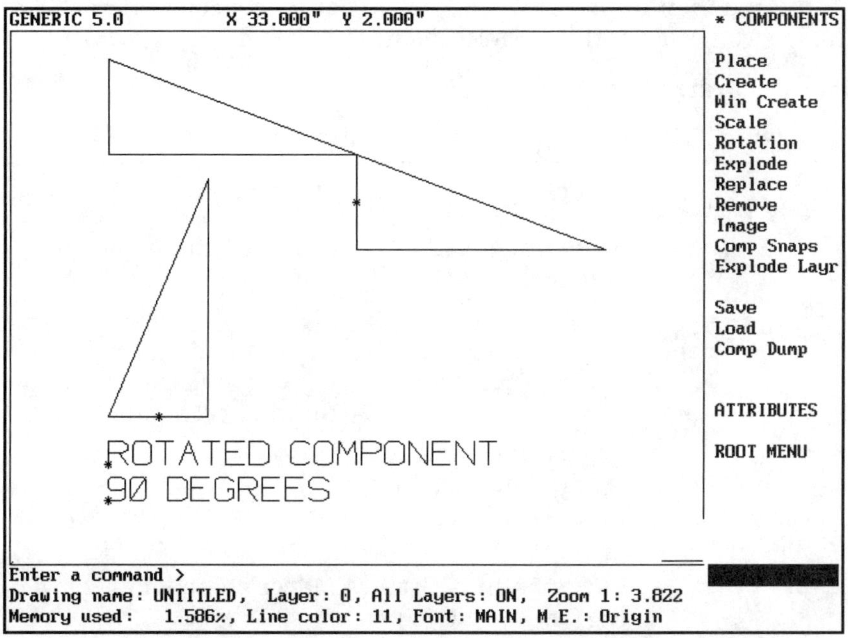

Figure 11.16: *JUNKSTUF with 90-degree rotation.*

Treating Component Parts as Individual Entities

Exploding components has both good and bad effects. The individual entities that make up the component can be edited. Exploded components, however, take up more memory than non-exploded components and cannot be globally edited. This will be demonstrated later in the chapter.

Three commands can be used to explode a component from a single entity into individual entities: Component Image (CI), Component Explode (CE), and Explode (EX). Another command, Component Explode Layer (XY), controls which layer exploded components go to. The Component Snaps command allows a component to be snapped to as if it was exploded.

Component Image (CI)

The Component Image command explodes components as they are inserted. No reference point and no attributes exist. The individual entities appear on the layer on which they were created unless you use the Explode Destination Layer (XY) command.

The command is a toggle. If it is on, components come into the drawing already exploded. If it is off, components come into the drawing as whole components. You then select Image from the COMPONENTS menu.

These points will be illustrated in the following exercise.

Using The Component Image Command

Prompt	*Input*	*Description*
`Command`	From Components side menu, pick Image	Starts Component Image command
`* [CI] Place component image is ON`		Components placed in the drawing from now on will be exploded
`Command`	From Components side menu, pick Place	
`Select component from side menu >> JUNKSTUF`	Press Enter	Selects JUNKSTUF
`Enter placement location`	Pick a point in drawing (see fig. 11.17)	Places component
The component's reference point did not appear on the screen. This indicates that the component is exploded into individual entities. In the next exercise on Component Explode (CE), you will test editing exploded and unexploded components. For now, complete the exercise.		
`Command`	**OO**	Undoes the last command
`Command`	**CI**	Toggles Component Image (CI) off

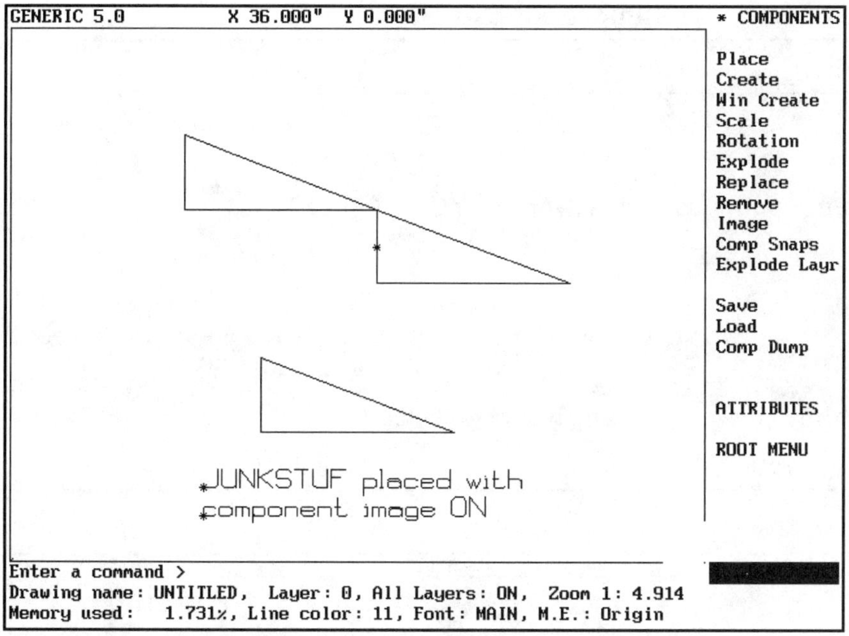

Figure 11.17: *JUNKSTUF placed with image on.*

Component Explode (CE)

The Component Explode command works on individual components. It returns them to individual drawing parts, allowing them to be edited.

You may pick Explode from the COMPONENTS menu, or type **CE**. The prompt will ask you to pick the component that you wish to explode. The Explode Destination Layer (XY) command helps control which layer the exploded parts will revert to.

In the exercise that follows, you will use the Erase command (ER) to test unexploded and exploded components.

Using the Component Explode Command

Prompt	*Input*	*Description*
`Command`	**ER**	Invokes the erase command
`Window, Object...`	**O**	Object
`Pick object`	Pick JUNKSTUF (see fig. 11.18)	Notice that the entire component is selected
	Press Esc	Cancels the command
`Command`	From Components, side menu, pick Explode	Starts the Component Explode command

Using the Component Explode Command

Prompt	*Input*	*Description*
`Pick object`	Pick JUNKSTUF	Selects the component (see fig. 11.20)

Now the reference point is gone, as you can see in figure 11.19.

Prompt	*Input*	*Description*
`Command`	**ER**	Starts Erase command
`Window, Object...`	**O**	Object
`Pick object`	Pick JUNKSTUF	Selects the component (see fig. 11.20)

Now see figure 11.21. Only one line has been selected.

Prompt	*Input*	*Description*
`Window, Object...`	Press Esc	Cancels the command

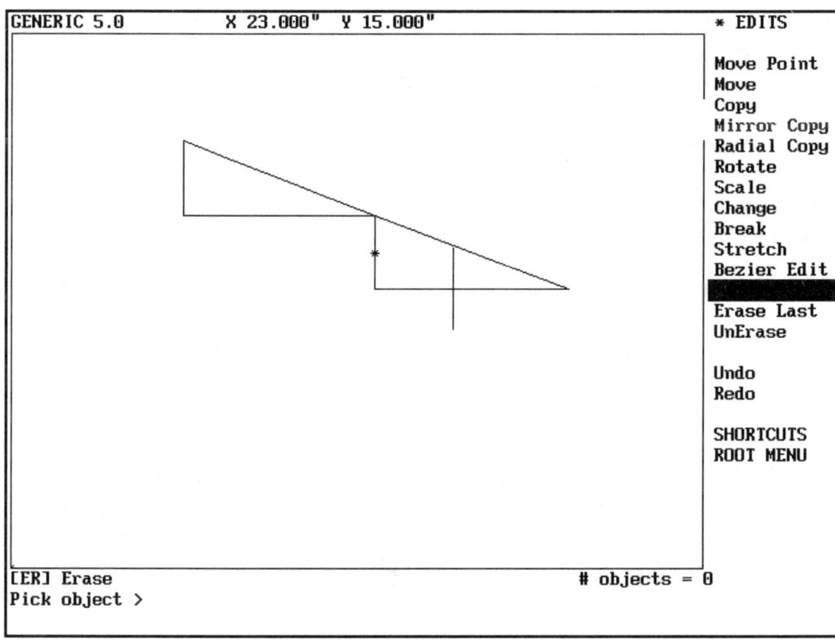

Figure 11.18: *Getting ready to pick a line on JUNKSTUF.*

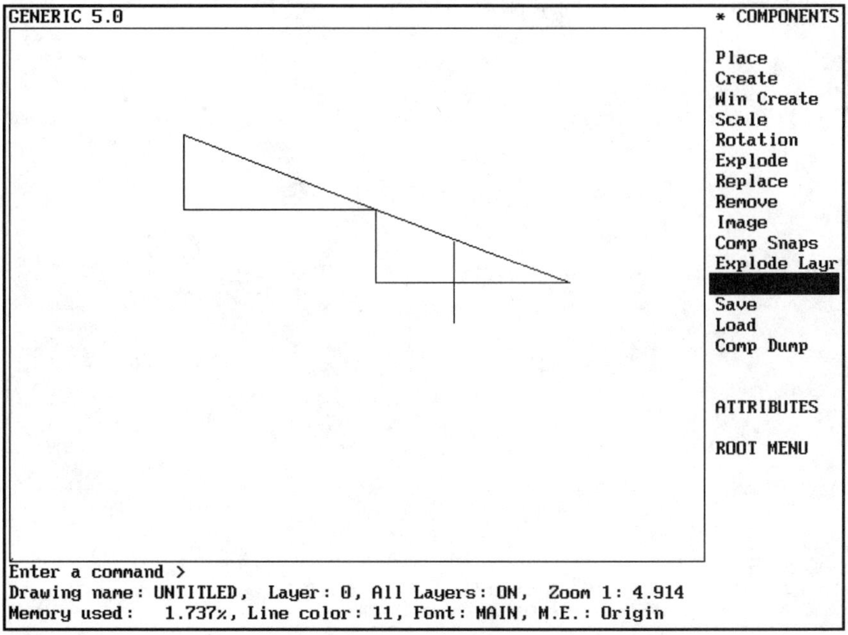

Figure 11.19: *The reference point is gone.*

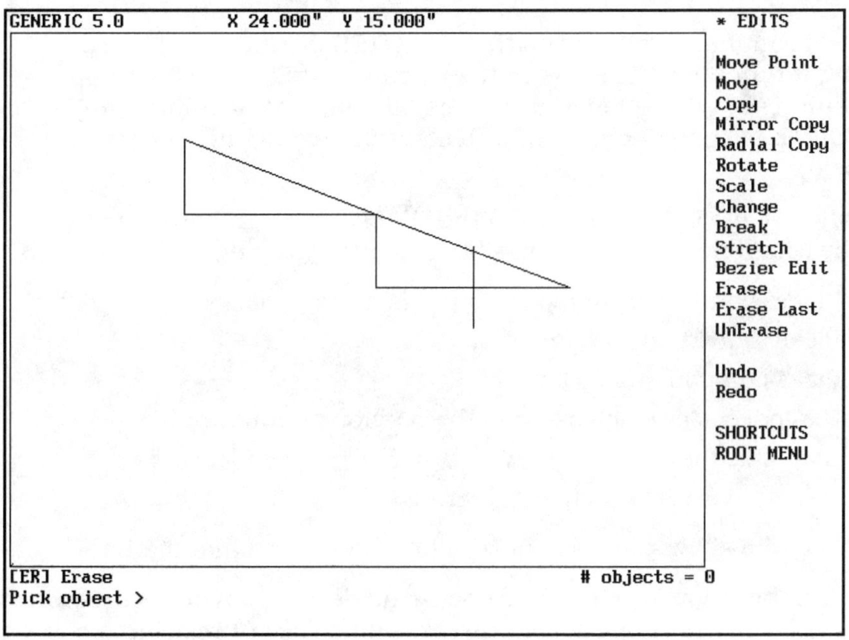

Figure 11.20: *Picking an object to erase.*

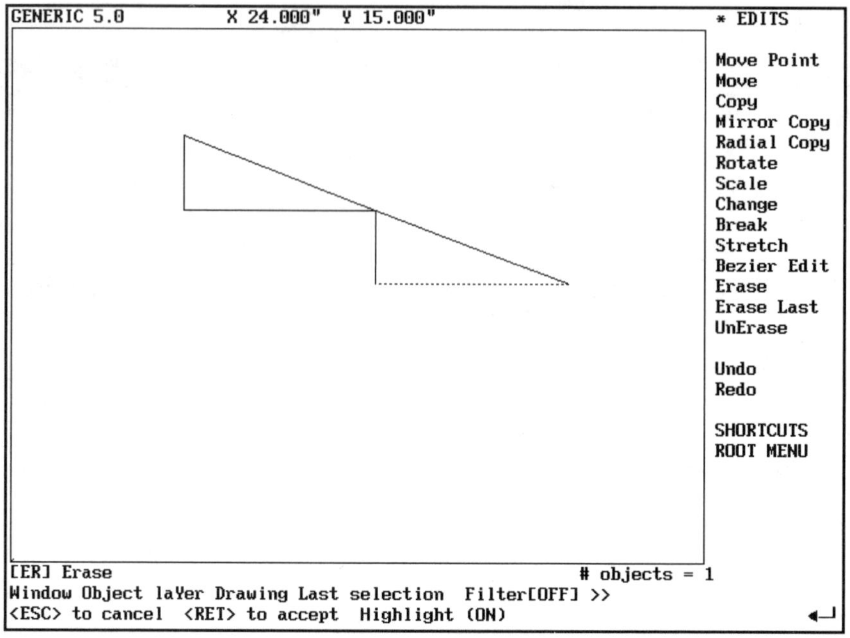

Figure 11.21: *Only one line of JUNKSTUF was selected.*

Explode Object (EX)

The Explode Object command is found on the UTILITIES menu, or can be initiated by typing **EX**. It functions the same as the Component Explode (CE) command, with two differences: it explodes attributes, dimensions, text lines, and text characters in addition to components, and you can select components using the options shown below.

You start the Explode Object command from the UTILITIES menu, or by typing **EX**. You select the components that you wish to explode by typing:

Window	Places window around component(s) to explode.
Object	Picks individual components.
la**Y**er	Picks components by layer.
Drawing	Explodes *everything* listed in the previous paragraph.
Last	Explodes the last selection.
Filter	Selection is initiated by characteristics.

Press Ctrl and any of the above letters to deselect entities using that method.

You may use any combination of selection devices and deselection devices. Once you are satisfied with what is on the screen, press Enter. The entire selection is exploded.

Component Snap (GC)

Normally, you only can snap to the reference point of a component. This can be a distinct disadvantage. To avoid exploding a component, Generic CADD 5.0 offers another option—the Component Snap command.

This toggle command is under the COMPONENTS menu, listed as Comp snaps, or it can be accessed by typing **GC**. Once it is turned on, all snaps work on the component.

The following exercise exhibits this useful command.

Using the Component Snap Command

Prompt	*Input*	*Description*
`Command`	Pick Place from the Components side menu	
`Select component from side menu >> JUNKSTUF`	Press Enter	Selects JUNKSTUF
`Enter placement location`	Pick a point in drawing (see fig. 11.22)	Places component
`Command`	**LI**	Starts the line command
`Starting point`	**SC**	Snaps to closest point
`Closest point to`	Pick a point on JUNKSTUF	Tries to use snap (see fig. 11.22)
Notice that no matter where you picked JUNKSTUF, the line jumps to the reference point. See figure 11.23.		
	Press ESC	Stops Line command
`Command`	From Components side menu, pick Comp snaps	Starts Component Snaps command
`* [GC] Component snaps is ON`	Press Enter	Components will now accept all the object snaps
`Command`	**LI**	Starts the line command
`Starting point`	**SC**	Snap to closest point
`Closest point to`	Pick a point on JUNKSTUF	Uses the snap (see fig. 11.24)
`Enter next point on line`	It worked! (see fig. 11.25)	Snaps to a point
	Press Esc	Cancels line command

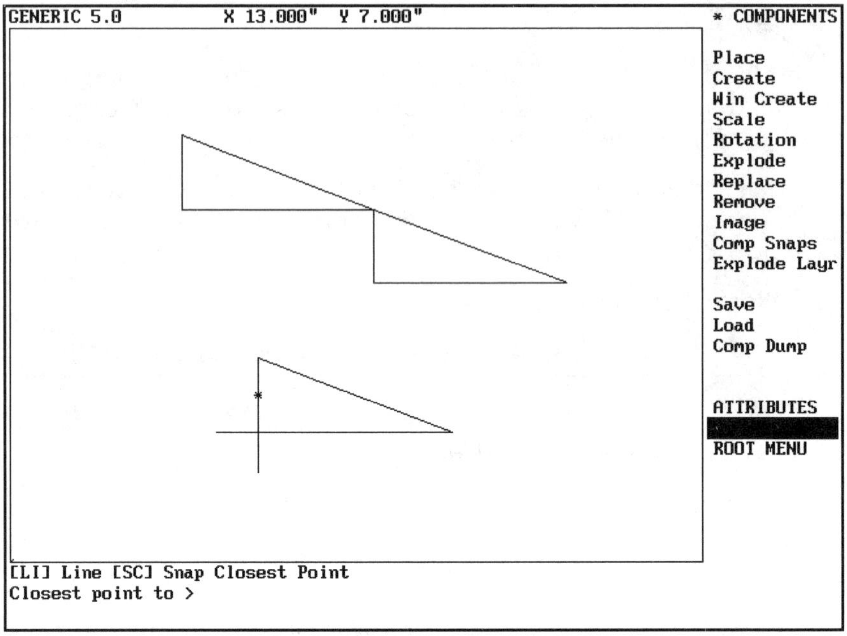

Figure 11.22: *Trying to pick a point on JUNKSTUF.*

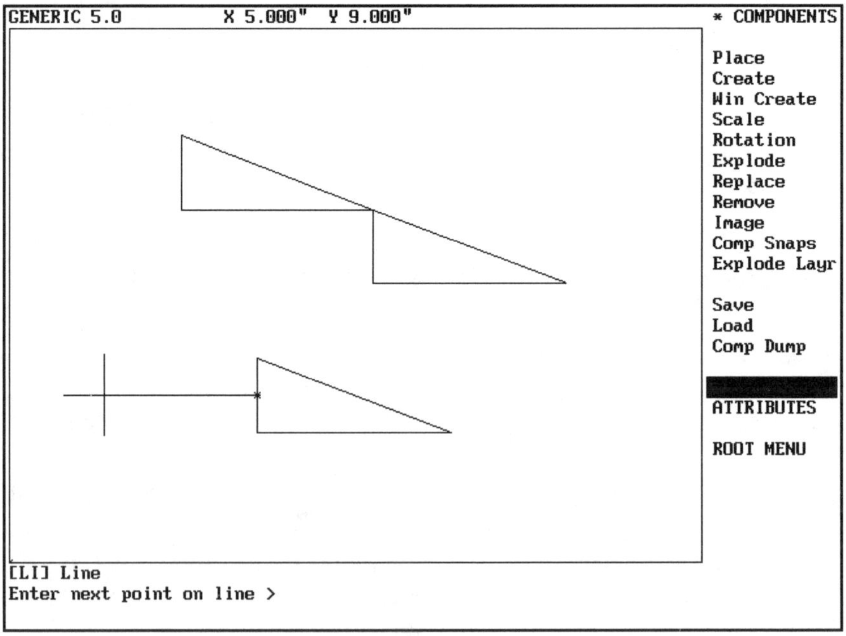

Figure 11.23: *The line has snapped to the reference point.*

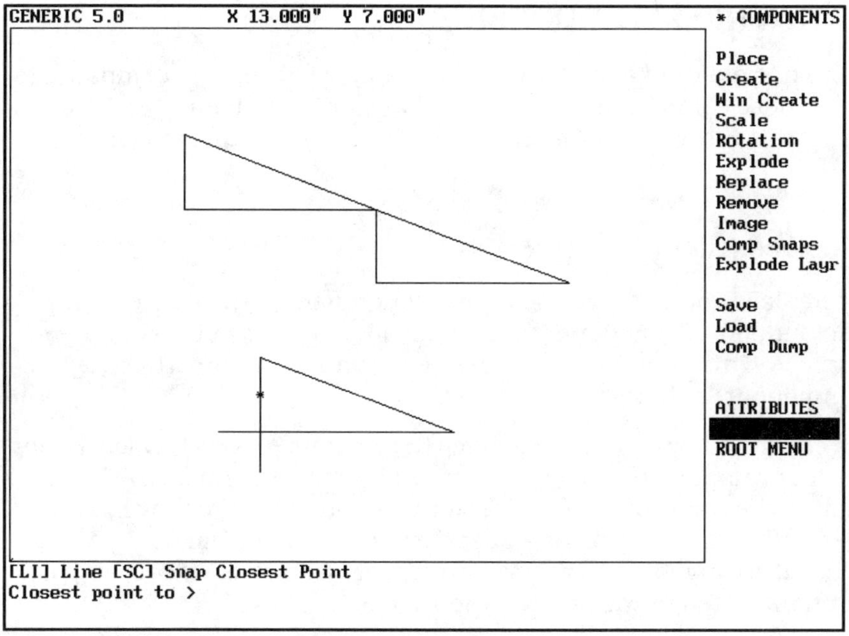

Figure 11.24: *Trying to pick an endpoint of JUNKSTUF.*

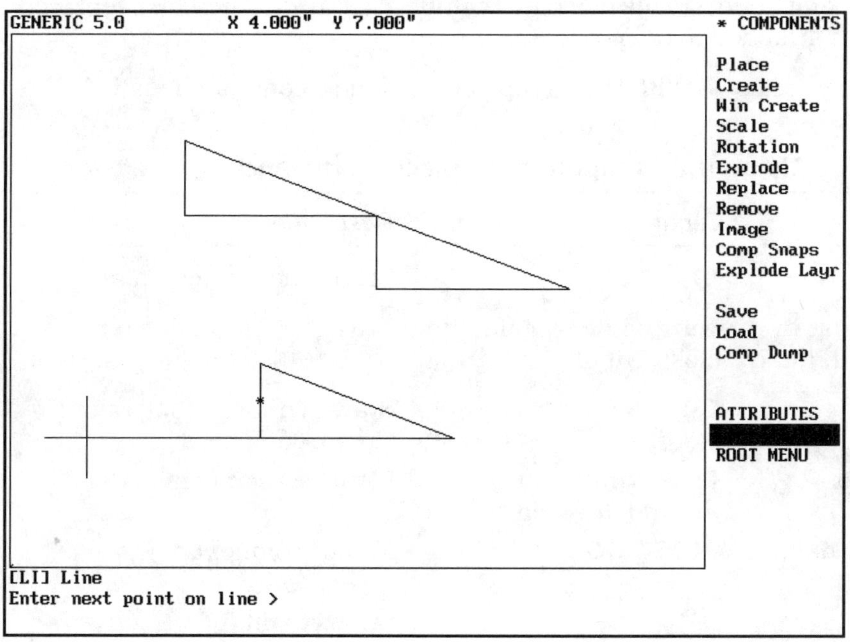

Figure 11.25: *It worked!*

Removing Unwanted Components

Generic CADD 5.0 has a pair of edit commands to remove or replace components within a drawing. These commands can work globally or by individual selection. The one exception is that these commands will not work with exploded components.

Component Replace (CN)

The Component Replace command replaces one component with another component. It can select individual components, or it can globally select every component of a certain type. This allows you to redefine a component, an attribute attached to a component, or both.

You initiate this command by selecting Replace in the COMPONENTS menu or by typing **CN**. The first prompt asks which component you wish to replace. The second prompt asks for the name of the replacement component. You now have a choice to replace all the components or a specific one. Selection can be by **W**indow, **O**bject, la**Y**er, **D**rawing, **L**ast or **F**ilter. You can also deselect by pressing Ctrl and one of the options listed in the previous sentence.

The selected components are replaced by the new components at the reference point. The new components take on all the characteristics of rotation, scale, and layer of the old components. This does not include attributes. These are replaced by the attributes attached to the new components.

In the following exercise, JUNKSTUF is replaced by a new component called JUNKTOO.

Using the Component Replace Command

Prompt	*Input*	*Description*
`Command`	**LI**	Starts the Line command
Create a square by drawing a line by going up 5", to the right 5", down 5", to the left 5" and, finally, closing it off.		
`Command`	**CW**	Starts Window Component Create command
`Place window`	Place window around drawing	Identifies component
`Enter component name>`	**JUNKTOO**	Names component
`Enter component reference point`	**SM**	Snaps to midpoint

Using the Component Replace Command—continued

Prompt	*Input*	*Description*
`Midpoint of`	Pick left vertical line	Sets reference point
`<RET> to complete`	Press Enter	Finishes command
`Command`	**CN**	Starts the Replace command
`Select component from side menu`	Pick JUNKSTUF	Selects component to be replaced
`Select component from side menu`	Pick JUNKTOO, replacing JUNKSTUF	Selects replacement component (see fig. 11.26)
`<RET>Replace all - S for selection`	Press Enter JUNKSTUF components	Accepts replacing all

Your screen should look like figure 11.27. The second JUNKSTUF was not replaced because it was exploded.

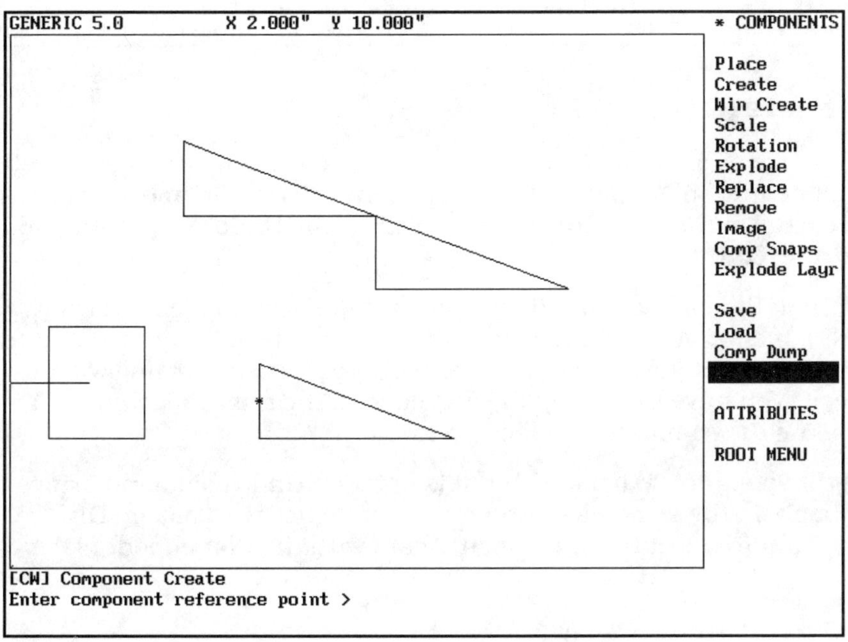

Figure 11.26: The new component JUNKTOO.

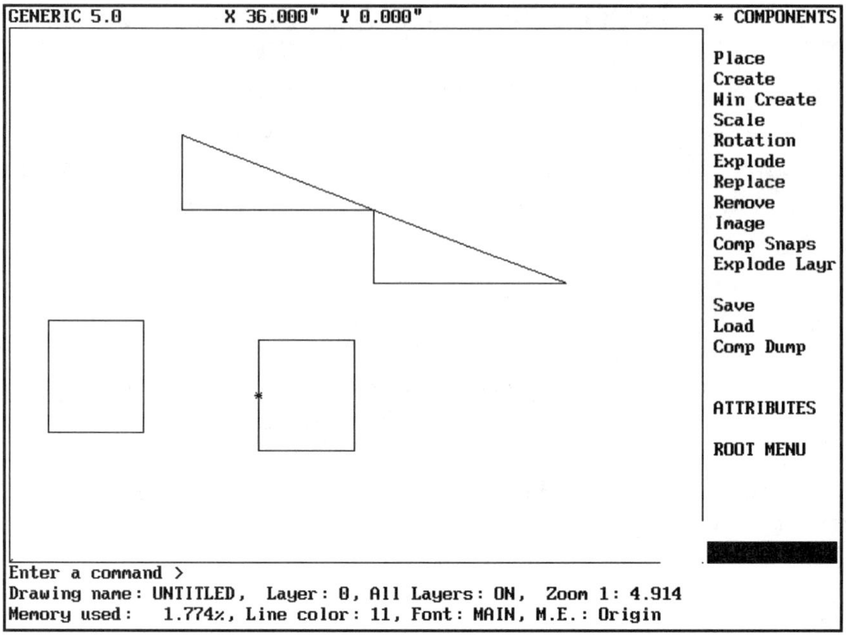

Figure 11.27: *JUNKSTUF replaced with JUNKTOO.*

Component Remove (CX)

The Component Remove command erases all the unexploded components, as well as the component definition. No part of the component will remain in the drawing, although it still exists on the hard drive if you saved it. The Undo (OO) command, however, will bring everything back.

Start the Component Remove command by typing **CX** or selecting Remove from the COMPONENTS menu. The first prompt asks for the name of the component to be removed. You can select it from the side menu or type it in. A warning will appear on the screen. You have the option to proceed with the removal by typing **Y** for yes, or cancelling the command by typing **N** for no.

The warning might appear catastrophic, but it is not. The Undo command brings the component back. In the worst case, you may need to use the Look on Disk option when you want to select the component again with the Component Place (CP) command.

JUNKTOO is removed in the following exercise.

Using the Component Replace Command

Prompt	*Input*	*Description*
`Command`	**CX**	Starts the Component Remove command
`Select component from side menu`	Pick JUNKTOO	Selects component to be removed
`** Warning ** the component "JUNKTOO" will no longer exist! Remove the component? (Y/N)`	**Y**	JUNKTOO is removed (see fig. 11.28)

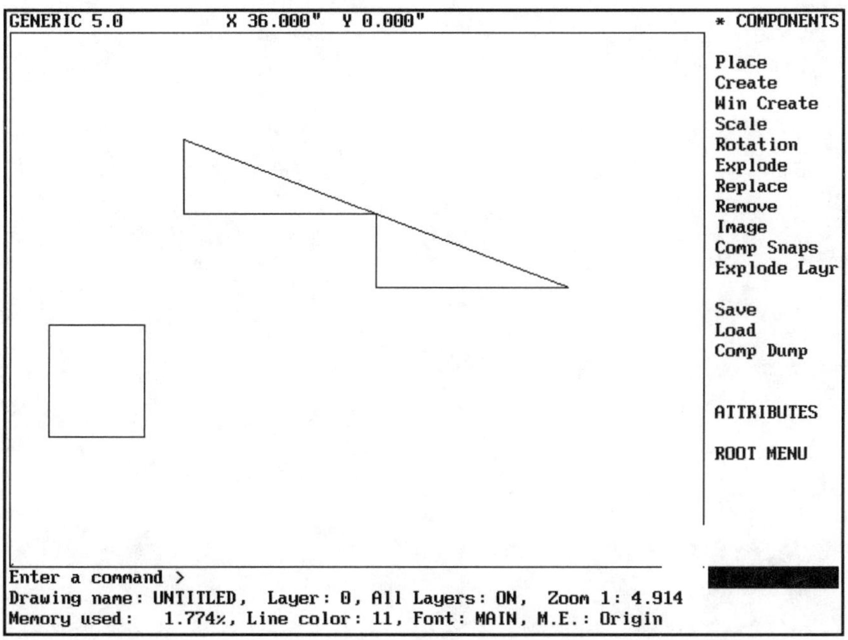

Figure 11.28: *JUNKTOO is replaced.*

Summary

This chapter covered a lot of ground on CADD's most useful tool—the component. In the beginning, illustrations and explanations covered what makes a good component and what makes a not-so-good component. With that background, you created a component with the Window Component Create (CW) command.

Bringing a component into a drawing has many variables that you can use to your advantage. Scale and rotation can be used a number of ways to produce a variety of effects.

Exploded components have advantages and disadvantages. You explored most of these with special exercises that you tackled throughout this chapter. After that you covered the Remove and Replace commands. Finally, you went through some practical uses for the Component Load (LO) command.

Components will be discussed again in Chapter 14, where you will learn to supercharge them with attributes. Read that chapter carefully, because it will enhance what you learned in this chapter.

12

Drawing Enhancements

The drawings used so far in this book have served their purpose, but they won't win any awards for elegance. This chapter shows you two ways to add visual interest to your drawings, by using hatches and fills. *Hatches* are repeating patterns of fine lines; *fills* are blocks of solid color.

Hatches and fills are often overlooked by the beginning CADD user as an unnecessary waste of time and computer resources. But the experienced CADD user has a different view. The thoughtful use of hatch patterns in a drawing can provide additional visual clues to the nature of the objects in the drawing. Many professionals have been trained to apply hatching manually to a drawing and already know the value of using hatch patterns in their designs.

Using Hatch Patterns

Hatches are repeating patterns of fine lines. They can be used to define certain objects, to provide shading, or to add interest to a drawing. Adding hatching to a drawing by hand is a tedious task but becomes relatively simple in Generic CADD 5.0. Hatching involves only a few rules and limitations.

All the commands for using hatches and fills are found on the HATCH/FILL menu.

Choosing a Hatch Pattern

Nineteen hatch patterns are supplied with Generic CADD 5.0, as illustrated in figure 12.1. In addition, several third-party vendors sell additional hatch patterns. You can even design your own, as detailed in the *Generic CADD 5.0 User Guide.*

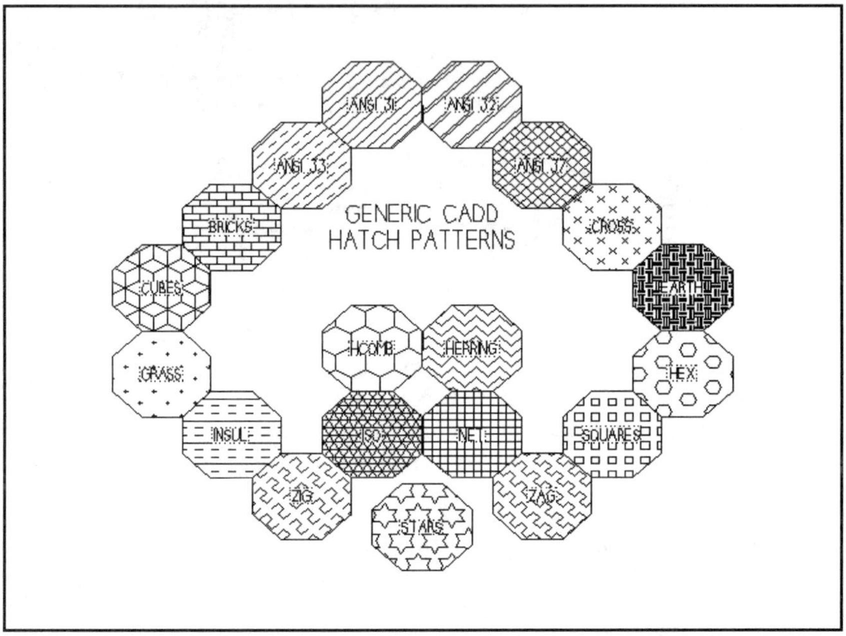

Figure 12.1: *Nineteen hatch patterns are included with Generic CADD 5.0.*

Some of the hatch patterns shipped with Generic CADD conform to professional standards (the ANSI hatches, for example). Most of the others represent patterns commonly used in many drafting environments.

Don't worry about which Line Type or Line Width to use for hatching. Generic CADD always uses Line Type and Line Width 0 for hatches. The color is not governed by the Line Color command, but by the Hatch Settings (HS) command, described below. Once a hatch pattern is drawn, it is considered one single object. Each hatch pattern placed in a drawing has its own reference point. To edit the hatch pattern (erase, rotate, rescale, and so on), select it by selecting only the reference point, as if it were a component.

Choosing Hatch Settings (HS)

The Hatch Settings (HS) command is used to adjust all the factors that affect hatches. To use the command, type HS at the prompt or select Hatch Settings from the HATCH/FILL menu. Some video display systems (including the one used to illustrate this book) cut off the last two or three letters of Hatch Settings in the menu.

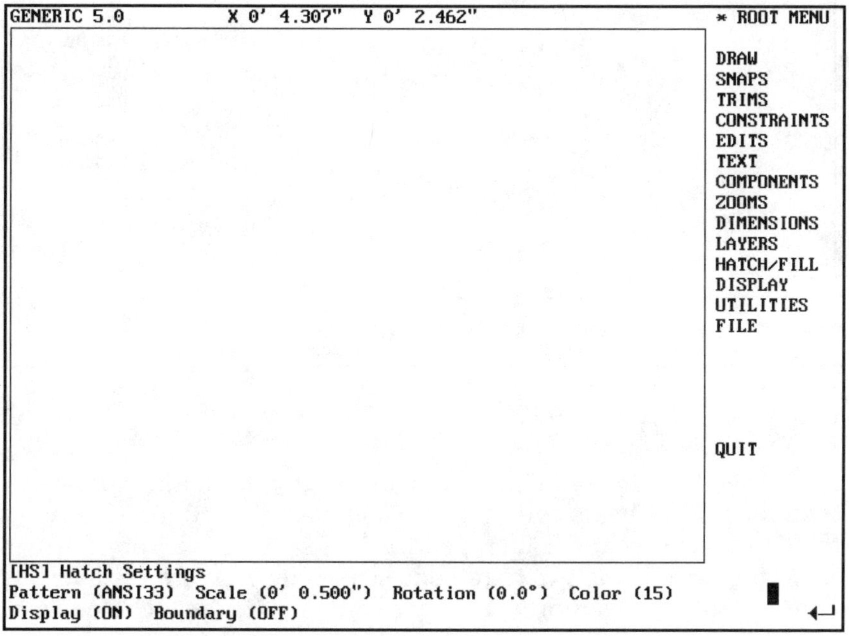

Figure 12.2: *The Hatch Settings command options.*

Select Hatch Pattern

The most important option in the Hatch Settings command is the name of the pattern. From the Hatch Settings list in the prompt line, type **P** to select a pattern. The list of patterns available appears in the menu on the side of the screen. Either type the name of the pattern or select it with the menu bar.

When you configured Generic CADD for the first time, a subdirectory was assigned for the storage of hatch patterns. Unless you changed it, that directory is C:/CADD5/HCH. Generic CADD looks in this directory when you select a pattern. If you acquire new hatch patterns, be sure to add them to this directory. If you don't, use the File Selector to view other directories containing hatch patterns.

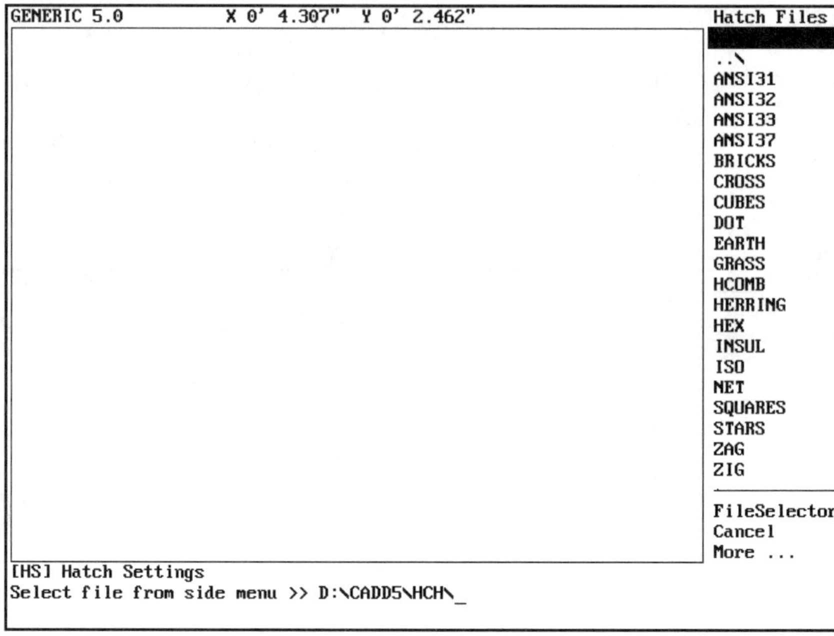

Figure 12.3: *Generic CADD's available hatch patterns.*

Select Hatch Scale

The Scale option controls the size of the individual elements that make up the hatch pattern. Examine any of the hatched objects shown in this chapter, and you see that all the hatches are made from repeating line segments arranged in various patterns. Figure 12.4 shows two hatch patterns at four different scale factors. The hatches are inside 1" squares. In these samples, the best choice for a scale factor is 1/4 (.25) because the drawings cover such a small area. The best scale factor for a drawing that covers an acre may be 10 or even 40 or more, depending on the look you need to achieve. Experiment in a drawing by hatching a small area first, to be sure the hatch scale is to your liking, before using it throughout the drawing.

Select Hatch Rotation

The default rotation for hatch patterns is 0 degrees, but the alignment of patterns in a drawing can be changed using the Rotation option. Figure 12.5 shows four possible rotations for two hatch patterns. Most of the time a rotation of 0 degrees is fine, but the option to change exists if you need it. As with everything else in Generic CADD, positive numbers refer to counterclockwise rotation; negative numbers refer to clockwise rotation.

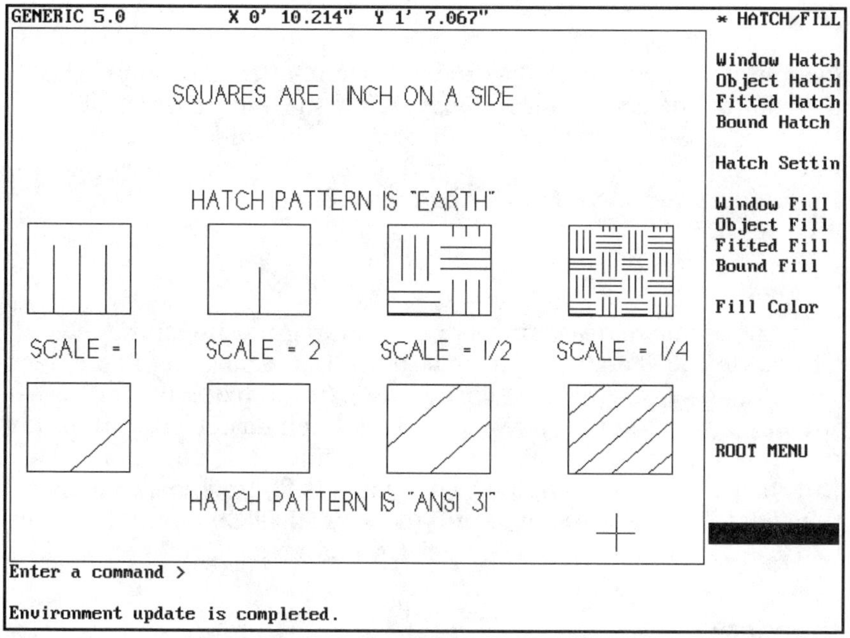

Figure 12.4: *How hatch patterns fill an area depends on the scale.*

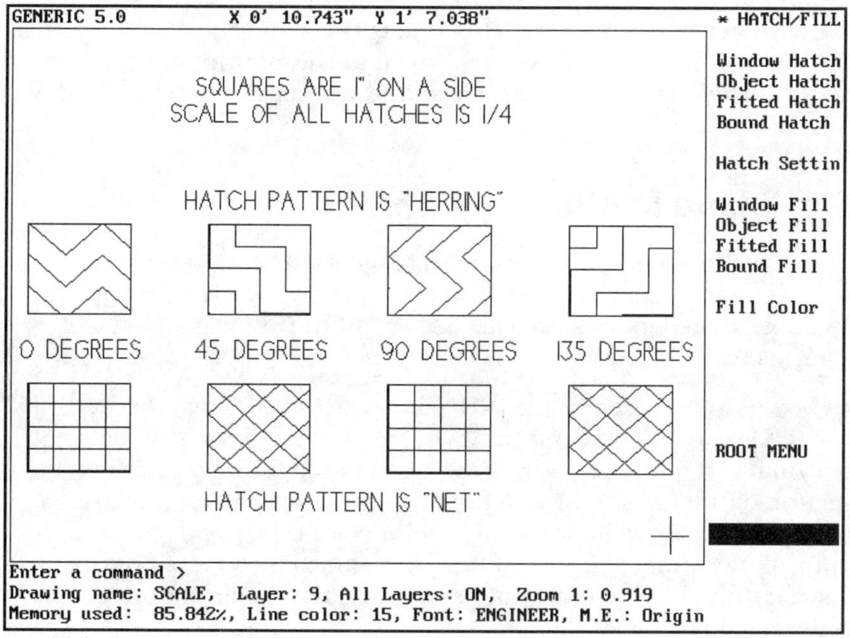

Figure 12.5: *Hatch patterns may be set at any angle of rotation.*

Select Hatch Color

To set the color of a hatch pattern, type **C** from the Hatch Settings prompt. You may choose from all of the line colors normally available in Generic CADD. For most systems, there are 16 colors; for a few high-performance video systems, 256 colors are available. If you print or plot to a color device, make sure the color you choose for hatching is one your output device can reproduce.

Select Hatch Display

Hatch patterns take more time to draw and redraw than regular lines; they redraw at about the same speed as text placed with the Text Character Placement (TC) command. If you have a large drawing with several hatch patterns and considerable text, you may want to set Display to off. The hatch pattern is still part of the drawing, and its reference point is still visible if you have reference point display turned on, but the pattern is not visible. The display of hatch patterns also can be set using the Fast Redraw (FA) command in the UTILITIES menu. If either command is used, the other command recognizes the change.

Select Hatch Boundary

When Generic CADD places a hatch pattern inside a boundary, it draws a line representing the boundary of the pattern. This line is the same color as the hatch pattern. If the line distracts from the drawing, type **B** at the Boundary option of Hatch Settings to shut the display off. This command is a toggle; to turn the display on again, type **B** again.

Choosing a Hatching Method

Generic CADD offers four methods when hatching objects. The method you choose depends on the items to be hatched and their proximity to other objects. The method you choose also depends on whether or not the objects you select come together to form closed boundaries.

When you draw a box using the Rectangle (RE) command, CADD draws four lines. The endpoints of each line touch the endpoints of another line, and the rectangle forms a closed boundary. If, however, you draw a box using four overlapping lines, the intersection of the lines defines a box, but the box is not considered a closed boundary for the purposes of hatching. (Solid color fills, to be considered after the discussion of hatching, generally follow the same rules.) It is possible to successfully place a hatch pattern inside an area defined by "open" boundaries. The technique is described below in the discussion of Fitted Hatches.

Some Generic CADD users do not take the time to draw with precision. They "eyeball" the connection of lines, for example. This lack of concern for precision can cause problems when hatching. If the endpoints of two lines come close but do not connect, Generic CADD may miscalculate the boundary of the object being hatched and do an incomplete job. To be considered a closed boundary, the lines that form an object must meet at the endpoints. It is still possible to add hatching to "open boundary" objects, but it is more time-consuming, and the likelihood of user error is higher.

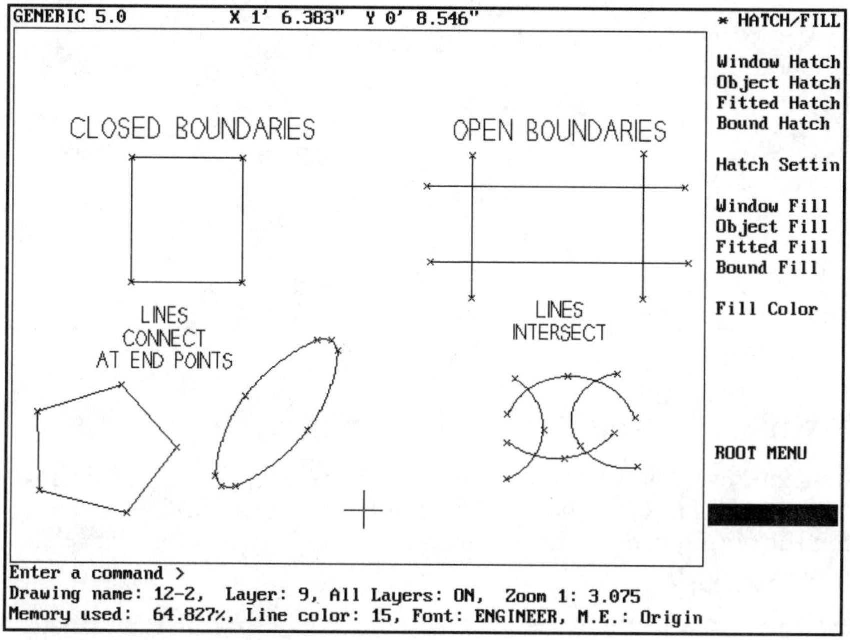

Figure 12.6: *Closed boundaries must meet the endpoints.*

To be hatched, an object must have been created with straight lines, circles, arcs, or ellipses (either true or construction). The Rectangle (RE) and Regular Polygon (RP) commands create objects using straight lines, so anything drawn using these commands can be successfully hatched. An ellipse drawn using the construction method also can be hatched, since it is defined using arcs. One exception to the above rule is that an object created using Bézier curves can be hatched using only the Window Hatch (WH) command. The object may be completely created from Bézier curves or from a mix of Bézier curves and other lines. The boundaries must be closed (the endpoints must connect). Under no circumstance can an object made from complex curves (CV) be hatched.

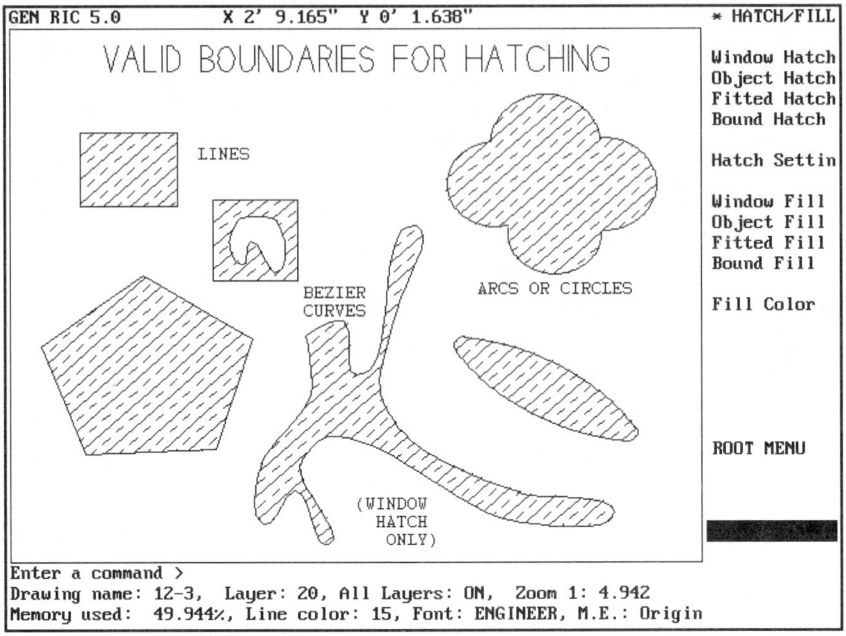

Figure 12.7: *Objects made from lines, circles, and arcs can be hatched.*

Window Hatch (WH)

The Window Hatch command is the easiest of the hatch commands to use and is the most commonly-used of the four hatch commands. But it can only be used successfully when the boundaries of the objects being hatched are closed (the endpoints of all lines connect).

When the window is drawn around items to be hatched, Generic CADD starts at the window and works its way in, identifying valid boundaries. If a second set of boundaries is found inside the first, hatching stops at the second boundary. This makes it possible to create hatches with open areas inside. This method was used to hatch the rectangle with the Bézier curves inside it in figure 12.7. Figure 12.8 shows how the Window Hatch command can identify several sets of boundaries, stopping and restarting the hatching as it works from the outside in. Window Hatch can identify multiple sets of boundaries if they are nested (each inside the next) and if they are otherwise valid boundaries for hatching.

However, Window Hatch is easily confused if the lines are not distinct as well as securely connected to each other. Although all the lines in the chart of hatch patterns in figure 12.1 form valid boundaries, Window Hatch cannot successfully hatch the chart. The sides of the octagons that are adjacent cause Window Hatch to become confused as to where one boundary stops and another begins. Object Hatch (OH) was used instead.

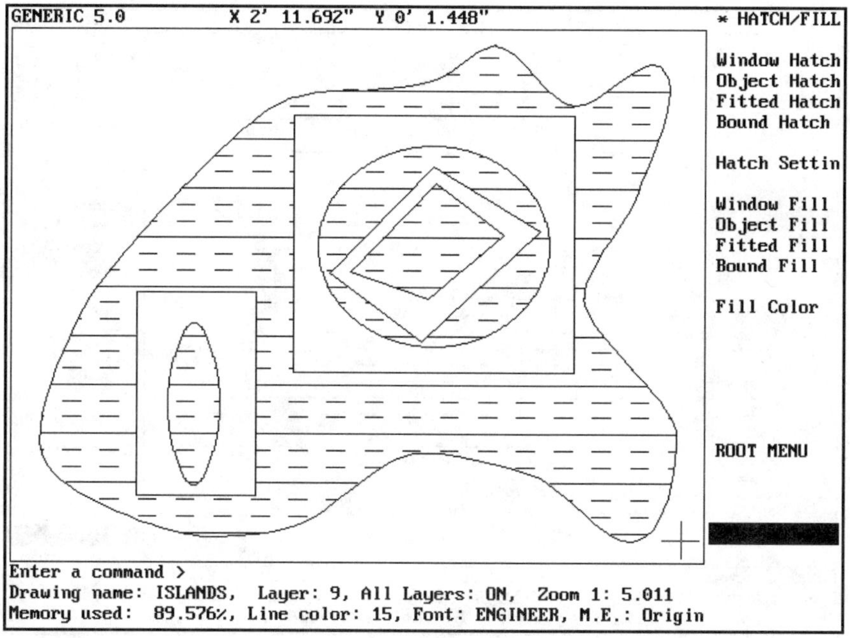

Figure 12.8: *Window Hatch can identify nested sets of boundaries.*

Object Hatch (OH)

Object Hatch can define an area to be hatched by selecting the lines one by one, instead of having Generic CADD determine the boundaries (as it does when Window Hatch is used). The main difference between this command and Window Hatch is that each line, arc, or other boundary must be selected. The entities used to create the boundaries must still follow the rules. Since the boundaries are individually selected, it is possible to hatch areas that would be left unhatched if Window Hatch were used. Figure 12.9 hatches the same objects as figure 12.8, but the hatching is different because only the circles, arcs, and Bézier curves have been selected as boundaries, not the straight lines.

As mentioned above, Object Hatch was used instead of Window Hatch to hatch the objects in figure 12.1. Although all the boundaries are legal, and there is a rectangle around each title (which would have kept the hatching off the text), Window Hatch became confused by the overlapping boundaries. For each hatch pattern, Object Hatch was used. The eight lines of each octagon and the four lines of each rectangle surrounding the text were selected at a time. To select the lines, the cursor was placed close to, but not directly on, each line. As illustrated in figure 12.10, one side of the crosshair intersected the object being selected, but the center of the crosshair did not touch the line. When lines overlap, as they do in figure 12.1, use this method of selection to ensure that the line closest to the others you are selecting is chosen.

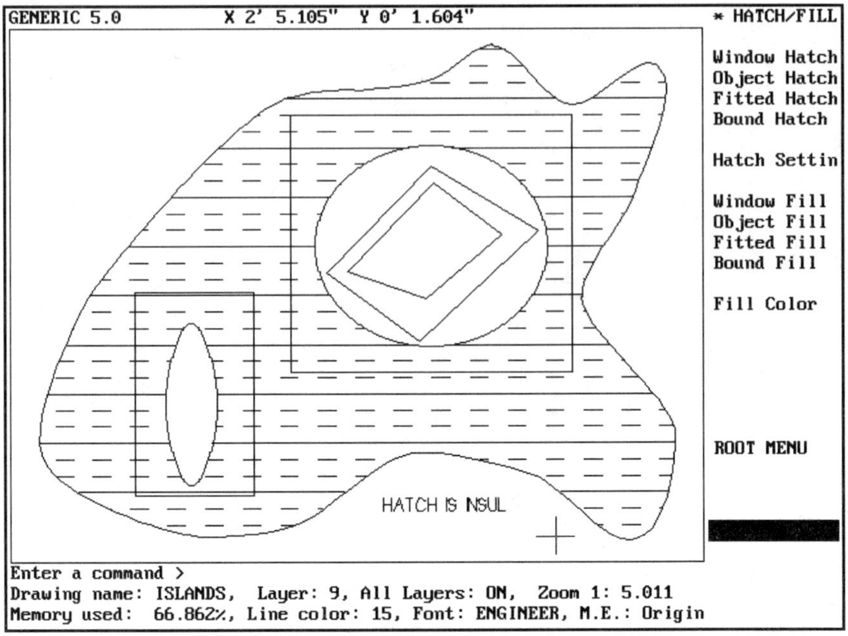

Figure 12.9: *Use Object Hatch to overwrite selected objects.*

As objects are selected, the counter used in the selection process in editing commands also appears. If you know how many lines there are in an object, this helps you to be sure you have selected them all. Another key to selecting all the required lines is to watch the screen for the appearance of construction points. As each line, arc, and so on is selected, its construction points appear (unless construction points are already on display for all objects). Making sure that every segment of a Bézier curve is selected is much easier if you check to see that construction points for every part of the curve are showing as you move along it. Always select the objects for Object Hatch in a circular fashion, from the outside in.

Fitted Hatch (FH)

If you take care as you draw, and create connecting boundaries, Window Hatch and Object Hatch works in most situations. But situations may still arise when you need to hatch an area that is not well-defined. Use the Fitted Hatch command in these situations.

Fitted Hatch works like Object Hatch. Objects that form the boundary for the hatch are selected one by one. The difference is that Generic CADD looks for intersections as it analyzes the boundaries you have selected and places the hatch accordingly.

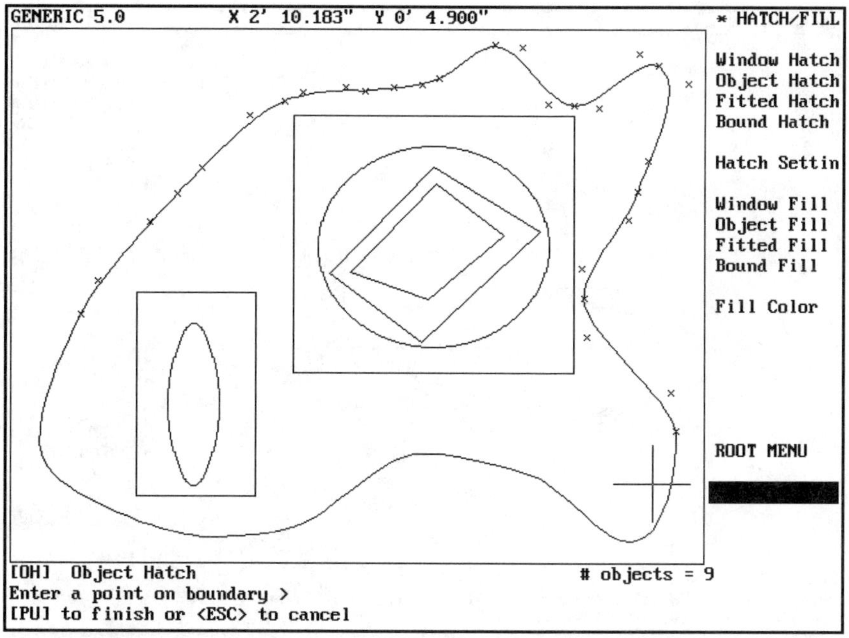

Figure 12.10: *Selecting the boundaries in a circular pattern.*

As you select objects for the boundary, place the cursor along the midpoint of an object, not near the endpoint or where one line intersects another (see fig. 12.11). If you select an object that you do not want to include in the definition of the boundary, press Ctrl-Backspace to remove the object from the list of selected items. Each time you press Ctrl-Backspace, the last object selected is deselected; you can continue deselecting items back to the start if you like.

As with the other hatch commands, only straight lines, circles, and arcs may be used with the Fitted Hatch command (Bézier curves, remember, are valid boundaries only if Window Hatch is used). At least three objects must be selected for the Fitted Hatch command to work. For example, this means that a circle, by itself, is ineligible for the Fitted Hatch command. If you need to hatch the space between two intersecting arcs, as illustrated in figure 12.12, use Object Break first to break one of the arcs into two. So that the boundaries are still connecting, use the same point for both the first and second selection in the Object Break command.

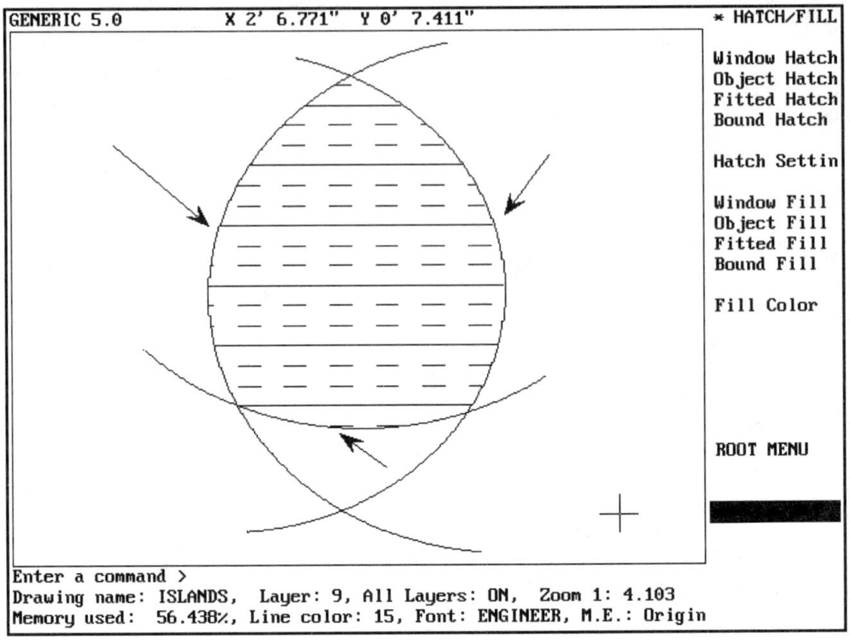

Figure 12.11: *Fitted Hatch hatches objects without valid boundaries.*

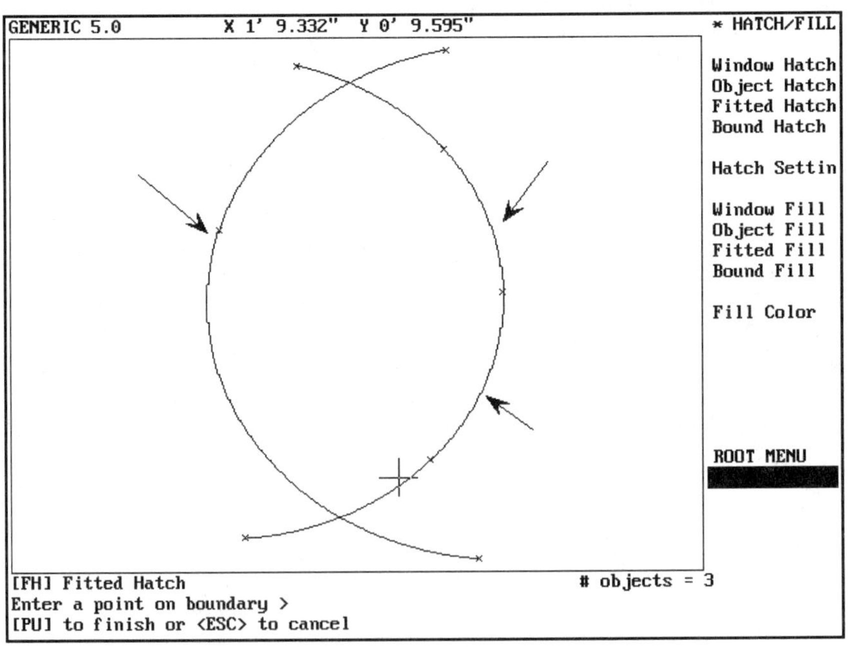

Figure 12.12: *At least three objects must be selected for Fitted Hatch.*

Boundary Hatch (BH)

If you want to place hatching in an area that is not defined by existing objects, use the Boundary Hatch command. It allows you to create a straight line boundary and hatch it at the same time. You can draw the lines in open space, on top of existing lines, or in any combination. You can use snaps to define the endpoints of the boundary if needed. The boundary lines drawn by the Boundary Hatch command are visible after the hatching is placed only if the Boundary option in the Hatch Settings command is on.

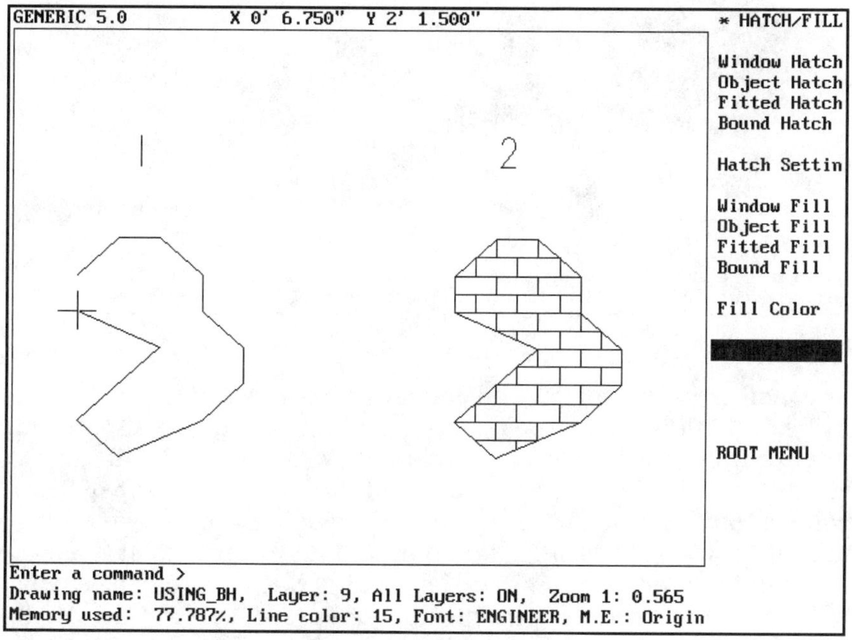

Figure 12.13: Boundary Hatch can be used to place a hatch pattern.

Using Solid Color Fills

Solid color fills follow the same rules as hatches. Only circles, arcs, and straight lines are valid boundaries, except that Bézier curves may be used with the Window Fill command. The color of the fill is selected using either the Color Settings (CS) command, found on the DISPLAY menu, or the Fill Color (FC or FK) command on the HATCH/FILL menu. To save time during redraws, the display of fills may be turned on or off, using the Fill display option of Fast Redraw (FA), on the DISPLAY menu, or the two-letter command DF to toggle the display of fills on or off. DF, for display fills, is not located on any menu. DF was left over from previous versions of Generic CADD that lacked the Fast Redraw command. It was included in version 5.0 primarily for the convenience of experienced users.

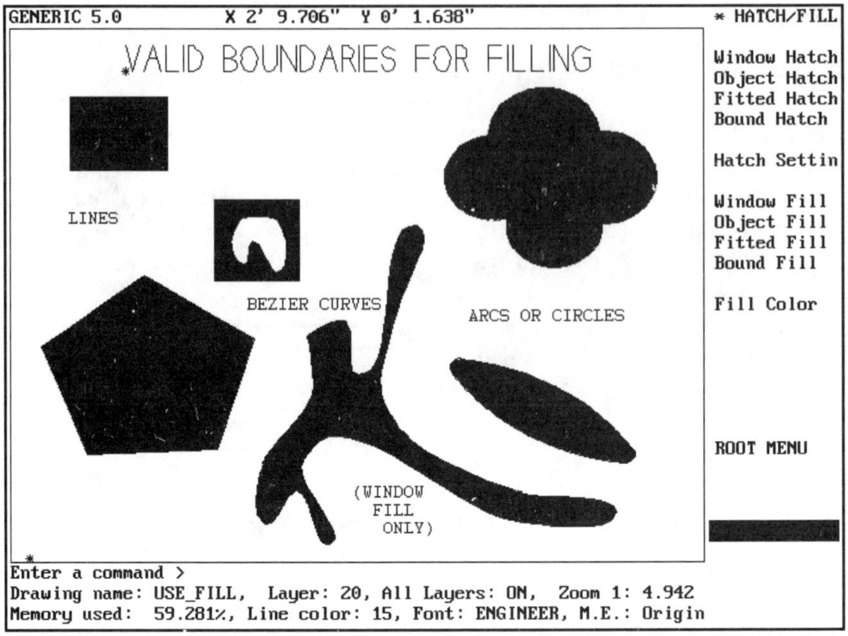

Figure 12.14: *Valid boundaries for solid color fills.*

A solid color fill is considered one object, and each fill has its own reference point. Sometimes it may be difficult to locate the reference point if the fill is complicated. In figure 12.14, for example, one Window Fill command was used to fill all the objects. The reference point is located in the center of the circle at the top of the drawing. If each object had been filled separately, each would have its own reference point. To make it easier to find the fill and hatch reference points, it is a good idea to put fills and hatches on their own layer. This way, they can be easily erased, if needed, without disturbing other objects. Just set All Layers Edit (AL) to off, switch the current layer to the hatch/fill layer (using Layer Current, YC), and erase the fills or hatches as required, using Layer selection inside the Erase (ER) command.

Using Window Fill (WF)

The Window Fill command works exactly like the Window Hatch command, except that a solid color is placed inside the boundaries selected. If there are nested boundaries, the solid color fill creates islands of filled and unfilled areas, depending on the number of boundaries found. The boundaries must connect at their endpoints, and they must be made from straight lines, arcs, circles, or Bézier curves.

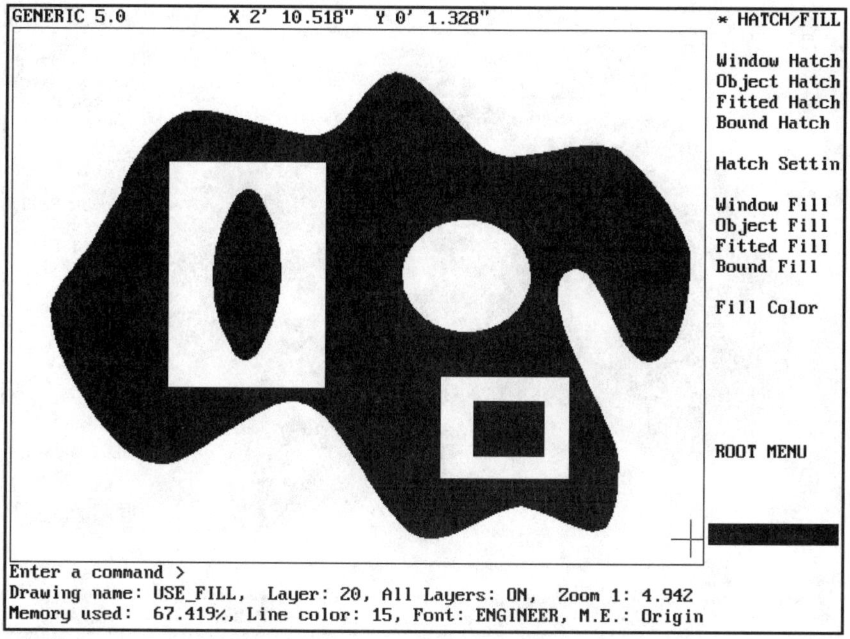

Figure 12.15: *Window Fill can identify nested sets of boundaries.*

Using Object Fill (OF)

The Object Fill command is used to define an area to be filled with a solid color by selecting the lines one by one, instead of having Generic CADD determine the boundaries (as it does when Window Fill is used). The main difference between this command and Window Fill is that each line, arc, or other boundary must be selected; the entities used to create the boundaries must still follow the rules. Since the boundaries must be individually selected, it is possible to add solid color fill to areas that would be left uncovered if Window Fill were used. Figure 12.16 uses the same objects as figure 12.15, but the shape of the fill is different because only the circles, arcs, and Bézier curves have been selected as boundaries, not the straight lines. Figure 12.16 has been modified to show the location of the straight lines; in normal use the fill would cover them.

Using Fitted Fill (FF)

If you take care as you draw and create connecting boundaries, Window Fill and Object Fill work in most situations. But occasions may still arise when you need to hatch an area that is not well-defined. If so, use the Fitted Fill command.

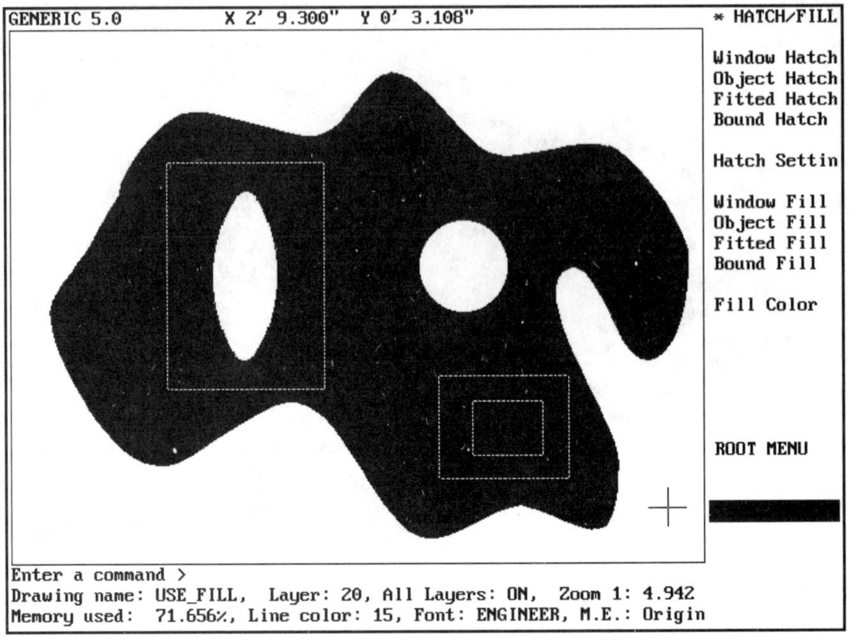

Figure 12.16: *Use Object Fill when the solid color should overwrite objects.*

The Fitted Fill command is used the same way as the Object Fill command is used. Objects that form the boundary for the fill are selected one by one. The difference is that Generic CADD looks for intersections as it analyzes the boundaries you have selected and places the solid color accordingly.

As you select objects for the boundary, place the cursor along the midpoint of an object, not near the endpoint or where one line intersects another (see fig. 12.11, on using this technique for Fitted Hatch). If you happen to select an object that you do not want to include in the definition of the boundary, press Ctrl-Backspace to remove the object from the list of selected items. Each time you press Ctrl-Backspace, the last object selected is deselected; you can continue deselecting items back to the start if you like.

As with the other hatch and fill commands, only straight lines, circles, and arcs can be used with the Fitted Fill command (Bézier curves, remember, are valid boundaries only if Window Hatch/Window Fill is used). At least three objects must be selected for the Fitted Fill command to work. This means, for example, that a circle, by itself, is ineligible for the Fitted Fill command. If you need to fill the space between two intersecting arcs, as illustrated in figure 12.18, use Object Break first to break one of the arcs into two. (Note in the illustration that `# objects = 3`.) So that the boundaries are still connecting, use the same point for both the first and second selection in the Object Break command.

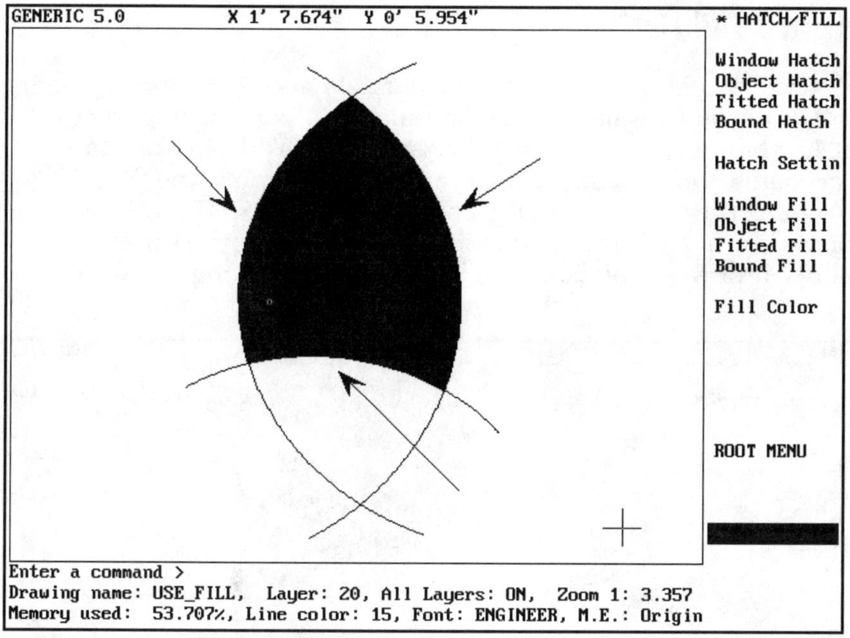

Figure 12.17: *Use Fitted Fill to fill objects without valid boundaries.*

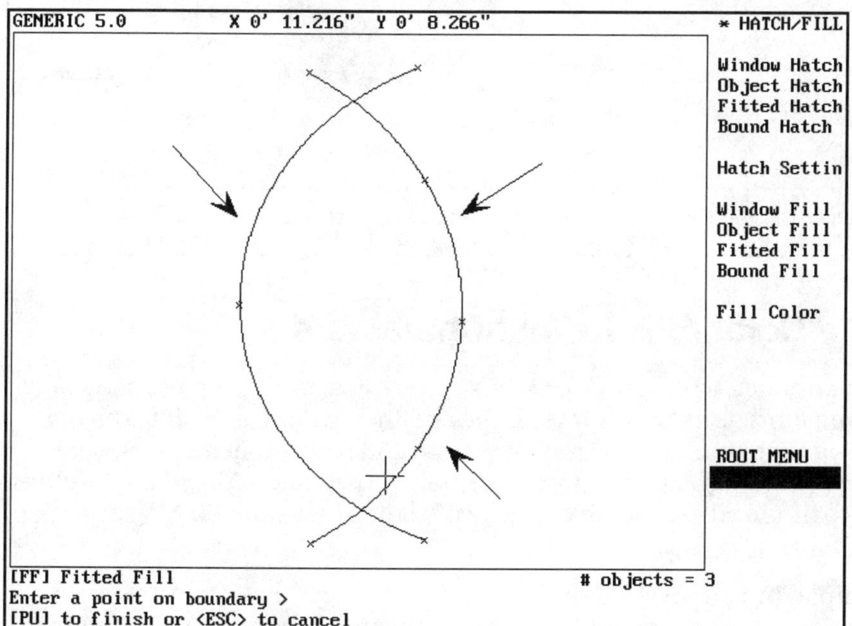

Figure 12.18: *At least three objects must be selected for Fitted Fill.*

Using Boundary Fill (BF)

If you want to place solid color in an area that is not defined by existing objects, use Boundary Fill. It works the same way as Boundary Hatch, allowing you to create a straight-line boundary and fill it at the same time. You can draw the lines in open space, on top of existing lines, or any combination of the two. You can use snaps to define the endpoints of the boundary if needed. Unlike Boundary Hatch, the boundary lines drawn by the Boundary Fill command are temporary and do not appear once the fill has been placed in the drawing.

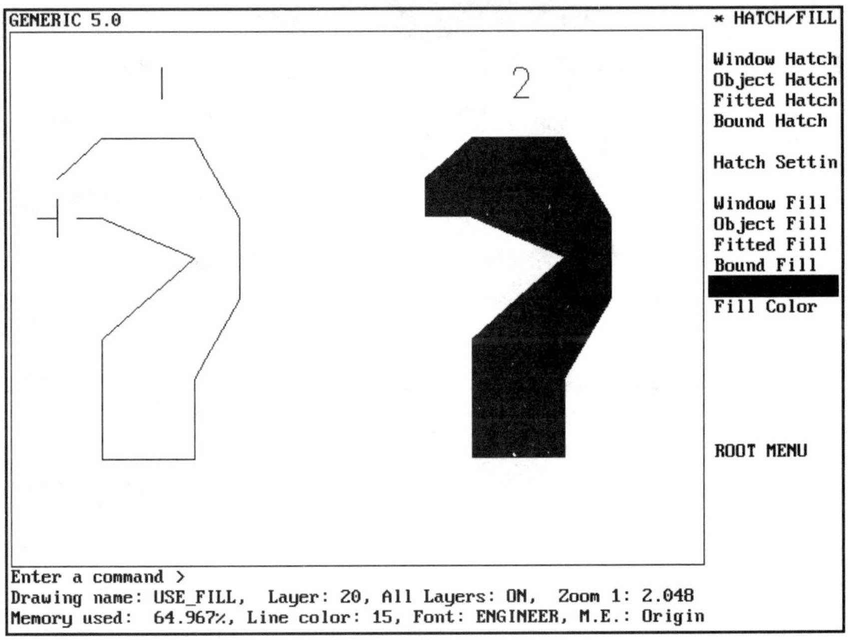

Figure 12.19: *Boundary Fill may be used to place a solid color fill anywhere.*

Adding Solid Color Fills to Text Characters

Two of the fonts supplied with Generic CADD 5.0, Italics and Complex, are not strictly single-line fonts, but have some shapes defined by outlines. If text from either of these two fonts is exploded (text lines have to be exploded twice), solid color fills can be placed in these outlines to enhance the look of the text (Hatching also can be used, but tends to look like solid color fill unless the text is very large.).

This sounds simple, but there is more than meets the eye. These fonts were not designed to be filled. Some of the lines don't meet at their endpoints, and many times the intersections are not clean. Complex curves, ineligible as hatch or fill boundaries, are used in some of the characters. Many invalid boundaries need to be fixed before these letters can be filled.

Figure 12.20 points out some of the potential pitfalls to watch for if you plan to add solid color fill to text. The numbers in the illustration refer to the points discussed below. Figure 12.21 shows the result when the problems are fixed and the letters filled.

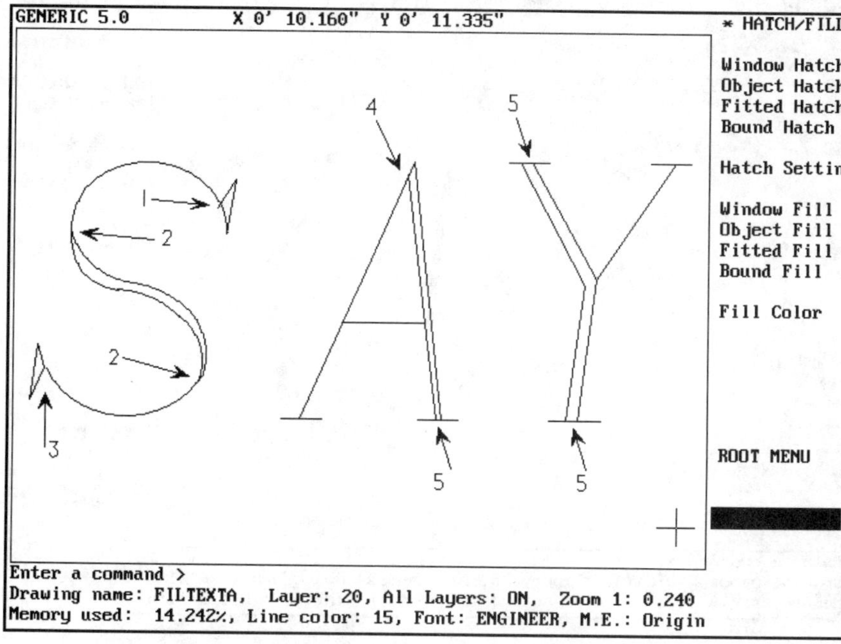

Figure 12.20: These outline fonts were not designed to be filled.

- ❑ 1. The line that forms the back side of the serif crosses over the main stem of the letter. To fix this, use Trim (RM) to cut the extending end of the serif line back to the arc. Then use Object Break to make a separate arc of the part of the stem that extends into the serif.
- ❑ 2. Although this portion of the letter is defined by arcs, the ends do not meet. Use Object Break to break the stem of the letter at each end. Use Snap to Nearest Point to identify both the first and second break points as the endpoint of the arc that forms the width of the letter.
- ❑ 3. This time the line of the serif does not intersect the stem. Use Object Break to break the stem, creating a new arc from the part of the stem that adjoins the serif.
- ❑ 4. This is a simple case of an improper boundary. Use Object Break to create a smaller line segment reaching from the tip of the A down to the intersection with the inside line of the right branch of the letter.

❑ 5. If you were to explode every character in Italics, the placement of the serifs shown here would be the most common problem to be corrected. Use Object Break to create a gap in each serif the width of the outline. Use Snap to Nearest Point to identify the endpoints of the outline as the location of each break. Then draw a new line in each gap to create a proper boundary for the fill command.

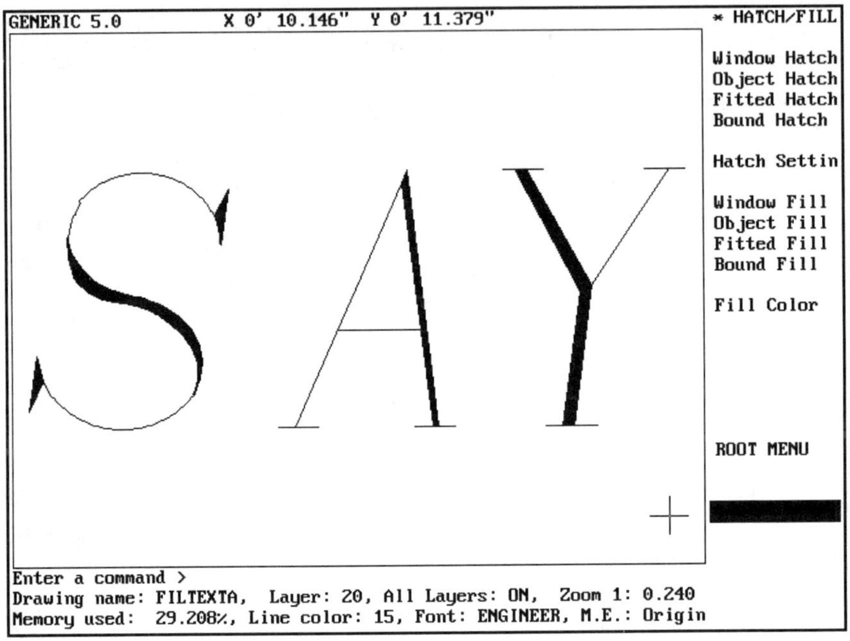

Figure 12.21: *All the boundary problems have been fixed.*

Summary

Placing hatches and fills in a drawing is a relatively simple procedure, but certain rules must be followed, and not all objects qualify as valid boundaries for hatches and fills. The wise Generic CADD user is always as precise as possible in the placement of endpoints and the connection of lines, not only to insure easy placement of hatches and fills, but also to take advantage of the program's ability to draw with precision.

13

Dimensioning

Drawings convey ideas. In past chapters, you learned how to create drawings with an electronic "drafting machine" called Generic CADD. Contained within the lines, arcs, circles, and other objects is a wealth of information. Layers, colors, line lengths, text starting points, center locations for arcs, and more are part of the drawing on the screen. Some of this data is plain to see, but other information is hidden until it is displayed by a series of keystrokes.

When you print a drawing, much of its information is hard to convey. A line created with an accuracy of .0001" on-screen is impossible to duplicate accurately on a piece of paper. In fact, a printed drawing is itself less exact because it is the product of a conversion of vectors to rasterized dots. These dots are placed on the paper by a printer that can only print in a predesignated pattern. In a plotter, the paper slips and the pens skip.

The solution is to use text to tell the story. Describe the length of the line. Label the location of the center of an arc. In other words, use dimensioning to place measurements in your drawings.

The Dimensioning Process

All types of objects can be dimensioned—arcs, circles, angles, and lines. Generic CADD offers many options and a wide variety of ways to accomplish these dimensioning tasks.

Learning about dimensioning can be challenging. The many terms and variables have only subtle shades of difference. As is frequently the case with technical terms, seeing is understanding.

To understand dimensioning, you need to understand the basic anatomy of a *dimension string.* A dimension string may include an arrowhead, dimension text, a dimension line, and extension lines (see fig 13.1).

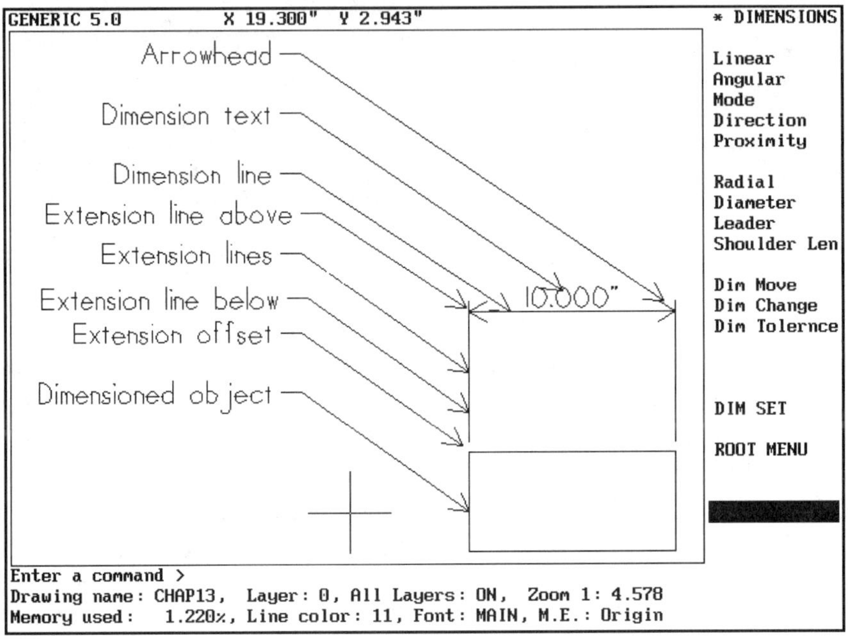

Figure 13.1: *The anatomy of a dimension string.*

Dimension Text

Dimension text is a crucial part of the dimension string. It specifies the exact size of the dimensioned object, and it can also specify a tolerance. Text can be generated automatically or input manually. Generic CADD also enables you to add additional clarifying text; for example, you might add "Dia" for diameter, or "O.C." for on center, or supply other text to convey a special meaning to the user.

Dimension Line

The dimensioned text sits above, or in the middle of, a *dimension line* (depending upon the type of drafting that you do). The line can be horizontal, vertical, angled, or arced. It often lies between extension lines, with particular arrowheads to indicate which extension lines pertain to which dimension text.

Arrowheads

Extension lines, visible when an object is selected, end in a wide variety of shapes: short open arrows, long filled arrows, filled and unfilled dots, and hash marks. Generic CADD offers a wide choice of options that enable you to indicate related extension lines and text.

Extension Lines

Extension lines define the boundaries of a dimension string. They usually extend from the dimensioned object to the dimension line and beyond. Consisting of three distinct parts—offset, line below, and line above—extension lines can be manipulated using the dimension settings commands. When you first start dimensioning objects, the results may not be exactly what you expect. Reworking the dimensions so that they match what you are used to seeing involves tapping Generic CADD's extensive library of dimension settings. This is covered later in the chapter.

Dimensioning Methods

Generic CADD 5.0 allows the user a wide range of dimensioning options. You can dimension horizontally, vertically, aligned, at an angle, and with or without tolerancing. You can dimension angles, circles, and arcs, and even add dimension notes.

Linear Dimension (LX)

The basic dimensioning command, Linear Dimension, dimensions the distance between two points. It creates dimension lines, arrowheads, extension lines, and text that indicates size. The user can, at the prompt, add additional text next to the displayed size.

Linear Dimension is selected from the DIMENSION menu or by its two-letter command, LX. Once it is selected, the prompt shows the current mode: Single, Partitioned, or Cumulative. (More about these modes later.) To begin to dimension, enter the first point, followed by the next point at the prompt. The prompt then displays the distance and asks if you want to add additional text. At this point, you have several options: press Enter to accept the text; use the backspace key to erase the "#" sign and replace the given text value with another value; or add additional text. To finish the command, enter the location of the dimension line. Generic CADD uses this information to construct the dimension.

The command is affected by the dimension variables, Dimension Direction (DD) and Dim Mode (UM). As you might guess from the command name, Dimension

Direction dimensions in different directions or orientations. Dim Mode allows you to dimension objects one at a time or in a string.

Dimension Direction (UD)

The Dimension Direction command works with the Linear Dimension command; it can also be selected from the DIMENSIONS menu. The two-letter command is UD. It allows you to dimension horizontally, vertically, aligned, or at an angle. When an object is aligned, the dimension line will be parallel to the selected object: if the object is at a 37-degree angle, the dimension line will also be at a 37-degree angle.

Once the object is selected, Generic CADD prompts you to pick a direction: horizontal, vertical, aligned, or at an angle. The current (or the default) setting is shown in parentheses.

The following exercise demonstrates the use of the Linear Dimension command. In it, you will go through a number of dimension setting commands. In particular, you will use Dimension Direction to draw differently oriented dimensions. Begin by drawing an object to dimension. Be sure that Tracking is on before you start the exercise.

Using Linear Dimension and Dimension Direction

Prompt	*Input*	*Description*
`Command`	**SG**	Turns Snap to Grid on
`Command`	**OR**	Turns Ortho off
`Command`	**ZO**	Zooms out
`Pick center of zoom`	Pick a point near midpoint of upper horizontal line	Centers zoom
`Command`	**LI**	Selects the Line command
`Starting point dimension`	Pick a point just above the center of the screen	Enters first point of line
`Enter next point on line`	Move cursor to right 6"	Enters second point of line
`Enter next point on line`	Move cursor down 6"	Enters third point
`Enter next point on line`	Move cursor to the left 10"	Enters fourth point
`Enter next point`	Connect last point with	Finishes four-sided

Using Linear Dimension and Dimension Direction—continued

Prompt	*Input*	*Description*
`on line`	the start point	polygon
`Command`	**A2**	Begins two-point arc
`Enter center of arc`	**SM**	Snaps to midpoint
`Midpoint of`	Pick right vertical line	Selects arc midpoint
`Enter start of arc`	Pick bottom of vertical line	Selects start of arc
`Enter end of arc`	Pick top of vertical line	Selects end of arc

The object you will dimension should look similar to the one in figure 13.2.

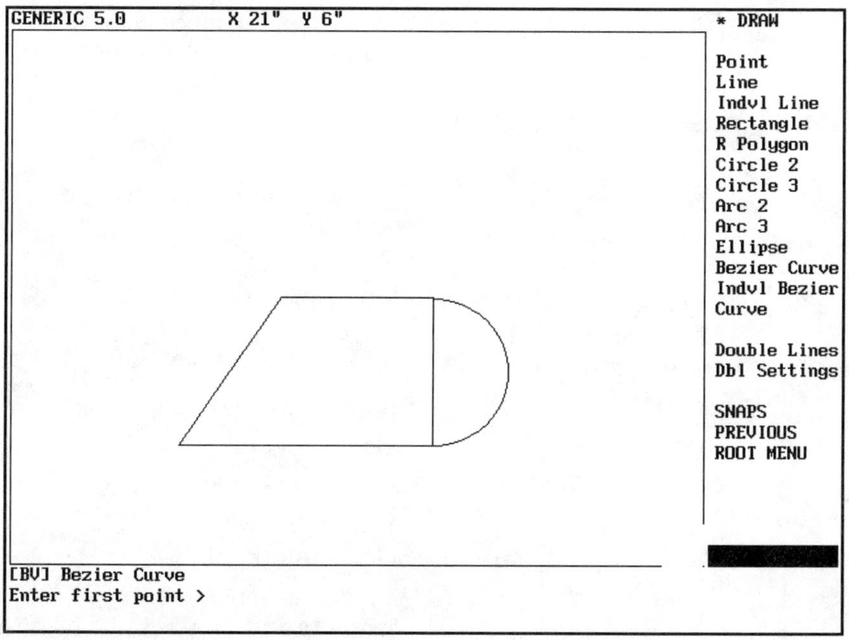

Figure 13.2: *Object to be dimensioned.*

Proximity Fixed (PF)

The Proximity Fixed command is toggled from the DIMENSIONS menu or invoked by typing **PF**. When PF is on, extension lines are automatically drawn the specified length. For this exercise, toggle PF off. Don't be concerned if you are instructed to try a few dimensioning commands in this next exercise sequence that haven't been discussed yet. Just follow along for now, and more details will be introduced later.

Horizontal Dimension

Prompt	*Input*	*Description*
`Command`	**NF**	Selects Numeric Format

`Angular (Degrees)`
`Linear (Decimal)`
`Decimal value (3)`
	D, 0	Shows dimensions as whole numbers, so 2.000 becomes 2

`Command`	**PF**	Selects Proximity Fixed command to check its setting
`* [PF] Proximity Fixed ON`	**PF** (omit if PF is already off)	Toggles PF from on to off
`Command`	**XS**	Selects Extension Stretch command to check its setting
`Offset (0.5") length`	If stretch is off, pick the word "Stretch" with your cursor	Turns XS from off to on
`Command`	**UD**	Selects Dimension Direction command
`Aligned (Horizontal)...`	**H**	Selects horizontal dimensioning
`Command`	**LX** or choose `Linear` from side menu	Starts a linear dimension
`Enter first point`	**SC**	Snaps to closest point
`Closest point to`	Pick left side of bottom horizontal line	Selects left side
`Enter next point`	**SM**	Snaps to midpoint of arc
`Midpoint of`	Pick midpoint of arc	Selects midpoint
`# = 13"`	Press Enter	Accepts dimension size without additional text
`Enter location of`	Pick a location on screen above object	Locates dimension line

Your first dimension should look like the one in figure 13.3.

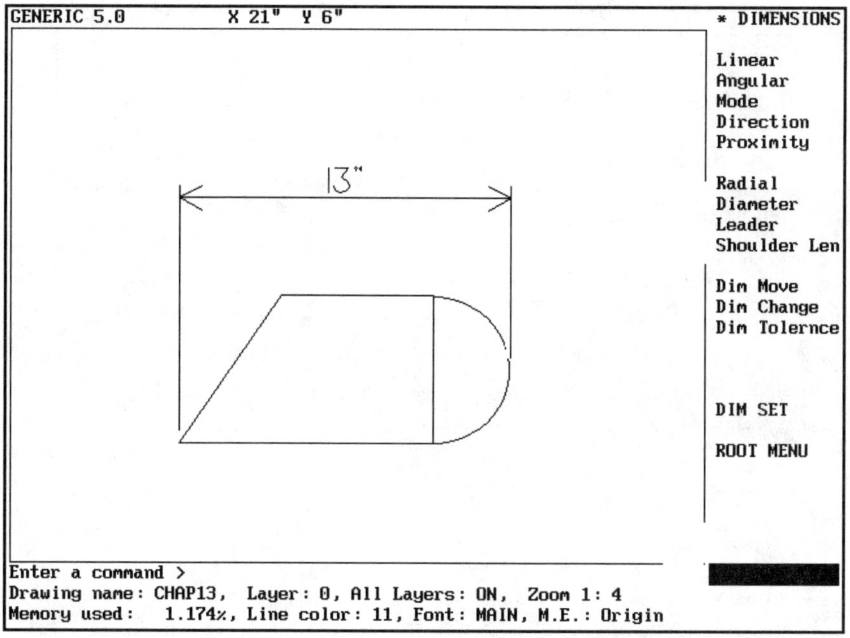

Figure 13.3: *Horizontal linear dimension.*

Vertical Dimensioning

Prompt	*Input*	*Description*
`Command`	**UD**	Starts Dimension Direction command
`Aligned...` `Vertical...`	**V**	Selects vertical dimensioning
`Command`	**LX** or pick `Linear` from side menu	Starts a linear dimension
`Enter first point`	**SC**	Snaps to closest point
`Closest point to`	Pick left side of bottom horizontal line	
`Enter next point`	**SC**	Snaps to closest point
`Closest point to`	Pick top of angled line	
`# = 6"`	Press Enter	Accepts dimension size without additional text
`Enter location of dimension`	Pick a location on screen left of object	Locates dimension line (see fig. 13.4)

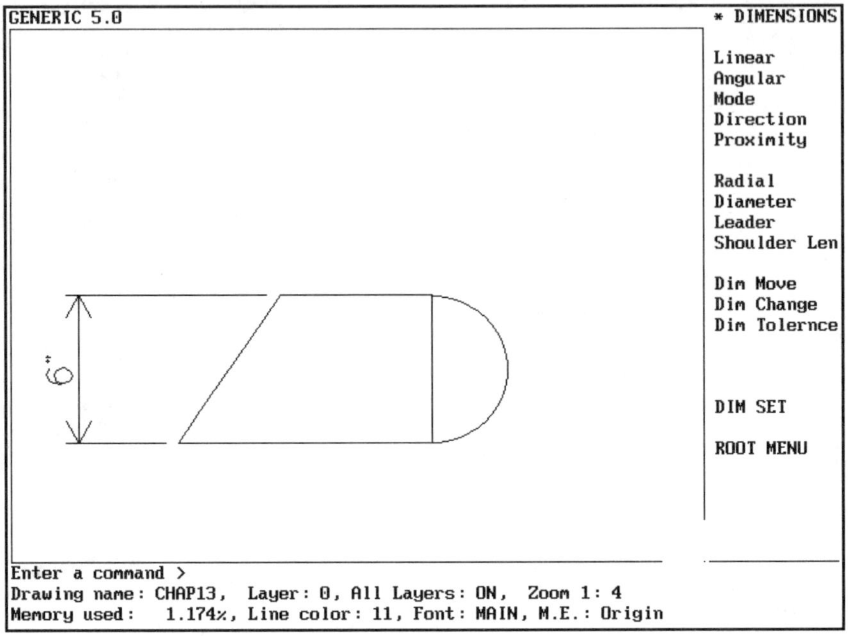

Figure 13.4: *Vertical linear dimension.*

Aligned Dimensioning

Prompt	*Input*	*Description*
`Command`	**OO**	Undoes last action
`Command`	**UD**	Starts Dimension Direction command
`...(`**`H`**`orizontal)` **`A`**`ligned...`	**A**	Does an aligned dimension
`Command`	**LX** or pick `Linear` from side menu	Starts a linear dimension
`Enter first point`	**SC**	Snaps to closest point
`Closest point to`	Pick left side of bottom horizontal line	Selects left side
`Enter next point`	**SC**	Snaps to closest point
`Closest point to`	Pick top of angled line	Selects top of line
`# = 7"`	Press Enter	
`> #`	Press backspace to erase the # and type **8"**	Erases the #
`Enter location of dimension`	Pick a location on the screen to left of object	Locates dimension line

This time, the dimension is at an angle. Your aligned dimension should look like figure 13.5 below.

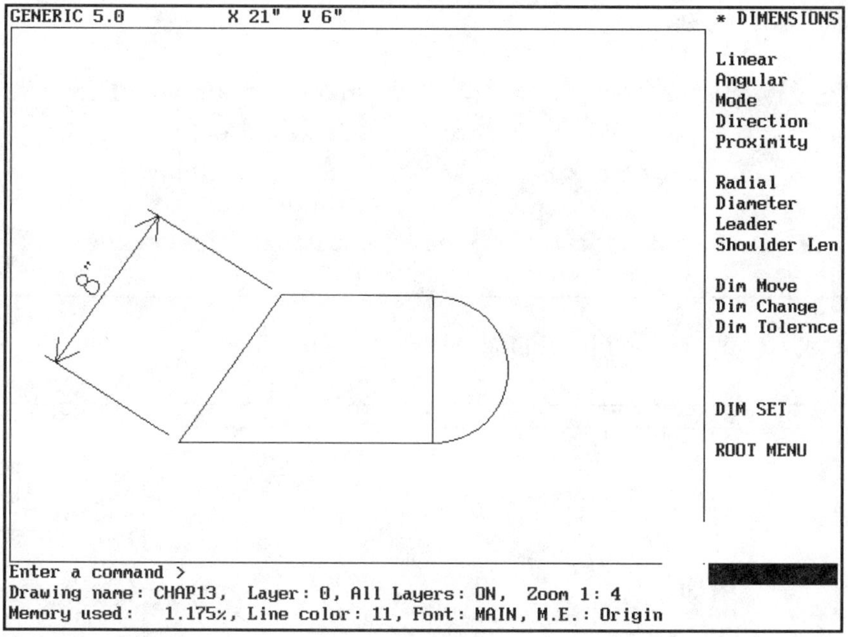

Figure 13.5: *Aligned linear dimension.*

The last dimension was angled but still aligned with a specific line. The next exercise shows you how to specify a dimension's angle.

Dimensioning at an Angle

Prompt	*Input*	*Description*
`Command`	**OO**	Undoes last action
`Command`	**UD**	Starts Dimension Direction command
`...Vertical, at an anglE...`	**E**	Starts dimensioning at an angle
`Change Angle (30) Limits: -360 to 360`	**10**	Gives dimension line a 10-degree angle
`Command`	**LX** or pick `Linear` from side menu	Starts a linear dimension
`Enter first point`	**SC**	Snaps to closest point

Dimensioning at an Angle—continued

Prompt	*Input*	*Description*
`Closest point to`	Pick left side of bottom horizontal line	Selects left side
`Enter next point`	**SM**	Snaps to midpoint of arc
`Midpoint of`	Pick midpoint of arc	Selects midpoint
`# = 13"` `> #`	Press Enter	Accepts dimension size without additional text
`Enter location of dimension`	Pick a location on the screen above the object	Locates dimension line

This time, your angled dimension should look like fig. 13.6 below.

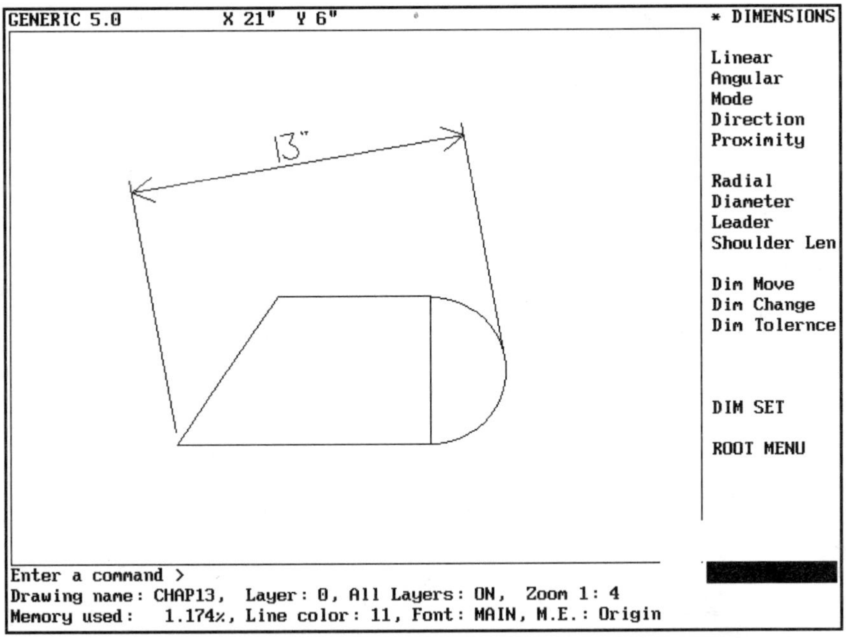

Figure 13.6:
Angled linear dimension.

Proximity Fixed is a toggle that works with most types of dimensions. You are most likely to use it with the linear dimension commands. In the preceding exercises, you placed the dimension line at various distances from the dimensioned object. This works well during practice, but in a real set of plans, this may look sloppy. Fixed distances between the dimensioned object and the dimension line and fixed distances between one dimension line and the dimension line above it look much more professional. Turn Proximity Fixed on again for the next exercise.

Dimension Extensions (XS)

The Dimension Extensions command controls four different options: offset distance; extensions above the dimension line; distance from the offset to the dimension line; and whether the extension lines stretch from the offset to the dimension line. You used this command earlier to turn Stretch on for the extension lines in the first exercise. Refer to figure 13.1 to refresh your memory of these terms. In figure 13.2, the left extension line stretches down to the first point, which would not happen if Stretch was turned off.

Once Dimension Extensions has been selected, four options are displayed with the default values shown: **O**ffset (0.5") length, **A**bove (0.5") length; **B**elow (0.5") length; and **S**tretch (off). To select these options, type the capitalized letter or choose it from the screen using the cursor.

Using Proximity Fixed and Dimension Extension

Prompt	*Input*	*Description*
`Command`	**OO**	Undoes last action
`Command`	**UD**	Starts Dimension Direction command
`Aligned (Horizontal)...`	**H**	Starts horizontal dimensioning
`Command`	**PF**	Selects Proximity Fixed command to check its setting
`* [PF] Proximity Fixed is ON`	If PF is on, skip next step	Retains PF setting
`* [PF] Proximity`	**PF**	Turns Proximity on
`Command`	From the side menu, choose `Dim Set`, then `Extensions`	Selects Dim Set
`Offset (0.5") length, Above (0.5") length, Below (0.5") length, Stretch (ON)`	**A, 1** **B, 4** **S**	Sets above length to 1", below length to 4", turns stretch off (offset is not changed)
`Command`	**LX** or pick `Linear` from side menu	Starts a linear dimension

Using Proximity Fixed and Dimension Extension—continued

Prompt	*Input*	*Description*
`Enter first point`	**SC**	Snaps to closest point
`Closest point to`	Pick left side of bottom horizontal line	Selects left side
`Enter next point`	**SM**	Snaps to midpoint of arc
`Midpoint of`	Pick midpoint of arc	
`# = 13"` `> #`	Press Enter	Accepts dimension size without additional text
`Enter location of dimension`	Pick a location on screen above object	Locates dimension line

Your latest dimension should look like figure 13.7.

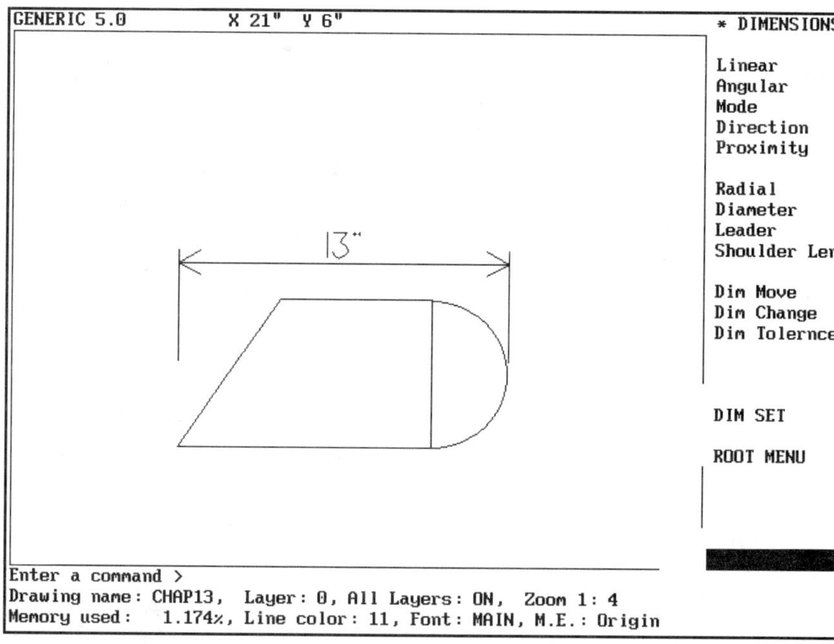

Figure 13.7: *Horizontal linear dimension with PF on and changed extension options.*

Dimension Tolerance (UT)

Dimension Tolerance is another facet of the Linear Dimension command, but it is also used occasionally with radial and diameter dimensioning. Just as tolerance implies that a certain amount of variance is acceptable, Dimension Tolerance allows the length of an object to vary by a certain value (usually within thousandths of an inch) and still be within acceptable limits.

Dimension Tolerance is located on the DIMENSIONS menu, and it can also be initiated by typing **UT**. Tolerance is expressed in three different ways: Fixed variance, Max/min variance, and Stacked variance, each explored in the exercise below. There is also a No tolerance option. To select options, use the cursor or type the capitalized, bold letter associated with each option. You can also select dimension tolerances with the Dimension Text command.

Each option has different prompts. Fixed variance requires a single tolerance value, with precision limits for tolerance ranging from 0 to 6 decimal places. With Max/min and Stacked variances, you must provide lower and upper tolerances.

The following exercise demonstrates how each type of tolerance changes the look of the dimension string.

Using Dimension Tolerance

Prompt	*Input*	*Description*
`Command`	**OO**	Undoes last action
`Command`	**PF**	Selects Proximity Fixed command to check its setting
`* [PF] Proximity Fixed is ON`	If PF is on, skip next step	Retains PF setting
`* [PF] Proximity`	**PF**	Turns Proximity on
`Command`	**UT** or pick `Tolerance` from side menu	Selects Dimension Tolerance command
`(`**`N`**`one)...`**`F`**`ixed variance`	**F**	Selects Fixed variance option
`Change tolerance value`	**.003**	Allows variance of plus or minus .003"
`Change decimal Limits: 0 to 6`	**3**	Sets 3 decimal place tolerance precision
`Command`	**LX** or pick `Linear` from side menu	Starts a linear dimension
`Enter first point`	**SC**	Snaps to closest point
`Closest point to`	Pick left side of bottom horizontal line	Selects left side
`Enter next point`	**SM**	Snaps to midpoint of arc

Using Dimension Tolerance—continued

Prompt	*Input*	*Description*
`Midpoint of`	Pick midpoint of arc	Selects midpoint
`# = 13"` `> #`	Press Enter	Accepts dimension size without additional text
`Enter location of dimension`	Pick a location on screen above object	Locates dimension line showing tolerance figure (see fig. 13.8)

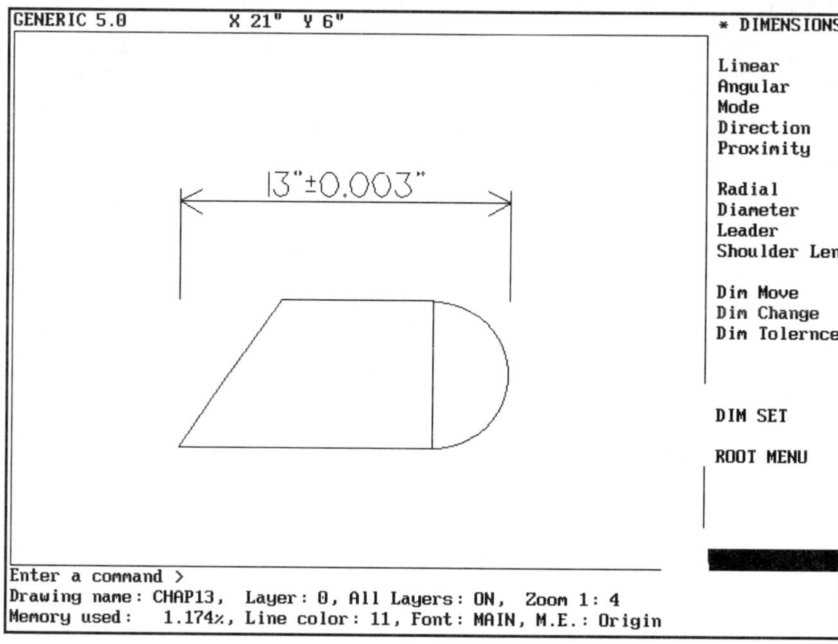

Figure 13.8: *Linear Dimension with a Fixed variance tolerance.*

Using the Max/Min Variance

Prompt	*Input*	*Description*
`Command`	**OO**	Undoes last action
`Command`	**UT** or pick `Tolerance` from side menu	Selects Dimension Tolerance command
`(`**`N`**`one) `**`M`**`ax/min...`	**M**	Selects Max/min variance
`Change lower tolerance`	**.003**	Allows variance of minus .003"

Using the Max/Min Variance—continued

Prompt	*Input*	*Description*
`Change upper tolerance`	**.001**	Allows variance of plus .001"
`Change decimal Limits: 0 to 6`	**3**	Sets tolerance precision to 3 decimal places
`Command`	**LX** or pick `Linear` from side menu	Starts a linear dimension
`Enter first point`	**SC**	Snaps to closest point
`Closest point to`	Pick left side of bottom horizontal line	Selects left side
`Enter next point`	**SM**	Snaps to midpoint of arc
`Midpoint of`	Pick midpoint of arc	Selects midpoint
`# = 13"` `> #`	Press Enter	Accepts dimension size without additional text
`Enter location of dimension`	Pick a location on the screen above the object	Locates dimension line

This dimension should look like the one in figure 13.9.

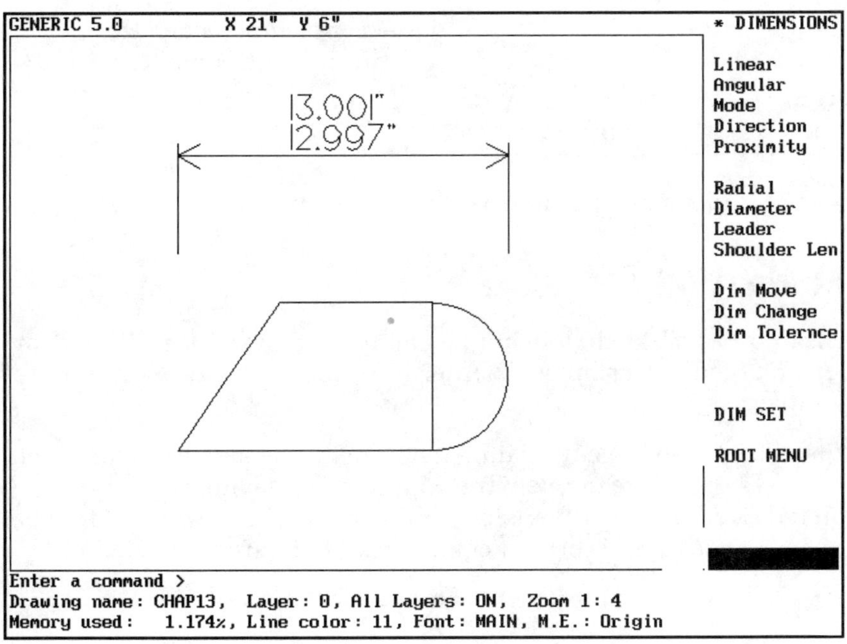

Figure 13.9: *Horizontal linear dimension with a Max/min variance.*

Using the Stacked Variance

Prompt	*Input*	*Description*
`Command`	**OO**	Undoes last action
`Command`	**UT** or pick `Tolerance` from side menu	Selects Dimension Tolerance command
`(None)... Stacked variance`	**S**	Selects Stacked variance option
`Change lower tolerance`	**.003**	Allows variance of minus .003"
`Change upper tolerance`	**.001**	Allows variance of plus .001"
`Change decimal Limits: 0 to 6`	**3**	Sets tolerance precision to 3 decimal places
`Command`	**LX** or pick `Linear` from side menu	Starts a linear dimension
`Enter first point`	**SC**	Snaps to closest point
`Closest point to`	Pick left side of bottom horizontal line	Selects left side
`Enter next point`	**SM**	Snaps to midpoint of arc
`Midpoint of`	Pick midpoint of arc	Selects midpoint
`# = 13" > #`	Press Enter	Accepts dimension size without additional text
`Enter location of dimension`	Pick a location on the screen above the object	Locates dimension line

Your stacked variance dimension should look like the one in figure 13.10.

Dimension Mode (UM)

Dimension Mode is another of the dimensioning commands that work with Linear Dimension. Dimension Mode determines whether the dimensions are Single, Partitioned, or Cumulative.

In the preceding exercises, you have been dimensioning in the single mode, which is the default setting. As the name implies, the command ends after a single dimension is completed. You did one dimension, and to do another, you had to type **LX** or press the space bar to repeat the last command. There are two other approaches.

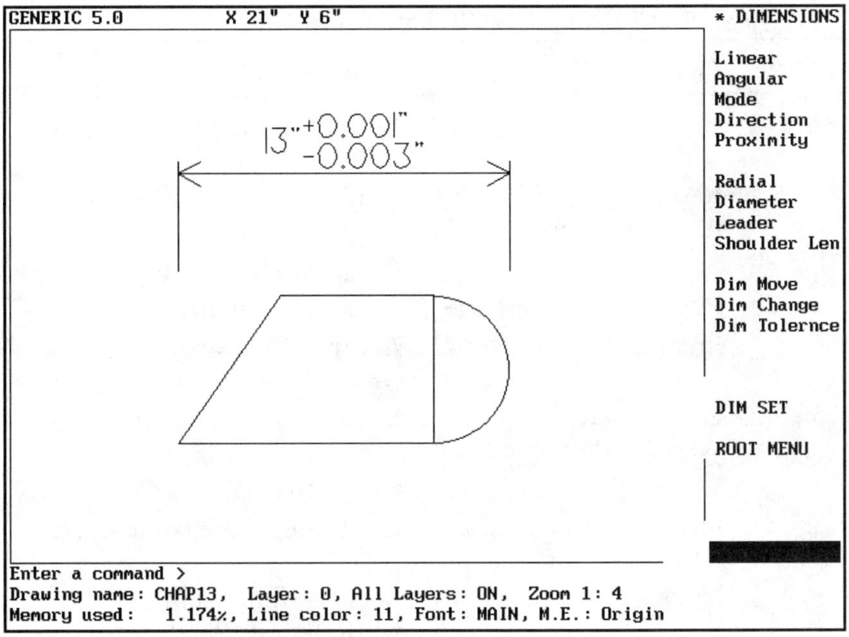

Figure 13.10: *Horizontal linear dimension with a Stacked variance.*

In the Partitioned mode, you are prompted for a next point after the first dimension is completed. In fact, you are prompted for points until you press Enter to end the command. This creates a continuous horizontal line made up with the various dimension lines.

The Cumulative mode is a combination of Single and Partitioned mode prompts. You pick a first point, a next point, and a dimension line location. Then you pick a next point and a dimension line location. This continues until you press Enter to end the command. The result looks like inverted stair steps. Each dimension will be a dimension from a base point rather than from point to point.

Since you have already completed several single mode dimensions, this exercise will demonstrate Partitioned and Cumulative modes.

Using the Partitioned Mode

Prompt	*Input*	*Description*
`Command`	**OO**	Undoes last action
`Command`	**UT** or pick `Tolerance` from side menu	Selects Dimension Tolerance command
`(`**`N`**`one) `**`M`**`ax/min...`	**N**	Selects No tolerance
`Command`	**UM** or pick `Mode` from side menu	Starts Dimension Mode command

Using the Partitioned Mode —continued

Prompt	*Input*	*Description*
`(Single) Partitioned...`	**P**	Selects Partitioned mode
`Command`	**LX** or pick `Linear` from side menu	Starts a linear dimension
`Enter first point`	**SC**	Snaps to closest point
`Closest point to`	Pick top of angled line	Selects top of line
`# = 4" > #`	Press Enter	Accepts dimension size without additional text
`Enter location of dimension`	Pick a location on screen above object	Locates dimension line
`Enter next point`	**SC**	Snaps to closest point
`Closest point to`	Pick right side of top horizontal line	Continues dimension string
`# = 6" > #`	Press Enter	Accepts dimension size without additional text
`Enter next point`	**SM**	Snaps to midpoint of arc
`Midpoint of`	Pick midpoint of arc	Selects midpoint
`# = 3" > #`	Press Enter	Accepts dimension size without additional text

Your partitioned dimension should look like the one in figure 13.11.

Using the Cumulative Mode

Prompt	*Input*	*Description*
`Command`	**UT** or pick `Tolerance` from side menu	Selects Dimension Tolerance command
`Command`	**OO**	Undoes last action
`Command`	**UM** or pick `Mode` from side menu	Starts Dimension Mode command
`...Partitioned Cumulative`	**C**	Selects Cumulative mode
`Command`	**LX** or pick `Linear` from side menu	Starts a linear dimension
`Enter first point`	**SC**	Snaps to closest point
`Closest point to`	Pick top of angled line	Selects top of line

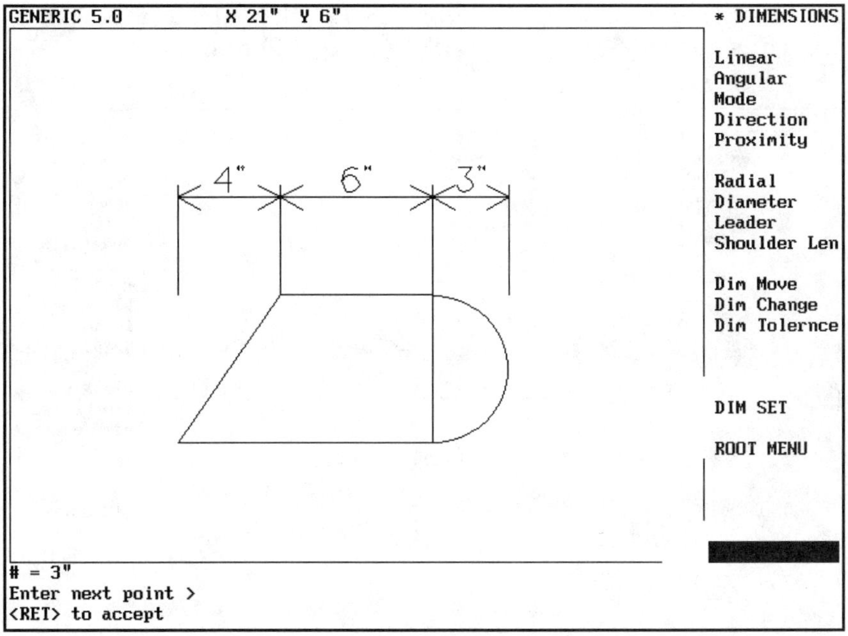

Figure 13.11: *Partitioned horizontal linear dimension.*

Using the Cumulative Mode—continued

Prompt	*Input*	*Description*
`# = 4"` `> #`	Press Enter	Accepts dimension size without additional text
`Enter location of dimension`	Pick a location on screen above object	Locates dimension line
`Enter next point`	**SC**	Snaps to closest point
`Closest point to`	Pick right side of top horizontal line	Continues dimension string
`# = 6"` `> #`	Press Enter	Accepts dimension size without additional text
`Enter next point`	**SM**	Snaps to midpoint of arc
`Midpoint of`	Pick midpoint of arc	Selects midpoint
`# = 3"` `> #`	Press Enter	Accepts dimension size without additional text

Your cumulative dimension should look like figure 13.12. Although it is like partitioned dimensioning in some ways, the end result is quite different.

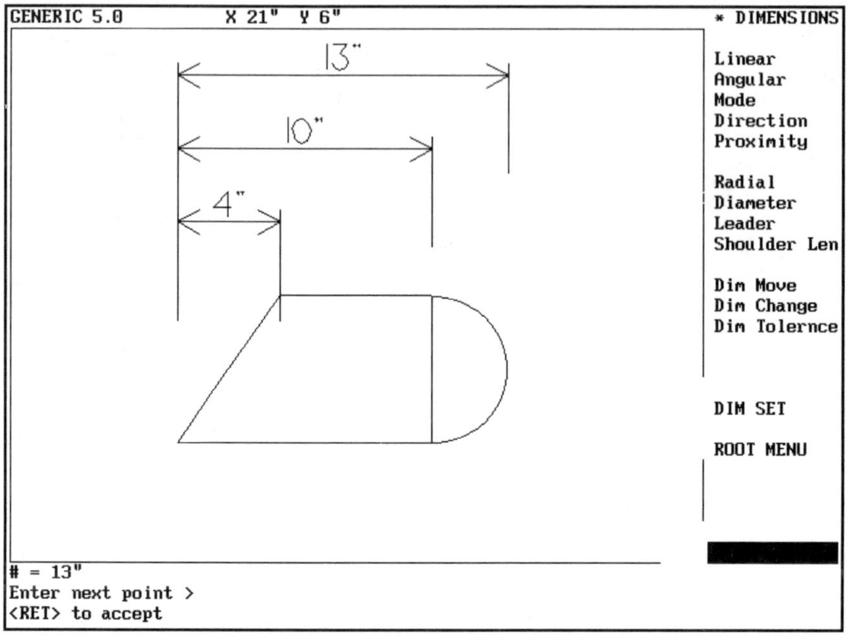

Figure 13.12: *Cumulative horizontal linear dimension.*

Angular Dimension (AX)

The Angular Dimension command dimensions the angle of two lines. The text is displayed in degrees or in degrees:minutes:seconds. This command accepts Dimension Mode (UD) and can show single, partitioned, or cumulative sets of dimensions.

Once Angular Dimension is selected, the first prompt asks for the center point. Further prompts allow you to pick the two angled lines and show the dimension location. Depending on how the cursor is placed, Generic CADD gives you the option to show either the small or large angle. When the actual angle is displayed, you can accept, modify, or add to this number.

In the next exercise, you will do an Angular Dimension (AX) to display the small angle dimension. Before you finally place the dimension line, you will be asked to move the cursor so that you can see how the CADD program can display the large angle dimension line as well.

Using the Angular Dimension Command

Prompt	*Input*	*Description*
`Command`	**OO**	Undoes last action
`Command`	**UM** or pick `Mode` from side menu	Starts Dimension Mode command
`(Single) Partitioned...`	**S**	Selects single mode
`Command`	**AX** or pick `Angular` from side menu	Starts an angular dimension
`Enter center point`	**SC**	Snaps to closest point
`Closest point to`	Pick left side of bottom horizontal line	Locates center point
`Enter point on first line`	Pick bottom horizontal line	First radius line
`Enter point on next line`	Pick top of angled line line	Second radius line
`Radius # = 56.310`	Press Enter	Accepts calculated radius
`Place dimension`	Move cursor from a point within the two lines to a point to the left; pick a point within the two lines	Shows both radius dimension lines

Your angular dimension should be similar to the one in figure 13.13.

Radial Dimension (RX)

The Radial Dimension command dimensions the radius of an arc or circle. Dimension Tolerance can be used with this command.

Select Radial from the DIMENSIONS menu or type **RX**. To use the command, you must select an arc or circle, then show the placement of the text. Radial Dimension displays the text within or outside the arc (or circle) depending on the location you pick on-screen.

The following exercise will take you through this straightforward dimension command.

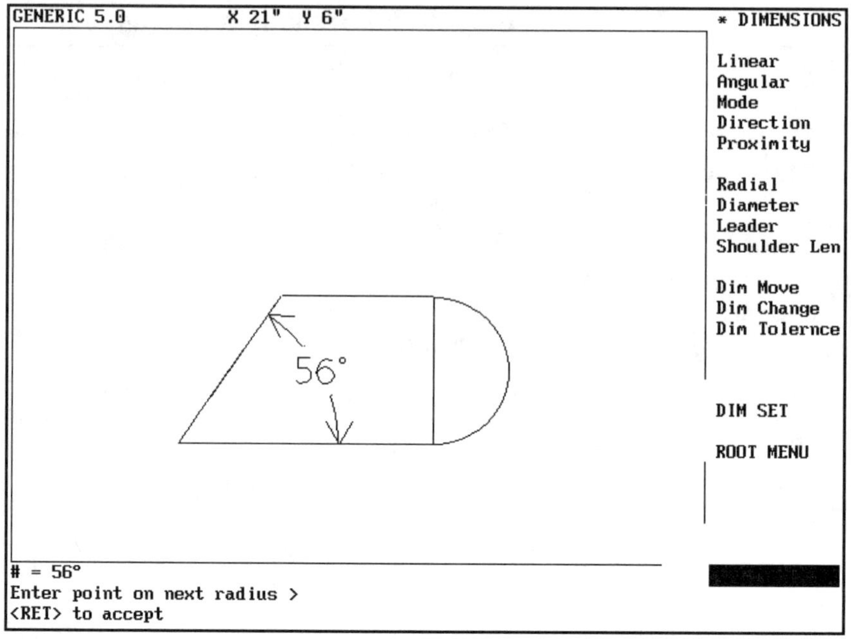

Figure 13.13: *An angular dimension.*

Using the Radial Dimension Command

Prompt	*Input*	*Description*
Command	**OO**	Undoes last action
Command	**RD**	Redraws screen
Command	**RX** or pick Radial from side menu	Starts Radial Dimension command
Select arc or circle	Pick the arc	Chooses the object
# = 3" > #	Press space bar once, then type **R**	Adds an R (for radius) to the dimension string
Place dimension	Move cursor to the left and right of arc; then pick a spot to the left of the arc	View the text placement options, then place text

Your radial dimension should be similar to the one in figure 13.14.

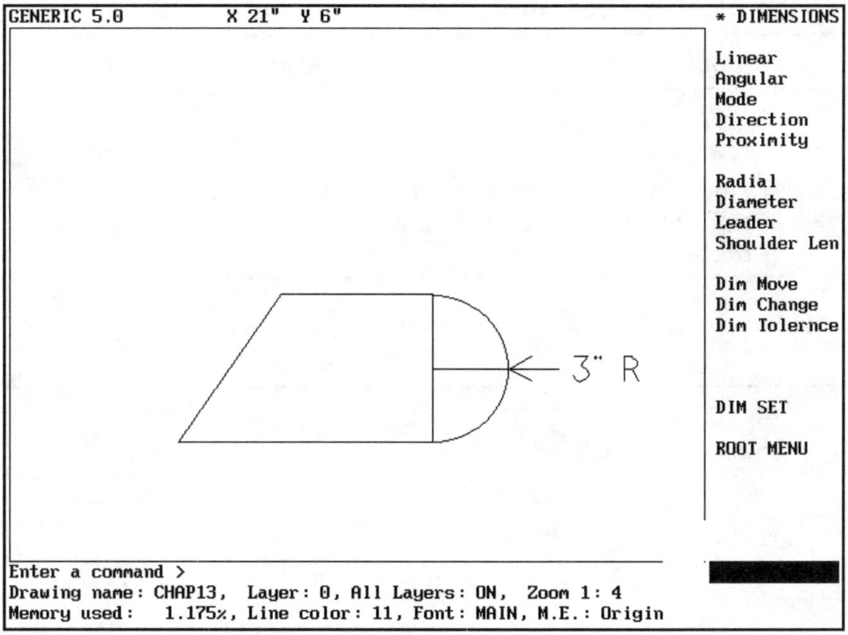

Figure 13.14: *A radial dimension.*

Diameter Dimension (IX)

The Diameter Dimension command dimensions the diameter of an arc or circle. It accepts the Dimension Tolerance (UT) command.

To start Diameter Dimension, select Diameter from the DIMENSIONS menu or type **IX**. After selecting an arc or circle, a default dimension is shown, which you can either accept or modify. The dimension text can be placed within the arc or circle or it can be placed on the outside of the curve.

The Diameter and Radial Dimension commands follow parallel sequences. It should not surprise you to find that this exercise is almost identical to the preceding exercise, except that it produces a diameter dimension.

Using the Diameter Dimension Command

Prompt	*Input*	*Description*
`Command`	**OO**	Undoes last action
`Command`	**IX** or pick `Diameter` from side menu	Starts Diameter Dimension command
`Select arc or circle`	Pick the arc	Chooses the object

Using the Diameter Dimension Command—continued

Prompt	*Input*	*Description*
`# = 6"` `> #`	Press space bar once, then type **Dia**	Adds DIa (for diameter) to the dimension string
`Place dimension`	Move cursor to the left and right of arc; then pick a spot to the left of the arc	View the text placement options, then place text

Your diameter dimension should be similar to the one in figure 13.15.

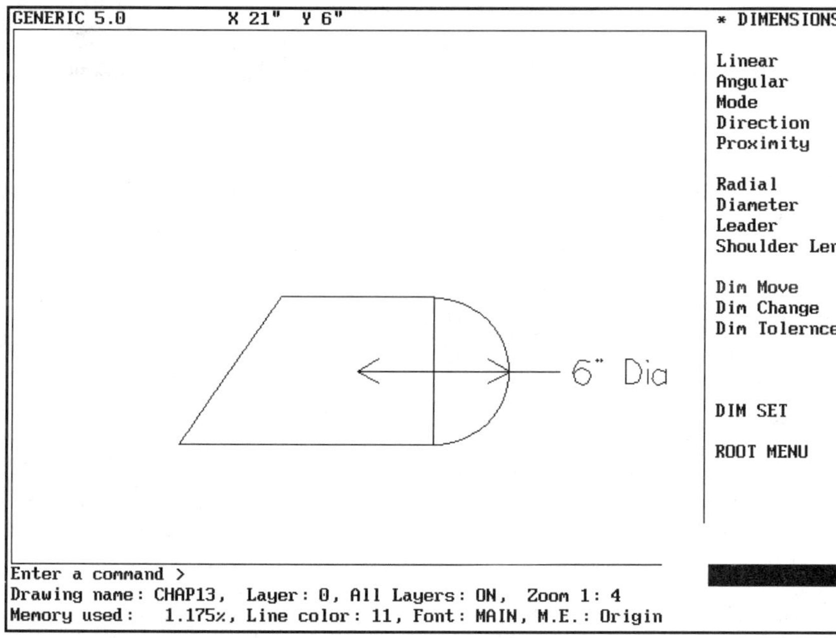

Figure 13.15: *A diameter dimension.*

Dimension Leader (LE)

The Dimension Leader command not only lets you add a note to a drawing, it lets you point to the object to which the note refers. The dimension leader entity is composed of an arrowhead, an angled line (also called the leader), a horizontal line known as the shoulder, and the text itself.

The Dimension Leader command is found under the DIMENSIONS menu, and it can also be started by typing LE. At the beginning of the command, you are prompted to enter the desired text. To draw the leader, you must pick a starting point and a terminal point and indicate the shoulder direction.

Shoulder Length (LL)

The Shoulder Length command is a modifier of the Dimension Leader command. It adjusts the length of the leader shoulder. It is found after the Leader command in the DIMENSIONS menu or it can be accessed by typing LL and inputting the desired leader shoulder size.

Using the Dimension Leader and Shoulder Length Commands

Prompt	*Input*	*Description*
`Command`	**OO**	Undoes last action
`Command`	**LL** or pick `Shoulder Length` from side menu	Starts Shoulder ength command
`Change leader shoulder size (1")`	**3**	Changes length of shoulder to 3"
`Enter string`	**TOP**	Enters text label
`Enter leader starting point`	Pick top horizontal line	tarts leader line
`Enter leader terminal point`	Pick point above and to left of object	Ends leader line
`Enter a point indicating shoulder direction`	Pick to the left	Allows text string to be to the left or right

Your dimension leader should be similar to the one in figure 13.16.

Dimension Move (UV)

Dimension Move is a unique and powerful command. With it, both the dimension line and the text can be moved. This allows you to adjust the dimensioning positions for easier reading.

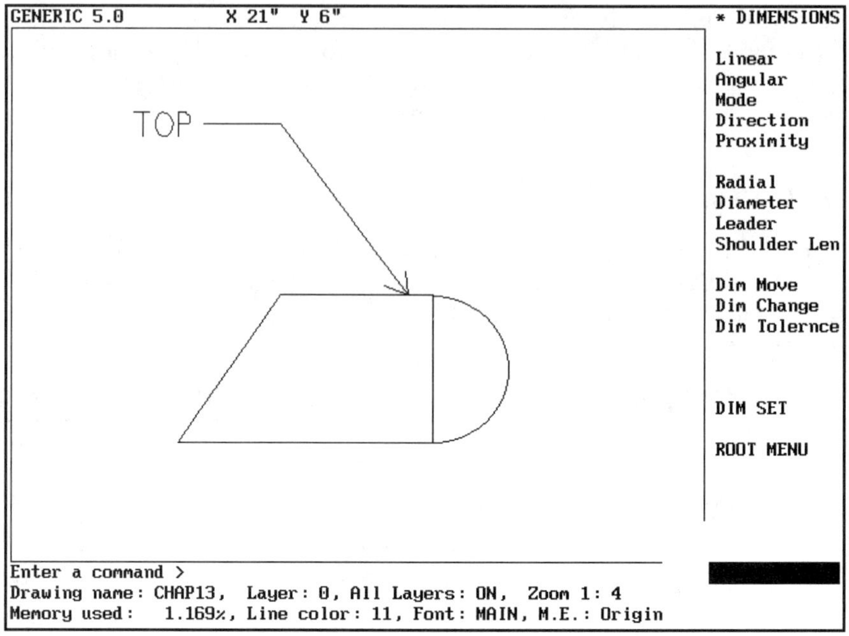

Figure 13.16: *The dimension leader.*

Using the Dimension Move Command

Prompt	*Input*	*Description*
`Command`	**OO**	Undoes last action
`Command`	**LX** or pick `Linear` from side menu	Starts a linear dimension
`Enter first point`	**SC**	Snaps to closest point
`Closest point to`	Pick left side of bottom horizontal line	Selects left side
`Enter next point`	**SM**	Snaps to midpoint of arc
`Midpoint of`	Pick midpoint of arc	Selects midpoint
`# = 13"` `> #`	Press Enter	Accepts dimension size without additional text
`Enter location of dimension`	Pick a location on screen above object	Locates dimension line
`Command`	**UV** or pick `Dim Move` from side menu	Starts Dimension Move command
`Point to portion of dimension to move`	Pick text	Selects text to be moved

Using the Dimension Move Command—continued

Prompt	*Input*	*Description*
`Enter new dimension point`	Pick a point to the left	Moves text to left
`Point to portion of dimension to move`	Pick the dimension line	Selects dimension line to be moved
`Enter new dimension point`	Pick a point above	Moves dimension line up

Your moved dimension should look like the one in figure 13.17.

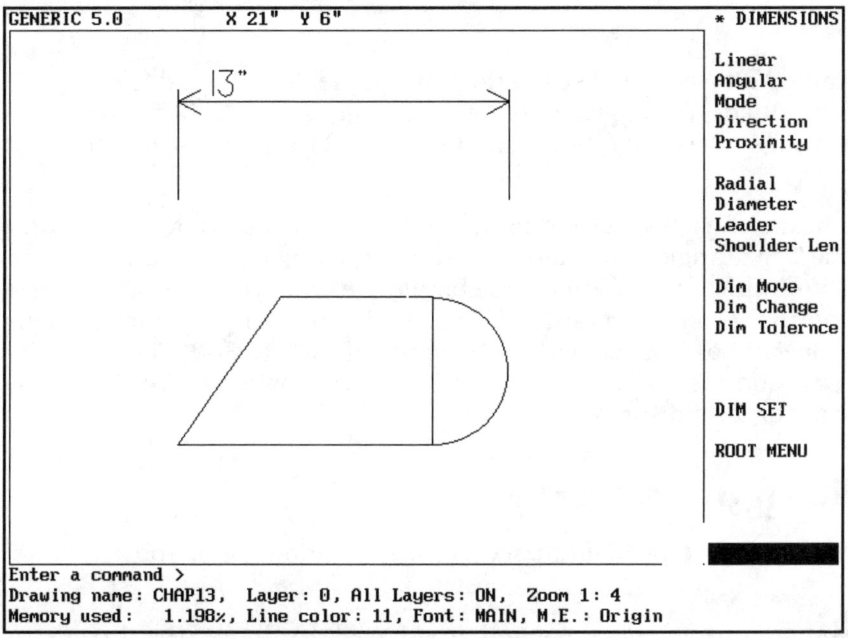

Figure 13.17: *Dimension Move command.*

Dimensioning Setup

You have considerable control over the appearance of the dimension string. Arrow size and type, text height, font, placement, dimension layer, and color can all be altered to suit your needs. You can even hide different elements of the dimension string.

Dimension Display (DD)

The Dimension Display command is a toggle that allows you to show or hide different elements of the dimension string. You can hide the left or right arrow, dimension line, left or right extension line, or the dimension text.

Dimension Display command can be selected from the DIM SET menu or accessed by typing **DD**. Once this is done, the different toggles show at the bottom of the screen. You can change a toggle by typing the appropriate capitalized letter or by selecting the word using the cursor.

Every dimension placed after you have changed the Dimension Display settings will reflect those changes. Dimensions placed before the change are not affected.

Arrows (AR)

The Arrows command allows you to select the type, angle, length, and location (pointing inside or outside) of arrowheads. As with Dimension Display, any changes to the settings affect only those dimensions and leaders placed after the changes.

Arrows is found under the DIM SET menu. It can also be accessed by typing **AR**. You can select the **T**ype, **A**ngle, **L**ength or l**O**cation by typing the capitalized letter or by selecting it with the cursor. When you change the type, you choose between normal-**C**losed, normal-**O**pen, normal-**F**illed, **N**otched, circle-**U**nfilled, circle-fIlled, or **S**lash. The angle can be changed within the limits of -360 to 360. The length option gives you the chance to change the length of the arrowheads. The location is a toggle for inside or outside arrows.

Font Selection (FS)

Font Selection controls the type of font used in the text, dimension, and attribute formats.

If you type **FS**, you are prompted as to whether you wish to change the text, dimension, or attribute font. After you have made a choice, the side menu will show all of the fonts available. (If you pick Font Selection from the DIM SETTINGS menu, it takes you directly to font selection.) Pick one and you have made a new font selection.

Text Size (TZ)

Text Size sets the height of the text and is covered in detail in Chapter 6.

After you pick Text Size from the DIM SET menu or choose text after typing **TS**, you can enter the text size that you desire.

Dimension Text Settings (DT)

The Dimension Text Settings command is a collection of toggles and choices that determine how the text will be shown.

Dimension Text Settings is under the DIM SET menu, or it can be initiated by typing **DT**. You will be presented with the following options: **P**lacement (above line), **D**irection (aligned), **C**entered (ON), **I**n-line offset ("), **A**bove offset (") and **T**olerance (none). Select the option by typing its capital letter or by picking it with the cursor.

Placement

Placement refers to text placement: above or dividing the dimension line. The toggle switches between above line and in line.

Direction

Direction controls whether text is parallel to the dimension line or if it always remains horizontal. The toggle switches between aligned and horizontal.

Centered

Centered determines whether or not text is centered on the dimension line. It toggles on and off.

In-line Offset

In-line offset is the gap between the text and the dimension line caused when the text sits in the middle of the dimension line. In-line offset specifies the gap size.

Above Offset

Above offset is the space between the text and the dimension line when the text sits above the dimension line. Above offset prompts for size of offset.

Tolerance

Tolerance was covered earlier in this chapter. It offers four choices: None, Stacked, Fixed, or Max/min variance.

Dimension Layer (UY)

The Dimension Layer command offers a convenient way to place dimension information on your choice of layers. After it is picked, the side menu displays the available layers.

Dimension Color (CS)

When selected, Dimension Color allows you to set the colors for lines, text, dimensions, attributes, hatches, and fills.

Summary

Dimensioning has so many options because of the two major types of drafting styles, architectural and mechanical. All other styles fit somewhere in between these two extremes. Generic CADD does an excellent job of catering to the varying needs of drafters and drafting techniques.

Dimensioning does, in fact, add dimension to your drawings. With dimension commands, components that make up the drawing are explicitly labeled. The power of dimension-related commands is that they provide concrete data: the length of a line, the location of a circle's center, or the number of degrees in an angle.

The basic dimensioning command is Linear Dimension (LX), which dimensions the distance between two points. As part of this labeling process, dimension lines, arrowheads, extension lines, and text are all used to indicate size.

Linear Dimension is affected by the dimension variables, particularly Dimension Direction and Dim Mode. These options allow you to dimension in different directions and to dimension more than one object at a time. Because CADD allows so much flexibility not only in how dimensioning can be accomplished, but in the visual effect, this chapter covers many other commands and options that are an integral part of using dimensioning commands effectively.

Once you become comfortable with dimensioning commands and concepts, think about combining that knowledge with the power of menus and macros (covered in Chapters 15 and 16). These advanced approaches streamline the drafting process and your personal drafting style. Macros can turn toggle commands, such as Proximity Fixed, off and on and set the extension size to various lengths. So much to do, so little time—but at least with CADD, you can do more in less time.

14

Attributes

Like their counterparts created at the drafting table, Generic CADD drawings often are used for recording and storing information. Because every line and object can be drawn with precision, the final drawing can be used as a visual database. Questions like "How many 2x8 floor joists are there?" and "How many feet of 12-gauge wiring are needed for this project?" can be answered by consulting the CADD drawing. The visual representation of objects in Generic CADD thus becomes a database of physical information and quantities.

Jobs such as the design of objects and the creation of working drawings are only a few of many tasks facing the average Generic CADD user. Some common tasks include creating job estimates, compiling a bill of materials, and maintaining inventory levels. Much of the information required for these jobs relates back to the objects depicted in the CADD drawings. But such facts as item number, price, brand names, hours of labor to produce, weight, and markup percentage don't lend themselves to being drawn the way size and quantity do. These pieces of information are non-graphic by nature, yet they also relate to items depicted in CADD drawings. Without a way to attach these kinds of information to the objects, a CADD drawing is an incomplete source of information.

Fortunately, Version 5.0 of Generic CADD includes a way to unite the graphic and non-graphic data generated by a drawing project. By using features called *attributes*, non-graphic data can be attached to objects in the drawing and made available for a variety of purposes.

How Attributes Work

Generic CADD attributes enable you to attach data to components in a drawing. The information can be prepared in advance and attached at will to components in the drawing. Attributes also may be created "on the fly" at any time and immediately attached to a component.

This book has implied that Generic CADD is a database-management program. That is not exactly correct. Attributes, in particular, are similar to the records generated by a database-management program, but the comparison won't hold if it's stretched too far. To understand the uses and limitations of attributes better, the following example compares the use of a database-management program and Generic CADD for recording information about a farmer.

Just last week the county tax collector drove by, looking at farms in the area. When he passed the land belonging to the farmer, the tax collector muttered to no one in particular, "There he is, standing in a field; he is of value to us. We have a record of that man. We keep it in our file." Although this tax collector is a bit eccentric, his muttering happens to be a good description of the database-management program the tax collector uses.

When the tax collector said, "There he is, standing in a field; he is of value to us," he was referring to the relationship between the farmer's name and its place in the tax collection database. The farmer's name is a piece of information. A single piece of information, called a *value*, is stored in a *field* in a database program. Other individual pieces of information (individual *values*) about the farmer—date of birth, address, telephone number, and so forth—are each kept in separate *fields*. For every farmer in the county, the tax collector uses the same *fields*; the *values* change for each farmer.

Next, the tax collector said, "We have a record of that man." All of the fields, with the values filled in, that describe the farmer are stored as one *record*. If the information in the computer were printed out, it would fit on one sheet of paper and would serve as a *record* of what the county knows about the farmer.

Finally, Mr. Taxman said of the record, "We keep it in our file." All of the records of all the farmers are kept in one computer *file*. Fields are filled with values, records, and files; these are the essential elements of a computerized database.

Compare this to Generic CADD and to attributes specifically. A *field* in Generic CADD would be an *entity*, such as a line, a circle, or a component. As you draw, you provide *values* to these fields. If the tax collector were to use Generic CADD to keep a record of the farmer, he would start by drawing a silhouette of the farmer (probably to real scale). The silhouette of the man can be considered a *field*; the height assigned to the outline the *value*. If the tax collector labeled the outline with the farmer's name, the line of text can be considered another *field* and the name typed in that line considered the *value*.

All the various fields reside together in one particular Generic CADD drawing. When saved on disk, it is referred to as a *file*. Note that we skipped the level of record. Perhaps each layer in the drawing is a record, or perhaps each object. As you can see, the comparison is not perfect. But then, we are dealing with only the visual representation of data at this point. The following section discusses the use of attributes with non-visual data.

If the tax collector were forced to use Generic CADD as his only database, it would be very limiting. Adding any more text would be unwieldy, creating a very large file. If, however, the tax collector creates an attribute to attach to the outline of the farmer, much more data can be stored with the drawing and be available for retrieval. As with the database manager, the attribute is made up of fields. "NAME:" would be one field; "TELEPHONE:" would be another. For each farmer, the tax collector can attach an attribute to the outline, filling in the values on each farmer as the attribute is placed. Figure 14.1 shows two silhouettes, representing two farmers. Each has an attribute attached.

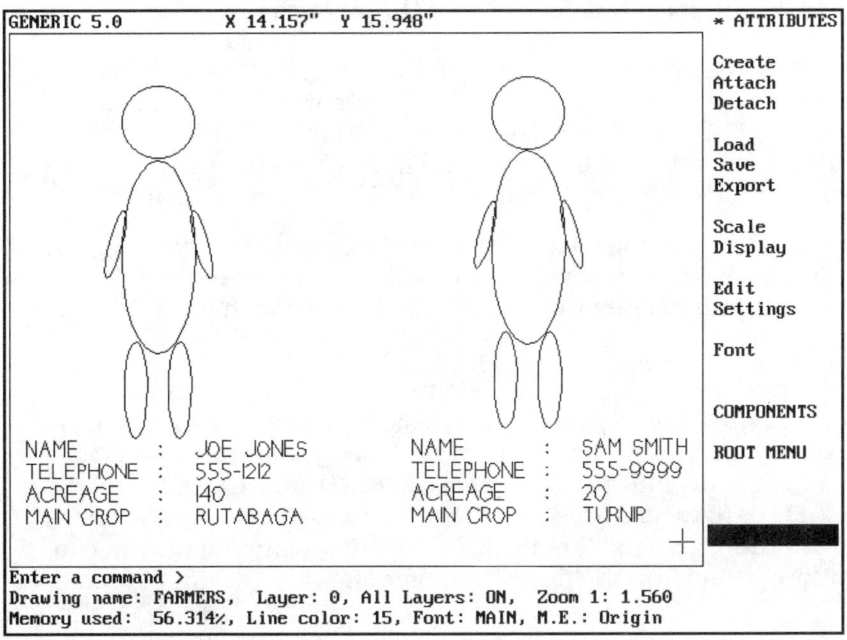

Figure 14.1: *Each outline is a component with an attribute attached.*

In the example shown, "NAME:" "TELEPHONE:" "ACREAGE:" and "MAIN CROP:" are fields; the data assigned to each field are the values. In Generic CADD 5.0, the set of fields is not called a record, but an attribute. Similar to a template, the same attribute (the same set of fields) is used for each farmer. The attribute "template" was attached to the component when it was created. Generic CADD knows to prompt the user to fill in the values each time the component is placed in a drawing.

Attributes have fields that hold values, and one attribute is the equivalent of one record in a database management program. Generic CADD attributes also can be assembled into a collection of attributes, equivalent to a collection of records in a database file. If you use a command called Attribute Export (XA), you can select some of the attributes on the screen or all the attributes in a drawing, and then save the data to a file. The file can be created in one of two formats: the first format can be read by Lotus 1-2-3 and compatible spreadsheets (WK1); the second format is designed for use by programs that read Comma Separated Values (CSV) files. Most database programs read the CSV file format, as do some programs in other application categories. The CSV file format is an ASCII text file, which can be read and edited in a word processor. Experienced programmers find it easy to write their own programs for data use in a CSV file created by Generic CADD 5.0.

How To Create and Place Attributes

This next section offers a step-by-step exercise for creating and using attributes. To follow the exercise, you need to use some of the components distributed with each copy of Generic CADD 5.0. If you removed them from your hard drive, you either can take the time to reinstall Generic CADD, which restores the components, or you can take a few minutes to create some simple components.

All attribute commands can be found in the ATTRIBUTES menu, which branches off the COMPONENTS menu (you won't find ATTRIBUTES listed in the ROOT menu). Most of the two-letter commands for attributes start with the letter "A," but there are exceptions.

Before you can create and place attributes, you first must know what kinds of data you are working with, and then you must design an attribute to match. This exercise creates an attribute "template," which is placed on four bathroom fixtures. To keep it simple, only four fields are recorded: "ITEM:" "COLOR:" "STOCK #:" and "COST$:". Three of the fixtures are components supplied with Generic CADD 5.0; you draw the fourth fixture. By drawing a new component, you can use the option to "pre-attach" an attribute to a component at the time the component is created.

If you need to create substitutes for the components supplied with Generic CADD 5.0, use the three components shown in figure 14.3 as examples. Your replacements don't have to match exactly, as long as you know which of your components replaces each one listed here.

When you do the exercises in this chapter, you place three components from the C:\CADD5\CMP directory: a sink, a tub, and a toilet. If you no longer have these components on your hard drive, draw substitutes for each. If the components supplied with Generic CADD 5.0 are still on your hard disk, follow these steps:

Placing Three Components: a Sink, a Tub, and a Toilet

Prompt	*Input*	*Description*
`Command`	**LS**	Selects Limits command
`Change height limit`	**90"**	Sets new default screen height of 90
`Change width limit`	**60"**	Gives new default screen width of 60
`Command`	**ZL**	Selects Zoom Limits command
`Command`	Move menu bar to `COMPONENTS` and press second mouse button or Home	Brings the COMPONENTS menu on-screen (see fig. 14.2)
`Command`	Move menu bar to `Place` and press second mouse button or Home	Selects the Component Place command
`Select component from side menu`	The menu should be empty. Move menu bar down to `Look on disk` and press second mouse button or Home	Looks in default directory for components
`Select file from side menu: C:\CADD5\CMP\`	The menu should list 10 components, as shown in figure 14.2. Move menu bar to `RSINK-PL` and press second mouse button or Home	Selects the component RSINK-PL to place in drawing

The components supplied with Generic CADD 5.0 appear in the menu when you select the Look on disk option from the Component Place command (see fig. 14.2).

`Enter placement location`	Move cursor to to upper right portion of screen and click	Places sink in drawing
`Command`	Press Space bar	Repeats last command, Component Place

Placing Three Components: a Sink, a Tub, and a Toilet—continued

Prompt	*Input*	*Description*
`Select component from side menu`	Move menu bar to `Look on disk` and press second mouse button or Enter	Looks in default directory for another component
`Select file from side menu`	Move menu bar to `STTUB-PL` and press second mouse button or Home	Selects the component STTUB-PL to place in drawing
`Enter placement location`	Move cursor so component fits along right side of screen and click	Places bathtub in drawing
`Command`	Press Space bar	Repeats last command, Component Place
`Select component from side menu`	Move menu bar to `Look on disk` and press second mouse button or Enter	Looks in default directory for another component
`Select file from side menu`	Move menu bar to `TLET2-PL` and press second mouse button or Home	Selects the component TLET2-PL to place in drawing
`Enter placement location`	Move cursor to lower right corner of screen and click	Places toilet in drawing (see fig. 14.3)

You will create one more component so that an attribute can be pre-attached. But first, you must create the attribute.

Attribute Create (AC)

The Attribute Create command is used to define an attribute that will be attached to one or more components. The attribute name must follow the rules of DOS file names (maximum of eight characters; certain characters not allowed) because it is saved on disk as a separate file, like a component or a drawing file.

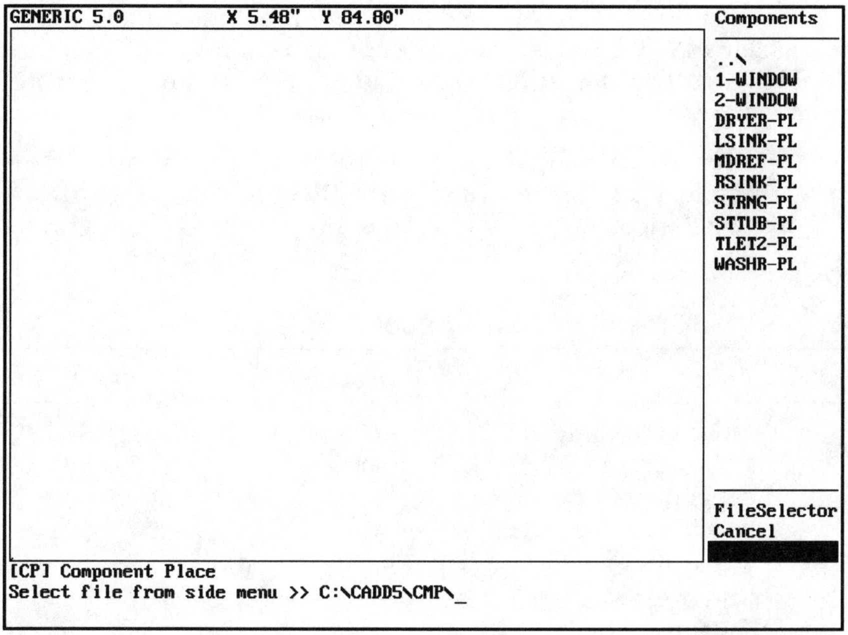

Figure 14.2: *Components appear when the Look on disk option is selected.*

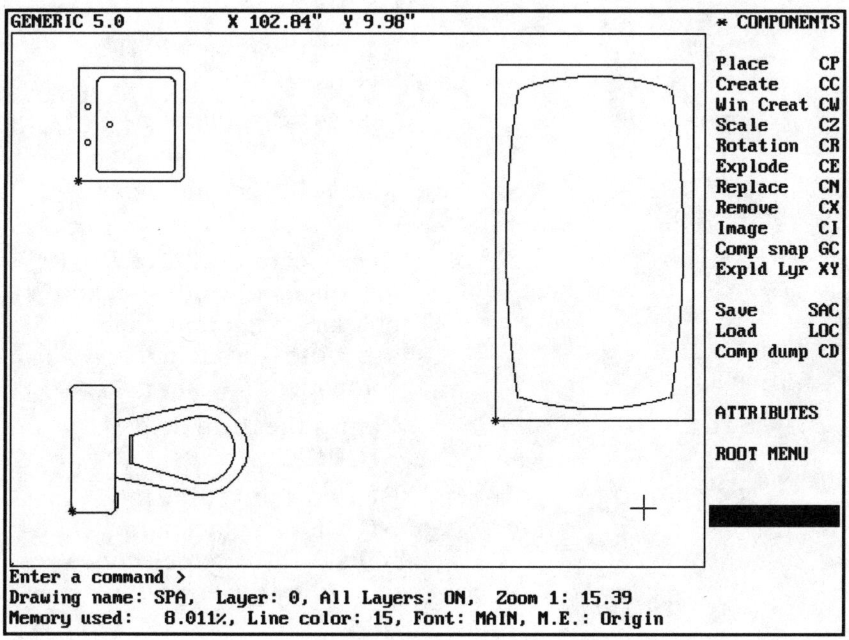

Figure 14.3: *Components placed from the C:\CADD5\CMP directory.*

An attribute can have up to 128 fields. The field names and their default values (or the values later assigned to the fields) also can contain as many as 128 characters. For each field in an attribute, Generic CADD asks for a default value. You may enter a value or leave the value blank by pressing Enter.

When an attribute is attached to a component, it can be set so that the attribute either is visible or not visible. Both the field names and their default values are displayed if the attribute is visible, so you may want to keep the field names brief.

Follow these steps to create a new attribute:

Creating a New Attribute

Prompt	*Input*	*Description*
`Command`	Move menu bar to `ATTRIBUTES` and press second mouse button or Home	Switches to ATTRIBUTES menu
`Command`	Move menu bar to `Create` and press second mouse button or Home	Selects Attribute Create command
`Enter attribute name`	**BATHROOM**	Names the new attribute BATHROOM
`Enter first field name`	**ITEM**	Names the first field ITEM (see fig. 14.4)
`Enter default ITEM`	Press Enter	Leaves value blank
`Enter next field name`	**COLOR**	Names the second field COLOR
`Enter default COLOR`	**WHITE**	Gives default value of WHITE for this field; value can be changed each time the attribute is attached to a component
`Enter next field name`	**STOCK #**	Names the third field STOCK #
`Enter default STOCK #`	**XXXX-000**	Gives default value for STOCK #, a placeholder that reflects future stock codes of four letters and three numbers

Creating a New Attribute—continued

Prompt	*Input*	*Description*
`Enter next field name`	**COST$**	Names the fourth field COST$
`Enter default COST$`	**100.00**	Puts in a value to show correct format for future entries
`Enter next field name`	Press **F10**	Finishes attribution definition; CADD prompt line reads `Attribute has been defined`

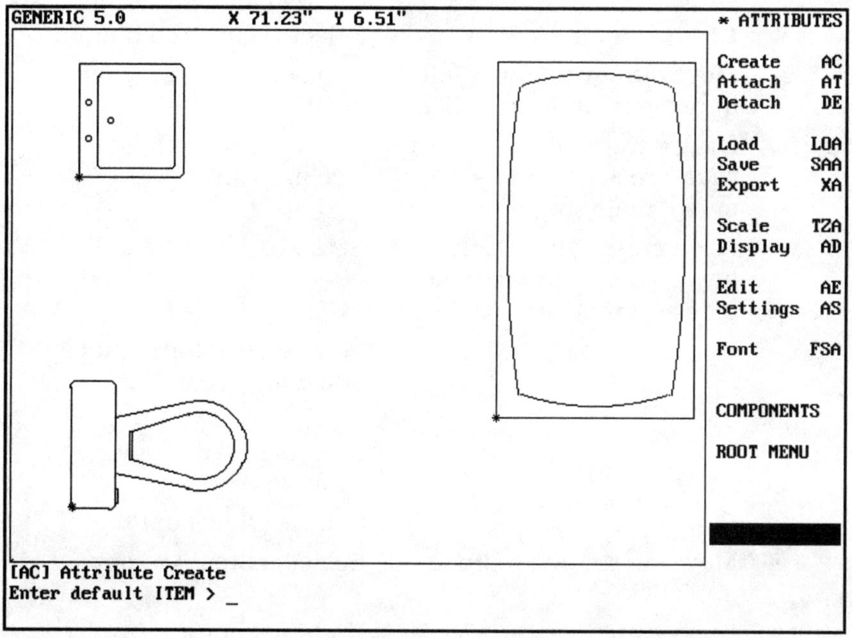

***Figure 14.4:** Generic CADD asks for a default value for each field.*

For the next exercise, draw one more object, a circle with three ellipses, to represent a drain cover. Save it as a component; you later will pre-attach an attribute to it.

Drawing a Circle with Three Ellipses

Prompt	*Input*	*Description*
`Command`	Move cursor to center of screen	Selects center of screen as location for cover
`Command`	**C2**	Selects Two-Point Circle command
`Enter center of circle`	Press Enter	Places center of circle (see fig. 14.5)
`Enter a point on the circle`	Nudge cursor in any direction, type **6"**	Uses direct distance to set radius of circle
`Command`	**ZW**	Selects Zoom Window command
`Place window`	Draw window around circle	Gives close up of circle
`Command`	**EP**	Selects Ellipse command
`Enter start of major axis`	Move cursor to upper left quarter of circle and click	Starts ellipse in top left portion of circle
`Enter end of major axis`	Drag cursor down and left, then press Enter to set end of major axis	Sets length of ellipse (see fig. 14.6)
`Enter an endpoint of the minor axis`	Move crosshair slightly away from center of major axis and press Enter	Sets width of ellipse
`True or Constructed ellipse?`	**T**	Makes true ellipse (not one made from arcs)
`Command`	**RC**	Selects Radial Copy command
`...Object...`	**O**	Selects Object option
`Pick object`	Move cursor onto ellipse and click	Selects ellipse to copy
`Window, Object...`	Press Enter	Ends selection
`Enter an axis point`	**SN**	Snaps to center of arc (see fig. 14.7)
`Center of`	Move cursor onto any part of circle and click	Snaps to center of circle
`Enter total degrees to span`	**360**	Copies objects in a full circular pattern
`Enter total number of items in span`	**3**	Creates three ellipses, including original (see fig. 14.8)

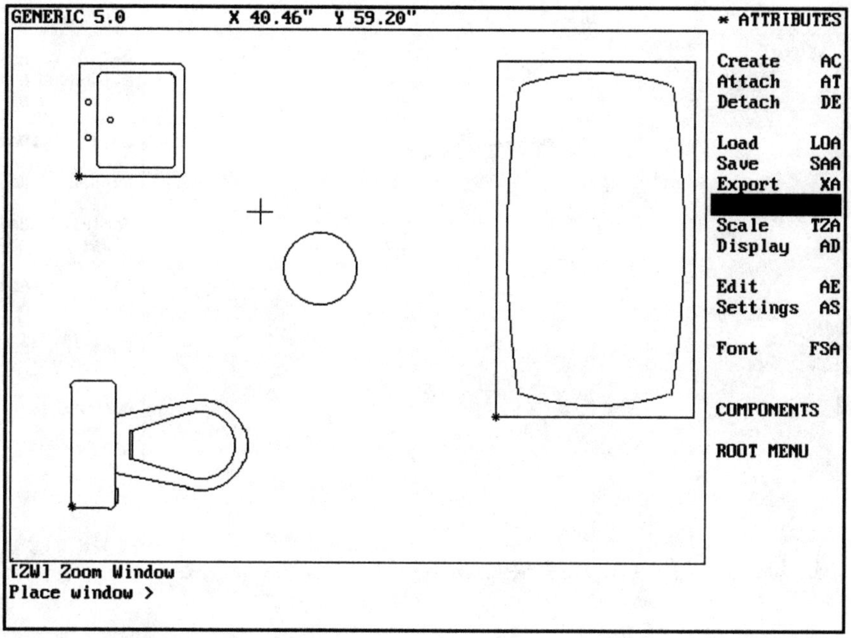

Figure 14.5: *Circle drawn in the center of the screen.*

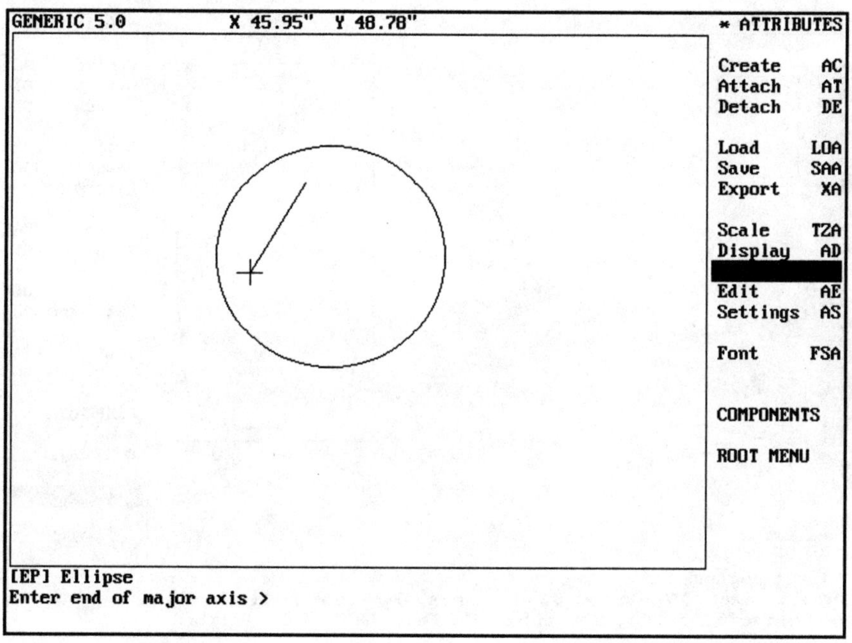

Figure 14.6: *End of the major axis set.*

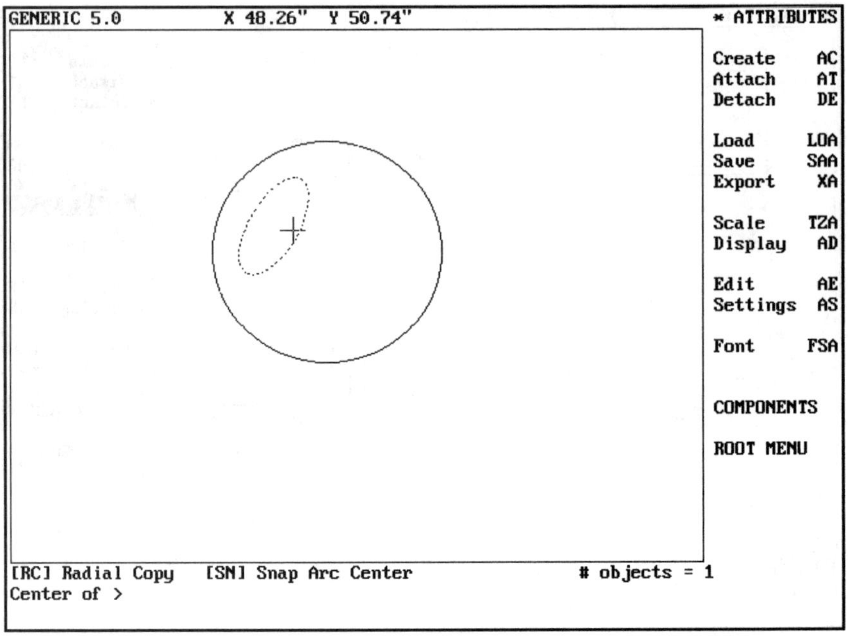

Figure 14.7: *Snap to Arc Center locates the center of the circle.*

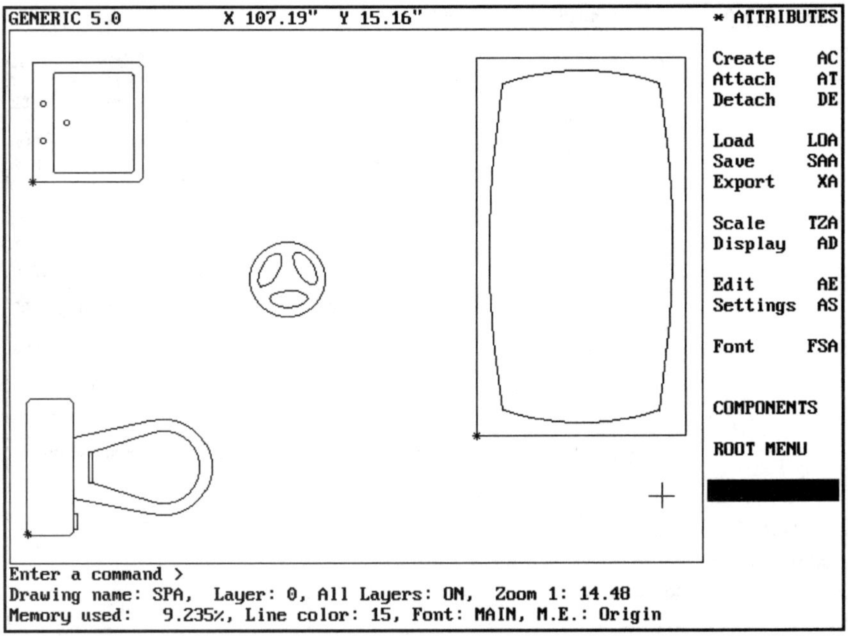

Figure 14.8: *Radial Copy adds two more ellipses.*

Now turn the drain cover into a component and attach the attribute defined earlier. Once the attribute is attached, Generic CADD gives you the option of displaying the attribute on-screen. Conclude the exercise by displaying the attribute next to the component, being careful not to obstruct the drain.

Displaying the Attribute On-Screen

Prompt	*Input*	*Description*
`Command`	**ZA**	Selects Zoom All command
`Command`	**CC**	Selects Component Create command
`Window...`	**W**	Selects Window option
`Place window`	Draw selection window around circle with ellipses	Selects object just drawn to save as a component
`Window...`	Press Enter	End selection process; `# objects = 4`
`Enter component name`	**DRAIN**	Names new component DRAIN (see fig. 14.9)
`Enter component reference point`	**SN**	Snaps to center of arc
`Center of`	Move cursor to any part of circle and click	Selects center point of circle as new component's reference point (see fig. 14.10)
`...Attach attribute...`	**A**	Attaches attribute to new component
`Select Attributes from side menu`	Move menu bar to `BATHROOM` and press second mouse button or Home	Selects an attribute defined earlier
`Display Attribute On oFf`	**O**	Attribute is displayed with component (see fig. 14.11)
`Enter default placement location`	Move cursor and box it is dragging, position just below drain and click	Sets location of the attribute
`Replace original`	**R**	Replaces current drawing of drain with component made from it
`Enter ITEM`	**DRAIN**	Selects DRAIN as value for ITEM field

Displaying the Attribute On-Screen—continued

Prompt	*Input*	*Description*
`Enter COLOR`	**BLACK**	Selects BLACK as value for COLOR field
`Enter STOCK #`	**BATP-013**	Selects BATP-013 as value for STOCK # field
`Enter COST$`	**4.95**	Selects 4.95 as value for COST$ field
`Enter placement location`	Press Enter	Accepts previously defined default location for attribute placement
`Command`	(No action required)	Attribute appears on-screen just below new component (see fig. 14.11)

Attribute Attach (AT)

Once an attribute is defined, a copy of the attribute can be attached to a component at any time. In the previous steps, you attached a copy of the BATHROOM attribute to the floor drain cover; now use the Attribute Attach command to link data with the other components on the screen.

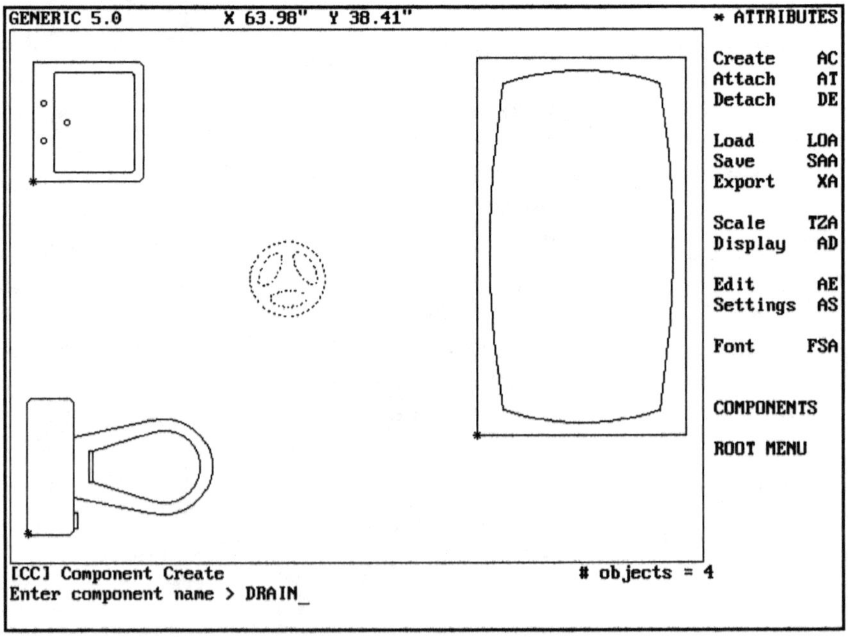

Figure 14.9: *Naming the object.*

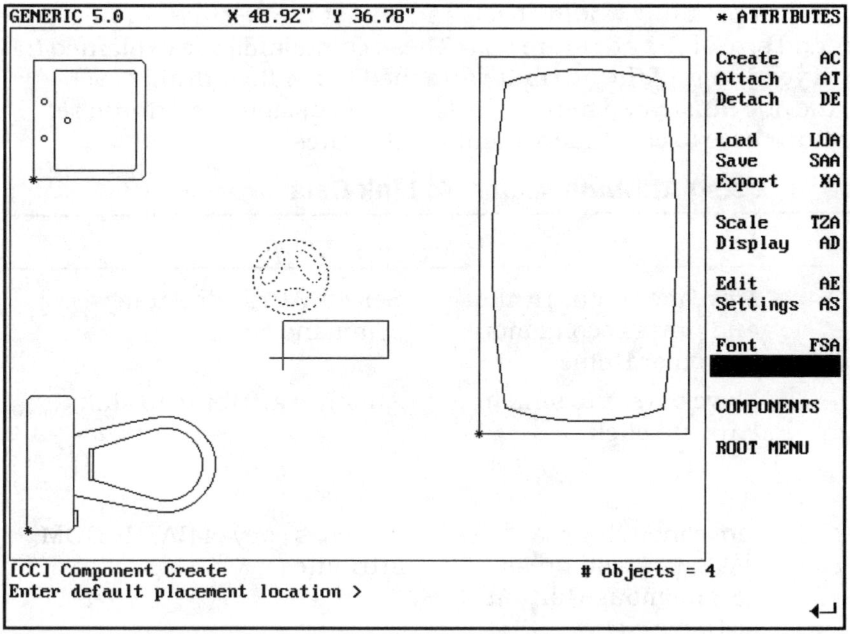

Figure 14.10: *Attribute placed so it is readable and non-obstructive.*

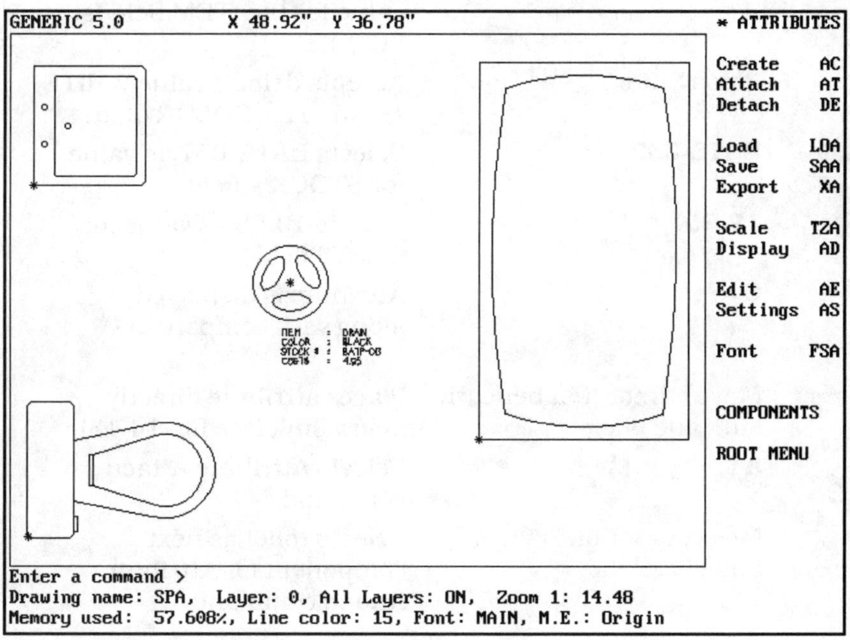

Figure 14.11: *New component with the attribute below.*

In regular practice, you probably would check and adjust the settings for items such as the color and size of the attribute text. These commands are explained in the next section. If your copy of the attribute attached to the floor drain cover doesn't look like the one illustrated here, refer to the discussion of attribute settings, and then return here to continue attaching attributes.

Using Attribute Attach To Link Data

Prompt	*Input*	*Description*
`Command`	Move menu bar to `Attach` and press second mouse button or Home	Selects Attribute Attach command
`Select a component to attach attribute to`	Move cursor to sink (top left) and click	Attaches attribute to sink
`Select Attribute from side menu`	Move menu bar to `BATHROOM` and press second mouse button or Home	Attaches copy of BATHROOM attribute
`Enter ITEM`	**ECONOMY BSINK**	Selects ECONOMY BSINK as value for the ITEM field (see fig. 14.12)
`Enter COLOR`	Press Enter	Accepts default value WHITE as value for COLOR field
`Enter STOCK #`	**BATS-057**	Selects BATS-057 as value for STOCK # field
`Enter COST$`	**19.95**	Selects 19.95 as value for COST$ field
`Display Attribute On oFf`	**O**	Attribute is displayed along with component
`Enter placement location`	Move cursor just beneath sink and click	Places attribute directly below sink (see fig. 14.13)
`Command`	**AT**	Selects Attribute Attach command
`Select a component to attach`	Move cursor onto toilet and click	Selects toilet as next component for Attribute Attach command

Using Attribute Attach To Link Data—continued

Prompt	*Input*	*Description*
`Select Attributes from side menu`	BATHROOM attribute should appear in prompt line; if so, press Enter. If not, select BATHROOM via menu bar or type in at the prompt line	Selects BATHROOM attribute
`Enter ITEM`	**ECONOMY WATER SAVER**	Selects ECONOMY WATER SAVER as value for ITEM field
`Enter COLOR`	Press Enter	Accepts default value WHITE as value for COLOR field
`Enter STOCK #`	**BATT-001**	Selects BATT-001 as value for STOCK # field
`Enter COST$`	**49.95**	Selects 49.95 as value for COST$ field
`Display Attribute On oFf`	**O**	Attribute is displayed along with component
`Enter placement location`	Move cursor just beneath bowl of toilet and click	Places attribute directly below toilet
`Command`	Press Space bar	Repeats last command, Attribute Attach
`Select a component to attach`	Move cursor to bathtub and click	Selects bathtub as next component for Attribute Attach command
`Select Attributes from side menu`	BATHROOM attribute should appear in prompt line; if so, press Enter. If not, select BATHROOM via menu bar or type in at the prompt line	Selects BATHROOM attribute again
`Enter ITEM`	**BUDGET TUB**	Selects BUDGET TUB as value for ITEM field
`Enter COLOR`	**PINK**	Accepts default value WHITE as value for COLOR field
`Enter STOCK #`	**BATB-127**	Selects BATB-127 as value for STOCK # field
`Enter COST$`	**199.95**	Selects 199.95 as value for COST$ field

Using Attribute Attach To Link Data—continued

Prompt	*Input*	*Description*
`Display Attribute On oFf`	**O**	Displays attribute along with component
`Enter placement location`	Move cursor toward center of tub and click	Places attribute inside tub; fig. 14.14 shows all components with attributes attached

Attribute Save (SA)

Remember from the discussion of components that merely creating a component does not mean it is safely stored on disk—saving is a separate process. The same is true for attributes. Although the BATHROOM attribute is placed in this drawing four times, it is not yet stored on disk as an attribute. To make it available for use in other drawings, it must be saved. Generic CADD automatically adds the file extension ATB when it saves attributes. Unless you specify otherwise, Generic CADD saves attributes to the default directory used to store components. (For most users, this will be the C:\CADD5\CMP directory.)

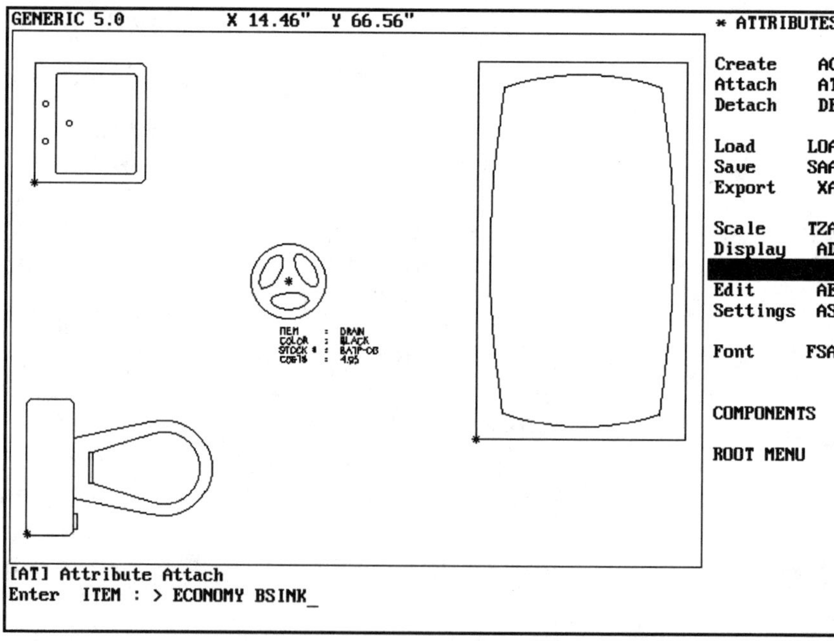

Figure 14.12: *Values entered for each field.*

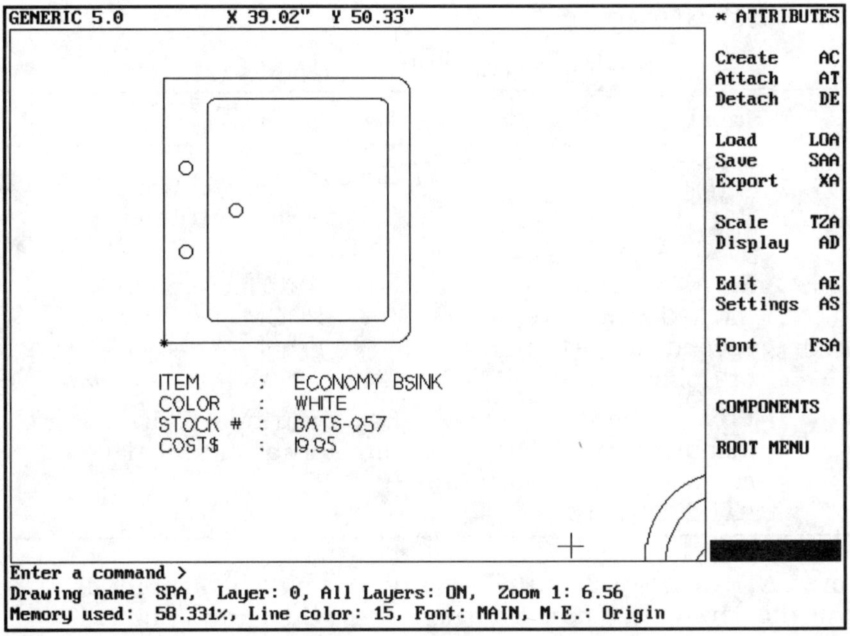

Figure 14.13: *Attribute placed directly beneath the sink.*

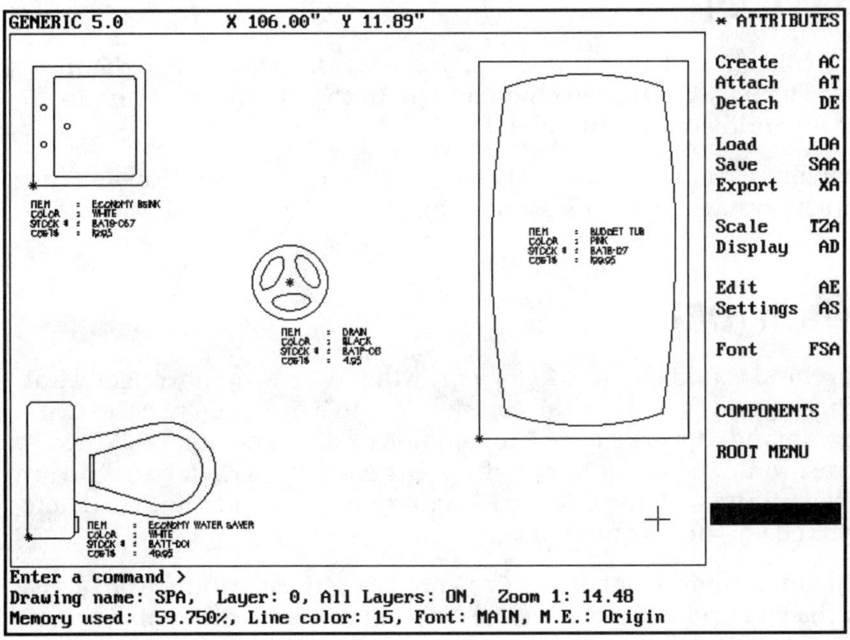

Figure 14.14: *All four components with attributes attached.*

Save the attribute in the next exercise.

Saving an Attribute

Prompt	*Input*	*Description*
`Command`	**SA**	Saves the drawing
(Save options appear)	**A**	Selects Save Attribute options
`Select Attributes from side menu`	Move menu bar to `BATHROOM` and press second mouse button or Home	Selects attribute BATHROOM
`Save file as`	Prompt line should show default directory for components, with attribute `BATHROOM` listed.	Saves attribute to drive and directory as indicated

Press Enter to save BATHROOM to default directory. To save to a different drive and directory, type the new path, type the file name, and then press Enter.

Attribute Load (LO)

As you build your collection of attributes, you probably will want to use them again in other drawings. Use the Load command, with the Attribute option, to load one or more attributes into active memory.

If you need to load more than one attribute for use with a particular drawing, use the File Selection option, which enables you to mark more than one file for selection.

Attribute Detach (DE)

Attributes add to the size and complexity of a drawing. When you no longer want attributes attached to one or more of the components in a drawing, use the Attribute Detach command. It works like a single-choice editing command. When you type **DE** at the prompt or select Detach from the ATTRIBUTES menu, you are prompted for the attribute to detach. Move the cursor onto the attribute to delete and press Enter or click. The attribute disappears.

Detaching an attribute from a component does not erase the attribute from active memory or from the disk, nor does it alter the existing values of other placements of the same attribute. It simply gets rid of the one attribute you select.

Attribute Edit (AE)

As some wag once said, "Just about the time you get two ends to meet, somebody moves the middle." In other words, things are always changing. If the data associated with a component changes after you attach an attribute to it, you can edit the attribute to maintain its accuracy. It also is possible to edit the "template" version of an attribute, which changes the default values so that all future placements of this particular attribute will be up-to-date.

When you type AE for Attribute Edit or select Edit from the ATTRIBUTE menu, the prompt asks you to select whether you will edit a definition (the "template" version of the attribute with default values), or edit a placement (an attribute already attached to a component). Type **D** for Definition or **P** for Placement, as required.

If you choose to edit the definition, you are asked to select the attribute to be edited; select it from the menu or type the name at the prompt line. Generic CADD prompts you to accept or edit each field name and value. Press Enter to accept an entry as is; type corrections and press Enter to make a change. To move faster through the fields and values, use up- and down-arrow keys. You need not go through every field and every default value. Once you have made all the necessary changes, press **F10** to complete the editing session. If you realize you'd rather not make any changes, press Escape to exit the Attribute Edit command without making changes to the attribute's definition.

If you choose to edit a particular placement of an attribute, Generic CADD asks you to pick the appropriate component. Next, you are asked whether you wish to edit the fields in this attribute or change the display status. If you type **F** for edit Fields, you are prompted to accept or change fields and values, as if you were editing the definition. Press Enter to accept current fields and values; type in changes and then press Enter to edit the fields and values. Press **F10** to finish; press Enter to abort the session. If you decide either to make no changes or to not make further changes, press Esc.

The Display default option of the Attribute Edit command is a toggle; if the attribute is set to display on, it will be shut off, and vice versa.

Attribute Settings Options

Like text, components, and dimensions, attributes appear in a specified size, font, color, and rotation. Each option of the Attribute Settings command controls the way attributes look.

Attribute Settings (AS)

The Attribute Settings command is three toggles combined under one title. When you type **AS** or select Settings from the ATTRIBUTES menu, the three toggles appear. They control the status of the default values when the attribute is placed (at Placement); the alignment of attributes (Direction); and the automatic placement of attributes with components (Auto placement).

The at Placement option allows you to choose whether the default values in an attribute are automatically accepted as the values for the new placement, or whether Generic CADD prompts for new values each time an attribute is attached to a component.

The Direction option enables you to choose whether attributes that are made visible are horizontal or set in the drawing at the same angle of rotation as the component.

The Auto placement option controls the placement of attributes that were "pre-attached" when the component was created. When Auto placement is on, the attribute location given when the component was created is automatically accepted. When Auto placement is off, you are prompted to select a location for the attribute, even though you designated one when you created the component. Figure 14.15 shows the prompt line when Attribute Settings is in use. To change any of these values, move the prompt line cursor over the choice and click or type the highlighted letter to toggle the option.

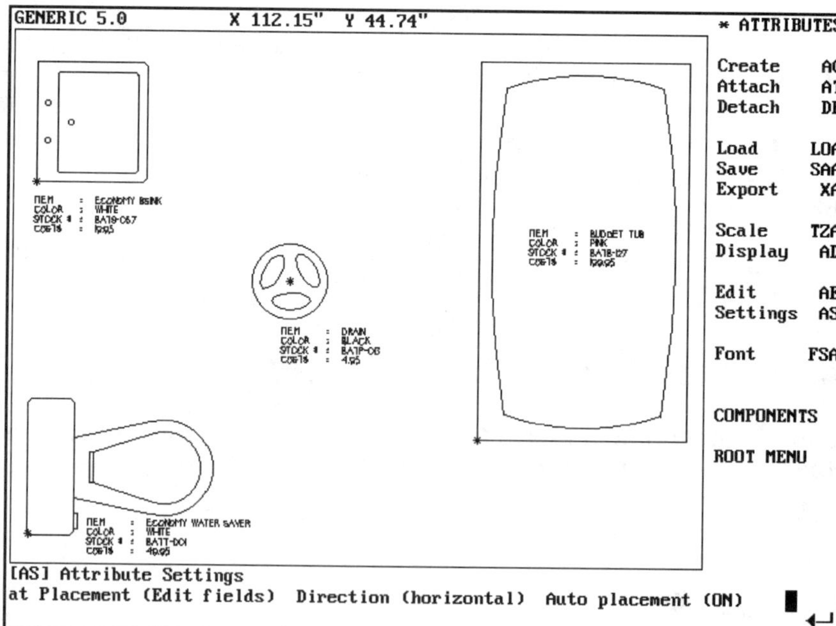

Figure 14.15: *Attribute Settings controls the look of attributes.*

Attribute Scale (TZA)

Attribute Scale controls the size of the text used to display attributes in the drawing. The default size is 1", which was the right size for the example in this chapter. Attribute Scale is user-friendly; you can press equals (=) and click on an object to set the text size equal to the size of the object. If you want to "eyeball" the size, draw a line onscreen that is the desired height of the attribute text. Type **TZA** for Text Size Attribute, then type = and click on the line. The size of attribute text is then equal to the length of this line. Of course, don't forget to erase the line when you are finished with it.

If the size of attribute text is changed after some attributes have been placed in the drawing, only newly-placed attributes display the new text size; the size of existing attribute text will not change.

Attribute Display (AD)

When attributes are first defined, you are asked to choose whether or not they should appear in the drawing when attached to a component. If you use a variety of attributes, some may have a default setting on (visible), others a default setting off (not visible). The Attribute Display command can override the default status of every component in a drawing. You can turn all attributes on, off, or simply let them be displayed according to their default status.

Extracting Information from Attributes

It is not uncommon for Generic CADD to enter into a professional's life through the back door. A contractor or consulting engineer may buy a computer to take care of the books and then discover the value of computer-aided design and drafting. If so, programs probably are already in use that can manipulate the same data as attributes. It is possible to pass the information from the attributes in a drawing to other programs using the Attribute Export command.

Attribute Export (XA)

Attribute Export uses the same selection process as multiple-object editing commands. When you type **XA** at the prompt, or select Export from the ATTRIBUTES menu, the list of selection options appears in the prompt line. This enables you to select the exact attributes you need for a special report. Perhaps you have a large floor plan filled with components and attributes and you need to prepare a bid estimate for only one room. By using Attribute Export, you can select the components in that room and have the attribute data saved to a file.

The file created by the Attribute Export command can take one of two formats. As mentioned earlier, the two formats are the WK1 file specification (for spreadsheets compatible with Lotus 1-2-3) and an ASCII text format called CSV (Comma Separated Values). This latter format commonly is used by database-management programs.

Follow these steps to save all the attributes in your drawing to a CSV-format file:

Saving Attributes to a CSV-Format File

Prompt	*Input*	*Description*
`Command`	Type **XA** or select Export from the `ATTRIBUTES` menu	Selects Attribute Export command
(Selection options appear)	**D**	Selects Drawing option; all components and their attached attributes are selected and highlighted
(Selection options appear)	Press Enter	Ends selection of attributes
`Export format: CSV Lotus`	**C**	Selects Comma Separated Values as file format for attributes file about to be created
`Save file as`	**SPA.CSV**	Saves attributes in file named SPA.CSV
`Command`	(Do nothing)	File is created; components (and their attached attributes) are no longer selected

The resulting file created by the Attribute Export command looks like the following:

```
/100,"RSINK-PL",  10.958137,  65.060249,   1.000000,     1.000000
/200,"BATHROOM"
/300,"ITEM","COLOR","STOCK #","COST$"
/400,"ECONOMY BSINK","WHITE","BATS-057","19.95"
/100,"TLET2-PL",  10.115203,   9.325302,   1.000000,     1.000000
/200,"BATHROOM"
/300,"ITEM","COLOR","STOCK #","COST$"
/400,"ECONOMY WATER SAVER","WHITE","BATT-001","49.95"
```

```
/100,"STTUB-PL",  78.814293,  24.722895,   1.000000,    1.000000
/200,"BATHROOM"
/300,"ITEM","COLOR","STOCK #","COST$"
/400,"BUDGET TUB","PINK","BATB-127","199.95"
/100,"DRAIN",  50.154549,  49.662655,   1.000000,    1.000000
/200,"BATHROOM"
/300,"ITEM","COLOR","STOCK #","COST$"
/400,"DRAIN","BLACK","BATP-013","4.95"
```

Each /100 item is the name of the component, followed by the coordinate location (two numbers), and the scale of the component (two numbers, for X-scale and Y-scale). Each /200 item is the name of the attribute. Each /300 item lists the names of the fields in the attribute and each /400 item provides the values for each field. For more information on how this information is used, consult the reference manual of the database-management program you plan to use. Check the index for "Importing" or "CSV files."

Summary

The addition of attributes to Generic CADD 5.0 has made it possible to deal with not only the design and drafting of objects, but the storage of data associated with these objects as well. By their nature, drawings can account for size and quantity. Certain items of information are non-visual, however, (cost, stock number, weight, and terms of warranty, for example) and do not lend themselves to being represented by drawing objects. Attributes can be used to attach such non-visual information to objects in a CADD drawing. The only restriction on the placement of attributes is that they must be attached to components, not individual lines.

The format of an attribute in Generic CADD is similar to that used by database management programs. Individual pieces of data, known as values, are grouped together to form one attribute, which can be created before anything is drawn on the screen. You then can re-use the attribute, like a template, making changes each time to accurately reflect new data.

Attributes can be created "on the fly" when needed. Attributes can be displayed on-screen, remain invisible, or be saved on disk for repeated use. Like other forms of text available in Generic CADD, attributes can be edited to correct errors. The data can be extracted from a CADD drawing and used in other software. Two formats are supported: the WK1 format, used by Lotus 1-2-3 and compatible spreadsheets; and the Comma Separated Values format (CSV) used by many database management programs.

15

Automating Repetitive Tasks with Macros

The real power in using a computer for drafting comes not so much from its speed and accuracy, but from its ability to automate repetitive tasks. Most CAD packages, including Generic CADD, enable users to automate tasks by grouping commands into strings. Commands that are grouped together in such a manner are called *macros*.

Using Generic CADD for fun or profit becomes more fun and certainly more profitable if you use macros. You almost can't avoid using them, in fact. A macro can be used for nearly every command, providing endless opportunities to save keystrokes. Macros, batch files, and custom menus make an already fast CADD program even faster.

Macros also improve accuracy. They reduce input errors because, once written properly, they do not make mistakes. Unlike people, macros never change a value, misspell a word, or get distracted by the telephone.

Macros can do just about anything that can be done manually, such as placing text, placing components, editing, and automatic drawing. If it can be done with the keyboard, digitizer, or mouse, it can be done with a macro.

This chapter teaches you how to write macros and gives you some sample macros to try.

Defining Macros

Macros can be as simple as stringing together one command and its single-letter option, such as FS,D (Font Scale, Dimension). This macro, for example, alerts the computer that a change is about to take place and what the change is going to be. A macro can include over 250 characters, and about 80 commands, which is enough to perform just about any environmental update that a user might require.

A macro's maximum length is determined by its use. Macros used within a menu are limited to 80 characters, minus the number of characters in the menu item name or line number. Macros assigned to a function key or pointer button are limited to 250 characters. Macros in the form of batch files are limited only by the computer's memory.

Macros can be made up of anything that can be typed on the keyboard. They may contain any Generic CADD command, any user response to a previous command, and even variables. (See Chapter 17 on batch files for more information.) Macros can perform most of the mundane drafting tasks that take up productive time; they can, in fact, be the most important tool in Generic CADD's toolbox.

Understanding How Macros Work

Basically, a Generic CADD macro works by temporarily redirecting to input a series of previously stored commands. The macro may be invoked by pressing a function key or pointer button, or by clicking on a menu selection. The CADD program reads the entire macro and then acts on each command in sequence until it reaches the end, signified by a semicolon.

The following macro sets a chamfer distance and then issues a command to chamfer:

```
CA,.25",.25",CH;
```

Why combine the two commands? Because setting the chamfer distance every time a chamfer is required is both redundant and uses CPU time. Using a macro saves at least one keystroke or click of the mouse, and the user always gets the correct chamfer size.

Writing and Saving Macros

Macros may be stored and used through four input methods: function keys, pointer buttons, menus, and batch files. Function keys and pointer buttons are discussed here; menus and batch files are explained in Chapters 16 and 17. All macros, however, are written in the same command language.

Understanding the Ground Rules for Writing Macros

Only a few rules are required for writing macros, but those rules most be followed to the letter. Leave out a single character, even just a comma, and the macro does not work. The following special characters are used in macros:

- The comma (,) separates commands, data, and other special characters. It also acts as an Enter key and causes problems with any command, such as the Filter command, that activates without the Enter key.
- The tilde (~) is used whenever the macro requires the user to type in a numeric value or a name (X and Y values count as one value each, that is (,~,~,)).
- The at sign (@) prompts the user to enter a point from the pointer or keyboard.
- The pound or number sign (#) acts as an Escape key and is used to end text placement within a macro.
- The semicolon (;) denotes the end of a macro. Anything after it is ignored; notes can be stored after the semicolon.
- The exclamation point (!) acts as an Enter key.
- The slash (/) deactivates a special character when placing text with a macro, so that a special macro character is read as text and not as part of a command. The slash is used prior to a special character. For example, put a slash before a comma, a number sign, or a slash that you want to appear as text (/,), (/#), or (//).
- The double plus (++) or double minus (--) signs set toggles on or off, in or out, and this or that. These symbols are used only after a toggle and have no effect if used anywhere else. Be prepared for a little trial and error when setting some toggles in macros.

Don't assume anything when you're writing macros. The only thing you should assume is that the settings your macro needs in order to run correctly may not be properly set. Use the double plus (++) or double minus (--) signs to set any toggles that are required in the macro.

Always use units when setting a value within a macro. Setting the units, for example, ensures that the macro returns a value of one inch instead of one millimeter. It is not necessary to use units for values of zero or when setting scale values.

Always set the Manual Entry Offset Relative (MR) mode when setting points. Unusual results can occur if the entry mode is not set properly.

Examining Macros

Many options are available when writing a macro. A detailed examination of two macros—one that places a component and one that draws a balloon—shows how they work.

Introducing the Component-Placing Macro

```
CR,A,@,@,GC,++,CZ,~,~,CI,++,CP,~,~,@,IP,@,@,@;
```

The first few characters control component rotation. There are actually three ways this section could have been written:

```
CR,A,@,@
```

This method enables the user to match the rotation with another line or direction. In most cases, the user should first snap to the leftmost or bottommost point and then to the second point.

```
CR,V,@,@,@
```

This method requires the user to select three points, following the prompt located in the status area of the screen. The three points selected form the angle that sets the component rotation.

```
CR,~
```

This method looks the simplest, but it requires the user to type the rotation from the keyboard (hence the tilde symbol). The zero degree angle is at the 3 o'clock position on the monitor.

The Component Snap command in the macro enables you to use other points within the component as construction or snap points rather than the defined reference point:

```
GC,++
```

Turns on the Component Snap command. This is very useful for insertion of screw heads, clamps, and so on.

```
GC,–
```

Turns off the Component Snap command.

The Component Scale (CZ) command should be included in every macro that places components because you probably won't know the scale setting when the macro is typed in:

```
CZ,~,~
```

This macro segment enables you to select X and Y scales that are either different from each other or are the same. Remember, circles and arcs within exploded components cannot have different scales. Actual values can replace ,~,~, if you want to lock in a certain scale.

The Component Image (CI) command is included to make sure that the command is turned on or off in the macro:

```
CI,++
```

Places components as images. Images should be used whenever you are sure that the component is to be edited or when the drawing is to be converted to a DXF file. Components cannot be inserted into an AutoCAD file when the ACAD.DWG (template drawing) is present.

```
CI,-
```

Places components as components. Components can be exploded for editing.

Placing the component is very simple within a macro. The user has two choices: "component name specific" or "user defined during execution of the macro." Either choice has its use and value, depending on the situation:

```
CP,name
```

Name-specific placement commands are used mostly in menus. They also can be used where special components used as drawings or dimensional symbols are employed.

```
CP,~,~,@
```

User-specified placement commands are used as generic macros. This command invokes the side bar menu and displays any components already loaded into memory. You also are enabled to look at the disk for components. You can click on one of these displayed components or type one from the keyboard. Digitizer users do not have the side bar option unless a video menu is loaded first. (See Chapter 16 for more information on loading video menus.)

The Insertion Point (IP) command, the last item in this macro, is used to reset the point of insertion of a macro. It enables you to temporarily set down the component and pick it up again. Then the components can be inserted with a different reference point and with more precision:

```
IP,@,@,@;
```

The first "@" symbol pauses the macro for you to choose a temporary resting place. The second "@" is for choosing another insertion point. The third "@" is for picking the placement point.

Introducing the Balloon Macro

The individual commands of the balloon macro are discussed in the following section. Make sure your program is set to Manual Entry Offset Relative (MR) before trying out this macro.

```
YC,~,LT,0,LC,3,C2,@,.281",0,L1,
-.562",0,.562",0,PO,-.281",.04",PO,0,-.205";
```

```
YC,~
```

Current layer is user-selectable. If it is on the desired layer, the user still is required to enter a layer number because entering a return without doing so makes Generic CADD return a value of -1. It may be possible to have a layer called -1, but it is not a good practice.

```
LT,0
```

Selects Line Type Zero (solid).

```
LC,3
```

Selects Line Color 3.

```
C2,@,.281",0
```

Draws a circle .562 in diameter and places it at the point you designate.

```
L1,-.562",0,.562",0
```

Draws a horizontal line through the center of the circle.

```
PO,-.281",.04"
```

Places a standard point for text insertion in the upper half of the balloon.

```
PO,0,-.205";
```

Places a standard point for text insertion point in the lower half of the balloon.

Using Macro Assign (MA)

The Macro Assign command enables you to create and save macros on the fly. It is accessed within CADD by typing **MA** or clicking on Macro Assign from the UTILITIES menu. The prompt area at the bottom of the screen displays the prompt `Press a function key or a pointer button to be assigned a macro >>`. The choices are as follows:

Pointer buttons B3 through B16 (B1 and B2 are reserved by Generic CADD)

Function keys F1 through F12

Ctrl + Function keys F1 through F12

Shift + Function keys F1 through F12

Alt + Function keys F1 through F12

It is possible to program up to 62 macros using the function keys and pointer buttons. How can you remember exactly which does what? A list of your macros can be viewed in at least two ways.

The least complicated way is to use the Screen Flip command (SF) and select the third item (`Display assigned macros`). The screen display lists the macros. A secondary menu appears under the list offering these choices:

Shift **A**lt Ctrl **F**unction_key - **P**ointer_button

Selecting any one of these secondary menu items displays another 12 function keys, except Pointer button which displays 16 button selections.

The second way to examine your macros is slightly more complicated, but it may prove easier to use. If the video driver supports images, a drawing can be made. Execute the Image Save (SA,I) command and call it Macro. Then edit the F1 function key as follows:

Using Macro Assign To Write and Save Macros

Prompt	*Input*	*Description*
`Command`	**MA**	Starts the Macro Assign command
`Press a function key or pointer button to be assigned a macro`	Press F1	Displays edit line for F1 at bottom of screen
`Edit macro [F1]>>`	Press backspace to delete until cleared: type **LO,I,**`path`****`macro`;	Saves the macro when you press Enter after typing the macro name

When using a mouse or the keyboard, the primary function keys should be programmed with snaps. This increases the input speed. When using a 16-button puck or a digitizer, the snaps should be assigned to the buttons.

When selecting the secondary function buttons for assignment, you must press Ctrl, Shift, or Alt along with the function keys because the menu only displays the current status of the function keys.

Using Screen Flip (SF)

The Screen Flip (SF) command assigns, edits, and saves macros. The command works in much the same way as the Macro Assign command. The primary difference is that the Screen Flip command displays a menu. Choosing #3 from the SF menu displays the choices as follows:

Shift **A**lt Ctrl **F**unction_key - **P**ointer_button

Editing is accomplished in the following example.

Using Screen Flip (SF) To Write and Save a Macro

Prompt	*Input*	*Description*
Command:	**SF**	Starts the Screen Flip command
`Enter Selection>`	**3**	Accepts `Display assigned macros`
`Press a function key or pointer button to be assigned a macro`	Press a function key and then use backspace until cleared	Shows any previously assigned macro and prepares line for new macro
`Edit macro [Fno.]>>`	**CA,.5",.5",CH;** and Press Enter	Establishes and saves new macro

When using a mouse or the keyboard, the primary function keys should be programmed with snaps. This increases the input speed. When using a 16-button puck or a digitizer, the snaps should be assigned to the buttons.

When selecting the secondary function buttons for assignment, you must press Ctrl, Shift, or Alt along with the function keys, because the menu only displays the current status of the function keys.

Creating Some Sample Macros

The best way to learn how to write macros is to try writing and using some of the following macros. These sample macros utilize component placement, environment settings, and editing sequences. The following macros can pre-set dimensional displays, set dimension offsets, place text, construct drawing elements, and select line color and type.

Setting Up Dimensional Display Macros

One of the major obstacles when finishing a drawing is selecting dimensional displays. How the dimension is displayed is not too important until the plot is finished. That is when all of the multiple lines that are in the same spot show up. Turning off different witness lines and arrows for each dimension can be a hassle. This is where the macro comes in. Chapter 13 discusses dimension setups in detail.

```
DD,L,++,R,++,D,++,E,—,X,—,T,++,!,AR,O,++,!;
```

Hides both extension lines and sets arrows outside pointing in (see fig. 15.1).

```
DD,L,++,R,++,D,++,E,—,X,++,T,++,!,AR,O,++,!;
```

Hides first extension line and sets arrows outside pointing in (see fig 15.1).

When almost every dimension requires a different setting, the macro becomes even more important.

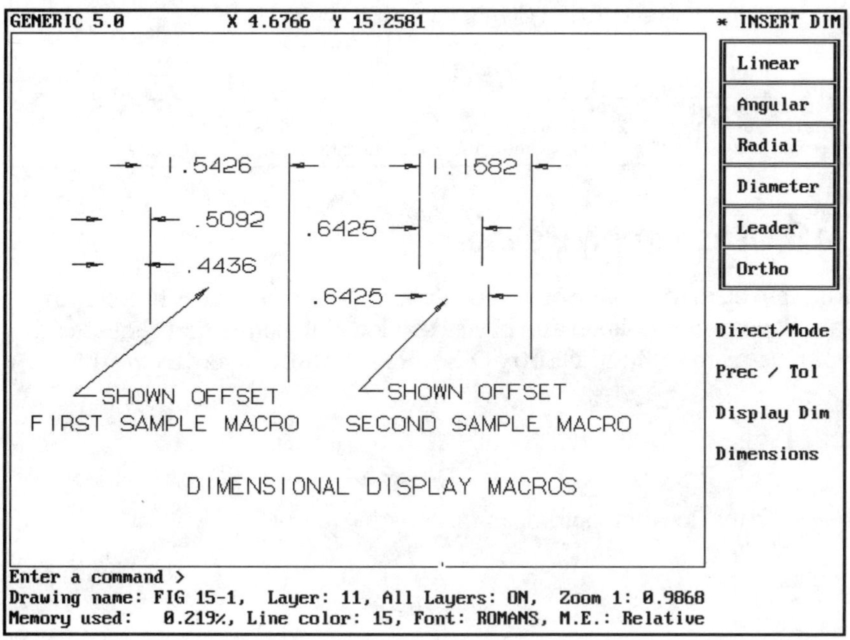

Figure 15.1: *Dimensional display presets.*

When returning to standard dimensioning from an ortho dimensional display, extension line offsets must be reset.

```
XS,O,.06",A,.12",B,.44",!,DT,P,++,D,—,!;
```

Sets line gap, above and below line distance, dimension text placement, and direction (see fig 15.2).

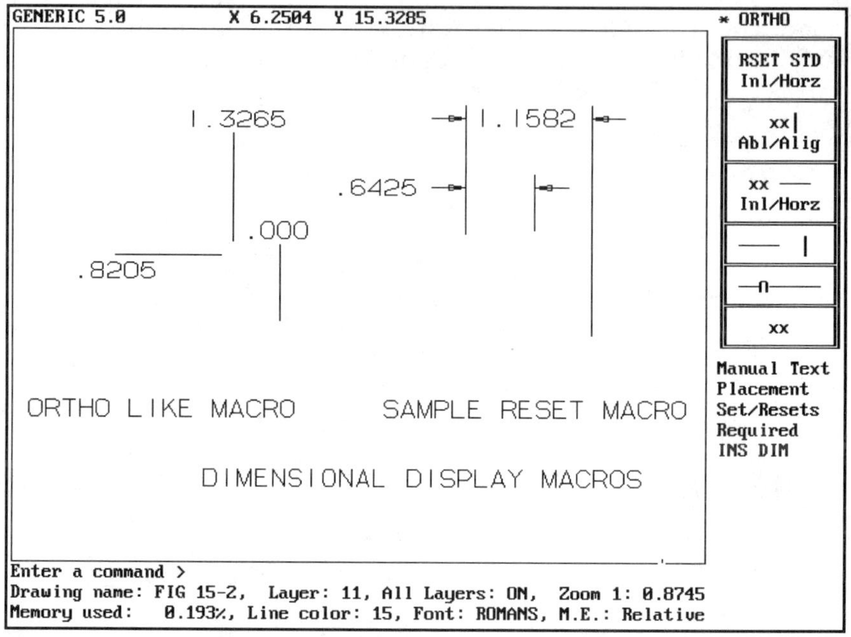

Figure 15.2: *Resetting offsets.*

Constructing a Split Assembly Balloon

Every drawing has certain elements that clarify the intent of the delineation. The following macro constructs a split assembly balloon and places text location points that center text. Remember to set your program to Manual Entry Offset Relative (MR) before trying this macro.

```
YC,~,LT,0,LC,3,C2,@,.281",0,L1,-.562",0,.562",0,PO,
-.281",.04",PO,0,-.205";
```

Figure 15.3 shows the text location points.

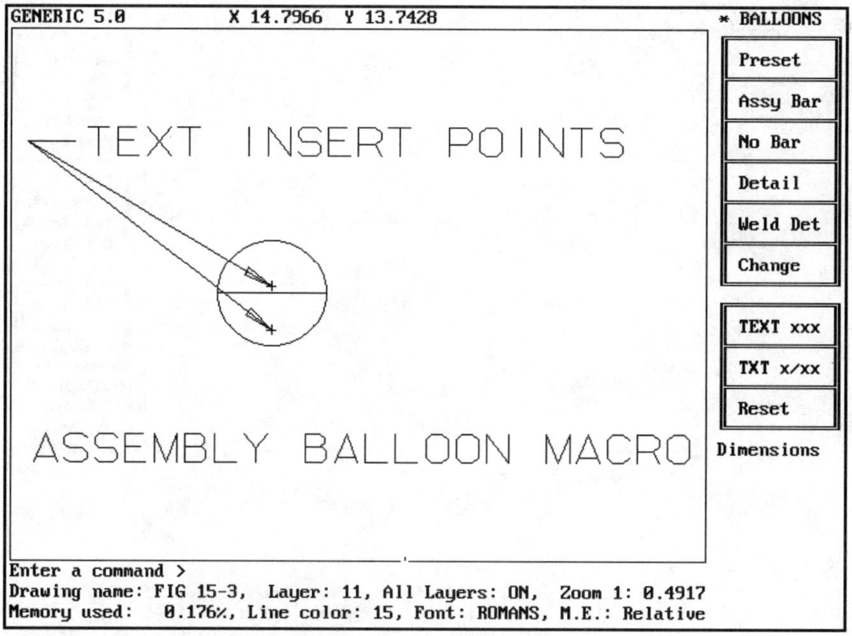

Figure 15.3: Assembly balloon with text location points.

Standardizing Text Input

Standardized text placement with macros speeds input. The following example demonstrates just how effective macros can be.

```
TL,@,TEXT PLACE,!,#;
```

Figure 15.4 shows the insertion point.

Standardized text, whether accessed through pointer buttons, function keys, or menus, can speed text input by a factor of 15.

Setting Line Type and Color

The following simple macro ties linetype to line color. The layer, width, scale, and so on also could be included.

```
LT,0,LC,1;
```

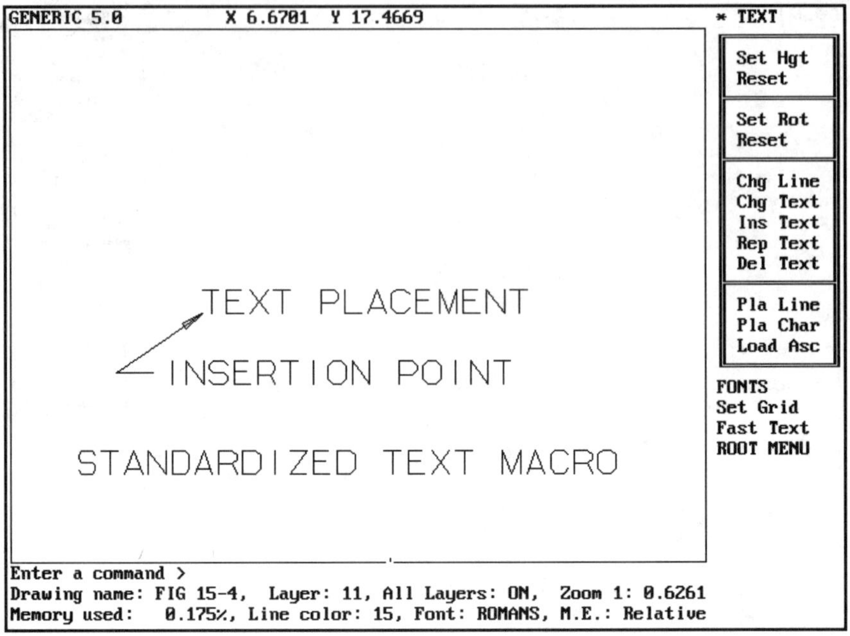

Figure 15.4: *Standardized text input.*

Placing Components

Macros should be used to place every component. All conditions can be set with a macro and are not forgotten, including scale, rotation, layer, image on/off, component snap, insertion point, and the component itself. The following macro includes all of these components:

```
CR,A,@,@,GC,++,CZ,~,~,CI,++,CP,~,~,@,IP,@,@,@;
```

The user must decide whether to use A or V after CR; ++ or -- after GC and after CI; O,C, or P after XY; and whether IP is to be used at all.

The macro above enables you to set the rotation by pointing to the ends of an existing line, setting the X and Y scale, naming the component, and changing the insertion point.

Setting Up the Environment

Macros can be written to set or reset any or all default values. When starting a drawing that is going to be plotted at half size, clicking on a macro that sets all affected defaults to double scale makes quick work of a very time-consuming process.

Text height, dimensional offsets, shoulder lengths, and arrowhead lengths are just a few items that can be included in a macro.

```
TZ,D,~,T,~,A,~,!,XS,O,~,A,~,B,~,!,AR,L,~,!,LL,~;
```

If the macro contains actual values instead of the tilde for user input, the process is even faster. Several macros could be written for all the different scales used.

Using Common Editing Sequences

Editing drawings takes more time than constructing them, so it is essential to reduce the number of keystrokes. Just as components reduce input time for drawing, macros can reduce editing time. Macros that select, chamfer, fillet radii, and change dimensions reduce key strokes. A few examples of editing macros follow.

```
CA,.25",.25",CH;
```

Sizes and places the command for chamfer

```
FR,.5",FI;
```

Sizes and places the command for fillet

```
UG,@,O,!;
```

Changes the location of dimension arrows (see fig. 15.5)

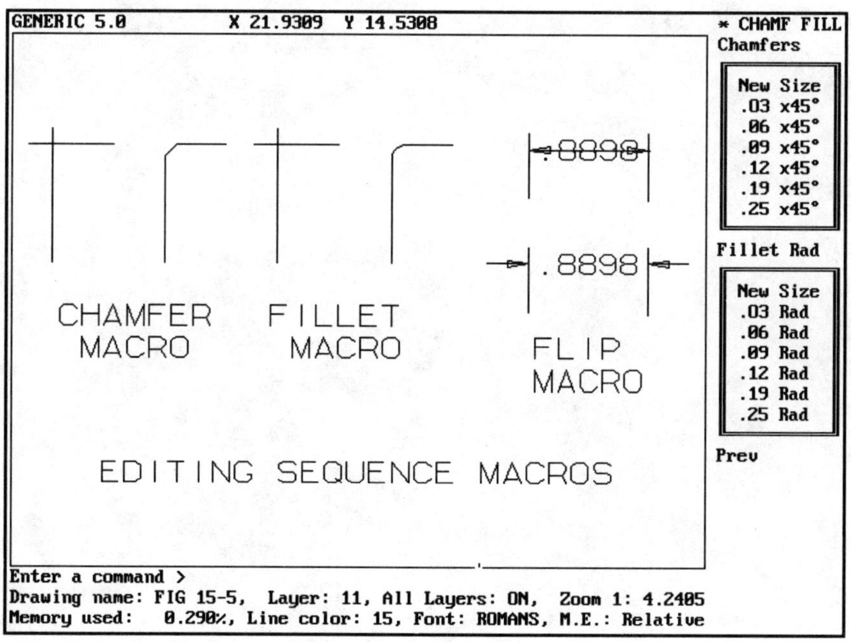

Figure 15.5: Sample editing sequences.

Hundreds of editing macros are possible, but you can get along nicely with about 24.

Summary

In this chapter, you learned many things about macros. You now know from examples that macros are nothing more than command strings that automate repetitive tasks. You learned about the maximum lengths of macros and how to use the Generic CADD commands to achieve greater ease and speed in your use of Generic CADD.

Learning how macros work and the rules that govern them is a good foundation for writing your first macros. Several macros were examined to show the various options available to you. You have been guided through several sample macros that covered subjects ranging from dimensional display macros to common editing sequence macros. These samples enabled you to expand your understanding of macros.

You learned through the Macro Assign (MA) and Screen Flip (SF) commands how macros can be written and saved. These two commands guide the user through the macro-writing process.

One final warning: although you could, through intentional errors, make macros do things the software wasn't designed to do, be warned that the next update may wipe out those macros. Avoid using any undocumented procedures because they may not be included in the next version.

16

Tailoring the Menu System

Of all the tools in Generic CADD's toolbox, menus, with their easy editing techniques, are the most important. Menus give you access to the user files in the order you require. The ability to find and access data is the backbone of any efficient CADD system.

The standard menu structure provided with Generic CADD is stored in a special ASCII text file called CADD5.MNU. The program looks for and loads this menu because it is listed in the environmental file. The menu is not simply a list of command choices, but a hierarchy that begins at the base menu, known as the ROOT menu. The ROOT menu lists the other menu choices. In this chapter, all other menus are referred to as submenus or pages. A *submenu* lists available commands, as well as other submenus or pages.

After Generic CADD boots and the first screen has been displayed, the program loads the menu system starting with a ROOT menu as shown in figure 16.1. `ROOT MENU`, the first item at the top of the menu, is followed by a blank line, below which is a list of items that can be selected to view the various submenus. The ROOT menu depicted in figure 16.1 is an edited version having the standard menu selections above the added options.

After one of these submenus is selected, the appropriate submenu is displayed. The first item indicates its submenu or page name, followed by a blank line which separates the submenu name from the command choices that are available. As figure 16.2 shows, the last three choices may be menu item names, such as Previous, ROOT menu, or More. Choosing the Previous option returns the menu to the last-displayed page, whereas choosing the More option advances the menu to whatever you have named as the next page. Some first-time users think that "More" means that there are more menu choices of the same type, but the More option actually can take you to any specified location in the file.

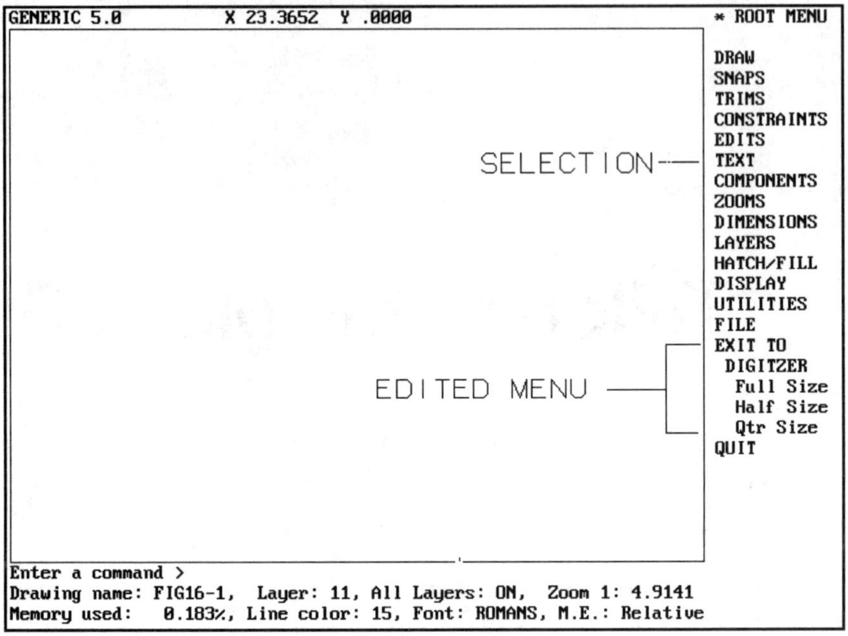

Figure 16.1: *ROOT menu.*

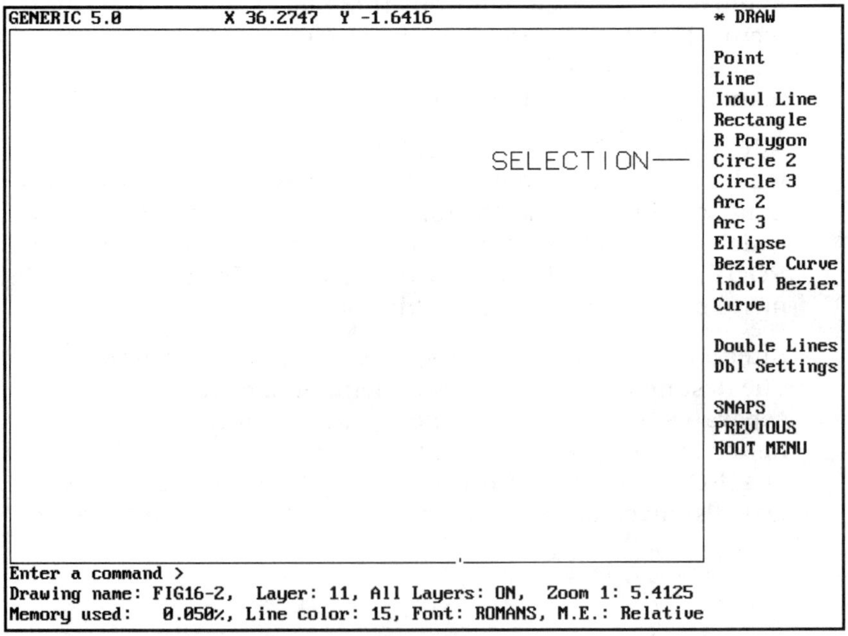

Figure 16.2: *Typical submenu.*

Certain commands, such as Hide, Display, Current Layer, call up a unique feature known as the *sidebar.* This feature is Generic CADD's answer to pull-down menus. The sidebar not only lists the current contents of the data base, but also enables you to browse through the hard disk and pick items to insert into the drawing file. When you select Cancel, the program returns to the submenu that was in use before browsing began. Figure 16.3 shows a sidebar menu that lists all the drawing files in the directory. Digitizer users cannot use this feature directly. They must write a macro that loads the video menu and calls for one of the commands to evoke the sidebar. They also must edit the video menu so it toggles back to the digitizer.

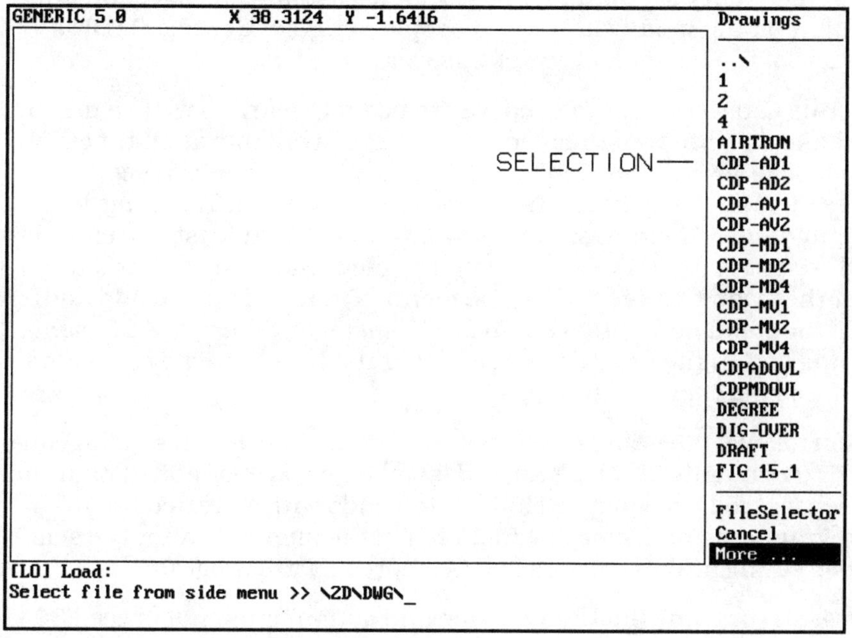

Figure 16.3: *Typical sidebar.*

The sidebar feature does much more than a simple pull-down menu. When selecting Line Type, Line Width, or Line Color, the sidebar displays the actual linetype, width, or color instead of displaying the corresponding numerical equivalent. The sidebar lists any file that is assigned one of the default paths for drawings, components, images, fonts, batches, and hatches. The user can set the current layer, hide or display layers, or set the display to show only those layers with data.

Unlike most other CAD programs, Generic CADD offers a unique menu system that has a command structure or user interface that enables you to do simple editing. You don't have to be a programmer to edit a Generic CADD menu, and the menu doesn't need compiling before it can be used. Few of the menu items in the Generic CADD video menu (CADD5.MNU), for instance, can be considered true macros. Generic CADD's menu system, however, enables the user to edit the menu to include macros, load batch file macros, or customize the menu in many ways.

Introducing the Anatomy of Generic CADD's Menu System

One of the best automobile engines ever developed probably was the Ford flat-head V-8. It delivered plenty of power and respectable gasoline mileage, and any shade-tree mechanic could modify it. It was a people's engine. Generic CADD's menu system is one of the flat-head V-8s of this world.

Viewing the existing CADD menu is a good way to begin to learn to write a menu. It also helps to make a printout of the menu so that it is available at all times for reference. If you look at your CADD5.MNU in your text editor, you can see, for example, that the menu has two parts: the name and the action. The name section displays menu names and notes. Names must consist of at least one character and are displayed with up to twelve characters; more than twelve characters can be used, but they won't be seen when the menu is in use. You can add additional text or instructional notes such as *Go to XYZ menu* or *Return to ABC menu.* All lines containing text in the menu name section must be followed by a comma or the program does not display that line.

The action section follows the name section's last comma. The action section consists of any CADD commands. Each command, symbol, or user-supplied name or value, must be separated by a comma. This section ends with a semicolon. Instructions or programming notes may be included in the menu file after the semicolon because everything after the semicolon is ignored by the program.

The total length of any one line (including name and action) must not exceed 80 characters, including the first character and the semicolon. Spaces count as characters.

Submenu names must begin with an asterisk (*), followed by a space, and then the name. To create a submenu named Draw, for example, you would type * **DRAW**. Similarly, a call to the same submenu is **DRAW,****. Returning to the ROOT menu would be **ROOT menu,****. Semicolons are not required, nor can they be used on submenu names or calls as in the **goto** call.

Another way to call the DRAW submenu is to use the Page command (PG). Thus, **Draw,PG,DRAW;** would display the submenu DRAW. The Page command **Prev,PG,0;** is used to recall the prior displayed page. If the submenu has more items than fit on a single page, * **DRAW2** adds a second page. The following list sums up the various methods for paging submenus.

Menu Line	*Action*
DRAW,**	* DRAW
Draw,PG,DRAW;	* DRAW
More,PG,DRAW2;	* DRAW2
Prev,PG,0;	* DRAW

Adding Items to a Menu

Adding a menu item is very simple in Generic CADD. As you develop a working knowledge of the CADD5.MNU, you undoubtedly will want to edit the menu. The Generic CADD menu is the logical place where you want to make those improvements; it is the platform on which to build the enhancements that are unique to you. The end result speeds up your drawing process. You can, if you wish, write a completely new menu uniquely tailored to your needs. Digitizer users, for instance, will need to write a menu before they can effectively use their tablet.

Editing an Existing Menu

Because CADD video menus are simply text files, you can edit them with a text editor (the DOS EDLIN command) or with a word processor that imports and exports ASCII text. Editing the existing menu is another good way to begin to learn to write a menu. You can examine and imitate the existing menu as a model. Be sure to make a backup copy of your CADD5.MNU before you try editing it.

You cannot add additional lines to a menu below the last effective line in a menu page (just above the bottom drawing screen line). If you do, they are not displayed, nor do they appear on the next page. In the following example, the Constraints submenu is being edited by adding a 1/8" grid setup selection on line 106. Figure 16.4 shows that line 106 is blank. (The DOS EDLIN text editor is being used here.) Type **106** and press Enter. This makes line 106 current and available to edit. Then type:

```
.125 Grid,gs,0,.125",!; or .125 Grid,gs,.125",.125";
```

The first approach is in the CADD5.MNU itself, and the second is a Level3 menu item (previous Generic CADD release) that works in Generic CADD 5.0 (see fig. 16.4).

After this editing is complete, the change is enacted when you exit the text editor. Reboot and you see the results of the edit: as figure 16.5 shows, a 1/8" grid choice has been added to the menu.

```
* CONSTRAINTS

Ortho Mode,or;
Ortho Angle,oa;

Tracking,tk;
Cursor Free,cf;

Grid On/Off,gr;
Snap Grid,sg;
Grid Size,gs;
Grid Reorgin,go;
Curs Move,cm;

1.0  Grid,gs,1,!;
.5   Grid,gs,0.5,!;
.25  Grid,gs,0.25,!;
*


ROOT MENU,**
* EDITS

Move Point,mp;
*
```

Figure 16.4: *CADD5 Constraints submenu.*

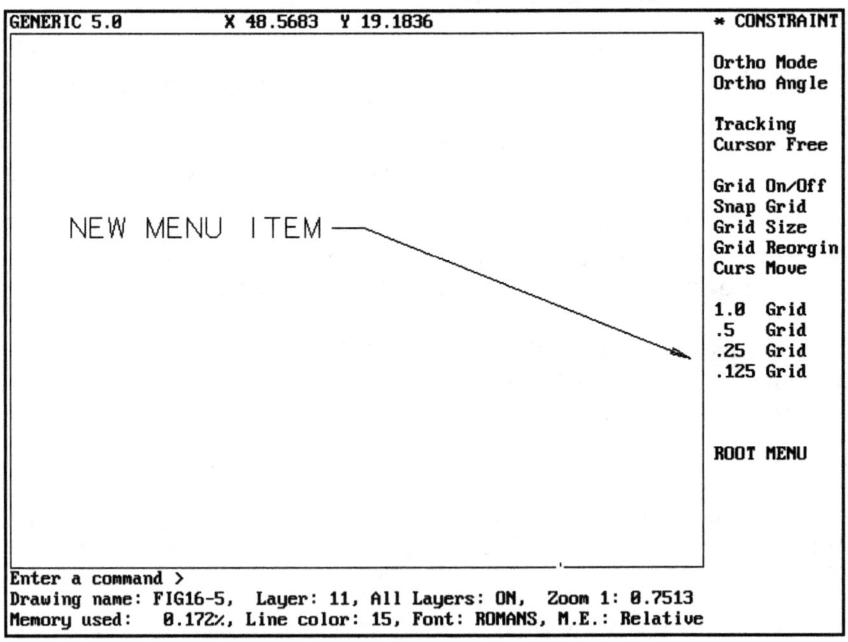

Figure 16.5: *Edited Constraints submenu screen.*

A digitizer menu is edited the same way a video menu is edited. Because the menu name is not displayed in a digitizer menu, however, the name may be shorter. Numbering schemes range from simple to elaborate, from 1,2,3,...,512 to M01L01B26 (menu 1, line 1, and box 26). It is acceptable to use just one character followed by a comma.

Writing a New Menu

At some point, you may discover that the CADD5 menu does not completely meet all your requirements. The CADD5 menu wasn't designed to be an all-encompassing, do-everything menu. It does cover all the commands, in a logical order. You may need several menus: one for your applications, another to plot scales, and another to meet individual client needs. The next two sections cover developing video and digitizer menus. Don't try to reinvent the wheel; print a hard copy of CADD5.MNU to use as a guide.

Video Menus

To write one menu that meets all your requirements might lead to a megamenu. A full-blown menu loaded with macros can require 19 to 20K, five to six times that of the CADD5.MNU file. Unless the memory capacity of your computer is above 1M, it would be better to have separate menus that accomplish different tasks.

For example, you could create three submenus: Main, Draw, and Dimension. Figure 16.6 depicts the Main ROOT menu page showing the Display, Setup, Utilities, Input, Output, Menu, as well as Go To Draw, Go To Dimension, and Quit choices. The Go To items toggle from the Main submenu to either the Draw or Dimension submenus. As part of your customized solution, you may choose different divisions and have as many of them as you need.

Part of the Main menu, the Display submenu, could contain Color, Points, Coordinates, Screen, and Misc. The Setup submenu could contain all items set to update the environment. Utilities could include Manual Entry, Measure, Drawing, and a Misc. category for other utilities. The Input submenu could contain all of the load commands; Output could have the plot and save commands. The Menu submenu could contain other menu toggles, trace commands, and so on. The Draw selection toggles out to the Draw submenu.

As figure 16.7 shows, the Draw menu's ROOT menu page could list the following: Draw (selects two or more submenu pages), Layers, Text, Fonts, Edits, Components, Attributes, Shortcuts, Units, as well as the Go TO Dimensions and Return To Main Menu toggles.

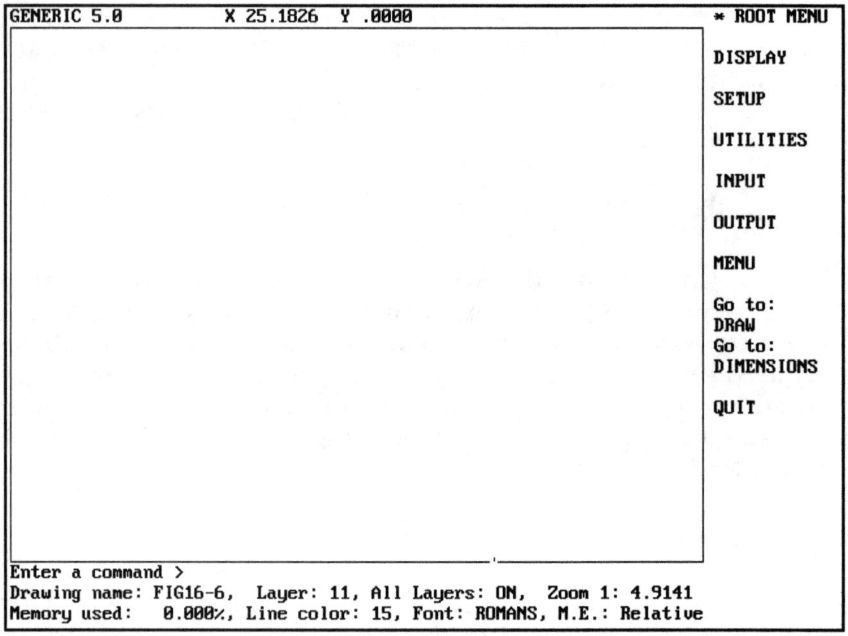

Figure 16.6: *ROOT menu of the Main menu.*

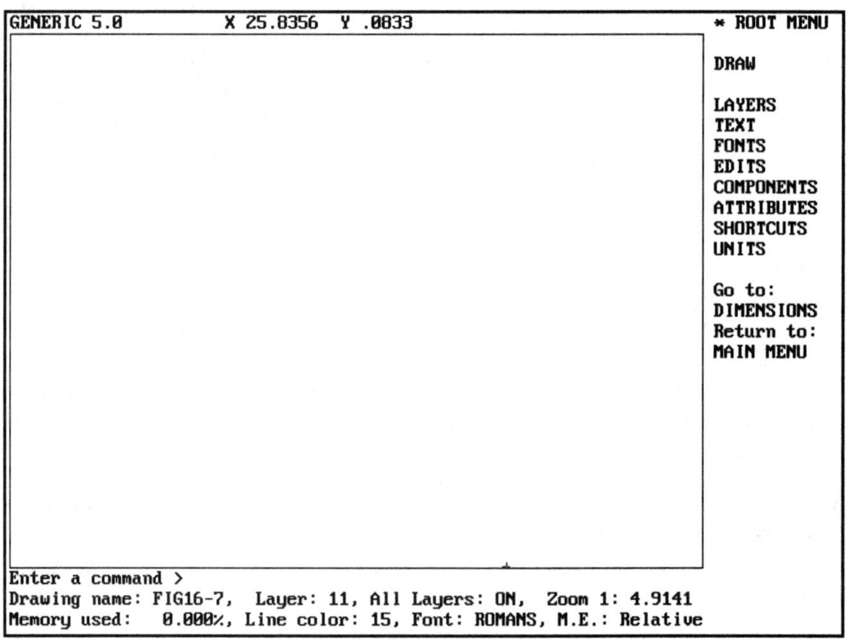

Figure 16.7: *ROOT menu page of the DRAW menu.*

The selection of Draw, as shown in figure 16.8, brings up the first drawing menu page. This page could access lines, arcs, circles, redraws, erase, zooms, linetype, and snaps menu pages.

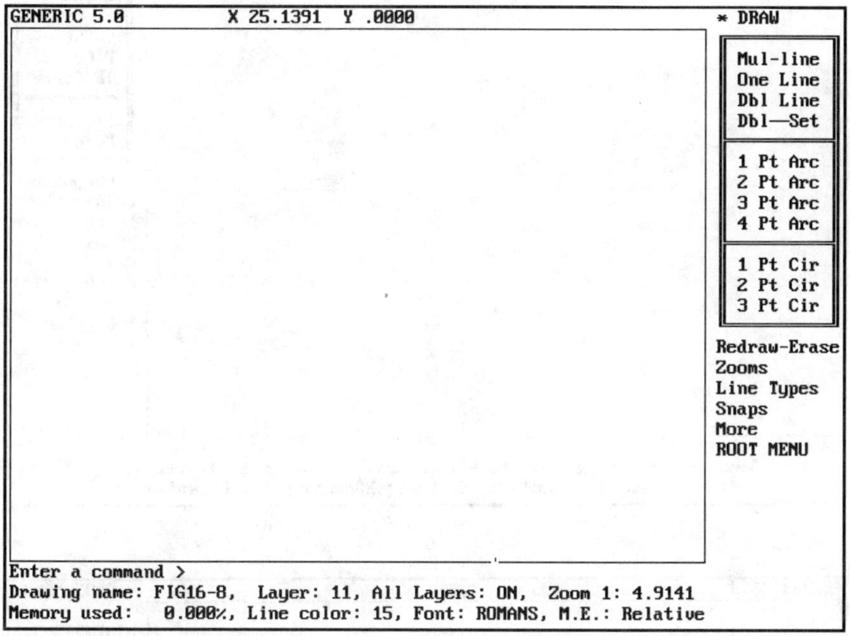

Figure 16.8: *First Draw menu page.*

Clicking on More displays the second Draw menu page as depicted by figure 16.9. In this example, the second page accesses (in addition to most of the Generic CADD entity commands) Standard Components (on line), Grids, Redraw, Erase, Zooms, Chamfers, Fillets, Hatches, and Fills. Notice the repeats in the menu selections. Switching pages can be a burden, and repeating selections in different locations reduces the need to switch. Selecting the Prev option returns you to the first drawing page, whereas choosing the Root menu returns you to the first menu page.

A return to the root menu page of the Draw submenu enables you to select Go To Dimensions. This toggles out to the Dimensions menu as depicted by figure 16.10. The selection options include: Dimensions, Layers, Text, Font, Zoom View, Redraw Era, Grid-Ortho, Go To Draw, and Return to Main Menu.

Selecting the Dimensions submenu calls up another page as shown by figure 16.11. The list of choices call up other menu pages. The Shoulder selection is for setting the leader shoulder length.

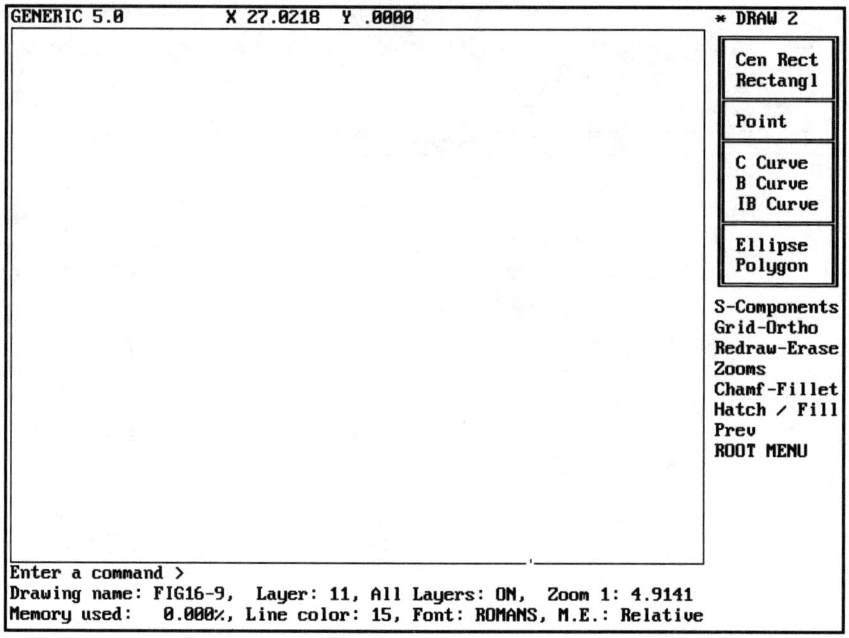

Figure 16.9: *Second menu page.*

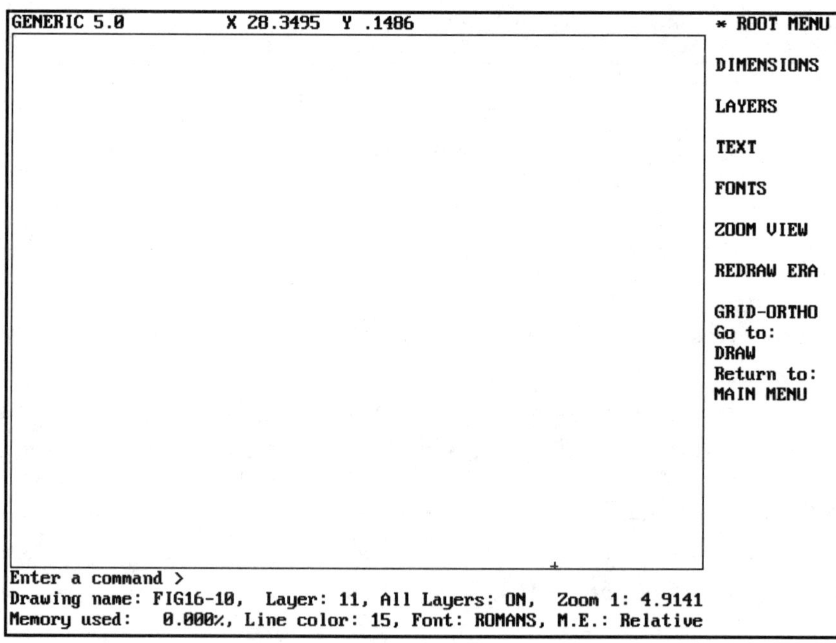

Figure 16.10: *Dimension Root menu.*

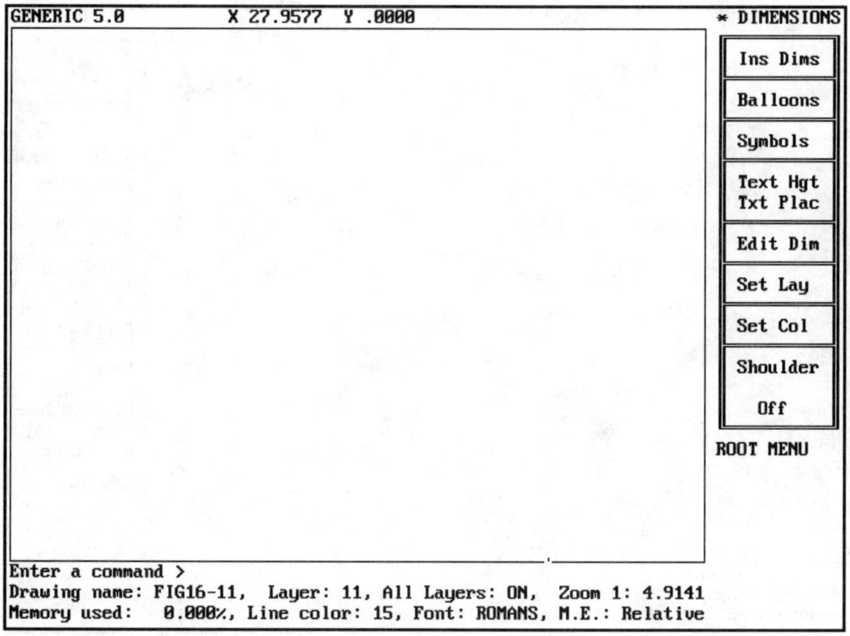

Figure 16.11: *Dimension submenu page.*

If you select the first choice, Ins Dims, a page is displayed, as shown by figure 16.12, from which you can select Generic CADD dimension commands. There also are selections that call up pages that offer Dimensions, Direction, Mode, Precision, Tolerance, and Display command choices.

As figure 16.13 shows, selecting Display Dim displays a page of Dimensional Display presets. The symbols displayed on the screen show the different dimensional settings used in the drawing process. With a little imagination, you can see the dimension that Generic CADD displays. Other pages show more presets and other variations.

You are not limited by the CADD5.MNU file when writing your own menu. Let your imagination run freely. Your menu can be as plain and simple or as complex as it needs to be. The important thing is that it fulfills your requirements. As you gain experience at editing and writing menus, more ideas present themselves. Editing is a continuing process in which you are always improving, always tailoring to specific needs.

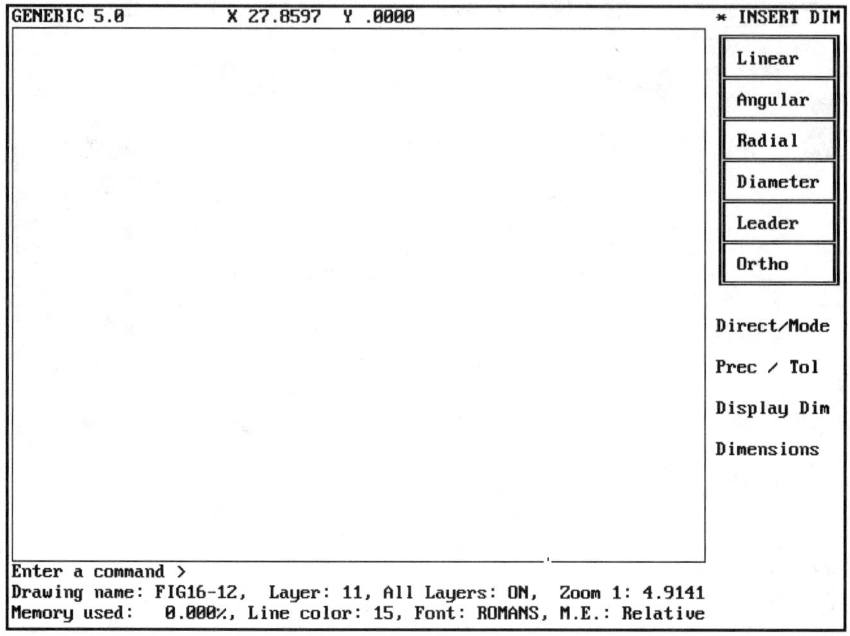

Figure 16.12: *Insert Dimension submenu.*

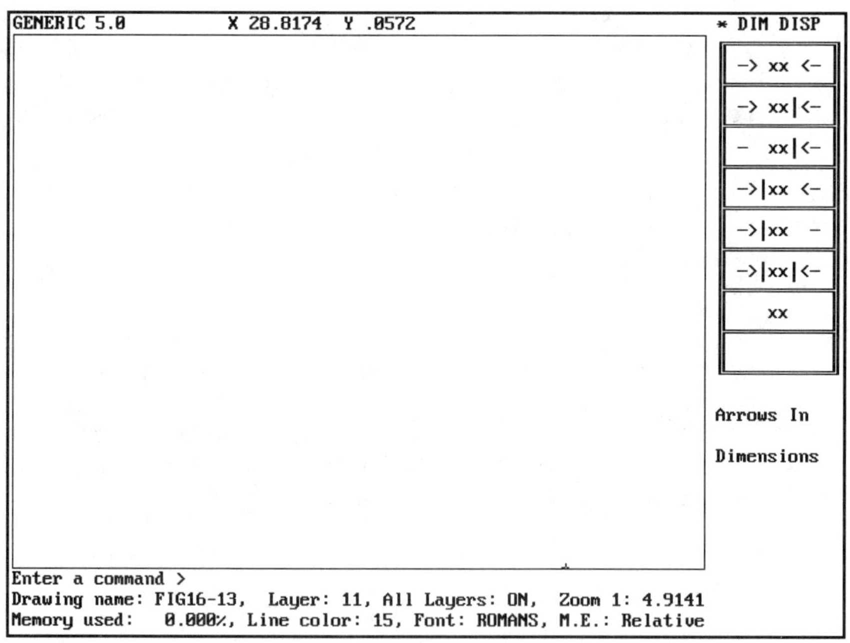

Figure 16.13: *Dimensional presets.*

Digitizer Menus

Digitizer menus are like video menus except they do not have submenus and do not display menu names. They require an overlay drawing, and the number of lines allowed is limited to 512. Digitizer menus are much faster to use than video menus, and video menus still can be accessed. Digitizer menus require a bit more work to set up. The overlay drawing must be well thought out, and it may take several attempts before a working model is perfected.

Generic CADD can display up to ten different digitizer menus at one time. These menus may be contained in the same file or in ten file names. At most, you probably will only use four or five. The digitizer menu requires an active area in addition to the enabled menus.

As in video menus, the maximum memory is limited only by the amount of memory that you are willing to allocate to digitizer menus. Unlike video menus, however, the line limit is 512. Each line can have 80 characters, including spaces.

Where do you start—with the menu file or the overlay drawing? Although it is actually a parallel process, you should start by developing your digitizer menu on a hard copy layout of the proposed overlay. How many squares are enough? The largest practical number for a 12 x 12 tablet is 26 x 26 = 676 squares. Of these, 164 are required for the active area. This leaves 512 squares or lines (the maximum allowed).

The menu file doesn't have submenus, but the overlay does. When designing the overlay, the shape of the squares as well as their number must be considered. The example in figure 16.14 demonstrates this treatment for text.

When designing the overlay, delete commands that have little or no relevancy to your application. Devote your planning time to the commands that actually are going to be used and consider carefully which of these remaining commands should or should not be combined into macros. In general, macros make the best use of any menu because they reduce the number of keystrokes necessary to carry out the commands.

As you write the menu file, take care to group similar commands in the spot that matches the overlay. Digitizer menus are numbered left to right, top to bottom. To avoid confusion, number the overlay hard copy with the proper number and the desired command. Refer to this reference for each line of the menu file to ensure that the commands and overlay match.

The numbering of the overlay squares must not only coincide with the menu file, but also include in its numbering all the menus enabled in the environmental file. Menu 1, for example, may have 286 squares numbered from 1 to 286. Menu 2 may have 90 squares numbered from 287 to 376. Menu 3 may have 75 squares numbered from 377 to 451, and menu 4 may have 60 squares numbered from 452 to 511. The user must keep all the active menus in mind when laying out the overlay.

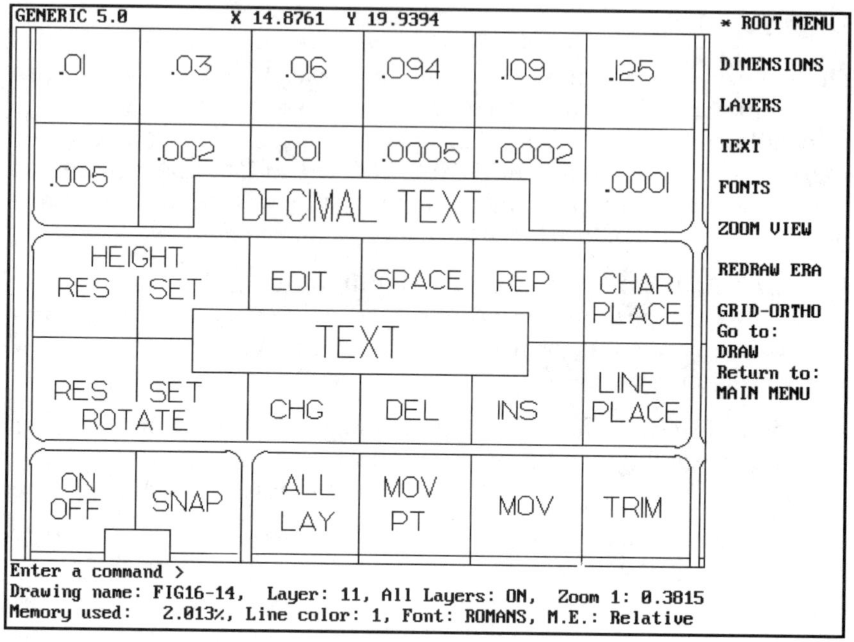

Figure 16.14: *Sample digitizer overlay.*

Another important overlay feature to consider is the active area. The smaller the active area, the faster the cursor moves on the screen. A good ratio to use is about 75 percent of the screen's drawing area. This gives the user good control for eye-hand coordination.

After the digitizer menu file and overlay is completed, there is still a series of steps to take before the overlay can be used by Generic CADD. The user must enable the digitizer menu in CADD. This is accomplished by the Select Digitizer command. Type **SD** and then select the Setup option. Follow the prompts for each menu area of the overlay. Then type **AA** for selecting the active area of the overlay and follow the prompts. Finally, the environment must be updated. Type **EN** and press Enter. This final step saves the digitizer setup.

What do you do when the list of commands is greater than the number of squares available? Starting over may not be necessary. Remember the second button on most calculators? The second calculator button enables you to add a second function to the 1 key. The following example uses this second-button principle.

You may find, for example, that your overlay has only eight squares left for 14 commands that are of the same type. Place the first seven commands in the normal area of the digitizer file and overlay, plus use a macro that toggles to a new menu. Then place the next seven commands at the end of the menu file, plus another macro that toggles back to the original commands (see example). The last eight commands in the menu file belong to a new menu, so you must tell Generic CADD that there is a new menu in the file. To do this, type **SD** and then **S**. Then follow the prompts and type **EN** (Environment Save).

Here are the macros for toggling the menus:

```
Menu toggle macro; line no.,SD,E,4,5,#;
Toggle back macro; line no.,D,E,5,4,#;
```

Remember that when a new menu is enabled over another, the original menu no longer functions. Also, make sure that the two toggle macros fall on the same square and that there are no more than 512 lines in the menu file.

If you are a new user or are under pressure to get work out, consider purchasing one of the industry-specific digitizer menus. They can save an enormous amount of time because the purchased menu and overlay can be edited to suit your work much faster than a custom menu can be written from scratch.

Linking Menus

There are three different ways to control the loading of menus in a multi-menu environment: load several small menus, one at a time; swap one menu for another; or toggle from video display menu to a digitizer menu and back. Each approach is outlined in turn in the following sections.

Adding Menus

Users with 1M or less of memory can save drawing space by adding menus. Memory requirements for menus are reduced when individual menus are kept small and when menus are added or deleted as necessary.

When one menu is loaded on top of another, Generic CADD appends the second menu to the first. This is known as *linking menus*. Menus can be linked until the space allocated in memory is full. The program then issues a warning that the menu memory space is full and that the loaded menu has been truncated. The program further suggests that the user allocate more space.

One of the drawbacks of using this method is that it generates a number of small menu files that must then be maintained. Generic CADD solves the problem of remembering the file names with the sidebar feature. But unless the menu file names indicate their function, you still won't know what each file does. Therefore, give each menu file a name that serves as a reminder of its function.

Chaining Menus

Chaining menus is an alternative to linking menus. Chaining enables you to replace one menu with another. This is useful because special-purpose menus, such as component library menus, can be quite large (a component menu may need more than 39K). If you can erase all other menus while that one is in use, the least amount of memory possible is used. Chaining accomplishes this objective.

The Component menu in the next example is a menu for inserting clamps into a drawing as depicted in figure 16.15. You can see the differences between the item choices and the chaining macros on the page shown. The chaining macros erase the current menu and replace it with another. The next menu can be chained to the first or to the last (fourth) menu. Only one menu is in the memory at any given time.

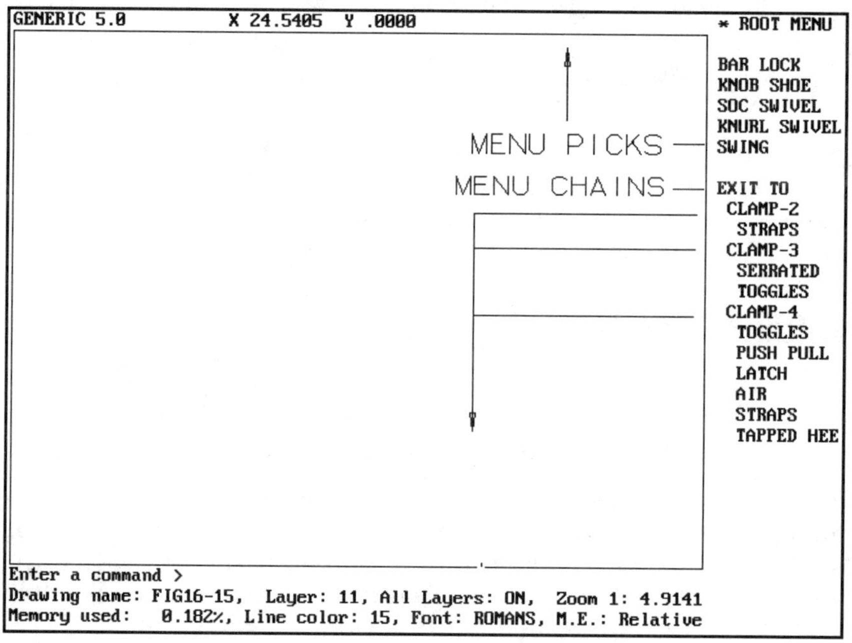

Figure 16.15: *Component menu with chain macros.*

The macros that chain or swap menus are as follows:

```
item name,VX,LV,new menu;     item name,VX,LV,old menu;
line no.,LV,Y,new menu;       item name,LD,Y,old menu;
```

Chaining within menus saves keystrokes, memory, and time. What's more, the procedure is done correctly every time.

Toggling between Video and Digitizer

The best way to tap into Generic CADD's power when using a digitizer is to devise a method of swapping between the digitizer and video menus. Because the sidebar feature is unavailable while a digitizer menu is loaded, the user must either swap out to a video menu or erase the digitizer menu and use the keyboard. Swapping out to a video menu is the best choice for most users.

To accomplish this procedure automatically, the digitizer menu must have a square or line in the menu file that erases the digitizer menu file and loads a video menu file. If these commands and the single-letter switch are included in the macro, the program loads the menu and switches to the proper sidebar. The following macro erases the digitizer menu, loads the video menu, and invokes the sidebar for loading components:

```
line no.,LV,Y,menu name,LO,C;
```

As figure 16.16 demonstrates, the video menus should include macros to return to the digitizer. The macro `VX,LD,Y,digitizer name;` erases the current menu and loads the digitizer menu.

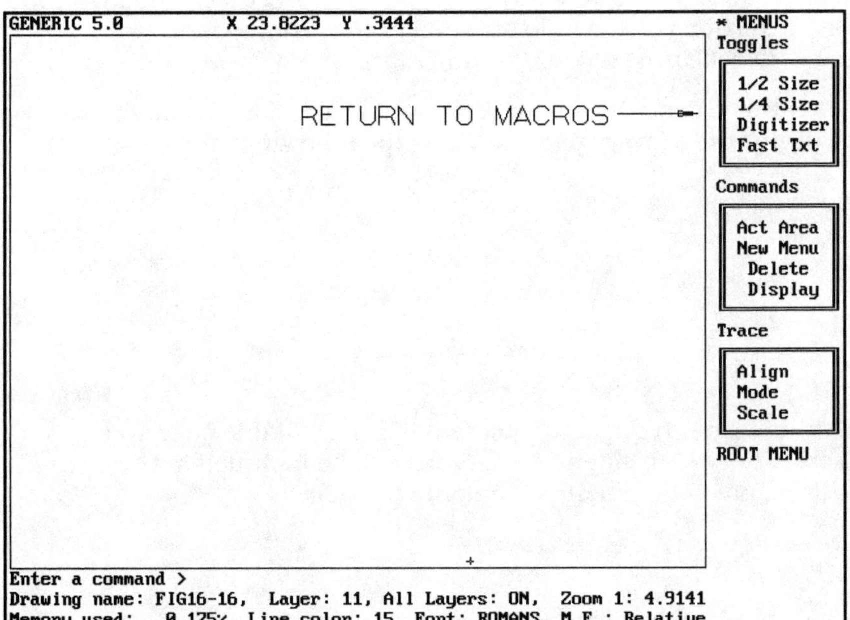

Figure 16.16: *Return to digitizer.*

Customizing Menus

Custom menus can encompass any type of menu for any purpose; they adapt Generic CADD's menu structure to meet your needs. Figures 16.4 through 16.16 are excerpts from custom menus. Custom menus can be used to access components, automate drafting, and for special purposes, such as inserting standardized text.

Making Menus for Component Libraries

If you have just a few components, you can get by without a special system for keeping track of them. The sidebar, for example, enables you to view a list of the components on the data base and to access the hard disk on the default path. This approach works adequately with a limited number of components, but with a few hundred or thousands of component names to choose from, the process slows considerably. The Custom menu offers the best path to speedy access.

The Custom menu can be as simple as a list of component file names with the command CP in front and a semicolon to finish: `item or line no.,CP,comp;`. This is not as effective as a menu that controls rotation, scale, explosion layer, snaps, images, and insertion point, while also placing the component. But a menu controlling all these features would be quite large.

One way to reduce the size of such a menu file would be to place the modifying commands at the beginning of every page, such as the following:

```
Rotation,CR;
Scale,CZ;
Snaps,GC;
Image on,CI,++;
   off,CI,—;
Exp Lay,XY,P;      C or O can be used also
Insert pt.,IP;
```

This list uses seven lines and requires 35 percent of the available page space, but it does save memory. These same menu items could all be included in the string to yield about a third more component placements per page:

```
menu name,CR,A,@,@,CZ,~,~,GC,++,CI,—,
XY,P,CP,name,IP,@,@,@;
```

Either method works just fine, as will any combination of the two as shown in figures 16.17 and 16.18. Although the examples used in these two figures are modified from Level3 menus, they also work.

```
** KNOB
SELECT,
    LAYER,YC,~;
    SCALE,CZ,~,~;
    ROTAT,CR,A,@,@;
    EXP-LAY,XY,C,!;

38BAR 131S P,CP,CL0014P;
38BAR 131S S,CP,CL0014S;
38BAR 231S P,CP,CL0015P;
38BAR 231S S,CP,CL0015S;
38BAR 331S P,CP,CL0016P;
38BAR 331S S,CP,CL0016S;
50BAR 162S P,CP,CL0017P;
50BAR 162S S,CP,CL0017S;
50BAR 262S P,CP,CL0018P;
50BAR 262S S,CP,CL0018S;
50BAR 462S P,CP,CL0019P;
50BAR 462S S,CP,CL0019S;

Prev,PG,0;
NEXT,PG,KN2;
* KN2

*
```

Figure 16.17: From a Component menu.

```
190,A4;
191,PO;
192,RP;
193,EP;
194,CZ,~,~,CR,A,@,@,XY,C,CP,HEXBOLTP;
195,CZ,~,~,CR,A,@,@,XY,C,CP,HEXBOLTZ,IP,@,@,@;
196,CZ,~,~,CR,A,@,@,XY,C,CP,HEXBOLTS,IP,@,@,@;
197,CZ,1,1,CR,A,@,@,XY,C,CP,TBALLS;
198,CZ,1,1,XY,C,CP,TBALLP;
199,CZ,~,~,CR,A,@,@,XY,C,CP,SPRINGS,IP,@,@,@;
200,CZ,~,~,CR,A,@,@,XY,C,CP,PLUGS;
201,CZ,~,~,CR,A,@,@,XY,C,CP,PLUGP;
202,CZ,~,~,CR,A,@,@,XY,C,CP,PHSS;
203,CZ,~,~,XY,C,CP,PHSP;
204,ZL;
205,ZA;
206,ZI;
207,ZM;
208,ZV;
209,GS,~,~;
210,GO;
211,CO;
212,MI;
213,RC;
*
```

Figure 16.18: From a Digitizer menu.

Using Menus for Automated Drafting

Automated drafting menus can access macros, batch files, and standard component files to perform drafting tasks.

Macros on a Menu

Macros can be used to draw small symbols for placement in a drawing file. This lends speed, and there are no disk files to contend with. Menued macros produce the same results every time they are used. As figure 16.19 shows, a menu page of detail balloons has been drawn by macros.

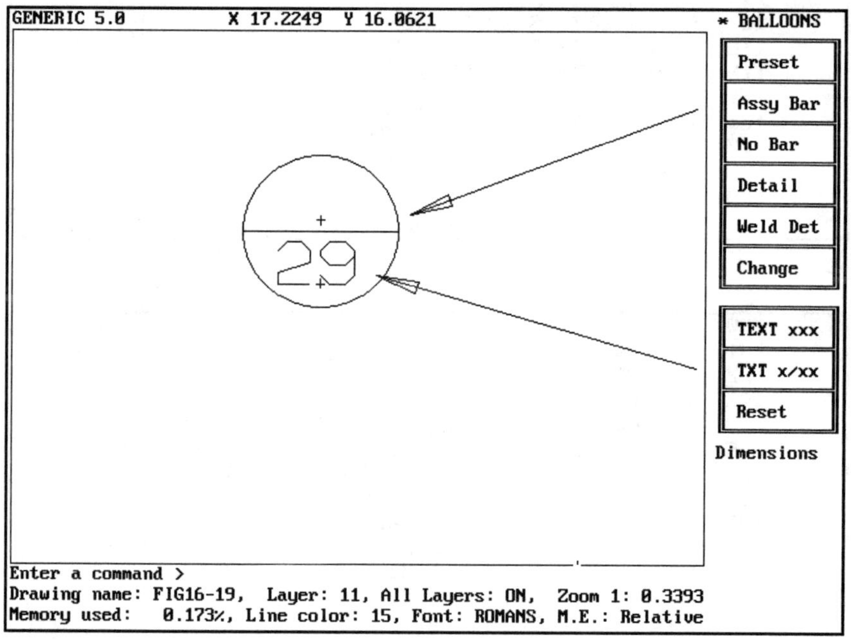

Figure 16.19: *Menu page of macros.*

Standard Components on a Menu

Standard components can be quickly placed into a drawing file. The process is fast, and there are no disk files to remember. When using menu components as when using a menu with macros, the user can expect the same results every time. Figure 16.20 shows a menu page of dimension symbols that can be inserted as components.

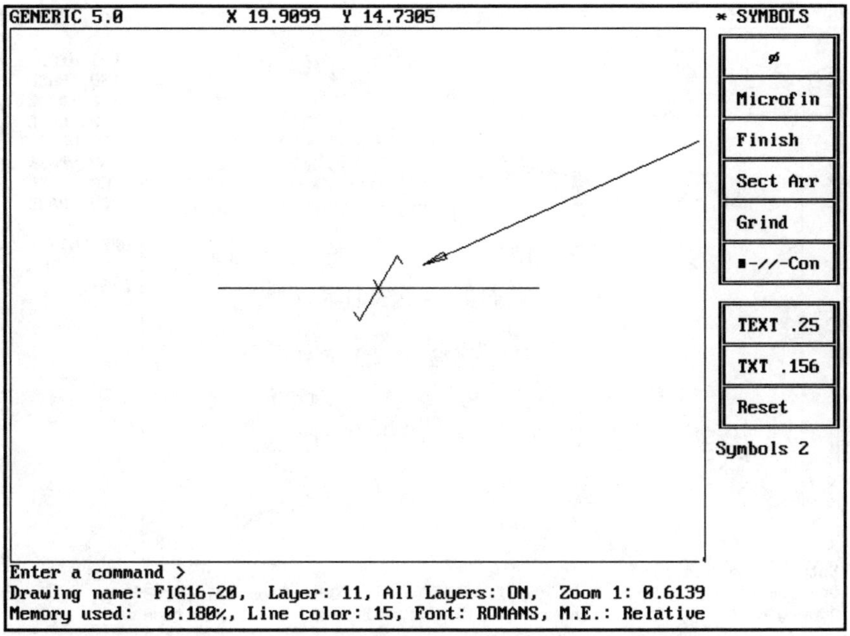

Figure 16.20: *Menu page of standard components.*

Submenus can be used as selective branches. A toggle clamp, for example, has several variations: solid or open bar, straight or tee handle, or vertical or horizontal bases. By creating a tree menu having submenus, the path can be narrowed to a single list of choices.

Standard Drawings on a Menu

After only a short time using Generic CADD, you'll find your collection of drawing files growing. These files soak up disk space with no way to access the data efficiently. Some of these drawings may be used again and again as standard items. Other drawings can be used as templates onto which minor changes can be made. To access these important drawings, build a menu and reap huge benefits. Such a menu enables you to cut and paste drawings, which reduces huge blocks of time from drawing tasks. The standard drawings obtained from the menu and used in figure 16.21 reduced a 4-hour drawing task to 15 minutes.

Complete drawings can be stored as drawings or text (batch) files, called up with a menu, and placed into a drawing. Figure 16.21 demonstrates how this approach can be used.

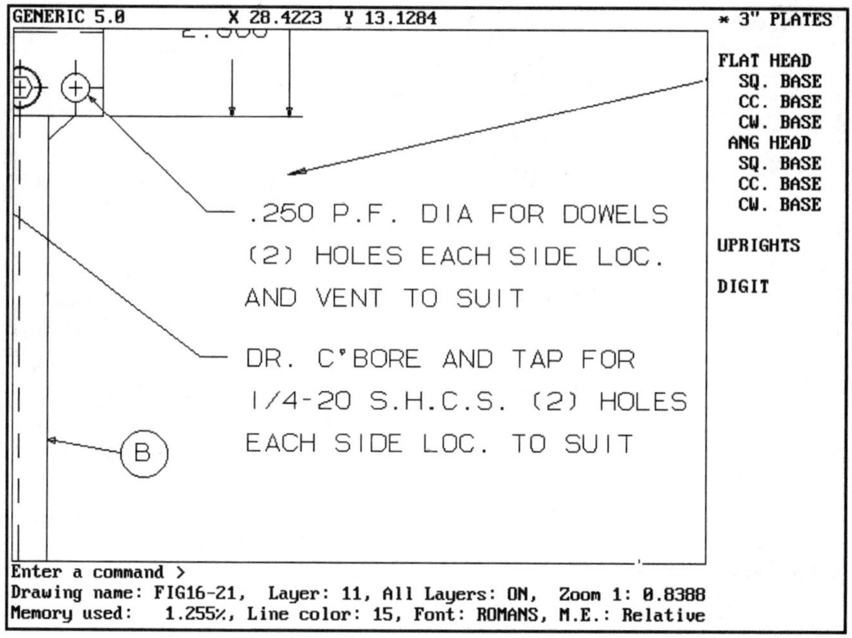

Figure 16.21: *Menu page of standard drawings.*

Creating Menus for Special Needs

Special needs menus are determined by the user; they are whatever the user needs. One such need could be a menu to place standardized text into a drawing. Because text placement by macro increases the speed of text input by a factor of 15, a text placement menu certainly fills the bill. Because fewer keystrokes are involved when using a text-placement macro, you can expect more accuracy and less fatigue.

One submenu could have key words that pertain to all text found on a floor plan; another could refer to foundations; and the next could deal with elevations. As figure 16.22 demonstrates, just page to the proper submenu to add text to a drawing.

Summary

This chapter explains how Generic CADD's menu system works. The menu supplied with the program is all that some users will need. Others, however, will need a little more and still others a lot more. Whatever your requirements, the ability to easily edit or write custom menus is what really sets this software apart from the others.

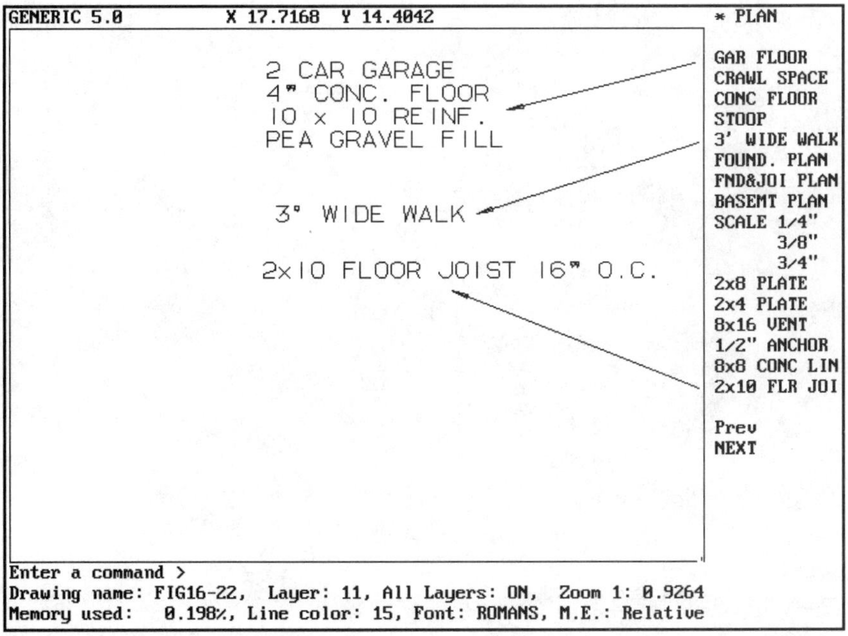

Figure 16.22: *Placing text.*

In this chapter, you have learned how to edit, what to edit, how to write, and what to write. As the user gains experience at editing and writing menus, more ideas will come forth. Editing is a continuing process, always improving.

Growing data files cause the user to write, link, and swap menus for efficient use of data. Menus are Generic CADD's way to keep track of user files.

As a final note, it is strongly recommended that the user read all of the material supplied by Generic CADD concerning custom menus. A helpful practice is to use this chapter simultaneously with Generic CADD's manuals.

17

Batch Files, Formulas, and Variables

A batch file is a series of CADD commands and parameters that execute automatically when you use the Load (LO) command's Batch option. A batch file is essentially a script, written in the language of two-letter commands, that Generic CADD follows to perform a task. A batch file can automate drawing tasks or act as an interface between Generic CADD and another program. It is an ASCII text file, so it can be used to extract data from a drawing or even to edit a drawing.

Generic CADD creates batch files using a text editor or word processor, or using any program that creates ASCII files. Batch files should be given the extension TXT to indicate they are text files. The structure of a batch file is similar to that of a macro assigned to a function key, except that macros are limited to one line while a batch file can consist of any number of lines.

Tools for Editing Batch Files

Viewing and editing batch files is ideally done with a text editor, a program similar to a word processor that uses ASCII text files as its native format. Many good text editors are available. The BRIEF and QEDIT programs are two of the most popular among programmers. Most utility packages, such as PC-Tools, Norton Utilities, and Mace Utilities, include a text editor program. DOS 5.0 also has the MS-DOS Editor.

If you do not have a text editor, you can use a word processing program. Most shareware word processors can save text in the ASCII format and are thus well-suited to editing Generic CADD batch files. Commercial word processing programs usually save files in a document format with special formatting codes. These formatting codes "choke" Generic CADD when it attempts to load the batch file, so learn how to save your text files in a simple ASCII text format. This sometimes is called "saving without formatting" or "saving as text." You can use EDLIN, a DOS program that enables you to edit files one line at a time. This program is very awkward to use, however, and is only recommended as a last resort.

Your text editing program, regardless of its type, will be referred to generically as an *editor* in this chapter.

An editor should be able to perform search and replace functions. This is particularly useful when using a batch file to edit a Generic CADD drawing. To complete the exercises in this chapter, you will need to know how to load, use search and replace, and save files with your editor.

Saving a Drawing as a Batch File

Generic CADD enables you to save an entire drawing as a batch file, or you can save portions of a drawing, using the selection process.

When you save a drawing as a batch file, Generic CADD "reverse engineers" the drawing and creates a batch file of the commands necessary to re-create your drawing in its current form. This will not necessarily be the same set of commands you used to create the drawing. For example, while you may have drawn a rectangle using the Rectangle (RE) command, the batch file will use four Line (LI) commands to re-create that same rectangle. Bézier curves are saved using the individual Bézier (BW) command.

Component definitions are not saved in the batch file. If your drawing contains components, the Component Place (CP) commands will be in the batch file. This is a problem only when you load the batch file. If the appropriate CMP files are not available in the current component directory, `Component not found` will flash on the screen and Generic CADD will continue with the next command in the batch file. Generic CADD cannot reverse engineer fills or hatches, and these entities are not saved in batch files.

NOTE

You can sometimes restore a corrupted drawing file by executing the Save Batch (SB), Drawing Remove (DX), and Load Batch (LO,B) commands, in order. You should first ensure that all components have been saved to disk so that they are not lost. Then use the Change and Filter commands to move all hatches and fills to an unused layer. Save this layer with the Layer Save (YS) command as a separate file, which then can be reloaded after the Load Batch operation is complete.

Save Batch (SB)

You can save your entire drawing as a batch file with the Save Batch (SB) command. You can also save a batch file with the Save (SA) command by choosing Batch (B) as the file to save. Generic CADD will prompt you for a name to use when saving the batch file and will suggest the name of the current drawing with the extension TXT. You can either press Enter to accept the suggested name or enter a new name. You do not need to add the extension when entering a new name; Generic CADD will do this for you automatically.

The following exercise shows you how to save a drawing as a batch file using the Save Batch command. Later, you will load this batch file and watch Generic CADD re-create your drawing by executing the commands in the batch file.

In preparation for this exercise, start Generic CADD and load a drawing. (It does not matter which one.) Use the Zoom All (ZA) command so that the entire drawing is visible on the screen, and then follow these steps:

Saving a Drawing as a Batch File

Prompt	*Input*	*Description*
`Command`	**SB**	Starts the Save Batch command
`Save file as: >> C:\CADD5\DRAWINGNAME.TXT`	**BATCH1**	Renames and saves the batch file

That's all there is to it. You have just created your first batch file.

Selection Save Batch (BS)

The Selection Save Batch (BS) command allows you to save a portion of a drawing as a batch file. After entering the command, you use Generic CADD's selection process to choose what parts of your drawing to save as a batch file. After you press Enter to confirm your selections, Generic CADD will prompt you for a name to use. As with the Save Batch command, Generic CADD will suggest the name of the current drawing; either press Enter to accept the suggested name or input a different name.

The following exercise displays the Selection Save Batch command. You will need to use Generic CADD's Selection interface to choose part of your drawing (about half of it is fine) to be saved as a batch file. Do not choose the whole drawing because that would be the same as using the Save Batch command.

Saving a Portion of a Drawing as a Batch File

Prompt	*Input*	*Description*
`Command`	**BS**	Starts the Selection Save Batch command
`Selection`	Type **W** or **O** or **Y**, etc.	Uses one or more selection methods to select parts of the drawing to be saved as a batch file
`Selection`	Press Enter	Confirms selection
`Save file as: >> C:\CADD5\drawingname.TXT`	**BATCH2**	Renames and saves the batch file

The simplicity of the process is deceptive. Enter only a few commands, and Generic CADD figures out which commands are needed to re-create your drawing. When you later look at the batch files you have just created, you will be amazed at all that Generic CADD takes into consideration when saving a drawing as a batch file.

Loading a Batch File

When you load a batch file, Generic CADD processes the commands in the file one by one, building the drawing with blinding speed right before your eyes. It's like watching Generic CADD run on autopilot. Watch closely, and you will see the commands flash by.

Choose the Batch (B) option under the Load (LO) command to begin loading a batch file. Generic CADD will prompt you for the name of the batch file to load. If the video menu is on, Generic CADD will list the available batch files in alphabetical order. You may either select a batch file by highlighting it with the menu bar and pressing the second button on your mouse, or by typing in the name and pressing Enter. As with all load commands, you may activate the file selector or use the side menu to look for files in other directories on your hard disk.

In the following exercise, you erase the drawing on your screen, and then re-create it from the batch file. Generic CADD automatically executes the Zoom Limits command when you remove the entire drawing from memory, so you will use the Zoom Previous command to reset the screen and watch as Generic CADD loads the batch file.

Re-Creating a Drawing from a Batch File

Prompt	*Input*	*Description*
`Command`	**DX**	Starts the Drawing Remove command
`Do you really want to remove the current drawing Y/N?`	**Y**	Removes the drawing
`Command`	**ZP**	Performs the Zoom Previous Command
`Command`	**LO**	Starts the Load Command
`Drawing Component Batch...`	**B**	Selects batch file
`Select file from side menu >>`	Move menu bar to BATCH1 and click second mouse button	Selects BATCH1 as file to load

Generic CADD re-creates your drawing piece by piece. Soon your drawing reappears just as it was before you erased it. If you want to see Generic CADD load the second batch file you saved, repeat the above steps, selecting BATCH2 as the file to load instead of BATCH1.

Creating a Batch File

Creating a batch file to export data from a drawing is useful and will be discussed in more detail later. The primary use for batch files in Generic CADD, however, is to automate the drawing process. As mentioned earlier, a text editor ordinarily is used to create batch files. When you use an editor, though, you must remember some rules and guidelines about creating batch files, as well as learn the special functions some characters have when used in a batch file.

Rules and Guidelines for Batch Files

When creating batch files, remember the following rules:

- ❑ Anything typed after a semicolon is assumed to be a comment, not part of the command.
- ❑ The command portion of each line *must* not exceed 80 characters.
- ❑ The command portion of each line *must* end with a semicolon, even if no comments follow.
- ❑ Commands and parameters *must* be separated by a comma.
- ❑ Toggles (such as AL) *must* be turned off or on by using "--" or "++" as parameters, respectively.
- ❑ If the first character of a line is a semicolon, the entire line is assumed to be a comment and is ignored.

Writing a batch file is like writing any program—instead of Pascal or C or Basic, the language is Generic CADD. As with other programs, you can make your work easier by following some basic guidelines.

Comment Everything

Write frequent comments into your batch files; don't worry about overdoing it. The commands in a batch file may make sense to you when you first write them, but you might be confused by them later. When writing a batch file, assume you will need to modify it at a later date and comment accordingly. If others will be using your batch files, remember the programmer's adage: "Comment unto others as you would have them comment unto you."

Use Structure for Clarity

You can put several commands on one line (up to 80 characters), but this can make your batch files look confusing. If several commands make sense together, group them on a line; otherwise, it is best to limit each line to one command. Your batch file will be easier to understand and edit.

Extra spaces in a batch file are ignored. You can use this to your advantage by placing spaces between coordinate pairs on the same line to make successive X,Y coordinates easy to see.

To illustrate this point, consider the following structures of the same batch file.

Written this way, the file is difficult to understand:

```
TS,C,25,L,160,S,10,A,1.25,J,C,P,-,!;  text settings
```

This example, which includes comments, requires more time and space to write, but is much easier to understand:

```
TS;         Starts Text Settings command
C,25;       Sets between character spacing by percentage
L,160;      Sets between line spacing by percentage
S,10;       Sets text slant by degrees
A,1.25;     Sets aspect ratio (>1=wide, <1=narrow)
J,C;        Sets justification (L=left, C=center, R=right
P,-;        Turns off Proportional Spacing command
!;          Ends Text Settings command
```

They both perform the same function, but one is much easier to read and understand than the other.

Never Assume Anything

A batch file can be loaded at any time, so you should never assume that any of Generic CADD's settings or toggles are already set correctly. Just imagine what would happen if the units in your batch file were based on inches and Generic CADD was set for meters. If you are familiar with programming, think of this as initializing all your variables. The following checklists cover most of the settings you will need to consider when making batch files.

If your batch file draws new entities, remember to set:

- ❑ Manual entry mode (Origin, MO; Relative, MR; Basepoint MB)
- ❑ Units (UN)
- ❑ Line Color (LC)
- ❑ Line Type (LT)
- ❑ Line Width (LW)
- ❑ Current Layer (YC)

If your batch file uses double lines, remember to set:

- ❑ Double Line settings (DB)
- ❑ Auto Fillet (AF)
- ❑ Fillet Radius (FR)

If your batch file places text, remember to set:

- ❑ Text Color (CS,T)
- ❑ Font Select (FS,T)
- ❑ Text Size (TZ,T)
- ❑ Text Settings (TS)
- ❑ Text Rotation (TR)

If your batch file draws dimensions, remember to set:

- ❑ Font Select (FS,D)
- ❑ Text Size (TZ,D)
- ❑ Dimension Layer (UY)
- ❑ Dimension Color (CS,D)
- ❑ Dimension Direction (UD)
- ❑ Proximity Fixed (PF)
- ❑ Dimension Display (DD)
- ❑ Extension Settings (XS)
- ❑ Arrow Settings (AR)
- ❑ Dimension Text Settings (DT)

If your batch file edits the current drawing, remember to set:

- ❑ All Layers Edit (AL)
- ❑ All Layers Snap (SY)
- ❑ Chamfer Distances (CA)
- ❑ Fillet Radius (FR)

Some settings are not critical to the proper operation of your batch files, but can slow the batch file operation when it is loaded into Generic CADD. Make sure these three settings are off:

- ❑ Rubber Banding (RB)
- ❑ Object Drag (OD)
- ❑ Highlighting (HI)

Generic CADD also follows this advice. If you look at a batch file created by Generic CADD (such as the two we just made), you will see that the first line in the batch file sets the units. The next line turns off the setting just mentioned and sets Manual Entry Relative to the origin.

Because there are a lot of text and dimension settings to worry about, you can let CADD take care of writing that part of the batch file for you. Simply make a drawing of a single text line or dimension. Adjust all the settings the way you like them and save that drawing as a batch file. Then you can simply clip out that portion of the batch file (created by CADD) and paste it into the batch file you're writing.

Special Characters in Batch Files

Batch files use the same special characters as macros, so you may already be familiar with them. If not, you need to know the function of the following symbols:

- **Semicolon (;).** The semicolon marks the end of a line of commands. Generic CADD assumes any text found on the same line after a semicolon is a comment and ignores it.
- **Comma (,).** The comma separates commands and parameters. It also performs the same function as pressing Enter when found after a parameter.
- **Plus signs (++).** Two plus signs turn on a toggle when they follow a toggle command. Commands that are either on or off, and commands that have only two settings, such as Dimension Text Placement (DT,P), are considered toggles.
- **Minus signs (—).** Two minus signs turn off a toggle when they follow a toggle command, such as Ortho Mode (OR).
- **At sign (@).** The at sign is used in place of a coordinate pair. Generic CADD pauses and prompts for a point. You can enter the point using any of the normal methods (a mouse or digitizer, the arrow and enter keys, or manual entry).
- **Tilde (~).** The tilde is used in place of a parameter other than a coordinate pair. It can be used any time Generic CADD expects a value or a name. As with the at sign, Generic CADD pauses and prompts for a parameter. You can respond by typing from the keyboard, or, when appropriate, by selecting "off" from the side menu.
- **Number sign (#).** The number sign performs the same function as pressing Esc. It is useful for exiting commands like Text Line (TL) and Text Place (TP).
- **Exclamation mark (!).** The exclamation mark acts as if you pressed Enter. It is useful for exiting selection functions or Text Settings (TS) commands.
- **Slashes (/).** The slash characters cause Generic CADD to treat the next character as if it were not a special character. They are used mostly for placing characters such as # and ! in a text line without their activating the Escape or Enter functions. Two consecutive slash marks are required for the slash to function.

Batch files might appear complicated because of all the rules and guidelines that accompany them, but don't be intimidated by them. Use the guidelines as a checklist while making your own batch files or as a troubleshooting guide when they do not work properly. You do not need to be a programmer to write a batch file. If you can use the two-letter commands to run Generic CADD, you can write a batch file.

Writing a Simple Batch File

In the next section, you will write a simple batch file that draws a square. Activate your editor and create a new file named DISK.TXT in your CADD5 directory. (Note that the batch file path is usually set to the CADD5 directory.) Type the following lines into your editor. You do not have to type the comments that appear after the semicolon on each line.

```
UN,I;               Sets units to inches
OD,-,RB,-,OR,-;     Turns off Object Drag, Rubber Band, and Ortho
MO;                 Sets manual entry relative to origin
YC,0;               Sets current layer to 0
LC,11;              Selects line color 11
LT,0;               Selects line type 0
LW,0;               Selects line width 0
RE;                 Draws 5.25" square
0,0;
5.25,5.25;
ZA;                 Performs the Zoom All command
```

Check your input carefully for typographical errors, such as omitting semicolons, and then save it. If you are using a word processor, save it in an ASCII text format. Then start Generic CADD. Once you are at the drawing screen, start the Load (LO) command and select Batch file (B). You should see DISK listed on the side menu; select it with the second button of your mouse and watch your batch file in action. (If you do not see DISK listed on the side menu, use the File Path command to check the path for batch files and make sure it is set to the same directory in which you saved the DISK.TXT file.)

The batch file you just typed and saved draws a centered rectangle on your screen, as shown in figure 17.1. If this is not what you see, exit Generic CADD and use your editor to check your batch file again. Most batch file problems are caused by a simple error, such as a missing semicolon or a comma instead of a period. After making any necessary corrections, load the batch file into Generic CADD and try again.

The following batch file creates a more complicated figure than a rectangle. Exit Generic CADD without saving the drawing, and start your editor again. Load the file DISK.TXT and add the following lines to the end of the file (after the Zoom All command):

```
C2;                 Draws a 1.5" diameter circle
2.625,2.625;
3.375,2.625;
LI;                 Draws three connected lines
5.25,4.0625;
5.125,4.0625;
```

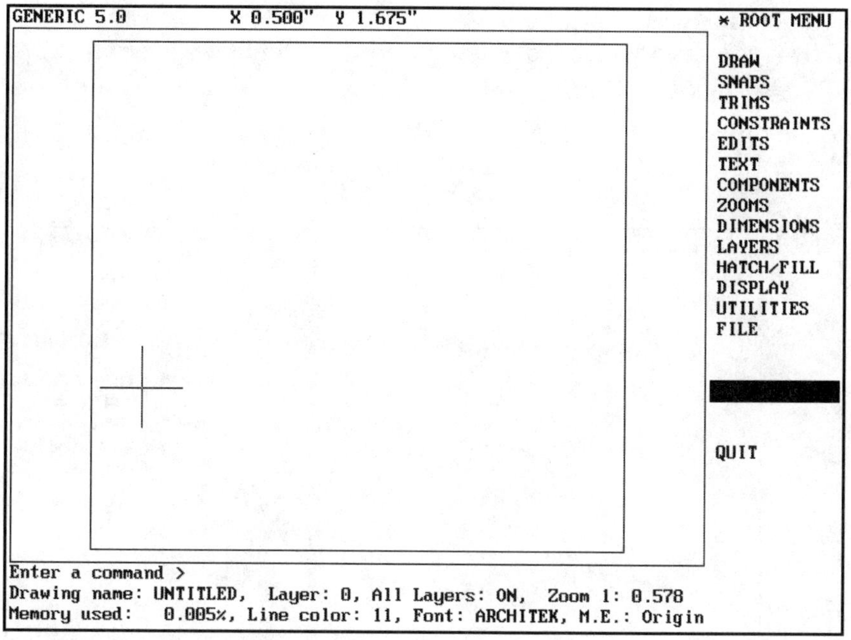

Figure 17.1: *Centered rectangle created by batch file.*

```
5.125,3.8125;
5.25,3.8125;
OB,5.25,3;          Breaks side of rectangle
5.25,4.0625;
5.25,3.8125;
C2;                 Draws a 1/4" diameter circle
3.625,2.375;
3.75,2.375;
L1;                 Draws a single line
2.375,1.25;
2.375,0.375;
L1;                 Draws a single line
2.875,1.25;
2.875,0.375;
A3;                 Draws a 3-point arc
2.375,1.25;
2.625,1.5;
2.875,1.25;
A3;                 Draws a 3-point arc
2.375,0.375;
2.625,0.125;
2.875,0.375;
RB,++,OD,++;        Turns on Rubber Band and Object Drag
```

Save this file after checking your work for accuracy. Then start Generic CADD and run the Load (LO) command again, choosing B for Batch file. Choose DISK from the side menu, as before.

The result should look like figure 17.2. Again, if the drawing does not appear as it should, use your editor to examine your batch file for mistakes.

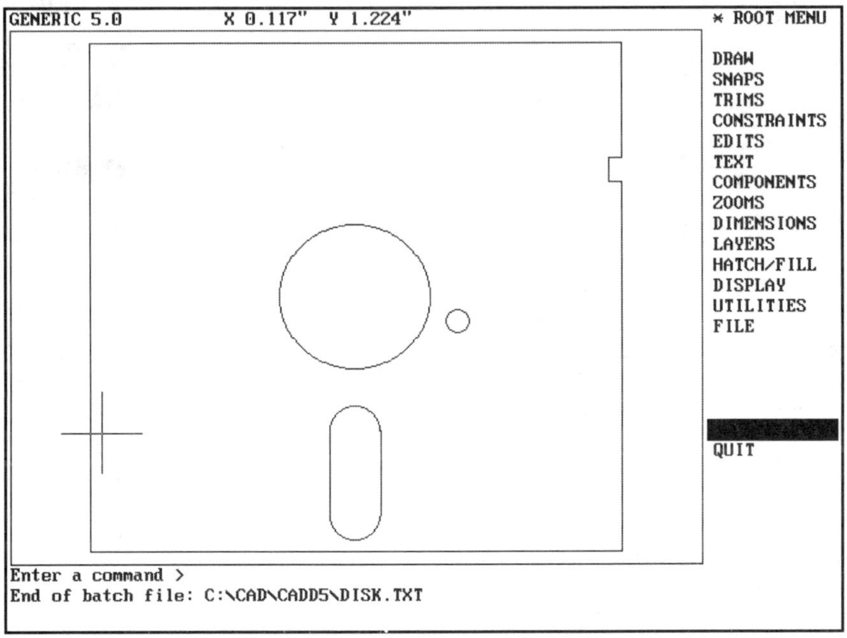

Figure 17.2: *Screen after loading DISK.TXT.*

The previous batch file was written with one point per line. You can condense the batch file somewhat by entering all points for a given command on the same line, separating the X,Y pairs with spaces to make it easier to read.

What follows is the same batch file in a more condensed format with generalized comments. The comments for sections of the batch file that draw objects precede the draw commands on a separate line. Both methods work equally well; go with your preference.

```
UN,I,OD,-,RB,-,OR,-,MO;          Performs standard setup
YC,0,LC,11,LT,0,LW,0;            Sets layer and line parameters
;                                Ends setup
;                                5.25" square (disk outline)
RE, 0,0, 5.25,5.25;
ZA;                              Starts the Zoom All command
;                                1.5" diameter circle (center hole)
C2, 2.625,2.625, 3.375,2.625;
```

```
;                                 3 lines and break right side
;                                 at lines (write protect notch)
LI, 5.25,4.0625,  5.125,4.0625,  5.125,3.8125,  5.25,3.8125;
OB, 5.25,3,  5.25,4.0625,  5.25,3.8125;
;                                 1/4" diameter circle (timing hole)
C2, 3.625,2.375,  3.75,2.375;
;                                 lines and arcs (R/W head slot)
L1, 2.375,1.25,  2.375,0.375;
L1, 2.875,1.25,  2.875,0.375;
A3, 2.375,1.25,  2.625,1.5, 2.875,1.25;
A3, 2.375,0.375,  2.625,0.125, 2.875,0.375;
RB,++,OD,++;                      Turns on Rubber Band and Object Drag
```

Writing an Interactive Batch File

So far, you have worked with batch files that are totally automatic. You will often need to interact with the batch file, however, to have more control over the drawing process. In the next section, you will create a batch file that pauses and prompts you for input.

The following example shows you how to automate the method for making pie charts shown in Chapter 4. This batch file pauses for you to enter the center of the pie chart. After it draws the basic pie chart, the file prompts you to label each section using a leader. You will use a basepoint as the center of the pie chart, and all coordinates will be entered relative to that basepoint. You will learn about the various lines as you go through the batch file, so that you better understand what each line in the batch file does.

Use your editor to create a file called PIE.TXT in your batch file directory (usually C:\CADD5). The first thing you should do in any batch file is to make your basic settings, such as the current layer, line type, and so on. The following lines do this. (The first several lines are identical to those at the beginning of DISK.TXT, so you can "borrow" them from that file to save time.)

```
UN,I;               Sets units to inches
OD,-,RB,-,OR,-;     Turns off Object Drag, Rubber Band, and Ortho
MO;                 Sets manual entry relative to origin
YC,0;               Sets current layer
LC,11;              Sets line color
LT,0;               Sets line type
LW,2;               Sets line width
```

This is a fairly standard beginning for a batch file. If you want to use a color other than 11 (bright cyan), simply substitute a different value. You might want to save this setup and use it as a beginning for all your batch files, changing the values when needed. Notice that the line width is set to 2; this is purely a matter of preference for the first several objects to be drawn in the batch file.

You will be using leaders to label the various wedges of the pie, so you also need to change some text and dimension settings:

```
TR,0;TS,C,30,L,150,S,0,A,1,J,L,P,++;     Text settings
```

This line sets the Text Rotation (TR) command to 0 degrees. It then invokes the Text Settings (TS) command to set the between-character spacing (C) to 30 percent, the between-line spacing (L) to 150 percent, the slant (S) to 0 degrees, the aspect ratio (A) to 1:1, and the justification (J) to left. Finally, it turns on proportional spacing (P). If you were placing text, you would want to select a text font, size, and color. Those commands are not included here because only leaders are being used.

The TS command does not end with an Enter (!), as it normally does. This is because Generic CADD deals inconsistently with toggle settings that are "under" another command, such as arrow position (under AR) and proportional spacing (under TS). A semicolon after such a toggle acts as a return to end the command (in this case, TS). If this inconsistency is fixed at a future date, which it may well be, you will need to insert an exclamation mark between the double plus sign and the semicolon.

The following lines adjust the dimension settings which affect leaders:

```
UY,0;                      Sets dim/leader layer
FS,D,engineer;             Sets font for dims
TZ,D,.25,!;                Sets text size for dims
AR,T,N,A,25,L,.5,!;        Makes arrow settings
LL,.25;                    Sets leader shoulder length
DT,I,.25,!;                Sets text inline offset
```

The lines above govern the setting that affects leaders. If you were placing dimensions, you would need to write commands for more settings. The Arrow Settings (AR) command sets the arrow type (T) to filled notched (N), the angle (A) to 25 degrees, and the length (L) to a half-inch. Again, an exclamation mark is used to end the Text Size and Arrow Settings commands. The inline offset determines the offset between the shoulder line and the leader text.

The final step in the settings portion of the batch file is to set the limits and issue the Zoom Limits command. This is not always necessary, but in this case it ensures that the screen will be an appropriate size for the pie chart. A "blank" line consisting only of a semicolon is an easy-to-see marker that denotes the end of the settings portion of the batch file.

```
LS,12,12,ZL;   Sets limits, starts Zoom Limits command
;              Ends setting portion
```

To draw the pie chart, you need to draw a number of objects based on a single location. The next two lines of the batch file prompt you for a basepoint and turn on manual entry relative to the basepoint:

```
BP,@;     Prompts user for basepoint location
MB;       Starts manual entry relative to basepoint
```

The at sign (@) pauses Generic CADD and prompts you for the X,Y coordinates needed for the basepoint command. This is the only true form of variable available in a batch file. It enables the user to enter a point and then have the batch file draw objects or carry out operations relative to the basepoint. For this technique to work, you must change the manual entry mode to be relative to the basepoint (MB), and not to the origin (MO) or last point (MR).

The following command draws a circle with a two-inch radius centered on the basepoint. If you want a larger circle, you need only alter the X value of the second coordinate (which is on the circumference of the circle):

```
C2, 0,0,  2,0; Draws 4" diameter circle
```

You then need to draw the lines necessary to divide the circle into four wedges. Each command starts the line at the center of the circle and uses a Snap Percentage (SR) command to end the line at the appropriate point on the circle's circumference. Because the percentage is always measured from the same point on the circle, the percentage for each wedge must equal the total for all wedges up to that point. Draw the first line (which is at 0 percent or 100 percent, depending upon your point of view) last. This is done so that the line will not cause Generic CADD to find two objects when you use the Snap Percentage command. The following commands draw the lines:

```
L1, 0,0, SR,2,0, 40;  Marks 40% wedge
L1, 0,0, SR,2,0, 70;  Marks 30% wedge
L1, 0,0, SR,2,0, 90;  Marks 20% wedge
L1, 0,0, 2,0;         Marks last wedge (10%)
```

If you adjust the diameter of the circle, you must also adjust the X value of the second coordinate pair for each line. You also can adjust the percentages to make differently numbered or sized wedges.

The following two commands set a finer line width and turn on the Rubber Band command so you can position the leaders:

```
LW,0;     Sets line width
RB,++;    Turns on Rubber Band command
```

You will need four leader commands to label each section of your pie:

```
LE,40% ~,@,@,@;
LE,30% ~,@,@,@;
LE,20% ~,@,@,@;
LE,10% ~,@,@,@;
```

The tildes pause Generic CADD while you edit the leader text. In each case, you've "pre-loaded" the leader text with the percentage of the wedge to be labeled. You can add to this percentage, or even backspace over it when the tilde transfers control of the leader text line to you. The three at signs pause Generic CADD and prompt you to input the three points needed to draw the leader (start, end, and shoulder direction).

Finish the batch file by turning on those options you may have turned off. This is a standard line for the end of a batch file that ensures you are not dragging a line from some point, and that both the Rubber Band and Object Drag commands are turned on after the batch file finishes. (The RB command in this example is redundant because you just turned it on above, but it doesn't hurt anything to turn it on again.)

```
PU,OD,++,RB,++;  Turns on the Object Drag command
```

Here is the entire batch file as it should appear on your editor's screen:

```
UN,I;                   Sets units to inches
OD,-,RB,-,OR,-;         Turns off Object Drag, Rubber Band, and
                        Ortho
MO;                     Sets manual entry relative to origin
YC,0;                   Sets current layer
LC,11;                  Sets line color
LT,0;                   Sets line type
LW,2;                   Sets line width
TR,0;TS,C,30,L,150,S,0,A,1,J,L,P,++;    Makes text settings
UY,0;                   Sets dim/leader layer
FS,D,engineer;          Sets font for dims
TZ,D,.25,!;             Sets text size for dims
AR,T,N,A,25,L,.5,!;     Sets arrow settings
LL,.25;                 Sets leader shoulder length
DT,I,.25,!;             Sets text inline offset
LS,12,12,ZL;            Sets limits and starts Zoom Limits com-
                        mand
;                       Ends settings portion
BP,@;                   Prompts for basepoint location
MB;                     Sets manual entry relative to basepoint
C2, 0,0,  2,0;          Draws 4" diameter circle
```

```
L1, 0,0, SR,2,0, 40;     Marks 40% wedge
L1, 0,0, SR,2,0, 70;     Marks 30% wedge (40+30=70)
L1, 0,0, SR,2,0, 90;     Marks 20% wedge (70+20=90)
L1, 0,0,  2,0;           Marks last wedge (10%)
LW,0;                    Sets line width
RB,++;                   Turns on Rubber Band command
LE,40% ~,@,@,@;          Labels section of pie chart
LE,30% ~,@,@,@;          Labels section of pie chart
LE,20% ~,@,@,@;          Labels section of pie chart
LE,10% ~,@,@,@;          Labels section of pie chart
PU,OD,++,RB,++;          Turns on Object Drag command
```

After checking your batch file for mistakes, save it and exit your editor. Then start Generic CADD and follow these steps:

Testing the Pie Chart Batch File

Prompt	*Input*	*Description*
`Command`	**LO**	Starts the Load command
`Drawing Component Batch file....`	**B**	Selects batch file as type of file to load
`Select file from side menu >>`	Type **PIE**, or select from side menu with second mouse button	Selects file to load
`Set a new basepoint (X,Y)`	Enter a point near center of screen	Centers pie chart and draws circle with four wedges (see fig. 17.3)
`Enter string> 40%`	Enter a label for the first wedge	Identifies wedge
`Enter leader starting point`	Click on circle near first wedge	Positions arrowhead of the leader
`Enter leader terminal point`	Point end of arrow at circle and click	Positions other end of arrow
`Enter a point indicating shoulder direction`	Move the cursor to left or right and click	Positions text left or right of leader arrow

Repeat these steps for the remaining three leaders, pointing to each wedge of the pie chart in turn. When you are finished, your results should look like figure 17.4.

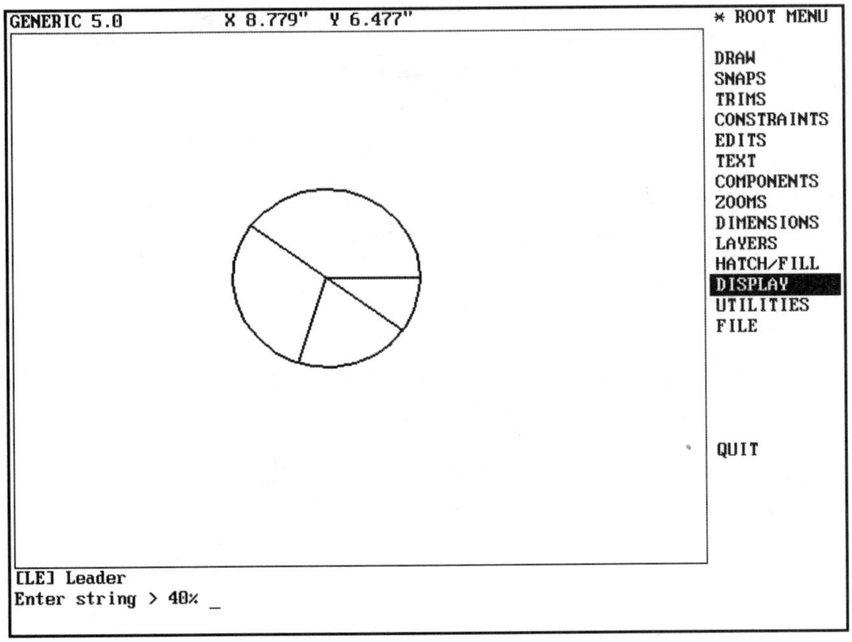

Figure 17.3 *The basic pie chart before leaders are inserted.*

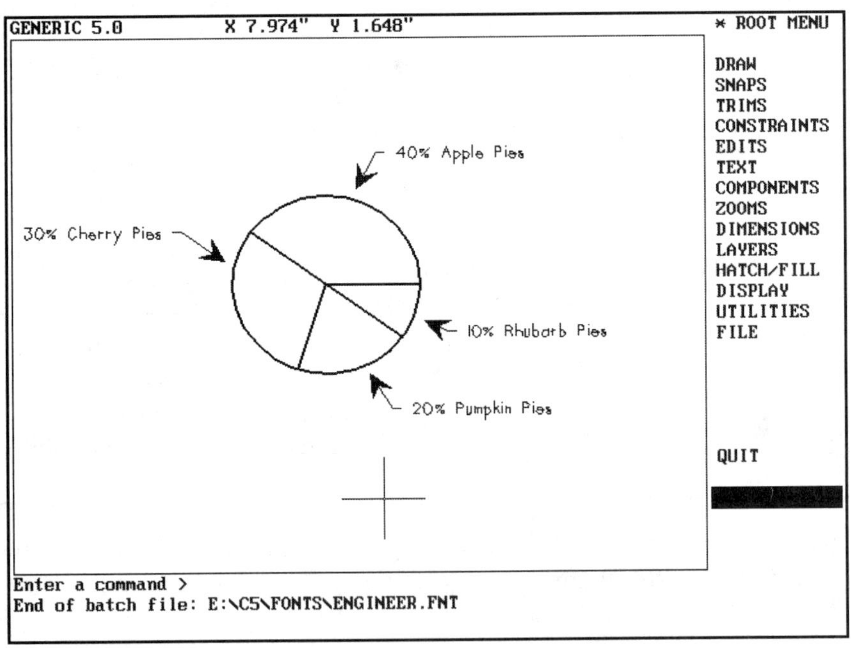

Figure 17.4 *The completed pie chart.*

Using Shell to Executable

The capability of Generic CADD 5.0 to shell out to other programs greatly expands the use of batch files. *Shell out* means that you leave the Generic CADD program and run another program. This is not like quitting Generic CADD because Generic CADD is still loaded in memory when you shell out.

Many programs simply remain loaded and allow you to use the available remaining memory, often 100K or less of free RAM. Generic CADD 5.0 uses all available memory, so it needs to perform a few tricks to shell out. Generic CADD writes all but a very small portion of itself and your drawing out to disk in a shell file, so this leaves a majority of your memory available in the shell. Unfortunately, you cannot load any software that remains resident in memory (such as TSR programs) and expect to return to Generic CADD.

You can shell out to a nearly unlimited number of programs, so this function can be used in a nearly unlimited number of ways. You can use the Shell to Executable (SH) command to help write and debug batch files, or to run an editor to make a text file that is then loaded using Generic CADD's Load ASCII (LA) command. You can even shell to a program that writes another batch file.

Generic CADD has a good text editor, but you may find that editing large blocks of comments can be done more easily with a dedicated editor or wordprocessing program. This can be easily facilitated with CADD's Shell to Executable (SH) and Load ASCII (LA) commands. The following batch file, for example, shells out to the PC-Write editor (ED.EXE) and edits a file called TEMP.DOC. The batch file invokes Generic CADD's Load ASCII command to load the file and then prompts the user for the placement in the drawing.

```
SH,ED.EXE,TEMP.DOC;
LA,TEMP.DOC,@;
```

You can also use the SH command to shell to a program that writes another batch file, then load that batch file when you return to Generic CADD. This can be used for what is sometimes called *parametric design*, in which the drawing process is automated by another program and Generic CADD serves mostly as a graphics engine programmed with batch files.

The Shell to Executable command is perhaps best used to shell to your editor program to edit and debug batch files. A single misplaced comma or semicolon can cause a batch file to fail, so batch files often fail on the first several attempts. Debugging a batch file may mean loading your editor, modifying the batch file, exiting the editor, running Generic CADD, testing the batch file, exiting Generic CADD, loading the editor again, and so on. It is a tedious process at best.

An alternative to that tedious process is use the Shell to Executable command to shell out of Generic CADD and run your editor. Once you finish editing the batch file, you exit your editor and automatically return to Generic CADD. You can make this even easier by putting the shell command on a macro. The following macro, for example, shells out to the PC-Write editor (ED) and edits a batch file called WORK.TXT:

```
SH,ED.EXE,WORK.TXT
```

Using Batch Files To Modify a Drawing

Batch files provide a way to alter a drawing when Generic CADD's editing and change commands fall short. A batch file created by the Save Batch (SB) command not only gives you access to all the commands required to construct a drawing but also allows you to alter those commands.

Say, for example, you have a drawing with a lot of dimensioning in it and you want to change the arrowhead style of all the dimensions. Whereas Generic CADD enables you to change individual dimensions with the Dimension Change (UG) command, it does not provide a way to change more than one dimension at a time. Changing all the dimensions in an entire drawing is a rather tedious task, even if you make a macro that only requires you to point at the dimension text.

An alternative approach is to start by using the Selection Save Batch (BS) and the Filter commands to save all the dimensions in the drawing as a batch file. Then shell out to your editor (or quit Generic CADD and run your editor) and call up the batch file. Use your editor to search for AR (the Arrow Settings command) and make the appropriate changes to alter the arrowhead style. The AR command will show up in the batch file only where dimensions or leaders were placed using a different arrowhead style. The AR command, therefore, might show up several times in a batch file, but it is almost certain to be fewer than the number of dimensions and leaders in the drawing.

After making the changes to the batch file, return to Generic CADD. Use the Erase and Filter commands to erase all the dimensions in the drawing. (If you have shelled out to your editor instead of quitting Generic CADD, you can select the last selection (L), which will be the same dimensions that were saved as a batch file earlier.) Then use the Load Batch (LB) command to load the batch file you just edited. The batch file will re-create all your dimensions, this time drawing them with the new style of arrows according to the changes you made to the batch file.

Using Batch Files To Extract Data from a Drawing

Batch files are saved in ASCII format, so they are an ideal medium for extracting data from your drawing. This function is useful primarily for programs that do not support formats such as DXF (Drawing Interchange Format), which are specifically designed for the interchange of drawing data between Generic CADD or CADD-related programs.

A batch file contains the exact coordinate data for every entity in a drawing—the endpoints of every line, a point in the center or on the circumference of every circle, and so on. It also contains other useful information, such as the name and location of every component in the drawing.

If you look at the batch files you saved earlier using Generic CADD's Save Batch (SB) and Selection Save Batch (BS) commands, you will see that they are highly ordered. Generic CADD places one command to a line and one pair of points to a line when it saves a batch file. This makes it fairly easy to write a program that will "parse" though a batch file for the information you wish to extract.

You need some experience with a programming language to write a program that reads and processes an ASCII file such as a Generic CADD batch file, but you don't need to be a wizard. Many users have been able to use batch files for a variety of tasks with languages such as Quick Basic and Turbo Pascal.

You could, for example, search a batch file for CP (Component Place) commands and note the name of each component. From this information you could construct a bill of materials list. Or, you could read in a batch file and re-order the entities and points to create a "cut path" to be used by a machine. The possibilities are limited only by your imagination and programming ability.

Linking CADD to Other Software with Batch Files

One of the more powerful uses of batch files is as a link to other programs. When software does not support more traditional methods of exchanging drawing data, batch files provide an effective way to create a drawing from other information. It generally is best to use a data exchange format that is specifically designed for Generic CADD data, such as DXF (Drawing Interchange Format). If another program supports reading and/or writing of DXF files, you can use Generic's AutoConvert program to translate DXF files to and from Generic's proprietary DWG and CMP formats.

Information from a number of sources can be imported into Generic CADD through batch files. If you have data that is in coordinates (X,Y) format, for example, it is relatively easy to translate it into batch file format and create a drawing based on that data. Ideally, another program (such as a spreadsheet) can be made to save data to disk in a Generic CADD batch file. This enables you to highly automate the drawing process and engage in *parametric design*, in which an entire drawing is created from a few parameters.

Massaging Raw Data into Batch File Format

Generic CADD is an excellent tool for plotting coordinate-based information such as statistical data. The challenge is to transpose the data from raw form into a format that means something to Generic CADD. This process is known as *massaging*, which means the material is put into a different form but the content is not altered.

An editor or word processor (preferably one with macro capability) ordinarily is used for this task, although a special program can be written. You should have to resort to writing a special program, however, only if the information is particularly diverse or esoteric.

Most statistical data takes a fairly regular form and can be edited with a word processor and a simple macro. Say, for example, you have information in X,Y format that represents measurements of three groups, and you want to create a graph to see how the groups relate to one another.

You do not need to worry about the size or scope of the numbers involved. X might range from 1 to 4, and Y could range from 200 to 20,000. When massaging data into a batch file, *never* alter the values of the original data. Make your alterations by placing the raw data in a formula within the batch file. The formula can be easily modified with the search and replace function, leaving the original data intact.

The following example assumes the data is listed one point to a line:

```
pppp g xx.xxxx yy,yyy.y
```

In this example, pppp is a point number, g is the group the point belongs to, xx.xxxx is one value, and yy,yyy.y is another value. As an additional twist, assume that the X and Y ranges are disparate, with X running from 0 to 100 and Y ranging from 0 to 100,000.

Assume you want to place a symbol at each point location that identifies the group to which that point belongs. You also want to be able to look at any point and get the point number so that you can look up other data related to that point. You can do this in Generic CADD by making three components, one to identify each group. Attach an attribute to each component, perhaps called "point," which contains a field for the point number. (The attribute could contain all the above information, but it would be a little more difficult to massage the data.)

You would want to follow these steps before you process the batch file:

1. Create an attribute named "point" which contains one field named "point #" with a default value of nothing (just press Enter).
2. Create three components to be used as symbols for the three groups: such as a triangle filled with green, a circle filled with blue, and a rectangle filled with red. The name of each component should be the same as the name for each group; this could even be a number such as 1, 2, or 3. You probably want the reference point to be in the center of each symbol.
3. Attach the "point" attribute to each component as it is created. Determine a default location for the attribute and leave the default value for "point #" blank. Set the display default to off. (You probably do not want the drawing cluttered with all the attribute text.)
4. Experiment with placing a few of the components manually. Pick a few points at random and place several symbols at the appropriate X,Y locations. This will allow you to experiment with component scales, text sizes, and so on to get a feel for what will work well. You might, for example, determine that you want to divide all Y values by 100 to make the graph more readable.

Always try a few dry runs manually to get a feel for how things will work when designing a batch file. Make notes along the way to determine what commands need to be issued and what information needs to be supplied to perform those commands. In this example, this would allow you to ascertain that the sequence needed to place one point of data would be:

1. Issue the CP (Component Place) command.
2. Supply the name of the component (the "group" in this case).
3. Enter the X and Y coordinates to place the component.
4. Enter the "point #" for the attribute.

Be sure to note which settings make things work properly, such as setting Attribute Settings to prompt you to edit field values at placement, and turning on Autoplacement.

Consider the format of the original data and how you want the resulting batch file line to appear. In this example you are starting with data in the following format:

```
pppp g xx.xxxx yy,yyy.y
```

You will want the resulting batch file line to look like this:

```
CP,g,x.xxxx,yyyyy.y/100,pppp;
```

The first step is to purge the comma in the middle of the Y value. You need to insert CP at the beginning of each line and a semicolon at the end of each line. You also need to insert /100 after the Y value and to change the spaces that separate everything into commas. Perhaps the most difficult step will be moving the point number to the end of the line, with a space between it and the Y value. You might be able to combine several of these steps into a macro, or you can tackle them one at a time.

Stripping the comma from the middle of the Y value can be done with a simple search (for a comma) and replace (with nothing). If you can arrange the data so that everything is separated with spaces (`CP g x.xxxx yyyyy.y/100 pppp;`), then another search and replace can easily place commas where they are needed.

If you can make a macro to take care of the other steps, massaging the data into a batch file will be easy. If your editor's macro facility supports self-repeating (or looping) macros, it will be almost painless.

A macro for the word processor PC-Write follows. It uses simple commands that most editors or word processors support. The general function for each command is noted so that you can follow the process, or create a similar macro for using your favorite editor or word processor.

Start with the cursor at the end of the first line of data. The insert mode should be turned on. Type the macro as follows:

In PC-Write, the asterisk key (the one by the key pad, not Shift-8) is the macro key. By pressing it when recording a macro, you automatically stop recording and create a self-repeating macro. Macro languages vary, but nearly all of them can create a macro which repeats until it reaches the end of the file.

Some word processors move text by using the mark-move-unmark sequence above, while others use a mark-cut-paste sequence. Nearly all editors or word processors have commands which will move the cursor to the beginning or end of the line, or to the first character of the "word" to the left or right. You do not have to depend on all values in data being the same length when you use such functions. The above macro would work, for example, if the "point number" is two digits or five digits, but pressing the left arrow would only work for four-digit numbers.

You may need to experiment to discover how your editor treats a series of numbers, such as 12.34 567.89. PC-Write, for example, treats 12.34 as one word. If the cursor was at the 1 in this nine-number sequence, pressing Ctrl and the right-arrow key would move the cursor to the 5. Microsoft Word, however, treats 12.34 differently; pressing Ctrl and the right-arrow key would move the cursor to the period, then to the 3, and then to the 5. Learn and anticipate your editor's characteristics when creating macros.

Table 17.1
Writing a Macro in a Word Processor

Input	*Description*
Ctrl-@	Starts recording a macro
/100	Inserts /100 after Y value
Space bar	Inserts a space after /100
Home	Moves cursor to beginning of line
CP	Inserts CP at beginning of line
F6	Begins marking text to be moved
Ctrl-Right Arrow	Moves cursor right one word
Left Arrow	Moves cursor left one space
F6	Ends marking text to be moved
End	Moves cursor to end of line
F6	Moves marked text to cursor
F5	Turns off marking
End	Moves cursor to end of line
;	Inserts ; at end of line
Down Arrow	Moves cursor down one line
End	Moves cursor to end of line
Asterisk	Stops recording macro, makes a "repeating macro"

Once you have massaged the data into a batch file, you need to insert a section only at the top of the file to account for any settings. In this batch file, for example, you would need to concern yourself with the following items:

- ❑ Component Scale (CS)
- ❑ Font Select (FS) for Attributes (A)
- ❑ Text Size (TZ) for Attributes (A)
- ❑ Attribute Settings (AS)

    Auto Placement on (A,++)

    Edit Fields at Placement (P,++)

Once you have loaded the batch file, you may discover that you want to make some adjustments — the components may be too large, for example, or the Y scale might need to be compressed to give the graph a more favorable appearance. You only need to go back and edit the batch file. It may be as simple as changing one line, or you may need to perform the search and replace function (replacing /100 with /200, for example). Once you have made the changes, return to Generic CADD and load the batch file again.

Parametric Design

Perhaps the most exciting use for batch files is as a link with another program (such as a spreadsheet) to create a highly automated drafting and design environment. Many drawings can be reduced to a generic design which can be compiled into formulas that describe the basic geometric relationships between its objects. Nearly anything can be drawn this way, from a camshaft in an engine to the cutting diagram for a cardboard box. This technique is called *parametric design.*

The formulas for a drawing can be placed into a program that calculates the coordinates for every point needed to create a batch file for Generic CADD. Spreadsheet programs are well-suited to this task because they are designed to work with large numbers of values and formulas. The spreadsheet is normally divided into three parts: a data entry section, a formulas section containing the formulas for each point, and a portion which is printed to disk to create a Generic CADD batch file.

A new design can be generated by simply changing a few variables that recalculate the spreadsheet and creating a new batch file. The final step is to load the batch file into Generic CADD to view the basic design. This enables you to rapidly perform "what if" experiments with your designs. In more advanced parametric designs, some values can be allowed to "float" while other values determine the design.

Consider the pattern for a cardboard box shown in figure 17.5. Every point needed to draw the lines for this pattern can be determined from four values: the height (H), width (W), depth (D), and the gap (G) needed between the flaps (a factor of the thickness of the cardboard). It is relatively simple to make a list of the lines needed to draw this pattern and to make the formula for the endpoints of each line.

The data entry portion of the spreadsheet contains areas for entering the height, width, depth and gap parameters from which the rest of the design is derived. The formulas section would contain the formula for each point needed to create the drawing. The batch file section contains the Generic CADD commands and references to the formulas section needed to create the batch file. The batch file is created by printing the batch file section to a disk file.

Figure 17.6 shows the left half of the box with the formulas for several of the points indicated. The lower left corner is duplicated at the right with four points (labeled 1, 2, 3, and 4) and three lines (A, B, and C).

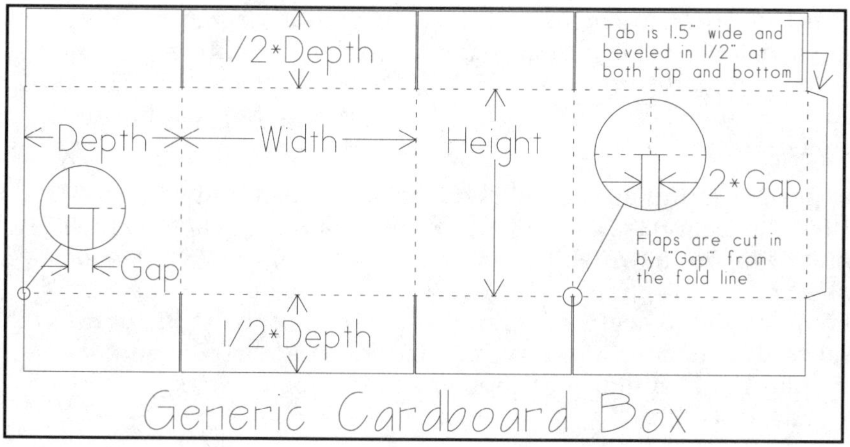

Figure 17.5: *Basic pattern for a cardboard box.*

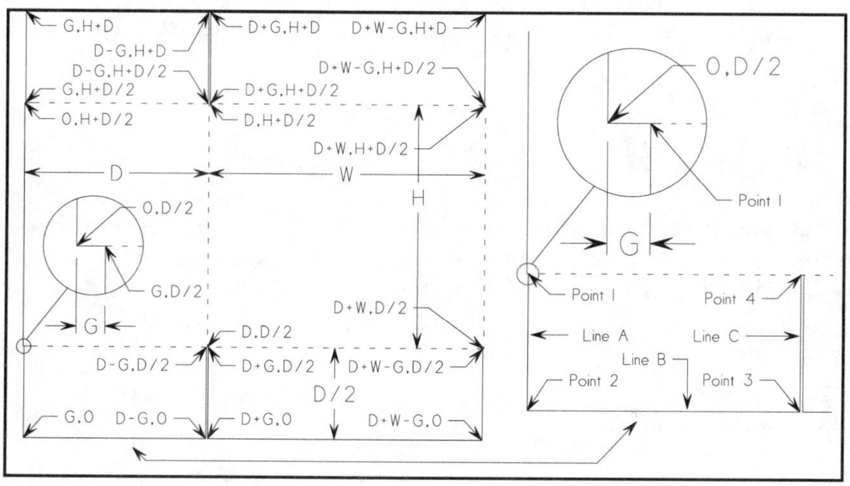

Figure 17.6: *Box Outline with formulas.*

Examine the three parts of the spreadsheet needed to draw the three lines. The data entry section would look something like this:

	A	*B*
1	Height	12
2	Width	16
3	Depth	8
4	Gap	0.0625

Column A contains the labels, and column B holds the values from which the rest of the spreadsheet is calculated. If your spreadsheet program enables you to name cells, rename cells B1 through B4 as H, W, D, and G, respectively. This will make filling in formulas much easier. More importantly, it makes reading and editing the formulas easier if you need to change your drawing template later.

A logical place to put the formulas section is to use columns X and Y in the spreadsheet to hold the formulas for the X and Y coordinates for each point. This allows a very intuitive layout in which the formulas for the X and Y values for point 1 are in cells X1 and Y1, point 2 in cells X2, Y2 and so on. Most spreadsheet programs require you to begin a formula with a number or a plus or minus sign so that the spreadsheet does not think you are entering text. Set your spreadsheet to display the formulas for this section (as opposed to the values) to make it easier to read and edit.

The formulas section for points 1 through 4 might appear as follows:

	X	*Y*
1	+B4	+B3/2
2	+B4	0
3	+B3-B4	0
4	+B3-B4	+B3/2

The section of the spreadsheet that you print to disk to make a batch file consists of cells which contain text for the Generic CADD commands needed to draw objects, as well as cells for X and Y coordinates that refer to cells in the formulas section. While creating the spreadsheet, set the display to show "formulas," and this section will appear as follows:

	D	*E*	*F*	*G*	*H*	*I*	*J*	*K*	*L*	*M*
1	Line A	LI,	+X1	,	+Y1	,	+X2	,	+Y2	;
2	Line B	LI,	+X2	,	+Y2	,	+X3	,	+Y3	;
3	Line C	LI,	+X3	,	+Y3	,	+X4	,	+Y4	;

The following is the same section with values displayed as they would appear prior to printing to disk:

	D	*E*	*F*	*G*	*H*	*I*	*J*	*K*	*L*	*M*
1	Line A	LI,	0.0625	,	4	,	0.0625	,	0	;
2	Line B	LI,	0.0625	,	0	,	7.9375	,	0	;
3	Line C	LI,	7.9375	,	0	,	7.9375	,	4	;

The D column of cells is for your reference and to make editing easier. It takes slightly more time to type them in, but if you have to make changes several weeks later, you will be glad you did. Columns G, I, K, and M are set to a width of 1 because they only contain single characters. This is done only to make viewing the spreadsheet easier. Remember, Generic CADD does not care about extra spaces in batch file lines, so this needs to be done only if the lines might be longer than the 80-character limit. The rows above this would contain standard setup commands such as line width, type, color, layer, and so on.

To create the batch file, configure your spreadsheet for the simplest printer it allows; this is usually labeled something like "text printer." Select DISK FILE as the destination for the printed output, and be sure to use TXT as the filename extension. Then simply select the range of cells (in this case, columns E through M) to be printed, and print them to a disk file. That file can then be loaded into Generic CADD to create the basic drawing. You can then add finishing touches such as comments, title blocks, and so on.

The template for the cardboard box you have worked with is an example of simple parametrics. In more advanced parametric designs, values are often interrelated. Some of them can be set to float, whereas others are fixed; the formulas are then solved for the floating values.

The automatic staircase generation in the GenCADD Architectural module (an add-on product for Generic CADD 5.0) is an example of more advanced parametrics. A number of variables determine the finished design of a staircase: the height and length of the staircase, the number of steps, and the tread and rise of each step. These variables, however, are interrelated; the number of steps is related to the height of the staircase and the rise of each step, for example. One of these values always can be found based upon the other two.

Using Formulas and Variables in Generic CADD

Generic CADD enables you to use mathematical expressions (formulas) to enter points or values. If you have ever entered fractional values, you may have used this ability already without knowing it. A fraction is really a simple division operation. For example, 1/4 is the same as 1 divided by 4.

Mathematical Functions

The following mathematical functions, variables, and rules can be used for macros, custom menus, batch files, or when entering values from the command line.

- **Basic arithmetic operations.** Addition (+), subtraction (-), multiplication (*) and division (/).

- **$SQR(X).** The square of X (X^2 or X*X, depending upon the notation you are accustomed to seeing.
- **$SQT(X).** The square root of X.
- **$ABS(X).** The absolute value of X. Absolute value returns the positive value of a number, as if it were multiplied by -1. (The absolute value of -3.14 is 3.14.)
- **$SIN(X).** The sine of angle X.
- **$COS(X).** The cosine of angle X.
- **$ATN(X).** The arctangent of value X. This function returns an angle whose tangent is the value X.
- **$LN(X).** The natural or "base *e*" logarithm of X. Usually referred to as the "natural log of X" ("*e*" is an indeterminate constant similar to pi).
- **$EXP(X).** *e* to the X power, sometimes expressed as *e*^X.

The following rules apply to these mathematical functions:

- X may be any real number or mathematical formula, and may include system variables.
- X must be enclosed in parentheses. The function $SIN32 will not work, while $SIN(32) will.
- Numbers must be expressed in decimal form. Degrees must be in decimal, not D:M:S (Degrees-Minutes-Seconds).
- Avoid mixed dimensions, such as 2'3".
- Spaces may be added for clarity; they are ignored when Generic CADD evaluates the expression.
- X to the Y power (X^Y) can be derived using the "natural log" and "*e* to the X" functions using the following formula: X^Y = $EXP(Y * $LN(X)).

When Generic CADD solves mathematical expressions, it does so in the following order:

1. Anything enclosed in parentheses. Deepest nested parentheses are evaluated first.
2. The various $ functions described above, such as $SQR.
3. Multiplication and division.
4. Addition and subtraction.

Here are some examples of how the equations are formatted in Generic CADD:

```
4 + 5 * 8 - 6       =  4 + 40 - 6  =  38       =  38
(4 + 5) * 8 - 6     =  9 * 8 - 6   =  72 - 6  =  66
4 + 5 * (8 - 6)     =  4 + 5 * 2   =  4 + 10  =  14
(4 + 5) * (8 - 6)   =  9 * 2       =  18       =  18
```

System Variables

Generic CADD 5.0 supports three system variables: $VAL, $PNTX, and $PNTX. These variables are automatically updated by certain program operations. You can use these variables in mathematical operations, or on their own. Use the variable $VAL whenever you need to specify a single value, such as a line color or rotation angle. The variables $PNTX and $PNTY work as a pair, and can be used to specify points or "paired" values (such as X and Y scales, or X and Y grid sizes).

The $VAL Variable

The $VAL variable is updated whenever a single value is entered. Whenever you use a command such as Line Color or Text Size, for example, $VAL is updated to whatever value you enter. You can set $VAL to the current value of any setting by activating the proper command and accepting the default (current) value for that setting. For example, if you issue the Component Rotation command and press Enter, no change is made to the component rotation setting, but $VAL is updated to reflect the current Component Rotation value.

This allows you to increment or alter any setting based on the current setting. You do this by issuing the proper command, accepting the default value (thus updating $VAL to equal that value), and then issuing the command a second time and using $VAL in a formula to enter a new setting.

For example, the following line in a macro, batch file, or custom menu will alter the Component Rotation by 90 degrees:

```
CR,!,CR,$VAL + 90;    Sets CR to CR+90 degrees
```

CR is the Component Rotation command. The exclamation mark acts as if Enter had been pressed to accept the current value, thus leaving CR unchanged and setting $VAL to the current component rotation. CR then issues a second Component Rotation command and sets the rotation to the current value (held in $VAL) plus 90 degrees.

You also can use this command to set one value equal to another. Use this to set two or more settings to the same value at the same time. Say, for example, you want the line color to be changed to match the layer number whenever you change the current layer, so that objects with color 1 will be drawn on layer 1, color 2 on layer 2, and so on.

Do this by using the following line instead of the YC command to set the current layer:

```
YC,~,LC,$VAL;   Sets current layer; color = layer #
```

In this line, YC starts the Current Layer command, and the tilde pauses for you to select the layer from the side menu. LC sets the Line Color to $VAL, which was updated to reflect the layer number that was selected. (This works even if the layer is named.) Note that because the Current Layer command, which can accept both names and numbers, interprets $VAL as a layer name, the reverse of this process will not work.

You also can set three text sizes at the same time:

```
TZ,T,~,D,$VAL,A,$VAL,!;
```

The $PNTX and $PNTY Variables

The $PNTX and $PNTY system variables work as a pair. Both are updated whenever you set a value that uses a pair of settings, as in the Component Scale or Grid Size commands. These variables are also updated whenever you use a Snap command such as Snap to Nearest Point or Snap Intersection. Points entered by clicking or manual entry do not update these two variables.

One potential use for these two variables would be to make a pair of macros that would either double or halve the current component scale. Consider the following four examples:

```
CZ,!!,CZ,$PNTX * 2,$PNTY * 2;      Doubles component scale
CZ,!!,CZ,$PNTX * .5,$PNTY * .5;    Halves component scale
CZ,!!,CZ,$PNTX * 2,$PNTY;          Doubles X component scale
CZ,!!,CZ,$PNTX,$PNTY * 2;          Doubles Y component scale
```

You may want to "store" one of these system variables on occasion. The easiest way to do this would be to use a setting that you rarely (if ever) use as a holding place for the value. Some users, for example, use the Line Scale (LZ) command as a holding place for $VAL. Because the basepoint takes a pair of values, some users employ it as a holding place for $PNTX and $PNTY. This is done as follows:

```
LZ,$VAL;            Puts $VAL into LZ
LZ,!;               Gets $VAL from LZ
BP,$PNTX,$PNTY;     Puts $PNTX and $PNTY into BP
BP,!!;              Gets $PNTX and $PNTY from BP
```

Summary

Batch files are one of Generic CADD's most powerful and versatile features. They enable you to automate your drafting and design tasks by writing a script of commands to perform any number of functions, from creating an entire drawing to selectively editing portions of a drawing.

You also can use batch files to create charts and graphs simply by altering the values in a standard batch file.

Batch files can export drawing data to other programs. You can use this function to create a bill of materials or schedules for items such as doors and windows. Batch files also can be used to export drawing data for CAM (Computer-Aided Manufacturing) applications.

Batch files provide a link to import data from other programs. Statistics and other information can be taken in raw form and massaged into a batch file to represent the data in graphical form. You can automate the design process and delve into parametric design by using a spreadsheet to create batch files, which convert the numbers into a nearly finished drawing.

Batch files enable you to put an A in front of Generic CADD, changing Generic CADD from a simple drawing tool to a means of performing Automated Computer-Aided Design and Drafting.

A

Using a Digitizer

Comparing Digitizers to Mice and Trackballs

Generic CADD supports two types of pointing devices: relative motion devices (mice and trackballs) and absolute position devices (digitizers). The primary difference between these two classifications is the nature in which they operate. Because a trackball is really just an upside-down mouse, this discussion refers to both devices as *mice.*

The mouse registers movement on the basis of a ball which rolls as the mouse is moved across a surface. The trackball uses the same principle but is stationary. Rolling the ball with your thumb or finger moves the cursor on the screen. Digitizers use a combination of a *tablet* and a *stylus* or *puck* (sometimes called a *cursor*). A stylus looks like a pen, while a puck resembles a mouse with a clear lens containing a fine crosshair. This discussion refers to both styles of pointers as a puck.

The puck senses its position relative to the tablet, often with a resolution as high as one thousand parts per inch. The digitizer sends a continuous stream of coordinates to CADD in an X,Y format that indicates the position of the puck.

Mice are called *relative motion devices* because they relay position information to CADD based on motion. A mouse does not know *where* it is on your desk. You can pick it up and move it without affecting the location of the cursor on your CADD drawing screen. Mice and trackballs only take notice when they are 'rolled' or a button is pressed. They report this information to CADD, which keeps track of the location of the cursor, updating it when you move the mouse.

In addition, many mice now support a feature called *ballistics*, which means that the mouse is sensitive to how fast it is moved. When this feature is used the mouse reports more or less movement to CADD depending on the rate at which it is moved. This enables you to move the cursor on the screen a great distance by making a small but rapid movement of the mouse. The primary advantages to a mouse are the small amount of space required to use it (consider the size of the average mouse pad) and its low cost.

Digitizers, on the other hand, report an *absolute position* to CADD based on the location of the puck. You can pick the puck up and wave it around as much as you want with no effect, but as soon as it is within sensing distance of the tablet, it reports its exact location relative to the tablet. In this sense the puck cannot get *lost*, it always knows where it is relative to its tablet. The puck does not care how fast it is moved. For a given position on the tablet's surface, it always reports the same X,Y coordinates.

Examining Digitizer Advantages

Because digitizers report an absolute position, they can be used for many tasks that would be difficult if not impossible for a mouse.

The most obvious use for a digitizer (from which its name stems) is for tracing or digitizing drawings. You can tape a drawing to the surface of the tablet and trace the drawing into CADD. This is made possible because the puck always reports the same coordinates for a given position on the surface of the tablet. This enables you to indicate the points needed to draw a line, circle, or other primitive to CADD with an accuracy that is limited only by your ability to center the crosshairs on the point you want.

The second advantage of a digitizer is that you can place a menu template on its surface. Thus, the digitizer can be used to enter CADD commands or macros by simply pointing to the appropriate command on the template and clicking the first puck button. This is more effective than using the screen menus because hundreds of commands can be placed on the surface of the tablet, whereas screen menus must be nested to save space. The use of a digitizer menu enables you to preform a wide range of commands in a *point & shoot* fashion.

If you are using a puck instead of a stylus, a third advantage of using a digitizer is that many digitizers come with multi-button pucks. Most digitizers can be ordered with a 12 or 16 button puck. The puck buttons can be programmed for commands or macros just as the third mouse button or your function keys can be programmed. By placing your most commonly used commands on the puck buttons, you can greatly increase your productivity. Most digitizer users soon memorize which functions are on which puck buttons, and with one hand on the puck and with eyes on the screen, they can draw and edit with amazing speed.

Installing a Digitizer

Installing a digitizer and configuring it for use with CADD is a fairly straightforward process. You configure the digitizer itself (if necessary), connect it the computer, and use the CONFIG program to configure CADD to use the digitizer for your pointing device.

Appendix A of *Generic CADD Users Guide* lists the configuration of most digitizers supported by CADD. Refer to this section to see if there are any switches that need to be set on the digitizer. These switches may be in the form of a physical dip switch or in the form of *soft switches* accessed by using the digitizer's puck or stylus. Other digitizers may have no switches at all and are controlled by setup codes established by CADD, a practice typical of digitizers which emulate the Summagraphics mm1201).

You also may want to check the file HARDWARE.DOC that comes with CADD 5.0 because it may contain information about digitizers which supplements the *User Guide*. If you do not see your digitizer listed in the manual, be sure to check the HARDWARE.DOC file before you panic.

If you do not see your digitizer listed, you may want to refer to the digitizer manual to see what emulations it supports. Two common cmulations arc Summagraphics Summasketch (model mm1201) and GTCO 'type 5'. Most digitizers can be supported by CADD 5.0 by emulating one of these two standards. Table A.1 summarizes some of the settings which are normally required for the digitizer to work properly with CADD in an emulation mode.

Table A.1
Digitizer Settings Used in Emulation Mode

Function	*mm1201*	*GTCO type 5*
Output Mode	"RUN"/"STREAM"	"RUN"/"STREAM"
Output Format	5 byte high resolution packed binary	6 byte high resolution packed binary
Resolution	500 lines per inch	1000 lines per inch
Report Rate	"Auto" or Maximum	"Auto" or Maximum
Baud Rate	9600 baud	9600 baud
Data bits	8	8
Stop bits	1	1
Parity	ODD	NONE

Although the nomenclature differs—some manuals refer to *run mode* and others to *stream mode*—they mean the same thing-*a continuous stream of data whenever the puck or stylus is within sensing distance of the tablet.*

Once you are sure that the digitizer is properly configured, hook it up to your computer (usually through a serial port) and plug in any power sources that are required (refer to your digitizer manual for details). In order to properly configure CADD, you need to know what *port* your digitizer is connected to. This normally is a *serial port* identified as either COM1 or COM2. Most digitizers are supplied with a cable to connect your digitizer to the computer. If a cable is not supplied, refer to *Generic CADD 5.0 Users Guide* for cabling information compatible with your digitizer. Most digitizers use a standard cable that is diagrammed in the *Users Guide* at the beginning of the digitizer section in Appendix A.

Change to your CADD directory (usually C:\CADD5) and run the CONFIG program. Press Enter to get to the main configuration menu. Select Option 2, `Select a Pointing Device`, from the main configuration menu. CONFIG displays a list of pointing devices. If you do not see your digitizer listed on the first page, press Enter to see the next page. CADD currently supports about 65 different pointing devices. Type the number representing your digitizer and press Enter.

If the type of digitizer you choose comes in more than one size, CONFIG displays a list of the available sizes. Type the number that represents the size of your digitizer and press Enter. CONFIG next asks you to identify which I/O (input/output) port your digitizer is connected to. Choose **1** for COM1 or **2** for COM2 and press Enter.

After choosing the COM port, CADD displays the default settings. Verify that the settings match those for your digitizer. If any of the settings appear to be different, change either the Digitizer or CONFIG so that the settings match. Press Esc to exit from the serial port setup menu and return to the main CONFIG menu. Press Esc a second time to exit from CONFIG and answer Yes when CONFIG asks if you want to save your changes.

Using a Digitizer as a Pointing Device

A digitizer may be used as an expensive but simple pointing device. The major difference between the digitizer and mouse is that the digitizer reports the absolute position of the puck on the tablet surface. Other than this, the puck operates in all respects just like a mouse. The first button is used to point to the screen, and the second button is used to pick from the video menu (or as Pen Up). Any additional buttons may be assigned to commands or macros using the Macro Assign (MA) command.

By default, CADD maps the entire surface of the digitizer to your drawing screen. Thus, if you want to point to the far upper right corner of the screen, you need to move the puck to the same corner on the digitizer. If you are used to using a mouse, this may be rather frustrating. *Stroking* the mouse, a common mouse technique, is done by moving the mouse, picking it up and setting it down near its original location, and moving it again. Many digitizer users try to stroke their digitizer rather than reach across the entire surface. As you might guess, stroking a digitizer is rather futile.

When using a digitizer as a pointing device, you may want to reduce the digitizer's *active area* which results in a much smaller portion of the digitizer's surface being mapped to the screen. Often, an active area of three to five inches square is sufficient and reduces the need to reach all over the digitizer in order to enter points on the drawing screen.

To set up your digitizer with a reduced active area, type **AA** at the `Command` prompt. Then move the puck to a comfortable location on the digitizer and click first button. This point becomes the lower left corner of the new active area of the digitizer. Ignore the location of the cursor on the screen when you do this. Now move the puck approximately 4 inches above and to the right of the first point and click. This point becomes the upper right corner of the new active area. Ignore the location of the cursor on the screen when you do this.

You have now re-defined the active area of the digitizer. While you move the puck about the digitizer surface, you notice that the drawing cursor *freezes* when the puck is outside the area you have defined. This is normal. Also, notice that a much smaller portion of the digitizer can now be used to control the on-screen cursor. Although the active area can be set very small, this is not recommended because finding a small active area is hard to do and controlling the cursor in a small active area can be difficult.

NOTE

> The upper right corner of the active area *must be* above and to the right of the lower left corner. If you define an invalid area, CADD simply ignores all input from the digitizer until you use the AA command to define a valid active area.

Tracing Drawings with a Digitizer

One of the primary uses for a digitizer is tracing existing drawings in order to turn them into CADD drawings. Tracing a drawing requires two steps: (1) setting up CADD and the digitizer for tracing and (2) tracing the drawing using CADD commands combined with coordinates input from the digitizer.

In order to accurately trace a drawing you must turn Trace Mode (TM) on. When Trace Mode is off, CADD maps the active area of the digitizer to the drawing screen at all times. If necessary, it *stretches* the coordinates so that the corners of the active area correspond to the corners of the drawing area on the screen. This makes it impossible to trace accurately.

When Trace Mode is on, CADD maps the surface of the digitizer to a corresponding portion of the drawing area. In order to trace accurately, the coordinates are not stretched to fit the screen but are multiplied by a Trace Scale. You can see this effect clearly if you turn Trace Mode (TM) on and then Zoom Out (ZO). Notice that your cursor only points to a part of the drawing area. When Trace Mode is on, any point you enter on the surface of the digitizer creates a point at the corresponding location in your drawing. This happens even if you are zoomed in and the cursor is not visible on the screen.

Setting Up for Tracing

The first step in setting up for tracing is to attach the original drawing to the digitizer surface in such a way that it does not shift or move. Usually, this means affixing the drawing to the tablet surface using tape. Some digitizers come equipped with a clear overlay for just this purpose. The drawing can be placed under the overlay which reduces the risk of it moving. It may be advisable to use a small amount of tape anyway just to make sure that the original does not shift in the middle of a tracing session.

Do not be overly concerned about making sure that the original is square to the digitizer surface. It's almost impossible to get the original 100% aligned with horizontal and vertical. For this reason, CADD provides a method to correct for any rotation of the original relative to the digitizer, so you don't need to worry if the original is at an angle. Because CADD can correct for any rotation error, if it fits better, you can even place the original sideways to the digitizer surface.

In order to verify the tracing scale and to correct for the rotation of the original, CADD needs at least two known points. These points can be anywhere on your drawing, but for the most accurate calculations, they should be as far apart as possible. You need to know the exact locations for these points. A good choice is to use the endpoints of a line of known length and angle, such as a property line or the long side of a building.

After choosing two points, enter them into CADD through Manual Entry. If the points are on a line, use the Line command. (The construction points on the ends of the line can be used to align the CADD drawing with the original.) Use the Zoom All (ZA) command if necessary so that both points can be seen on the screen.

If you are tracing artwork or a logo which does not have scale, you can use the corners of the paper to do the Draw Align command. Simply draw a rectangle in CADD to the exact size of the paper. Then you can align corners of the rectangle with the corners of the paper taped to the digitizer.

If you have reduced the Active Area (AA) of the digitizer in order to use a smaller area of the digitizer for pointing to the screen, the Active Area needs to be reset. (See the previous section in this appendix titled "Using a Digitizer as a Pointing Device.") You should use the AA command to reset the active area so that you can point to the entire original you are tracing.

Next, you need to use the Drawing Align (DA) command to align the original on the digitizer surface. Even if you think you know the scale of the original, it's a good idea to let CADD calculate the scale to be sure it agrees with your information. When you enter points on the digitizer, hold the puck at the same angle, this minimizes any errors caused by the crosshairs being slightly off center.

For the purposes of the next exercise, tape a standard 8.5" x 11" piece of paper to your digitizer so that the long edge of the paper runs side to side. To demonstrate how CADD corrects for rotation angles, center the paper under the digitizer, but place it at a slight angle. In this exercise, you draw a rectangle to represent the paper, and then you align the drawing with the paper taped to the digitizer.

Tracing a Rectangle

Prompt	*Input*	*Description*
`Command`	**MO**	Sets Manual Entry mode relative to the origin
`Command`	**UN I**	Sets display units to inches
`Command`	**RE**	Sets Rectangle command
`Enter one corner...`	Type **0,0** and press Enter	Sets first corner of the rectangle at 0,0
`Enter opposite corner`	Type **11,8.5** and press Enter	Draws an 11 by 8.5 inch rectangle
`Command`	**ZA**	Makes sure that you can see the whole rectangle
`Command`	**DA**	Establishes Drawing Align command
`Is this the correct tracing scale? (Y/N)`	**N**	Gives you the ability to have CADD calculate the scale
`Do you know the scale ? (Y/N)`	**N**	Calculates the scale

If you answer yes at the last prompt, CADD asks you for the proper scale.

You now use the NP command to enter any point on the screen. Move the cursor close to the lower left corner of the rectangle and type **NP**. You must snap to the point, or the alignment is not accurate. Next, center the puck crosshairs on the lower left corner of the paper taped to your digitizer and click the first puck button. Take great care entering this point to be sure you are exactly on the corner of the paper.

To enter a different point on the screen, use the NP command again. First, move the cursor close to the upper right corner of the rectangle and type **NP**. You must snap to the point or the alignment is not accurate. Now, center the puck crosshairs on the corresponding point on your original and click. Take great care entering this point to be sure it is exact.

CADD then displays the calculated trace scale (which should be close to 1:1) and the rotation angle (which it automatically corrects for). CADD's calculated scale factor may be slightly larger or smaller than the exact scale of the original. This may indicate an error in your original, or, more often, it may indicate a slight error when digitizing the points on the drawing.

For best results, note the calculated scale and rotation and repeat the process. It is recommended that you repeat the drawing alignment at least three times to get a statistical average for the scale factor. Then repeat the command one last time, but answer yes when CADD asks if you know the scale and then input the average of the calculated scales. This allows CADD to calculate the rotation angle.

NOTES

- If you are digitizing a copy of an original, you may expect the scale to be slightly off. It is not uncommon for xeroxed copies to be approximately 5% less than the original.
- The information that CADD uses in its digitizer configuration assumes that the CADD database is set for inches. If your database unit is other than inches, you can expect that the scale factor enlarges or reduces accordingly. For example, if your database unit is set for Feet, the scale is off by a factor of .083333 (1/12th), while if the database unit is set for Centimeters, the scale is off by a factor of 2.54. The traced drawing is still the proper size. You can contact Generic's Technical Support department for instructions on how to edit the digitizer configuration file so that the scale factor is expressed correctly.

After you complete the Drawing Align (DA) command, CADD does several things for you automatically. It sets the Trace Scale (RZ), begins correcting the coordinates coming in from the digitizer for the rotation angle, and it turns Trace Mode on. In this sense, the Drawing Align (DA) command is a one-step process that sets up CADD for tracing.

Tracing a Drawing

It should be noted that tracing should only be used for elements in the drawing that are not of known position and size. If you have a dimensioned floorplan, it's usually easier to re-create the drawing in CADD using manual entry. Manual entry is not only faster but also more accurate. Often, however, only scale drawings are available. These drawings are not completely or accurately dimensioned. This is especially true of maps and charts.

Learning to accurately trace a drawing takes time. You do not actually trace the drawing by dragging the crosshairs over the items to be digitized. This technique makes it entirely too easy to slip and create errors. In addition, the output is extremely difficult to edit.

The process of tracing (or more properly *digitizing*) a drawing consists of using CADD commands combined with points from the digitizer which are used to define primitives. This is similar to drawing on screen except that you have the original drawing for reference.

To trace a line, for example, issue the LI command from the keyboard or with a puck button. Carefully center the crosshairs of the cursor over one end of the line and click and then do the same thing for the other end of the line. Arcs are usually traced using a 3 point arc (A3), and circles are usually traced using a 3 point circle (C3).

Tracing curves takes a little practice. In sections where the curve is slight, you can usually get away with only placing a few points. On the other hand, in tight corners, you may have to place several points in order to define the location of the curve before the corner, the shape of the corner, and the location of the curve after the corner. You can think of this process as a little like driving. On the straighter sections, you can go faster, but on the corners, you must slow down. Likewise, when tracing, you put the points further apart in straighter sections and put the points closer together at a curve.

The primary factor contributing to poor-quality traced drawings is human error in positioning the puck. Fortunately, CADD provides several tools that reduce human error. In addition, there are some tricks that help to create more accurate digitized drawings.

Considering Tips for Digitizing

- Use a puck not a stylus. The tip of a stylus tends to obscure what you are trying to trace, and the angle of the stylus can sometimes make a difference in the coordinates transmitted.
- Hold the puck at the same angle; don't spin it around. The crosshairs are rarely at the exact center of the sensing loop. If the puck is always held at the same angle, any error is consistent and has minimum effect on your finial product.
- Set up an appropriately-sized grid. Most objects created by man are sized in regular increments. By using snap to grid, you can ensure that the coordinates you trace are nice even numbers.
- Use Ortho a lot. Man likes right angles, and this ensures that if you trace 90 degree lines, the angle comes out that way.
- When using Ortho, use Snap Object (SO) to start lines out that are attached to other lines or objects.
- When using Ortho, use Cursor Free (CF) or Snap Object (SO) to end lines at other lines or objects. (This way you don't have to go back and trim them to meet later.)
- Draw anything that is of known location and size using manual entry. These objects can then be used as starting points or ending points of other objects. Think of them as landmarks.
- Use symmetry to your advantage. If something is symmetrical, draw half and then use a mirror command to create the other half.
- If you have a multi-button puck, consider putting commands such as LI, C3, A3, BV, CV, OR, CF, SO, NP, ZW, ZP on the buttons. These are likely to be your most frequently used commands.
- Use Zoom Window to see an area in larger detail. Your digitizer is usually more accurate than your screen. Trace mode is not affected by zooming. Use Zoom Previous to return to the prior view.
- When you are Zoomed In (ZI or ZW) on a section of your tracing, you can use Pan (PA) to look at another portion without zooming out first. Just issue the PA command and point using the puck in the center of the area you want to see.

Creating Digitizer Menus

Digitizers make excellent menu devices. Because the puck always knows where it is relative to the tablet surface, you can declare portions of that surface to function as a menu. This is done by placing a menu template on the surface of the digitizer and then by configuring CADD to associate various commands or macros with the portions of the digitizer that correspond with the template. To accomplish this, two parts are necessary: the template itself and a menu file for CADD that contains the commands associated with the template. You can either make your own template and menu or purchase a pre-made template which comes with a menu file.

The primary advantages of pre-made templates are convenience and quality. Someone else has already drawn the template, figured out the arrangement, and created the menu file. Also, pre-made templates are usually laminated or printed on sturdy plastic. Commercial templates are usually well illustrated with fairly intuitive icons that enable even a beginner to operate CADD with relative ease. Generic's newsletter "The Generic Software News" (which is sent to all registered users in the U.S. and Canada) often contains advertisements for inexpensive digitizer templates. The template comes with instructions and with all you need to get the digitizer set up and running.

Pre-made templates have the disadvantage of being made for a large group of users and are, therefore, not likely to be as well-suited to your individual needs as templates you make yourself. In addition, pre-made templates mostly emphasize basic CADD commands, rather than macros. Experienced users usually reserve the tablet menu for macros, pointing out that they can use the keyboard to type two-letter commands just as fast as someone can point to a command on a pre-made digitizer template.

Digitizer menus are used to quickly place symbols (components) on a drawing. You can place a miniature version of each symbol on the template and assign a macro to that location which places the appropriate component. Because component names often get rather cryptic, this visual reference menu enables you to select your symbols visually instead of by name (which you would have to do if picking the component off the side menu in CADD).

Whether you are a novice or advanced user, consider purchasing a ready-made digitizer template. Because a lot of thought has gone into most existing templates, they are a good source of ideas for icons and layout when designing a personal template customized to your own needs.

The process of creating a digitizer template and menu file is discussed in Chapter 16. Chapter 16 also includes information on how to set up and configure CADD to use a digitizer menu.

B

Generic CADD Commands

This appendix is a list of all the Generic CADD 5.0 commands. The first part of the appendix categorizes the commands by menu; the second part of the appendix shows you which commands are covered in each of this book's chapters. You can use these lists as a quick reference when you want to find a command in Generic CADD or in this book.

Commands Categorized by Menu

The following sections list Generic CADD's commands as they appear in the program's menus. The full command name is provided, along with its two-letter command name. In this appendix, an asterisk (*) indicates commands that do not appear in the Generic CADD menu. Two asterisks (**) indicate commands that can be issued only from a digitizer.

DRAW Menu Commands

Full Command Name	*Two-Letter Command*	*Full Command Name*	*Two-Letter Command*
Point	PO	Four-Point Arc*	A4
Line	LI	Ellipse	EP
Individual Line	L1	Bézier Curve	BV
Rectangle	RE	Individual Bézier	BW
Regular Polygon	RP	Complex Curve	CV
Two-Point Circle	C2	Double Lines	L2
Three-Point Circle	C3	Double Lines Settings	DB
Two-Point Arc	A2	Double Line Offsets*	TH
Three-Point Arc	A3		

SNAPS Menu Commands

Full Command Name	*Two-Letter Command*	*Full Command Name*	*Two-Letter Command*
Snap Closest Point	SC	Snap Perpendicular	SP
Snap Nearest Point*	NP	Snap Tangent	ST
Snap Object	SO	Snap Arc Center	SN
Snap Midpoint	SM	Snap to Grid	SG
Snap Percentage	SR	Component Snaps	GC
Snap Intersection	SI	Snap to All Layer	SY
Snap Parallel	SL	Tolerance	TO

TRIMS Menu Commands

Full Command Name	*Two-Letter Command*	*Full Command Name*	*Two-Letter Command*
Trim	RM	Chamfer	CH
Extend	XT	Chamfer Distance	CA
Fillet	FI	Intersection Trim	IT
Fillet Radius	FR	Multi-Trim	MT
Autofillet	AF		

CONSTRAINTS Menu Commands

Full Command Name	*Two-Letter Command*	*Full Command Name*	*Two-Letter Command*
Ortho Mode	OR	Snap to Grid	SG
Ortho Angle	OA	Grid Size	GS
Tracking	TK	Grid Origin	GO
Cursor Free	CF or KF	Cursor Move	CM
Grid Display	GR		

EDITS Menu Commands

Full Command Name	*Two-Letter Command*	*Full Command Name*	*Two-Letter Command*
Move Point	MP	Object Break	OB
Move	MV	Stretch	SS
Copy	CO	Bézier Edit	BE
Mirror Copy	MI	Erase	ER
Radial Copy	RC	Erase Last	EL
Rotate	RO	UnErase	UE
Scale	SZ	Undo	OO
Change	CG	Redo	UU

SHORTCUTS Menu Commands

Full Command Name	*Two-Letter Command*	*Full Command Name*	*Two-Letter Command*
Object Copy	OC	Window Rotate	WR
Window Copy	WC	Drawing Rotate	DR
Object Erase	OE	Window Scale	WZ
Window Erase	WE	Drawing Scale	DZ
Object Move	OM	Object Change	OG
Window Move	WM	Window Change	WG
Window Stretch	WS	Drawing Change	DG

TEXT Menu Commands

Full Command Name	*Two-Letter Command*	*Full Command Name*	*Two-Letter Command*
Text Line Placement	TL	Font Select	FST
Text Change	TG	Text Line Spacing	TS
Text Line Edit	TE	Text Color	CST or TC
Text Character Placement	TP	Text Size	TZT
Text Insert	TI	Text Rotation	TR
Text Delete	TD	Window Create Text Font	WT
Text Replace	TX	Load ASCII	LA

COMPONENTS Menu Commands

Full Command Name	*Two-Letter Command*	*Full Command Name*	*Two-Letter Command*
Component Place	CP	Component Remove	CX
Component Create	CC	Component Image	CI
Window Component Create	CW	Component Snap	GC
Component Scale	CZ	Explode Layer	XY
Component Rotation	CR	Save Components	SAC
Component Explode	CE	Load Components	LOC
Component Replace	CN	Comp Dump	CD

ATTRIBUTES Menu Commands

Full Command Name	*Two-Letter Command*	*Full Command Name*	*Two-Letter Command*
Attribute Create	AC	Attribute Text Scale	TZA
Attribute Attach	AT	Display Attributes	AD
Attribute Detach	DE	Edit Attribute	AE
Load Attribute	LOA	Attribute Settings	AS
Save Attribute	SAA	Attribute Font Select	FSA
Export Attribute	XA		

ZOOMS Menu Commands

Full Command Name	*Two-Letter Command*	*Full Command Name*	*Two-Letter Command*
Zoom All	ZA	Backwards Redraw	BR
Zoom Window	ZW	Window Redraw	WD
Zoom In	ZI or ZU	Zoom Limits	ZL
Zoom Out	ZO or ZB	Zoom Value	ZM
Pan	PA	Zoom View	ZV
Zoom Previous View	ZP	Name View	NV
Redraw Screen	RD	Delete View	NX

DIMENSIONS Menu Commands

Full Command Name	*Two-Letter Command*	*Full Command Name*	*Two-Letter Command*
Linear Dimension	LX	Diameter Dimension	IX
Angular Dimension	AX	Leader	LE
Dimension Mode	UM	Shoulder Length	LL
Dimension Direction	UD	Dimension Move	UV
Proximity	PF	Dimension Change	UG
Radial Dimension	RX	Dimension Tolerance	UT

DIMENSION SETTINGS Menu Commands

Full Command Name	*Two-Letter Command*	*Full Command Name*	*Two-Letter Command*
Display Dimensions	DD	Dimension Text Size	TZD
Extension	XS	Dimension Text	DT
Arrows	AR	Dimension Layer	UY
Dimension Font Select	FSD	Dimension Color	CSD

LAYERS Menu Commands

Full Command Name	*Two-Letter Command*	*Full Command Name*	*Two-Letter Command*
All Layer	AL	Layer Rotate	YR
Layer Current	YC	Layer Scale	YZ
Layer Display	YD	Layer Change	YG
Layer Name	YN	Dimension Layer	UL
Layer Hide	YH	Layer Load	YL
Layer Erase	YE or YX	Layer Save	SVY

HATCH/FILL Menu Commands

Full Command Name	*Two-Letter Command*	*Full Command Name*	*Two-Letter Command*
Window Hatch	WH	Window Fill	WF
Object Hatch	OH	Object Fill	OF
Fitted Hatch	FH	Fitted Fill	FF
Boundary Hatch	BH	Boundary Fill	BF
Hatch Setting	HS	Fill Color	FC or FK

DISPLAY Menu Commands

Full Command Name	*Two-Letter Command*	*Full Command Name*	*Two-Letter Command*
Line Color	LC or LK	Display Screen	DI
Line Type	LT	Reference Points	PR
Line Width	LW	Construction Points	PC
Line Scale	LZ	Standard Points	PS
Color Settings	CS	Redraw	RD
Fast Redraw	FA	Object Drag	OD
Coordinate Display	DC	Rubberband	RB
Numeric Format Display	NF	Highlight	HI
Units	UN		

MENUS Menu Commands

Full Command Name	Two-Letter Command	Full Command Name	Two-Letter Command
Load Menu	LV	Select Digitizer Menu**	SD
New Menu	VXLV	Drawing Align**	DA
Remove Menu	VX	Active Area**	AA
Display Menu	VM	Trace Mode**	TM
Load Digitizer Menu**	LD	Trace Scale**	RZ

UTILITIES Menu Commands

Full Command Name	Two-Letter Command	Full Command Name	Two-Letter Command
Manual Entry Origin	MO	Selection	SE
Manual Entry Relative	MR	Limits	LS
Manual Entry Basepoint	MB	Match Parameters	MH
Set Basepoint	BP	Shell to Executable File	SH
Explode	EX	View Fast Text	TV
Measure	ME	Drawing Origin	DO
Measure Distance*	MD	Save Batch	SB
Macro Assign	MA	Select Batch	BS
Screen Flip	SF	Load Batch	LB
Entity Filter	EF		

FILE Menu Commands

Full Command Name	Two-Letter Command	Full Command Name	Two-Letter Command
Load	LO	Print	DP12
Save	SA	Postscript	DP13
Select Save	SV	Select Plot	PL
Drawing Rename	DN	Pack Data	PD
Drawing Remove	DX	Definition Unload	DU
File Path	FP	Update Environment	EN
Load ASCII	LA	Quit	QU
Plot	DP11		

(The Update Environment command also is available during the Quit command. After you issue the Quit command, you can press **E** when Generic CADD prompts you to press **C** for Continue or **Q** for Quit.)

Commands Listed by Chapter

The following sections show you which Generic CADD commands are introduced in each chapter of this text. Use this list as a quick guide when you want to learn about any Generic CADD command.

Chapter 1

Full Command Name	*Two-Letter Command*	*Full Command Name*	*Two-Letter Command*
Rectangle	RE	Selection Save Drawing	SV
Zoom All	ZA	Layer Save	YS
Undo	OO	Load	LO
Redo	UU	Drawing Load	DL
Erase Last	EL	Layer Load	YL
UnErase	UE	Remove Drawing	DX
Save	SA	Drawing Rename	DN
Drawing Save	DS	Quit	QU

Chapter 2

Full Command Name	*Two-Letter Command*	*Full Command Name*	*Two-Letter Command*
Limits	LS	Numeric Display Format	NF
Current Layer	YC	Coordinate Display	DC
All Layers Edit	AL	Reference Points	PR
Name Layer	YN	Construction Points	PC
Line Color	LC or LK	Standard Points	PS
Line Width	LW	Object Drag	OD
Line Type	LT	Rubberbanding	RB
Line Scale	LZ	Highlight	HI
Color Settings	CS	Display Menu	VM
Screen Display	DI	Remove Menu	VX
Units	UN	Environment Save	EN

Chapter 3

Full Command Name	*Two-Letter Command*	*Full Command Name*	*Two-Letter Command*
Line	LI	Bezier Curve	BV
Individual Line	L1	Individual Bezier	BW
Two-Point Arc	A2	Complex Curve	CV
Three-Point Arc	A3	Rectangle	RE
Four-Point Arc	A4	Regular Polygon	RP
Two-Point Circle	C2	Double Line Settings	DB
Three-Point Circle	C3	Double Lines	L2
Ellipse	EP		

Chapter 4

Full Command Name	*Two-Letter Command*	*Full Command Name*	*Two-Letter Command*
Grid Size	GS	Snap Perpendicular	SP
Grid On/Off	GR	Snap Intersection	SI
Snap To Grid	SG	Snap Parallel	SL
Snap To Nearest Point	NP	Snap Object	SO
Snap To Closest Point	SC	Component Snaps	GC
Snap To Midpoint	SM	Snap to Non-Editable Layers	SY
Object Move	OM	Redraw	RD
Cursor Free	KF or CF	Backward Redraw	BR
Snap Percentage	SR	Window Redraw	WD
Snap Tangent	ST	Fast Redraw	FA
Snap To Arc Center	SN		

Chapter 5

Full Command Name	*Two-Letter Command*	*Full Command Name*	*Two-Letter Command*
Manual Entry Relative	MR	Ortho Angle	OA
Display Coordinate	DC	Tracking	TK
Manual Entry Basepoint	MB	Cursor Free	KF or CF
Ortho Mode	OR	Cursor Movement	CM

Chapter 6

Full Command Name	*Two-Letter Command*
Font Select	FS
Text Size	TZ
Between Character Space	TSC
Between Line Space	TSL
Proportional Spacing	TSP
Slant	TSS
Aspect	TSA
Justification	TSJ
Text Rotation	TR
Text Color	TC

Full Command Name	*Two-Letter Command*
Text Line Placement	TL
Text Character Placement	TP
Text Edit	TE
Text View	TV
Text Change	TG
Text Insert	TI
Text Replace	TX
Text Delete	TD
Load ASCII	LA
Window Create Text	WT

Chapter 7

Full Command Name	*Two-Letter Command*
Zoom All	ZA
Zoom Limits	ZL
Zoom Window	ZW
Zoom Previous	ZP
Zoom In	ZI or ZU
Zoom Out	ZO or ZB
Zoom Value	ZM
Name View	NV

Full Command Name	*Two-Letter Command*
Zoom View	ZV
Delete View	NX
Pan	PA
Layer Hide	YH
Layer Display	YD
Grid Re-Origin	GO
Drawing Re-Origin	DO

Chapter 8

Full Command Name	*Two-Letter Command*
Drawing Plot	DP

Chapter 9

Full Command Name	*Two-Letter Command*
Object Copy	OC
Object Break	OB
Trim	RM
Extend	XT
Tracking	TK
Intersection Trim	IT
Fillet	FI
Chamfer	CH
Fillet Radius	FR

Full Command Name	*Two-Letter Command*
Autofillet	AF
Chamfer Distances	CA
Object Erase	OE
Object Change	OG
Object Move	OM
Move Point	MP
Bezier Edit	BE
The Like Option	=
Match Parameters	MH

Chapter 10

Full Command Name	*Two-Letter Command*
Selection	SE
Entity Filter	EF
Screen Flip	SF
Stretch	SS
Scale	SZ
Move	MV
Copy	CO
Change	CG
Rotate	RO
Mirror Copy	MI
Multi-Trim	MT
Radial Copy	RC

Full Command Name	*Two-Letter Command*
Explode	EX
Window Copy	WC
Window Scale	WZ
Window Erase	WE
Window Move	WM
Window Rotate	WR
Drawing Rotate	DR
Drawing Change	DG
Layer Scale	YZ
Layer Erase	YE
Layer Rotate	YR
Layer Change	YG

Chapter 11

Full Command Name	*Two-Letter Command*	*Full Command Name*	*Two-Letter Command*
Component Create	CC	Component Explode	CE
Window Create	CW	Component Snaps	GC
Component Place	CP	Component Save	SAC
Component Scale	CZ	Component Load	LOC
Component Rotation	CR	Component Dump	CD
Component Insertion Point	IP	Component Replace	CN
Component Image	CI	Component Remove	CX

Chapter 12

Full Command Name	*Two-Letter Command*	*Full Command Name*	*Two-Letter Command*
Hatch Settings	HS	Window Fill	WF
Window Hatch	WH	Object Fill	OF
Object Hatch	OH	Fitted Fill	FF
Fitted Hatch	FH	Boundary Fill	BF
Boundary Hatch	BH		

Chapter 13

Full Command Name	*Two-Letter Command*	*Full Command Name*	*Two-Letter Command*
Linear Dimension	LX	Dimension Display	DD
Angular Dimension	AX	Dimension Extension	XS
Radial Dimension	RX	Arrows	AR
Diameter Dimension	IX	Dimension Font Select	FSD
Leader Lines	LE	Dimension Text Size	TZD
Dimensioning Mode	UM	Dimension Text	DT
Dimension Direction	UD	Dimension Layer	UY
Proximity	PF	Dimension Colors	CSD

Chapter 14

Full Command Name	*Two-Letter Command*	*Full Command Name*	*Two-Letter Command*
Attribute Create	AC	Attribute Edit	AE
Attribute Attach	AT	Attribute Settings	AS
Attribute Save	SAA	Attribute Scale	TZA
Attribute Load	LOA	Attribute Display	AD
Attribute Detach	DE	Attribute Export	XA

Chapter 15

Full Command Name	*Two-Letter Command*	*Full Command Name*	*Two-Letter Command*
Macro Assign	MA	Screen Flip	SF

Chapter 16

Full Command Name	*Two-Letter Command*	*Full Command Name*	*Two-Letter Command*
Load Menu	LV	Remove Menu	VX
New Menu	VXLV	Display Menu	VM

Chapter 17

Full Command Name	*Two-Letter Command*	*Full Command Name*	*Two-Letter Command*
Save Batch	SB	Shell To Executable	SH
Select Save Batch	BS		

Appendix A

Full Command Name	*Two-Letter Command*	*Full Command Name*	*Two-Letter Command*
Load Digitizer Menu	LD	Active Area	AA
Select Digitizer Menu	SD	Trace Mode	TM
Drawing Align	DA	Trace Scale	RZ

How Generic CADD and Generic 3D Work Together

Generic 3D is a three-dimensional wireframe modeling and shading program that works in conjunction with Generic CADD. Generic 3D is a stand-alone program, which is designed to provide Generic CADD users with three-dimensional drafting capabilities. The great majority of people who use Generic 3D also own and use Generic CADD.

Generic 3D is closely modeled after Generic CADD. The two programs' interfaces do differ, however, because of the distinction between two-dimensional drafting and three-dimensional drafting. Generic CADD, as you will recall, uses a double-axis drawing cursor because it needs to represent only two drawing planes (the X and Y planes). In Generic 3D, the drawing cursor has three axes, representing the X, Y, and Z axes that are available in 3D drawing.

Reviewers have given Generic 3D high marks for the way it helps the user navigate the cursor through what appears to be three dimensions, when the cursor really exists on the flat video monitor. Generic Software achieved this solution by developing two tools—called Tracking and Cursor Free—specifically for Generic 3D. These two tools (which also are available in Generic CADD 5.0) enable you to easily identify locations in a drawing. You can limit Generic 3D's cursor to two dimensions (XY, YZ, or XZ), and rotate the cursor to realign the three axes' direction. This last feature is especially helpful when you import two-dimensional Generic CADD drawings into Generic 3D because Generic CADD drawings have only the X and Y axes. If Generic CADD had a third dimension (Z), it would lie at a right angle to the XY plane. By rotating the 3D cursor, you can position Generic CADD's 2D objects so that they lie at any rotation and angle in space within a Generic 3D drawing.

Using Generic CADD Files with Generic 3D

Generic 3D can read drawings created by Generic CADD, for the purposes of turning them into three-dimensional models. Generic 3D, however, was released before the latest update of Generic CADD (version 5.0). With version 5.0, Generic Software modified Generic CADD's file format. This means that you need to take extra steps if you want to use a Generic CADD 5.0 file with Generic 3D.

To use a Generic CADD 5.0 drawing with Generic 3D, you must save the drawing in the format used by a previous version of Generic CADD. In the Generic CADD 5.0 Save (SA) menu, you will find an option that enables you to save a drawing in "Level 3" format. This option saves the drawing file under the old Generic CADD DWG format, which Generic 3D can read. Figure C.1 shows the floor plan, drawn earlier in this book, about to be saved in Level 3 format for use in Generic 3D.

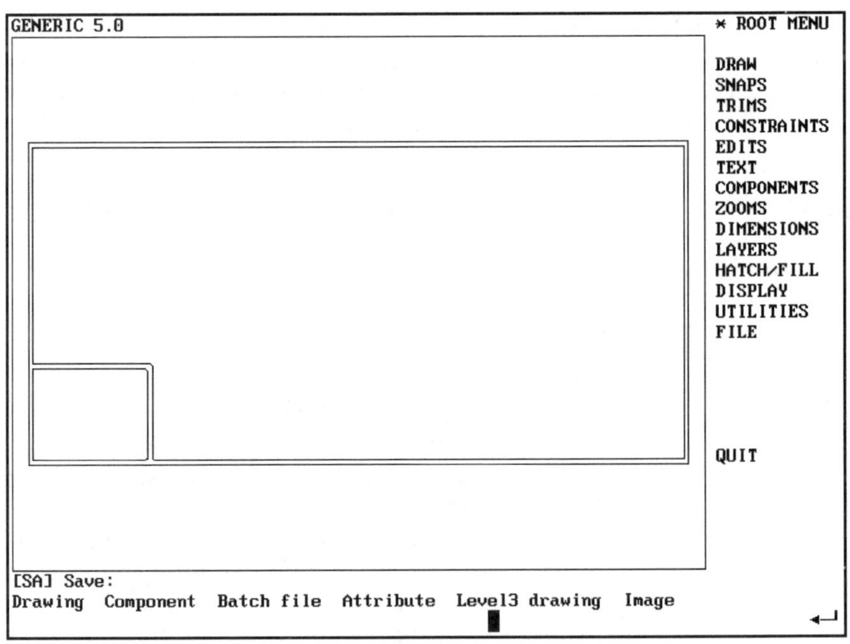

Figure C-1: Using the Save as Level 3 Drawing option in Generic CADD 5.0.

You can save Generic 3D drawings in a flat, two-dimensional format that is directly readable by Generic CADD. No special conversion of the file is necessary because Generic CADD 5.0 can read DWG files.

Using Generic 3D To Modify a 2D Drawing

When installed on the same computer, Generic CADD and Generic 3D exist independently of each other. By issuing the Shell to Executable (SH) command in Generic CADD 5.0, you can temporarily exit from Generic CADD, use Generic 3D, and return to CADD. Generic 3D does not currently offer the Shell to Executable command.

You can use Generic 3D to create drawings from scratch, or you can start drawings in Generic CADD and turn them into three-dimensional drawings in Generic 3D. The 3D program's extrusion capabilities can give three-dimensional features to a two-dimensional drawing from Generic CADD.

The following paragraphs describe the steps involved in changing a two-dimensional drawing created in Generic CADD into a three-dimensional model in Generic 3D. Figure C.2 shows the house plan (from fig. C.1) after being imported into Generic 3D.

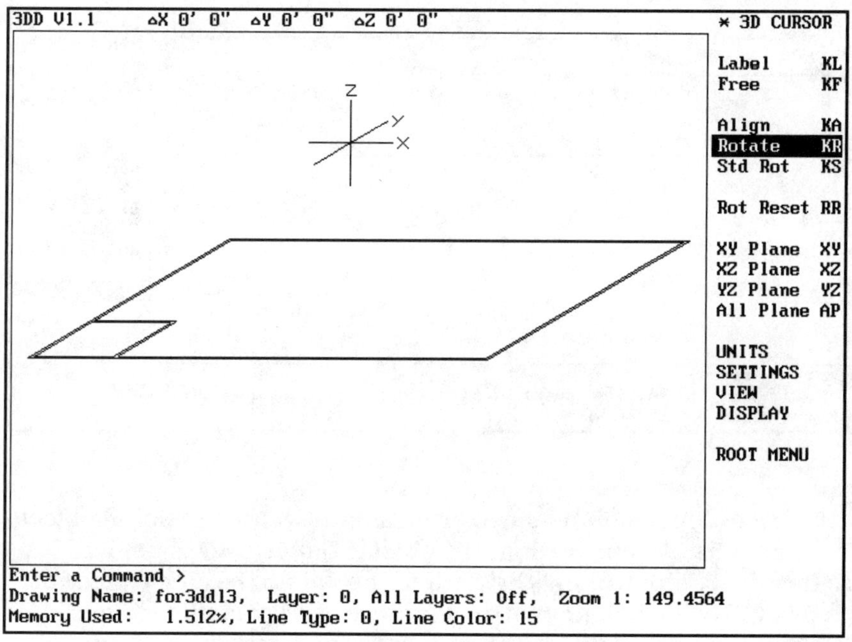

Figure C.2: *The house plan from fig. C.1, after being loaded into Generic 3D.*

In this example, the Generic 3D cursor is rotated so that the Z axis points up and down. (By default, the cursor rotation is set so that the X and Y axes lie on the plane of the screen, while the Z axis projects outward.) By rotating the cursor in this manner before loading the drawing into Generic 3D, you can load the 2D drawing as shown in figure C.2. This is because all two-dimensional drawings brought into Generic 3D line up with the cursor's X,Y heading.

Adding 3D Characteristics to 2D Objects

The two-dimensional floor plan is now a series of connected lines floating in space in Generic 3D. Before you can extrude the floor plan into a true three-dimensional object, you must convert the floor plan into polygons, a process that identifies a group of connecting lines as a single object. The next step is to extrude the polygons, as illustrated in figure C.3.

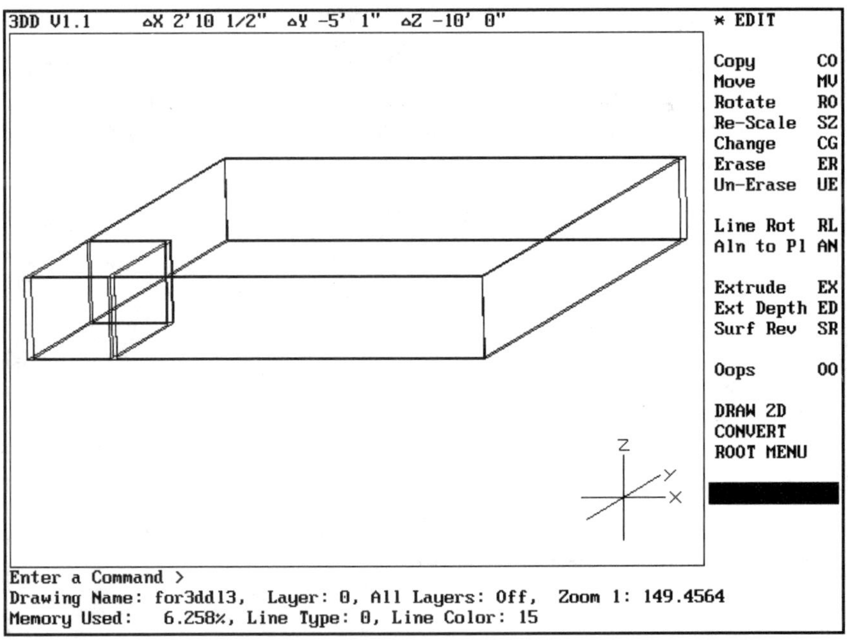

Figure C.3: *The floor plan, after being extruded to create three-dimensional walls.*

You also can create three-dimensional objects from a flat, two-dimensional object by spinning it about an axis. When you spin the object, Generic 3D considers each place where the object stops along the path of the spin to be a new piece of the object. This type of 3D object is known as a *surface of revolution.* Figure C.4 shows a flat, two-dimensional arc; figure C.5 shows the arc transformed into a hemisphere, after being treated by Generic 3D's surface-revolving feature.

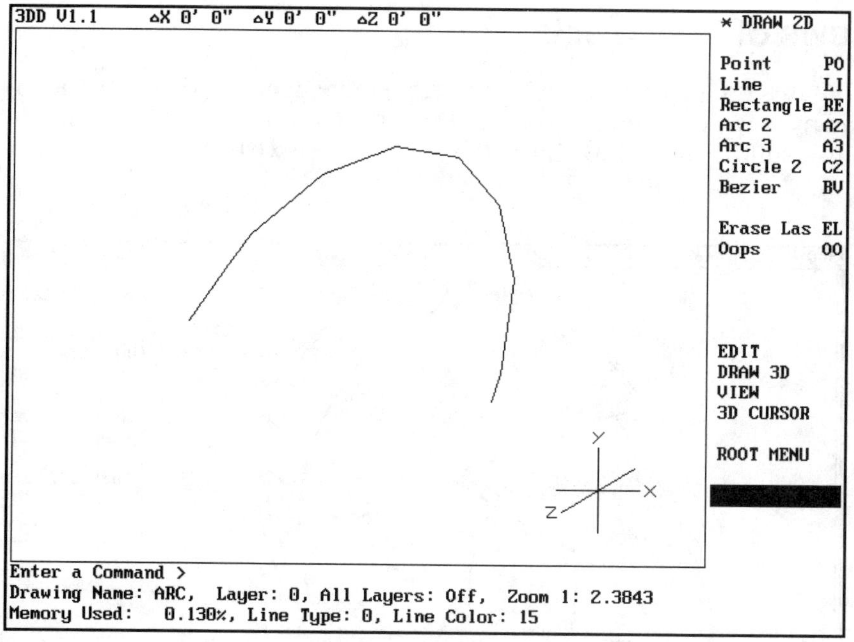

Figure C.4: *A flat arc, created in Generic 3D.*

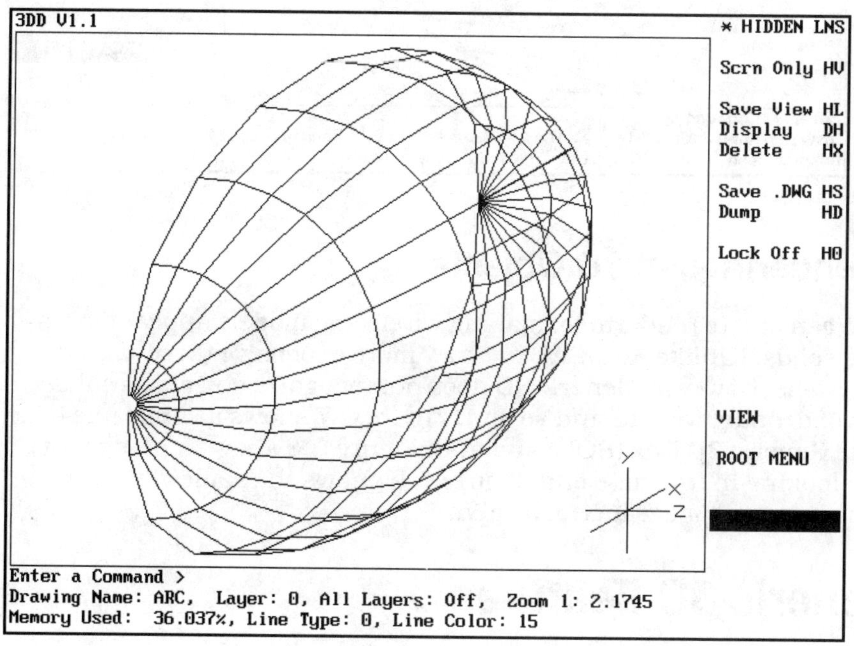

Figure C.5: *The arc, after being spun about an axis to create a hemisphere.*

Creating Views of 3D Objects

Generic 3D automates the process of creating perspective, isometric, and orthogonal views. From any view, you can remove the lines that would be hidden if the object were really a solid. Figure C.6 shows the hemisphere with the hidden lines removed.

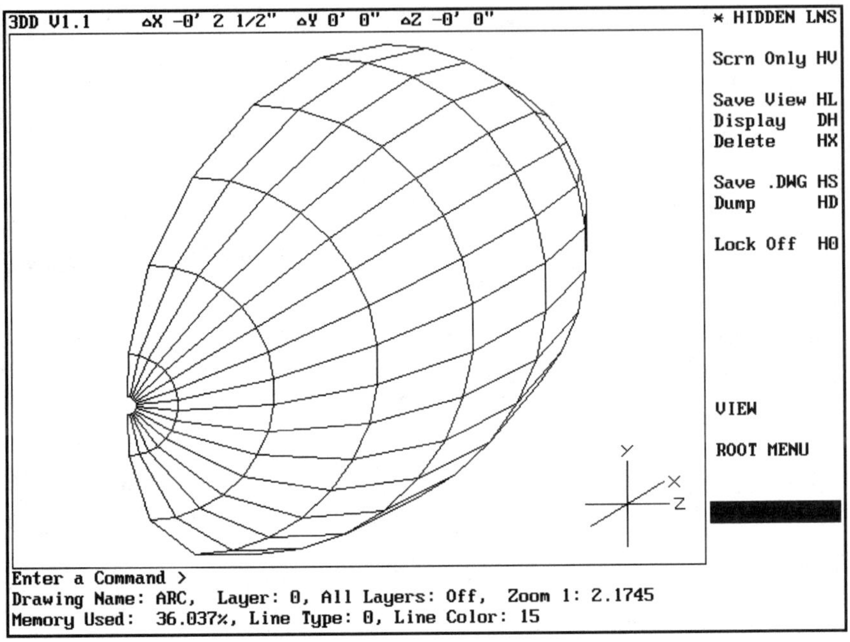

Figure C.6: *A view of the hemisphere, with hidden lines removed.*

Creating Renderings of 3D Objects

Generic 3D also can create renderings, making wireframe models appear as though they are solids. (Unlike AutoCAD or other more expensive three-dimensional CAD programs, however, Generic 3D does not recognize objects as solids, with properties of density, weight, and so on.). Figure C.7 shows a wireframe box, drawn using the Generic 3D Box (BO) command. Figure C.8 shows a perspective view of the box, looking in from one end. Figure C.9 shows the same view, rendered to give the box the appearance of a solid.

Other Generic 3D Features

Like Generic CADD, Generic 3D enables you to create and save components that you use often, to automate the repeated use of common objects. You also can purchase symbol libraries directly from Generic Software.

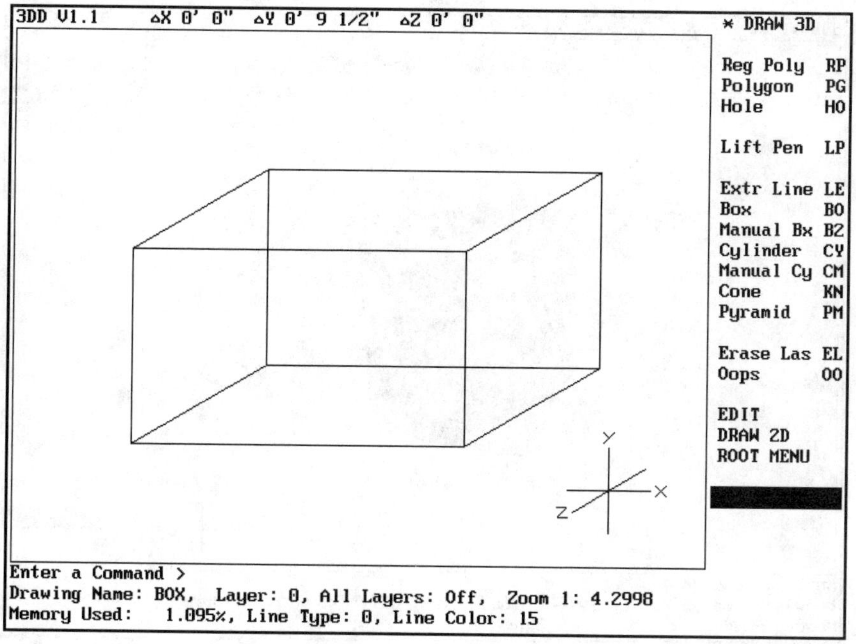

Figure C.7: *A simple box, drawn in Generic 3D.*

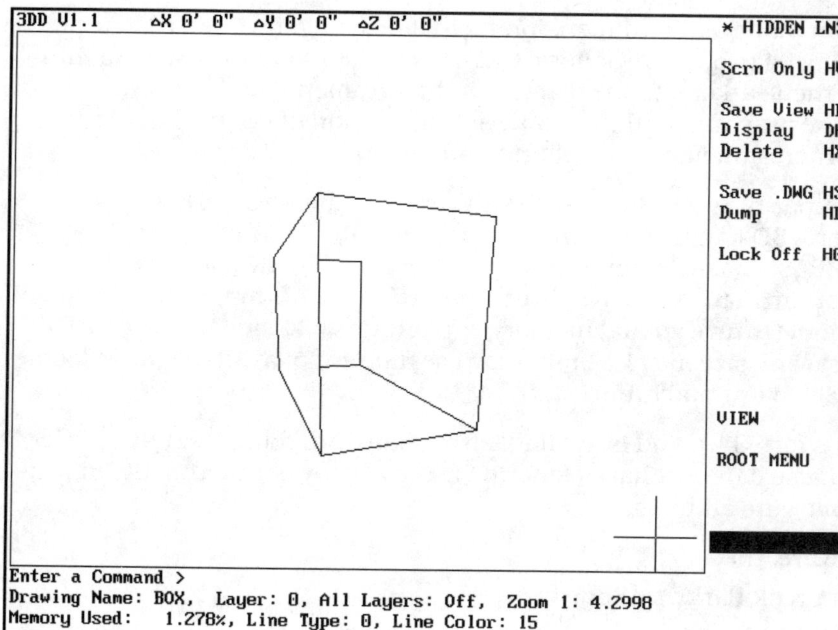

Figure C.8: *The box, after being rotated to provide a perspective view.*

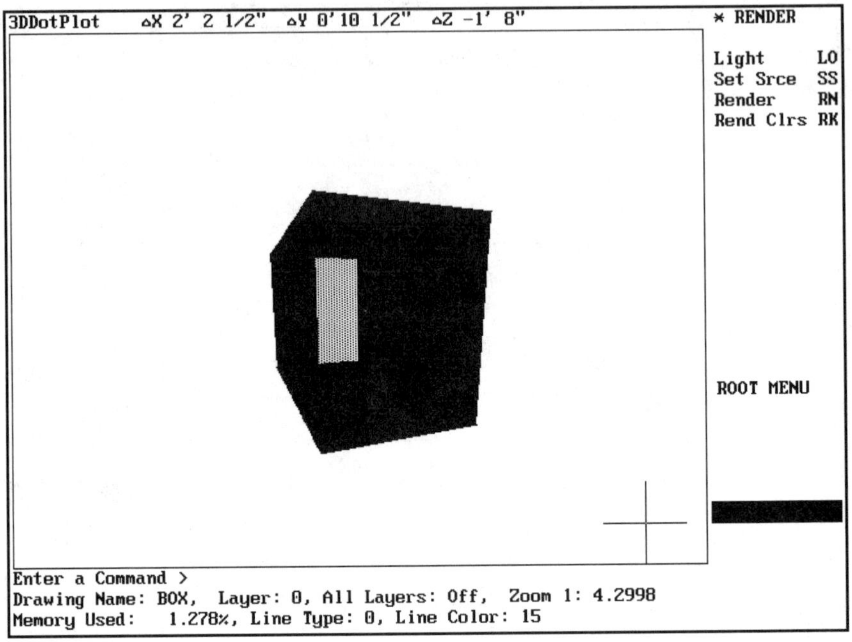

Figure C.9: *The box, after rendering.*

Generic 3D cannot place text or dimensioning in a drawing. If you use Generic CADD, you can start a project in Generic CADD and then take the drawing into Generic 3D. You then can create the drawing's three-dimensional aspects, save special views of the drawing, and then take a final version of the file back into Generic CADD, where you can add text and dimensions.

Generic 3D is compatible with the same hardware as Generic CADD, which means that Generic 3D can be used on budget-level XT computers as well as state-of-the-art 80486-based computers. Used together, the two programs are a cost-effective alternative to expensive three-dimensional CAD programs. Because Generic 3D does not feature virtual memory capabilities (as does Generic CADD 5.0), however, drawing size may be limited by the amount of available RAM (conventional or EMS) in your machine.

Generic 3D retails for $349, and is available from software retailers that sell Generic CADD. You also can purchase Generic 3D directly by contacting the manufacturer at the following address:

Generic Software, Inc.
11911 North Creek Parkway South
Bothell, WA 98011
(800) 228-3601 (U.S. and Canada)
(206) 487-2233 elsewhere

D

Translating Generic CADD Files for Use with AutoCAD

Generic CADD is the most popular under-$500 CAD program on the market. Of all CAD programs, only AutoCAD outsells Generic CADD. With so many people using these two programs, it is not uncommon for Generic CADD users and AutoCAD users to share drawing files and components.

To allow for the transfer of data in and out of AutoCAD, Autodesk (the makers of AutoCAD and the parent company of Generic Software) developed the DXF format. The file-name extension *DXF* stands for Drawing eXchange Format, and has become the de facto standard for the transfer of data among all CAD programs, not only those published by Autodesk. Many other graphics programs also read and write the DXF format, adding to its appeal.

AutoConvert 5.0, published by Generic Software, can convert Generic CADD and Generic 3D drawing files into the DXF format, and can convert DXF-format files into the DWG format used by Generic CADD or the 3DD format used by Generic 3D. Because AutoCAD can create three-dimensional drawing files, the DXF standard supports both two-dimensional and three-dimensional data structures.

AutoConvert 5.0 can adjust to support AutoCAD Releases 9, 10, and 11. AutoConvert 5.0 also supports Generic CADD 5.0 and Generic CADD Level 3, which is the predecessor to version 5.0.

AutoConvert provides a wide variety of default responses, to account for variations between AutoCAD and Generic CADD. These defaults affect the selection of fonts, choices in the translation of linetypes not used by both programs, and the translation of colors between programs.

AutoConvert 5.0 retails for $99.95, and is available from most software retailers that sell Generic CADD. You also can purchase AutoConvert directly from Generic Software, by contacting:

Generic Software, Inc.
11911 North Creek Parkway South
Bothell, WA 98011
(800) 228-3601 in the US and Canada
(206) 487-2233 elsewhere

Index

Symbols

A

B

C

D

E

F

G

H

M

N

O

P

Q-R

S

T

U

V

W

X-Z

To order: Fill in the reverse side, fold, and mail

NO POSTAGE NECESSARY IF MAILED IN THE UNITED STATES

BUSINESS REPLY MAIL

FIRST CLASS PERMIT NO. 6008 INDIANAPOLIS, IN

POSTAGE WILL BE PAID BY ADDRESSEE

NEW RIDERS PUBLISHING
P.O. Box 90
Carmel, Indiana 46032